LYTLE
莱特尔

Psychotherapy
with Deaf Clients
from Diverse Groups

Psychotherapy with Deaf Clients from Diverse Groups

Irene W. Leigh, Editor

Gallaudet University Press / Washington, D.C.

Gallaudet University Press, Washington, D.C. 20002

Printed in the United States of America

Library of Congress Cataloging-in-Publication Data

Psychotherapy with deaf clients from diverse groups / Irene W. Leigh, editor.
p. cm.
Includes bibliographical references and index.
ISBN 1-56368-083-1 (casebound : alk. paper)
1. Deaf—Mental health. 2. Psychotherapy. I. Leigh, Irene.
RC451.4.D4P79 1999
616.89'14'0872—dc21 99-40434
CIP

The tables in chapter 16 are reprinted by permission of The Minnesota Chemical Dependency Program for Deaf and Hard of Hearing Individuals from *Clinical Approaches: A Model for Treating Chemically Dependent Deaf and Hard of Hearing Individuals*, published by Deacones Press in 1994.

∞ The paper used in this publication meets the minimum requirements of American National Standard for Information Sciences—Permanence of Paper for Printed Library Materials, ANSI Z39.48-1984.

Contents

Part Three/The Ethnic Dimension

Part Four/Special Issues within the Deaf Community

Foreword

People are complex. We bear, demonstrate, or are influenced by an immense variety of characteristics. Ethnicity, gender, religion, cultural heritage, sexual orientation, national identity, health status, political persuasion, primary language, education, social affiliation, and family constellation are just a few of them. Psychologists, sociologists, and politicians frequently point to these or other characteristics in their efforts to understand and explain human behavior. Of course, attempts to describe or understand human beings on any one, two, three, or ten of these dimensions always fall short of capturing the rich diversity that an individual, much less a group of individuals, present.

But this doesn't stop people from trying. Perhaps that's human nature. We have a great desire to understand things that strike us as puzzling or different, especially other people. Those who experience life differently than we do or who behave differently than we do command our attention and cause us to seek "explanations." We tend to seek the simplest explanations first, before the weight of additional data forces us to abandon previously held beliefs. That is the nature of human curiosity and how we advance our knowledge, especially in the social and physical sciences. Perhaps it is also our nature (or at least the nature of those born to the privilege of majority status) to assume that we are at the top of the evolutionary chain and that "different" ways of living or behaving are "worse" ways of living or behaving.

In long-ago times, evolutionary inferiority or demonic possession were simple and sufficient explanations for most forms of unfamiliar behavior or manners of living. Over time, the sciences of medicine and psychology created new frameworks for understanding puzzling behavior, some of which were set aside in the newly-conceived category of mental illness or *psychopathology*. Explanations for psychopathological human characteristics were usually postulated to lie in one or a combination of easily observed human characteristics—race, gender, birth order, the pattern of lumps on one's head, and so on. These and other assumptions about what makes people with mental illness think or behave the way they do frequently reflected the author's (or prevailing group at hand's) *own* defining characteristics, that is, their physical and experiential basis for framing normalcy and, therefore, deviations from it.

While psychology and psychiatry have certainly made remarkable advancements in this century, one can still see evidence of the search for more simplistic, characteristic-based explanations for human psychopathology. One need look no further than the preponderance of writings that focus on deaf people, at least those writings appearing prior to 1970 or thereabouts—and still quite a few thereafter.

Prior to the 1970s, thc typical individual who wrote about the topic of deaf people and psychopathology was a hearing individual who knew little about how life as a deaf person could possibly be lived in any "normal" way. The idea that a different way of experiencing the world, one that did not heavily involve audition and speech ("a different center" as Carol Padden and Tom Humphries later termed it[1]), might also be psychologically normal (even though it differed from the "usual") was simply not considered. Thus, the presumption of deaf abnormality was a given, and it was a short leap from there to presumptions or "evidence" of psychopathology. I have previously suggested that the shift from a presumption of psychopathology toward the consideration of psychological normalcy in the lives of deaf individuals sprang from pioneering linguistic research on American Sign Language (ASL):

> [William Stokoe] and his deaf coauthor Carl Croneberg had effectively reframed sign language and, by extension, the Deaf community itself in as permanent and profound a way as Galileo or Einstein had reframed the thinking of their day. ASL's recognition as a language had the effect of bringing legitimacy to the Deaf community in the eyes of many hearing persons, including those in the mental health field. Psychologists' earlier, negative views of the linguistic, intellectual, and psychological characteristics of deaf people were suddenly cast in a new light, reconsidered, and frequently abandoned. Stokoe made the premise of deaf psychological health a far more viable one than it had ever been before.[2]

Since 1970, writings and conferences about psychopathology and deaf people have increasingly reflected the view that hearing loss does not automatically lead to mental disorder. Instead, intervening variables thought to promote psychological health vs. psychopathology in the deaf population have been explored and debated with increasing frequency. The primary foci of this phase of scholarship have been sign language use by the deaf individual and/or his or her family and the nature of the deaf individual's education and socialization experiences. Another post-1970s branch of research has been examining mental health services that deaf people receive, identifying diagnostic accuracy and complications, as well as service access and quality of care issues.

While the expanded research agenda of the past three decades has helped us appreciate the contributions that communication modality, education, Deaf culture affiliation, and other characteristics make toward defining and treating mental illnesses in deaf people, much of this work could be criticized for treating the deaf population as rather homogeneous. Yes, distinctions have been made between those who use sign language and those who do not, those born deaf and those whose hearing loss occurred later in life, those with and without complicating physical and mental disabilities, those educated in mainstream programs and those educated in schools for the deaf, and those affiliated with Deaf culture and those who are not. However, it was not until this publication that a major mental health text has addressed the nonphysical, nonlinguistic, non-educational, non-Deaf culture types of diversity represented in the deaf population.

Psychotherapy with Deaf Clients from Diverse Groups suggests that we are entering a new era in the deafness and mental health field—one where our understanding of the psychological experiences of deaf individuals and the treatment modalities best suited to addressing their mental health needs are informed not only by factors that differentiate

1. Padden, C., & Humphries, T. (1988). *Deaf in America: Voices from a culture.* Cambridge, MA: Harvard University Press.

2. Pollard, R. Q. (1993). 100 years in psychology and deafness: A centennial retrospective. *Journal of the American Deafness and Rehabilitation Association, 26* (3), 32–46.

deaf people from hearing people but by a variety of nontraditional (i.e., non-deaf-related) factors that differentiate deaf people from one another (and even link them to hearing people in some ways). Each chapter of this ground-breaking text elucidates previously underappreciated aspects of human diversity in the deaf population and the implications for conceptualizing and conducting psychotherapeutic treatment.

As if the search for adequate explanations for the causes and manifestations of psychopathology were not complicated enough, the nature of psychotherapeutic treatment is even more complicated. Up to this point, I have been talking about individual diversity in the deaf population and how it complicates the prediction and understanding of psychopathology. In psychotherapy, there is an additional layer of complexity—the human variability embodied in the therapist. The therapist's own characteristics or manifestation of human diversity is no less important than that of the consumer. An interpersonal encounter, psychotherapy is thus complicated by the individual variations of both parties involved plus the meta-complications of their interactions with one another (e.g., cross-cultural or cross-linguistic interactions). It's enough to make your head spin, even before you add a sign language interpreter into the picture!

The psychotherapeutic journey is a marvelously mysterious, uniquely human encounter that begins with the great diversity of experiences and perspectives that both the therapist and the consumer bring to it, and goes from there toward a goal of greater psychological health for the consumer. Along the way, this intimate interpersonal journey navigates through corridors of the most complex of interactions between the past and the present influences of both brave travelers (and others who may join in the encounter). This book lays out previously unaddressed critical aspects of the psychotherapeutic terrain when working with deaf consumers. It is a fine guide for the therapist who seeks to appreciate the diversity that deaf individuals bring to this encounter and it will increase your familiarity and skills in negotiating at least some of that interpersonal complexity.

Robert Pollard, Ph.D.

Associate Professor of Psychiatry (Psychology)
University of Rochester Medical Center

Preface

In the mental health arena, every book published is a stepping stone in the endeavor to understand human nature and the forces that shape it. Ultimately, this understanding should elucidate the process of human development, facilitating the ability of mental health service providers to enhance the quality of life for individuals struggling with mental health issues. The field of mental health is increasingly affirming mental health treatment processes that are culturally relevant and culturally sensitive. Recent publications such as *Culturally Affirmative Psychotherapy with Deaf Individuals*[1] challenge readers to internalize the affirmation of Deaf culture in psychotherapy practice. This book, *Psychotherapy with Deaf Clients from Diverse Groups*, takes this concept one step further. It is groundbreaking in that it is the first single volume to present a compendium of perspectives on mental health work with diverse constituents of the deaf community within a multicultural framework.

As Aponte, Rivers, and Wohl assert, "To note that the practitioner must take into account clients' social, ethnic, racial, linguistic, and other culturally defining characteristics has become almost a banality of the trade. Developing the particular skills and sensibilities necessary to make that axiom not just a cliché but a vital part of clinical training and practice is imperative."[2] Taking on the mantle of cross-cultural therapy requires the understanding that cultures manifest themselves differently in features such as attitudes, forms of emotional expression, patterns of relating to others, and ways of thought. To do this, practitioners need to learn how to step outside the traditional Euro-American academic and professional conceptualizations which are comfortable because of their own backgrounds and training and confront unfamiliar worldviews and expectations that may defy their traditional assumptions in doing therapy.

In the case of deafness, this process facilitates a therapy paradigm shift from dealing with deafness as pathology to dealing with deafness as a way of life. Sensitivity to all of these components is integral to the evolution of the psychotherapeutic process; and developing this sensitivity is a necessary part of becoming "culturally literate."

To be culturally literate in working with deaf people is to acknowledge the concept that "deaf" in and of itself does not always presuppose certain ways of communicating, certain ways of functioning, and certain ways of "being." Deaf and nondeaf individuals who feel connected with the deaf community—a complex entity of which Deaf culture is one component, albeit a significant one—acknowledge the common bond of audiological deafness or cultural Deafness.[3] Feelings of connection are based on individual

1. Glickman, N. S., & Harvey, M. A. (1996). *Culturally affirmative psychotherapy with deaf persons.* Mahwah, NJ: Lawrence Erlbaum Associates.

2. Aponte, J., Rivers, R., & Wohl, J. (Eds.) (1995). *Psychological interventions and cultural diversity.* Boston: Allyn & Bacon, pp. x–xi.

3. For the sake of consistency, "deaf" refers to the audiological condition of hearing loss and "Deaf" refers to Deaf people as a cultural group.

life experiences rather than auditory status per se. People choose to be deaf or Deaf in different ways. Deaf people who choose to be oral can feel their own way of being deaf deep down in the inner core of their being, not necessarily in a pathological sense, just as culturally Deaf persons feel deaf or specifically Deaf when they search for their own inner essence. To complicate the issue, not all individuals are Deaf in the same way. Deaf people come from diverse cultures and live varying cultural lifestyles. They engage in an ongoing struggle to shape the relationship between the cultural background they were born into and contemporary Deaf culture without losing their unique heritage. All these considerations differently shape the cultural and linguistic worlds of these deaf individuals.

The Deaf culture paradigm, as defined in recent literature, merely acknowledges the existence of cultural differences. The literature generally has not yet incorporated the inherent complexities of these differences into basic Deaf culture imperatives. Multiculturalism as represented by different ways of life and different ethnic cultures in and of itself will influence Deaf culture as we know it in the United States and expand the ways in which this Deaf culture manifests itself.

Psychotherapists working with deaf clients from diverse groups should attune not only to relevant group attributes, but also the ways in which the interaction between these attributes and the deafness dimension play themselves out during the therapeutic process. This premise has influenced the direction I have chosen for this book, specifically one which focuses on psychotherapeutic approaches within a diversity framework. Using this paradigm, I have asked all the contributing authors to reflect on the specific cultures and lifestyles of clients within the deaf community with which they feel an affinity. The ultimate goal of these reflections is to explore the authors' perspectives of the deaf/Deaf constituencies they work with, their mental health issues, the consequences for individual life directions, and the treatment approaches that work best. This sets the foundation for the entire book. In each chapter, readers will see differences in how "deaf" and "Deaf" are used, as based on the authors' views of deaf/Deaf culture. These differences reflect the evolving nature of both terms.

Increasing numbers of deaf professionals are now joining the ranks of their nondeaf colleagues as mental health service providers and have begun to take their places as authorities in the mental health arena.[4] *Psychotherapy with Deaf Clients from Diverse Groups* reflects this change. This book is part of the current effort to turn to members of host communities who have the type of life experiences that can influence the effectiveness of mental health service delivery. While all the contributing authors have different and credible perceptions of the deaf/Deaf experience, eight of us are deaf or have some form of hearing loss, thus bringing an added dimension to this book in terms of identification issues with the populations we write about (see the contributor list for more information).

Allen E. Sussman and Barbara A. Brauer introduce the book with a personalized overview of what being a psychotherapist with deaf clients is all about. As psychologists who are deaf and who have served as direct witnesses to the history of mental health services for deaf individuals, they have seen both successes and failures.

Without knowing deaf consumer perspectives on mental health aspects, we are shortchanged in our ability to change the course of service delivery for the better. Annie G. Steinberg, Ruth C. Loew, and Vicki Joy Sullivan provide us with these perspectives

4. Leigh, I. W. (1991). Deaf therapists: Impact on treatment. *Proceedings, XI World Congress of the World Federation of the Deaf: Equality and self-reliance* (pp. 290–297). Tokyo, Japan: World Federation of the Deaf.

based on dialogue with Deaf individuals. Irene W. Leigh and Jeffrey W. Lewis then present an analysis of considerations for deaf therapists who may live as well as work within the deaf community and Deaf culture. They explore the inherent complexities of the therapy process as deaf therapists confront boundary issues and encounter culturally different members of the deaf community.

At this point, the focus of the book shifts to an exploration of diverse constituencies within the deaf community. Tovah M. Wax begins with an exploration of how psychotherapy with deaf women has evolved in a more affirmative way using a constructivist approach as a foundation. Next, Virginia Gutman provides a perspective of therapy issues for deaf lesbians, gay men, and bisexual men and women, within the context of culture and lifestyle. In so doing, she takes into account the ambivalent role therapy has played in gay and lesbian lives because of societal attitudes toward the meanings of sexual orientation. Shirley Shultz Myers, Randall R. Myers, and Alan L. Marcus illustrate how hearing children of deaf parents may positively connect with the deaf/Deaf community and simultaneously deal with the mixed feelings that can emerge when hearing and deaf worlds collide.

The next section of this book consists of four chapters covering the ethnic dimension. Carolyn A. Corbett describes the mental health issues that affect African Americans who are deaf and struggling with racism and identity concerns—concerns that are magnified by historical and current oppression. She presents a home-based psychotherapy approach that encompasses culturally validating features for this population. Nancy M. Eldredge explores the cultural issues of American Indians who are deaf, and indicates how therapists can be culturally responsive to this population. Because those who are Asian, American, and deaf are not a homogenous entity due to linguistic and cultural differences related to country of origin, Cheryl L. Wu and Nancy C. Grant devote primary attention in their chapter to deaf people and their families with Chinese heritages. Those heritages are not easy to generalize because Chinese individuals from different areas within and outside of China bring with them diverse cultural and linguistic experiences. For this population, therapy needs to be family-centered in reverence to tradition. Lastly, Margarita Hernández describes deaf Latino immigrant adolescents who are confronted with migration-related issues, which greatly impact their ability to adjust to life in a new country and also, therefore, impact their mental health. She recommends a group-based model of intervention that is culturally and linguistically sensitive. Throughout all four chapters, the authors acknowledge that the process of integrating nondominant ethnic cultures and cultural aspects of deafness within the United States forces a confrontation with critical identity issues as deaf individuals explore group affiliations and define their sense of self in culturally affirmative ways.

The book concludes with a group of chapters that focus on special issues within the deaf community—issues that create subgroups of deaf individuals. One such subgroup consists of those living with the diagnosis of HIV/AIDS. For them, life becomes an ongoing struggle with health and social complications that are more likely than not to be stigmatizing. Daniel J. Langholtz and Richard Ruth have taken the psychotherapeutic journey with them and share their notes with us.

Deaf persons who have experienced sexual abuse represent another such subgroup, a vulnerable one that tends to remain hidden because of society's avoidance of the topic. Florrie Burke, Virginia Gutman, and Patricia Dobosh look at some of the information related to sexual abuse and illustrate ways in which therapists can facilitate the healing process for survivors.

People who rely on their eyes and not their ears for contact with the world face painful psychological adjustments when they lose their eyesight due to Usher syndrome. Ilene D. Miner describes this syndrome and how its fluctuating nature impacts affected individuals throughout the life cycle. She then offers guidance to therapists who work with this small, and thus traditionally underserved, population. Kathleen Duffy addresses another traditionally underserved group: people struggling with factors such as mental illness, trauma, cognitive impairment, illiteracy, and economic disadvantage. Her clinical case management approach encompasses therapeutic interventions that can validate the lives of these adults. Lastly, those in the deaf community who are chemically addicted require strategic interventions that are rarely available. Debra Guthmann, Katherine Sandberg, and Janet Dickinson present a treatment model for these individuals that could potentially be more broadly applied.

The contributors dedicated untold hours in the effort to create chapters that present newly integrated information appearing in book form for the first time. They have had to draw from the literature for general information about the specific groups of people they specialize in, apply this information to deaf/Deaf people, and analyze the implications vis-à-vis their work with these individuals. They have also drawn from within themselves and their life experiences, as well as from their experiences in working with the populations they write about. For many of them this was a daunting task, but one they accepted because it was a task whose time had come. They recognized their responsibility to convey accurate pictures of human beings within specific contexts and the nature of their work with these individuals. Out of this integrative effort came new meanings and implications for mental health professionals. I leave it to you to judge their success in conveying the complexity and diversity of the deaf community and its impact on current psychotherapy paradigms.

Acknowledgments

I would like to express my gratitude to those who have taught, supported, and sustained me in the work to which I have devoted my professional career. As a deaf woman, as a teacher, as a psychologist, and as a mother, I have had different opportunities for exposure to the various facets of the deaf community, as well as the community's frustrations and its triumphs. These opportunities have forged my efforts to be sensitive regarding cultural influences on the lives of deaf individuals. To this community I owe thanks.

The enthusiasm demonstrated by the authors who agreed to be part of this book was an inspiration to me. Some of them struggled to overcome personal adversity so that they could complete their chapters. Without them all, this book could not have come to fruition. To them I owe heartfelt thanks and enduring gratitude.

Ivey Pittle Wallace, managing editor at Gallaudet University Press, encouraged me to develop the proposal that formed the foundation for this book. She has been a source of help that allayed my fears as I encountered the various challenges attendant upon completing the book. Christina Findlay, editor, carried this book smoothly to fruition. I thank them as well.

To all those on the home front who gave me the time and space to shape this book, I express my love. Their acceptance of my need to immerse myself in the process of producing a meaningful piece of work sustained me through the times of sacrifice.

My last words are for Larry G. Stewart, Ph.D. Larry was a deaf pioneer who contributed to the definition of mental health service delivery for deaf people. I knew him from afar because of his national prominence. When I became his colleague in the Department of Psychology at Gallaudet University, I was confronted with his astute intelligence and his ability to get at the heart of unresolved issues related to the definition of who and what deaf people are. He was a man who loved challenges, who was never afraid of controversial issues, and who felt very strongly that deaf people should be deaf in their own ways. In that spirit, I initiated the challenge of putting together a book that reflects the diversity of deaf people in the hopes that mental health services for deaf people would benefit from the contents. Larry's untimely death was a significant loss to the field. This book is a testament to his influence on my ongoing development as a professional who is deaf.

Contributors

Barbara A. Brauer, Ph.D., is a deaf pioneer in mental health and deafness. She was an assistant research scientist at the New York State Psychiatric Institute, which had the first mental health program for the deaf in the United States. She obtained her doctorate from New York University. After postgraduate training in clinical psychology at St. Elizabeths Hospital in Washington, D.C., she served as staff psychologist there for ten years before coming to Gallaudet University as research scientist with the Mental Health Research Program at the Gallaudet Research Institute. She is currently at Gallaudet as executive director of the Mental Health Center and professor in the Department of Counseling (graduate level). Additionally, she maintains a private practice.

Florrie Burke, M.A., spent fourteen years as a certified teacher of the deaf. She then served as a clinician and clinical director of the University of California Center on Deafness before becoming executive director of the Lexington Center for Mental Health Services (an affiliate of the Lexington School for the Deaf/Center for the Deaf). She is licensed as a Marriage, Family, and Child Counselor, and holds master's degrees in Clinical Psychology from John F. Kennedy University and in Special Education (Deafness). Currently, she is a mental health and disabilities consultant; an adjunct faculty member at New York University.

Carolyn A. Corbett, Ph.D., received her clinical psychology degree from Pennsylvania State University in 1991 and worked at the Gallaudet University Counseling Center as a staff psychologist before coming to the Department of Psychology. She is currently associate professor in the clinical psychology doctoral program. Her clinical and research interests are ethnic and racial issues in deafness. Her private practice involves providing in-home services to African American children and their families.

Janet E. Dickinson, Ph.D., is the director of community affairs at the Marie H. Katzenbach School for the Deaf in New Jersey. Previously, she was the deputy director of the Newark Target Cities Project, a federally funded drug treatment program. At the New Jersey Division of Alcoholism, Drug Abuse, and Addiction Services, she was responsible for developing substance abuse prevention and treatment services for the state's deaf and hard of hearing people.

Patricia Dobosh recently received her Ph.D. from Gallaudet's clinical psychology program. She has clinical and research interests in trauma and sexual abuse survivors; her dissertation research involved the effects of childhood sexual abuse on Deaf adults.

Kathleen Duffy, M.S., is a licensed Marriage and Family Therapist and Certified Rehabilitation Counselor. She obtained her degree from San Francisco State

University, and also holds a C.S.C. from the Registry of Interpreters for the Deaf (RID). She formerly worked at the University of California Center on Deafness as a clinical social worker and was the center's first case manager. Currently she teaches at San Francisco State University.

Nancy Eldredge, Ph.D., is in private practice as a psychologist in Tucson, Arizona. She formerly was director of the Mental Health/Deaf Program in Oregon and director of the Rehabilitation Counseling/Deafness Program at the University of Arizona. Previous research work covers the cognitive developmental and social/emotional development of deaf children in the United States and China. She has conducted research on both Australian Aborigines and American Indians who are deaf, in addition to doing evaluations and therapy with the latter group.

Nancy C. Grant, M.S.W., has family members with late onset deafness. She founded the Big Brothers/Big Sisters Hearing Impaired Program in 1982 for multicultural deaf and hard of hearing individuals. "HIP" moved to the Hearing Society for the Bay Area in 1995. Under her direction, the program provides developmental group activities and family support services (parent education, home-school liaison, social work, and mental health).

Debra S. Guthmann, Ed.D., directs pupil personnel services at the California School for the Deaf in Fremont. She is the former director of the Minnesota Chemical Dependency Program for Deaf and Hard of Hearing Individuals and continues to manage several of the program's training grants. She develops international substance abuse outreach activities, teaches at San Francisco State University and the University of Minnesota, and is an officer for the National Association of Addiction Drugs and Disability and the American Deafness and Rehabilitation Association.

Virginia Gutman, Ph.D., is the founder and director of Gallaudet's doctoral program in clinical psychology, and is a professor in the Department of Psychology. She was director of the Gallaudet Counseling Center for five years, and has over twenty years of clinical experience. She earned a doctorate in clinical psychology in 1974 from Duke University. She conducts a private practice in Virginia and the District of Columbia.

Margarita Hernández, C.S.W., obtained her master's degree in social work from New York University. She is currently a clinical social worker at the Jackson Developmental Center, a special education preschool, in New York City. She was formerly a senior clinical social worker and family therapist at the Lexington Center for Mental Health Services (an affiliate of the Lexington School for the Deaf/Center for the Deaf). At the Lexington Center, she primarily worked with Latino people who were deaf or hard of hearing, and their immediate family members. She has presented nationally on her group work with deaf Latino adolescents who have immigrated, as well as with groups of parents of deaf Latino children.

Daniel J. Langholtz, L.C.S.W., who is deaf, coordinates HIV services at the University of California Center on Deafness in San Francisco. He also consults and presents in the areas of accessibility, gay/lesbian, HIV/AIDS, interpreting, mental health, and community relationship issues with a focus on deafness. Additionally, he counsels deaf youth at a mainstream program. He received his master's degree in social work from New York University.

Irene W. Leigh, Ph.D., was the third deaf teacher at the Lexington School for the Deaf in New York City before obtaining her master's degree in rehabilitation counseling and her doctorate in clinical psychology, both from New York University. She has served at the Lexington School for the Deaf/Center for the Deaf as director of Guidance Services and as assistant director of the center's Mental Health Services affiliate. Currently at Gallaudet University, she is a professor in the Department of Psychology with primary responsibility in the doctoral program in clinical psychology. She also maintains a private practice and presents nationally and internationally on various issues related to parenting, socialization and identity, multiculturalism, and mental health.

Jeffrey W. Lewis, Ph.D., is a professor in the Department of Counseling and director of the graduate-level Mental Health Counseling Program at Gallaudet University. He maintains a private practice in metropolitan Washington, D.C., and Frederick, Maryland. A second-generation Deaf person, Dr. Lewis received his doctorate in counseling psychology from New York University. He presents workshops nationally and internationally on issues related to mental health.

Ruth C. Loew, Ph.D., received her doctoral degree in linguistics from the University of Minnesota and her M.A. in education of the hearing impaired from Northwestern University. She is an associate examiner with Educational Testing Service in Princeton, New Jersey where she develops graduate school admissions examinations and serves as an internal consultant on deafness-related issues. She was involved in research on deaf consumers' attitudes toward mental health services at Children's Seashore House in Philadelphia and has taught at the National Technical Institute for the Deaf and the Pennsylvania School for the Deaf.

Alan L. Marcus, Ph.D., a hearing son of deaf parents, received his doctorate in counseling psychology from Temple University. He became director of Community Services at Gallaudet University's Mental Health Center in 1996 after serving as staff psychologist at the university Counseling Center. In addition to maintaining a private practice, he has made numerous presentations on issues related to mental health and deafness. He serves on the CODA (Children of Deaf Adults International) Board of Directors as well as the Board of the Maryland School for the Deaf.

Ilene D. Miner, C.S.W., A.C.S.W., consulted for the Helen Keller National Center in Sands Point, Long Island, and several state children's deaf-blind programs. She developed a deaf services program at Bellevue Hospital Center in New York City, which provided staff education, health education, and mental health intervention for deaf individuals. She has lectured widely on psychosocial aspects of the impact of Usher syndrome on people who are deaf and hard of hearing. Currently, she director of Mental Health Services at the League for the Hard of Hearing in New York City.

Randall R. Myers, L.C.S.W.-C., a hearing son of deaf parents, received his master's degree from the School of Social Welfare at the University of California, Berkeley.

He has extensive direct, administrative, and consulting experience in providing mental health services to deaf and hard of hearing people. He has served as the state coordinator of Deaf and Hard of Hearing Services in the Illinois Department of Mental Health and Developmental Disabilities and as adjunct professor for Gallaudet's master's program in social work. Currently he provides therapy for deaf and hard of hearing clients at the Jewish Social Services Agency in Rockville, Maryland.

Shirley Shultz Myers, Ph.D., a hearing daughter of deaf parents, is a professor of English at Gallaudet University. She obtained her doctorate from Emory University in 1984 in modern drama, with a special interest in psychology and American literature. In addition to having taught seriously mentally ill deaf people as part of the Thresholds Bridge Program in Chicago, she also holds a certificate from a two-year program in psychodynamic psychology at the Washington School of Psychiatry.

Richard Ruth, Ph.D., is a clinical psychologist with postgraduate training in psychoanalysis, neuropsychology, and family therapy. He maintains a private practice in Wheaton, Maryland. He also is a member of the medical staff at CPC Health/ Chestnut Lodge Hospital in Montgomery County, Maryland; an adjunct professor in the graduate programs in counseling at Trinity College, Washington, D.C.; and a faculty member of the Washington School of Psychiatry. Since 1986 he has been chair of the Disability Interest Group of the American Orthopsychiatric Association. He has worked for many years with men, women, and children with HIV/AIDS.

Katherine A. Sandberg, B.S., L.A.D.C., is program manager of the Minnesota Chemical Dependency Program for Deaf and Hard of Hearing Individuals. She also assisted in the development of a specialized version of the Drug Abuse Resistance Education (D.A.R.E.) curriculum and has provided material development, outreach, and training in the area of substance abuse with deaf and hard of hearing individuals on a national basis.

Annie G. Steinberg, M.D., a former Robert Wood Johnson scholar, is the director of Psychiatry at Children's Seashore House and co-director of the Deafness and Family Communications Center at the Philadelphia Child Guidance Center. She is an assistant professor in both pediatric and psychiatric departments at the University of Pennsylvania School of Medicine, and has completed training in pediatrics, adolescent medicine, and adult and child psychiatry. Her areas of research include multiculturalism, access to health care, and linguistic barriers to health care.

Vicki Joy Sullivan, M.A., R.D.T. who is deaf serves as a research associate and communication specialist at the Deafness and Family Communication Center at Children's Seashore House in Philadelphia. She is currently researching cultural and linguistic barriers to mental health service access, as well as loneliness and social isolation in the workplace during transition years. Additionally, she is a community outreach coordinator and creative arts facilitator of a support group for deaf adults in recovery at Signs of Sobriety, Inc. She obtained her master's degree in drama therapy from New York University, and has a certificate in therapeutic recreation for children with disabilities.

Allen E. Sussman, Ph.D., is a deaf pioneer in mental health and deafness. He obtained his doctorate from New York University before proceeding to postgraduate training in clinical psychology at Maimonides Medical Center in New York City, where he eventually became director of the center's Mental Health Program for the Deaf. He has held positions at NYU as an assistant professor and research scientist at the university's Deafness and Research Training Center, at Gallaudet University as dean of Student Affairs and as the Counseling Center director, and at the Albert Witzke Medical Center in Baltimore as an affiliate of the Deaf Services Program. Currently he is a professor at Gallaudet's Department of Counseling, where he teaches graduate students in the Mental Health Counseling Program. He has held a private practice for over thirty years.

Tovah Wax, Ph.D., C.S.W., is a deaf professional who holds a doctorate in psychology from the University of Delaware (Newark), an M.S.W. from the University of Maryland (Baltimore), and an additional doctorate from the State University of New York (Buffalo) in counseling psychology (respecialized). She is currently director of the Deaf Services Unit at Dorothea Dix Hospital in Raleigh, North Carolina. Her previous positions include associate professor of psychology at the Rochester Institute of Technology, staff chair for NTID Psychological Services, coordinator of Washington State's mental health services for deaf and hard of hearing people, and assistant professor in Gallaudet's Department of Counseling.

Cheryl L. Wu, M.A., who has a fluctuating hearing loss due to Ménière's Disease, obtained her master's degree in mental health counseling from Gallaudet University. She is currently in a doctoral program in clinical psychology at California School of Professional Psychology (Alameda). Her clinical experience with multicultural deaf people and families has been in both Taiwan and the United States. Since 1989 she has provided clinical counseling to deaf and hard of hearing children and families in the Hearing Impaired Program, or "HIP," at the Hearing Society for the Bay Area in San Francisco.

Part One

Overview

1

On Being a Psychotherapist with Deaf Clients

ALLEN E. SUSSMAN AND BARBARA A. BRAUER

As a result of the human potential movements of the 1960s and 1970s, society experienced a "psychotherapy boom" and the burgeoning of consciousness-raising groups. The explosion and tremendous growth of counseling and psychotherapy, and the preeminence of therapists, became a social phenomenon. A compendium of psychotherapies from that time lists more than 250 "brand-name therapies," running the gamut from analytically oriented to insight-developing, cognitively oriented, behaviorally oriented, and eclectically oriented approaches that included various forms of couples, marital, family, sex, and group therapies (Herink, 1980). Psychotherapy was no longer limited to people who were "sick," maladjusted, neurotic, or mentally ill. A growing number of relatively well-adjusted individuals entered psychotherapy because they wanted to understand themselves better, function at the highest levels of their potential, improve their relationships with others, face the world more confidently, and live more satisfying, productive, self-actualizing, and meaningful lives (Wolberg, 1995).

This smorgasbord of psychotherapies was, however, not accessible to deaf individuals for a variety of reasons, including the relatively late entry of the behavioral sciences and mental health disciplines in the field of deafness and the acute shortage of qualified therapists. The slow progress in psychotherapy with deaf people was further exacerbated by negative attitudes of mental health professionals and avowed experts in deafness regarding the ability of deaf individuals to benefit from psychotherapy (Stewart, 1981; A. E. Sussman, 1988). The prevailing attitude at the time was that deaf people, due to their traditionally imputed deficiencies such as language difficulties, communication problems, lack of English skills, inability to reason on the abstract level, and personality issues, were not appropriate or feasible candidates for in-depth, insight-developing, affectively oriented, psychoanalytically oriented, and cognitively oriented psychotherapies. It was believed that only the highly educated, the highly verbal, postlingually deafened individuals could benefit from such forms of therapy.

Historically, professionals involved in the lives of deaf people were teachers, athletic coaches, members of the clergy, social workers, and in later years, vocational rehabilitation counselors (Vernon, 1971). For years these people filled the mental health void for deaf people, providing whatever assistance or words of wisdom they could. The type of assistance given to deaf individuals was usually straightforward: advice, directions, instructions, lectures, admonishments, and so on. Because of the limited perceptions regarding the capabilities of deaf individuals, psychotherapy for deaf people was pretty much mired in outdated and anachronistic directive approaches, the nature of which is antithesis to personal growth and independent functioning. This occurred while the field of psychotherapy was growing by leaps and bounds and gaining in scientific credibility.

The situation improved with the arrival and growth of counselors and caseworkers in the field of deafness during the 1970s. However, the brand of counseling that emerged continued to be largely directive, presumably fitting the attributed personality, language, and cognitive limitations of deaf clients, leaving little room for their growth and development. In this approach, the counselor is judgmental, telling the client what is wrong and what is right, and advising the client how to correct the problem. Essentially, most counselors believed, as the following quote demonstrates, that counseling with deaf clients had to be concrete:

> Successful counseling with most deaf persons and perhaps with people in general must be related to the here and now. . . . It means environmental manipulation, talking to employers, getting the family to help, and giving support instead of abstractly discussing super ego problems, displacement of unconscious drives, and other valid but intangible therapeutic concepts. The immaturity and the communication limitations of many deaf clients often made abstract procedures a useless tour de force. (Vernon, 1967, p. 10)

No mention was made of the highly heterogeneous nature of the deaf population, many of whom would benefit as much from psychotherapy as their hearing counterparts. Minimal attention was given to promoting counseling approaches that encourage the client to express feelings and thoughts, to reflect on these, and then to assume responsibility for them. Similarly, counselors who encouraged problem exploration (by the client) were largely ignored.

The concrete, here-and-now approach was reinforced in professional journals that continued to feature articles by influential authors who argued against the use of affectively oriented, analytically oriented, insight-developing, and in-depth counseling and psychotherapy approaches (Rainer et al., 1963; Vernon, 1967). During the 1960s, prominent psychoanalysts who worked with deaf patients maintained that psychoanalytic therapy with deaf people was not possible because of the level of abstract reasoning required and because of the need for the deaf patient to face the therapist, which cannot be accomplished while lying on the couch (Rainer et al., 1963). The fact that there are other approaches within the psychoanalytic camp was not mentioned. Further, there was no mention of the fact that psychoanalysis also does not work with many hearing people.

Arguments were also advanced against the newer rational, cognitive, and client-centered approaches on the grounds that they required high intellectual, logical, and abstract functioning and hence were not suitable for deaf people. According to Vernon, "Rogerians attempting to reflect affective overtones or responding with 'humms' which cannot be lipread and for which there is no sign soon see their technique as inappropriate with the average deaf client" (1967, p. 10). This particular reasoning has been proven to be patently absurd. Stewart (1981) and A. E. Sussman (1988) note that many counselors and therapists trained to work with "average" deaf clients have successfully used therapist characteristics such as communicating unconditional positive regard, accurate empathic understanding, congruence, and other classic core conditions promulgated by Carl Rogers and his client-centered counseling and psychotherapy. The "humms" and all client-centered cornerstone approaches, such as active listening, attending, reflection, and clarification, can be effectively conveyed via signed languages, including American Sign Language (ASL). In fact, many aspects of the Rogerian approach are made to order for ASL! Much can also be conveyed nonverbally, using mannerisms, gestures, body language, and facial expression. Many therapists skilled in working with deaf clients are skilled in various forms of the Rogerian "humm" with deaf clients.

Differences between client and therapist do not automatically make basic psychotherapy an inappropriate choice. "What is needed is for the therapist to know *how to conduct psychotherapy* with groups of people who differ from [the therapist], and *not* to conclude that it is inapplicable" (Weiner, 1975, p. 21, emphasis in original). To decide simply on the basis of deafness that a particular deaf client will be unsuitable for a "talking therapy" or a therapy involving some degree of self-scrutiny is analogous to what Wohl says "constitutes by itself an insult and, if the issue is ethnicity, an ethnic slur" (Wohl, 1995, p. 76). The propensity to stereotype deaf people as difficult and high-risk candidates, as is done with poor, disadvantaged, disabled, old, and nonverbal populations, served only to thwart psychotherapeutic opportunity for deaf clients' emotional growth and psychological enhancement. The therapist's qualifications, skills, and sign language competencies were hardly addressed as part of the psychotherapy equation.

It took years to recognize that the reported and observed difficulties and failures in psychotherapy with deaf clients often reflected the therapist's skills and attitudes rather than the imputed or stereotyped limitations of the deaf client. The therapists themselves generally did not possess a working knowledge of deafness and its psychosocial concomitants. Also, they were not able to communicate effectively and meaningfully with their deaf clients.

A small pool of pioneers, particularly psychologists who themselves were deaf and often isolated from one another, gamely attempted to place psychotherapy in its proper place in the field of deafness. They claimed that the nature and basic principles of psychotherapy with deaf individuals were not different from those of psychotherapy with nondeaf individuals. Nor was a new theoretical orientation needed despite earlier literature advocating a separate, psychopathologically oriented, and disputable "psychology of deafness" (Levine, 1960; Myklebust, 1960; Vernon & Andrews, 1990). As based on the perspectives of these few pioneering deaf psychologists, many deaf people representing various educational, economic, social, ethnic, cultural, and communication backgrounds did respond to and benefit from the various forms of psychotherapy used with hearing people when conditions for effective psychotherapy were present (A. E. Sussman, 1988). It is the implementation that may differ. For example, in addition to a therapist's skills and attitudes, proficiency with the communication mode preferred by the deaf client is one of the obvious conditions for effective psychotherapy.

A new, more promising era began to emerge in the 1980s and 1990s. Increasing numbers of young people—hearing and deaf—began to look to careers in deafness mental health (Leigh, 1991). Those already in clinical practice began to take an interest in working with deaf people. Contributing to this significant increase of clinicians in deafness mental health was the establishment of training programs such as Gallaudet University's master's programs in mental health counseling and social work, and its doctoral program in clinical psychology. Additionally, the number of local, regional, national, and international conferences, workshops, training institutes, and continuing education programs related to deafness mental health, including psychotherapy, also increased. From "the psychological and social problems of deaf people and their mental health needs" stage, the deafness mental health field has moved to the "what and how to do" stage. Current practitioners and graduate students are now focusing on the pragmatic aspects of psychotherapy with deaf clients. The question has changed from "Does psychotherapy work with deaf clients?" to "How is theory translated into practice with deaf clients and how does psychotherapy work with deaf clients?" Emergent is the healthy desire to learn from practicing psychotherapists representing a wide variety of theoretical orientations on how various approaches and techniques of psychotherapy are applied to deaf clients.

Another aspect of this movement is the growth of literature on the subject of counseling and psychotherapy with deaf clients, offering different theoretical and treatment perspectives. While not directly contradicting earlier authors advocating the more simplistic and directive approaches, this literature demonstrates that earlier contentions as to the inapplicability of various approaches for deaf individuals are without merit, provided that conditions for effective therapy exist (Brauer, 1980; Brauer & Sussman, 1980; Sussman & Stewart, 1971).

The psychoanalytic approaches are no longer summarily ruled out or restricted. For example, Levin (1981) and Rayson (1985) have demonstrated that some psychoanalytic therapies are possible, feasible, and useful with many deaf clients—as long as they are conducted in the client's preferred mode of communication. Approaches heretofore considered off-limits for deaf clients, such as the humanistically oriented therapies, Adlerian therapy, cognitive therapy, and rational-emotive therapy, have made their appearance in the therapist's office and in the literature (Anderson & Watson, 1985; Gough, 1990; Sussman, 1988). Especially helpful are case studies, excerpts of therapy dialogue between the deaf client and therapist, case vignettes, and therapist commentaries (Corker, 1994; Harvey, 1989; Stewart, 1981). This new literature provides the needed encouragement for practitioners to try traditional and new approaches and techniques that are known to be effective with hearing clients but have been rarely or never used with deaf clients.

The implementation of effective psychotherapeutic practices clearly depends on the therapist. The role, characteristics, attributes, attitudes, skills, and competencies of the clinician comprise the most pivotal element in the psychotherapy relationship (American Psychological Association, 1992, 1993). When therapists understand and appreciate all the differing factors that make up the disparity between themselves and their deaf clients, they are then equipped to become culturally sensitive practitioners. And by building appropriate characteristics and skills upon this sensitivity, competency can be achieved. The therapist is increasingly becoming a major focus in psychotherapy process and outcome research and in the general literature (e.g., Rutan, 1992). The following section explores those characteristics essential to successful psychotherapy with deaf clients.

Characteristics of Effective Psychotherapists

Psychotherapy is an intricate process of interaction between two complex personalities. The client seeks help with problems of an emotional nature from a trained professional who, by establishing a positive and trustworthy relationship with the client, helps the client mature and grow. Psychotherapy can also be seen as a healing process during which a psychotherapist helps a client learn new perceptions about the "self" (Amada, 1985). There have been many models and analogies used to describe the essence of psychotherapy, each deserving respectful recognition. The efficacy of psychotherapy, irrespective of theoretical orientation, depends on meaningful communication between client and therapist. Communication often is a deciding factor in the match between client and therapist.

COMMUNICATION SKILLS

A cardinal tenet in psychotherapy is for the therapist to communicate in ways that the client understands. Communication plays a pivotal role in the social chemistry or "fit" between client and therapist. Difficulty in communication drastically reduces the effectiveness of psychotherapy. In fact, communication alone can make or break psychotherapy.

In order for psychotherapy to work for a majority of deaf people, they must be accorded the rightful opportunity to use the mode of communication they prefer, usually use, and through which they best understand and are understood. It is the therapist's responsibility to follow the deaf client's communicative lead, whether expressed in sign, pantomime, gesture, body language, facial expression, speech, or any combination thereof.

It is essential for the therapist to astutely and as seamlessly as possible ascertain the client's mode of communication at the initial encounter. The therapist must never make assumptions about the communication modes that deaf clients will use. It is also important, while ascertaining the client's linguistic style, to employ vocabulary, language, and concepts within the client's conceptual sphere that are clearly understandable to the client. This involves knowing when to use or when not to use figures of speech and the like. This does not necessarily mean that they cannot be used for some clients. Rather, the therapist should have the communicative skills and the ability to "translate" them into forms that the client can comprehend. Clients who are deaf, irrespective of their communication mode and level of comprehension, do respond well to the use of colloquialisms, metaphors, similes, figures of speech, Aesopian-type examples, and axioms, which are often useful tools in psychotherapy (Isenberg, 1996), as long as they are communicated in ways the client can understand. Again, here the focus is on the therapist's competencies rather than the client's so-called shortcomings.

This compendium of the therapist's communication competencies includes an astute awareness of deaf clients' nonverbal behavior and body language. While these complement sign language very well, deaf people in general make more use of nonverbal behavior and body language, including pantomime, gesture, and facial expression. From a psychotherapy standpoint, these facilitate expression and serve as valuable indices of some of the most important conflicts, defenses, resistances, hidden meanings, and nuances. They also serve as indices of the clients' strengths, assets, and inner resources that can be marshaled to help clients with their problems.

The difficulty, failure, and pessimism reported by psychotherapists who work with deaf clients is often related to the therapists' inability to use sign language or to match the sign language used by the client. This gives rise to high levels of discomfort, stress, and fatigue for both client and therapist. Without appropriate sign language skills, it is also difficult to gain the client's confidence, arouse expectations of help, clarify whatever misconceptions the client may have of psychotherapy and the role of the therapist, and motivate the client to accept the conditions of therapy. Without fluent, smooth communication between client and therapist, there can be little or no movement into the exploratory and working-through phases of therapy. Further, the deaf client will be less apt to handle anxieties associated with recognizing and facing conflicts. This, unfortunately, is too often the case. Many deaf clients are able to express their deepest feelings and thoughts only through ASL, but these feelings and thoughts are left frustratingly unexpressed or bottled-up with a therapist who is not able to communicate in ASL.

In many psychotherapeutic situations, the deaf client is forced to accommodate the therapist's communication shortcomings or preference for signed English instead of the therapist accommodating the client's mode of communication. When clients accommodate their therapist's sign language limitations, it entails an added, superimposed, induced, exogenously generated, and unnecessary stress for both client and therapist. There is nothing more demoralizing in therapy than to feel misunderstood or to struggle to understand while already in distress. When the therapist is able to communicate with deaf clients according to their mode of communication, effectiveness and success in psychotherapy are more likely to occur than difficulties and failures.

Consumerism in psychotherapy advises that if the match between client and therapist seems to be a bad one, which is not unusual, then the client should terminate the relationship and seek a better one. A client-therapist relationship with communication difficulties is a bad match. Unfortunately, with the shortage of qualified therapists able to communicate with deaf people and competent in treating them, deaf clients often endure difficult, frustrating, unproductive, even noxious psychotherapy experiences.

On the positive side, several university-based graduate degree granting and professional preparation programs in counseling, psychology, and social work require intensive and extensive credit courses in sign language and cultural aspects of deafness. It is now considered unconscionable and irresponsible *not to* include such a requirement in the professional preparation and training programs in deafness mental health. Consequently, we can expect an increasing number of mental health professionals who are qualified and competent to work and communicate with much larger numbers of deaf people (Pollard, 1996).

THERAPIST CREDIBILITY

People who are deaf who rely on ASL or another form of sign language base their evaluation of a therapist's credibility on the therapist's fluency in sign language. For deaf clients, sign language competency is as important, if not more so, than the therapist's advanced degrees and years of clinical experience. Many deaf people are realistic in that, while they consider the therapist's understanding of Deaf culture to be desirable, this is not a competency that all therapists have. However, sign language competency and familiarity with Deaf culture enhances therapist credibility. Therapists who do not use sign language or those whose skills are inadequate are regarded with suspicion and doubt. Deaf clients are forced to tolerate this situation because they rarely have alternative choices. To deaf clients, therapists who do not sign or do not take the time, effort, and even expense to improve their sign language skills, and still call themselves specialists in deafness have no business in the field of deafness mental health.

BELIEF IN DEPATHOLOGIZING DEAFNESS

An important characteristic of effective therapists working with deaf clients is their awareness and working knowledge of the characteristics of relatively psychologically healthy, well-adjusted deaf individuals and their experience with them. Such therapists are familiar with the general criteria of mental health and their applicability to deaf people as well as to the general population. While these therapists are experts in psychopathology and treatment, they also operate from the wellness standpoint. In contrast, many therapists still adhere to the medical model or the psychopathology viewpoint of deafness and deaf people, thus potentially reducing their effectiveness with deaf clients.

Historically, research and interventions with deaf children and adults have been based on the medical, or pathology, model (Marschark, 1993; Paul & Jackson, 1993; Schlesinger & Meadow, 1972; Vernon & Andrews, 1990). When psychology and psychiatry entered the field of deafness, they characteristically applied the psychopathological perspective (Myklebust, 1960; Rainer et al., 1963). Emphasis was placed on dysfunction, disability, deficit, and deviance. Psychologists with this viewpoint can give an impressive discourse on psychopathology, but might have difficulty when asked to describe a healthy deaf personality. The field of deafness for too long has been preoccupied with what is *wrong* with deaf people rather than with what is *right* with them. This unfortunate preoccupation with pathology leads to a distorted view of deaf people and the deaf community.

There are vastly more well-adjusted, psychologically healthy, and effective deaf people than there are not. These deaf individuals are busy living productive, eventful, and generally satisfying lives (Lane et al., 1996). They are adaptively and effectively dealing and coping with the everyday problems of living. Many professional people have never seen these deaf individuals, nor are they aware of their existence. Having a standard or a model against which to measure a deaf individual for psychological health, personal effectiveness, and adjustment—all within the context of the deaf person's life, culture, group membership, socioeconomic status, communication persuasion, and social opportunities and constraints—is critical for therapists working with deaf clients in terms of truly comprehending how psychologically healthy deaf individuals may manifest themselves. After all, psychopathology can only be appropriately interpreted within the context of normality (Offer & Sabshin, 1991).

The Wellness Model

In the process of depathologizing and normalizing deafness, we should follow the lead of Abraham Maslow (1968), who was instrumental in developing the humanistic trend in psychology. Criticizing the early Freudian preoccupation with the sick and crippled side of human nature, he contended that if we base our findings on a sick population, we will have a sick psychology. Too much attention has been given to hostility, aggression, neuroses, and immaturities; likewise, too little attention has been given to love, creativity, joy, and "peak experiences" (Maslow, 1968).

This humanistic view of human nature has significant implications for the development of wellness models (Myers, 1991; Offer & Sabshin, 1991; Seeman, 1989) as well as the practice of psychotherapy in general and with deaf people in particular. It is based on the belief that the individual has an inherent capacity to move away from maladjustment toward psychological health. Seeing deaf people in this light means that the therapist focuses on the constructive side of human nature, on what is right with the deaf client, and on the assets the client brings to therapy, in addition to the reasons for referral. Therapy therefore becomes more than a process of diagnosis and treatment of psychological disorders. It becomes a process of growth that proceeds according to the client's capabilities and potential.

Wellness models that are based on sociocultural components that enhance the psychological integrity of deaf people can also serve as primary and secondary preventive mental health guides in psychotherapy. These models focus on normality within the paradigms of deafness.

VALIDATING DEAF CLIENTS' EXPERIENCES

Because the condition of deafness often forms the crux of therapy sessions, the therapist has to recognize that deafness itself denotes the physical inability to hear. It becomes a handicap due to the limitations and restrictions society places on the deaf person. Deafness seen as a handicap is akin to racism, sexism, and other "isms" associated with minority groups, and as such lends itself to stereotypical responses on the part of society in general. "Handicappism" was first coined in 1978, and is the most pervasive mental health problem confronting deaf individuals (Sachs, 1978). It is not endemic to the deaf community. It is generated, operated, and perpetuated by the nondeaf community and its institutions. Even in this day of enlightenment, Deaf people endure daily insults, often from early childhood. Thus the oft-quoted statement by deaf people to the effect that rather than the hearing disability per se, the attitudes of society toward deaf people is the handicapping factor (Williams & Sussman, 1971).

These stereotypical attitudes can have a telling effect on the deaf individual's psychological makeup and integrity. It is not surprising that the handicapping aspect of deafness is a common theme in psychotherapy with many deaf clients. Given this context of "handicappism," it is therefore imperative for the therapist not only to have an understanding of deafness, but also sensitivity to societal attitudes toward deaf people as experienced by the deaf client. The therapist must avoid stereotypical pictures of deafness and focus on the individual within. Conversely, hearing therapists must be aware of possible transference reactions by deaf clients because such therapists may symbolize or represent the population group responsible for the negative attitudes and behaviors experienced by the client (Harvey, 1996). Many deaf individuals have developed a way of life that dismisses the existence of a handicap, a way that is self-validating. Therapists need to understand and respect this. With this understanding, these therapists and their clients should be able to productively work through the clients' confrontations with handicappism.

REFUSAL TO LABEL DEAF CLIENTS

Labeling deaf clients according to imputed deficits is a form of scapegoating. An oft-used and abused label, concocted by rehabilitation professionals in the field of deafness, is the "low-functioning deaf person" (Long & Alvares, 1995). This label was created to classify deaf people with developmental disabilities purportedly for placement in appropriate rehabilitation evaluation, training, and sheltered workshop programs. Unfortunately, this label became a semantic convenience, a wastebasket category assuming a life of its own in the process of diagnosing otherwise normal deaf individuals with whom professionals had difficulty communicating and working. These individuals may not have had a complete education. They may have come from culturally disadvantaged environments and may have low reading and writing skills. Nevertheless, they might possess average or better intelligence. Importantly, they are largely fluent in their own form of ASL. Labeling these people as "low-functioning" has been damaging in more ways than one, and it has become a cloak behind which therapists hide their lack of competencies and skills.

The issue here is whether such labels as "low-functioning deaf person" or "impossible client" are justifiable much of the time. A large number of deaf clients have demonstrated their responsiveness to psychotherapy. Deaf clients are not necessarily impossible. At present, the "low-functioning" label is gradually being replaced by the term "traditionally underserved" that Duffy (this volume) defines in a more positive frame. Her approach in providing psychotherapeutic services to this population is based on the premise by Duncan, Hubble, and Miller (1997) that success can occur even with the most challenging and difficult cases when conditions of effective psychotherapy are present.

Perhaps due to the passion for classification in our society, another unfortunate label is used in education, rehabilitation, and mental health to describe and group those deaf people with "minimal language skills" (MLS). An unfortunate misnomer, MLS all too often refers to those deaf individuals with minimal English skills, while ignoring other language skills, such as ASL, that they might possess. MLS is often used by therapists as a reason for difficulty or failure in psychotherapy with deaf clients. However, it is the therapists who may not possess the necessary language skills to match the linguistic needs of these "MLS" deaf clients. They have been sardonically labeled as "MSLS" therapists: therapists with Minimal Sign Language Skills. They are the ones who are linguistically incompetent in this context.

The various client labels used to exonerate the therapist's contribution to difficulties and failures in psychotherapy are harmful in two ways. The first is that the client can become worse off from experiencing frustration, disappointment, stress, and a sense of incompleteness in such a relationship with the therapist. The second is the attitude conveyed to deaf clients that therapy is not successful because of their shortcomings and liabilities. If fortunate enough, these clients may be referred to or find therapists who can undo this psychological damage.

RECOGNIZING COUNTERTRANSFERENCE ISSUES

Recent literature increasingly recognizes the importance of the therapist's characteristics, attributes, role, and contributions to the therapeutic process. Of particular interest is the psychology of the therapist (Goldberg, 1991; Roth, 1990; M. B. Sussman, 1992). The classic definition of *countertransference* is a therapist's unconscious emotional response to a client that is likely to interfere with objectivity. Unresolved conflicts and attitudes of the therapist are projected onto the client (Corey, 1996). Countertransference has been attributed as a cause in relationship difficulties between therapist and client and may as a consequence influence process and outcome. Contemporary approaches view countertransference as an inevitable product of the therapeutic interaction that can be used constructively and as an important means of understanding the therapist, as well as the client (M. B. Sussman, 1992).

The extent to which countertransference is managed depends on a therapist's clinical astuteness, understanding of deafness and its cultural aspects, and, of course, sign language competency. Some therapists do recognize the crucial factor of countertransference and its management in psychotherapy with deaf clients (Harvey, 1996, 1997). Other therapists may continue to experience difficulty in psychotherapy with deaf clients due to unaddressed and unresolved countertransference reactions and hence may engage in the scapegoating of deaf clients' characteristics and limitations. These therapists should look to the possibility of countertransference as a cause of the difficulty of therapy with deaf clients. Incidentally, countertransference reactions are not limited to hearing therapists working with deaf clients. There are deaf therapists with countertransference issues of their own that often are manifested during sessions with their deaf clients, as noted by Leigh and Lewis (this volume).

The personal qualities and style of the therapist seem to have a more significant effect on therapeutic outcome than the therapist's particular theoretical orientation to psychótherapy (Lambert & Bergin, 1994; Wolberg, 1982) and cannot be underestimated in the countertransference process. The therapist's personality and attitude toward deaf clients, their clients' hearing status, and deafness in general is crucial to the social chemistry of the relationship between therapist and client and the therapeutic outcome. Characteristics that may influence the process of change and thus therapeutic outcome are nonpossessive warmth, friendliness, genuineness, interpersonal style, beliefs, values, and attitudes.

These personal qualities have special meaning in the practice of psychotherapy with deaf clients. They would encompass, for example, a willingness to learn about deafness and deaf people and about what it means to exist as a deaf person; unconditional positive regard for deaf clients no matter what their limitations are, including their difficulties with the English language or their inability to use speech; acceptance of the clients' sign language or mode of communication as part of the clients' being and existence; freedom from traditional, stereotypic, negative, and derogatory attitudes toward deaf individuals; the ability to see deaf clients as people with worth and value; and an understanding and respect for deaf clients' values, even though they may be at variance with those of the therapist. Above all, therapists should be aware of their own feelings, biases, blind spots, and limitations (that may delay, interfere with, or impede progress in therapy), rather than yield to temptations to blame all problems and difficulties in psychotherapy on the deaf client. With these attributes in the picture, the chances for inimical countertransference reactions are lessened or at least become more recognizable and manageable.

AVOIDING BURNOUT

It is important to recognize that burnout is a potential occupational hazard in the profession of psychotherapy in general (Farber & Heifetz, 1982) and in work with deaf clients in particular (Heller et al., 1986). Burnout is a state of emotional exhaustion, depersonalization, and reduced personal satisfaction that is experienced by professionals whose work involves helping others with their problems (Maslach & Jackson, 1986). Rather than having a single cause, burnout results from a combination of factors—individual, interpersonal, and organizational, manifesting itself through various symptoms.

Few studies have been done on the incidence of burnout among psychotherapists. However, we note that some therapists leave the field of deafness mental health and continue to practice therapy with nondeaf clients. This is a defection from deafness mental health, not mental health in general, that may be attributed to the fact that these professionals find work with deaf people too demanding or too challenging, or that they lack the personal characteristics or flexibility in communication styles that render them suitable for work with deaf clients. Perhaps they are also dealing with some of the "savior" type syndromes referred to in Hoffmeister & Harvey (1996) that collide with the reality of providing services to deaf clients in general.

BELIEF AND FAITH IN MODE OF THERAPY

Contemporary accounts of therapeutic schools and approaches reveal a plethora of different types of psychotherapy (Wolberg, 1995). Whether therapists consider themselves psychodynamic, existential, gestaltist, behavioral, cognitive, rational-emotional, constructivist, eclectic, or integrative, they all believe in their approach and, given favorable conditions, achieve favorable results: clients get relief and are often enough cured of their difficulties (Patterson & Hidore, 1997). Allegiance to a specific theoretical orientation or approach appears necessary for the confidence and professional identity of the therapist (Karasu, 1996).

In the 1960s, experts in deafness mental health believed that deaf clients were not suitable for various modes of psychotherapy because of their limitations and other characteristics. This belief is largely responsible for the inordinately slow progress in the practice of psychotherapy with deaf people. Therapists who worked with deaf and hearing clients would apply a double standard—using their preferred mode of therapy with hearing clients but, with deaf clients, abandoning that mode for approaches that were outmoded, ineffectual, and possibly harmful. This double standard resulted in therapeutic failure with deaf clients "even in the hands of highly skilled therapists" (Rainer et al., 1963; Vernon, 1967).

Today we know that deaf people in general, like their hearing counterparts, respond to and benefit from various modes of psychotherapy. Therapists who possess the characteristics, competencies, and skills necessary for effective psychotherapy with deaf clients use their preferred mode of therapy with all of their clients, thus maximizing the chances for effective outcomes.

LEARNING FROM FAILURE

All therapists experience some degree of failure in their work (Kottler & Blau, 1989). This can range from a minor misjudgment to the premature termination of therapy or the unsuccessful outcome of a case. Common sense tells us that failure in therapy is sometimes a function of the client, sometimes a function of the psychotherapist, and sometimes both. While it is easy to blame deaf clients' unwillingness to change as the cause of failure, many therapy failures occur because of the therapist's limitations. However, of the various factors that cause failure in psychotherapy, the one that can be remedied most easily is the therapist (Chessick, 1971).

One of the essential characteristics for a successful therapist is the willingness to admit mistakes (Corey, 1996). As Fritz Perls contends, one never learns from one's successes but only from one's failures. Although therapists should not be overburdened with guilt over how they could or should have acted, they learn from mistakes, either by themselves or with the assistance of colleagues or supervisors. An abiding consolation is that there is much to learn from critical reviews of one's therapeutic work with deaf clients.

EMPATHY

The term *empathy* derives from the German word *Einfühlung*, implying a "feeling oneself into" another's experience (Jenkins, 1997; Korchin, 1976; Margulies, 1989). It refers to the ability to "put oneself in another person's shoes" emotionally, while maintaining one's own identity and perspective. In psychotherapy, empathy can mean different things, but all definitions include the therapist's efforts to sense, perceive, share, or conceptualize how another person experiences the world (Bohart & Greenberg, 1997).

Therapeutic empathy consists of an attitude or stance toward the client, including regard for the client, a genuine respect for the client's point of view, and a belief that there is validity to clients' feelings, behaviors, and experience when seen from their frames of reference. Empathy occurs when therapists directly perceive and experience the client in relationship to themselves, themselves in relationship to the client, and the relationship itself. Thus, therapists' communicative as well as attitudinal capacities play crucial roles in their attempts to enter the psychological world of people who are different from themselves (Bohart & Greenberg, 1997). Deaf clients report higher levels of empathic understanding among deaf therapists than hearing therapists (Brauer, 1979). This finding points to the need for hearing therapists to recognize the different valid cultural ways of addressing life problems. As Karl Meninger pointed out in 1952:

> The psychiatrist as a person is more important than the psychiatrist as a technician or scientist. What he *is* has more effect upon his patient than anything he *does*. Because of the intimate relationship between patient and psychiatrist, the value systems, standards, interests, and ideals of the doctor becomes important. (quoted in Wolberg, 1982, p. 366)

JUDICIOUS USE OF HUMOR

Having a sense of humor and being able to use humor in psychotherapy are important characteristics of effective therapists (Corey, 1996). Having a sense of humor enables a therapist to put problems and imperfections in perspective. Effective therapists know how, when, and where to use humor with clients. Some go as far as to maintain that therapy tends to fail when, among other things, the therapist fails to use humor.

There is much within the deaf population that lends itself to humor. Deaf culture, for instance, is a virtual cornucopia of humor. This is attested to by the growing number of publications relating to humor and deafness (see Glickman, 1986; Holcomb, 1985). These accounts and compilations recount anecdotes, jokes, blunders, and *faux pas* made by deaf as well as hearing people in relation to deafness. They poke fun both at deaf and hearing people. This literature on deafness and humor can, along with training and experience, educate and sensitize therapists about some of the life experiences of deaf people and thus enhance their effectiveness with deaf clients.

Psychotherapy and Interpreters

Using a sign language interpreter in psychotherapy sessions with deaf people has a direct impact on the therapeutic process (Leigh et al., 1996). The use of an interpreter facilitates communication when the therapist lacks the requisite sign language skills. It also may convey to the client the therapist's acceptance of the reality of their mutual communication difficulties, as well as the therapist's sincere desire to understand and to be understood freely. There are, however, aspects that noticeably alter or hinder therapy.

Recent research calls into question the traditional assumption that it is possible for the interpreter to function as a neutral, passive conduit. Metzger (1999) indicates that interpreter neutrality is a myth. This is now reflected in interpreter-training programs that focus on the ways interpreters influence interaction.

Astute therapists have known for a long time that interpreters, despite their professionalism, skills, and efforts at neutrality, nevertheless influence the psychotherapeutic process and outcome. The therapist needs to be aware of this natural occurrence and utilize it appropriately. Therapists who have used interpreters acknowledge that it dilutes and distorts the usual one-to-one relationship, especially because of the loss of visual contact between therapist and client. The shift of attention from both sides to the interpreter delimits the influence of the therapist's personal characteristics and technical skills on the therapeutic relationship and prevents the therapist from integrating the client's nonverbal behavior with what is being said simultaneously due to interpreter lag. Moreover, there is always the potential problem of the interpreter being the central focus of the triadic relationship. As Wohl puts it, "the therapy itself requires a substantially shared language and the interaction of the participants alone together. The interpreter's presence creates a triangular situation with many potential complications" (1995, p. 81).

An additional complication is the fact that health insurance for psychotherapy usually does not cover interpreter fees. Further, depending on location, deaf clients and therapists are often hard-pressed to recruit a highly skilled or certified interpreter for the psychotherapy situation. Interpreting in psychotherapy is one of the most challenging and formidable tasks for the interpreter. Hence, it takes only the very best of interpreters with top-notch voice and sign skills. There are many competent interpreters with appropriate certification and expertise, but only a minority have the "right stuff" to be interpreters in the psychotherapy setting.

This is not to be construed as a polemic against the use of interpreters in therapy. While a one-to-one relationship with a fully communicating therapist is ideal and preferred by deaf people, realistic recognition is given to the fact that the day is still distant when deaf people will have a sufficient number of fully qualified therapists. Deaf individuals themselves acknowledge that in locations where fully communicating therapists are still in short supply or nonexistent, they would accept interpreted access to psychotherapy (Steinberg et al., this volume). Deaf people may be tolerant of the therapist who has just begun to work with deaf clients and generally do tolerate the temporary use of interpreters while the therapist undergoes training in sign language, particularly of the type appropriate to psychotherapy. Such therapists are expected, in due time, to gain mastery sufficient to strike out on their own without an interpreter. Without the crutch of an interpreter, these therapists cannot help but increase their mastery of sign language and thereby enhance their credibility as service providers.

Technical Competence

Competency in psychotherapy with deaf people is not achieved simply through academic psychological training, medical training, postgraduate training in psychotherapy, or in terms of degrees, certification, licensure, or diploma status. Psychotherapists who treat deaf clients must also possess skills over and above those normally required for their respective disciplines. This involves specialized, additional, and supplementary education and training and clinical supervision. Such training for mental health professionals working with deaf individuals should include the competencies outlined in figure 1.

TRAINING NEEDS FOR MENTAL HEALTH PROFESSIONALS

1. A thorough pedagogical grounding in the historical, educational, social, cultural, linguistic, vocational, economic, and demographic aspects of deafness, with emphasis on the heterogeneity and diversity of the deaf population. This includes a working knowledge of the psychologically healthy, well-adjusted deaf individual.

2. Successful completion of studies in the psychological, developmental, and mental health aspects of deafness, involving all life stages from infancy to old age.

3. Principles, practices, and approaches in psychological evaluation and psychodiagnostics with deaf children and adults.

4. Principles, practices, and approaches in psychotherapy with deaf children and adults, including application of current theoretical orientations in working with deaf clients.

5. Principles, practices, and approaches in crisis intervention with deaf individuals.

6. Supervision by or consultation with a psychotherapist, preferably deaf, experienced in psychotherapy with deaf clients. This is best done by watching videotapes, observing client-therapist interaction through a two-way mirror, consulting meetings, and case conferences. Supervision sessions make it possible for countertransference issues to be addressed.

7. Professional development based on attendance at continuing education programs, training institutes, seminars, and workshops, and active participation in professional organizations in the field of deafness.

8. Communication competence in the broad communicative spectrum presented in deaf clients, from exclusively oral communication to American Sign Language. In between there is a dizzying array of variations and combinations, often influenced by geographical, educational, socioeconomic, ethnic, and cultural factors. These variations require that the therapist develop a working knowledge of the historical, philosophical, developmental, psychosocial, attitudinal, and linguistic aspects and implications of communication modes used by deaf individuals from all walks of life. This versatility renders the therapist accessible to a much larger number of deaf children and adults.

Figure 1. Training Needs

Some Caveats

While the number of mental health service programs for deaf people in the United States has grown, such programs remain in short supply, particularly in the more sparsely populated areas (Willigan & King, 1992). Budget cuts, reduction in services, and the closing of some programs serve only to accentuate this problem. But the most telling problem is the acute shortage of therapists who are competent to work and communicate with deaf individuals. Many of the existing programs are in state hospitals. They cater to the very disturbed and mentally ill, many of whom are in custodial care. There remains a general neglect of deaf individuals who are not disturbed enough to be hospitalized but who nonetheless are in need of psychotherapy and are likely to benefit from it (Pollard, 1994). These deaf people need psychotherapy to keep themselves out of the hospital, and they represent the majority of deaf people in need of outpatient preventive and rehabilitative mental health services. The consequences of this shortage of services are cases of misdiagnoses, nontreatment, improper treatment, malpractice, and clients committing suicide.

A majority of mental health services provided to deaf people via a public agency or private practice are by managed health care organizations. It is the organizations themselves that often credential or "qualify" mental health professionals to provide therapy to patients. The basis for selection is often on specific educational requirements and licensure in the discipline. Very little screening, if any, is involved in assigning therapists to deaf clients. Interpreters usually are not provided for those therapists lacking sign language skills.

One of the results of this shortage of therapists and programs is the prescription of psychotropic medication without psychotherapy or referral to an appropriate therapist competent to treat deaf people. While medication can and does facilitate treatment where it is clearly indicated, it should not be used as a substitute for psychotherapy. The deaf client must be given to understand that while medication may offer symptom relief, it does not solve problems and it is not a magic pill. Ideally, when medication is indicated, it is employed in tandem with psychotherapy, and the medication aspect of treatment should be under the supervision of a psychiatrist if psychotherapy is provided by a nonmedical therapist.

Concluding Remarks

Despite inherent problems associated with the practice of psychotherapy in general, such as the constraints imposed by managed health care, we believe these are exciting times in the profession of psychotherapy with deaf people. It is especially rewarding to us, as psychotherapists, teachers, clinical supervisors, and mentors in psychotherapy, to witness firsthand the steady growth in the number of competent and skilled therapists in the field of deafness mental health. Particularly encouraging is the greater and wider representation of the various theoretical orientations and approaches in psychotherapy, thus enabling an even larger number of deaf individuals to gain access.

In order to advance the practice of psychotherapy with deaf clients, it is essential to gain a clear understanding of the therapist's characteristics and competencies and the pivotal role these play in effective psychotherapy with deaf clients. The mark of successful therapists is not that their clients stay forever, but that they leave with what they came to acquire. This means that deaf clients are getting the most out of psychotherapy. Further, the practice of psychotherapy with deaf people can be a creative endeavor, one in which psychotherapists can grow and transform themselves.

As a final comment, here is an excerpt from M. B. Sussman's book, *A Curious Calling: Unconscious Motivations for Practicing Psychotherapy:*

> Therapists may be forgiven if at times they look back wistfully on the days when the clinical focus was squarely on the client, and the psychodynamics of the therapist were largely overlooked.... Nostalgia aside, those of us who choose to practice psychotherapy can no longer afford not to explore our own motivations to heal. Our opening questions to clients—"What brings you here"—must be posed to ourselves as well. Granted, this does not come easily. And that is why it is best that the role of psychotherapist remain a calling, and not just a vocation. (1992, p. 259)

References

Amada, G. (1985). *A guide to psychotherapy.* Lanham, MD: Madison Books.

American Psychological Association. (1992). Ethical principles of psychologists and code of conduct. *American Psychologist, 47,* 1597–1611.

———. (1993). Guidelines for providers of psychological services to ethnic, linguistic, and culturally diverse populations. *American Psychologist, 48,* 45–48.

Anderson, G. B., & Watson, D. (Eds.). (1985). *Counseling deaf people: Research and practice.* Little Rock, AR: Arkansas Rehabilitation Research and Training Center on Deafness and Hearing Impairment, University of Arkansas.

Best, H. (1943). *Deafness and the deaf in the United States.* New York: Macmillan.

Beutler, L. E., Machado, P. P. P., & Neufeldt, S. A. (1994). Therapist variables. In A. E. Bergin & S. L. Garfield (Eds.), *Handbook of psychotherapy and behavior change* (4th ed.) (pp. 229–269). New York: Wiley.

Bohart, A. C., & Greenberg, L. S. (1997). Empathy: Where are we and where do we go from here? In A. C. Bohart & L. S. Greenberg (Eds.), *Empathy reconsidered: New directions in psychotherapy* (pp. 419–449). Washington, DC: American Psychological Association.

Brauer, B. A. (1979). The dimensions of perceived interview relationship as influenced by deaf persons' self-concepts and interviewer attributes as deaf or nondeaf. Abstract in *Dissertation Abstracts International, 40* (3-B), 1352.

———. (1980). Perspectives on psychotherapy with deaf persons. *Mental Health in Deafness, Experimental Issue, NIMH, 4,* 4–8.

Brauer, B. A., Braden, J. P., Pollard, R. Q., & Hardy-Braz, S. T. (1999). Hearing. In J. H. Sandoval (Ed.), *Test interpretation and diversity: Achieving equity in psychological assessment* (pp. 297–315). Washington, DC: American Psychological Association.

Brauer, B. A., & Sussman, A. E. (1980). Experiences of deaf therapists with deaf clients. *Mental Health in Deafness, Experimental Issue, NIMH, 4,* 9–13.

Chessick, R. D. (1971). *Why psychotherapists fail.* New York: Science House.

Corey, G. (1996). *Theory and practice of counseling and psychotherapy* (5th ed.). Pacific Grove, CA: Brooks/Cole.

Corker, M. (1994). *Counseling—the deaf challenge.* London: Jessica Kingsley.

Duncan, B. L., Hubble, M. A., & Miller, S. D. (1997). *Psychotherapy with "impossible" cases.* New York: W. W. Norton.

Engler, J., & Goleman, D. (1992). *The consumer's guide to psychotherapy.* New York: Simon and Schuster.

Erting, C. J., Johnson, R. C., Smith, D. L., & Snider, B. D. (Eds.). (1994). *The deaf way: Perspectives from the international conference on Deaf culture.* Washington, DC: Gallaudet University Press.

Farber, B. A., & Heifetz, L. J. (1982). The process and dimensions of burnout in psychotherapists. *Professional Psychology, 13,* 293–301.

Glickman, K. P. (1986). *Deafinitions for signlets.* Silver Spring, MD: DiKen Products.

Glickman, N. S. (1996). The development of culturally deaf identities. In N. S. Glickman & M.A. Harvey (Eds.), *Culturally affirmative psychotherapy with Deaf persons* (pp. 115–153). Mahwah, NJ: Lawrence Erlbaum.

Goldberg, C. (1991). *On being a psychotherapist.* Northvale, NJ: Jason Aronson.

Goldenberg, M. M. (1990). *Pharmacology for the psychotherapist.* Muncie, IN: Accelerated Developments.

Gough, D. L. (1990). Rational-emotive therapy: A cognitive-behavioral approach to working with hearing impaired clients. *Journal of Rehabilitation of the Deaf, 23* (3), 96–104.

Harvey, M. A. (1989). *Psychotherapy with deaf and hard-of-hearing persons: A systemic model.* Hillsdale, NJ: Lawrence Erlbaum.

———. (1996). Utilization of traumatic transference by a hearing therapist. In N. S. Glickman & M. A. Harvey (Eds.), *Culturally affirmative psychotherapy with Deaf persons* (pp. 155–167). Mahwah, NJ: Lawrence Erlbaum.

———. (1997). Utilization of a traumatic transference by a hearing therapist. *Journal of the American Deafness and Rehabilitation Association, 30* (2 and 3), 1–8.

Heller, B., Langholtz, D., & Acree, M. (1986). Effective psychotherapy with deaf persons: Therapist and client characteristics. In D. Watson, G. B. Anderson, & M. Taff-Watson (Eds.), *Integrating human resources, technology, and systems in deafness, Monograph No. 13* (pp. 46–74). Silver Spring, MD: American Deafness and Rehabilitation Association.

Herink, R. (Ed.). (1980). *The psychotherapy handbook.* New York: New American Library.

Hoffmeister, R., & Harvey, M. (1996). Is there a psychology of the hearing? In N. S. Glickman & M. A. Harvey (Eds.), *Culturally affirmative psychotherapy with Deaf persons* (pp. 73–97). Mahwah, NJ: Lawrence Erlbaum.

Holcomb, R. (1985). *Silence is golden, sometimes.* Berkeley: Dawn Sign Press.

Isenberg, G. (1996). Storytelling and the use of culturally appropriate metaphors in psychotherapy with deaf people. In N. S. Glickman & M. A. Harvey (Eds.), *Culturally affirmative psychotherapy with Deaf persons* (pp. 169–183). Mahwah, NJ: Lawrence Erlbaum.

Jenkins, A. H. (1997). The empathic context in psychotherapy with people of color. In A. C. Bohart & L. S. Greenberg (Eds.), *Empathy reconsidered: New directions in psychotherapy* (pp. 321–341). Washington, DC: American Psychological Association.

Karasu, T. B. (1996). *Deconstruction of psychotherapy.* Northvale, NJ: Jason Aronson.

Kassau, L. D. (1996). *Shrink rap.* Northvale, NJ: Jason Aronson.

Kleinke, C. L. (1994). *Common principles of psychotherapy.* Pacific Grove, CA: Wadsworth.

Korchin, S. J. (1976). *Modern clinical psychology.* New York: Basic Books.

Kottler, J. A., & Blau, D. S. (1989). *The imperfect therapist.* San Francisco: Jossey-Bass.

Kottler, J. A., & Hazler, R. J. (1997). *What you never learned in graduate school.* New York: W. W. Norton.

Lambert, M. J., & Bergin, A. E. (1994). The effectiveness of psychotherapy. In A. E. Bergin & S. L. Garfield (Eds.), *Handbook of psychotherapy and behavior change* (4th ed.) (pp. 143–189). New York: Wiley.

Lane, H., Hoffmeister, R., & Bahan, B. (1996). *A journey into the Deaf-world.* San Diego: Dawn Sign Press.

Lazarus, A. A., & Beutler, L. E. (1993). On technical eclecticism. *Journal of Counseling and Development, 7* (4), 381–385.

Lefcourt, H. M., & Davidson-Katz, K. (1991). The role of humor and the self. In C. R. Snyder & D. R. Forsyth (Eds.), *Handbook of social and clinical psychology* (pp. 41–46). New York: Pergamon.

Leigh, I. W. (1991). Deaf therapists: Impact on treatment. In *Proceedings of the eleventh world congress of the World Federation of the Deaf: Equality and self-reliance* (pp. 290–297). Tokyo: World Federation of the Deaf.

Leigh, I. W., Corbett, C. A., Gutman, V., & Morere, D. A. (1996). Providing psychological services to deaf individuals: A response to new perceptions of diversity. *Professional Psychology, 27,* 364–371.

Levin, F. M. (1981). Insight-oriented psychotherapy with the deaf. In L. K. Stein, E. G. Mindel & T. Jabaley (Eds.), *Deafness and mental health* (pp. 113–132). New York: Grune and Stratton.

Levine, E. S. (1960). *The psychology of deafness.* New York: Columbia University Press.

Long, G., & Alvares, R. (1995). The development of a communication assessment paradigm for use with traditionally underserved deaf adults. *Journal of the American Deafness and Rehabilitation Association, 29,* 1–16.

Margulies, A. (1989). *The empathic imagination.* New York: W. W. Norton.

Marschark, M. (1993). *The psychological development of deaf children.* New York: Oxford University Press.

Maslach, C., & Jackson, S. E. (1986). *Maslach Burnout Inventory Manual* (2d ed.). Palo Alto: Consulting Psychologists Press.

Maslow, A. (1968). *Toward a psychology of being* (rev. ed.). New York: Van Nostrand Reinhold.

Metzger, M. (1999). *Sign language interpreting: Deconstructing the myth of neutrality.* Washington, DC: Gallaudet University Press.

Moores, D. F. (1996). *Educating the deaf: Psychology, principles and practices.* Boston: Houghton Mifflin.

Mosak, H. H. (1987). *Ha ha and aha: The role of humor in psychotherapy.* Muncie, IN: Accelerated Development.

Myers, J. E. (1991). Wellness as *the* paradigm for counseling and development: The possible future. *Counselor Education and Supervision, 30* (3), 183–193.

Myklebust, H. (1960). *The psychology of deafness.* New York: Grune and Stratton.

Offer, D., & Sabshin, M. (Eds.). (1991). *The diversity of normal behavior.* New York: Basic Books.

Padden, C. (1980). The deaf community and the culture of deaf people. In C. Baker & R. Battison (Eds.), *Sign language and the deaf community* (pp. 89–103). Silver Spring, MD: National Association of the Deaf.

Padden, C., & Humphries, T. (1988). *Deaf in America: Voices from a culture.* Cambridge, MA: Harvard University Press.

Patterson, C. H., & Hidore, S. (1997). *Successful psychotherapy.* Northvale, NJ: Jason Aronson.

Paul, P., & Jackson, D. (1993). *Toward a psychology of deafness: Theoretical and empirical perspectives.* Boston: Allyn and Bacon.

Pollard, R. Q. (1994). Public mental health services and diagnostic trends regarding individuals who are deaf or hard of hearing. *Rehabilitation Psychology, 39,* 147–160.

———. (1996). Professional psychology and deaf people: The emergence of a discipline. *American Psychologist, 51,* 389–396.

Rainer, J. D., Altshuler, K. Z., Kallmann, F. J., & Deming, W. E. (Eds.). (1963). *Family and mental health problems in a deaf population.* New York: New York State Psychiatric Institute.

Rayson, B. C. (1985). Psychodynamic psychotherapy with deaf clients. In G. B. Anderson & D. Watson (Eds.), *Counseling deaf people: Research and practice* (pp. 123–144). Little Rock, AR: Arkansas Rehabilitation Research and Training Center on Deafness and Hearing Impairment, University of Arkansas.

Richman, J. (1996). Points of correspondence between humor and psychotherapy. *Psychotherapy, 33* (4), 560–566.

Roth, S. (1990). *Psychotherapy: The art of wooing nature.* Northvale, NJ: Jason Aronson.

Rutan, J. S. (1992). *Psychotherapy for the 1990s.* New York: Guilford Press.

Sachs, B. (1978). The mental health needs of deaf Americans: Report of the special populations subpanel on mental health of physically handicapped Americans. Report of the Task Panel on Special Populations: Minorities, Women, Physically Handicapped (Report No. PCMH/P-78/14). In *Task Panel Reports Submitted to the President's Commission on Mental Health. Vol. III, Appendix.* Washington, DC: U.S. Government Printing Office.

Schlesinger, H., & Meadow, K. (1972). *Sound and sign: Childhood deafness and mental health.* Berkeley: University of California Press.

Seeman, J. (1989). Toward a model of positive health. *American Psychologist, 44,* 1099–1109.

Stewart, L. G. (1981). Counseling the deaf client. In L. K. Stein, E. G. Mindel, & T. Jabaley (Eds.), *Deafness and mental health* (pp. 133–159). New York: Grune and Stratton.

Stokoe, W. (1978). *Sign language structure.* Silver Spring, MD: Linstok Press.

———. (1989). Dimensions of difference: ASL and English based cultures. In S. Wilcox (Ed.), *American Deaf culture: An anthology* (pp. 49–60). Silver Spring, MD: Linstok Press.

Sussman, A. E. (1988). Approaches in counseling and psychotherapy revisited. In D. Watson, G. Long, M. Taff-Watson, & M. Harvey (Eds.), *Two decades of excellence 1967–1987: A foundation for the future* (pp. 2–15). Little Rock, AR: American Deafness and Rehabilitation Association.

———. (1990). Let the buyer beware. *Gallaudet Today, 20* (3), 22–29.

———. (1992). *Characteristics of the well-adjusted deaf person.* Keynote address presented at the Statewide Conference on Deafness and Hard of Hearing, Raleigh, North Carolina.

Sussman, A. E., & Brauer, B. A. (1981). Epilogue. In E. S. Levine (Ed.), *The ecology of early deafness* (pp. 349–351). New York: Columbia University Press.

Sussman, A. E., & Stewart, L. G. (Eds.). (1971). *Counseling with deaf people.* New York: New York Deafness and Research Training Center, New York University School of Education.

Sussman, M. B. (1992). *A curious calling: Unconscious motivations for practicing psychotherapy.* Northvale, NJ: Jason Aronson.

———. (Ed.). (1995). *A perilous calling: The hazards of psychotherapy practice.* New York: Wiley.

Szaz, T. S. (1973). *The second sin.* Garden City, NJ: Anchor Press.

Vernon, M. (1967). Counseling the deaf client. *Journal of Rehabilitation of the Adult Deaf, 1* (2), 3–16.

———. (1971). Current status in counseling with deaf people. In A. E. Sussman & L. G. Stewart (Eds.), *Counseling with deaf people* (pp. 30–42). New York: New York Deafness and Research Training Center, New York University School of Education.

Vernon, M., & J. Andrews. (1990). *Psychology of deafness.* New York: Longman.

Weiner, I. B. (1975). *Principles of psychotherapy.* New York: Wiley.

Williams, B. R., & Sussman, A. E. (1971). Social and psychological problems of deaf people. In A. E. Sussman & L. G. Stewart (Eds.), *Counseling with deaf people* (pp. 13–29). New York: New York Deafness and Research Training Center, New York University School of Education.

Willigan, B. A., & King, S. J. (Eds.). (1992). *Mental health services for deaf people: 1992 edition.* Washington, DC: Gallaudet Research Institute, Mental Health Research Program, Gallaudet University.

Wohl, J. (1995). Traditional individual psychotherapy and ethnic minorities. In J. F. Aponte, R. Y. Rivers, & J. Wohl (Eds.), *Psychological interventions and cultural diversity* (pp. 74–91). Boston: Allyn and Bacon.

Wohl, J., & Aponte, J. F. (1995). Common themes and future prospects. In J. F. Aponte, R. Y. Rivers, & J. Wohl (Eds.), *Psychological interventions and cultural diversity* (pp. 301–316). Boston: Allyn and Bacon.

Wolberg, L. R. (1982). *The practice of psychotherapy.* New York: Brunner/Mazel.

———. (1995). *The technique of psychotherapy.* Northvale, NJ: Jason Aronson.

2

The Diversity of Consumer Knowledge, Attitudes, Beliefs, and Experiences: Recent Findings

ANNIE G. STEINBERG, RUTH C. LOEW,
AND VICKI JOY SULLIVAN

Attitudes toward health care influence the ways in which individuals in any community seek, utilize, and benefit from services. Consequently, the provision of accessible and compassionate health care demands that clinicians possess an acute understanding of the beliefs and viewpoints prevalent in the communities in which they work (Groce & Zola, 1993; Helman, 1984; National Public Health and Hospital Institute, 1994). There is an urgent need for increased awareness in the medical community of the concerns of deaf consumers, particularly given the evidence that these individuals may have altered health care utilization patterns—seeing physicians more frequently, having more bed days due to illness, and rating their health as poorer than do their hearing peers (Ries, 1982). Although it may be that deaf individuals suffer from more serious health problems than their hearing counterparts, it is more likely that utilization patterns result primarily from cultural differences and poor communication between clinician and client, leading to misdiagnoses and inappropriate care (Phillips, 1996; Zazove et al., 1993).

This need for sensitivity to the values and attitudes of deaf consumers is particularly crucial for those providing mental health services to the deaf population, a minority that is traditionally underserved and seriously over-represented in the populations of correctional institutions and mental health inpatient facilities (Freeman, 1989; Misiaszek et al., 1985). Deaf and hard of hearing clients may have less access to basic clinical services than their hearing peers, receiving disproportionate amounts of case management and continuing treatment services; and clinicians, prevented by communication barriers from conducting full diagnostic interviews, are apt to misdiagnose deaf clients (Freeman, 1989; Misiaszek et al., 1985; Pollard, 1994). Only recently, in keeping with the movement toward development of standards of care for minority populations (National Latino Behavioral Health Workgroup, 1996), have there been professional efforts to establish standards of mental health care for deaf consumers (Myers, 1995). Still, few mental health service providers possess knowledge of deafness or appropriate communication skills for working with deaf clients (Heller, 1987; McEntee, 1993; Steinberg, 1991). Even of those currently providing services to deaf consumers, 85–87% did not address deafness during their training, and roughly half cannot sign (McEntee, 1993). Despite this shortage of specialized professionals, referral networks have not been established to ensure that clients are connected with qualified providers (Ebert & Heckerling, 1995; McEntee, 1993). The diversity of the deaf population in socioeconomic status, educational attainments, communication skills

Table 1. Participant Characteristics

Characteristic	Percentage $N = 54$
Gender	
male	43%
female	57%
Racial/ethnic identity	
non-Hispanic white	81.5%
Hispanic	7.4%
African-American	11.1%
Age	
18–29	18.5%
30–45	24%
46–60	26%
61 and over	31.5%
Highest educational level completed	
grade 11 or below	5%
high school completed	42.5%
some post-secondary education	42.5%
NA	9%

and preferences, and racial/ethnic identity argues against a one-size-fits-all solution, and it makes the need for consumer input all the more urgent.

This chapter draws from the findings of a two-year study in which fifty-four deaf adults were interviewed about their knowledge, attitudes, and beliefs about mental health and mental health services. Participants were encouraged to tell stories of their own or other deaf individuals' experiences with mental health care and to relate Deaf community folklore on the subject. Personal experience with mental health services was not a requirement for participation in the study.

Most, though not all, of the participants in this study identified with the signing Deaf community. The researchers endeavored to recruit a sample as varied as possible in age, racial/ethnic background, educational attainments, and socioeconomic status. However, because the objective of the study was to obtain qualitative, and often highly personal, data on a potentially sensitive topic, deaf individuals willing to be interviewed were not eliminated on the basis of demographic characteristics. Therefore, the sample is not a representative cross-section of the deaf population. Table 1 summarizes some of the demographic characteristics of the participants.

A deaf member of the research team conducted semistructured interviews in both individual and group settings; twenty-two participants were interviewed individually, and thirty-two were interviewed in groups of two to four. The findings reported here focus on three particularly pertinent topics: concepts of the causation of mental health problems; communication issues in therapeutic settings; and knowledge and beliefs about mental health services and resources.

Concepts of Mental Health

Health care providers and their patients frequently hold divergent beliefs about the origin and best treatment of an illness (Chrisman, 1977; Fabrega, 1974; Groce & Zola, 1993; Helman, 1984; Kleinman, 1980, 1988). Clinician and client typically construct different explanatory models, or "cognitive maps," of an illness, including the nature of the problem, its causes, its treatment, and the anticipated outcome (Kleinman, 1988).

In mental health care, acknowledging the differences between the provider's and consumer's explanatory models is a crucial step in attaining a common ground for therapeutic engagement. Both symptom expression and help-seeking behaviors can vary from one ethnic group to another. Although it is vital to recognize individual variation and to avoid stereotyping a given ethnic group's mental health characteristics and beliefs, understanding local explanatory models can facilitate the clinician's response both to psychological problems and to their social consequences (Dinges & Cherry, 1995; Malgady et al., 1987).

EXPLANATORY MODELS: CAUSES OF MENTAL HEALTH PROBLEMS

The need for cultural awareness and attunement, well documented in the mental health literature (Foster et al., 1996; Kakar, 1995; Kendall, 1996; Kleinman, 1988), is as pressing for clinicians working with deaf clients as it is for those working with any other culture. It is only with sensitivity to the social and cultural context of the client's presenting symptoms that the clinician may avert inappropriate judgments and the misdiagnosis of pathology or deviance.

Much of the older literature on deafness and mental health treats deafness as pathogenic (Altshuler, 1971; Basilier, 1964; Grinker, 1969; Rainer et al., 1969). The American Deaf cultural community, on the other hand, propounds a view of deafness as a healthy and positive condition (Kannapell, 1980; Padden, 1980; Padden & Humphries, 1988). From this perspective, many of the psychological deficiencies commonly attributed to deaf individuals can be attributed instead to the communication difficulties that result from deafness and to the oppression and misunderstanding of deaf people and their culture by the hearing majority (Freeman, 1989; Lane, 1988, 1992; Linderman, 1994; Misiaszek et al., 1985; Phillips, 1996).

As no existing literature addresses the beliefs of deaf individuals regarding mental health and mental illness, the study asked participants for their beliefs about the cause of mental health problems. Overwhelmingly, participants maintained that mental health problems in any individual, hearing or deaf, typically arose from external factors, such as upbringing, poor communication, or family problems.

The lifelong concern with communication figured prominently in their explanatory models for mental health problems in deaf individuals. Deafness per se was not seen as pathogenic: 92% of the participants expressed the belief that a mental health problem "was because of your life, not the deafness. . . . The deafness just adds to the frustration; it doesn't cause all of the frustration." However, 40% asserted that the communication problems, family stresses, and societal prejudice that accompany deafness could have this effect: "People aren't lonely because of being deaf. They're lonely because of communication problems, which happen because they're deaf. . . . If deaf people have mental health problems, it's not because of deafness. It's because of their family experiences growing up." In fact, communication breakdowns were cited as the causal agents of mental health problems ranging from suicidal depression to substance abuse and violent behavior.

For many deaf individuals, this concern with communication arises from experiences with their own families, from which they received minimal or no information (Mindel & Vernon, 1971; Nelson, 1990). Some participants blamed communication failures in their families for their own addictions or psychological problems. One man, for example, began his alcohol abuse at age fourteen after a particularly traumatic revelation. Mystified by his father's absence whenever he returned home for vacation from a residential school for the deaf, he finally discovered the explanation: his brother had fatally shot his father two years earlier. His family had never transcended the communication barrier to inform him of this tragic event. Stunned and embittered, he not only began drinking heavily, but terminated all contact with his family for twenty-three years.

Communication difficulties between the deaf individual and the hearing family often develop in early childhood. The adjustment to having a deaf child is often a traumatic one for hearing families, particularly the parents, who typically do not know initially how their child will be able to function in society. Parents often have difficulty making the adjustments in their lives that a deaf child demands (Koester & Meadow-Orlans, 1990; Mindel & Vernon, 1971; Nelson, 1990). Some deaf adults recall a strong childhood awareness that their parents were ashamed of them and their deafness: "My mother brushed me away and was so ashamed of me. Every time I greeted my mother, she disappeared fast with my sisters without looking at me or saying a word. Gosh, she was so ashamed." Some participants expressed the opinion that hearing families, in their fear and embarrassment at having a deaf child, may keep the child isolated from the rest of the world, which leads to mental instability. This forms the central image of a recurrent bit of folklore: the deaf person who suffers severe mental disturbance as a result of isolation, typically enforced by hearing family members. One participant cited the case of an energetic ringleader at a school for the deaf, who returned to his family's isolated farm following graduation. After residing there for a decade or so, his mischievous behavior vanished, and he became totally passive and uncommunicative. Another man attributed a deaf woman's suicide to her seclusion at her family's rural home. Because isolation represents communication deprivation taken to an extreme, these observations provide further evidence of deaf individuals' tendency to attribute mental health problems to communication failures.

Although clinicians experienced in working with deaf clients are aware of the significance of communication issues for this population, these comments are powerful testimony to the centrality of communication in deaf individuals' notions of mental well-being.

Language Issues

The deaf population is not unique in experiencing communication difficulties in medical and mental health settings. Even for members of the majority culture, medical terminology can be an obstacle because "physicians generally overestimate what their patients have understood" (Charney, 1972, p. 268). The potential for communication failure is of course even greater if practitioner and client lack a common language, particularly in a stressful situation such as a mental health interview, where second-language fluency may deteriorate (Malgady et al., 1987; Oquendo, 1996). Furthermore, a client's moderate skill in the majority language can at first appear to be full fluency, thus deceiving the clinician into believing communication to be more successful than it truly is.

In many cases, a clinician unfamiliar with a given culture can perceive typical mannerisms and conversational styles as normal as pathological (Dinges & Cherry, 1995). With regard to deaf individuals, many aspects of their communication and associated behavior are readily misinterpreted. For example, the tendency to answer a question with a story may be perceived by a naive clinician as evidence of evasiveness or inability to focus, and the facial expressions that are crucial grammatical components of ASL can be misconstrued as inappropriate expressions of affect (Phillips, 1996). The deaf population's heterogeneity in language skills and preferences make it particularly vital for the provider to be sensitive to communication issues.

LANGUAGE: BRIDGE OR BARRIER?

The English vocabulary of medical and mental health care is an impediment to service access for many deaf individuals (Ebert & Heckerling, 1995). It is difficult even to ask or search for services if one doesn't know what words to use. Many providers, lacking experience in working with deaf consumers, mistake deficiencies in English knowledge for conceptual shortcomings. The study revealed that although some English mental health terms were commonly recognized ("addiction" by 80% of participants, "depression" by 87%), others had far lower recognition rates (46% for "psychiatrist," 22% for "psychosis").

Sometimes the content *is* the issue, whatever language is used. For example, few participants could explain the difference between a psychologist and a psychiatrist in either ASL or English; of the more than half who failed to recognize the English word "psychiatrist," many also did not recognize the corresponding ASL sign.

In other instances, however, the language is the obstacle. Some individuals who could discuss such concepts as "depression" or "addiction" quite perceptively in ASL with the deaf interviewer were totally unfamiliar with the corresponding English vocabulary. One participant, for example, shown a flash card of the English word "addiction," eventually signed "ADDITION? ACTION??" Not recognizing the word, he evidently retrieved from memory others with similar sequences of letters. In the course of the interview, however, he described the consequences of alcohol abuse; discussed the experiences of friends who had gone through therapy for alcohol and cocaine addiction; and recommended Alcoholics Anonymous, based on his friends' experiences. His ability to discuss, in ASL, many facets of substance abuse and addiction attested to his grasp of the content; in English, he simply lacked the appropriate vocabulary.

Even for those familiar with the complexities of ASL/English interactions in deaf individuals' language usage, accurately assessing the relationship between linguistic and conceptual knowledge is often difficult. One example is the varied interpretations and associations of the phrase "mental health." For many participants in the study, the connotations of the English expression "mental health" were powerfully negative. This parallels Galloway's (1969) observation that if the expression "mental health" meant anything at all to the typical deaf person, it meant "insanity." The phrase was used only to refer to mental health service agencies or mental illness, not to a condition of well-being. Deaf individuals may associate the phrase with the situation in which they encounter it (e.g., on medical insurance forms or in the name of an agency to which they are referred), rather than analyzing the English expression to discern that it can refer to a kind of health. In these contexts, the focus is on mental health *problems*. Thus, in one interview group, three participants defined "mental health" solely in terms of psychological problems or mental health service agencies. The course of this discussion was dramatically changed by the fourth participant's observation that "good mental health means that a person is happy and at peace with himself," which came as a revelation for the other group members. In this instance, there being no single, conventional way to sign "mental health" in ASL, the interviewer had introduced the notion by fingerspelling the English words "mental health." It is therefore virtually impossible to ascertain whether it was the concept of mental health or the English phrase that bore the negative connotations.

This kind of partial comprehension may lead to serious communication gaps between provider and client. Although utter failure to comprehend English may elicit alternative communication strategies, a client who recognizes an English expression but associates it with a meaning that does not precisely match the standard definition may instead appear to be making irrelevant or inappropriate observations. Sensitivity to the language status of many deaf Americans is therefore critical for the mental health practitioner working with this population.

DEAF CONSUMERS' PERCEPTIONS OF THEIR COMMUNICATION SKILLS

Many deaf individuals, acutely conscious of their limited English skills, approach medical and mental health settings expecting to encounter communication barriers. Some, due to educational background or other variables, have limited grasp of either ASL or English and have impoverished world knowledge. Others are aware that they possess conceptual knowledge that they can express eloquently in ASL but which is not adequately reflected in their command of English. Still others, unable to articulate this distinction, erroneously regard their limited English ability as an indication of their "basic" language skills and, perhaps, their general ignorance (Padden & Humphries, 1988).

This discomfort with English can itself represent an obstacle to communication: "Many deaf people lack confidence . . . because they lack English skills. They are ashamed to write." In medical settings, deaf individuals' expectation of being addressed in a language they do not understand, coupled with the language attitudes outlined above, leads to such comments as, "Doctors use advanced words," "Deaf people don't understand," "They need to use basic language with Deaf people." Although such descriptors as "basic" may not be an objectively accurate characterization of these individuals' ASL skills, these comments reflect the insight that communication must be tailored to meet the client's needs.

COMMUNICATION PREFERENCES AND EXPERIENCES

Many individuals, whether hearing or deaf, who can communicate competently orally or in writing when the subject matter and vocabulary are familiar (e.g., name and address), may be unable to continue when the topic changes to medical terminology or insurance regulations. If the clinician and the client share a language, there is a reasonable likelihood that the clinician will recognize when this occurs or that the client will be willing and able to ask for an explanation. However, some deaf clients have enough superficial facility with English—whether read, written, spoken, and/or speechread—to mislead the naive clinician into overestimating the client's grasp of the language. Health care professionals often erroneously expect oral or written communication to suffice with deaf clients, not realizing just how difficult it is for someone who has never heard to fully master a spoken language (Ebert & Heckerling, 1995).

Deaf individuals who use sign language commonly view fluent sign language skills as essential for mental health professionals and are skeptical of those who rely on speech and writing. The overriding emphasis on sign language skills is sometimes linked with a deep mistrust of hearing professionals (Freeman, 1989). Several study participants maintained that professionals with negligible sign skills are willing to settle for a minimal level of communication with deaf clients that they would never tolerate with hearing patients. For example, one woman reported on a therapy session she had witnessed as a hospital volunteer. The clinician asked deaf inpatients rudimentary, poorly signed questions ("Did you eat?" "Did you sleep well?") and was satisfied with their apparent comprehension. "If I were the patient," the woman said, "I would have been tempted to slap him!" She felt strongly that in this case communication differences had distracted the clinician from providing deaf patients with the same level of therapeutic services that their hearing peers received.

There is a common perception that signing Deaf people are in danger of being misunderstood, perhaps even institutionalized, by hearing clinicians ignorant of deafness. "Sometimes a professional who doesn't want to deal with deaf people sends them to the mental hospital. . . . There they are ruined because they don't have interpreters."

Even programs explicitly designed for deaf consumers may not meet the diverse communication needs of their clientele. One deaf man, who had limited formal education and came from a Spanish-speaking home, reported on his experience in a residential substance-abuse program for deaf individuals: "It was not successful, because I had a hard time understanding them [the other patients]. We were not on the same communication and intelligence level. They were more advanced than I am. Group sharing was hard for me to follow, especially talking about past experiences in relation to addiction—that's even harder to understand." The diversity of the deaf population in language and educational background dictates that programs for deaf clients must be flexible in their communication strategies.

USING INTERPRETERS

Similar issues arise whether interpreters are employed with signing deaf clients or with users of minority spoken languages. Although legal mandates have encouraged the training and use of interpreters for spoken as well as signed languages, their employment in health care has lagged behind their use in other venues, such as legal settings (Putsch, 1985; Woloshin et al., 1995). Furthermore, practitioners often do not know how to effectively use an interpreter.

They may speak too fast or may address and interview the interpreter rather than the client (Stansfield, 1981; Vernon, 1965). The interpreter's role in mental health settings is particularly sensitive, where confidentiality and the therapist's and client's mutual comfort with the interaction are crucial (Frishberg, 1986; Vernon, 1965). For deaf mental health clients, an additional complication is that the guiding and controlling role of therapist-client eye contact is disrupted by communication routed through an intermediary (Frishberg, 1986).

Clinicians and clients are often forced to depend either on their own linguistic abilities or on those of family members or other ad hoc interpreters pressed into service on the spot (Ginsberg et al., 1995; Woloshin et al., 1995). The use of such interpreters, who typically have no training in interpreting, introduces additional complexities. Out of concern with privacy or propriety, a family member acting as an impromptu interpreter may edit the messages conveyed or answer the clinician's questions him or herself, thereby jeopardizing the clinician's ability to diagnose and treat the client (Malgady et al., 1987; Marcos, 1979; Vasquez & Javier, 1991). Additionally, the client's confidentiality is directly compromised when family members act as interpreters.

Deaf consumers strongly appreciate good interpreting in mental health settings. In the study, there was general consensus that therapy involving a qualified interpreter was far preferable to uninterpreted therapy with a non-signing therapist: "Well, if a deaf person has a problem and is committed, if there are interpreters there, that will be fine." "If I was given the name of a hearing counselor, no way—they can't communicate. Unless an interpreter is provided; then I'd be satisfied."

Nonetheless, participants repeatedly expressed ambivalence toward interpreters in therapeutic settings. Some of the negative reactions pertained to confidentiality: "I might see the interpreter again in a different situation, and she'd know about my personality and background." Given the limited number of qualified interpreters in many geographic areas, this concern is well-founded. Another reason for this ambivalence was a preference for direct communication with a signing professional: "With an interpreter, there has to be three-way communication. It confuses things." One woman clearly articulated the ambiguity of the interpreter's role: "I am not for interpreters [in mental health settings] because the patient may focus on the interpreter as if he or she is the psychologist."

A number of participants in the study also had serious misgivings about interpreters' skills, particularly their comprehension of ASL. One woman observed that in her experience, many sign-to-voice interpreters were unable to capture all the nuances of her signing, including information conveyed via posture and facial expression, which would be crucial in therapy. Another participant emphasized the importance of coordination between therapist and interpreter, indicating that she would consider a therapist with an interpreter over a signing therapist only if the therapist and interpreter were able to form a smoothly functioning team. Although deaf consumers appreciate the interpreter's role in facilitating communication, they also acknowledge the advantages of direct, unmediated communication with a signing therapist.

Deaf consumers' acute sensitivity to communication leads them to attribute mental health problems to communication failures; to place high priority on a mental health practitioner's signing skills, or on the presence of a qualified interpreter; and to be deeply concerned about communication failure in therapeutic settings, as a result of either their own or the clinician's skills. The lifelong struggle of most deaf individuals to achieve satisfactory communication can thus be seen to pervade their attitudes toward mental health and mental health services.

Services and Resources

The lack of information about existing resources can be a substantial obstacle for ethnic minorities (Hoberman, 1992; Schensul & Schensul, 1982; Solis et al., 1990), as well as deaf consumers, many of whom have little or no conception of where or how to locate accessible mental health services (Nelson, 1990). In the interview study, 56% of the participants, when asked where one could find mental health services for deaf consumers, responded, "I don't know." One woman responded, "I have no idea. For hearing people, it's easy to find places, but for deaf people requiring special treatment and sign language, I don't know where they can go." In another interview, when asked where deaf people could see a psychologist, a participant replied, "There is none, but they should have one." Even those living within ten miles of a regional mental health program for deaf clients often were unaware of its existence.

Many participants in the interview study identified the Yellow Pages as a resource in the quest for services. This reflects ignorance both of those accessible services that may exist and of such resources as the *TDI National Directory and Guide* (published annually by Telecommunications for the Deaf, Inc.), which includes listings for a wide range of services accessible to deaf consumers. It also reflects an assumption that all facilities will have the resources and staff to provide services for deaf consumers. Not infrequently, deaf consumers in need of mental health services go to a local medical hospital in the expectation that it will have services accessible to deaf clients, or at least assuming that a prompt and appropriate referral will be available.

In the absence of suitable mental health resources, some individuals take advantage of any linguistically accessible programs, even if these do not meet their needs. Thus, two participants in the study, seeking an environment in which they could communicate with other adults, attended a local literacy program for deaf clients, although they both were in need of mental health services. In some Deaf communities, substance abuse and self-help programs are better known than are other mental health services, and community leaders encourage others to attend interpreted meetings: "AA, NA [Alcoholics Anonymous, Narcotics Anonymous], they are good places to go, you don't need to be an alcoholic, go, you'll learn a lot."

INFORMATION PATHWAYS: HOW DEAF PEOPLE LEARN ABOUT MENTAL HEALTH

The avenues through which deaf individuals obtain information about mental health resources reveal the structure and values of the community. Participants in the study relied almost exclusively upon Deaf community resources rather than outside sources. Underscoring the significance within Deaf culture of bonds among deaf peers, participants cited deaf services agencies and their newsletters; friends; and schools for the deaf, which often serve as headquarters of Deaf community activity, as valued elements of the communal information network. In general, those most knowledgeable about mental health issues, resources, and vocabulary were (a) those who had extensive experience with mental health care (either for themselves, family members, or friends), and (b) those who had worked or volunteered in mental health settings, such as halfway houses or inpatient units.

Furthermore, individuals over the age of sixty frequently had greater knowledge of mental health care than did their younger counterparts. This may be due in part to changing confidentiality standards. The stories some individuals recounted suggested that thirty or forty years ago professionals sometimes shared information that would probably be divulged more cautiously now. Another factor in older deaf individuals' knowledge of mental health issues is the changing structure of the Deaf community itself. Many older individuals, educated before mainstreaming became popular, attended residential schools for deaf students (Moores et al., 1990), where professionals familiar with deafness were available and where information about services accessible to the Deaf community was freely shared (Vernon, 1995). Furthermore, before TTYs (telecommunications devices for people who are deaf) were widely available, deaf individuals waited eagerly for the nights when they could congregate at Deaf clubs to socialize and exchange information. Even more then than now, personal information was shared freely, and medical and psychological concerns were fair game for discussion. Some older deaf individuals have gained much of their knowledge from this spontaneous sharing among members of the Deaf community. These factors further underscore the importance of the community in educating its members about mental health issues.

An understanding of these existing community information pathways can be valuable in planning informational outreach for this population. Because deaf individuals seek information about mental health resources from schools for the deaf, deaf service agency newsletters, and the Yellow Pages, for example, efforts to ensure that adequate information is in fact available from these sources could improve awareness of existing resources.

STEREOTYPICAL IMAGES OF MENTAL HEALTH CARE

If deaf individuals are to seek and utilize mental health services, they must perceive the value of these services. Deaf community folklore, however, presents a less favorable outlook. Padden (1995) observes that one theme of deaf folklore is the deaf person as victim, in danger of wrongful imprisonment as a consequence of communication gone awry. Hence, deaf folklore abounds with tales of deaf individuals imprisoned because a police officer misconstrued their indistinct speech as an indication of drunkenness or thought that the individual's claim of deafness was a ruse. In a subtype of this folktale, abundantly attested to in the interview study, the deaf individual is incarcerated in a psychiatric hospital rather than a prison. This theme demonstrates a common image of the mental health facility in the Deaf community—it is a place to be feared, a place where people are taken and abandoned, a place where a hapless, unsuspecting deaf person might be sent if misunderstood. For many deaf individuals, these images of institutionalization and insanity are the only images the expression "mental health" conjures up (Galloway, 1969).

Although such images represent one extreme, the study revealed a generally negative, stereotypical view of mental health institutions and mental health practitioners, who were regarded as authoritarian, restrictive, and prejudiced. In some cases, ASL vocabulary itself reveals negative attitudes toward mental health facilities. Colloquial signs for "psychiatric hospital" include PRISON, STRAITJACKET, CRAZY-HOUSE, and BUG-HOUSE. In the study, one participant differentiated MENTAL HEALTH from the CRAZY-HOUSE by explaining that the former included clinics one might attend for treatment, and the latter was a place where patients were incarcerated with no hope of improvement. The study participants often compared psychiatric hospitals with penal institutions: "A mental hospital is like a prison. You stay; you're left there; you can't go out; you're not free." One woman shrugged, "From a Deaf person's point of view, a jail and a mental hospital are the same."

Mistrust of hearing professionals also contributes to deaf clients' negative images of mental health care. Participants in the interview study commonly considered deaf patients in mental health settings to be totally at the mercy of hearing authorities. One participant gave a definition of mental health services that was particularly forceful on this point: "You mean hearing people think deaf people are mentally ill and have them committed? Mental health services—yeah, it means putting someone away."

The deaf person, unable to communicate and erroneously committed to a psychiatric facility, represents another recurrent image in community folklore. One woman who took her seriously depressed husband to a hospital felt that "if I hadn't been there to interpret for him, he would have been in restraints and locked up." Another observed, "Even if I were just asking directions at the information desk [of a psychiatric hospital], miscommunication could lead to my being committed by mistake, with no explanation. . . .You have to watch out. . . . I'd be stuck there, and how would I contact the outside world? . . . I don't want to go there, even for a visit."

These descriptions exemplify the common perception that in mental health settings, authority resides with the hearing caregivers, and the deaf clients are essentially powerless to make decisions about their own care. If mental health care utilization by deaf individuals is to be improved, the pervasive negative images of mental health providers and facilities must be addressed.

COMMUNITY ATTITUDES: SUPPORT AND STIGMA

Mental health concerns cannot be divorced from their social context. Community attitudes toward mental illness and the recipient of mental health services have a powerful impact on the utilization and efficacy of these services (Groce & Zola, 1993; Helman, 1984). Social support can have positive effects on mental health, both by directly enhancing well-being and by aiding the individual in coping with stressful events (Cohen & Syme, 1985; Kessler & McLeod, 1985). On the other hand, if mental health problems are heavily stigmatized, an individual in need of services may be less likely to seek them out or to participate in an ongoing treatment plan. Little information is available on the stigmatization or support of mental health care recipients within the Deaf community.

As demonstrated in the study, deaf consumers' expectations of others' responses to mental health needs reflect both the frequent tension between deaf individuals and their hearing families and the tendency of these individuals to seek support from deaf peers. Fewer than half the participants in the interview study believed that families would be supportive of a family member seeking therapy. This expectation was often rooted in personal experience or communal folklore about the difficulties of growing up deaf in a hearing family. Those who anticipated negative responses from family members frequently cited the stereotypical case of an unresponsive hearing family failing to comprehend the needs of its sole deaf member. Participants were considerably more optimistic, however, about receiving support from friends. The vast majority (92%) maintained that a friend would encourage another to seek necessary therapy: "I'd feel it's up to them [my friends]. . . . I'd try to be supportive and encouraging. . . . If it were me, my friends would support me." Some felt that the Deaf community would be neutral or supportive toward a member who sought mental health services: "They would approve. Well, at first, maybe they wouldn't care one way or the other, but if the person improved and changed, they'd approve." This parallels Gutman's observation that her survey did not reveal particularly strong negative attitudes toward mentally ill individuals (1992).

The social intimacy of the Deaf community, however, engenders concerns about confidentiality and privacy that limit deaf individuals' willingness to share information about mental health service use with other deaf people. Keeping information about one's mental health care private, which the hearing majority tends to take for granted, is difficult in the small, intimate Deaf community (Guthmann & Sandberg, 1995; Nelson, 1990; Vernon, 1965). A majority of participants in the study maintained that the Deaf community shouldn't be informed about a member's use of mental health services. As one woman observed, "The Deaf community is like a family. One thing can spread to everyone, and all the world knows about it. With Deaf people, it's never a secret." Others commented that a deaf person known to be receiving mental health care would be shunned: "In general, it's a private issue and would cause the person to become a social outcast from the Deaf community. The community ought not to know of the mental problems." Of those who felt that the Deaf community should know, however, the usual rationale was that increased information sharing could be beneficial, both by raising people's levels of knowledge and by dispelling stigma. "People should tell others that they are going to mental health services, because that way the word gets out that there are services available," said one participant. "Perhaps a friend will hear that you are going to a clinic and knows another person who has the same problem as you do. Then they can refer the person to a place that can help them."

COMMUNITY AS A RESOURCE

In many ethnic groups, nuclear and extended family members, folk healers, and other respected community members are often sought out for assistance with mental health problems (Akutsu et al., 1996). In the case of the Deaf community, Deaf people have a tradition of taking care of their own; this tradition yields internal resources for addressing mental health issues (Griggs, personal communication). Often deaf individuals seek out the better-educated members of the Deaf community for help with their personal problems (Galloway, 1969). The interview study reveals that there are also certain respected deaf individuals, not necessarily highly educated but held in high regard in the Deaf community for their sensitivity, common sense, and life experience, who become informal peer counselors. In the case of one older couple who fulfill this role, neither has any education beyond high school. The experience they have garnered through weathering family rifts, poverty, and alcoholism has won them the respect of their deaf peers, who turn to them for informal counseling, moral support, and sometimes even shelter. One man with extensive formal substance-abuse counseling experience said of this couple, "Whenever I am bothered by a problem or have an argument, I go to Sam and Helen [pseudonyms]. They help me by explaining the nature of the problem and teach me to ignore the people causing it."

Other deaf people carry out the tradition of Deaf community self-sufficiency by taking mentally ill deaf individuals into their homes. Over the years, one couple permitted several individuals to board with them, some for extended periods of time. Another couple befriended a younger deaf neighbor with some psychological difficulties and became, in effect, her surrogate parents, providing her with meals, transportation, and advice. These anecdotes reflect this community's longstanding pride in its self-sufficiency and its utilization of nonprofessional resources for the informal provision of mental health services.

Client Expectations of Professional Behavior: Boundary Issues

Training programs for mental health professionals emphasize professional boundaries. It is a general Western, or at least American, assumption that information revealed to a doctor or therapist will go no farther, and that the professional transactions between therapist and client do not carry over into the private lives of either (Rubanowitz, 1987).

The boundaries between public and private realms blur for those working with a small and close-knit population such as the Deaf community, in which clinician and client will almost inevitably encounter one another outside the therapeutic setting. This is especially true because of the value of information exchange in Deaf culture. Many of the ordinary ways in which hearing individuals acquire information are difficult or impossible for deaf individuals to access. Information, and the opportunities to share it, are therefore welcomed and cherished, and secrecy is regarded as antisocial (Hall, 1989). A therapist's professional training in regard to boundaries can conflict with Deaf people's openness with information that hearing society considers highly personal. Achieving a balance between professional ethical standards and the norms of the client population is a challenge for therapists, both hearing and deaf.

A key question is how deaf consumers themselves view the boundary between professional and personal spheres. The study reveals that Deaf consumers are quite conscious of these boundary issues, although there is considerable variation in individual responses.

First, for some deaf consumers, the intimacy of the Deaf community is a consideration in choosing a therapist, despite the limited number of specialized professionals. Nearly half of the participants preferred that a therapist be part of the local Deaf community, feeling greater comfort with someone who associated with that community rather than remaining at arm's length. However, a substantial proportion (29%) felt more at ease receiving mental health services from someone outside the community, preferring to relax in the knowledge that the therapist was unlikely to intrude on their personal lives. One woman expressed discomfort about receiving services from a therapist who was a friend of her deaf sister, preferring instead to maintain boundaries between personal and professional spheres by selecting a psychologist outside her social circle. A well-known American deaf writer felt that therapists familiar with the Deaf community were unable to set aside what they already knew of an individual's achievements in order to focus on the issues raised in therapy.

Once a therapist has been selected, issues of boundaries between Deaf and hearing cultures figure prominently in consumers' expectations of professionals' behavior in social contexts. For example, although participants in the study considered familiarity with Deaf culture and Deaf organizations to be essential for hearing professionals, a desire to retain control over their own social groups led several participants to indicate that hearing therapists were welcome at Deaf clubs only if they had been invited or if they notified their clients in advance, not if they were motivated solely by curiosity. The vast majority (95%) nonetheless agreed that a therapist encountering a client at such a gathering should behave like a friend. This expectation may run counter to a hearing therapist's inclination to maintain a strong distinction between the professional and the personal.

It is important for mental health practitioners to recognize that although Deaf cultural values thus permit more mingling of the professional and the personal than clinical training ordinarily suggests, boundaries do exist. Thus, behaving like a friend with a client encountered in a social setting does not extend to discussing professional matters there. One participant cited with distaste an incident in which a therapist embarrassed a client by questioning her at a social event about a missed appointment.

Although the core values of their culture often lead deaf consumers to expect less rigid boundaries between therapist and client than hearing consumers might assume, the deaf population is far from unanimous on this point. Because deaf individuals vary in their expectations of professionals' behavior, a therapist working with this population needs to be attuned to these differences. To increase the likelihood that these expectations can be met, therapists can discuss with new clients how to behave in the event of chance encounters outside the therapy setting.

Client Preferences in Choosing a Therapist

Studies in recent years have generally found a preference on the part of African-American clients for African-American therapists (Atkinson, 1985; Copeland, 1982; Tien & Johnson, 1985). However, there is little evidence that other populations have ethnic preferences for mental health care providers, nor has outcome research shown conclusively that racial or ethnic pairings lead to more satisfactory outcomes (Atkinson, 1985). There is evidence that ethnically matched therapists are more likely than ethnically mismatched therapists to rate clients as high-functioning, which suggests that therapists who are ethnically similar to their clients may be better able to understand behaviors within their cultural context (Russell et al., 1996). Consumers, however, judge cultural sensitivity to be crucial (Copeland, 1982; Pierce & Pierce, 1991; Tien & Johnson, 1985), regardless of whether counselor and client share the same ethnic background.

DEAF VS. HEARING THERAPISTS

There has been little research on deaf clients' preferences for deaf or hearing therapists. As mentioned earlier, deaf consumers' concepts of mental health care frequently involve negative images of hearing professionals, featuring ignorant hearing providers exercising control over powerless deaf clients (Freeman, 1989). These images, however, do not necessarily translate into a preference for deaf therapists. Many deaf consumers, having little or no exposure to deaf professionals of any kind, automatically envision therapists as hearing. Thus, although participants in the study tended to express a preference for deaf therapists, some of these respondents regarded this as merely a fantasy.

This preference for deaf therapists was stated in terms of both language and experience. Familiarity with ASL and Deaf culture, which in principle a hearing person can attain, were regarded as essential, but so was the life experience of deafness: "A Deaf counselor knows the language, the culture; knows what deafness means. Hearing people don't know that." "The deaf person is like me." Some maintained that although a hearing therapist might be distracted by the communication issues presented by a deaf client, a deaf clinician would be able to address the therapeutic issues more directly.

The preference for deaf therapists is far from uniform. Some deaf consumers, believing hearing people to be better educated than deaf individuals, assume that a deaf therapist will be less qualified than a hearing counterpart (Lala, 1995). For one participant in the interview study, he justified his ambivalence about the relative merits of deaf and hearing therapists by expressing his belief that a hearing therapist would have the professional advantage of ready access to informational resources: "A hearing leader has more access to . . . the media, so he would have more resources to offer to the group members, while the deaf leader . . . may miss important information that may be beneficial to clients." For another man, his own desire to limit the information shared in therapy led him to prefer the safety and distance afforded by hearing clinicians: "With a deaf person, I'm afraid I'd open up and spill everything."

GROUP THERAPY: ALL-DEAF VS. MIXED DEAF/HEARING

In group therapy, deaf consumers have expressed strong preferences for all-deaf settings. Lala (1995) states that those who favor all-deaf substance abuse peer counseling groups assert that only fellow deaf participants can credibly challenge behavioral ploys and excuses a deaf individual might use in therapy. Interview study participants overwhelmingly preferred all-deaf (or deaf/hard of hearing) groups over integrated deaf/hearing situations, even if interpreting services were available. The ability of all members of the group to share equally in the communication was seen as critical: "I think a deaf group would be better. Everybody would sign and be comfortable." The support that deaf individuals could obtain from one another in a group setting was equally vital: "A deaf hospital program is better because the deaf understand where the person is coming from." One woman felt that deaf patients would receive more attention in an all-deaf group: "A deaf group is better because in a mainstream program, the staff would give more attention to the hearing patients and leave deaf patients isolated and doing nothing. In a deaf group, they have something in common; they can at least communicate and interact." Another participant felt so strongly about the need for communication and common ground among group members that she expressed a preference for joining an all-deaf group that included mentally retarded deaf participants over an integrated deaf/hearing group.

THERAPIST QUALIFICATIONS

The preference for culturally sensitive and linguistically accessible services was accompanied by a concern for the quality of therapy, although there was considerable variation in how individual participants in the study weighted these considerations. The majority of participants (56%) maintained that sign communication skills were a more important factor in choosing a therapist or facility than excellent counseling skills: "It's the same as if it were the Russian language or an African language—if people don't understand the language, then putting a person in an institution is a waste of time." However, given the reality that most mental health professionals are not skilled signers, a significant proportion of the participants (36%) stated that they would value excellent counseling skills over sign communication ability in choosing a therapist, provided that interpreting services were available, particularly if the clinician offered special expertise that a client required. Nor are communication ability and measurable therapy skills the only considerations in selecting a professional. One woman prioritized the rapport between therapist and client over either hearing status or cultural awareness as the most crucial factor in a therapeutic relationship.

Deaf individuals themselves are generally well aware of the diversity of their community. Along with sign language skills and knowledge of Deaf culture, participants in the study ranked familiarity with deaf people from diverse backgrounds as an important qualification for a mental health professional. Both an understanding of the core values of Deaf culture, and an appreciation and respect for the uniqueness of each deaf individual, are essential for a therapist working with this population.

OTHER PREFERENCES

The availability of a skilled therapist with sign language expertise thus does not guarantee that the requirements of all deaf consumers will be satisfied. In addition to the need for appropriate communication, deaf individuals have reasons similar to those of their hearing counterparts for preferring one therapist over another. Some prefer a counselor of the same gender. The personality and approach of a particular therapist may be a good match for one deaf client, but not for another. One study participant who expressed a strong individual preference was a single mother whose teenage sons had been molested as children. Desiring family therapy and convinced of the value of continuity, she insisted on returning to the social worker who had counseled the children at the time of the abuse. Although the dearth of trained professionals and the economics of referral systems do not always permit deaf consumers a great deal of choice, health care administrators need to consider the diversity of consumer preferences and needs in restructuring delivery systems.

Conclusion

The values and attitudes prevalent among deaf individuals contain essential information for the mental health practitioner. Among the themes that emerge from deaf consumers' observations on mental health are the value placed on communication, the existing informational networks of the Deaf community, and the diversity of the deaf population.

The experiences of deaf consumers attest to the strong beliefs about mental health, mental illness, and related services held by members of this minority community. Clinicians working with deaf individuals must incorporate the consumer's perspectives, values, and preferences in order to enhance the quality of mental health service delivery and to provide more respectful and meaningful care.

References

Altshuler, K. Z. (1971). Studies of the deaf: Relevance to psychiatric theory. *American Journal of Psychiatry, 127,* 1521–1526.

Akutsu, P. D., Snowden, L. R., & Organista, K. C. (1996). Referral patterns in ethnic-specific and mainstream programs for ethnic minorities and whites. *Journal of Counseling Psychology, 43* (1), 56–64.

Atkinson, D. R. (1985). A meta-review of research on cross-cultural counseling and psychotherapy. *Journal of Multicultural Counseling and Development, 13,* 138–153.
Basilier, T. (1964). Surdophrenia. *Acta Psychiatrica Scandinavica, 40,* 362–374.
Charney, E. (1972). Patient-doctor communication: Implications for the clinician. *Pediatric Clinics of North America, 19,* 263–279.
Chrisman, N. J. (1977). The health seeking process: An approach to the natural history of illness. *Culture, Medicine, and Psychiatry, 1,* 351–377.
Cohen, S., & Syme, S. L. (1985). The study and application of social support. In S. Cohen & S. L. Syme (Eds.), *Social Support and Health* (pp. 6–9). Orlando, FL: Academic Press.
Copeland, E. J. (1982). Oppressed conditions and the mental health needs of low-income black women: Barriers to services, strategies for change. *Women and Therapy, 1,* 12–25.
Dinges, N. G., & Cherry, D. (1995). Symptom expression and the use of mental health services among American ethnic minorities. In J. Aponte, R. Y. Rivers, & J. Wohl (Eds.), *Psychological interventions and cultural diversity* (pp. 40–56). Boston: Allyn and Bacon.
Ebert, D. A., & Heckerling, P. S. (1995). Communication with deaf patients: Knowledge, beliefs, and practices of physicians. *JAMA, 273,* 227–229.
Fabrega, H. (1974). *Disease & social behavior: An interdisciplinary perspective.* Cambridge, MA: MIT Press.
Folio Corporation (1995). *FolioVIEWS Infobase Production Kit.* Provo, UT: Folio.
Foster, R. P., Moskowitz, M., & Javier, R. A. (Eds.). (1996). *Reaching across boundaries of culture and class: Widening the scope of psychotherapy.* Northvale, NJ: Jason Aronson.
Freeman, S. T. (1989). Cultural and linguistic bias in mental health evaluations of deaf people. *Rehabilitation Psychology, 34,* 51–63.
Frishberg, N. (1990). *Interpreting: An introduction.* Rockville, MD: RID Publications.
Galloway, V. H. (1969). Mental health: What it means to the typical deaf person. In K. Z. Altshuler & J. D. Rainer (Eds.), *Mental health and the deaf: Approaches and prospects* (pp. 51–61). Washington, DC: U.S. Department of Health, Education, and Welfare.
Gerteis, M., Edgman-Levitan, S., Daley, J., & Delbanco, T. L. (Eds.). (1993). *Through the patient's eyes: Understanding and promoting patient-centered care.* San Francisco: Jossey-Bass.
Ginsberg, C., Martin, V., Andrulis, D., Shaw-Taylor, Y., & McGregor, C. (1995). *Interpretation and translation services in health care: A survey of U.S. public and private teaching hospitals.* Washington, DC: National Public Health and Hospital Institute.
Grinker, R. R. (Ed.). (1969). *Psychiatric diagnosis, therapy, and research on the psychotic deaf.* Washington, DC: U. S. Department of Health, Education, and Welfare.
Groce, N. E., & Zola, I. K. (1993). Multiculturalism, chronic illness, and disability. *Pediatrics, 91,* 1048–1055.
Guthmann, D., & Sandberg, K. A. (1995). Clinical approaches in substance abuse treatment for use with deaf and hard of hearing adolescents. In M. D. Garretson (Ed.), *Deafness: Life and culture II. A Deaf American monograph, 45* (pp. 55–59). Silver Spring, MD: National Association of the Deaf.
Gutman, V. (1992, July). *Views of deafness and mental health: Stigma, helping, and help-seeking.* Paper presented at the Breakout! conference, Washington, DC.
Gutman, V., & Stewart, L. (1991, May). *Community attitudes toward mental health services: A survey of deaf adults.* Paper presented at American Deafness and Rehabilitation Association meeting, Chicago.

Hall, S. (1989). TRAIN-GONE-SORRY: The etiquette of social conversations in American sign language. In S. Wilcox (Ed.), *American deaf culture: An anthology* (pp. 89–102). Burtonsville, MD: Sign Media/Linstok Press.

Heller, B. (1987). Mental health assessment of deaf persons: A brief history. In H. Elliott, L. Glass, & J. W. Evans (Eds.), *Mental health assessment of deaf clients* (pp. 9–20). Boston: Little, Brown.

Helman, C. (1984). *Culture, health, and illness: An introduction for health professionals.* Bristol, England: Wright.

Hoberman, H. M. (1992). Ethnic minority status and adolescent mental health services utilization. *Journal of Mental Health Administration, 19,* 246–267.

Holt, J. A., & Hotto, S. A. (1994). *Demographic aspects of hearing impairment: Questions and answers* (3rd ed.). Washington, DC: Gallaudet University Center for Assessment and Demographic Studies.

Jeter, I. K. (1976). Unidentified hearing impairment among psychiatric patients. *Journal of the American Speech and Hearing Association, 18,* 843–845.

Kakar, S. (1995). Clinical work and cultural imagination. *Psychoanalytic Quarterly, 44,* 265–281.

Kannapell, B. (1980). Personal awareness and advocacy in the deaf community. In C. Baker & R. Battison (Eds.), *Sign language and the deaf community: Essays in honor of William C. Stokoe* (pp. 105–116). Silver Spring, MD: National Association of the Deaf.

Kendall, J. (1996). Creating a culturally responsive psychotherapeutic environment for African American youths: A critical analysis. *Advances in Nursing Science, 18* (4), 11–28.

Kessler, R. C., & McLeod, J. D. (1985). Social support and mental health in community samples. In S. Cohen & S. L. Syme (Eds.), *Social support and health* (pp. 219–240). Orlando, FL: Academic Press.

Kleinman, A. M. (1980). *Patients and healers in the context of culture.* Berkeley: University of California Press.

———. (1988). *The illness narratives: Suffering, healing, and the human condition.* New York: Basic Books.

Koester, L., & Meadow-Orlans, K. (1990). Parenting a deaf child: Stress, strength, and support. In D. F. Moores & K. Meadow-Orlans (Eds.), *Educational and developmental aspects of deafness* (pp. 299–320). Washington, DC: Gallaudet University Press.

Lala, F. J. J., Jr. (1995). Substance abuse among deaf people: A discussion. In M. D. Garretson (Ed.), *Deafness: Life and culture II. A Deaf American monograph, 45* (pp. 67–72). Silver Spring, MD: National Association of the Deaf.

Lamb, L. E., & Graham, J. T. (1962). Audiometric screening in a psychiatric hospital. *Audiological Research, 2,* 338–349.

Lane, H. (1988). Is there a "psychology of the deaf"? *Exceptional Children, 55,* 7–19.

———. (1992). *The mask of benevolence: Disabling the deaf community.* New York: Alfred A. Knopf.

Leigh, I. W., Corbett, C. A., Gutman, V., & Morere, D. A. (1996). Providing psychological services to deaf individuals: A response to new perceptions of diversity. *Professional Psychology: Research and Practice, 27,* 364–371.

Linderman, A. (1994). Oppression, culture of poverty, and deaf people. In M. D. Garretson (Ed.), *Deafness: Life and culture. A Deaf American monograph, 45* (pp. 75–79). Silver Spring, MD: National Association of the Deaf.

Lopez, S., & Hernandez, P. (1986). How culture is considered in evaluations of psychopathology. *Journal of Nervous and Mental Disease, 176* (10), 598–606.

Malgady, R. G., Rogler, L. H., & Costantino, G. (1987). Ethnocultural and linguistic bias in mental health evaluations of Hispanics. *American Psychologist, 42,* 228–234.

Marcos, L. R. (1979). Effects of interpreters on the evaluation of psychopathology in non-English-speaking patients. *American Journal of Psychiatry, 136,* 171–174.

McCoy, D., & Plotkin, W. H. (1967). Audiometric screening of a psychiatric population in a large state hospital. *Journal of Auditory Research, 7,* 327–334.

McCrone, W. F. (1982). Serving the deaf substance abuser. *Journal of Psychoactive Drugs, 14,* 199–203.

McEntee, M. K. (1993). Accessibility of mental health services and crisis intervention to the deaf. *American Annals of the Deaf, 138,* 26–30.

Mindel, E. D., & Vernon, M. (1971). *They grow in silence.* Silver Spring, MD: National Association of the Deaf.

Misiaszek, J., Dooling, J., Gieseke, M., Melman, H., Misiaszek, J. G., & Jorgensen, K. (1985). Diagnostic considerations in deaf patients. *Comprehensive Psychiatry, 26,* 513–521.

Moores, D. F., Cerney, B., & Garcia, M. (1990). School placement and least restrictive environment. In D. F. Moores & K. Meadow-Orlans (Eds.), *Educational and developmental aspects of deafness* (pp. 115–136). Washington, DC: Gallaudet University Press.

Munoz, R. F. (1982). The Spanish-speaking consumer and the community mental health center. In E. E. Jones, & S. J. Korchin (Eds.), *Minority mental health* (pp. 362–398). New York: Praeger.

Myers, R. (Ed.). 1995. *Standards of care for the delivery of mental health services to deaf and hard of hearing persons.* Silver Spring, MD: National Association of the Deaf.

National Center for Health Statistics. (1994). *Data from the national health interview survey,* series 10, no. 188, table 1. Washington, DC: U. S. Government Printing Office.

National Latino Behavioral Health Workgroup. (1996). *Cultural competence guidelines in managed care: Mental health services for Latino populations.* Boulder, CO: Western Interstate Commission for Higher Education Mental Health Program.

National Public Health and Hospital Institute. (1994). *Cross-cultural competence in health care.* Unpublished manuscript.

Nelson, P. (1990). *Mental health service needs in the deaf, hard of hearing, and deaf/blind community: Report on a community outreach process.* Vancouver: Greater Vancouver Mental Health Service Society.

Oquendo, M. (1996). Psychiatric evaluation and psychotherapy in the patient's second language. *Psychiatric Services, 47,* 614–618.

Padden, C. (1980). The deaf community and the culture of deaf people. In C. Baker & R. Battison (Eds.), *Sign language and the deaf community* (pp. 89–103). Silver Spring, MD: National Association of the Deaf.

———. (1995). *Folklore and symbolism in deaf culture.* Lecture at Pennsylvania School for the Deaf, Philadelphia.

Padden, C., & Humphries, T. (1988). *Deaf in America: Voices from a culture.* Cambridge, MA: Harvard University Press.

Phillips, B. A. (1996). Bringing culture to the forefront: Formulating diagnostic impressions of deaf and hard of hearing people at times of medical crisis. *Professional Psychology: Research and Practice, 27,* 137–144.

Pierce, R. L., & Pierce, L. H. (1991). The need for cultural competencies in child protective service work. In R. L. Hampton (Ed.), *Black family violence: Current research and theory* (pp. 175–186). Lexington, MA: Lexington Books.

Pollard, R. Q. (1994). Public mental health service and diagnostic trends regarding individuals who are deaf or hard of hearing. *Rehabilitation Psychology, 39,* 147–160.

Putsch, R. W., III. (1985). Cross-cultural communication: The special case of interpreters in health care. *Journal of the American Medical Association, 254,* 3344–3348.

Rainer, J. D., Altshuler, K. Z., & Kallman, F. J. (Eds.). (1969). *Family and mental health problems in a deaf population* (2d ed.). Springfield, IL: Charles C. Thomas.

Reeves, K. (1986). Hispanic utilization of an ethnic mental health clinic. *Journal of Psychosocial Nursing, 24* (2), 23–26.

Rehabilitation Services Administration. (1977). *Third annual conference on deafness.* Washington, DC: U. S. Department of Health, Education, and Welfare.

Ries, P. W. (1982). Hearing ability of persons by sociodemographic and health characteristics: United States 1977. *Vital Health Statistics 10,* 140.

Robinson, L. D. (1978). *Sound minds in a soundless world,* pub. ADM 77–560. Washington, DC: U.S. Department of Health, Education, and Welfare.

Rubanowitz, D. E. (1987). Public attitudes toward psychotherapist-client confidentiality. *Professional Psychology: Research and Practice, 18,* 613–618.

Russell, G. L., Fujino, D. C., Sue, S., Cheung, M-K., & Snowden, L. R. (1996). The effects of therapist-client ethnic match in the assessment of mental health functioning. *Journal of Cross-Cultural Psychology, 27* (5), 598–615.

Schensul, S. L., & Schensul, J. J. (1982). Helping resource use in a Puerto Rican community. *Urban Anthropology, 11,* 59–79.

Schlesinger, H. S., & Meadow, K. P. (1972). *Sound and sign: Childhood deafness and mental health.* Berkeley: University of California Press.

Solis, J. M., Marks, G., Garcia, M., & Shelton, D. (1990). Acculturation, access to care, and use of preventive services by Hispanics: Findings from HHANES 1982–84. *American Journal of Public Health, 80* (supplement), 11–19.

Stansfield, M. (1981). Psychological issues in mental health interpreting. *RID Interpreting Journal, 1,* 18–31.

Steinberg, A. (1991). Issues in providing mental health services to hearing-impaired persons. *Hospital and Community Psychiatry, 42,* 380–389.

Telecommunications for the Deaf, Inc. (1996–99). *TDI national directory and guide.* Silver Spring, MD: Telecommunications for the Deaf, Inc.

Tien, J. L., & Johnson, H. L. (1985). Black mental health clients' preference for therapists: A new look at an old issue. *International Journal of Social Psychiatry, 31,* 258–265.

Trybus, R., & Karchmer, M. (1977). School achievement scores of hearing-impaired children: National data on achievement status and growth patterns. *American Annals of the Deaf, 122,* 62–69.

Vasquez, C, & Javier, R. A. (1991). The problem with interpreters: Communication with Spanish-speaking patients. *Hospital and Community Psychiatry, 42,* 163–165.

Vernon, M. (1965). Interpreting in counseling and psychotherapeutic situations. In S. P. Quigley (Ed.), *Interpreting for deaf people: A report of a workshop on interpreting* (pp. 94–103).Washington, DC: U. S. Department of Health, Education, and Welfare.

———. (1995). Psychology and deafness: Past and prologue. *Gallaudet Today, 25* (3), 12–17.

Willigan, B. A., & King, S. J. (1992). *Mental health services for deaf people.* Washington, DC: Gallaudet Research Institute; American Deafness and Rehabilitation Association, Mental Health Section; University of California—San Francisco Center on Deafness.

Woloshin, S., Bickell, N. A., Schwartz, L. M., Gany, F., & Welch, H. G. (1995). Language barriers in medicine in the United States. *JAMA, 273,* 724–728.

Woodward, J. (1972). Implications for sociolinguistics research among the deaf. *Sign Language Studies, 1,* 7.

Zazove, P., Neimann, L. C., Gorenflo, D. W., Carmack, C., Mehr, D., Coyne, J. C., & Antonuccci, T. (1993). The health status and health care utilization of deaf and hard-of-hearing persons. *Archives of Family Medicine, 2,* 745–752.

3

Deaf Therapists and the Deaf Community: How the Twain Meet

IRENE W. LEIGH AND JEFFREY W. LEWIS

Deaf therapists are a unique and visibly growing presence within the community of mental health providers serving the deaf community. Deaf therapists consistently confront life experiences related to how their deafness affects their lives and those of their clients.

Today's deaf therapists are in essence part of a new group of professionals (Pollard, 1992–1993, 1996; Vernon, 1995). They became more than mere anomalies when training programs increasingly welcomed deaf applicants in response to laws such as Section 504 of the Rehabilitation Act of 1973 and the Americans with Disabilities Act of 1990 (Leigh et al., 1991; Pollard, 1992–1993, 1996). Rehabilitation counselor training programs such as those at New York University and the University of Arizona produced a number of deaf counselors who went into mental health work. Data from several 1986 surveys indicate that 20% of mental health professionals working with deaf and hard of hearing populations were themselves deaf or hard of hearing (Heller et al., 1986; Pray et al., 1986). Currently the American Deafness and Rehabilitation Association (ADARA), an organization composed of professionals who focus on service delivery to deaf and hard of hearing people, boasts that 30% of its 750 members are deaf, and many of these are mental health professionals (Pollard, 1996).

Another source of newly trained therapists is Gallaudet University, which in recent years has established a clinical psychology Ph.D. program (accredited by the American Psychological Association), a mental health counseling M.A. program (accredited by the Council on Accreditation of Counseling Related Educational Programs), and a master's of social work program (accredited by the Council on Social Work Education). These programs have put major emphasis on recruiting and training deaf and hard of hearing people. These new deaf and hard of hearing professionals have had the opportunity to receive mentoring from seasoned academicians and clinicians who are versatile in their understanding of mental health issues and the deaf community. This differs from the previous generation of deaf professionals who received their training from programs that had faculty with very little or no experience with deaf people and the deaf community.

The dramatic change in the number of deaf therapists is in part attributable to the 1988 Deaf President Now movement at Gallaudet University (Christiansen & Barnartt, 1995; Gannon, 1989), during which deaf students, faculty, and staff on campus staged a collective protest against the selection of a hearing university president. The result of their protest was the elevation of I. King Jordan, a deaf man. This was a seminal movement in the empowerment of deaf people that proved their ability to take their lives and destinies into their own hands. One consequence of this protest has been a change in perspectives of what it means to be deaf, influencing all areas related to deafness, including mental health work.

By virtue of who and what they are, deaf therapists have different levels of expectations in terms of therapeutic parameters. At the very least, there is an expectation, true or not, that deaf therapists are experientially aware of what it really means to be deaf, and, by extension, they have better insight, more commitment, and greater rapport with deaf clients (Anderson & Rosten, 1985; Harvey, 1989; Heller et al., 1986; Langholtz & Heller, 1986; Leigh et al., 1991; Lewis, 1987; Stewart, 1981; Vernon, 1971). Brauer (1979) conducted interviews with students at a college for the deaf and found a preference for deaf over nondeaf interviewers despite the fact that all interviewers were equally proficient in American Sign Language.

This preference was corroborated by Lewis's (1987) research with a sampling of the same population, in which he showed that deaf subjects, regardless of parental hearing status or school background, had a significantly more positive interviewer rating when told that the interviewer was deaf. In a study by Langholtz and Heller (1986), some deaf therapists reported significantly lower deaf client drop-out rates compared to nondeaf clinicians. It is therefore plausible that those who are connected to the deaf community might view a deaf therapist as more credible. This is consistent with findings from research done on minority group counselor preferences and perceptions of counselor credibility (Beutler et al., 1994).

Therapists struggle to establish the conditions in which their interventions take place, taking into account issues of continuity, therapist activity, degree of client support, and reality constraints on client behavior change (Ursano & Fullerton, 1991). These conditions enter into the crux of the therapeutic alliance, a core process that significantly influences therapeutic outcome (Krupnick et al., 1996). In the therapeutic process, one other component, namely "the person of the psychotherapist" (Mahoney, 1995a, p. 483), is increasingly viewed as critical in predicting the course of psychotherapy. What this means is that the ways and means in which a therapist shares as a human being with a client has profound implications for the therapy process (Harvey, 1993; Jourard, 1971; Kottler, 1993; Leitner, 1995; Mahoney, 1995a). Hence, the client will have specific responses to a therapist who is deaf, and these responses will emerge within the process of therapy, influencing that process. At the same time, the deaf therapist will also be reacting both as a person and as a professional to those perceptions. While there are complex variables that enter into the making of a therapist, we take the position that genetics, biology, personality, physical attributes, family and cultural influences, and other attributes notwithstanding, the deaf experience will certainly be one of the variables that colors what each therapist brings to each session. Therefore, the implications of the deaf experience need to be explored in terms of how these play out in the therapy process. The following vignette offers a good example.

* * *

> Clara was a deaf woman who came for help with depression.[1] She spoke about feeling ashamed when signing with deaf people in public and drawing attention to herself despite the fact that signing was her typical way of communicating. She was unable to stare back at nondeaf individuals who gazed intrusively at her. Through a gradual process of internalizing the therapist's comfort as a deaf person, she was eventually able to ignore the curious glances of nondeaf people at a basketball game. She recognized how her feelings had been imposed on her by

1. All identifying information has been altered for purposes of confidentiality.

the majority nondeaf culture. Once that was acknowledged, therapy progressed rapidly.

In this vignette, despite the client's feelings of shame about her deafness, she is able to accept a deaf therapist, idealize the therapist, and internalize a positive reframing of herself as a deaf woman. The deaf therapist is able to frame the client's reaction within a normalized context as a dilemma that emanates from a pattern of discrimination and shaming rather than as a purely idiosyncratic social anxiety problem. This resolution comes out of the therapist's own history of struggles to invalidate society's frequently negative perceptions of her deafness. Her comfort with this process, her understanding of the implications, and who she is as a person all have an impact on the client in therapy.

Sometimes the therapist's deafness has a negative influence on the client, as the following two examples illustrate.

* * *

A male oral deaf college student came to a mental health center serving deaf and hard of hearing people. The therapist he was assigned to was deaf. His communication was oral-auditory and the therapist easily followed that mode. This client's entire life was in the mainstream. He struggled to be just like everyone else and avoid "looking stupid" when he couldn't understand others. To him, deafness meant failure and inadequacy. He did not know the therapist was deaf until after a few sessions, when she divulged it. His negative reaction paralleled his expectations about how others would react to his deafness. He claimed that the therapist's speech impeded the therapy dialogue despite the fact there had been no complaints prior to the disclosure. His negative attitude eventually necessitated a transfer to a nondeaf therapist.

This client cannot feel safe with a deaf therapist who challenges his stereotypical worldview of deafness as a burden. The therapist herself has to deal with what it means to be rejected simply because she is deaf. It can be painful to be the victim of someone who reveals his anger at his deafness by discriminating against other deaf people. How the therapist frames the response has implications for the termination phase, as well as for one's continuing work as a deaf therapist.

* * *

A college student who became deaf through neurofibromatosis and expressed interest in learning more about the deaf community was referred to a deaf therapist to help him adjust to hearing loss. He had also taken one sign language class. The client did not know that the therapist was deaf until he came to the first session and met the therapist. The client's reaction to the therapist was one of astonishment and then discomfort. The client physically pushed his chair back to the wall and understood less and less of the conversation as the hour went by, even though communication was not laborious at the beginning. The client insisted on a transfer to a hearing therapist.

This client likewise felt very unsafe with a deaf therapist, even though the client had taken a sign language class and was interested in learning more about the deaf community. It may be that the client found it too painful yet to work with someone who lived with and was comfortable with being deaf. It may well be that the client was also dealing with his own stereotypes about deaf people. The next vignette illustrates a different sort of dynamic.

* * *

> A deaf young adult who felt he was not culturally Deaf enough chose a culturally Deaf therapist because, in the client's own words, "By working with you, you can tell me when I am 'culturally Deaf enough' because you are the expert in this."

Here we have a deaf client who has been frustrated in his repeated attempts to become an accepted member of the culturally Deaf core within the deaf community. This client seeks a culturally Deaf therapist for several reasons: to work with someone who is where this client wants to be; who is qualified to pass judgment on when this client is sufficiently enculturated; and who, perhaps, possesses the magical key that this client desires to obtain.

These vignettes illustrate several factors important to the therapeutic outcome. Therapists who are deaf have to understand the implications of deafness in their own lives, how society at large perceives their deafness, how they have used their "being" to deal with that, and the message that "being" conveys to the client. In addition, therapists must remember that clients have their own reactions and intentions regarding the hearing status of their therapists. Even when the issues the client brings to treatment are not related to being deaf per se, the entire being of the therapist, including the deaf part, will play a fundamental role in the therapy process.

Societal Perceptions of Deafness

The prevailing view in the hearing world is that deafness equals disability (Humphries, 1993, 1996). Typically, hearing parents go through a period of mourning when their children are diagnosed with deafness (Koester & Meadow-Orlans, 1990; Luterman, 1979; Paul & Jackson, 1993; Vernon & Andrews, 1990). These parents mourn the loss of the child they expected to raise. Yet deafness as a disability becomes overt only when communication takes place. The personal meaning of being deaf is not constructed in isolation. One's connection or nonconnection to others directly influences social integration and identity. For many deaf people, the nature of these connections leads to common life experiences, including varied experiences of liminality and marginality in the larger American hearing society that play out when the individual recognizes that not fully hearing what is going on casts him or her into a position of differentness.

The notion of *liminality* is a recently identified social construct in the conceptualization of what disability means (Goldin & Scheer, 1995; Murphy, 1990; Scheer, 1994). It expresses the ambiguity of who one is and what defines one's place in society. In essence, the disabled person has no clear niche within particular social groups and instead is on the fringe. The deaf person is not hearing, and what it means to be deaf is not necessarily clearly specified by the dominant hearing society other than the essence of "not hearing." Because the deaf person is not fully accepted as complete, he or she is stigmatized. The meaning of being deaf evolves in response to the deaf person's unique experience in adjusting to, adapting to, or overcoming the communication consequences of being deaf.

The construct of *marginality* goes beyond the notion of liminality. It incorporates not only the idea of being stigmatized and made less credible, but also the sense of being diminished or lacking in the power to define personal and structural relations in comparison to others (Phillips, 1996; Prilleltensky & Gonick, 1994). This often places the deaf person in a position of relative helplessness in managing individual or community interactions. For example, if a deaf person asks what is going on and is told "Nothing important," that person is rendered helpless in terms of the discourse taking place at that moment. Multiplying such incidents many times over in different settings will lead deaf people to feel marginalized within the dominant hearing society.

The deaf therapist, by virtue of being deaf, will most likely have experienced this process toward a self-definition of *deaf,* albeit in varying degrees depending on individual strengths and weaknesses and the kind of experiences that occur. Therefore, he or she will be that much more attuned to deaf clients' efforts to define the meaning of their deafness within social contexts and will be able to deal with their perceptions regarding their liminality/marginality status. How the therapist projects that self-definition and attunement becomes a force within the therapeutic relationship that cannot be ignored because of its impact on transference and countertransference reactions when the deaf client encounters a deaf therapist (Asch & Rousso, 1985; Bliss, 1994; DeWald, 1994; Leigh, 1991; Melgoza et al., 1980). The astute deaf therapist will respond to that realization in a way that facilitates the making of the working alliance, joining the client in terms of the connection of deafness and differentiating in terms of recognizing the deaf client's unique experiences.

The common experiences of liminality and marginality that occur as a consequence of communication difficulties with hearing society tend to encourage kinship bonding among deaf people. For these reasons, deaf individuals have historically come together to form their own community within the larger communities in which they live (Higgins, 1980; Neisser, 1983; Schein, 1989; Stewart, 1992). The relationship between the deaf therapist (who wishes to attend to her or his needs as a deaf person) and the deaf community (to which the therapist may be connected) has profound repercussions on the therapist's life outside the professional setting. This relationship determines what the deaf therapist brings to the therapy encounter with a deaf client and how the therapist and client will perceive one another. To understand the community is to understand the forces and influences that affect the lives and intrapsychic dynamics of the community members (Franklin et al., 1993). Therefore, we now turn to an exploration of the deaf community.

The Deaf Community

The deaf community has existed in the United States for at least the last two centuries (Schein, 1989; Van Cleve & Crouch, 1989). It is a very diverse entity representing a broad spectrum of deaf and hearing individuals, all of whom are connected to varying degrees because of the meaning of deafness in their lives. For many, if not all, deaf people, entry into the deaf community often means finding a niche, a sense of belonging. The liminality and marginality that one struggles with in hearing society recedes as the roots in the deaf community strengthen. However, within this complex entity there are social, political, cultural, linguistic, religious, regional, and ethnic communities (Corker, 1994; Higgins, 1980; Humphries, 1993; Padden, 1980; Paul & Jackson, 1993; Schein, 1989). Despite the commonality of deafness, these diverse constituencies within the deaf community do not always coexist in harmony, just as the various hearing or nondeaf constituencies in American society often coexist in uneasy ways. To recognize the complexity of this deaf community entity is to acknowledge the enormity of the task of the deaf therapist, or of any therapist working with people who are deaf.

Not every deaf person feels connected to the deaf community. Deaf individuals who choose to relate only to hearing society or who have been deafened later in life may see the deaf community as an alien entity. These individuals rarely come to the attention of a deaf therapist unless there is some emotional crisis related to the deafness experience that leads them to search for the meaning of deafness, or unless provider panels connected with HMOs so dictate.

Deaf Culture

The emergence of Deaf culture as an entity worthy of serious consideration took place in the 1970s and 1980s when American Sign Language (ASL) gained recognition as a legitimate language (Baker & Battison, 1980; Padden, 1980; Padden & Humphries, 1988; Paul & Jackson, 1993; Regan, 1990; Schein, 1989). In essence, Deaf culture "is the view of life manifested by the mores, beliefs, artistic expression, understandings, and language particular to Deaf people" (Paul & Jackson, 1993, p. 218). Padden (1980) writes about a Deaf culture that deaf people are either born into, particularly if they have Deaf parents, or enculturated into, depending on how they are exposed to Deaf influences (in school or within social contexts). According to Padden and Humphries (1988), the people of this culture do not see themselves as having a pathological condition (i.e., not hearing); their deafness is a way of life.

For those who identify with Deaf culture, American Sign Language (ASL) is the heart and core, the language that binds them together. As such, ASL is a manifestation of how deaf people have demonstrated their talents for adaptation, for finding ways to work with and move around barriers (Schein, 1989). Their adaptation and their values reflect differences from the majority hearing culture that enable deaf people to develop an inner sense of normality. Deaf people see themselves as individuals who develop as others develop, for whom language and culture are learned spontaneously, and thus there is no "handicap" to overcome except for what society has imposed on them (Davis, 1995; Humphries, 1993, 1996; Lane et al., 1996). When they have problems requiring mental health intervention, these problems are not necessarily "because they are deaf"; rather, the problems may be biologically based, a consequence of society's inability to find a good interface with people who are deaf, problems of daily living, communication difficulties, or the like (see Steinberg et al., this volume).

Value judgments enter into how any group of people is perceived. In this case, Deaf culture is the medium through which Deaf people have attempted to define their own "voice" and their conceptualization of normality in the process of moving toward self-determination. It is an expression of collective consciousness of what it is to be deaf (Barnartt, 1996). Within this context, voice is used as a metaphor for the ability and desire to express choices, opinions, or perceptions that may not mesh with those of the majority society (Phillips, 1996; Reinharz, 1994; Sampson, 1993). The expression of voice is a means of self-determination that enables one to affirm a personal identity despite being different from dominant societal norms (Prilleltensky & Gonick, 1994). As such, it reflects the process of empowerment. The task of psychologists and mental health professionals is one of listening to that voice and understanding the relationship between that voice and the life of the person expressing it.

How the deaf therapist listens to that voice depends on the extent to which the therapist's own Deaf culture identity has been internalized. Stewart (1981) believes that no one, hearing or deaf, can genuinely be "with" the deaf client without understanding sign language and the experience of deafness and its ramifications. However, while all therapists can only partially, never fully, enter the world of any client, the deaf therapist has the opportunity for a more intimate awareness of the deaf experience and of Deaf culture. The therapist's Deaf culture identity then becomes a factor in the therapeutic interaction, subject to how it is projected to the deaf client and how the client perceives it and chooses to relate to it.

Glickman (1986, 1993, 1996) has identified four different types of deaf identity. It is a model equally applicable to deaf therapists, deaf clients, and nondeaf people intimately connected with the deaf community, such as the hearing children of deaf couples (see figure 1).

Glickman (1993) theorizes that these cultural identities are developmentally related in that culturally hearing or marginal individuals eventually become enamoured of Deaf culture, immerse themselves within that culture, and eventually move toward an integrative, bicultural stance. This developmental sequence is one that many deaf individuals experience, particularly those with hearing parents. However, one must not lose sight of the various possibilities in terms of cultural identity development (Aponte & Barnes, 1995). Core identity changes can occur in any direction, depending on life circumstances and opportunities for acculturation. For example, there are individuals who emerge from immersion within Deaf culture and move toward a culturally hearing orientation. Additionally, Aponte and Barnes (1995) caution that such classifications should not be used rigidly to classify any one person; rather they should enhance understanding, taking into account individual dynamic variations relative to environmental imperatives.

TYPES OF DEAF IDENTITY

1. *Culturally hearing.* Hearing norms are the reference point for normality, health, and spoken communication. The role of deafness in one's identity is not emphasized. Rather, deafness is viewed through the lens of medical pathology as a situation to be rectified.

2. *Culturally marginal.* Those who do not fit into either hearing or Deaf societies as demonstrated through their behaviors. Their identities emerge as confused, without clear notions of hearingness or deafness. They may often state they do not feel as if they belong in either society, or their loyalties may shift without evidence of true solidity.

3. *Immersed in Deaf culture.* A positive and uncritical identification with Deaf people. Hearing values are denigrated and the Deaf world is idealized. Anger at hearing people will often be expressed.

4. *Bicultural.* The ability to comfortably negotiate hearing and Deaf settings. These people embrace Deaf culture and also value hearing contacts. They recognize the strengths and weaknesses of both Deaf culture and the hearing communities.

Figure 1. Deaf Identity

Deaf Therapist/Deaf Client Considerations

Many deaf clients are more likely to select a deaf therapist if one is available because of the bond of deafness and the perceived commonality of the Deaf experience. This perceived commonality may facilitate the initial therapeutic alliance. However, differences become apparent when one considers the various meanings and perceptions of deafness (Harvey, 1989). The deaf therapist is not just deaf; he or she has uniquely defined perceptions of being deaf that may or may not parallel the deaf client's perceptions. Added to this are all the other factors (temperament, socioeconomic status, ethnicity, etc.) that sabotage any effort to frame the therapist-client interaction solely in terms of the deafness dimension or deaf cultural identification parameters.

Nonetheless, Deaf culture identity parameters do affect therapist-client attunement. The deaf client may either consciously or unconsciously choose a deaf therapist whose cultural orientation reflects where the client might eventually like to be (Harvey, 1989; Lewis, 1987; Lytle & Lewis, 1996). It is highly unlikely that a culturally hearing deaf person would select a culturally Deaf therapist because of the difficulties in juxtaposing the goal orientations subsumed within each identity category. Unfortunately, the relative scarcity of deaf therapists in many geographic locations renders the possibility of choice moot.

In their analysis of the interface between multiculturalism and psychology, Fowers and Richardson (1996) remind us that, as agents of sociocultural change, therapists need to understand where a client is located in any culture, where that client wishes to be, and how the client's goal might contrast with the therapist's perspective of where the client needs to be. In other words, the therapist has the duty to figure out how to decide when to "match" the client's culture and when to see that perspective as inappropriate. This raises difficult questions, such as, How does the culturally Deaf therapist deal with a client who is culturally hearing? and, Can a culturally hearing deaf therapist comfortably enable a deaf client to consider immersion within Deaf culture in the process of exploring identity issues?

Not every deaf therapist is similarly acculturated into Deaf culture. This is a factor that is easily overshadowed by the bond of deafness when deaf therapists are few and far apart. To be aware of this is to be aware that professionals working within the deaf community can fall into the trap of being naive about the complexity of cross-cultural issues with reference to Deaf culture (Anderson & Rosten, 1985; Harvey, 1989; Pollard, 1996). To complicate matters, there are numerous situations where Deaf culture norms do not go hand in hand with the process of therapy. The following vignette illustrates this point.

* * *

A culturally Deaf client seeking personal growth challenges chose to begin therapy. She was referred to a therapist that she did not know. In the first session, she asked the therapist whether he was deaf or hearing. The therapist invited her to explore this issue (her guess, how she would feel regarding the therapist's hearing status, etc.) before divulging his hearing status. The therapist believed that this process would allow the client to experience uncontaminated feelings about deaf/hearing issues that would allow for greater self-exploration. This client

> reacted with initial resistance, saying that Deaf culture rules allowed for people to ask and receive an immediate answer regarding others' hearing status. The therapist concurred and explained that two different issues were at hand: the client's cultural expectation that she could ask and receive a prompt answer about whether the therapist was deaf or hearing, and the therapist's belief that the client would benefit more by exploring this issue before he answered her question. This explanation satisfied the client and she became willing to engage in this therapeutic process.

A second vignette illustrates another cultural phenomena that is at odds with what usually is seen in therapy.

* * *

> A culturally Deaf woman chose to see a deaf therapist that she previously knew on a casual basis. At the beginning and end of the first session, the woman hugged the therapist as she was arriving and leaving. This was awkward for the therapist and the client picked that up. The woman explained to the therapist that because both she and he were members of the deaf community, she felt it was appropriate to hug him upon arrival and departure, and she would want to greet him with a hug at the beginning of the next session (Deaf culture norm). At the next session, the client entered the room and went to her chair without hugging the therapist. She began the session by stating that she had given some thought to the issue of greeting with a hug and felt it would be better to define her relationship with her therapist in a more professional way. She appeared to be comfortable with this decision and the therapist did not pursue it any further.

Here we see how the cultural pull on the deaf client and the deaf therapist can be played out. This highlights the critical need for therapists to understand cultural norms and expectations and devise ways to address them, also taking into account situations when ethnic culture becomes an added factor in the interaction between therapist and client.

Cultural Competence

Cultures are understood by examining various aspects, including attitudes, forms of emotional expression, patterns of relating to others, and ways of thought (Aponte et al., 1995). These aspects are all integrated in ways that separate one particular culture from the larger culture and yet in many ways still reflect that larger culture. Adding yet another culture, specifically Deaf culture, to the picture heightens the degree of complexity and the need to consider the interactive aspects of each of the cultures involved. In view of all this, cultural sensitivity and cultural competency are essential if the therapist is to be seen as credible.

The concept of culturally affirmative psychotherapy with deaf people is now gaining prominence (Glickman & Harvey, 1996). This therapeutic approach has two components: *cultural sensitivity* and *cultural competence.* Cultural sensitivity must precede cultural competence (Dana, 1993); cultural sensitivity stems from knowledge and first-hand acquaintance with another culture, which allows one to willingly accommodate another culture. In order to be culturally competent, the therapist must go beyond the level of cultural sensitivity not only to acknowledge and accept cultural differences, but to internalize the meanings of behavior within specific cultural contexts and make them part of the therapy dialogue. These meanings reflect the multiple levels of the human psyche that influence cross-cultural relationships (Leong, 1996).

ISSUES FOR THE DEAF THERAPIST

Therapists who wish to become competent in a specific culture must be aware of how their own culture influences their thinking and behavior. They must then analyze this influence for how it affects their interactions with clients from different cultures. Hearing therapists grow up unconsciously internalizing their hearingness; it is very much a part of them, not an "issue" that they discuss with other hearing people. Those deaf therapists who grow up outside of Deaf culture have a very different experience. Their relationships to other deaf people involve exploring the similarities and differences in the way they interpret "deafness." In order to be sensitive to the therapeutic process, they must therefore explore and define their unique interpretation of deafness and their relationships to the deaf community, to the different constituencies within the deaf community, and the extent of their own acculturation into Deaf culture. This is an ongoing process that becomes part of their "being" as people and as therapists. The more they are aware of the different aspects of who they are and what they represent vis-à-vis where their deaf clients are in terms of cultural identification, the more they will understand the subtleties of their own and their clients' reactions within the framework of their differing deaf/Deaf perceptions. This ability will then enhance the deaf therapist's cultural competency with respect to Deaf culture.

In order to be culturally competent and therapeutically connected with deaf clients, therapists must be able to linguistically match their deaf clients (Corker, 1994; Harvey, 1989; Paul & Jackson, 1993; Stewart, 1981). This is the linchpin that determines whether therapists are credible within the deaf community. Because deaf clients express themselves in a variety of ways, the truth is that knowledge of ASL is essential but not sufficient for competency. By virtue of their communication backgrounds, deaf clients demonstrate a large variety of idiosyncrasies in their communication systems. For example, some deaf clients sign in straight English format, some mix ASL with English grammatical structure, some incorporate gestures into their communication system, some mouth words not necessarily in English order and interpose signs here and there, and some rely entirely on oral communication. Without flexibility in adjusting to all these varied communication paradigms, therapy dialogue will falter. Any therapist working with this population needs and is expected to have this flexibility to ensure some modicum of success (Leigh et al., 1991).

This expectation can be either conscious or unconscious. It differs from expectations for the typical hearing therapist who has to prove communication competency before being deemed culturally competent and whose skills likely will be questioned until proven otherwise. Deaf therapists appear to be significantly more skillful in the use of manual communication, and they use more ASL than do hearing therapists (Heller et al., 1986). It is logical to assume that the deaf therapist who cannot demonstrate flexibility in communication becomes much less credible within the deaf community. The "Deafness" of the deaf therapist will be questioned. If a client has negative or ambivalent feelings about Deaf culture and sign language and communicates orally, then sign skills will diminish in importance, but the ability to match the client's communication needs continues to be critical for joining in therapy.

An additional dimension that deaf therapists need to incorporate into their cultural competence armamentarium is an awareness of hearing cultural behavior and the implications that behavior may hold for their deaf clients. The ways deaf therapists acculturate to the majority hearing society depend in part on the evolution of their deaf/Deaf identities. Whatever the status of their relationship to hearing society, deaf therapists will find it difficult to do their clients justice unless they can claim some competency in the area of hearing cultural behavior. Understanding the structure, mechanisms, and dynamics of hearing interactions ensures that deaf therapists will be that much more attuned to the various cultural frameworks within which their deaf clients function. Therefore, they will be that much more competent in pinpointing client issues that emerge, whether these issues are framed in terms of differences in behavior, perceptions, or worldviews.

The extent to which deaf therapists are familiar with hearing paradigms tends to be a function of their personal experiences. Formal coursework on "hearing norms" for those who may need it appear to be practically nonexistent. While this may be a commentary on the minimization of "hearing values" in relation to the deaf community, or an assumption that everyone automatically knows/understands hearing norms, the need to understand the larger hearing society cannot be denied.

The recent proliferation of publications on cross-cultural interventions for treatment efficacy (e.g., Aponte et al., 1995; Dana, 1993; Ramirez, 1991; Sue & Sue, 1999; Yutrzenka, 1995) emphasizes the need for cultural understanding and cultural competency due to the relative scarcity of ethnic mental health personnel (Allison et al., 1994; Bernal & Castro, 1994; "Sex, Racial/Ethnicity Data Available," 1995). Needless to say, deaf ethnic therapists are even more scarce (Heller et al., 1986; Langholtz & Heller, 1986, 1987). Because of this scarcity, therapists may encounter scenarios such as those detailed in the following vignettes.

* * *

A Japanese deaf man came for help with social relationships. He was anxious to establish a relationship with a woman. During one session he animatedly described a chance encounter with an attractive deaf Korean female. The White deaf therapist encouraged him to follow up on that chance encounter, but he refused. His rationale was that Korean women were not suitable for Japanese men. He appeared irritated that the therapist was not sensitive to this cultural perception.

* * *

An African deaf student came to seek advice and was referred to a White deaf therapist. In this session, nondirective suggestions were offered to this student in response to specific questions about what he should do in making several decisions. The client became increasingly frustrated with the therapist and explained that in his African culture, young men sought out and received directive counsel from older wise men, and this was what he was seeking.

In order to develop a successful therapeutic alliance, White deaf therapists need to recognize that minority deaf people are members of at least three communities: the deaf community, their ethnic minority community, and their ethnic minority deaf community (Corbett, this volume; Leigh et al., 1996). Each separate membership has unique implications in terms of issues that are colored by the interactions of deafness, ethnicity, and culture, and, in particular, the dynamics of dual minority status (Pape & Tarvydas, 1993).

To truly comprehend the intricacies of this situation, many deaf therapists must examine not only the meaning of their being deaf/Deaf, but also of being White within the context of American society. The White deaf therapist is not only part of the dominant White society, but also simultaneously part of a deaf community/Deaf culture struggling with self-definition and empowerment issues within the dominant (hearing, American) society. By the same token, the dominant White society is still in the throes of acknowledging the voices and empowerment efforts of minority groups. All of these aspects enter into the therapeutic dialogue. How the persona of the White deaf therapist influences the responses of culturally and ethnically different deaf clients in terms of dominance, oppression, and recognition of differences is a process that calls for intensive scrutiny on a session-by-session basis.

Ultimately, to maintain credibility as a therapist, the deaf therapist must be able to see, comprehend, and connect with the "voices" that are uniquely expressed by diverse entities within the deaf community. In addition to the voices of ethnic cultures, we have the voices of those who differ in terms of sexual orientation, the voices of women, the voices of those who are both deaf and blind, the oral deaf, and so on. These voices have social, historical, and political roots (Lane, 1992; Sampson, 1993; Wrigley, 1996) arising out of the way deaf people have been perceived from the beginning of time. Deaf therapists may identify differently with these voices depending on the nature of their connections with the groups giving rise to these voices. To be professionally competent in handling these diverse voices demands the ability to respect diversity and develop boundaries that permit safe joining and separation. This includes situations where the therapist confronts personal fears and may wish for distance from the client. The following example illustrates this dilemma.

* * *

> A deaf client sought therapy to deal with impending vision loss due to retinitis pigmentosa, and chose to work with a deaf therapist. During the course of therapy, which extended over two years, this client experienced significant vision loss and consequently had several significant periods of depression. The therapist experienced many strong feelings about the trauma of vision loss, the process of accepting one's own deaf-blindness, and the pain of watching a client slip more into darkness while searching for some illumination.

Such confrontations highlight the type of countertransference and boundary issues that deaf therapists who live, work, and play within the greater deaf community—a community in which "everyone knows everyone"—often need to work through. Because such issues have their roots within the "self" or the "being" of the deaf therapist and implicitly have the power to influence and direct the process of therapy, we cannot leave this chapter without considering the therapist's persona in terms of countertransference and boundaries.

Countertransference and Boundary Issues within the Deaf Therapist

The way that therapists perceive clients' behavior shapes their intervention strategies (Goncalves, 1995). These perceptions, which essentially reflect intentions or "meanings," are influenced by the therapists' procedural and declarative knowledge structures, as well as by their cognitive-processing mechanisms. These structures and mechanisms are essentially a manifestation of the self/being of the therapist.

When therapists intervene, they frame meanings in different ways that enable the client to reconstruct perceptions (Carlsen, 1995; Clarke, 1996; Rosen, 1982). Throughout this process, the therapist's and the client's voice, or being, will influence each other in the course of therapy (Kegan, 1982; Mahoney, 1995b; Rosen, 1982). Because of the intense nature of this process, therapists will experience countertransference, which is "the emotional reactions of the therapist in response to the patient's (client's) behavior in the therapy relationship" (Cashdan, 1988, p. 155). These emotional reactions to the voices or constructions of clients are influenced by the therapist's past and ongoing relationships outside the therapy session. The therapist will construct the meanings attached to his or her emotional reactions in ways that will influence the client's therapy. The following example illustrates this process.

* * *

> While in therapy with a culturally Deaf therapist, a deaf client expressed a strong desire to blend into the deaf community and into Deaf culture. He idealized the therapist as a member of Deaf culture. Despite his intensive efforts to join, the client recognized that he was subtly being rejected by the Deaf group into which he was trying to enculturate, and he could not achieve a sense of belonging. He desperately wanted to keep on trying to assimilate and defined the meaning of his own experience as rejection. The therapist worked with the client to find some sort of resolution while inwardly the therapist was aware of and dealing with his own countertransference issues.

If the therapist basks in the glow of the idealization experience and frames his responses accordingly, this will diminish his objective ability to respond to the client's construction of the rejection experience. The client's idealization of the therapist as a personification of successful enculturation into Deaf culture may be spilling over into idealization of Deaf culture. If that process is a function of the therapist's countertransference, it will mean the client potentially could perceive himself as a failure unless the therapist frames the cultural aspects differently, reconstructs the meaning of the client's experiences, and minimizes the idealization.

Because deaf clients typically have hearing families in which communication is greatly hampered (Levine, 1981; Marschark, 1993; Meadow, 1980; Vernon & Andrews, 1990), there is a strong possibility that they may latch on to their deaf therapist as the deaf parent or family member that they never had and wished for (Corker, 1994; Leigh et al., 1991). The process by which the deaf therapist relinquishes that particular role imposed by the client, as indeed she or he eventually must for therapeutic resolution and client independence, relies heavily on the nature of the countertransference manifestation. How much the therapist wishes to fill the client's void in part depends on how the therapist's own family history is construed and the extent to which the therapist may identify with the client's own family history. The idealized parent syndrome can feed into the therapist's narcissistic needs to take care of others and evolve into a critical countertransference issue.

Deaf clients will at times perceive deaf therapists as inadequate or "disabled" in comparison to hearing therapists (see the second and third vignettes earlier in this chapter;

Harvey, 1989; Lytle & Lewis, 1996). While covert feelings about being deaf clearly are the critical factor, clients will overtly rationalize by relying on negative stereotypical perceptions of deaf people. Examples might include observations that deaf people have less access to current information and therefore are less knowledgeable, or that the deaf therapist's communication (whether based on signs or speech) is deficient for the client's purpose. This issue becomes a serious liability for deaf therapists if they are uncomfortable with their own deafness or become aware of their own feelings of inadequacy (Leigh et al., 1991). Deaf therapists are "supposed" to be comfortable with their being deaf. If therapists with unresolved issues surrounding their deafness avoid the pain of discomfort and disavowal of an integral part of their being, there may be potentially disaffirming consequences for their deaf clients.

Overidentification with clients in terms of issues related to being deaf emerge in many different ways; therapists who deny what is happening do their clients a disservice. For example, deaf therapists who frequently have encountered incidences of discrimination and marginality may overidentify with deaf clients struggling with feelings of oppression by hearing society. Their clients' struggles then become *their* struggles, to the point where client empowerment may be at stake. Late-deafened therapists who see clients that have recently lost their hearing may reenact the pain of their own hearing loss and the pace of their adjustment to the loss. This can give rise to therapist expectations for client adjustment, thereby inadvertently invalidating client progress that is not in tune with these expectations (Leigh et al., 1991). What happens to a deaf gay therapist going through the throes of HIV testing when he encounters a deaf client going through the same experience and complaining about the lack of interpreters? His countertransference reactions may resonate with those of the client, perhaps to the point that the client cannot utilize his frustrations in an effective manner.

Countertransference issues force therapists to search within themselves and understand who and what they are. These issues highlight the need to maintain boundaries in order to enable client growth. For deaf therapists connected to the deaf community, boundary issues take on additional significance because of difficulties in distancing the therapy encounter from encounters that take place outside the therapy room (Patterson & Stewart, 1971; Stewart, 1967; Thoreson & Tully, 1971). Even though hearing therapists working in the deaf community encounter similar boundary problems, they do not live within the deaf community to the extent that many deaf therapists do. Deaf therapists continually wrestle with the dilemmas caused by the juxtaposition of their professional and personal lives (Gutman et al., 1995; Lybarger & Langholtz, 1995). This leads to excruciatingly sensitive issues of safety and confidentiality. It is very common for deaf therapists to be told deaf clients do not wish to see them because the clients fear chance encounters outside of therapy and loss of privacy.

While all therapists must discuss confidentiality with their clients in terms of ethical and legal paradigms (Swenson, 1993), deaf therapists often need to go the extra mile in order to enhance their deaf clients' feelings of safety (Falberg, 1985; Harvey, 1989). Lytle (1995) recommends going through possible scenarios with every deaf client to define the client's wish in terms of how unexpected encounters should be handled. Agreement should be reached on issues having to do with whether the client wishes to be acknowledged by the therapist in public, how acceptable acknowledgment is defined, and how the therapist can maintain the client's trust.

Despite such precautions, the unexpected can happen, thereby putting the therapist in a quandary, as the following vignette demonstrates.

* * *

> A deaf therapist inquired about the nature of a Halloween party to be given by a local deaf community organization. After ensuring that it would be appropriate for young children to attend, she brought her two children along. When the festivities were well underway, she suddenly encountered a deaf client of hers whose costume was very sexually revealing. The client was also acting in a sexually exhibitionistic way. There was a shock of recognition when the client made eye contact with the therapist who at that moment was holding her two children by the hand. No dialogue took place. Even though the children were enjoying themselves, the therapist made the decision to leave very shortly thereafter.

In this vignette, confidentiality and boundary issues are entwined. While we can speculate on the internal state of the client who inadvertently has been exposed in this type of encounter, the boundary dilemmas for the therapist, whose privacy has been invaded, force a renegotiation of the therapeutic alliance and a reevaluation of the approach to therapy. New meanings about each of the participants have been constructed that alter the old meanings and expectations set within therapy sessions. For the therapist, the new meanings are shaped by several factors: emotional feelings about the deafness connection that brought both to the same place, loss of personal freedom, inadvertent disclosure of private information, the exhibitionism of the client, and professional safety. Working through these countertransference reactions here enables the therapist to expand his or her self-awareness in ways that potentially can facilitate client growth.

Not all deaf clients fear loss of privacy. Some want to be friends with their therapist, whom they feel is the only one who truly understands them, and they do not comprehend the nature of the therapy relationship (Langholtz & Heller, 1986). When deaf therapists put limits on the relationship with these clients to maintain neutrality and then encounter them in social settings, it becomes difficult for the therapists to minimize client feelings of rejection. The dilemma of "betraying" the socially hungry client by not gratifying the client or betraying the profession has to be resolved in ways that encourage the client to understand therapeutic imperatives, painful as it may be for the deaf therapist struggling with compassion and the desire to nurture the client.

Within the therapy situation, therapists are expected to maintain closed self-boundaries by divulging minimal information about themselves (Derlega et al., 1991). The focus, after all, is on the client. However, self-disclosure can be used as a therapeutic tool, depending on the client's specific problem and the content of the disclosure. In the case of the deaf therapist, perceived similarity (i.e., being deaf) has a greater probability of enhancing the therapist's influence, at least initially (Anderson & Rosten, 1985; Brauer, 1979; Harvey, 1989; Lewis, 1987). The deaf therapist's mantle of authority will also be enhanced by positive client perceptions of the therapist's cultural competence vis-à-vis where the client is positioned culturally. Self-disclosure on the part of the deaf therapist related to "deaf" issues entails some risk in that it will of necessity reveal differences that do not match client perceptions about the bond of deafness. This increases the likelihood of differentiation and may even distance the deaf client who labels the differentiation as nonsimilar (Harvey, 1989). For example, when a deaf therapist disclosed that she could hear on the telephone, albeit in a very limited manner, her oral deaf, culturally hearing client screamed, "You're NOT deaf!" In such situations it is very easy for the deaf therapist to lose boundaries and feel a sense of invalidation as a deaf person in the process of this exchange. When the deaf therapist can reconstruct the meaning of this scenario in terms of her or his inner sense of being deaf/Deaf and focus on the client issues, the negative countertransference interference diminishes in saliency.

Conclusion

The state of being deaf permeates the fabric, the being, the persona, the inner essence of deaf therapists in terms of life structure and ways of relating to the societies surrounding them. This deafness strongly influences therapy, and imposes a significant burden on the deaf therapist who works within the deaf community because the intricacies of living within this small community place the deaf therapist in a fishbowl for all to see. Understanding how deaf therapists can juxtapose public and private lives in ways that will foster the growth of their deaf clients will also contribute to the therapists' professional success.

References

Allison, K. W., Crawford, I., Echemendia, R., La Vome, R., & Knepp, D. (1994). Human diversity and professional competence: Training in clinical and counseling psychology revisited. *American Psychologist, 49,* 792–796.

Anderson, G. B., & Rosten, E. (1985). Towards evaluating process variables in counseling deaf people: A cross-cultural perspective. In G. B. Anderson & D. Watson (Eds.), *Counseling deaf people: Research & practice* (pp. 1–22). Little Rock, AR: Arkansas Rehabilitation Research and Training Center on Deafness and Hearing Impairment, University of Arkansas.

Aponte, J. F., & Barnes, J. M. (1995). Impact of acculturation and moderator variables on the intervention and treatment of ethnic groups. In J. F. Aponte, R. Y. Rivers, & J. Wohl (Eds.), *Psychological interventions and cultural diversity* (pp. 19–39). Boston: Allyn and Bacon.

Aponte, J. F., Rivers, R. Y., & Wohl, J. (Eds.). (1995). *Psychological interventions and cultural diversity.* Boston: Allyn and Bacon.

Asch, A., & Rousso, H. (1985). Therapists with disabilities: Theoretical and clinical issues. *Psychiatry, 48,* 1–12.

Baker, C., & Battison, R. (1980). *Sign language and the deaf community.* Silver Spring, MD: National Association of the Deaf.

Barnartt, S. (1996). Disability culture or disability consciousness. *Journal of Disability Policy Studies, 7,* 1–19.

Bernal, M. E., & Castro, F. G. (1994). Are clinical psychologists prepared for service and research with ethnic minorities? Report of a decade of progress. *American Psychologist, 49,* 797–805.

Beutler, L., Machado, P., & Neufeldt, S. (1994). Therapist variables. In A. Bogin & S. Garfield (Eds.), *Handbook of psychotherapy and behavior change* (4th ed.) (pp. 229–269). New York: Wiley.

Bliss, S. (1994). Perfection or preconception: Some thoughts on reactions to disability in the therapist. *British Journal of Psychotherapy, 11,* 115–119.

Brauer, B. A. (1979). The dimensions of perceived interview relationship as influenced by deaf persons: Self-concepts and interviewer attributes as deaf or nondeaf. (Ph.D. dissertation, New York University, 1979). *Dissertation Abstracts International, 40,* 1352B.

Carlsen, M. B. (1995). Meaning-making and creative aging. In R. A. Neimeyer & M. J. Mahoney (Eds.), *Constructivism in psychotherapy* (pp. 127–154). Washington, DC: American Psychological Association.

Cashdan, S. (1988). *Object relations therapy: Using the relationship.* New York: W. W. Norton.

Christiansen, J. B., & Barnartt, S. N. (1995). *Deaf president now! The 1988 revolution at Gallaudet University.* Washington, DC: Gallaudet University Press.

Clarke, K. M. (1996). Change processes in a creation of meaning event. *Journal of Consulting and Clinical Psychology, 64,* 465–470.

Corker, M. (1994). *Counseling: The deaf challenge.* London: Jessica Kingsley.

Dana, R. H. (1993). *Multicultural assessment perspectives for professional psychology.* Needham Heights, MA: Allyn and Bacon.

Davis, L. (1995). *Enforcing normalcy: Disability, deafness, and the body.* London: Verso.

Derlega, V. J., Hendrick, S. S., Winstead, B. A., & Berg, J. H. (1991). *Psychotherapy as a personal relationship.* New York: Guilford Press.

DeWald, P. A. (1994). Countertransference issues when the therapist is ill or disabled. *American Journal of Psychotherapy, 48,* 221–230.

Falberg, R. M. (1985). Maintaining confidentiality when counseling deaf adults in rehabilitation facilities. In G. B. Anderson & D. Watson (Eds.), *Counseling deaf people: Research and practice* (pp. 105–120). Little Rock, AR: Arkansas Rehabilitation Research & Training Center on Deafness and Hearing Impairment, University of Arkansas.

Fowers, B. J., & Richardson, F. C. (1996). Why is multiculturalism good? *American Psychologist, 51,* 609–621.

Franklin, A. J., Carter, R. T., & Grace, C. (1993). An integrative approach to psychotherapy with Black/African Americans. In G. Stricker & J. R. Gold (Eds.), *Comprehensive handbook of psychotherapy integration* (pp. 465–479). New York: Plenum Press.

Gannon, J. (1989). *The week the world heard Gallaudet.* Washington, DC: Gallaudet University Press.

Glickman, N. (1986). Cultural identity, deafness, and mental health. *Journal of Rehabilitation of the Deaf, 20,* 1–10.

———. (1993). Measuring Deaf cultural identities: A preliminary investigation. *Rehabilitation Psychology, 38,* 275–283.

———. (1996). The development of culturally Deaf identities. In N. S. Glickman & M. A. Harvey (Eds.), *Culturally affirmative psychotherapy with Deaf persons* (pp. 115–153). Mahwah, NJ: Lawrence Erlbaum.

Glickman, N. S., & Harvey, M. A. (1996). *Culturally affirmative psychotherapy with Deaf persons.* Mahwah, NJ: Lawrence Erlbaum.

Goldin, C. S., & Scheer, J. (1995). Murphy's contributions to disability studies: An inquiry into ourselves. *Social Science and Medicine, 40,* 1443–1445.

Goncalves, O. F. (1995). Hermeneutics, constructivism, and cognitive-behavioral therapies: From the object to the project. In R. A. Neimeyer & M. J. Mahoney (Eds.), *Constructivism in psychotherapy* (pp. 195–230). Washington, DC: American Psychological Association.

Gutman, V., Leigh, I. W., Corbett, C. A., & Morere, D. A. (1995, August). *Ethical issues in a small community: Models for deafness.* Paper presented at the meeting of the American Psychological Association Convention, New York, NY.

Harvey, M. A. (1989). *Psychotherapy with deaf and hard of hearing persons: A systemic model.* Hillsdale, NJ: Lawrence Erlbaum.

———. (1993). Cross cultural psychotherapy with Deaf persons: A hearing, White, middle class, middle aged, non-gay, Jewish, male, therapist's perspective. *Journal of the American Deafness and Rehabilitation Association, 26,* 46–55.

Heller, B. W., Langholtz, D., & Acree, M. (1986). Effective psychotherapy with deaf persons: Therapist and client characteristics. In D. Watson, G. B. Anderson, & M. Taff-Watson (Eds.), *Integrating human resources, technology and systems in deafness, Monograph No. 13* (pp. 46–74). Silver Spring, MD: American Deafness and Rehabilitation Association.

Higgins, P. O. (1980). *Outsiders in a hearing world: A sociology of deafness.* Beverly Hills, CA: Sage Publications.

Humphries, T. (1993). Deaf culture and cultures. In K. M. Christensen & G. L. Delgado (Eds.), *Multicultural issues in deafness* (pp. 3–15). White Plains, NY: Longman.

———. (1996). Of deaf-mutes, the strange, and the modern deaf self. In N. S. Glickman & M. A. Harvey (Eds.), *Culturally affirmative psychotherapy with Deaf persons* (pp. 99–114). Mahwah, NJ: Lawrence Erlbaum.

Jourard, S. M. (1971). *The transparent self.* New York: Van Nostrand Reinhold.

Kegan, R. (1982). *The evolving self: Problem and process in human development.* Cambridge, MA: Harvard University Press.

Kisor, H. (1990). *What's that pig outdoors? A memoir of deafness.* New York: Hill and Wang.

Koester, L. S., & Meadow-Orlans, K. P. (1990). Parenting a deaf child: Stress, strength, and support. In D. F. Moores & K. P. Meadow-Orlans (Eds.), *Educational and developmental aspects of deafness* (pp. 299–320). Washington, DC: Gallaudet University Press.

Kottler, J. A. (1993). *On being a therapist.* San Francisco: Jossey-Bass.

Krupnick, J. L., Sotsky, S. M., Simmens, S., Elkin, I., Watkins, J., & Pilkonis, P. A. (1996). The role of the therapeutic alliance in psychotherapy and pharmacotherapy outcome: Findings in the National Institute of Mental Health Treatment of depression collaborative research program. *Journal of Consulting and Clinical Psychology, 64,* 532–539.

Lane, H. (1992). *The mask of benevolence.* New York: Alfred A. Knopf.

Lane, H., Hoffmeister, R., & Bahan, B. (1996). *A journey into the Deaf-world.* San Diego: Dawn Sign Press.

Langholtz, D., & Heller, B. (1986). Deaf and hearing psychotherapists: Differences in their delivery of clinical services to deaf clients. In D. Watson, G. B. Anderson, & M. Taff-Watson (Eds.), *Integrating human resources, technology and systems in deafness, Monograph No. 13* (pp. 34–45). Silver Spring, MD: American Deafness and Rehabilitation Association.

———. (1987). Effective psychotherapy with deaf persons: Therapists' perspectives. In D. Watson, G. Long, M. Taff-Watson, & M. Harvey (Eds.), *Two decades of excellence: A foundation for the future: Monograph No. 14* (pp. 54–67). Little Rock, AR: American Deafness and Rehabilitation Association.

Leigh, I. W. (1991). Deaf therapists: Impact on treatment. *Proceedings, XI World Congress of the World Federation of the Deaf: Equality and self-reliance* (pp. 290–297). Tokyo, Japan: World Federation of the Deaf.

Leigh, I. W., Clark, B., Cohen, C., Lewis, J., & Wax, T. (1991). Deaf therapists in mental health: Perspectives. In D. Watson & M. Taff-Watson (Eds.), *At the crossroads: A celebration of diversity, Monograph No. 15* (pp. 305–312). Little Rock, AR: American Deafness and Rehabilitation Association.

Leigh, I. W., Corbett, C. A., Gutman, V., & Morere, D. A. (1996). Providing psychological services to deaf individuals: A response to new perceptions of diversity. *Professional Psychology: Research and Practice, 27,* 364–371.

Leitner, L. M. (1995). Optimal therapeutic distance: A therapist's experience of personal construct psychotherapy. In R. A. Neimeyer & M. J. Mahoney (Eds.), *Constructivism in psychotherapy* (pp. 357–370). Washington, DC: American Psychological Association.

Leong, F. (1996). Toward an integrative model for cross-cultural counseling and psychotherapy. *Applied and Preventive Psychology, 5,* 189–209.

Levine, E . S. (1981). *The ecology of early deafness: Guides to fashioning environments and psychological assessments.* New York: Columbia University Press.

Lewis, J. W. (1987). *Counselor attitude influences on the counselor preferences and perceptions of counselor characteristics held by female deaf college students.* Ph.D. dissertation, New York University.

Lewis, J., & Lytle, L. (1987, October). *Therapeutic relationship: When the therapist is deaf, when the therapist is hearing.* Paper presented at the National Training Institute for Mental Health Professionals, Mental Health and the Postsecondary Deaf Student, New Orleans, LA.

Luterman, D. (1979). *Counseling parents of hearing-impaired children.* Boston: Little, Brown.

Lybarger, R., & Langholtz, D. (1995, May). *Crossing the line: Ethical dilemmas in deafness.* Workshop, American Deafness and Rehabilitation Association Convention, Kansas City, MO.

Lytle, L. (1995, 22 September). *Ethical dilemmas in the delivery of psychological services to deaf/hard of hearing adults and children.* Discussion, Department of Psychology Seminar, Gallaudet University, Washington, DC.

Lytle, L., & Lewis, J. (1996). Deaf therapists, deaf clients, and the therapeutic relationship. In N. S. Glickman & M. A. Harvey (Eds.), *Culturally affirmative psychotherapy with Deaf persons* (pp. 261–276). Mahwah, NJ: Lawrence Erlbaum.

MacDonald, R. J. (1994). Deaf-blindness: An emerging culture? In C. J. Erting, R. C. Johnson, D. L. Smith, & B. D. Snider (Eds.), *The deaf way: Perspectives from the International Conference on Deaf Culture* (pp. 496–503). Washington, DC: Gallaudet University Press.

Mahoney, M. J. (1995a). The modern therapist and the future of psychotherapy. In B. Bongar & L. E. Beutler (Eds.), *Comprehensive textbook of psychotherapy* (pp. 474–488). New York: Oxford University Press.

———. (1995b). The psychological demands of being a constructive therapist. In R. A. Neimeyer & M. J. Mahoney (Eds.), *Constructivism in psychotherapy* (pp. 385–399). Washington, DC: American Psychological Association.

Marschark, M. (1993). *Psychological development of deaf children.* New York: Oxford University Press.

Meadow, K. P. (1980). *Deafness and child development.* Berkeley: University of California Press.

Melgoza, B., Roll, S., & Baker, R. C. (1980). Transferential aspects in therapy: The therapist with a physical impairment. *The Clinical Psychologist, 33,* 11–12.

Murphy, R. (1990). *The body silent.* New York: W. W. Norton.

Neisser, A. (1983). *The other side of silence: Sign language and the deaf community in America.* New York: Alfred A. Knopf.

Padden, C. (1980). The deaf community and the culture of deaf people. In C. Baker & R. Battison (Eds.), *Sign language and the deaf community* (pp. 89–103). Washington, DC: National Association of the Deaf.

Padden, C., & Humphries, T. (1988). *Deaf in America: Voices from a culture.* Cambridge, MA: Harvard University Press.

Pape, D. A., & Tarvydas, V. M. (1993). Responsible and responsive rehabilitation consultation on the ADA: The importance of training for psychologists. *Rehabilitation Psychology, 38,* 117–131.

Patterson, C. H., & Stewart, L. G. (1971). Principles of counseling with deaf people. In A. E. Sussman & L. G. Stewart (Eds.), *Counseling with deaf people* (pp. 43–86). New York: Deafness Research and Training Center, New York University School of Education.

Paul, P. V., & Jackson, D. W. (1993). *Toward a psychology of deafness.* Boston: Allyn and Bacon.

Phillips, B. A. (1996). Bringing culture to the forefront: Formulating diagnostic impressions of deaf and hard of hearing people at times of medical crisis. *Professional Psychology: Research and Practice, 27,* 137–144.

Pollard, R. Q. (1992–1993). 100 years in psychology and deafness: A centennial retrospective. *Journal of the American Deafness and Rehabilitation Association, 26,* 32–46.

———. (1996). Professional psychology and deaf people: The emergence of a discipline. *American Psychologist, 51,* 389–396.

Pray, J., Pollard, B., & Wax, T. (1986). Social work practice with hearing-impaired persons: A profile. In D. Watson, G. B. Anderson, & M. Taff-Watson (Eds.), *Integrating human resources, technology, and systems in deafness: Monograph No.13* (pp. 2–14). Silver Spring, MD: American Deafness and Rehabilitation Association.

Prilleltensky, I., & Gonick, L. S. (1994). The discourse of oppression in the social sciences: Past, present, and future. In E. J. Trickett, R. J. Watts, & D. Birman (Eds.), *Human diversity: Perspectives on people in context* (pp. 145–177). San Francisco: Jossey-Bass.

Ramirez, M. (1991). *Psychotherapy and counseling with minorities.* New York: Pergamon.

Regan, T. (1990). Cultural considerations in the education of deaf children. In D. F. Moores & K. P. Meadow-Orlans (Eds.), *Educational and developmental aspects of deafness* (pp. 73–84).. Washington, DC: Gallaudet University Press.

Reinharz, S. (1994). Toward an ethnography of "voice" and "silence". In E. J. Trickett, R. J. Watts, & D. Birman (Eds), *Human diversity: Perspectives on people in context* (pp. 178–200). San Francisco: Jossey-Bass.

Rosen S. (Ed.). (1982). *My voice will go with you: The teaching tales of Milton H. Erickson, M.D.* New York: W. W. Norton.

Rutherford, S. (1988). The culture of American deaf people. *Sign Language Studies, 59,* 129–147.

Sampson, E. E. (1993). Identity politics: Challenges to psychology's understanding. *American Psychologist,* 48, 1219–1230.

Scheer, J. (1994). Culture and disability: An anthropological point of view. In E. J. Trickett, R. J. Watts, & D. Birman (Eds.), *Human diversity: Perspectives on people in context* (pp. 244–260). San Francisco: Jossey-Bass.

Schein, J. D. (1989). *At home among strangers.* Washington, DC: Gallaudet University Press.

Schildroth, A. N., & Hotto, S. A. (1996). Annual survey of deaf and hard of hearing children and youth: Changes in student and program characteristics, 1984–85 and 1994–95. *American Annals of the Deaf, 141,* 68–71.

Sex, race/ethnicity data available. (1995, Winter). *Trends in Education: APA Education Directorate News, 2,* 2–3.

Stewart, L. G. (1967). The social dilemma of the deaf professional counselor. *Journal of Rehabilitation of the Deaf, 1,* 21–25.

———. (1981). Counseling the deaf client. In L. K. Stein, E. D. Mindel, & T. Jabaley (Eds.), *Deafness and mental health* (pp. 133–159). New York: Grune and Stratton.

———. (1992). Debunking the bilingual/bicultural snow job in the American deaf community. In M. Garretson (Ed.), *Viewpoints on deafness: A deaf American monograph, 42* (129–142). Silver Spring, MD: National Association of the Deaf.

Sue, D. W., & Sue, D. (1999). *Counseling the culturally different: Theory and practice* (3rd ed.). New York: Wiley.

Swenson, L. C. *Psychology and law for the helping professions.* Pacific Grove, CA: Brooks/Cole.

Thoreson, R. W., & Tully, N. L. (1971). Role and function of the counselor. In A. E. Sussman & L. G. Stewart (Eds.), *Counseling with deaf people* (pp. 87–107). New York: Deafness Research and Training Center, New York University School of Education.

Ursano, R. J., & Fullerton, C. S. (1991). Psychotherapy: Medical intervention and the concept of normality. In D. Offer & M. Sabshin (Eds.), *The diversity of normal behavior* (pp. 39–59). New York: Basic Books.

Van Cleve, J. V., & Crouch, B. (1989). *A place of their own: Creating the deaf community in America.* Washington, DC: Gallaudet University Press.

Vernon, M. (1971). Current status of counseling with deaf people. In A. E. Sussman & L. G. Stewart (Eds.), *Counseling with deaf people* (pp. 30–42). New York: Deafness Research and Training Center, New York University School of Education.

———. (1995). An historical perspective on psychology and deafness. *Journal of the American Deafness and Rehabilitation Association, 29,* 8–13.

Vernon, M., & Andrews, J. (1990). *The psychology of deafness.* New York: Longman.

Wohar Torres, M. T. (1995). A postmodern perspective on the issue of deafness as culture versus pathology. *Journal of the American Deafness and Rehabilitation Association, 29,* 1–7.

Woodward, J. (1972). Implications for sociolinguistics research among the deaf. *Sign Language Studies, 1,* 1–7.

Wrigley, O. (1996). *The politics of deafness.* Washington, DC: Gallaudet University Press.

Yutrzenka, B. A. (1995). Making a case for training in ethnic and cultural diversity in increasing treatment efficacy. *Journal of Consulting and Clinical Psychology, 63,* 197–206.

Part Two

Diverse Constituencies

4

The Evolution of Psychotherapy for Deaf Women

TOVAH M. WAX

The act of singling out a relatively specific group—deaf women—for therapeutic consideration reveals the extent to which the American mental health profession, not to mention society as a whole, has essentially ignored or minimized the complex experiences of traditionally disenfranchised groups.[1] Those characterized by more than one type of disenfranchisement (e.g., being both female and deaf) have been particularly left out. Very little has been published about mental health issues of deaf women in the pertinent journals on deafness (e.g., *Gallaudet Today* and *Journal of the American Deafness and Rehabilitation Association*). Similarly, relatively little has been written about mental health issues of women, or even multicultural issues in mental health, within flagship journals of psychology. Most recently, articles about mental health issues of deaf people have been published in *American Psychologist* and *Rehabilitation Psychology*, but none have appeared about deaf women specifically.

Substantially more has been written about parallels identified between Deaf culture and other minority cultures (Brubaker, 1994; Glickman & Zitter, 1989; Sligar, 1995). The promotion of feminist, multicultural, and disability/deafness interests in mental health has come largely from the women's movement (Brown & Brodsky, 1992; Walsh, 1994) and from the civil rights movement (Rittenhouse et al., 1991; Sieber & Cairns, 1991). Interest in mental health issues of people with disabilities has also been influenced by more pervasive rehabilitation and disability legislation (e.g., the Americans with Disabilities Act of 1990) as well as by the rehabilitation field (e.g., Bowe, 1978). These movements have been accompanied by a corresponding increase in the number of specialty professional journals (e.g., *Women and Therapy, Feminism and Psychology*, the *Journal of Multicultural Counseling and Development*, and the *Journal of Cross Cultural Psychology*).

While there has been some increase in published scholarship about the mental health issues of several significant disenfranchised groups, there has been almost no movement at all regarding mental health research and practice with deaf women in particular. This chapter addresses briefly the reasons for the near absence of attention to this group and explores multicultural and constructivist therapeutic approaches that offer the most potential for effective treatment of mental health issues of deaf women.

1. In this chapter, disenfranchised individuals are those belonging to groups that experience sociopolitical discrimination, which is being disadvantaged in the form of lack of equal or equitable access to things considered rights or privileges for the larger society (education, employment, health or mental health care, etc.). See, for example, Atkinson & Hackett, 1995.

Women and Psychology: A Brief Review

Early psychometric research was characterized by an androcentric, maximalist, and "alpha-biased" approach. Gender differences were usually measured against male traits as valued norms (Bohan, 1993), with an overemphasis on the personalities of men and women and underemphasis on historic and cultural forces (Mowbray et al., 1992). Some gender differences have proven robust, a popular example being the greater frequency of depression among women (Katz et al., 1993). However, improved research methods have led to the revision of other findings, such as a gender-based influence on intelligence.

As a theoretical focus for mental health studies, sexism, racism, handicapism (e.g., Brauer, 1978), and even audism (Padden & Humphries, 1988) are largely concerned with the sociopolitical disenfranchisement of these groups within an overall society essentially dominated by the values of middle-class nondisabled Whites and/or males (Atkinson & Hackett, 1995; Sieber & Cairns, 1991). Among the elements of disenfranchisement are restriction or lack of access to common socioeconomic rights or privileges, such as education, employment, and medical and mental health care. Disenfranchised groups experience restriction of equal access to power and status (e.g., Schaef, 1985). Factors such as lack of empowerment, oppression, and victimization are cited as additional explanatory contributors to poor mental health (Atkinson & Hackett, 1995; Denmark & Paludi, 1993).

Socioeconomic status continues to be one of the strongest correlates of mental health for both men and women across all ethnic/minority groups (Pugliesi, 1992). Interaction between socioeconomic status and gender persists across racial/ethnic (Pugliesi, 1992) and disability populations (Nagler, 1993), with relatively higher proportions of women represented in certain diagnostic categories of psychopathology and in outpatient mental health treatment services.

A "beta-biased" approach posits that men and women are fundamentally similar and that observed gender differences are the result of restriction of opportunities or negative/devaluing perceptions (Kahn & Yoder, 1989). Rather than treat gender as an independent phenomenon, constructivist psychologists view it as a context-dependent socially constructed agreement in which participants carry out classes of transactions deemed to be appropriately "masculine" or "feminine" by those involved (Bohan, 1993). Work relationships, for example, are less defined by gender than by relative power and status—the behaviors of women and men tend to be more similar in the work context than in nonwork contexts (Major, 1987). In fact, all behaviors could ultimately be defined in terms of whether they are appropriately context-based: mental health could be operationalized through determining the number of contexts in which individuals are able to adopt pertinent behaviors, as well as by determining the extent and range of such appropriate behaviors throughout development (e.g., successfully navigating the multiplicity of roles; Simon, 1995). In their study of deaf women in the San Francisco Bay area, Becker and Jauregui (1981) observed that many of the women behaved "deferentially" toward their husbands at home, or toward men in general at Deaf community events, even as they performed in leadership or supervisory roles at work; these modifications in behavior could be interpreted as adaptive contextual responses to societal expectations or norms.

More recent methodologies and explanations involve the ways in which men and women perceive themselves in their multiple roles in different contexts, with gender differences deriving from the meanings attached to these perceptions. Simon (1995) found that sex differences in mental well-being were related to how men and women evaluated their roles as spouses, parents, and workers. For example, when both spouses were employed outside of the home, men experienced more congruence and less role conflict between their roles of provider and spouse/parent than did women. These differences in the meanings attributed to work and family roles by men and women were offered as explanation for the gender gap in mental health, at least within heterosexual marriages.

Among deaf people, gender differences in education have become minimal, but significant disparities continue to exist in occupational choice and status, as well as in income (Barnartt & Christiansen, 1985; MacLeod-Gallinger, 1992). A constructivist interpretation would suggest that educational contexts of deaf people are relatively more similar than those of the work force; therefore, the behaviors of men and women are also relatively more similar in the former than in the latter. Achievement-oriented gender differences in occupational choice and status are influenced by continued traditional key role expectations within the Deaf community (Kelly-Jones, 1984). Thus deaf women are more likely than deaf men to acutely experience the discrepancies between educational achievement and under- or unemployment than deaf men.

ETHNIC/MINORITY/CROSS-CULTURAL PSYCHOLOGY

In the United States, studies of cross-cultural psychology have largely focused on Black and Hispanic ethnic minorities (Betancourt & Lopez, 1993). Until the recent increasing globalization of psychology (Mays et al., 1996), multicultural and cross-cultural studies had not been considered part of the field's mainstream epistemology. Studies of differences among races or ethnic minorities paralleled those of gender differences in postulating that observed racial/ethnic differences were most likely confounded by differences in socioeconomic status.

By the 1970s, growing dissatisfaction with mainstream psychology, with its implicit and explicit attempts to fit all individuals into a generic White, middle-class model of psychosocial development, mental health, and psychopathology, gave rise to the formulation of cross-cultural psychological approaches (Atkinson et al., 1979).

Anchoring mental health issues in different psychosocial contexts and the application of constructivist psychological approaches can be extended to the minority perspective on deafness, with deaf women construed as a minority within a minority. As with other minority group members, deaf women's overall lower socioeconomic status is related to sociopolitical disenfranchisement, the experience of which in turn produces apparent differences in psychological functioning and mental health.

Comas-Diaz (1992) describes five stages of the development of cross-cultural psychotherapeutic approaches with ethnic minority groups: reactive, inquisitive, revisionist, integrationist, and pluralistic. The first two, *reactive* and *inquisitive,* focus on application of dominant culture psychological treatment; the next two stages, *revisionist* and *integrationist,* focus on incorporating ethno-cultural variables into psychotherapy. Comas-Diaz recognizes, however, that these stages of cross-cultural psychotherapeutic approaches reinforce the paradox that mental health for minority clients means subsuming their values in favor of those more congruent with the larger culture (Sue, 1983). As a corollary, psychotherapy has often amounted to acculturation (read: assimilation or subjugation) of ethnic minority clients to the dominant culture (Berry & Kim, 1988). The fifth stage, *pluralistic,* focuses on addressing clients' needs more directly in their own contexts, sometimes at loggerheads with the context(s) of the dominant culture.

While more responsive to the actual needs of ethnic and minority clients, current psychology nevertheless faces a growing challenge of helping therapists and clients balance *etic* (cross- or extracultural) and *emic* (within- or intracultural) concerns (Essendoh, 1996). It must also help therapists and clients to resist the pressure both to maintain one's own culture and adopt that of the dominant group(s) (Betz & Fitzgerald, 1993). Imagine, therefore, the multiple dilemmas of deaf women: within the Deaf community, they are challenged as women; in the context of hearing women they are disenfranchised as deaf people; finally, among hearing people in general, they are disenfranchised as both deaf and women. Imagine adding to that mixture additional ethnic or minority status, and the challenges of mental health service to this population become increasingly evident.

By acknowledging that all human action is shaped by cultural and historical forces, a hermeneutic approach to multicultural psychotherapy offers a promising resolution to most of these etic and emic dilemmas. Fowers and Richardson (1996) offer the following five areas of interpretation that can potentiate the psychotherapeutic process between clients and therapists from different cultures:

1. Identification of a shared context (for psychotherapeutic work);
2. Understanding of traditions and social practices;
3. Determining truth and morality claims;
4. Clarifying a vision of the "good life"; and
5. Sustaining cultural dialogue.

The common thread throughout these hermeneutic principles is that of constructing shared meaning about elements of culture through a psychotherapeutic process of ongoing dialogue and revision of narratives (feed-forward and feedback mechanisms, Lyddon, 1993). While conjecturing that such mutual construction of meaning/rapport would be maximized when both client and therapist share similar characteristics (e.g., both deaf and female), there is also the risk that both would bring similar negative or destructive perspectives to the therapeutic encounter. If the therapist is aware of, and has worked through, these risks, then he or she can serve as a model for helping the client undergo a similar process of deconstructing these undermining experiences and reframing them more constructively.

A Psychology of Deafness

Psychological perspectives on the development and mental health of deaf people have evolved in ways similar to those concerning women and ethnic/minority groups. Lane (1990, 1992) discusses the infirmity perspective of deaf people that has prevailed in the field of psychology until very recently, when cultural models began to have more impact (Lane, 1990; McDougall, 1991; Pollard, 1996). Given the view of deafness as a deviation from the norm of hearing, the deviance model, derived from the work of Becker (1963), places deaf people at a disadvantage because of the tendency of society to equate deviancy with deficiency (Moores, 1987). Early studies of the psychology of deafness (e.g., Levine, 1960; Myklebust, 1964) focused primarily on adjustment to or coping with deafness. This approach reinforced the acceptance of hearing status as a valued or preferred norm and forced deaf people into a fundamental dilemma: to be mentally healthy is to be at odds with one's own identity, and the solution is to become as "hearing" as possible. For deaf women, this meant become as "hearing" and as "male" (and in some cases, as "White") as possible. A summary of traits attributed to deaf people in the professional literature (Lane et al., 1996) is remarkably reminiscent of now-classic research comparing attributes of mental health and mental illness by gender (e.g., the finding that attributes of mentally healthy adult women were similar to those of mentally ill males; Broverman et al., 1970); similarly, attributes of deaf people were consistently considered unfavorable.

Therapists who rely on attribution research run the risk of misdiagnosing clients who are culturally Deaf or identified with the Deaf community. Behaviors that are socially acceptable among deaf people may be construed as mental illness, while actual psychopathological behaviors might be overlooked (Lane et al., 1996; Vernon & Andrews, 1990). Incidence and prevalence studies of psychopathology indicate few, if any, differences between deaf and hearing adults (Vernon & Andrews, 1990), but studies of differences in emotional/behavioral problems in deaf and hearing children suggest a higher percentage of deaf children evidencing psychopathology (e.g., Hindley et al., 1994). These data must be interpreted with caution, for a number of reasons detailed elsewhere (Corker, 1994), but particularly because differences observed in childhood essentially dissolve by adulthood (Sheetz, 1993). But any actual differences in mental health status of deaf and hearing people may be especially confounded by communication and other environmental barriers (Pollard, 1993).

The shift in psychological perspectives about deaf people is also reflected in the evolution of the concept of the "psychologically healthy deaf person" originally formulated by Sussman (1991). The predominant theme of his conceptualization is one of effectively coping with the oppression of being deaf in a hearing world. More recent conceptualizations suggest that mental health of deaf people is reflected in the ability to negotiate or construct deaf- or hearing-related contexts (Wax, 1994, 1996). By extrapolation, mental health of deaf women is related to their ability to construct or negotiate both deaf-hearing and male-female contexts, often simultaneously. In one sense, the relatively more robust mental health of deaf women (like that of disabled women in general; see Vernon & Andrews, 1990), could be related to the sustained ability to juggle more than one such negotiation at a time.

MENTAL HEALTH ISSUES UNIQUE TO DEAF WOMEN

Despite the shift in perspectives about mental health issues in general, few advances have been made in addressing the unique mental health issues of deaf women. Both women and deaf people experience social discrimination based on presumed lower intellectual and cognitive skills (Parasnis, 1996); other assumptions have been made about the additive effects of being both deaf and female (Hanna & Rogovsky, 1993b; MacLeod-Gallinger, 1992; Wax & Danek, 1984). In the way that shared gender unifies a variety of women, the experience of deafness unifies this population (Higgins, 1980; Parasnis, 1996). While gender and race differences among deaf people are consistent with those among other population groups, studies illustrate that the mental health effects of deaf-hearing differences tend to supersede those of gender and race (Barnartt & Christiansen, 1985; MacLeod-Gallinger, 1992).

Among the few studies that touch on mental health issues in deaf women, most have studied multiple jeopardy postulations about combined adverse effects of disadvantages or oppressions (Wax & Danek, 1984). Studies of relative mental health status of deaf women compared with that of either women or deaf people in general have been either poorly conducted or are simply not available. Peterson (1952) did provide fruitful demographic information about a population of mentally ill deaf female inpatients in St. Elizabeth's Hospital in Washington, D.C., one of the few extant inpatient treatment programs focused on treatment of deaf people. Including comparative data about deaf male inpatients and the inpatient population in general would have strengthened the study and perhaps revealed possible gender differences in mental health treatment needs. More recently, a study of gifted deaf adults revealed not only that a higher than expected percentage (40%) of participants were receiving mental health services, but also that deaf men fared worse than deaf women across diagnoses of psychopathology (Vernon & LaFalce-Landers, 1993). This finding is consistent with data showing that gender differences in mental health among people with disabilities generally favor women over men, in that women are described as having better mental health than men (Vernon & Andrews, 1990).

Studies of mental health in deaf women that touch on contextual or constructivist variables include that of Magilvy (1982), who found that social support was the most relevant contribution to the mental health status of deaf women with respect to maintaining satisfactory quality of life, particularly for those with late-onset deafness. In spite of some methodological paradoxes, Dee's (1993) study of deaf women and their hearing female siblings is significant for incorporating both contextual (differing educational and socialization experiences) and constructivist (meaning systems of gender socialization) variables into her interviews. The women in her study were asked not only about their upbringing, but also how they interpreted and understood their experiences as deaf or hearing women, respectively.

Still another study (Joseph, 1993) used the narratives of deaf women interviewed in focus group format to understand psychotherapeutic issues from a feminist perspective. For the participants in her study, the salience of deaf-hearing politics generally overrode that of gender differences; in addition, the construct of what Davis (1987) in her study of disabled women calls "boundary living" was of some concern among the deaf women participants. Boundary living describes the experiences of women attempting to maintain autonomous selves in the face of interventions or intrusions by patriarchal or dominant institutions. As inferred from Joseph's study, deaf women struggle to maintain a sense of autonomy and identity in the face of paternalism not only from the larger society, but also from within the Deaf community; in other words, the boundaries (of both freedoms and constraints) are relatively more stringently circumscribed for deaf women.

Deaf women are unique to the extent that they continuously encounter the intersection of common gender and deafness experiences. That encounter may be experienced as one of multiple identities, oppressions, diversities, contexts, and/or constructions of meaning. The choice and direction of psychotherapeutic treatment can therefore be significantly influenced by the frame of reference shared by the deaf woman client and her therapist. Appropriate psychotherapeutic approaches to deaf women have to be inferred from research about mental health intervention with disenfranchised people, women, and deaf people in general, as well as improved psychotherapy techniques, with those of constructivist psychology showing particular promise.

Psychotherapeutic Approaches with Deaf People

Going beyond the strictly intrapsychic model of deafness as some form of psychopathology (Farrugia, 1986; Rayson, 1985), theoretical frameworks addressing a "psychology" of deafness have paralleled those developed to explain a "psychology" of women and ethnic/minority groups. Current theoretical approaches to the psychotherapeutic treatment of deaf people can be grouped into three major areas: multiple identity or role development, multiple oppressions, and multiple diversities and/or contexts.

Multiple Identity/Role Development

A paradox often experienced by both ethnic minority and disabled women is the conflict between the societal myth of the multiplex superwoman (e.g., African American women) and the expectation that minority and disabled people are somehow incapable of fulfilling their role obligations (e.g., disabled women; Hanna & Rogovsky, 1993a). Most models of identity development in disenfranchised individuals propose stages through which individuals progress as they come to terms with conflicts such as sexism (McNamara & Rickard, 1989), racism (Berry & Kim, 1998), and audism (Brubaker, 1994; Glickman & Carey, 1993). Generally, these models show disenfranchised individuals progressing from initial stages of unawareness or ignorance to middle stages of realization/reaction and separation, and a final stage usually characterized by the adoption of a multicultural/multilinguistic attitude toward the dominant society (Comas-Diaz, 1992; Reynolds & Pope, 1991). Studies of the identity development of deaf people focus more on modes of acculturation rather than stages (Glickman, 1996a; Glickman & Zitter, 1989; Wax, 1993). Deaf people have been most popularly identified as assimilated or culturally hearing, segregated or immersed in Deaf culture, bicultural, or marginal, as noted in the Leigh and Lewis chapter in this volume. The development of a cultural orientation toward deafness is influenced by many factors, including age of onset, severity, family, education, and social experiences (see Glickman, 1996a, for a fuller discussion). The common flaw of all of these models of identity development is the assumption that disenfranchised individuals are the ones needing to acculturate. In the extant studies about deaf women (e.g., Becker and Jaugerui, 1981; Women and Deafness, 1984), there is no substantive discussion about the need for deaf *men* to acculturate to the community of deaf women.

Multiple Oppressions

Therapists are often assumed to be members of a dominant group and clients members of the oppressed (Ridgeway, 1994). The various interpretations of oppression discussed in the literature include those that center on the concepts of power (on colonization, see Lane, 1992; on powerlessness, see Gibbs & Fuery, 1994; Jankowski, 1995; Perkins, 1991; Schlesinger, 1987; Skodra, 1992) and attitudinal biases (on sexism, see Bohan, 1993; Katz et al., 1993; on handicapism, see Brauer, 1978; Hanna & Rogovsky, 1993a, 1993b; on fundamental negative attitudes, see Livneh, 1988, Wright, 1988). For deaf clientele, iatrogenic biases constitute an especially pernicious risk of negative treatment effects because of ignorance or malpractice (on counselor "types," see Corker,

1994a; on misdiagnosis, see Heller & Harris, 1987; Vernon, 1978; on medicalization, see Lane, 1990; on pathologization, see Sussman & Stewart, 1971).

Although oppression as an interpretation of mental health problems in individuals provides useful insights into the sociopolitical contexts of functioning, it is essentially a "no win" approach for clientele. As Lane (1992) frankly discusses, the "mask of benevolence" is but another mechanism used by professionals to keep deaf clients in a subordinate and manageable position with respect to the dominant hearing society. This issue is more onerous for deaf women in the face of continuing traditional gender role expectations within the Deaf community.

Multiple Diversity/Multiple Context

Psychological studies of cultural diversity among deaf people generally focus on identity and identification (Brubaker, 1994; Glickman & Carey, 1993; Glickman & Zitter, 1989; Sligar, 1995). Glickman and Carey (1993) note that deaf people with marginal identities tend to be those born deaf into an inaccessible hearing context, whereas those with immersion or bicultural identities tend to have been born into deaf families or spent developmental years in a deaf context (e.g., deaf school).

The increasing salience of context in mental health treatment has led to the development of different psychotherapeutic strategies with deaf clients, moving from intrapsychic approaches (Edelstein, 1978; Marr, 1983; McCrone, 1983; Quedenfield & Farrelly, 1983; Scott, 1978; Sussman & Stewart, 1971), to systemic approaches that focus more on modification of the environment (e.g., Glickman & Zitter, 1989; Harvey, 1984, 1990), to formulations that are increasingly contextualist (Glickman, 1996b; Harvey, 1985) and constructivist (Freedman, 1994).

Understanding environmental influences on the behavior of deaf individuals (e.g., Levine, 1981) has fostered two significant directions in developing mental health treatment for deaf people, especially in family therapy. Earlier family therapy approaches with deaf clients tended to focus on deaf members as cause or symptom (e.g., Baum, 1981; Mendelsohn & Rozek, 1983; Shapiro & Harris, 1976). Subsequent approaches to family therapy de-emphasized the focus on deaf family members in favor of more systemic issues such as patterns of communication (Sloman et al., 1987; Sloman & Springer, 1987). Harvey (1985) has been instrumental in "equalizing" deaf and hearing participants by distinguishing psychological from technical-linguistic paradigms of communication. Consideration not only of family context but also of other contexts involving deaf individuals (e.g., educational, vocational rehabilitation) is another important feature of Harvey's (1990) paradigmatic approach, in which, by minimizing or eliminating duplication, conflicts among strategies of treatment can be mitigated, similar strategies can be reinforced, and services can be made more cost-effective.

Constructivist Existentialist Developmental Psychology: Emerging Applications for Deaf Women

A significant outcome of context-based mental health treatment with deaf (as with nondeaf) people has been the recognition not only of the impact of contextual variables, but also the meanings or interpretations attributed to these variables by the participants in the situation. The foundation of constructivist psychology lies in uncertainty about the true nature of reality (Neimayer, 1993) and, therefore, about the true nature of gender or even deaf-hearing differences (Bohan, 1993; Corker, 1994a). Individuals are viewed as active agents who not only interpret and construct realities internally (or develop a culture of the mind, Rogers & Kegan, 1991), but also individually and collectively create or constitute relevant consensus realities (Neimeyer, 1991). Thus individual development is a process not so much of discovering a free-standing objective reality, but of formulating truths through a series of social interchanges.

Bohan (1993) illustrates that gender is simply the term given to a set of behavioral-environmental interactions that are consensually considered masculine or feminine. Extrapolation to the experiences of deaf individuals would suggest that deafness is less an intrinsic individual characteristic than it is a product of particular behavioral-environmental interactions or experiences. Consider that within a context of deaf people only (say, a Deaf club gathering), deafness is often an irrelevant or "invisible" variable, leaving only the question of possible gender differences. In most contexts involving interactions between deaf and hearing individuals, deafness, or at least the attendant issue of communication, assumes salience.

Principles of Constructivist Developmental Theory

Constructivist developmental theories borrow extensively from the principles of cognitive and existential-humanist psychologies. According to Kegan (1982), individuals construct meanings from their experiences and use these meanings both in response to environmental contexts and for generating more adaptive interpretations of self, objects, others, and events (Rosen, 1991). Neimeyer (1993) suggests that developing individuals are like complex systems models in which thought, feeling, and behavior are interdependent expressions of increasingly complex interactions between the self and its significant contexts, mediated by the "centralized" mechanism of core ordering processes. While stage theories of development have not really materialized in existential psychology beyond May's (1983) or Deurzen-Smith's (1988) formulations of existence modes, some unifying conceptual existential themes across the life span can nevertheless be discerned (see table 1).

Overall, individuals construct, and are embedded within, increasingly complex and ultimately universalized structures of meaningful relationships (Kegan, 1982; May & Yalom, 1984). Individual development is an accumulation of experience (or existence/essence relationships) through an application of an individual's awareness (being/participating/doing) in one "direction" and knowledge (spectating/interpreting/meaning-making) in the other "direction," as diagrammatically represented in figure 1.

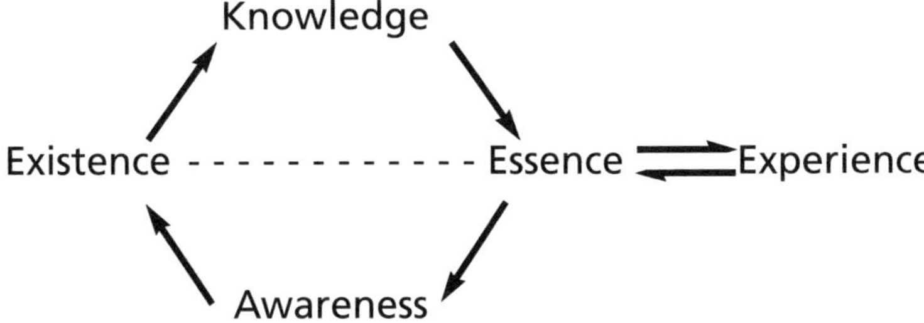

Figure 1. The Meaning-Making Cycle of Individual Development

Table 1. Resonance Among Developmental Theories

Erikson	Piaget	Kohlberg	Rogers	Maslow	Kegan	May	Proposed
Infancy	Sensorimotor		Organismic Valuing Process	Survival	Incorporative	Umwelt	Existence
		Instrumental Relativism					
Toddler	Pre-Operational			Safety	Impulsive		Awareness
		Personal Concordance					
Childhood	Concrete Operations	Social Contract	Positive Regard	Mastery	Imperial	Mitwelt	Essence
Adolescence	Formal Operations			Love, Belonging	Interpersonal	Eigenwelt	Experience
			Self Regard		Instrumental		
Adult/Aged	Post-formal Operations	Individual Principles		Esteem, Self-Actualization			
					Inter-individual	Uberwelt	Transcendence

Note. The placement of the stage names reflects the relative positions of the developmental stages according to each theorist. These theories can be reviewed in Newman and Newman, 1992; Kegan, 1982; Kramer, 1990; May, 1983; Rogers, 1973.

Table 2. Constructivist Existential Developmental Evolutions

Proposed Stages or Levels	Proposed Epiphanic Evolutions	Proposed Revision of Meaning
Existence	Being	Living
Awareness	Knowing	Learning
Essence	Reasoning	Mastering
Experience	Doing	Committing
Transcendence	Becoming	Satisfying

This experience—or meaning-making—cycle (Malm, 1993), activated developmentally with the emergence of awareness, reaches maximum strength in adulthood, when "sufficient experiencing" data (autobiography and biography; Bujold, 1990) is acquired. Eventually, one's own existence can be transcended through acknowledging the circumscription of experience by ultimate nothingness or meaninglessness. Succinctly put, transcendence consists of simultaneously finding meaning in life (love, work, leisure, etc.) while coming to terms with its loss (death).

Core ordering processes are a key mechanism of movement or transition through these stages of constructivist-existential development (Neimeyer, 1993). They reflect conscious epiphanic perceptions of symbolic or metaphorical dimensions of immediate experience significant enough to invoke a new level or growth of being (epiphanic evolutions; see table 2). Commitment to and/or responsibility for choices and their consequences is facilitated by epiphanies of transition from reasoning to doing; becoming (being = doing) characterizes the epiphanies associated with adulthood transitions. As Malm (1993) might put it, the individual becomes increasingly fluent in repeatedly reconstituting the self, therefore becoming increasingly congruent or authentic.

Psychotherapeutic Applications

Within the constructivist psychotherapeutic framework, understanding psychopathology is largely phenomenological, with modification of meaning-making mechanisms of individuals the primary focus of treatment. Constructivist therapists are less concerned with specific diagnoses of mental illness and more concerned with understanding the constructs of a patient's world (Kelly, 1977; Rogers & Kegan, 1991). Individuals develop "cultures of the mind" over time that shape experiences (Rogers & Kegan, 1991). If these mind cultures are sufficiently at odds with those of others around them, if they do not feel integrated within the self, or if they provide neither satisfactory resolution of problems or obstacles nor discernible movement toward desired goals, then the individual may experience mental or emotional distress. A major goal of constructivist psychotherapy is to help individuals revise and/or expand the repertoire of their core ordering processes, enlarging their "culture menu" (DeCarvalho, 1990), using feedback (assimilative) and feed-forward (accommodative) strategies (Lyddon, 1993). Resistance is considered to be an attempt by the client's threatened or challenged core ordering processes to maintain a familiar continuity of the known meaning-making self (Mahoney, 1991).

In the most "cognitive" of constructivist psychotherapeutic approaches, the person is viewed as scientist, constructing hypotheses about the world on the basis of experiences

(Kelly, 1977; Neimeyer, 1993). Several clinical applications have been found useful with this approach, including repertory grids amenable to mathematical probability analysis (Landfield & Epting, 1987). Other applications of the personal construct approach to therapy include the work of Berg-Cross and Zoppetti (1991), who developed a "person-in-culture" interview to explore personal-cultural values and meanings of individuals, and that of Maher and Tetreault (1993), who focus on understanding an individual's cultural-relational stance ("positionality"). Similarly, Glickman and Carey's (1993) deaf identity development scale may help define the identity and identification of deaf people with respect to different contexts of the Deaf community. It would be of interest to determine what this instrument would reveal about gender differences in identity development in this population. Farrugia (1986) and Padden (1996) have both discussed the centrality of deafness among the experiences of deaf individuals, both for the purpose of establishing appropriate communication strategies within therapeutic sessions and for maintaining a dialogue about the meaning of deafness experiences. For deaf women, this dialogue would also have to include the meaning of gender and the interaction of deafness and gender experiences.

According to structural-developmental constructivist therapeutic approaches, core ordering processes are formulated early in life based on interpretation of early experiences (Guidano & Liotti, 1983). Among the therapeutic techniques used by proponents of this approach are life review or lifeline graphs, in which clients are asked to identify important events or experiences as far back as they can remember (Mahoney, 1991). Freedman (1994), among others, has used the lifeline intervention technique with deaf clients. For deaf women clients, deaf/hearing and gender-related events can be expected to emerge as salient life themes (Dee, 1993; Joseph, 1993).

Another major psychotherapeutic approach adopted by constructivist practitioners is that of narrative reconstruction (Neimeyer, 1993). Clients are encouraged to tell stories about significant life experiences and are asked to respond to stories that contain moral situational dilemmas (Freedman, 1994). Through these stories, therapists can discern psychopathology by the extent to which the stories of individuals reflect deviations from the formulations of reality developed within the cultures in which those individuals are embedded (Howard, 1991). Psychotherapy, then, is a process of helping clients "repair" their stories through what is essentially considered a cross-cultural experience of converging the life stories of both therapist and client (Beutler et al., 1990). In the case of therapists working with deaf women clients, this will often mean creating consensus from divergent perspectives of multiple oppressions on the part of the client and multiple dominances on the part of the therapist (Ridgeway, 1994). One technique used to facilitate narrative psychotherapy involves having the therapist share progress notes with the client in the form of inquiry or challenge. In other cases clients may be asked to "externalize" or "objectify" their stories and then challenge them as a way of revising negative, destructive, or self-defeating scripts to more growth-enhancing ones (Neimeyer, 1993).

The value of using storytelling as a therapeutic tool with deaf people is gaining increasing recognition (Freedman, 1994; Isenberg, 1996) due to the popularity of storytelling and drama in the Deaf community (Corker, 1994b; Isenberg, 1996). In addition to inviting storytelling and lifeline constructions, Freedman (1994) and Isenberg (1996) use illustrative metaphorical and allegorical situations to help deaf clients deal more effectively with their issues. Content analysis of stories from deaf women, however, depends to a great extent on therapists' expertise on deaf/hearing and gender issues in the Deaf community context, with respect to the meanings of metaphors and allegories used (Glickman & Harvey, 1996). Conceivably, the content of daydreams from deaf women and men may be different; specifically, for example, the daydreams of highly educated deaf women may reflect more frustrations with deafness-related and/or gender-related issues affecting occupational and other life choices than those of less highly educated deaf women (Anthony & Gibbins, 1992).

Developmental-Existential-Affirmative-Formulative (D.E.A.F.) Therapy

The blending of constructivist approaches results in a developmental-existential-affirmative-formulative approach, or D.E.A.F. therapy. The developmental-existential aspects of this therapeutic approach are a distillation of common elements from stage or level theories of cognitive, behavioral, and affective development, mediated by core ordering processes. Psychological growth occurs through a constructive web of cultural and personal development (Bidell, 1992).

Culturally affirmative psychotherapies (Browning et al., 1991; Eldredge, 1993; Glickman & Zitter, 1989; Martin & Hall, 1992) recognize the parameters of one or more sociocultural contexts that influence a client's identity and identifications or affiliations. Therapeutic effectiveness depends on the degree to which therapist and client can come to consensus about communication style (Sue, 1990), shared context (e.g., acquisition of context; Coleman 1995), and shared vision(s) of reality (Andrews, 1989).

Finally, the formulative considerations of psychotherapy emerge from the encounter between therapist and client. The therapist-client alliance permits a dialogue (Dwyer, 1987) of reciprocity (Davis, 1987) that in turn fosters development of an intersubjective culture (Benjamin, 1992; DeCarvalho, 1990; Howard, 1991), from which new or alternative ways of being and doing can be inspired in the client.

Case Illustration: Evolution of a Multifaceted Deaf Woman

* * *

Petra is a twenty-five-year-old deaf Caucasian female who was born deaf and raised in a large metropolitan area of New York.[2] She has three siblings, including an older half-sister, an older brother, and a younger brother; one sibling died before she was born. Her younger brother and several other family members are also deaf, suggesting a genetic factor contributing to deafness. When Petra was two years old, her mother left her father and subsequently married another man. Her father was an alcoholic, and Petra maintained a relationship with him until she was a teenager, after which they became estranged. She perceived her mother to be caring but "strict," and her stepfather to be "soft" and a "listener."

Before matriculating at the National Technical Institute for the Deaf (NTID) in Rochester, New York, Petra attended several schools for the deaf. Although trained in oral communication skills, Petra prefers almost exclusive use of American Sign Language—an observation linked to the evolution of her identity as a Deaf person (see later discussion). Petra reported being a "rebellious, troublesome teenager," with few friends among her peers. Believing herself to have

2. The name of this client and some other identifying information have been altered in order to protect her privacy and to maximize confidentiality.

more in common with her teachers than with her peers, Petra preferred to hang out with selected favorite teachers throughout her high school years.

Petra initiated psychotherapy with me shortly after her arrival at NTID; attendance at sessions was sporadic for several months before becoming more consistent. After two years, therapy was terminated, with the client feeling "more in touch with who I *am*." Following a two-year hiatus with sporadic contacts, therapy was resumed, interrupted only by school and summer breaks, for one year.

Although college students are treated typically through the use of brief psychotherapy models, this case is exceptional in that therapist and client sustained a therapeutic dialogue spanning several years of college/life experiences. Therefore, the evolution of Petra's ability to integrate several apparently disparate aspects of her identity toward the woman she is today are substantively documented. As the client evolved, so did the therapist, with therapeutic approach and intervention continually being modified by the increasing complexity of Petra's articulated experiences and the therapist's own professional growth. The following composite narrative illustrates this process of mutual (deconstructive, reconstructive) evolution.

CLIENT PRESENTATION (1990–1991)

Petra initially came to therapy because of dissatisfaction with her interpersonal style, which she acknowledged was openly rebellious, angry, and controlling. Petra had few friends and generally strained relationships with family members; she felt it was time to change her behaviors and try a different approach. Petra's father was an alcoholic who she described as "good to us kids" although unreliable; yet, she told one story of an occasion when he "nearly choked" her. Petra both rebelled against and appreciated her mother's strict disciplinarian approach; they still maintain an ambivalent relationship. As a rule, angry confrontations appeared to be the most direct form of communication among family members, with feelings of closeness and solidarity inferred from ability to be "frank" with each other. As an example, Petra once visited her sister, who was engaged to be married. During the visit, Petra witnessed an affair between her sister and a live-in boarder. When Petra confronted her sister with this observation, her sister reacted with anger that became physical and resulted in Petra's being "thrown out."

Positive and affectionate communications were significantly more awkward and tended to take indirect forms (e.g., a family member might discover that he or she was praised or defended to someone else). Petra spent a significant amount of time with her brothers, and the three of them frequently teased and provoked one another. The quality of these interactions suggests that Petra tried to be accepted as "one of the guys," a factor that may have worked against the more feminine aspects of her nature.

Through course work about self-awareness and substance abuse, Petra began to discover that "rules" operating in her family governed much of her behavior. She realized that in her family, overt expressions of love or appreciation were somehow less acceptable than expressions of anger, and that troublesome behavior received more attention than accomplishments. A theme running throughout Petra's stories about interactions with her family involved situations in which she got into some kind of attention-getting "trouble" (e.g., nearly missing her own high school graduation party; being accused of fooling around with her sister's boyfriend). She apparently preferred negative attention to perceived indifference, and perhaps related it to her role in distracting the family from dealing with issues of her father's alcoholism. That is, many of the family rules related to coping with alcoholism, with Petra taking on the role of clown or scapegoat (e.g., Bepko & Kreston, 1985).

Several themes characterized Petra's preoccupations about unsatisfactory interpersonal interactions beyond those with family members. One area of concern was what Petra perceived to be persistent allusions to and rumors about her sexuality and sexual orientation. She found her few dating and sexual experiences with men generally uncomfortable, and somewhat disgusting. Petra professed disinterest in dating peers, preferring instead the company of older or married men; one affair with a married man ("everything but penetration") left her feeling primarily guilty and anxious, but Petra did recognize that these types of situations kept her from having to get seriously involved with anyone.

Another interpersonal issue concerned Petra's consistently getting into situations that could be characterized as triangulations among herself and two friends or groups of friends. In these situations, Petra perceived herself as being the focus of conflicting loyalties, always having to choose between one faction or the other. These observations are consistent with Petra's reports of being in related situations in which she was somehow perceived as "special," such as being the oldest or youngest, most sophisticated or naive, or otherwise standing out in some significant way. Her friendships are also characterized by an all-or-nothing style of extreme emotional attachments or or alienations, with closeness characterized by idealization and conflict characterized by condemnation of the designated other.

THERAPIST OBSERVATIONS AND INTERVENTIONS (1990–1991)

Throughout this period of therapy, Petra seemed preoccupied with family relationships, especially her family's perceptions of her progress in college and her own sense of inadequacy about meeting those expectations. In comparison with her brothers, who both graduated from college, Petra felt she was taking longer and having a more difficult time. At this point, she was still significantly enmeshed in her family relationships—particularly in comparing herself to, and competing with, her brothers. One task of therapy was to help Petra "disembed" herself from her original family and develop new "family" contexts. A more specific aspect of this task was for Petra to identify less with her brothers (and presumably "masculine" perspectives and activities) and more with herself as a woman and individual in her own right.

Equally preoccupied with her deaf and hearing contacts, Petra tended to assume major or sole responsibility for the difficulties she was experiencing. These concerns were associated with Petra's tendency toward perfectionism and to some rigidity about her expectations of others. Typically she would comment, "I know this is so bad/horrible/evil of me, and I shouldn't do/feel/be this way, but . . . " As indicated earlier, her reactions to people and events tended toward extremes of idealization or condemnation, and her most frequent response style was one of anger and and attempts to control others or situations.

During this phase of therapy, the therapist spent several months establishing rapport with Petra, who attended sessions sporadically and avoided addressing issues directly. Once attendance became more regular and Petra became more articulate, cognitive approaches were applied. Because Petra tended to develop singular interpretations of events and experiences, one therapeutic focus was to help her develop alternative hypotheses. For example, Petra once came in appearing devastated because someone she thought was a "true friend" dumped her in response to rumors of Petra's lesbianism. When asked how she knew this was the case, she acknowledged that she never confronted the friend or discussed it with her (largely, of course, because Petra had never yet confronted the issue in herself). The therapist helped her to develop alternative hypotheses about the friend's change of behavior, including other reasons besides this rumor such as unknown circumstances in the friend's life.

Another aspect of cognitive restructuring in this case was to help Petra revise her emotional reactions to more manageable proportions (e.g., from devastation to disappointment, or anger to frustration/annoyance, using Ellis's [1989] A-B-C approach). We also worked on identifying which aspects of interactions or situations were under her control and which were not ("boundary living"; Davis, 1987). A third aspect of this approach was to help Petra collect and rely as much as possible on empirical evidence (e.g., directly ask the friend about the apparent change in behavior), rather than rely on assumptions, in order to develop more realistic or functional interpretations of events and subsequent responses.

CLIENT PRESENTATION (1992)

As Petra became more detached from her family relationships, the focus of therapy shifted away from concern about family expectations to reflection about her academic and career interests, and to her social/sexual lifestyle. During this time Petra's struggle for personal happiness/fun vs. duty became more acute, and there was considerable discussion about whether or not to take an academic leave of absence from NTID. After considering several options ("moratorium"; Newman & Newman, 1992), Petra decided to remain at NTID. Her decision was influenced by three significant issues: recognition of her habit of procrastination and how that affected her choices in life; her attachment to her therapist and anxiety about losing therapeutic contact (transference); and a desire to deal more directly with her emerging awareness about her sociopolitical deaf identity and sexual orientation.

THERAPIST OBSERVATIONS AND INTERVENTIONS (1992)

Petra's desire to remain connected to the therapist appeared to reflect both the latest in a pattern of attachments to parental figures and a movement to learn about/establish intimacy in adult relationships (isolation vs. intimacy; Newman & Newman, 1992). As a simultaneous developmental and therapeutic transference issue, Petra began to explore her own perspectives on intimate relationships, including lifestyle choices with respect to involvement with both Deaf culture and lesbianism. Anxiety about her relationship to her hearing and deaf brothers became more evident, as she became more "radical" about her political and social involvement in Deaf culture. For example, Petra was concerned that her deaf brother functioned in ways more typical for a person who is hard of hearing, and that their increasing political and cultural differences might create more alienation between them. During this time, Petra's attraction/attachment to the therapist became apparent from comments Petra made during therapy. Petra also sent the therapist written notes and e-mails, in which she expressed appreciation for the intervention and a desire to maintain a friendship after/beyond therapy. The transference issues seemed to include elements of identification with the therapist as a deaf woman and psychosexual attraction.

Cognitive restructuring and some existential approaches were the hallmark of therapeutic intervention at this time. Significant use was made of the therapeutic encounter, using the relationship itself as both illustration and direct experience ("spectator" and "participant"; Cochran, 1990). To Petra, being "oneself" meant having nearly absolute congruence among thought, feeling, and action. Her interactions with people, therefore, were governed by the extent to which she believed this congruence existed; inevitably, such interactions continued to be characterized by an all-or-nothing approach.

An important aspect of treatment at this time was to illustrate how thought, feeling, and action were interdependent yet discrete units of psychological analysis. For example, as therapist and client each discussed feelings about the other, the therapist was able to illustrate that feelings of "solidarity" (e.g., both being deaf and female) are not necessarily acted upon, and that this knowledge did not make the relationship any less genuine or meaningful. Petra would comment about whether or not the therapist was present and/or involved in political activities on campus related to the issues of deaf women.

Extrapolation of this kind of understanding to other experiences was reflected, for example, during the process Petra went through "coming out" as both lesbian and as a culturally Deaf person. At first, it seemed essential that she reveal and act upon these identities to everyone with whom she interacted in order to minimize her sense of hypocrisy and "make up for lost time." She wanted nothing to do with hearing or straight (heterosexual) people, believing that the only way to be fully herself was to be with others exactly like her. Since then, and as a result of interventions facilitating "second culture acquisition" (Coleman, 1995, p. 726), Petra has been learning that total self-revelation is neither required nor relevant for authentic living. With Petra's increased self-acceptance and clearer sense of direction regarding academic goals, therapy was terminated, with the proviso that she could return in the future if necessary.

CLIENT PRESENTATION (1996)

Concomitant with difficulties Petra was experiencing in some of her courses, she was referred for psychoeducational testing for possible attention and learning deficits. Following assessment recommendations and her own interest in further personal development, Petra resumed counseling after a hiatus of nearly two years. In the interim, Petra had become more comfortable identifying herself as a Deaf feminist, particularly after exposure to and identifications with larger communities (e.g., visiting friends out of town, attending conferences) beyond her immediate college environment. Petra's ability to communicate directly with family members about her changes in academic/career plans and cultural-political and sexual orientations was a source of vast relief and contributed to her sense of liberation. Though internally more congruent, Petra had yet to translate her identifications into sustained intimate relationships with like-minded (e.g., other Deaf) individuals. Discussion of this issue revealed Petra's impatience about some of the ways Deaf people interact with each other and conduct organizational affairs. With some anxiety and guilt, Petra admitted feeling somewhat "superior" to many of her deaf peers, with respect to general knowledge, developmental maturity, and perceived understanding of social and/or political issues.

As Petra assumed a stronger Deaf cultural identity, she became preoccupied with experiences of oppression and increasingly expressed indignation about instances of perceived or actual injustices or inequities against deaf people in her classes and during other campus activities (consistent with experiences of people experiencing initial stages of acculturative stress; Brubaker, 1994).

THERAPIST OBSERVATIONS AND INTERVENTIONS (1996)

Developing intimacy and interpersonal relatedness became predominant concerns at this time. Therapeutic intervention was directed at exploring obstacles to intimacy, which largely included fear of rejection—both of the consequences of rejecting others and of being herself rejected. Petra was concerned that if after becoming sexually involved with someone, she decided not to continue the relationship, then the other person would feel "taken advantage of" and a bad reputation would result. She also felt confused about the dynamics of becoming intimately involved with either deaf or hearing partners, with concern about finding an "intellectually compatible" deaf partner or a hearing partner conversant in ASL and knowledgeable about Deaf culture issues. Intervention at this time was focused on helping Petra assess what was under her control in given situations or interactions.

With the changes in Petra's identifications and interests, she began to feel increasingly confined by the limitations of the campus and community environment. Petra was encouraged to consider various options for finding an environment more compatible with her self-concept, including transferring to a different college, leaving school to relocate to a different city, or staying one or two more years to finish her degree. Therapeutic intervention was directed toward exploring possibilities for remaining "authentic" by revealing aspects of herself that were pertinent and appropriate in different contexts. Examples included using different methods of oral or signed communication among different groups of deaf and hard of hearing people, keeping a low sexual orientation profile among heterosexuals, or choosing to socialize with people who think, feel, and behave similarly to herself. Petra ultimately decided to remain in school and finish her degree, recognizing that after graduation she could seek out environments more broadly congenial with her intended way of life.

Given Petra's increasing ability to distinguish and negotiate among individual, contextual, and intersubjective (Neimeyer & Mahoney, 1995) variables in any given situation, the process of termination was initiated. Sessions became characterized by Petra's narrations of experiences that were supported and reinforced by the therapist with little or no need for intervention.

Petra also became able to navigate more than one situation (context) involving the therapist. In the early stages of therapy, she studiously avoided any extrasession situations that might involve contact or interaction with the therapist; subsequently, she seemed more comfortable being in the same situation (e.g., at the theater or other campuswide events). Most recently, she had to complete a class project that involved using resources in the counseling center area, which meant interacting with the therapist. That she was able to interact with the therapist as a peer/colleague in this situation and yet maintain a client-therapist relationship in the next session was a reflection of her increasing ability to be different aspects of herself within different contexts in appropriate ways. In constructivist terms, when Petra was faced with a different context that included the therapist, she was able to "deconstruct" the therapist-client relationship and to "reconstruct" a different, more peerlike, relationship. Effective functioning in this new situation, of course, means that the therapist has to undertake a similar or parallel deconstruction-reconstruction process, in order to relate to the client in a more peerlike or collegial fashion.

Petra terminated therapy feeling more internally well-integrated while recognizing the need to continue practicing different ways of negotiating personal and professional situations in a more directly overt fashion. A major unresolved issue remained the choice of career/lifestyle, in that Petra would like to find work in environments compatible with and/or supportive of her preferred lifestyle. One source of ambivalence was the desire to succeed in the relatively more privileged and powerful "mainstream" world versus the desire to exist as a fully congruent Deaf feminist lesbian, which would probably mean seeking out and living within more circumscribed contexts (e.g., agencies and organizations focused on deaf women and/or lesbians). One therapeutic goal for mitigating this conflict would be to teach skills both of navigating multiple contexts and of making choices of different contexts for different life activities (e.g., work, home, leisure).

Evolution of D.E.A.F. Therapy

As discussed earlier, D.E.A.F. (developmental-existential-affirmative-formulative) therapy is a compilation of stage or level theories of cognitive, affective, behavioral development mediated by core ordering processes, recognition/affirmation of one or more sociocultural contexts influencing a client's identity, and the intersubjective dialogue between therapist and client (mutual formulation). Applying these concepts to the therapeutic process with Petra, the following can be noted. From the developmental perspective, Petra's maturation can be charted through a progressively advanced series of epiphanic moments. One such moment occurred when she was asked what she would do about taking a leave of absence if her family were all dead (disembedding from family context). At that moment, Petra was forced to realize the necessity of making a decision largely outside of the family context. In existential terms, she moved from undifferentiated "being" to "knowing," as suggested in table 2.

Petra had another epiphanic moment when she became aware of several aspects of her identity as a Deaf woman, a feminist, and a lesbian: she learned that "knowing" (self-awareness) about all of these aspects of herself did not necessarily require that all be present or acted upon at once ("doing"). Recognition of the ability to select and apply pertinent facets of one's being ("reasoning," table 2)—that is, to develop and appropriately enact deafness-related, feminist-related, or lesbian-related, behavioral episode schemas—is probably characteristic of the kind of epiphany involved at this stage of development. At the most progressive level of existential development, Petra would be able to maintain a consistent sense of integrated self (core ordering process) as a Deaf feminist lesbian while navigating and negotiating different contexts of experience ("becoming," table 2).

With respect to the culturally affirmative aspects of therapeutic intervention, Petra was encouraged to explore her experiences within the Deaf (as well as lesbian and lesbian deaf) communities. Multicultural and feminist strategies were applied to help Petra understand and make sense of the sociopolitical contexts in which these aspects of her identity formation occur and in which she will make decisions about the depth and extent of her various personal-political identifications. For example, after one class in which Petra became angry about perceived discrimination against deaf people by the teacher, we discussed different strategies for dealing with this situation, including withdrawal from the class, confronting the teacher and/or the department chair, and petitioning other deaf members of the class and/or the college Deaf community to raise protest. Each of these strategies was analyzed in terms of personal, social, and political consequences. In this instance, Petra decided to let the situation go, preferring to focus her energy on passing the course and graduating to a position of increased professional/personal credibility, a strategy of particular importance to multiply disenfranchised individuals, who often have to compete with, or exceed, the qualifications of more privileged peers.

Finally, Petra's therapy also included several elements of formulative (constructivist) therapy to help her understand the meanings of her experiences and choices; be able to choose and create, as well as respond to, different contexts or situations; and to negotiate different "visions" of reality (Andrews, 1989) while maintaining a central and reliable sense of self. If Petra chose, she could introduce into situations contributions of her own "meaning-making." As an example, sign language interpreters are traditionally viewed as being available to help deaf people communicate with hearing people. But some deaf people, Petra included, point out that in fact sign language interpreters help hearing people communicate with deaf people, because deaf people know the language that hearing people don't. This requires a paradigmatic shift in the meaning of the power relationship between deaf and hearing people in those contexts.

Conclusions

Overall, constructivist therapeutic interventions seem to offer the most unifyingly comprehensive approach to mental health treatment of deaf women, because they encompass not only the interplay of individual (intrapsychic) variables, but also intersubjective (interpersonal) and contextual variables developmentally over time. In particular, the "meaning-making" aspect of constructivist-existentialist therapy offers deaf women, and other similarly disenfranchised individuals, a specific opportunity to express, analyze, and integrate the unique characteristics of their experiences.

References

Andrews, J. (1989). Integrating visions of reality. *American Psychologist, 44* (5), 803–817.

Anthony, S., & Gibbins, S. (1992). Characteristics of the daydreams of deaf women. *Journal of Mental Imagery, 16* (3 & 4), 73–78.

Atkinson, D., & Hackett, G. (Eds.). (1995). *Counseling diverse populations.* Madison, WI: Brown and Benchmark.

Atkinson, D., Morten, G., & Sue, D. (1979). *Counseling American minorities.* Dubuque, IA: William C. Brown.

Barnartt, S., & Christiansen, J. (1985). The socioeconomic status of deaf workers: A minority group perspective. *Social Science Journal, 32,* 19–32.

Baum, V. (1981). Counseling families of deaf children. *Journal of the Rehabilitation of the Deaf, 15* (1), 16–20.

Becker, G., & Jaugerui, J. (1981). The invisible isolation of deaf women: Its effect on social awareness. *Journal of Sociology and Social Welfare, 8* (2), 249–262.

Becker, H. (1963). *Outsiders: Studies in the sociology of deviance.* London: Free Press of Glencoe.

Benjamin, J. (1992, Fall). Discussion. *Contemporary Psychology Review, 7,* 82–96.

Bepko, C., and Kersten, J. (1985). *The responsibility trap.* New York: Free Press.

Berg-Cross, L., & Zoppetti, L. (1991). Person-in-culture interview: Understanding culturally diverse students. *Journal of College Student Psychotherapy, 5* (4), 5–21.

Berry, J., & Kim, U. (1988). Acculturation and mental health. In P. Dasen, J. Berry, & N. Sartorius (Eds.), *Health and cross-cultural psychology: Toward applications* (pp. 207–236). London: Sage Publications.

Betancourt, H., & Lopez, S. (1993). The study of culture, ethnicity, and race in American psychology. *American Psychologist, 48* (6), 629–637.

Betz, N., & Fitzgerald, L. (1993). Individuality and diversity: Theory and research in counseling psychology. *Annual Review of Psychology, 44,* 343–381.

Beutler, L., Clarkin, J., Crego, M., & Bergan, J. (1990). Client therapist matching. In C. Snyder & D. Forsyth (Eds.), *Handbook of social and clinical psychology* (pp. 78–101). New York: Pergamon.

Bidell, T. (1992). Beyond interactionism in contextualist models of development. *Human Development, 35,* 306–315.

Bohan, J. (1993). Regarding gender: Essentialism, constructionism, and feminist psychology. *Psychology of Women Quarterly, 17,* 521.

Bowe, F. (1978). *Handicapping America.* New York: Harper and Row.

Brauer, B. (1978). Mental health and deaf persons: A status report. *Gallaudet Today, 9* (1), 1–4.

Browning, C., Reynolds, A., & Dworkin, S. (1991). Affirmative psychotherapy for lesbian women. *Counseling Psychologist, 19* (2), 177–196.

Broverman, I., Broverman, D., Clarkson, F., Rosenkrantz, P., & Vogel, S. (1970). Sex-role stereotypes and clinical judgments of mental health. *Journal of Consulting and Clinical Psychology, 34,* 1–7.

Brown, L., & Brodsky, A. (1992). The future of feminist therapy. *Psychotherapy, 29* (1), 51–57.

Brubaker, R. (1994). Acculturative stress: A useful framework for understanding the experience of deaf Americans. *Journal of the American Deafness and Rehabilitation Association (JADARA), 28* (1), 1–14.

Bujold, C. (1990). Biographical-hermeneutical approaches to the study of career development. In R. Young & W. Borgen (Eds.), *Methodological approaches to the study of career* (pp. 57–69). New York: Praeger.

Cochran, L. (1990). Narrative as a paradigm for career research. In R. Young & W. Borgan (Eds.), *Methodological approaches to the study of career* (pp. 71–86). New York: Praeger.

Coleman, H. (1995). Strategies for coping with cultural diversity. *Counseling Psychologist, 23* (4), 722–740.

Comas-Diaz, L. (1992). The future of psychotherapy with ethnic minorities. *Psychotherapy, 29* (1), 88–94.

Corker, M. (1994a). *Counselling—the deaf challenge.* Bristol, PA: Jessica Kingsley.

———. (1994b). The methodological challenge—moving beyond a "talking through." In M. Corker (Ed.), *Counselling—the deaf challenge* (pp. 124–156). Bristol, PA: Jessica Kingsley.

Davis, B. (1987, June). Disability and grief. *Social Casework, 68* (2), 352–357.

DeCarvalho, R. (1990). The growth hypothesis and self actualization: An existential alternative. *The Humanistic Psychologist, 18* (3), 252–258.

Dee, T. M. (1993). *Exploring gender with deaf women and their hearing sisters.* Unpublished master's thesis, University of Michigan.

Denmark, F., & Paludi, M. (Eds.). (1993). *Psychology of women.* Westport, CT: Greenwood Press.

Deurzen-Smith, E. (1988). *Existential counseling in practice.* Newbury Park, CA: Sage Publications.

Dwyer, P. (1987). The clinical application of contextual therapy. *American Journal of Family Therapy, 15* (2), 169–171.

Edelstein, T. (1978). Development of a milieu intervention program for treatment of emotionally disturbed deaf children. *Mental Health in Deafness, 2,* 25–36.

Eldredge, N. (1993). Culturally affirmative counseling with American Indians who are deaf. *Journal of the American Deafness and Rehabilitation Association, 26* (4), 1–18.

Ellis, A. (1989). Rational-emotive therapy. In R. Corsini & D. Wedding (Eds.), *Current psychotherapies,* (4th ed., pp. 197–238). Itasca, IL: F. E. Peacock.

Essendoh, P. (1996)., Multicultural counseling as the "fourth force": A call to arms. *Counseling Psychologist, 24* (1), 126–137.

Farrugia, D. (1986). An Adlerian perspective for studying deafness. *Individual Psychology, 42* (2), 201–213.

Fowers, B., & Richardson, F. (1996, June). Why is multiculturalism good? *American Psychologist, 51* (6), 609–621.

Freedman, P. (1994). Counseling with deaf clients: The need for culturally and linguistically sensitive interventions. *Journal of the American Deafness and Rehabilitation Association, 27* (4), 16–28.

Frick, W. (1987). The symbolic growth experience: Paradigm for humanistic-existential learning theory. *Journal of Humanistic Psychology, 27* (4), 406–423.

Gannon, J. (1981). *Deaf heritage.* Silver Spring, MD: National Association of the Deaf.

Gibbs, J., & Fuery, D. (1994). Mental health and well-being of Black women: Toward strategies of empowerment. *American Journal of Community Psychology, 22* (4), 559–582.

Ginsburg, H., & Opper, S. (1979). *Piaget's theory of intellectual development.* Englewood Cliffs, NJ: Prentice-Hall.

Glickman, N. (1996a). The development of culturally Deaf identities. In N. Glickman & M. Harvey (Eds.), *Culturally affirmative psychotherapy with Deaf persons* (pp. 115–154). Mahwah, NJ: Lawrence Erlbaum.

———. (1996b). What is culturally affirmative psychotherapy? In N. Glickman & M. Harvey (Eds.), *Culturally affirmative psychotherapy with Deaf persons* (pp.1–56). Mahwah, NJ: Lawrence Erlbaum.

Glickman, N., & Carey, J. (1993). Measuring deaf cultural identities: A preliminary investigation. *Rehabilitation Psychology, 38* (4), 275–283.

Glickman, N., & Harvey, M. (1996). *Culturally affirmative psychotherapy with Deaf persons.* Mahwah, NJ: Lawrence Erlbaum.

Glickman, N., & Zitter, S. (1989). On establishing a culturally affirmative psychiatric inpatient program for deaf people. *Journal of the American Deafness and Rehabilitation Association, 23* (2), 46–59.

Grosjean, F. (1982). *Life with two languages.* Cambridge, MA: Harvard University Press.

———. (1996). Living with two languages and two cultures. In I. Parasnis (Ed.), *Cultural and language diversity and the deaf experience* (pp. 20–37). New York: Cambridge University Press.

Guidano, V., & Liotti, G. (1983). *Cognitive processes and emotional disorders.* New York: Guilford Press.

Hanna, J., & Rogovsky, E. (1993a). On the situation of African-American women with physical disabilities. In M. Nagler (Ed.), *Perspectives on disability* (pp. 149–159). Palo Alto, CA: Health Markets Research.

———. (1993b). Women with disabilities: Two handicaps plus. In M. Nagler (Ed.), *Perspectives on disability* (pp. 109–120). Palo Alto, CA: Health Markets Research.

Harvey, M. (1984). Systemic treatment of a deaf adolescent with a rehabilitation counselor for the deaf. In G. Long & M. Harvey (Eds.), *Facilitating the transition of deaf adolescents to adulthood* (pp. 83–117). Little Rock, AR: Rehabilitation Research and Training Center of Deafness and Hearing Impairment.

———. (1985). Toward a dialogue between the paradigms of family therapy and deafness. *American Annals of the Deaf, 130* (4), 305–314.

———. (1989). *Psychotherapy with deaf and hard-of-hearing persons: A systemic model.* Hillsdale, NJ: Lawrence Erlbaum Associates.

———. (1990). Linguistic and systemic family interventions. In G. Long & M. Harvey (Eds.), *Facilitating the transition of deaf adolescents to adulthood* (pp. 65–81). Little Rock, AR: Rehabilitation Research and Training Center of Deafness and Hearing Impairment.

Heller, B., & Harris, R. (1987). Special considerations in the psychological assessment of hearing impaired persons. In B. Heller, L. Flohr, & L. Zegans (Eds.), *Psychosocial interactions with sensorily disabled persons* (pp. 53–79). New York: Grune and Stratton.

Higgins, P. (1980). *Outsiders in a hearing world.* Beverly Hills, CA: Sage Publications.

Hindley, P., Hill, P., McGuigan, S., & Kitson, N. (1994). Psychiatric disorder in deaf and hearing impaired children and young people: A prevalence study. *Journal of Child Psychology and Psychiatry, 35* (5), 917–934.

Howard, G. (1991). Culture tales. *American Psychologist, 40* (3), 187–197.

Isenberg, G. (1996). Storytelling and the use of culturally appropriate metaphors in psychotherapy with deaf people. In N. Glickman & M. Harvey (Eds.), *Culturally affirmative psychotherapy with Deaf persons* (pp. 169–184). Mahwah, NJ: Lawrence Erlbaum.

Jankowski, K. (1995). Empowerment from within: The deaf social movement providing a framework for a multicultural society. In C. Lucas (Ed.), *Sociolinguistics in deaf communities* (pp. 307–329). Washington, DC: Gallaudet University Press.

Joseph, D. (1993). *Deaf female clients give voice: A feminist perspective and counseling implications.* Ann Arbor, MI: University Microfilms International.

Kahn, A., & Yoder, J. (1989). The psychology of women and conservatism: Rediscovering social change. *Psychology of Women Quarterly, 15,* 7–14.

Katz, P., Boggiano, A., & Silvern, L. (1993). Theories of female personality. In F. Denmark & M. Paludi (Eds.), *Psychology of women* (pp. 133–159). Westport, CT: Greenwood Press.

Kegan, R. (1982). *The evolving self.* Cambridge, MA: Harvard University Press.

Kelly, G. (1977). The psychology of the unknown. In D. Bannister (Ed.), *New perspectives in personal construct theory.* San Diego: Academic Press.

Kelly-Jones, N. (1984). Can a woman ... Deaf kids respond. *Gallaudet Today, 14* (4), 9–11.

Kramer, D. (1990). Development of an awareness of contradiction across the life span and the question of postformal operations. In M. Commons, J. Sinnott, F. Richards, & C. Armon (Eds.), *Adult development: Vol. 1. Comparisons and applications of developmental models* (pp. 133–159). New York: Praeger.

Krippner, S., & Easton, H. (1972, August). Deafness: An existential interpretation. *American Annals of the Deaf,* 440–445.

Landfield, A., & Epting, F. (1987). *Personal construct psychology.* New York: Human Sciences Library.

Lane, H. (1990). Cultural and infirmity models of deaf Americans. *Journal of the American Deafness and Rehabilitation Association, 28,* 11–26.

———. (1992). *The mask of benevolence: Disabling the deaf community.* New York: Alfred Knopf.

Lane, H., Hoffmeister, R., & Bahan, B. (1996). *A journey into the Deaf-world.* San Diego: Dawn Sign Press.

Lang, H. (1994). *Silence of the spheres.* Westport, CT: Bergin and Garvey.

Lang, H., & Meath-Lang, B. (1995). *Deaf persons in the arts and sciences.* Westport, CT: Greenwood Press.

Levine, E. (1960). *Psychology of deafness: Techniques for appraisal for rehabilitation.* New York: Columbia University Press.

———. (1981). *The ecology of early deafness.* New York: Columbia University Press.

Livneh, H. (1988). A dimensional perspective on the origin of negative attitudes toward persons with disabilities. In H. Yukor (Ed.), *Attitudes toward persons with disabilities* (pp. 35–46). New York: Springer.

Lyddon, W. (1993). Developmental constructivism: An integrative framework for psychotherapy practice. *Journal of Cognitive Psychology: An International Quarterly, 7* (3), 217–224.

Magilvy, J. (1982). *Deaf and hearing-impaired older women, influences on quality of life.* Masters Thesis, University of Colorado.

MacLeod-Gallinger, J. (1992). The career status of deaf women. *American Annals of the Deaf, 137* (4), 315–324.

Maher, F., & Tetreault, M. (1993). Frames of positionality: Constructing meaningful dialogues about gender and race. *Anthropological Quarterly, 66,* 118–126.

Mahler, M. (1973). Symbiosis and individualism: The psychological birth of the human infant. *The Psychoanalytic Study of the Child, 28,* 89–106.

Mahoney, M. (1991). *Human change processes.* New York: Basic Books.

Major, B. (1987). Gender, justice, and the psychology of entitlement. In P. Shaver & C. Hendrick (Eds.), *Review of personality and social psychology: Vol. 7. Sex and gender* (pp. 124–148). Beverly Hills, CA: Sage Publications.

Malm, E. (1993). The eclipse of meaning in cognitive psychology: Implications for humanistic psychology. *Journal of Humanistic Psychology, 33,* 67–87.

Marr, J. (1983). Behavior modification: Applications for hearing impaired people. In D. Watson, G. Anderson, S. Ouellette, N. Ford, & P. Marut (Eds.), *Adjustment of services for hearing impaired persons* (pp. 65–75). Little Rock, AR: Rehabilitation Research and Training Center of Deafness and Hearing Impairment.

Martin, J., & Hall, G. (1992). Thinking black, thinking internal, thinking feminist. *Journal of Counseling Psychology, 39,* 509–514.

May, R. (1983). *Discovery of being.* New York: W. W. Norton.

May, R., & Yalom, I. (1984). Existential psychotherapy. In R. Corsini (Ed.), *Current psychotherapies* (pp. 354–391). Itasca, IL: F. E. Peacock.

Mays, V., Rubin, J., Sabourin, M., & Walker, L. (1996). Moving toward a global psychology. *American Psychologist, 51* (5), 485–487.

McCrone, W. (1983). Reality therapy with deaf rehabilitation clients. *Journal of the Rehabilitation of the Deaf, 17* (2), 13–16.

McDougall, J. (1991). Current issues in deafness: A psychological perspective. *Canadian Psychology, 32* (4), 612–627.

McNamara, K., & Rickard, K. (1989). Feminist identity development: Implications for feminist therapy for women. *Journal of Counseling and Development, 68,* 184–189.

Mendelsohn, M., & Rozek, F. (1983). Denying disability: The case of deafness. *Family Systems Medicine, 1* (2), 36–49.

Moores, D. (1987). *Educating the deaf: Psychology, principles, and practices* (3rd ed.). Boston: Houghton-Mifflin.

Morrow, L., & Kondritz, B. (1984). Use of a self-control procedure to extinguish hallucinating with a hearing impaired behavior disoriented adolescent. *Journal of the Rehabilitation of the Deaf, 17* (4), 5–9.

Mowbray, C., Herman, S., & Hazel, K. (1992). Gender and serious mental illness. *Psychology of Women Quarterly, 16,* 107–126.

Myklebust, H. (1964). *Psychology of deafness: Sensory deprivation, learning, and adjustment.* New York: Grune and Stratton.

Nagler, M. (1993). *Perspectives on disability.* Palo Alto, CA: Health Markets Research.

Neimeyer, R. (1993). An appraisal of constructivist psychotherapies. *Journal of Consulting and Clinical Psychology, 61 (2),* 221–234.

Neimeyer, R., & Mahoney, M. (1995). *Constructivism in psychotherapy.* Washington, DC: American Psychological Association.

Newman, P., & Newman, B. (1992). *Development through life.* (5th ed.). Pacific Grove, CA: Brooks/Cole.

Padden, C. (1996). From the cultural to the bicultural: The modern deaf community. In I. Parasnis (Ed.), *Cultural and language diversity and the deaf experience* (pp. 79–88). New York: Cambridge University Press.

Padden, C., & Humphries, T. (1988). *Deaf in America: Voices from a culture.* Cambridge, MA: Harvard University Press.

Parasnis, I. (Ed.). (1996). *Cultural and language diversity and the deaf experience.* New York: Cambridge University Press.

Perkins, R. (1991). Women with long term mental health problems, issues of power and powerlessness. *Feminism and Psychology, 1* (l), 131–139.

Peterson, J. (1952). A study of the deaf and/or hard-of-hearing female patients at St. Elizabeth's Hospital, Washington, DC. In *Student Theses, 182.* Masters thesis, Gallaudet University.

Pollard, R. (1993). Public mental health service and diagnostic trends regarding individuals who are deaf or hard-of-hearing. *Rehabilitation Psychology, 38* (4), 3–14.

———. (1996, April). Professional psychology and deaf people: The emergence of a discipline. *American Psychologist, 51* (4), 389–396.

Pugliesi, K. (1992). Women and mental health: Two traditions of feminist research. *Women and Health, 19* (2/3), 43–68.

Quedenfield, C., & Farrelly, F. (1983). Provocative therapy with the hearing impaired client. *Journal of Rehabilitation of the Deaf, 17* (2), 1–12.

Rayson, B. (1985). Psychodynamic psychotherapy with deaf clients. In G. Anderson & D. Watson (Eds.), *Counseling deaf people: Research and practice* (pp. 123–143). Little Rock, AR: Rehabilitation Research and Training Center of Deafness and Hearing Impairment.

Reynolds, A., & Pope, R. (1991). The complexities of diversity: Exploring multiple oppressions. *Journal of Counseling and Development, 70,* 174–180.

Ridgeway, S. (1994). The deaf alliance. In M. Corker (Ed.), *Counselling—the deaf challenge* (pp. 214–224). Bristol, PA: Jessica Kingsley.

Rittenhouse, R., Johnson, C., Overton, B., Freeman, S., & Jaussi, K. (1991). The Black and Deaf movements in America since 1960. *American Annals of the Deaf, 136* (5), 392–400.

Rogers, L., & Kegan, R. (1991). Mental growth and mental health as distinct concepts in the study of developmental psychopathology. In D. Keating & H. Rosen (Eds.), *Constructivist perspectives on developmental psychopathology and atypical development* (pp. 103–147). Hillsdale, NJ: Lawrence Erlbaum Associates.

Rosen, H. (1991). Constructivism: Personality, psychopathology, and psychotherapy. In D. Keating & H. Rosen (Eds.), *Constructivist perspectives on developmental psychopathology and atypical development* (pp. 149–171). Hillsdale, NJ: Lawrence Erlbaum Associates.

Schaef, A. (1985). *Women's realities: An emerging female system in a White male society.* New York: Harper and Row.

Scott, W. (1978). Counseling with deaf persons: An overview of literature dealing with definitions, situations, and types of approaches used. *Journal of Rehabilitation of the Deaf, 11* (4), 161–168.

Schlesinger, H. (1987). Effects of powerlessness on dialogue and development: Disability, poverty, and the human condition. In B. Heller, L. Flohr, & L. Zegans (Eds.), *Psychosocial interventions with sensorially disabled persons* (pp. 1–27). New York: Grune and Stratton.

Shapiro, R., & Harris, R. (1976). Family therapy in treatment of the deaf: A case report. *Family Process, 15* (1), 83–96.

Sheetz, N. (1993). *Orientation to deafness.* Needham Heights, MA: Allyn and Bacon.

Sieber, J., & Cairns, K. (1991). Feminist therapy with ethnic minority women. *Canadian Journal of Counseling, 25* (4), 567–580.

Simon, R. (1995, June). Gender, multiple roles, role meaning, and mental health. *Journal of Health and Social Behavior, 36,* 182–194.

Skodra, E. (1992). Ethnic/immigrant women and psychotherapy: The issue of empowerment. *Women and Therapy, 13* (4), 81–98.

Sligar, S. (1995). Managing tortillas, pitas, matzo, and mano when you grew up on White bread. *Journal of the American Deafness and Rehabilitation Association, 28* (4), 39–46.

Sloman, L., Perry, A., & Frankenburg, F. (1987). Family therapy with deaf member families. *The American Journal of Family Therapy, 15* (3), 242–252.

Sloman, L., & Springer, S. (1987). Strategic family therapy interventions with deaf member families. *Canadian Journal of Psychiatry, 32* (7), 558–562.

Sue, S. (1983). Ethnic minority issues in psychology. *American Psychologist, 38* (5), 583–589.

Sue, D. (1990). Culture-specific strategies in counseling: A conceptual framework. *Professional Psychology: Research and Practice, 21* (6), 424–433.

Sussman, A. (1991). *Depathologization of deafness: Ingredients for psychological effectiveness, equality and self reliance.* Plenary Lecture. XI World Congress of the World Federation of the Deaf, Tokyo, Japan.

Sussman, A., & Stewart, L. (Eds.). (1971). *Counseling with deaf people.* New York: New York University Deafness Research and Training Center.

Vernon, M. (1978). Deafness and mental health: Some theoretical views. *Gallaudet Today, 9* (1), 9–13.

Vernon, M., & Andrews, J. (1990). *Psychology of deafness.* New York: Longman.

Vernon, M., & Lafalce-Landers, E. (1993). A longitudinal study of intellectually gifted deaf and hard-of-hearing people. *American Annals of the Deaf, 138* (5), 427–434.

Walsh, M. (1994). Psychology and feminism. In C. Kramarae & D. Spender (Eds.), *The knowledge explosion* (pp. 291–302). New York: Teachers College Press.

Wax, T. (1993). Matchmaking among cultures: Disability culture and the larger marketplace. In R. Glueckhauf, L. Sechrest, G. Bond, & E. McDonel (Eds.), *Improving assessment in rehabilitation and health* (pp. 156–175). London: Sage Publications.

———. (1994). Unpublished manuscript.

———. (1996). Unpublished manuscript.

Wax, T., & Danek, M. (1984). Deaf women and double jeopardy. *Gallaudet Today, 14* (4), 13–15.

Wilber, K. (1986). The spectrum of development. In K. Wilber, J. Engler, & D. Brown (Eds.), *Transformations of consciousness* (pp. 65–105). Boston: New Science Library.

Women and Deafness [special issue]. (1984). *Gallaudet Today,* 14 (4).

Wright, B. (1988). Attitudes and the fundamental negative bias: Conditions and corrections. In H. Yuker (Ed.), *Attitudes toward persons with disabilities* (pp. 3–21). New York: Springer.

5

Therapy Issues with Deaf Lesbians, Gay Men, and Bisexual Men and Women

VIRGINIA GUTMAN

In the past twenty-five years, the literature on psychotherapy with lesbians, gay men, bisexual men and women, and other sexual minorities has grown remarkably. This increase is often traced to the removal of the diagnostic category of "homosexuality" from the American Psychiatric Association's *Diagnostic and Statistical Manual* in the early 1970s. Since then, discussion of sexuality and sexual identities has increasingly de-emphasized pathology and instead provided a wealth of information on "affirmative psychotherapy" with gay men and lesbians (Gould, 1995; Isay, 1996; Silverstein, 1991).

The news is not all good, however. Sexual orientation conversion therapies continue to be practiced, despite considerable evidence that they are ineffective, stigmatizing, and possibly harmful (Haldeman, 1994; Stein, 1996). Lesbians, gay men, and bisexual men and women in therapy still encounter both conscious and unconscious expressions of heterosexism that view nonheterosexual sexual behavior as second-best or indicative of psychopathology (Garnets et al., 1991). While many gay men and lesbians have found therapy to be helpful, others have had negative and personally damaging experiences with mental health professionals (Hancock, 1995; Isay, 1996; Nystrom, 1997); thus they may approach psychotherapy with caution, wishing to ascertain a therapist's attitudes about and comfort with gay themes, experiences, and issues before "opening up" and committing themselves to the psychotherapeutic process.

To work effectively with any individual, a psychotherapist must have an idea of the developmental experiences the client is likely to have had, stressors the client is likely to have encountered (understood in social and cultural context), and the support systems available to the client. Psychotherapists also must be able to comprehend what a client has to say about his or her life, especially the nuances of tone and vocabulary that reveal the inner world of the client. Few professional resources are available to practicing therapists or those in training who wish to learn about deaf clients who are gay, lesbian, bisexual, transsexual, or transgendered. Without appropriate information, therapists may underestimate the importance of certain experiences, while overestimating the impact of others.

Sexual Identity and Its Development

Identity issues are a major concern to members of minority groups. Gay men, lesbians, and other sexual minorities struggle with attaining or developing a sense of identity, as do deaf people and cultural and racial minorities (Glickman, 1996; Paradis, 1997; Trujillo, 1997). Heterosexuals are not expected to wonder how or when they became heterosexual, any more than hearing people are asked how they became hearing and what hearing identity means to them. The deaf person who is also gay, lesbian, or bisexual must develop several minority identities. Trying to find the community that can provide a comprehensive sense of identification may be extremely difficult when multiple minority status is involved. When the minority status and the identities associated with it are also disparaged or devalued (as deafness and gay/lesbian/bisexual orientations are in many contexts), attaining a positive self-concept and sense of self-worth and relatedness to others can be extremely challenging. Little is known about the relationship between gay and deaf identity development, although parallels have been suggested (Glickman, 1996; Hecht & Gutman, 1997).

Sexual identity is a complex phenomenon. The labels we apply to ourselves and others are highly individualized and sometimes idiosyncratic. These labels are influenced not only by an internal sense of who one is, but also by messages from family, friends, and culture as to who one should be. Different aspects of sexual identity may develop at different rates; some aspects may stay constant throughout life, while others change as the individual develops (Garnets & Kimmel, 1993; Patterson, 1995a; Weinrich, 1987).

Gender identity, the stable sense that one is either a boy or a girl, develops very early in life for most people. Gender conformity or nonconformity (behavior that appears to others to be "masculine" or "feminine") can be noticed when children begin to make choices. Children who are interested in activities, toys, and friendships not considered typical may be called "sissy" or "tomboy" and may receive intense pressure from adults and other children to conform to sex-role expectations. Often gay men and lesbians recall gender-nonconforming childhoods; however, interests and personality traits (such as gentleness for boys and aggressive competitiveness for girls) that do not conform to traditional masculine/feminine definitions are generally not sufficient for labeling oneself "gay." Many gender-nonconforming children who are called "sissy" or "tomboy" become heterosexual adults. Similarly, many gay or lesbian adults had traditional gender-typed interests and experiences in childhood. For most people, the label gay or lesbian is more specifically a statement about to whom one is attracted as a sexual partner than about one's gender conformity.

The emergence of an awareness of lesbian or gay identity most often occurs in late adolescence or young adulthood. Many gay men or lesbians are aware of feeling "different" earlier but do not yet know how to label the difference or how to integrate such a disparaged trait into their identity (D'Augelli, 1994). Bisexual identities tend to be recognized later, in early adulthood (Fox, 1995). Recognizing a gay, lesbian, or bisexual identity may occur much later in life as well.

The following examples illustrate how sexual identity can be puzzling to those who do not conform to generally expected behaviors:

- "My best friend says I'm 'not feminine.' She says I'm a lesbian and is mad that I won't admit it. How can I know for sure?"
- "When I told my father I was gay, he said I was just confused and would grow out of it. He said I was getting the wrong idea from my deaf friends and should spend more time at home."
- "My lover and I got into a big fight. When she found out I had slept with Joe, she said that I am not a lesbian and I am just using her and should not call myself a lesbian."
- "I've known I was gay since I was seven years old. But I thought for many years I was the only person in the world who had these feelings."

- "I never felt I fit in. I was never comfortable with the dating scene and always felt closer to other girls than to boys my age. Yet I can't be a lesbian because I am very feminine and have no doubt that I am a woman."
- "It's hard to believe that after seventeen years of a happy marriage, and raising two children, I'm suddenly in love with a woman. I don't know how it happened, but I know in my heart this is right and somehow I've always been a lesbian. I've been looking for this all my life and didn't know it."

Sexual activity and sexual identity are not necessarily the same, especially in adolescents. Gay youths and adults often have heterosexual experiences, and vice versa. On the other hand, some people achieve a stable sense of gay or lesbian identity without having any sexual contact with members of their own sex (Savin-Williams, 1995, 1996).

Gay men, deaf or hearing, tend to identify their sexual orientation earlier than women. They are more likely to feel that they have been gay from birth and that there was no choice or preference involved at any point (Gonsiorek, 1995). While some lesbians also feel this way, others experience their sexual identity as more fluid or mutable, or as having been chosen, or as being a preferred identity but not the only possible one (Brown, 1995). Some individuals develop a bisexual identity after experiences with partners of both sexes (Matteson, 1996; Siegal & Walker, 1966). However, one can have an opposite-sex partner and still identify as gay or lesbian, just as one can have same-sex experiences and identify as heterosexual.

Children and youth learn attitudes about homosexuality from their culture, school, media, family, and friends. Attitudes toward same-sex sexual involvement are most often negative (Herek, 1994; Kite, 1994), although members of the Deaf community may be less likely to cut off contact with a lesbian or gay member (Langholtz & Rendon, 1991–1992; Zakarewsky, 1979). Deaf people are likely to have known each other since childhood and to have many ties; the community is small and bonds are not easily broken even when relationships involve serious disagreements, animosity, or disapproval.

When a youth adopts or is assigned a gay or lesbian label, the frequent results are verbal and physical abuse, ranging from rejection and neglect to ridicule to assault (Klinger & Stein, 1996; Savin-Williams, 1994, 1995, 1996). Gay and lesbian teens are at risk for being thrown out of their homes and told to find their own way. The high school years constitute a particularly difficult and dangerous period for those who are identified as gay or lesbian (Savin-Williams, 1994, 1995). While no statistics on deaf gay and lesbian youth are available, deaf children and youth are thought to be at higher risk for all kinds of physical and sexual abuse (Dobosh and Gutman, 1998). A survey by Swartz (1995) suggested particularly high risk for sexual assault among deaf gay teenagers.

In many cases, adolescents fear that revealing the abuse or harassment may reveal their sexuality, leading to increased problems at home or at school. Anti-gay harassment is believed to be underreported for this reason. For deaf youth, who may have a limited number of adults with whom they can communicate in the best of circumstances, abuse may be even more hidden.

Coming Out

An important aspect of sexual identity development for gay, lesbian, and bisexual people is the process and events referred to as "coming out," in which the individual explores sexual identity; finally adopts a self-label as gay, lesbian, or bisexual; and reveals this identity to others. This can be seen as a process of either identity discovery or identity creation (Rust, 1993). The coming out process can begin at widely varying ages and proceed at different rates. In some respects it is a lifelong process. In some cases identity development appears to progress linearly, in stages. Other individuals may move among two or more identities more fluidly. Savin-Williams (1995) reports that the age of coming out appears to be decreasing; recent studies have found that youth of both sexes first disclose their sexual identity to others at about age sixteen, although same sex attractions, fantasies, and behaviors may have been occurring for several years. Hard of hearing youth tend to identify their sexuality somewhat later than hearing or deaf youth (Swartz, 1995), possibly reflecting their greater social isolation, which can make sexual exploration and experimentation difficult. Fox (1995) reports that a "bisexual" identity may precede or follow an identity as gay or lesbian.

Lesbian and gay youth often first disclose their sexual orientation to peers or siblings. Bisexual men and women report first disclosing their sexuality to a relationship partner or friend. For many gay, lesbian, and bisexual clients, the first disclosure is to a therapist or counselor. However, the coming out process does not end with the first disclosure.

In the hearing community, each new situation and each new individual encountered requires a new decision about disclosure. In the Deaf community, information is more likely to be shared so that with a few disclosures everyone in the community knows of the individual's sexual identity. This removes the burden of constant decisions about disclosure, but also leaves individuals with limited privacy as they explore very personal aspects of their identity. Romantic and sexual relationships, whether serious or casual, can quickly become common knowledge, following the individual anywhere he or she goes within the deaf community (Zakarewsky, 1979).

Thus it is extremely difficult for a deaf person to be both sexually active and "in the closet" unless sexual activities are confined to hearing partners with no connections to the Deaf world. The hearing youth can choose to tell some people (friends, for example) but not others (such as parents or teachers). The Deaf youth may not have such a choice, especially if his or her parents are deaf, for they will inevitably find out. Thus the hearing individual has the luxury of working on identity and building social relationships, networks, and support systems gradually over a number of years, coming out only to trusted people. Deaf children of Deaf families cannot assume that their social world will be separate from their parents'. To tell anyone may be to tell everyone, making the initial disclosure much more momentous and often frightening.

Deaf or hard of hearing individuals who do not attend schools for the deaf may be more able to maintain the "separate worlds" strategy that many hearing gay men and lesbians use to manage the coming out process throughout their lives. They may have deaf friends and hearing friends, and the two circles may not overlap. Their parents, if they are hearing and not involved in the Deaf community, may be insulated from information about their adolescent and adult children's activities to the same extent as hearing parents of hearing children.

The combined experiences of being deaf or hard of hearing in a hearing world, and gay/lesbian/bisexual in a primarily heterosexual world, may lead to profound feelings of isolation, alienation, and disconnectedness. Adolescents in this situation may have no one to talk with who can both provide free and easy communication and accept the deaf youth's attempts to develop a healthy and strong gay or lesbian identity. Consequently, concerns about sexuality are often raised obliquely, with much hinting and little direct discussion with adults or peers. Adults who are approached for help may miss the point, "reassure" the youth that he is not gay (when he knows he is and wants to know whether it is possible to be a good/happy/mature gay adult), or respond in a judgmental or rejecting manner to any hints of sexual concerns.

When communication is tenuous (as it may be in mainstreamed settings when a counselor who primarily works with hearing students serves a few deaf ones), misunderstandings can easily occur on both sides with disastrous consequences. The deaf gay or lesbian youth, already wondering if he or she is outside the pale of the human family, concludes "I was right . . . . My concerns are too disgusting for anyone to be able to understand." Inability to access the resources of either the hearing gay and lesbian communities or the Deaf community leaves some youths or young adults in a very vulnerable psychological position.

Deaf Gay Men and Lesbians in the Community

Gay and lesbian communities exist all over the country. In large cities these may be politically active and sophisticated, with various formal and informal social groups for people of different ages and interests. In areas with smaller populations, the community may not be so differentiated, but while there is a lesser range of options, a feeling that "we all have to stick together" is common and mutual support can be strong. Larger cities have organized resources to help high school and college-age youth deal with sexual identity concerns. Wherever there is a gay community, gay or lesbian youth can begin to meet gay and lesbian adults and peers and receive advice and assistance with integrating themselves with the community.

Major metropolitan areas in the United States have both organized and informal Deaf lesbian and gay communities, which tend to be separate from the hearing lesbian and gay communities (except for participation in major community events such as Pride celebrations). The decision to be visible within the Deaf community as an openly gay or lesbian individual and as an activist requires considerable courage: snide comments still are made and rumors whether based on fact or fiction, are repeated over and over. It is important for gay and lesbian deaf youth to see that successful role models do exist. For deaf youth raised outside of the Deaf community, information on how to find local deaf gay people and activities literally can be lifesaving.

Deaf gay men and lesbians must have skills for navigating a number of communities and subcommunities. The work world, the primarily heterosexual hearing and deaf worlds, any ethnic minority community with which the person identifies, and both hearing and deaf gay/lesbian communities all have resources that a deaf gay or lesbian adult may need. The different communities, however, may expect or demand incompatible behaviors. For example, the Deaf community may expect that deaf professionals will use their knowledge and resources for the betterment of the lot of deaf people. The hearing lesbian and gay community may expect that lesbian and gay professionals will serve the community by coming out, being role models to youth, and giving time and financial support to the struggle of lesbians and gay men against discrimination. A lesbian or gay man who is a member of an ethnic minority group may also face a third set of expectations regarding attention to family and community responsibilities (Chan, 1995; Espin, 1993; Greene, 1994; Greene & Boyd-Franklin, 1996; Liu & Chan, 1996; Loiacano, 1993; Morales, 1996).

A study by Hecht and Gutman (1997) suggested high levels of self-esteem, deaf identity, and involvement in the Deaf community among a national sample of deaf lesbians.

Within this sample, the subjects' self-esteem varied according to both internalized images of deaf people and of lesbians, but appeared more strongly correlated with specific views of deafness and deaf people. Those who reported the most positive internalized images of deaf people also reported the highest self-esteem. Self-esteem also appeared to vary with amount of social contacts, whether these were with deaf or hearing people. Thus this preliminary study suggested that experiences within the Deaf community may be the most crucial element of self-esteem for Deaf lesbians, with experiences within the lesbian community of slightly lesser importance. Confirmation of these findings is needed, as is extension of this research to deaf gay men and deaf bisexual individuals.

Home and Family

In most cases gay men and lesbians have heterosexual parents (Bailey et al., 1995; Strommen, 1993). Considering the fact that most deaf people have hearing parents, gay or lesbian deaf people in most cases come from hearing heterosexual families. A smaller number have deaf heterosexual parents, and virtually none have families in which one or both parents is both deaf and gay.

The hearing literature on the process of disclosing a gay or lesbian sexual orientation to parents and other family members implies that the disclosure usually evokes negative reactions on the part of the parents, whether these feelings are revealed to the gay/lesbian child or not (Herschberger & D'Augelli, 1995; Savin-Williams, 1996). A process of coming to accept the revised image of the gay or lesbian child is required. Sometimes parents are unable to come to this resolution, and a permanent estrangement may result. In the worst cases, angry parents may behave abusively toward the gay or lesbian child and/or throw a teenager out of the house to fend for him or herself. In the best cases, the parent is already sufficiently aware of the child's "difference" that the disclosure does not really present new information and the parent is able to accept it with statements such as "I was waiting for you to tell me." Even when the parent's response is supportive and accepting, however, internal feelings of guilt and disappointment are common. In hearing families, parents are often among the last to be told, as the youth first shares identity questions with friends, lovers, a trusted counselor, and perhaps a sibling. When the parents are informed, often the parent seen as most understanding and accepting will be told first and asked to help in the disclosure to the other parent.

The coming out process for deaf gay men and lesbians parallels that of hearing people in some ways, but not in all. The deaf youth who thinks he or she may be gay may be able to explore this possibility with deaf or hearing peers without the family initially finding out, if the family is hearing and not much involved with the Deaf community. With luck, the disclosure of identity can be made when the gay or lesbian person is prepared to do so, and when he or she feels the family is best able to handle the information. Long-standing difficulties in communication with parents, however, may create a situation in which explaining such a personal issue as sexual orientation may be extremely difficult, especially in face-to-face conversation (Langholtz & Rendon, 1991–1992; Rosenbaum, 1995). Revealing the information in a TTY (telecommunications device for people who are deaf) conversation, a letter, or e-mail may give the gay son or lesbian daughter more control over what is communicated and a better chance of making himself or herself understood to the hearing parents, while assuring that their response (hopefully also in writing) will be more fully accessible as well.

Some parents go through a grieving process upon finding out that their child is gay or lesbian; they grieve for the heterosexual future they envisioned for their child. This process is similar to what hearing parents experience when they learn their child is deaf. The impact of this earlier experience upon the child's coming out is unknown. However, some deaf children in hearing families may grow up believing that their deafness has disappointed or burdened their parents and may wish not to contribute to further parental worries. For deaf or hard of hearing adolescents whose parents have battled for years to obtain education and services for them, feelings such as gratitude and obligation may make leading a life the parents disapprove of virtually unthinkable. In other families a deaf child becomes isolated and estranged within the family network, communicating mostly with peers at school and feeling like a stranger at home (Rosenbaum, 1995). In these situations, revelation of gay or lesbian identity may simply push the child further out of the family circle.

For deaf children with culturally Deaf parents, the parents may be actively involved in local, state, national, or international Deaf communities. If they have ongoing contact with the school for the Deaf that their child attends, their involvement with and knowledge of every facet of the child's life may be profound. Thus a youth who is teased as a sissy at school, or who wishes to explore same-sex relationships with other deaf people or with hearing people related to the Deaf community, or who appears in public with a same-sex partner, hearing or deaf, must expect that his or her parents will quickly be told about it. The youth beginning to develop an adult identity that includes same-sex attractions must in many cases "have it out" with parents long before the identity is clearly developed or confidently embraced. Deaf parents' reactions may include not only the revision of their hopes and fantasies for a heterosexual life for their child, but also concern about the reactions of others in the Deaf community, the impact on their child's future of "double minority" status as both deaf and gay, and the possible reflection on the Deaf community at large if the child behaves in a way that might be embarrassing or could be used to discredit deaf people. Pressure to "be normal" may be intense and may seem to be coming from all sides.

While deaf children from Deaf families may be able to seek relationships, support, and privacy in the Deaf or hearing lesbian or gay communities, their Deaf parents have fewer resources available for dealing with their feelings and managing their own and their families' position and reputation within the Deaf community. Finding resources for parents of lesbians and gay men that are also accessible to deaf participants can be difficult. PFLAG (Parents and Friends of Lesbians and Gays), a major support organization with chapters nationwide, does not generally have sign language interpreting, and their resources are not well known in the Deaf community. A few local support groups for parents of deaf gay people have recently been developed (FLASH e-mail newsgroup, 3 September 1996); however, most communities do not have such resources. Even when they are available, deaf and hearing parents are unlikely to use support programs such as PFLAG to deal with their child's coming out (Swartz, 1995).

Partners/Lovers

No one label is universally accepted for the participant in a lesbian or gay relationship: lover, partner (or life partner), companion, spouse, husband, wife, girlfriend, and boyfriend all are sometimes used. Different couples and different communities have their own preferences, which counselors would be wise to ask about and then use when working with the couple. Studies cited in Peplau (1993), Kurdek (1995a, 1995b), and Slater (1995) indicate that stable, close relationships are sought by large percentages of both lesbians and gay men, and that long-lasting relationships are not uncommon. Blumstein and Schwartz (1983) and Green, Bettinger, and Zacks (1996) followed samples of lesbian and gay couples for eighteen months to two years and found that most couples in both groups were still together at the end of the study period, particularly if they had been together for more than 10 years prior to the study.

Some Deaf adults prefer and seek out Deaf lovers/partners, liking the open communication and the mutual understanding that comes from sharing many past and current experiences. Many Deaf gay or lesbian adults are willing to enter relationships with hearing partners, especially if communication is adequate. Some may take pride in having high-level skills for quickly making hearing acquaintances, although communication may be very difficult (Luczak, 1993). Deaf gay men and lesbians may see hearing partners or friends as providing an opportunity to relax away from a feeling of constant accountability, or the perception of being observed, evaluated, or commented on within the Deaf community.

For the therapist working with same-sex couples in which one or both members are Deaf, the challenge is to understand all cultures that are important to each member of the couple, including Deaf culture and any ethnic minority cultures that may be relevant. The therapist must understand enough about the background experiences of both members of the couple (as gay men or lesbians, and as Deaf, deaf, hard of hearing, or hearing people) to be able to provide a neutral ground for the two to work on their communication with each other.

To accomplish this, a therapist must be able to note communication breakdowns and misunderstandings that may be invisible to the couple. This requires the therapist to be fluent in various communication modes. The therapist can introduce communication clarity as an important foundation for therapeutic progress and not something that can be overlooked when strong emotions make communication difficult or because slowing down and focusing on communication seems burdensome or cumbersome.

This requires the therapist to find ways to promote communication between partners who may have unequal levels of proficiency in written or spoken English, sign language, and other languages and modes. Establishing ground rules for couples or family therapy such as "I don't care how you communicate but everyone in the room must understand everything that is said or signed" can be a useful approach with couples who have become accustomed to missing parts of their partner's discourse. Although they may be accustomed to "getting the gist of it," or "understanding the important parts," or "already knowing how she feels about this," an experience of full communication may add some very different information.

Comparable communication issues can be found in both heterosexual and same-sex couples. What is unique, however, in working with same-sex couples are pervasive myths about the inherent instability and unsatisfying nature of gay and lesbian relationships. To provide a framework of hope rather than despair, the therapist must be able to help the partners believe that good communication, commitment, intimacy, and satisfaction are reasonable goals for the relationship, or for other relationships each may have in the future.

Many lesbian and gay couples have full or partial responsibility for raising children. In the past, these were usually children of previous heterosexual relationships. Currently, growing numbers of gay men and women are choosing to raise children acquired in different ways, including adoption, alternative insemination methods, parenting agreements between gay men and lesbians (or with heterosexual friends), and surrogacy arrangements. Considerable information about these families and their children has been published, in part in response to several highly publicized court cases concerning issues of adoption and custody involving gay parents and/or their same-sex partners (American Psychological Association, 1995; Bailey et al., 1995; Flaks et al., 1995; Patterson, 1995b; Slater, 1995).

So far, however, there has been little discussion of this issue for deaf gay or lesbian parents. The small number of community programs providing peer support and parenting education for gay and lesbian families may be inaccessible for deaf parents because of communication barriers. Fears about losing custody of a child if one's sexual orientation becomes known may prevent full participation in the very few parent support services for deaf parents that are available. Thus tremendous pressure is on the nuclear family unit (the gay parents and their child or children) to deal with all their family and child-rearing issues in privacy, even in secrecy. Therapists providing help to deaf gay fathers and lesbian mothers may find that resources and information about child development, education options, discipline, sibling rivalry, and so on, can be valuable and necessary adjuncts to psychotherapy for increasing the client's effectiveness and sense of competency as a parent.

Psychotherapy and Counseling

Therapists who help clients develop a sense of pride and wholeness in themselves as gay or lesbian deaf people are practicing "affirmative therapy," regardless of the theoretical approach the clinician uses (Downey & Friedman, 1996). A number of excellent discussions of gay-affirmative therapy issues and techniques are available, including Falco (1991), Glassgold and Iasenza (1995), Gonsiorek (1985), Isay (1989, 1996), Rothblum (1994), and Silverstein (1991). Therapists who don't know or can't imagine a healthy, mature, successful, well-adjusted (or other relevant positive adjectives) deaf gay adult will have difficulty helping a client with these issues and may inadvertently lead the client to feel more hopeless and demoralized. The goal is to help clients find ways to be true to their own perception of who they are, and at the same time find intimate and satisfying relationships, a sense of pride and self-respect, and a productive work and community life.

A 1986 survey of psychologists indicated that 99% had worked with gay or lesbian clients (Garnets et al., 1991). The National Lesbian Health Care Survey found approximately 75% of the lesbians they surveyed had received psychotherapy or counseling (Ryan & Bradford, 1993). Nystrom (1997) reported that 41.6% of a sample of lesbians and gay men had seen a mental health provider within the previous twelve months. Thus, it is reasonable to assume that any clinician will have gay, lesbian, or bisexual clients at some point. Yet many clinicians report that they have little or no training in working with gay men and lesbians. In fact, despite numerous studies demonstrating that gay men and lesbians achieve equivalent scores to heterosexuals on measures of mental health and adjustment, many clinicians still believe that members of these groups are inherently more likely to manifest psychological disturbance (Gould, 1995; Hancock, 1995; Meredith & Riester, 1980).

Simply finding a gay-affirmative therapist may not lead to a positive psychotherapy experience for a Deaf gay or lesbian individual. Deaf clients who seek out gay-affirmative therapy in the hearing community may receive help with sexual identity development issues, but their therapists may misperceive them as deficient or handicapped because of their deafness (Glickman, 1996).

Commonly Reported Therapist Errors

Therapists who assume all clients are heterosexual until clearly told otherwise may unwittingly discourage self-disclosure. A related error is assuming that a gay client's primary goal is to emulate or be accepted by heterosexual society (Brown, 1996). Several additional therapist errors were identified in research done by Garnets et al., 1991, and Nystrom, 1997 (see figure 1).

Another type of therapist error is collaboration with and endorsement of institutions or programs that practice or support homophobia (Brown, 1996). This can pose dilemmas for therapists practicing in institutional settings whose policies or practices are hostile to gay men and lesbians, such as the military. Additionally, some treatment programs (for example, certain substance-abuse treatment programs for youth) actively punish same-sex romantic relationships while tolerating or encouraging cross-sex relationships. Some self-help programs for sexual addiction do not permit any sexual activity outside of a legal marriage, thus defining all same-sex relationships as incompatible with sexual sobriety.

1. Being uninformed or having inaccurate information about gays and lesbians and their development; or relying on the client to educate the therapist about gay or lesbian issues;
2. Believing that homosexuality is per se pathological, or that all a client's problems are attributable to sexual orientation; insisting that sexual orientation should be a focus of therapy;
3. Failing to recognize the influence of external or internalized homophobia or displaying insensitivity to the prejudice and discrimination faced by gay men and lesbians (and their families and friends);
4. Assuming all clients are heterosexual or want to be; discouraging development of a gay or lesbian lifestyle;
5. Expressing demeaning, trivializing, or disrespectful attitudes toward different sexual orientations;
6. Not understanding the possible positive and negative ramifications of "coming out" in various settings;
7. Underestimating the importance of intimate relationships and friendships; using a heterosexual frame of reference for relationships;
8. Assuming gay men, lesbians, or same-sex couples cannot be adequate parents;
9. Abruptly terminating or transferring a client because the therapist is uncomfortable with gay issues;
10. Treating a gay or lesbian identity as a "phase" or "fad";
11. Making derogatory or dismissive comments about sexual orientation;
12. Trying to change a client's self-identified sexual orientation.

Figure 1. Commonly Reported Therapist Errors

It is noteworthy that many of these types of therapeutic errors, especially those based on therapist ignorance of the population, stereotyped negative attitudes, and inability to change frames of reference, also are frequently encountered by deaf clients seeking therapy (Glickman, 1996). With deaf and hard of hearing clients, therapists' lack of information or training in hearing loss, deafness, and Deaf culture, as well as difficulties in communication, will often sabotage the therapeutic process.

Multiple Minority Status of Deaf Gay and Lesbian Clients

A number of issues should be explored with clients who have multiple minority status (Gibbins, 1995). Foremost are identity issues. For example, how far along in the coming out process is the client, and how consolidated are the client's other identities (e.g., as a Deaf person, as an African American, etc.)? Do "competing identities appear to the client to be mutually exclusive?" (p. 11). The therapeutic goal may be the development and integration of several positive identities.

A related area is the availability to the client of positive role models showing affirmative identity possibilities. Cultural, linguistic, geographic, socioeconomic, or other factors can all isolate clients from possible role models. Finding support for or positive models of all aspects of one's identity can be particularly difficult for bisexual clients, who may face animosity from heterosexuals as well as gay men and lesbians (Matteson, 1996).

Other identity-related concerns include whether the client must contend with negative attitudes regarding deafness in his or her gay/lesbian friends or community (Gibbins, 1995). Moreover, does the client have access to services within the gay/lesbian/bisexual community or are there communication or attitudinal barriers? Does the client know how to advocate for needed service accessibility? And, importantly, does the client have access to information about HIV, AIDS, and high risk vs. safer sexual behaviors (Doyle, 1995)? In major cities, deaf AIDS service agencies provide treatment coordination, support, and preventive education programs whose principal consumers are deaf gay and bisexual men. However, in other parts of the country access to accurate information for gay youth and adults may be minimal.

A particularly complex focus of therapy involves an exploration of the family of origin, including communication/language difficulties between the client and hearing family members, and family norms (or norms of the culture within which the family exists) that may make revelations about sexual identity especially difficult (Morales, 1996; Greene & Boyd-Franklin, 1996; Liu & Chan, 1996). Adolescents may not be able to predict how their parents will react. Therapists must help youth anticipate and plan for positive and negative reactions when discussing coming out and disclosure issues within families (Gibbins, 1995).

Confidentiality

Confidentiality issues in working with gay and lesbian deaf or hard of hearing clients are extremely thorny and there are many more questions than answers. Deaf clients experienced with the efficient news grapevine of the Deaf community may have difficulty fully believing in confidentiality in psychotherapy, especially because not all the information that passes along the grapevine is accurate. Even if the therapist main-

- Does the client want to acknowledge and briefly greet the therapist if they encounter each other in public?
- How much casual conversation will be engaged in?
- Will companions be introduced?
- If someone asks if you know each other and how you know each other, what will each party say?
- If someone attempts to seat client and therapist next to one another at a social event, what will they do?
- Will client and therapist try to plan in advance to avoid running into each other at certain events?

Figure 2. Confidentiality Issues

tains complete confidentiality, information about therapy can "leak" in other ways; for example, if the Deaf client talks to a friend who then passes the information on, or if the client is seen entering or leaving the therapist's office. Psychotherapists who work with deaf clients and those who work with gay and lesbian clients make it a rule early in therapy to discuss how to manage chance social encounters and how to avoid being thrown together in more than casual interaction outside the therapeutic setting (fig. 2; see also Leigh et al.,1996; Zitter, 1996).

For clients and therapists within the same small community (Deaf, lesbian, gay, or all of these) the special privacy, safety, and neutrality of the counseling/therapy relationship will be sacrificed if too much outside contact or too many mutual relationships occur; however, protecting the special nature of the therapy relationship may require either the therapist or client or both to sacrifice community activities that he or she might normally wish to participate in.

Clients can attempt to control information about themselves, their lives, or their counseling/psychotherapy in several ways. Some simply avoid counselors or therapists who have any connections in the Deaf community, preferring to deal with communication difficulties rather than possible confidentiality breakdowns. Other clients seek therapists who are knowledgeable about deafness (which usually means having at least some ties in the Deaf community) but rigorously avoid discussing anything about their counseling experiences with anyone but the counselor. If rumors (true or embellished) begin, they may routinely ignore or deny them.

A third approach to information control is for the client to provide enough accurate information to enough friends so that serious misunderstandings can be corrected, at the cost of some compromise to the client's (and perhaps the therapist's) overall privacy. A further cost of this approach is the burden of continuously monitoring the stories about oneself in the community and always being ready to take action to correct misinformation.

The issues raised here are considerably more complex than confidentiality considerations encountered in the general hearing community. Confidentiality and related issues, like rumor or gossip, not only raise difficult ethical questions, but also can challenge therapists' personal and professional well-being. Not only the client, but also the therapist may become the target of gossip. Maintaining an appropriate therapeutic stance can be difficult under such circumstances. To deal successfully with these issues, therapists need access to peers and supervisors who are knowledgeable about the communities and the dilemmas involved and are able to help the therapist find individual solutions that attend to the welfare of the client without ignoring the needs and development of the therapist.

Coming Out Issues in Therapy

The coming out process is a time of enormous turmoil, creativity, joy, self-discovery, and danger. Minimizing the impact of this process can lead to serious misunderstandings between therapists and clients (Greene, 1997; Siegal & Walker, 1996). The coming out process, which can involve intense positive and negative relationships with others and redefinition of who one is, must from time to time take precedence over other issues (Siegal & Walker, 1996). The following interaction was reported by a client in her late twenties who had seen the same therapist since her college days.

> Client: The most wonderful but terrifying thing has happened. I have fallen in love with Betty [her best friend]. We spent all night talking about it. I feel I am walking on air. But neither of us are lesbians.
>
> Therapist: Of course you are not a lesbian. This is a feeling you are having, but I have known you for a long time and you are not a lesbian, so let's be clear about that. I think it is important we don't get away from the issues with your boss that you have been working on with me lately.

The therapist's surprise at the client's sudden "falling in love" experience, which contradicted his view of her as a heterosexually active young woman, led him to prematurely cut off her exploration of the meaning of these new feelings for her identity. The therapist may also have lacked information about the different rates at which aspects of sexuality can develop, and the fact that coming out as gay or bisexual can happen at any stage of life.

Therapists' assumption that all clients are heterosexual (or that heterosexual clients will remain heterosexual) can also interfere with therapy. This is especially problematic during intake and first interviews, when the client does not know the therapist well and may be hesitant to reveal a gay or lesbian identity, as in the following example:

> Therapist (after getting basic background information and finding that the client is a twenty-three-year-old single female with a college education working in a clerical job): Can you tell me what made you decide to come here today?
>
> Client: I have been feeling depressed and not much interested in anything. I think it is because of a break-up, I can't seem to get over it.
>
> Therapist: How long ago did you and your boyfriend break up?

In this case the interviewer's well-intended question had the effect of putting the client in a difficult position. She either had to (a) tell the intake worker "no, I had a girlfriend, not a boyfriend," which she was reluctant to do because she assumed the interviewer was naïve about same-sex relationships or (b) pretend that the relationship had been heterosexual. Because both options seemed too difficult for her at that time, she simply never kept her next appointment.

Therapists can avoid this inadvertent heterosexism by being alert to any comments in which a client is ambiguous about the sex of a friend or partner, or is vague about the nature of a relationship. The therapist can then follow up with questions that are deliberately sex-neutral or that encourage the client to make further disclosure, depending on the therapist's approach and view of the client's readiness to discuss such issues. This area can be opened by questions or comments such as:

Male client: I've been trying to develop more dating skills, but it's not going well.

Therapist (unsure of sex of desired partners): Who were you thinking you might want to date? (or, more affirmatively) I don't want to make assumptions about what you mean. You didn't say if you were talking about meeting men or women.

Female client 1: Sandy took care of me when I was so sick. Then she suddenly was gone. I thought I would go crazy.

Therapist (unsure of the relationships between client and Sandy): It is hard to lose someone you love.

Female client 2: (arrives and places car keys on desk. A fob on key ring says *Angela,* which is not client's name)

Therapist: I just noticed your key ring says "Angela."

Client: Yeah, my girlfriend gave it to me.

Therapist (unsure of what is meant by girlfriend, but wanting to encourage client to feel free to disclose to her): Oh, that's nice, I didn't know you had a girlfriend. Tell me about her.

For clients in the early stages of wondering/fearing if they are gay/lesbian, these comments may not lead immediately to any additional information regarding same-sex partners. However, these kinds of comments do let the client know that the therapist is interested in hearing about such issues when the client is willing to talk about them.

Because of the complexity of issues involved in coming out (such as what to disclose to particular people, how to disclose, how to deal with positive or negative reactions to disclosure, and goals of disclosure or nondisclosure in particular instances), therapists and clients can easily fall back on the idea that there are "right" and "wrong" ways to manage this information. For example, assuming that everyone "should" come out because secrecy is destructive and debilitating can lead to underestimating the financial, physical, and emotional risks of disclosure in certain situations. Instead of encouraging or discouraging coming out, the therapist can assist the client to assess his or her own circumstances, resources, risks, and goals, in order to make the best coming out decisions for this person at this time in this situation (Green et al., 1996). Most clients engage in varying degrees of disclosure with different people in their lives, and this changes with changing circumstances (Falco, 1996).

Therapists may also misconstrue the client's goals in a particular coming out decision. Consider the following example, which took place between a therapist in training and his clinical supervisor:

Trainee: You know I am gay. I wonder how you think I am managing that with my clients and the other trainees?

Supervisor: I think you are managing it very well. I don't think any of them know.

The supervisor in this case assumed that the trainee's goal was to avoid having others find out he was gay. Actually, he was looking for help with appropriate forms of disclosure in a professional setting, as he wished to be "out" to some of his fellow students. After this exchange the student was understandably hesitant to seek further guidance from the supervisor.

Client Reactions to Therapist Characteristics and Behavior

Client preferences about the sexuality of their therapist vary. Some prefer a therapist they assume is heterosexual, others seek one who is gay or lesbian. A gay, lesbian, or bisexual therapist can provide a hopeful role model and information about community resources, lifestyle choices, and development of identity. A heterosexual therapist, on the other hand, may be able to show a client that not all heterosexuals have homonegative feelings and beliefs. A client just beginning to explore same-sex feelings may be too frightened or ashamed to work with a gay-identified therapist and may want encouragement from someone believed to be heterosexual in order to take the first steps to explore a gay or lesbian identity (Siegal & Walker, 1996).

Unless the client has specifically sought out a therapist known to be gay or lesbian, the client may assume the therapist to be heterosexual. The client often also assumes that the therapist endorses common belief systems that heterosexuality is best and that other sexualities are immature, defective, sick, sinful, or wrong (Gabriel & Monaco, 1995; Isay, 1996). While no evidence suggests that only gay therapists can effectively treat gay patients, similarity in lifestyles and belief systems has shown some moderate relationship to therapeutic outcome. One study showed lesbian clients could be expected to have poorer outcomes with therapists who hold traditional beliefs about gender roles (Beutler et al., 1994).

Deaf clients will often ask a therapist directly about hearing status. Lytle and Lewis (1996) discuss how therapists might respond to this question. Few clients, however, will ask their therapist directly about his or her sexuality, especially early in the process when the therapeutic relationship is being established. Indirect questions about marital status or children may help the client form an impression about the therapist's sexuality and life circumstances, but the impression may be erroneous.

Because of personal preferences, therapeutic approach used, or possible fear of repercussions, therapists differ in their willingness to inform clients about their personal lives. As a matter of practicality, however, therapists may want to deal directly with the client's assumptions about the therapist's attitudes about gay and lesbian issues. Framing comments about sexuality in a way that affirms gay, lesbian, and bisexual feelings, relationships, and lifestyle choices is crucially important. For clients who have been exposed to consistently negative reactions to their sexuality, however, such comments may be too subtle for the client to be able to really absorb their affirmative implications. To illustrate, the following interaction followed an exchange in which a Deaf client complained about negative comments a friend made about gay people being promiscuous. The therapist, trying to indicate gay-affirmative beliefs, said "I know many people think that, but really many gays and lesbians have very committed long-term relationships."

Client: Can I ask you a question?

Therapist: Yes, go ahead.

Client: Are you prejudiced?

Therapist: I'm not sure what you mean.

Client: Do you think gays are bad?

Therapist: No, I think gays are as good as everyone else. Can I ask what made you ask that question?

Client: Most people think gays are bad.

This opened the way for further discussion of what the client had in mind by the phrase "gays are bad," her own doubts about her possibilities for happiness, and her concerns about what would become of her if she decided to consider herself a lesbian, something she was experiencing great conflict about.

If this client had not been bold enough to probe further, the therapist could have felt she clearly expressed her gay/lesbian affirmative beliefs, while the client was left wondering what she really meant. Many clients are very reluctant to discuss much about attitudes, beliefs, or perceptions of sexual identities out of fear that they will offend or embarrass the therapist, or, worse, will discover that the therapist really does see the client's sexuality as evidence of damage or defect. They fear the possibility of insulting a heterosexual therapist if they hope or suspect he or she is gay or lesbian. They fear shaming a gay or lesbian therapist who they think may not want his or her sexual identity known. A therapist who can comfortably entertain and discuss questions about his or her sexuality (whether or not the therapist decides to answer such questions) can encourage client openness and allow clients to explore experiences, fears, fantasies, and perhaps shame about revealing or acknowledging their own sexual identity. Whether the therapist is heterosexual, lesbian, gay, or bisexual, it is important to state clearly the therapist's disagreement with homophobic and homonegative beliefs (Brown, 1996). However, many clients who are struggling with the "who am I/what am I" issues of coming out, as well as clients who identify themselves as gay or lesbian, still have feelings of negativity, distress, even contempt for same-sex relationships, based upon years of exposure to such attitudes from family, peers, and society at large. Such clients may find a therapist's affirmative statements confusing, even alarming (Downey & Friedman, 1996).

Client: I saw E. again last night.

Therapist: You care a great deal about him.

Client: It's sick and I really want to avoid being around him.

Therapist: Can you tell me what you mean when you say it is sick?

Client: If you don't know what sick means, why are you a counselor?

A client mired in feelings of self-disgust and self-criticism may not be able to accept gay-affirmative ideas, and in such cases the therapist may decide not to challenge the client's homophobic beliefs (while also not appearing to agree with them). It is important that such comments be genuine and nonintrusive (Stein & Cabaj, 1996). The therapist might continue the above dialogue with a statement such as:

Therapist: I usually think that feelings of caring and interest in another person are healthy, no matter who the two people are. But maybe your experiences give you a different feeling about it. I really would like to know how you see it.

This allows the client the opportunity to express and explore his or her own feelings, without feeling forced to accept the therapist's beliefs (Downey & Friedman, 1996; Stein & Cabaj, 1996).

Clients who believe their therapist is heterosexual may also be concerned with "protecting" the therapist from information that might be shocking to the therapist about the client's sexual experiences, and therefore refrain from discussing important people or interactions. For example, a Deaf lesbian client with a heterosexual therapist frequently went to leather bars and picked up hearing strangers for S&M (sadomasochistic) sexual activities. She thought these encounters were unacceptable and they frightened her, yet at the same time she felt compelled to pursue them. She refrained from telling her therapist about these concerns. The therapist, puzzled about what was going on, asked a gay colleague about the bar that the client mentioned, learned that it was considered a cruising place for finding partners for S&M and B&D (bondage and discipline) activities, and asked the client about this directly. The client, although initially embarrassed, was ultimately very relieved to have "permission" from her therapist to discuss these experiences.

This case illustrates the importance of heterosexual therapists being well-informed about issues of importance to lesbian, gay, or bisexual clients, and having sources of information about these issues other than their gay clients (Brown, 1996; Falco, 1996; Siegal & Walker, 1996).

Sexual Feelings in Therapy

An additional issue for therapists working with gay and lesbian clients is how to work with sexual feelings that may come up between the therapist and client. A client may be especially hesitant to reveal such feelings to a heterosexual therapist, fearing that the therapist will be shocked, embarrassed, or revolted, and therefore abandon the client. Unfortunately, when therapists are not comfortable with their client's sexuality and their own responses to it, these reactions can indeed happen, with devastating consequences for the client. When the therapist is seen as gay/lesbian, the client may both hope and fear that his or her feelings will be returned, and that the therapist will become a lover. The therapist must make it clear that the therapeutic boundaries will not change and sexual attractions will not be acted on, but that these feelings can be discussed openly in the therapeutic context. Tact, empathy, and firmness about the therapeutic role are required.

Brown (1996) recommends supervision whenever these issues enter into a therapeutic relationship. She further recommends that therapists struggling themselves with coming out (or closely related issues such as a spouse's coming out) should not see gay, lesbian, or bisexual clients in therapy until these personal issues are resolved.

Touch between therapist and client, whatever their cultures, can have many ramifications, and, because it is nonverbal, it can be interpreted very differently by therapist and client. With gay and lesbian clients, this can be an especially difficult issue because many are fearful of being accused of sexual overtures when hugging or otherwise expressing affection for heterosexual friends. For either gay or heterosexual clients, a hug from a therapist to whom a client feels attracted may be interpreted as a sign of sexual interest by the client. Clients who have been sexually abused may interpret hugging as a demand from the therapist for sexual contact. Zitter (1996) recommends that therapists working with deaf clients consider their own comfort with touch and its implications as well as what it means to the client. This means making a conscious decision in each therapeutic situation regarding the advisability of touching a client.

The therapist must also be able to attend to less obvious reasons why a client may discuss an attraction to the therapist. For example, a client may intentionally or unconsciously use discussion of sexual topics to keep the therapist off balance or distracted from other issues that feel more threatening to the client. Peer and supervisory arrangements where these issues can be openly discussed are essential, so that therapists do not either fall into an overt or covert romance with the patient, or reflexively reject the patient's loving feelings or sexual provocations (sometimes to the point of terminating the therapy because the therapist has become too uncomfortable).

Shame and Secrecy

Having a gay or lesbian therapist does not necessarily resolve all the client's potential concerns about sexuality. Deaf clients who choose to go into therapy with an openly lesbian or gay therapist who knows nothing of deafness may not only face communication barriers, but will spend therapeutic time teaching the therapist about the Deaf or Deaf/gay community. Clients with an openly gay or lesbian therapist may also use the therapist as a model. They may also fear that their ideas or doubts about their relationships or their sexual orientation will appear homophobic and thus insulting to the therapist and shameful to themselves. Many gay and lesbian clients' lives have been replete with shaming experiences (Kaufman & Raphael, 1996). Thus, providing a therapeutic environment in which the client feels able to bring up any topic with little fear of shaming, attack, or abandonment by the therapist is a major achievement.

In some cases clients with gay or lesbian therapists may develop the belief that the therapist's sexual orientation is a secret between the two of them and that they must try to protect the therapist from anyone finding out. An example follows:

> Client (frowning): Why are you wearing that pin? (referring to a pink triangle)
>
> Therapist: You seem to be feeling a reaction to it.
>
> Client: You should be more careful! You will take it off when you leave here, won't you?

A client burdened with a "secret" can also feel guilty if he or she reveals it (the parallels to old memories that may be present of incest or sexual abuse are apparent).

> Client: I feel bad about something. I told M. [another of the therapist's clients] that I thought you were gay. I'm so sorry. I feel very nervous about it. I guess she said she felt uncomfortable with you and I wanted to make her feel more comfortable. Is it all right? I wouldn't tell just anyone.
>
> Therapist: You seem very uncomfortable telling me this. Can you tell me how you are feeling?
>
> Client: I feel guilty. I wanted to help M., but I shouldn't have done it.

Such an exchange is likely to provoke the therapist's own fears about professional coming out decisions, which may be residual if he or she is generally open about his or her sexuality, or quite current if he or she is indeed trying to limit who knows this information. A number of the responses that come to mind, such as "How do you imagine I might feel about that?" or "What made you decide to tell her?" while superficially neutral have the potential of echoing their more negative counterparts ("And how the hell did you expect me to feel about that?" "What in the world made you tell her?"). A more direct response, which still allows the client freedom to explore feelings about the matter, might be something like "You seem to feel that you have broken some sort of rule, or fear that you have. Could you tell me about that?"

Therapist Hearing Status

A final but important therapist issue, which has been mentioned previously, is hearing status (Lytle & Lewis, 1966). Clients come to therapy with an idea in mind of the ideal therapist's characteristics (deaf, Deaf, or hearing; old or young; gay, lesbian, bisexual, or heterosexual). The client's bicultural comfort and experiences, negative or positive, with deaf and hearing professionals in the past are also a factor. As therapists, sometimes we have the pleasure of knowing we are exactly what the patient wanted. In other cases, we know we are the best the client could do, a compromise with what he or she really wanted. With economic factors dictating short-term therapy for many clients, client and therapist must quickly develop rapport so they can proceed to the real issues that bring the client to therapy. Direct discussion of the client's hoped-for therapist compared to the real one may allow the client to deal with any disappointment or concerns and allow rapport building to proceed.

Conclusion

Therapists working with lesbian, gay, and bisexual deaf clients must be aware of issues pertaining to deafness and Deaf culture and must know about and be comfortable with sexual identity issues. They must also be able to treat sexual identity and hearing status as background or foreground, as needed, and to work on issues the client identifies as troublesome rather than those the therapist might (rightly or wrongly) believe need attention. Success in these efforts requires a great deal of personal flexibility, self-knowledge, and comfort with one's own sexuality and sexual feelings, in both same-sex and opposite-sex relationships. Access to a support network of other professionals working with deaf and hard of hearing clients, on the one hand, and lesbian/gay/bisexual clients, on the other, is crucial for dealing with the very complex personal and therapeutic challenges that arise in working with these multifaceted social, cultural, and mental health issues. Opportunities for unexpected personal and professional growth are the reward.

References

American Psychological Association. (1995). *Lesbian and gay parenting: A resource for psychologists.* Washington, DC: American Psychological Association.

Anthony, S. (1992). The influence of personal characteristics on rumor knowledge and transmission among the deaf. *American Annals of the Deaf, 137* (1), 44–47.

Anthony, S., Gibbins, S., & Longo, D. (1997). *Outcome relevance and hurricane-related rumors among the deaf.* Presented at Eastern Psychological Association, Washington, DC, 2 April.

Bailey, J., Bobrow, D., Wolfe, M., & Mikach, S. (1995). Sexual orientation of adult sons of gay fathers. *Developmental Psychology,* 31, 124–129.

Beutler, L., Machado, P., & Neufeldt, S. (1994). Therapist variables. In A. Bergin & S. Garfield (Eds.), *Handbook of psychotherapy and behavior change* (4th ed.) (pp. 229–269). New York: Wiley.

Blumstein, P., & Schwartz, P. (1983). *American couples: Money, work, sex.* New York: Morrow.

Brown, L. (1995). Lesbian identities: Concepts and issues. In A. D'Augelli & C. Patterson (Eds.), *Lesbian, gay, and bisexual identities over the lifespan: Psychological perspectives* (pp. 3–23). New York: Oxford University Press.

———. (1996). Ethical concerns with sexual minority patients. In R. Cabaj & T. Stein (Eds.), *Textbook of homosexuality and mental health* (pp. 897–919). Washington, DC: American Psychiatric Press.

Chan, C. (1995). Issues of sexual identity in an ethnic minority: The case of Chinese American lesbians, gay men, and bisexual people. In A. D'Augelli & C. Patterson (Eds.), *Lesbian, gay, and bisexual identities over the lifespan: Psychological perspectives* (pp. 87–101). New York: Oxford University Press.

D'Augelli, A. (1994). Lesbian and gay male development: Steps toward an analysis of lesbians' and gay men's lives. In B. Greene & G. Herek (Eds.), *Lesbian and gay psychology: Theory, research, and clinical applications* (pp. 118–132). Thousand Oaks, CA: Sage Publications.

DeVine, J. (1984). A systematic inspection of affectional preference orientation and the family of origin. *Journal of Social Work and Human Sexuality, 2,* 9–17.

Dobosh, P., and Gutman, V. (1998). *Assessment and individual treatment issues with Deaf survivors.* Paper presented at the World Conference on Mental Health and Deafness, Gallaudet University, Washington, D.C.

Doyle, A. G. (1995). AIDS knowledge, attitudes, and behaviors among deaf college students: A preliminary study. *Sexuality and Disability, 13,* 107–134.

Downey, J., & Friedman, R. (1996). The negative therapeutic reaction and self-hatred in gay and lesbian patients. In R. Cabaj & T. Stein (Eds.), *Textbook of homosexuality and mental health* (pp. 471–484). Washington, DC: American Psychiatric Press.

Espin, O. (1993). Issues of identity in the psychology of Latina lesbians. In L. Garnets & D. Kimmel (Eds.), *Psychological perspectives on lesbian and gay male experiences* (pp. 348–363). New York: Columbia University Press.

Falco, K. (1991). *Psychotherapy with lesbian clients: Theory into practice.* New York: Brunner/Mazel.

———. (1996). Psychotherapy with women who love women. In R. Cabaj & T. Stein (Eds.), *Textbook of homosexuality and mental health.,* (pp. 397–412). Washington, DC: American Psychiatric Press.

Flaks, D., Ficher, I., Masterpasqua, F., & Joseph, G. (1995). Lesbians choosing motherhood: A comparative study of lesbian and heterosexual parents and their children. *Developmental Psychology, 31,* 105–114.

FLASH e-mail newsgroup. (3 September, 1996).

Fox, R. (1995). Bisexual identities. In A. D'Augelli & C. Patterson (Eds.), *Lesbian, gay, and bisexual identities over the lifespan* (pp. 48–86). New York: Oxford University Press.

Gabriel, M., & Monaco, G. (1995) Revisiting the question of self-disclosure: The lesbian therapist's dilemma. In J. Glassgold & S. Iasenza (Eds.), *Lesbians and psychoanalysis: Revolutions in theory and practice* (pp. 161–172). New York: Free Press.

Garnets, L., Hancock, K., Cochran, S., Goodchilds, J., & Peplau, L. (1991). Issues in psychotherapy with lesbians and gay men: A survey of psychologists. *American Psychologist, 46,* 964–972.

Garnets, L., & Kimmel, D. (1993). Lesbian and gay male dimensions in the psychological study of human diversity. In L. Garnets & D. Kimmel (Eds.), *Psychological perspectives on lesbian and gay male experiences* (pp. 1–52). New York: Columbia University Press.

Gibbins, S. (1995). Who am I? Multiply minority identity and its implications for working with deaf gay patients. Unpublished paper.

Gibson, P. (1989). Gay male and lesbian youth suicide. In ADAMHA, *Report of the Secretary's Task Force on Youth Suicide* (DHHS Publication No. ADM 89–1623; vol. 3, pp. 110–142). Washington, DC: U.S. Government Printing Office.

Glassgold, J., & Iasenza, S. (Eds.). (1995). *Lesbians and psychoanalysis: Revolutions in theory and practice.* New York: Free Press.

Glickman, N. (1996). The development of culturally deaf identities. In N. Glickman & M. Harvey (Eds.), *Culturally affirmative psychotherapy with Deaf persons* (pp. 115–153). Mahwah, NJ: Lawrence Erlbaum Associates.

Gonsiorek, J. (Ed.). (1985). *Homosexuality and psychotherapy: A practitioner's handbook of affirmative models.* New York: Haworth Press.

———. (1995). Gay male identities: Concepts and issues. In A. D'Augelli & C. Patterson (Eds.), *Lesbian, gay, and bisexual identities over the lifespan: Psychological perspectives* (pp. 24–47). New York: Oxford University Press.

Gould, D. (1995). A critical examination of the notion of pathology in psychoanalysis. In J. Glassgold & S. Iasenza, (Eds.), *Lesbians and psychoanalysis: Revolutions in theory and practice* (pp. 3–17). New York: Free Press.

Green, R-J, Bettinger, M., & Zacks, E. (1996). Are lesbian couples fused and gay male couples disengaged? In J. Laird & R-J Green (Eds.), *Lesbians and gays in couples and families: A handbook for therapists* (pp. 185–230). San Francisco: Jossey-Bass.

Greene, B. (1994). Ethnic-minority lesbians and gay men: Mental health and treatment issues. *Journal of Consulting and Clinical Psychology, 62,* 243–251.

———. (1997). Ethnic minority lesbians and gay men: Mental health and treatment issues. In B. Greene (Ed.), *Ethnic and cultural diversity among lesbians and gay men* (pp. 216–239). Thousand Oaks, CA: Sage Publications.

Greene, B., & Boyd-Franklin, N. (1996). African American lesbians: Issues in couples therapy. In J. Laird & R-J Green (Eds.), *Lesbians and gays in couples and families: A handbook for therapists* (pp. 251–271). San Francisco: Jossey-Bass.

Haldeman, D. (1994). The practice and ethics of sexual orientation conversion therapy. *Journal of Consulting and Clinical Psychology, 62,* 221–227.

Hancock, C. (1995). Psychotherapy with lesbians and gay men. In A. D'Augelli and C. Patterson (Eds.), *Lesbian, gay and bisexual identities over the lifespan: Psychological perspectives* (pp. 398–432). New York: Oxford University Press.

Hartstein, N. (1996). Suicide risk in lesbian, gay and bisexual youth. In R. Cabaj & T. Stein (Eds.), *Handbook of homosexuality and mental health* (pp. 819–838). Washington, DC: American Psychiatric Press.

Hecht, A., & Gutman, V. (1997). *Identity formation and self-esteem in D/deaf lesbians.* Paper presented at the annual meeting of the American Psychological Association, Chicago, August.

Herek, G. (1994). Assessing heterosexuals' attitudes toward lesbians and gay men: A review of empirical research with the TLG Scale. In B. Greene & G. Herek (Eds.), *Lesbian and gay psychology: Theory, research, and clinical applications* (pp. 206–228). Thousand Oaks, CA: Sage Publications.

Herschberger, S., & D'Augelli, A. (1995). The impact of victimization on the mental health and suicidality of lesbian, gay, and bisexual youths. *Developmental Psychology, 31,* 65–74.

Isay, R. (1989). *Being homosexual: Gay men and their development.* New York: Farrar, Straus, Giroux.

———. (1996). *Becoming gay: The journey to self-acceptance.* New York: Pantheon Books.

Kaufman, G., & Raphael, L. (1996). *Coming out of shame: Transforming gay and lesbian lives.* New York: Doubleday.

Kimmel, D., & Sang, B. (1995). Lesbians and gay men in midlife. In A. D'Augelli & C. Patterson (Eds.), *Lesbian, gay and bisexual identities over the lifespan: Psychological perspectives* (pp. 190–214). New York: Oxford University Press.

Kite, M. (1994). When perceptions meet reality: Individual differences in reactions to lesbians and gay men. In B. Greene & G. Herek (Eds.), *Lesbian and gay psychology: Theory, research and clinical applications* (pp. 25–53). Thousand Oaks, CA: Sage Publications.

Kitzinger, C., & Wilkinson, S. (1995). Transitions from heterosexuality to lesbianism: The discursive production of lesbian identities. *Developmental Psychology, 31,* 95–104.

Klinger, R., & Stein, T. (1996). Impact of violence, childhood sexual abuse, and domestic violence and abuse on lesbians, bisexuals, and gay men. In R. Cabaj & T. Stein (Eds.), *Textbook of homosexuality and mental health* (pp. 801–818). Washington, DC: American Psychiatric Press.

Kurdek, L. (1995a). Developmental changes in relationship quality in gay and lesbian cohabiting couples. *Developmental Psychology, 31,* 86–94.

———. (1995b). Lesbian and gay couples. In A. D'Augelli & C. Patterson (Eds.), *Lesbian, gay and bisexual identities over the lifespan: Psychological perspectives* (pp. 243–261). New York: Oxford University Press.

Langholtz, D., & Rendon, M. (1991–1992). The deaf gay/lesbian client: Some perspectives. *Journal of the American Deafness and Rehabilitation Association, 25,* 31–34.

Leigh, I., Corbett, C., Gutman, V., & Morere, D. (1996). Providing psychological services to deaf individuals: A response to new perceptions of diversity. *Professional Psychology: Research and Practice, 27* (4), 364–371.

Liu, P., & Chan, C. (1996). Lesbian, gay, and bisexual Asian Americans and their families. In J. Laird & R-J Green (Eds.), *Lesbians and gays in couples and families: A handbook for therapists* (pp. 137–152). San Francisco: Jossey-Bass.

Luczak, R. (1993). *Eyes of desire: A deaf gay and lesbian reader.* Boston: Alyson Publications.

Lytle, L., & Lewis, J. (1996). Deaf therapists, deaf clients, and the therapeutic relationships. In N. Glickman & M. Harvey (Eds.), *Culturally affirmative psychotherapy with Deaf persons* (pp. 261–276). Mahwah, NJ: Lawrence Erlbaum.

Matteson, D. (1996). Psychotherapy with bisexual individuals. In R. Cabaj & T. Stein (Eds.), *Textbook of homosexuality and mental health* (pp. 433–450). Washington, DC: American Psychiatric Press.

Meredith, R., & Riester, R. (1980). Psychotherapy, responsibility, and homosexuality: Clinical examination of socially deviant behavior. *Professional Psychology, 11,* 174–193.

Morales, E. (1996). Gender roles among Latino gay and bisexual men. In J. Laird & R-J Green (Eds.), *Lesbians and gays in couples and families: A handbook for therapists* (pp. 272–297). San Francisco: Jossey-Bass.

Morgan, K., & Brown, L. (1993). Lesbian career development, work behavior, and vocational counseling. In L. Garnets & D. Kimmel (Eds.), *Psychological perspectives on lesbian and gay male experiences* (pp. 267–286). New York: Columbia University Press.

Nystrom, N. (1997). *Mental health experiences of gay men and lesbians.* Paper presented at American Association for the Advancement of Science, Detroit, MI.

Paradis, B. (1997). Multicultural identities and gay men in the era of AIDS. *American Journal of Orthopsychiatry, 67* (2), 300–307.

Patterson C. (1995a). Sexual orientation and human development: An overview. *Developmental Psychology, 31,* 3–11.

———. (1995b). Lesbian mothers, gay fathers, and their children. In A. D'Augelli & C. Patterson (Eds.), *Lesbian, gay, and bisexual identities over the lifespan: Psychological perspectives.* New York: Oxford University Press.

Peplau, L. A. (1993). Lesbian and gay relationships. In L. Garnets & D. Kimmel (Eds.), *Psychological perspectives on lesbian and gay male experiences* (pp. 396–419). New York: Columbia University Press.

Ratner, E. (1993). Treatment issues for chemically dependent lesbians and gay men. In L. Garnets & D. Kimmel (Eds.), *Psychological perspectives on lesbian and gay male experiences.* New York: Columbia University Press.

Rosenbaum, J. (1995). Issues pertaining to gay and lesbian development: Social isolation and the role of the family (Applications to deafness). Unpublished paper.

Rothblum, E. (Ed.). (1994). Special section: Mental health of lesbians and gay men. *Journal of Consulting and Clinical Psychology, 62,* 211–269.

Rotheram-Borus, M., Rosario, M., Van Rossem, R., Reid, H., & Gillis, R. (1995). Prevalence, course, and predictors of multiple problem behaviors among gay and bisexual male adolescents. *Developmental Psychology, 31,* 75–85.

Rust, P. (1993). "Coming out" in the age of social constructionism: Sexual identity formation among lesbians and bisexual women. *Gender and Society, 7* (1), 50–77.

Ryan, C., & Bradford, J. (1993). The National Lesbian Health Care Survey: An overview. In L. Garnets & D. Kimmel (Eds.), *Psychological perspectives on lesbian and gay male experiences* (pp. 541–556). New York: Columbia University Press.

Savin-Williams, R. (1994). Verbal and physical abuse as stressors in the lives of lesbian, gay male, and bisexual youths: Association with school problems, running away, substance abuse, prostitution, and suicide. *Journal of Consulting and Clinical Psychology, 62,* 261–269.

———. (1995). Lesbian, gay male, and bisexual adolescents. In A. D'Augelli & C. Patterson (Eds.), *Lesbian, gay, and bisexual identities over the lifespan* (pp. 165–189). New York: Oxford University Press.

———. (1996). Self-labeling and disclosure among gay, lesbian, and bisexual youths. *Lesbians and gays in couples and families: A handbook for therapists* (pp. 153–184). San Francisco: Jossey-Bass.

Siegal, S., & Walker, G. (1996). Connections: Conversations between a gay therapist and a straight therapist. In J. Laird & R-J Green (Eds.), *Lesbians and gays in couples and families: A handbook for therapists* (pp. 28–68). San Francisco: Jossey-Bass.

Silverstein, C. (1991). Psychotherapy and psychotherapists: A history. In C. Silverstein (Ed.), *Gays, lesbians, and their therapists* (pp. 1–14). New York: W. W. Norton.

Silverstein, C. (Ed.). (1991). *Gays, lesbians, and their therapists.* New York: W. W. Norton.

Slater, S. (1995). *The lesbian family life cycle.* New York: Free Press.

Stein, T. (1996). A critique of approaches to changing sexual orientation. In R. Cabaj & T. Stein (Eds.), *Textbook of homosexuality and mental health* (pp. 525–538). Washington, DC: American Psychiatric Press.

Stein, T., & Cabaj, R. (1996). Psychotherapy with gay men. In R. Cabaj & T. Stein (Eds.), *Textbook of homosexuality and mental health* (pp. 413–432). Washington, DC: American Psychiatric Press.

Strommen, E. (1993). "You're a what?": Family member reactions to the disclosure of homosexuality. In L. Garnets & D. Kimmel (Eds.), *Psychological perspectives on lesbian and gay male experiences* (pp. 248–266). New York: Columbia University Press.

Swartz, D. (1995). Cultural implications of audiological deficits on the homosexual male. *Sexuality and Disability, 13,* 159–181.

Trujillo, C. (1997). Sexual identity and the discontents of difference. In B. Green (Ed.), *Ethnic and cultural diversity among lesbians and gay men* (pp. 266–278). Thousand Oaks, CA: Sage Publications.

Weinberg, G. (1972). *Society and the healthy homosexual.* New York: St. Martin's Press.

Weinrich, J. (1987). *Sexual landscapes.* New York: Charles Scribner's Sons.

Zakarewsky, G. (1979). Patterns of support among gay and lesbian deaf persons. *Sexuality and Disability, 2,* 178–191.

Zitter, S. (1996). Report from the front lines: Balancing multiple roles of a deafness therapist. In N. Glickman & M. Harvey (Eds.), *Culturally affirmative pscyhotherapy with Deaf persons* (pp. 185–246). Mahwah, NJ: Lawrence Erlbaum.

6

Hearing Children of Deaf Parents: Issues and Interventions within a Bicultural Context

SHIRLEY SHULTZ MYERS, RANDALL R. MYERS,
AND ALAN L. MARCUS

It may seem strange that a book about psychotherapy and deaf people should give space to hearing people. From a biological perspective, hearing children of deaf parents (hcdp) are not deaf and therefore not part of the deaf community or Deaf culture. From anthropological, sociological, and developmental perspectives, however, they are born into the deaf community, and many are acculturated to Deaf ways. In fact, while most deaf people learn about Deaf culture from Deaf peers (Becker, 1980; Meadow-Orlans et al., 1987; Padden & Humphries, 1988), their children—90% of whom are hearing—learn it the way anthropologists like hcdp Paul Preston say is usual: within the family (1994, p. 7).

Prevailing deaf community views indicate that deaf members do not embrace hearing offspring as full members, especially as adults. Alex Fleischman (1996) suggests that adult hearing children are members only if they perform a service or make some other contribution to the deaf community; other ties, such as marrying a deaf individual or parenting deaf children, may also qualify one for membership. Higgins (1980) and others posit that, even with fluency in signs and even as an adult active in the community, membership is marginal or courtesy. Padden and Humphries (1988) echo this view in their assertion that hcdp represent an "ongoing contradiction" in Deaf culture: "they display the knowledge of their parents—skill in the language and social conduct—but the culture finds subtle ways to give them an unusual and separate status" (p. 3). Bahan's (1994) definition of Deaf culture, based on two functional conditions, provides a possible rationale for this separate status: one condition is understanding deaf life from the direct experience of the physical reality of being deaf, which excludes hcdp, and the other is being a part of the Deaf world; hcdp meet this latter condition because they have acquired the "ways and nuances of interacting unique to this world—that is, they have 'Deaf World Knowledge'" (p. 243).

Membership is much more problematic in adulthood, especially for those who do not work or socialize with deaf people and must rely on special occasions or chance encounters. Those who have little interaction feel "as if we were raised in a foreign country with its own unique culture and language, and now we have moved to a new country where everything is different; every now and then we run into someone from the 'homeland' and the 'old ways' come flooding back" (Myers, 1991, p. 66). The very title of an excellent Australian videotape, *Passport Without a Country* (1992), indicates the identity dilemma and

For many helpful comments on earlier partial drafts of this article, we would like to thank Sandra G. Hershberg, M.D., P.C. For his careful reading, editorial help, and thoughtful comments on an earlier draft, we are also indebted to Russell H. Astley, Ph.D.

the sense of unrecognized membership in the deaf community: "It's like you were born in a country, and you have a passport to that country, but no one will recognize your passport." Looking solely at the physical difference—ears that hear—therapists and others, hearing and deaf, may overlook that an hcdp's most intimate, experiential knowledge is of a deaf family.

Unlike many deaf people, who often remain close to their hearing families of origin but who intrinsically know they are most at home in the deaf community, hcdp often experience confusion or other mixed feelings about where they belong, especially when they make the transition from adolescence to adulthood and when the deaf world feels warmer or more comfortable than the hearing world.

Therapists would do well to understand that these mixed feelings occur. However, there is a dearth of mental health knowledge about these offspring despite the fact that 90% of deaf couples have hearing children. The few published case studies provide some helpful information, but too many also inaccurately generalize in alarming ways. Children of Deaf Adults (CODA), several autobiographies, newspaper and magazine articles, and Paul Preston's (1994) study provide very helpful information, but a lack of accurate, useful information in the professional literature on the psychosocial impact of growing up hearing with deaf parents continues.

Although Preston's *Mother Father Deaf* is the best study to date, his assertion that "explaining family phenomena through medical or psychological explanatory models reinforces an aberrant perspective of deafness" (p. 229) derives from a rather circumscribed view of what a psychological perspective might include. That is, the psychological explanations his informants related to him dealt only with those found in "the popular literature on adult children of other types of parents," most often "children of alcoholics and adult children from dysfunctional families" (p. 226). Thus, Preston cannot go into any detail regarding relevant psychological explanations, because his informants did not supply them.

Acknowledging that his criticism of "psychological repercussions of deafness" is not absolute, Preston's main objective in this criticism is to counteract "a long history of explanations and responses to deafness [that] has reflected biases of the dominant Hearing culture and continues to overshadow the understandings of deaf people themselves" (p. 232). Moreover, Preston himself expresses a psychological perspective when he observes that, for an hcdp, "the drama of belonging and of being different unfolds within oneself" (p. 237). Taking a cue from Sheila Jacobs' cross-culturally sensitive therapy (Jacobs, 1993), the authors of this chapter provide a non-pathologizing—but definitely psychological—understanding of the hcdp experience.

We, hearing children of deaf parents, have constructed a biopsychosocial approach to understanding the experiences of hearing children with deaf parents wherein two main themes emerge: mediation and identity formation (Myers & Marcus, 1993). The issues we highlight will manifest differently depending on where a person is in terms of developmental stages, but our focus is on the issues per se that clinicians need to be sensitive to in working with hcdp. Seeking to avoid pathologizing physical and cultural differences, we nevertheless cannot apologize for dealing with the times when the two cultures not only enrich our lives but effect psychological conflicts as well, when neither world has the corner on truth. Our aim is to help therapists understand and respect the potential challenges of hearing children with deaf parents.

Setting the Context for Treatment: A Biopsychosocial Approach and Family Dynamics

The biopsychosocial approach (Engel, 1977, 1980) has been discussed in a variety of medical and mental health clinical contexts, for example, exploring the mind-body problem (Goodman, 1991), clinical problem solving (Sadler & Hulgus, 1992), and family therapy with adolescents (Matorin & Greenberg, 1992). The biopsychosocial model "is now the most coherent, comprehensive, and empirically valuable conceptual framework within which to understand the human being in health and in illness" (Goodman, 1991, p. 554). It addresses the relationship between mind and body and their social environment, evolving from studies in general systems theory. With this model, clinicians focus on at least three elements, biological or constitutional, psychological, and social, that influence human behavior. Moreover, this model helps correct the naive tendency on the part of clinicians to note the parents' deafness as the cause for the child's behavior and problems in the family. Clinicians need to explore each element, as well as consider interactions among the three, before an effective intervention may begin.

For the biological realm, a range of organically based disorders—for example, Attention Deficit Hyperactivity Disorder (ADHD), anxiety, panic disorder, or depression—should be considered first at the intake interview. With regard to the child's behavior patterns, a biopsychosocial approach might suggest that the child's temperament in interaction with environmental conditions may give rise to the behavior we see. Inquiries about temperament can then reveal the salient familial and social behaviors that interact with temperament or constitution to produce certain problem behaviors in the child.

For our purposes, it is helpful to take into account constitutional factors so as to understand better the challenging intrapsychic world of hearing children with deaf parents; the more innate individual resilience an hcdp has, the better able to cope with this psychosocial experience Preston describes so well:

> Hearing children of deaf parents move the schism between those who are different and those who are not to its ultimate setting. Here, the confrontation and the dialogue are not between those separated by geographic boundaries or political allegiances, between parent and child, or between Deaf and Hearing. Here, the drama of belonging and of being different unfolds within oneself. (1994, pp. 236–237)

As Preston's portrayal of the psychosocial reality of hearing offspring suggests, the clinician must recognize that this kind of family has enormous potential for stress and conflict. The hearing child is *born* into a family of differences—hearing abilities, communication mode preferences, language preferences, stigmatizing or empowering attitudes (of the parents, grandparents, siblings, and other extended family members)—and that range of attitudes is mirrored among hearing people in the outside world.

Another structural factor that creates stress and division is vocal communication between grandparents and children, as it potentially isolates the deaf parents from some family interactions (Harvey, 1989). Other psychosocial stressors are roles and responsibilities that hearing children assume (for example, communication facilitator, information provider, and advocate). These roles and responsibilities also occur in families of other cultures (Lynch, 1992). In unique and individual ways, hearing children of deaf parents adapt to, manage, and mediate myriad differences simultaneously, in their interactions with both immediate and extended family members and with people outside the family who can hear.

As the hearing child moves into adulthood, he or she renews, or creates anew, his or her own strategies and beliefs to manage these issues of diversity, difference, and disability. Expressing his or her own unique sensitivities and insights into family life, the hearing adult with deaf parents then integrates these often hard-won insights and strategies into his or her adult roles and identities.

INTRAFAMILIAL DYNAMICS

To set the context for hcdp's psychological development, we now introduce two models that have been used in related contexts (handicapped parents, in Thurman, 1985; other deaf family members, in Harvey, 1989) which might help explain the intrafamilial dynamics of deaf parent/hearing child families. The first model focuses on the process within the family (ecological congruence); the second focuses on the process between the family and the outside environment (cybernetic).

Ecological Congruence

The model of ecological congruence "stresses the need to change both the individual *and* the environment or setting with which an individual interacts" (Thurman, 1985, p. 39). The model is valuable for our purposes because it presents three dimensions in its framework: *deviancy* (attribute of individuals), behavior that is judged according to the context in which it occurs; *competency* (attribute of individuals), which defines certain sets of functional behaviors that lead to the completion of a task within that setting; and *tolerance for difference* (attribute of system or individuals), which "determines the goodness of fit between the individual and the environmental-social context" (p. 39). Ultimately this model encourages the development of interventions that develop more harmonious and tolerant ecologies.

How can these three dimensions be applied to the hearing child of deaf parents and his or her family? We can postulate that the deviancy dimension might refer to how the individual and family view the child's ability to hear. When some deaf parents state their wish for deaf children, their hearing children receive a troubling message about their hearing. On the other hand, three hcdp autobiographers report that their parents placed emphasis on their ability to hear and, in fact, relied on them for environmental auditory information as well as cultural or social information about hearing ways (Crowe, 1993; Sidransky, 1990; Walker, 1986). Competency might be viewed as the child's ability, or even willingness, to perform certain functions related to his or her ability to hear, such as informing deaf family members of environmental sounds, interpreting, and even brokering cultures. Although some hcdp like this special role, others become aware of lacking a sense of self that had been suppressed to meet the needs of communication between deaf and hearing worlds, as will be discussed later. Tolerance for differences might be viewed from the family's perspective or the individual's: "How well does the hearing child fit within the Deaf family system?" Such an ecology has a profound effect on family functioning as well as on the psychodynamic development of the child, especially once the child reaches adolescence and young adulthood.

Cybernetic Theory

Ecological congruence can operate as a tool in the analysis of family systems in cybernetic theory. Cybernetic theory is used to visualize how groups and systems remain stable even though changes may occur within them and in their interaction with the surrounding environment (Bateson, 1972; Schwartzman, 1982; Watzlawick et al., 1967; Watzlawick et al., 1974). We apply cybernetic theory as a way to examine and interpret the systemic and cross-cultural context and dynamics of the family with deaf and hearing members. Cybernetic theory proposes that a family needs to have the same cultural expectations for its members as the community of which it is a part, so that dependence and autonomy are not difficult developmental processes. From this perspective, Schwartzman (1982) explains that "each family's interaction creates the context for individual family members' own unique solutions to universal problems, and its cultural context provides the broad outlines for that defined as normal" (p. 395). Families are adaptive and self-correcting systems that provide the most pervasive context of learning and are parts of a more inclusive cultural system. Individuals and families must be able to adapt and function within and between hierarchies of systemic contexts, for example, between members in their immediate families, between families, and between other institutions in the environment.

In our case, many deaf parent/hearing child families are part of the deaf community, a Deaf culture, and a Deaf world. The family functions in this Deaf world when the hearing child is young and dependent. The family's culture and community are also embedded in a larger world that can hear: "Deaf parents have developed a wealth of know-how about successfully negotiating the challenges of being minority members of a hearing culture. In-group jokes and communications patterns make the hearing world the alien factor and reinforce the strengths of deaf culture" (Rayson, 1987, p. 109). The deaf community acts as a buffer between the family and the (generally) hostile hearing world, and it is in this environment that the child spends the first fifteen to twenty years of life. Living in this Deaf culture within a mainstream hearing culture may not be the case for parents who are late deafened or hard of hearing, however, because the perspective is different—the family functions in a predominantly hearing world. In this case, the hearing child *still* contends with the communication and related issues of having a parent who has a hearing loss, but here it is within the broader "cultural" context of people who can hear. In either situation, the child might compare his or her parents to parents who can hear, and see how the deafness might be a disability; but in the deaf community, this comparison occurs in an affirmative Deaf cultural context.

It is interesting to note that hearing children and their deaf parents may, in fact, have the common experience of growing up in a family where there are hearing, language, and cultural differences. However, the complex interplay of stigmatized and stigmatizing differs profoundly for deaf people and their hearing offspring.

Prime Issues in Therapy

Being born and growing up in an *intimate setting of difference* offers numerous possibilities for stress, growth, and strength in family members and in family life. We do not mean hcdp necessarily will develop psychological problems because of the stresses, any more than we would suggest that no one can navigate the turbulent waters of adolescence or the oedipal phase without becoming neurotic and in need of therapy. On the other hand, there should be no shame in looking at problems. Within a clinical focus, we are bound to look at them. Therefore, we discuss pathology not as a given, but as a possibility, the same possibility as would accompany any psychosocial stressor.

Certainly we suggest having deaf parents is an additional psychosocial stressor, as studies of bilinguals suggest. For therapists, we present the following prime clusters of issues to be sensitive to in treating hcdp: communication and connection, parentification, mediating different values and managing stigma, intergenerational dynamics, and identity formation.

COMMUNICATION AND CONNECTION ISSUES

Signing ability seems to have something to do with communication and connectedness. Despite growing up in the deaf community, some hearing children do not sign very well. There are several ways to interpret this behavior. Speaking from a family mental health perspective, Harvey (1989) suggests that the inability to sign may be seen as a "linguistic disengagement" and a linguistic barrier caused by rigid patterns of enmeshment between the child's parents who are deaf and grandparents who can hear. Indeed, Preston (1994) says that some of his informants (all hcdp) reported that their deaf parents did not teach them to sign; instead, they encouraged their children to use the dominant language while the parents paid more attention to their deaf friends. Harvey and Preston suggest that it may very well be the manner in which these deaf parents were raised that established this language and communication pattern as a norm within the family (i.e., no communication between parent and child in a common language). Rienzi (1990) also notes that the stability of the family can be affected when deaf and hearing members do not communicate using the same modality and language. Cybernetic theory might interpret this communication differential as a lack of uniformity of cultural expectations in the family to join with the deaf community. Instead, such hearing children may feel they are on their own, prefer to communicate orally, and end up having ineffective communication with their parents. When deaf parents themselves are oral and do not use sign language, hearing children will not need to learn a totally different form of communication. Although there is more connection with the hearing world and *perhaps* communication with parents is a less stressful event, mediating deaf and hearing worlds and managing stigma still predominate.

Meeting the challenge of communication, rather than being a detriment, in some instances stimulates increased autonomy and creative problem-solving ability. For example, in almost any family with deaf and hearing members, whether oral or signing, reliance on a usually well-developed skill in visual (and also tactile) contact, as well as visual communication, begins developing early. Some hearing children remember having to seek out their mothers instead of calling to them; others found innovative solutions when they were sick, such as throwing shoes to get the mother's attention or tying a piece of string to the mother's big toe.

The impetus to create these clever adaptive strategies reflects an early-developed and acute awareness of difference and separateness. Such unusually heightened sensitivity may be the hearing child's legacy. Moreover, such a legacy potentially has profound effects. For example, because of the difference in sensory input between the deaf parent and the hearing child, the hearing child often, if not always, seems to develop what has been termed a kind of "hypervigilance" or acute and early sensitivity to the environment, particularly sounds. One dramatic example in *Passport Without a Country* is the adult son's story of his hospital stay during WWII, when he panicked at the sound of an air raid siren because he was not at home to alert his deaf parents. The ways hcdp learn to handle separateness, closeness, autonomy, and dependency

(Kramer & Akhtar, 1988, as cited in Tyson & Tyson, 1990) all imprint upon their individual characters and affect their adult intimate relationships.

Deaf parents know they live in a world of sound, know that sounds can be important, and communicate that knowledge to their children at the earliest ages. Indeed, the parents are often glad when the child, even a toddler or younger, can tell them that someone is yelling angrily outside their window, the music is too loud, the toilet is making an odd sound, or the horn is stuck. The timing of awareness of hearing ability and its meanings, albeit at first largely unconscious, occurs in the first year or so of life as an unavoidable ontological reality. Soon thereafter, some hcdp as young as toddlers are interpreting for their parents. Robert Brody, for example, first did phone interpreting at the age of three (Brody, 1990); such interpreting requires some understanding of hearing and deaf differences. Ruth Sidransky illustrates this point in her autobiographical memoir, *In Silence: Growing Up Hearing in a Deaf World* (1990); her mother told her,

> "You were eleven months old in a crib bed when you say your first words to me. You told me someone was ringing a doorbell!"
>
> "Momma," I challenged, "babies don't say whole sentences."
>
> "You did. Your left hand was closed and your thumb was out. You push the air with your thumb over and over again. You look at me strong, shake your head and push the air some more. Your smart eyes so big and black look at me. I went to the door and the laundry man was there. I forget to leave the door open for him on Monday morning like always...."
>
> ...I did not speak, I signed. (p. 72)

Padden and Humphries (1998) say hcdp would not be puzzled that their parents did not respond to a loud noise because "there is not yet space for contradictions" (p. 23); in fact, it is because hcdp know, probably on some preverbal and unconscious level, that their parents won't respond. Furthermore, Padden and Humphries's explanation of why an hcdp named Joe does not remember feeling he was different from his deaf family members (namely, that his "parents' world gave him no reason to identify with sound as a primary cause of events" [p. 22]), does not seem to hold true in clinical and other anecdotal evidence. Other hcdp writers acknowledge this awareness of sensory difference; some even say they knew they needed to supply auditory information to their parents at early ages: Doris Crowe at fourteen months (1993, p. 18) and Lou Ann Walker at age two (1986, p. 54). Hence, we question the assumption that Joe's reported memory of no difference is the whole story.

In making this point, we are not implying other often mistakenly assumed ideas. The first of these ideas is that parents must avoid any and all dependence on the child's hearing. Certainly when the tasks are not taken up voluntarily, the child can chafe at the responsibility to be hearing. Although Sidransky could wake up without an alarm clock, as her father did, and although he enjoyed this part of her that was deaf like him, he admonished her to use the clock: "remember you are hearing girl, not deaf. You must listen to life, for you, for me, for Momma. Important you understand time in hearing world" (1990, p. 17). Sidransky often felt she could not voice her anger about this responsibility to be hearing in a deaf family. The few times she felt free were when her parents were with other deaf people or when she was playing with other children of deaf parents (pp. 95–99). Nevertheless, as Jacobs (1996) points out, an absolute or universal prohibition against any interpreting is unrealistic. Spontaneous and momentary business transactions, in a store for example, and even some emergencies and family gatherings, are examples of exceptions, particularly when a child shows a willingness to help. Furthermore, it is possible to appreciate occasional help as a healthy experience of the parents' promoting a sense of competence in the child and modeling adaptability to their children.

The second idea we do not wish to imply by insisting on the awareness of difference is that such awareness inevitably causes psychological problems. Nevertheless, this awareness can and has caused problems: one hearing daughter recovered in therapy a mournful sense of being "pushed out of the nest prematurely" and a marked need in relationships to diminish or even deny differences that threatened disconnection or loss, even to the point of suppressing (and losing pleasure in) a love of music. Sidransky (1990) also suppressed an attraction to music, although others have certainly delved into it as Walker's sisters (1986) and Crowe (1993) herself did. Indeed, as the 1997 German film *Beyond Silence* portrays, music can be a litmus test of an hcdp's management of the hearing/deaf dichotomy. Whether minimizing or accentuating differences, children will need to resolve the meanings of this sensory difference and the communication/connection challenges it entails.

THE ISSUE OF PARENTIFICATION

When the responsibilities of interpreting involve brokering two cultures and making decisions, parentification becomes an issue. Parentification not only involves overuse of interpreting but also tutoring, such as providing cultural and English language information. Furthermore, in the form of protection against hearing insults, it also relates to an aspect of managing stigma, the next issue.

Preston found that many of the hcdp he interviewed experienced their responsibilities within a deaf family as both a badge of honor and a burden (1994, p. 164). The gratification of this role is the sense of importance and sometimes of power; the burden is the loss of a carefree childhood along with a loss of a sense of self that is separate from the role of helper. This role especially intensifies and complicates adolescent separation when the hcdp faces the prospect of leaving home.

Like so many other hcdp, Walker (1986) interpreted, ordered at restaurants, explained to store clerks what her parents wanted, and, at the age of eight, began correcting her parents' letters. She concedes that although she enjoyed feeling important (p. 21), she was also embarrassed that she was doing things she thought all other parents could do (p. 81). Echoing Walker, Brody (1990) not only liked feeling special in his "job of liaison," he also "minded such chores" because of the effort and patience he had to muster for oral communication. Expressing a sense of duty and resentment about it, Linda Konner remembers, "on the way to the supermarket with Mommy, I'd gently push her back toward the curb when I heard a car approaching. I may have been an eight-year-old, but I never once forgot my primary role in life: to be my parents' 'hearing-ear-dog' in ordinary as well as potentially dangerous situations" (Konner, 1987, p. 230). Certainly the image of herself as a dog betrays some resentment. Even the article's title, "I was my parents' radio," suggests she did not even consider herself animate. Konner is fortunate in being able to express her resentment; others are inhibited by guilt and remorse: "How can I complain about something they cannot help?" or, "How could I betray my parents like that?"

Children become most tired of interpreting when they are the only one of several siblings asked to interpret. Most often, although not always, the oldest child is the interpreter in the family. Sometimes, it is the oldest girl. Some have no choice because they are only children. Walker, Sidransky, Crowe, and Brody, as well as some of the clinical examples, are all eldest children. The child's age, as well as the amount and types of interpreting, also affects the child's feelings. The younger the child, the more interpreting is seen as fun or helpful; as they begin to form peer relations in school, older children grow more tired of it (Buchino, 1988).

Most important, interpreting can mean more than the role prescribed for professional interpreters. Many adult children recall having to explain the underlying meaning of what a hearing person said and to work out what to do or reply to a hearing person. Sidransky's father called her his "dictionary" (1990, p. 15) and even asked her to pray to God for him because God would understand what he meant through her (p. 11). At the tender age of fifteen, with no more knowledge of the law than she had gotten from "movie courtroom scenes," Ruth represented the family in court over an altercation with apartment neighbors. Perhaps the most common traumatic experience of interpreting involves interpreting at funerals of parents or other close relatives and friends so that the "interpreter" has to grieve alone, afterwards, and, as a result, not always adequately.

Many hcdp feel a sense of gratification in being needed and important. However, they pay a high price for this gratification: a sense of isolation, of being on one's own, even of being abandoned, from which they seek escape. Of course, other children have a need to escape, too, but what the hcdp seeks to evade is unique. Some literally hide from their parents (Walker, 1986). Crowe invented an imaginary friend to keep her company and help define her situation. While imaginary friends are not uncommon to four- or five-year-olds, it is important to note that "Bobo" took care of Crowe, never let her do bad, and "was not deaf" (1993, p. 29). Sidransky retreated from both deaf and hearing worlds into the world of fantasy, where she in fact replayed the deaf/hearing themes. One alter-ego on the hearing side was the beautiful "Romaine, the shoemaker's daughter with her glorious singing voice, listened to by an [appreciative] audience." Sidransky indicated her identity through Romaine, whose father had the job a number of deaf men in that generation had. Another alter ego that erased the stigma of deafness was "Pocahontas, the Indian princess attended to by my tribe; my ladies spoke to me in royal sign, a language reserved for the high born" (1990, p. 152).

Although there can be escape from mediating between deaf and hearing worlds and parentified roles in fantasy, a more serious problem is the lack of a clear sense of self. Sidransky elegiacally mourns this lack in a number of places, but the most dramatic expression is this poem, written when she was eight years old:

No Self

Cross eyed cross faced little girl
Sad, bad little girl
Eared, heared little girl
Give me your ear
Give me your voice
Give me your tongue, your mouth
I gave you life
Your life is mine

I did not have ears
I made a pair
Be me, be me, be my dream
Be me, sad bad little girl
You are lost and I am lost
I love you for you are mine
Little girl, little girl. (1990, pp. 186–187)

When in her twenties, Walker (1986) also realized the price of her lack of separation and parentification: "The more you get to know me, the less there is to know. I was a black void." In a moment of horrible insight, when a psychiatrist during an interpreting job confuses a deaf patient's delusions for Walker's, she screams silently within, "This isn't me. It's her! I have talked and listened and heard and there is no me! I have heard and hidden the insults so long, I have been the conduit so long that I am disappearing!" (pp. 180–181). Transparency becoming vacancy would be any mediator's nightmare.

The double-edged sword of gratification and sacrifice involved in these childhood responsibilities complicates the meaning of leaving home in adolescence and young adulthood. Two siblings, Eve Barash Dicker and Harvey L. Barash (1991), write touchingly of their worries about "the inevitable separation from our parents that would take place when we were older. Unlike the average hearing family, whose concerns are focused on whether the children will be able to manage on their own after leaving the home's protected environment, our situation was reversed" (p. 146). Both siblings suffered tremendous guilt, so much so for the daughter that she developed psychosomatic symptoms. To compensate, they tried to "upgrade" their father's reading level and prepared notes to flight attendants for their parents. Although Dicker realized that her parents had gotten along fine before she and her brother were old enough to help, it wasn't until much later, as Barash explains, that they realized "separation was as much our problem as it was our parents'" (p. 151).

Note that Barash says it was a problem for both children and parents; certainly hearing parents might show reluctance in letting go of their children, but we are here concerned with a particular reaction of deaf parents. In acknowledging that "the idea of complete separation from both children became another source of sadness for my parents" (p. 158), he echoes Abel, the father in *In This Sign,* who mourns losing his soon-to-be-married daughter and his "mouth" (Greenberg, 1970, as cited in Bunde, 1976, p. 1).

Once hcdp give up their special role in the family, who can they be in the hearing world? For hcdp adolescents, the disjunction is more severe than the already difficult move from their families to the larger society to which their parents also belong. For hcdp, leaving the family also means leaving the society to which their parents belong, unless the person takes a deaf mate, nurtures other adult deaf peer relationships, or works professionally with deaf people. Even with these links, the person must come to terms with being a hearing adult, alone in the hearing world, where yet the mediation between worlds continues intrapsychically.

ISSUES OF MEDIATING DIFFERENT VALUES AND MANAGING STIGMA

At all times, we should keep in mind that the mediation between deaf and hearing values involves the interaction between a stigmatized minority and a majority that presumes the superiority of its values and ways of behaving. Thus, even the child who treasures his or her family's values will be hit with stigmatization, which in turn can exacerbate difficulties navigating between the deaf and hearing worlds, batter his or her vulnerable self-esteem, and again complicate the process of separation.

Protecting the deaf parents from insensitive remarks and questions from hearing people relates both to parentification and to managing stigma. Preston reports that "informants assumed a role of protection and advocacy on behalf of their parents, including responsibilities of impression management and disavowal of deviance" (1994, p. 149). Walker provides this example:

> I could never bring myself to tell Mom and Dad about the garage mechanic who refused to serve them because they were deaf, or the kids at school who made obscene gestures, mocking our sign language. Not once did I convey the questions asked literally hundreds of times: "Does your father have a job?" "Are they allowed to drive?" Those questions carried an implicit insult to a family such as ours, which was proud and hard-working and self-sufficient. I reworded the questions if I had to interpret them. And I never allowed myself to think about the underlying meaning. (1986, p. 21)

When values of the two worlds are very different, the hcdp must manage the stigmatization, even the pathologizing, of patterns that are healthy and adaptive in the deaf community. Rienzi (1990) provides the best example in her study of deaf families; she notes that these families allow more flexibility in authority. In situations where a decision was being made, deaf fathers appeared to express disagreement and then negotiate with family members. These deaf fathers seemed very attentive to their hearing children's communications: they had good eye contact with their children, used encouragement to keep them involved, and never excluded them from conversation. On the other hand, in the hearing families Rienzi observed, the hearing fathers appeared more authoritarian, and their expressions of disagreement often seemed to end the family's debate. Rienzi concluded that deaf-parented families support the involvement of the hearing child; this may be considered appropriate and realistic depending on the communication needs of the situation.

These findings appear consistent with the ecological congruency model, which describes a mechanism that maintains the family's *internal* balance. Rienzi suggests the term "adaptive dependency," which might be defined as a deaf parent relying on the child's ability to hear, for example, during an emergency. Deviancy, competency, and tolerance for difference dimensions are used to describe an open, flowing communication system encouraging the expression of opinion and feelings by all family members (Thurman, 1985). In deaf-parented families, this open or flexible system can be recognized as a healthy adaptation. Rienzi's study suggests that deaf parents are able to adapt to meet the communication needs in situations by relinquishing some power to the children when the children have skills that are needed, such as the ability to hear. This flexibility in communication offers family members an opportunity to practice and develop skills in changing their roles in family relationships in response to situational demands. Rienzi concludes that this flexibility should enhance the deaf family's efficiency. But it may create difficulties for hcdp in predominantly hearing settings (for an example in a public school classroom, see the section, "Structure of Therapy with Children and Adults," below).

Many hearing children are acculturated in the deaf community and do not have appropriate role models for interaction with hearing people until teenage or even adult years. Wilbur and Fristoe (1986) discuss responses from hearing children regarding interpersonal relationships and their feeling that their parents taught them how to interact in the deaf community, but not with hearing people. When these hearing children interacted with other hearing people, they found they were talking too loudly and exaggerating physical expressions of emotions, both of which may be of benefit to those who do not hear well, but do not fit modes of interaction with hearing people. The subjects in Wilbur and Fristoe's study felt they had deficiencies in social skills, tact, knowledge of etiquette, touch, gesture, as well as personal space problems, suspiciousness of hearing people, poor sense of time, and acceptance of authority without question. These difficulties with interaction may not be universal, but they are a potential cause for stress and concern. On the other hand, while ignorance of hearing ways may hold back some hcdp from successful interactions with the hearing world, others compensate for their stigmatized family ways and gain respect by excelling in school. Both Sidransky (1990) and Walker (1986) report working hard to succeed in school.

To help their hearing children feel comfortable with hearing activities and pleasures, as well as deaf ones, parents need to encourage their children's exposure to the hearing world. For example, they need to attend their children's school events, even musical ones (Bunde, 1979).

Some hearing offspring may avoid success in the hearing world out of guilt in surpassing their parents. Such is the case with the hearing daughter in Hallie Frank's (1978–1979) case study. Frank's patient feared that success with verbal skills was too easy a victory and superficial. In addition, she became aware that she evoked her parents' envy and believed her parents turned away from her as a result. Even more painful was the realization that her own desire to succeed simultaneously diminished her parents "in her eyes, and consequently . . . it was she who had sentenced herself to total isolation and abandonment." According to Frank, "success was all the more conflictual for this patient" because her successes were also a "source of considerable parental pride" because they were "a means of conferring status on the family" (pp. 311–312). The patient found herself in a no-win situation.

Additional stigmatizing conditions, such as low socioeconomic status, might be yet another source of stress that confuses and intensifies difficulties in understanding hcdp experience (Jacobs, personal interview, 12 August 1996). As the novel *In This Sign* (Greenberg, 1970) shows, sometimes it is not easy to separate what one can attribute to deafness and what belongs to other stigmas.

As a final comment on this issue, we suggest that parents be encouraged to tolerate their children's intermittent frustrations with the occasional disadvantages of stigmatization. Otherwise, children could turn the frustration and anger upon themselves—after all, the distorted thinking goes, "I must be very bad to be feeling these bad feelings that could hurt them." The difficulty of coming to terms with anger is common to all three hcdp autobiographies. Guilt over these feelings, without the possibility of full reparation, may linger indefinitely (Frank, 1978–1979, p. 314).

IMPACT OF INTERGENERATIONAL DYNAMICS

It is no accident that the autobiographers give over a large part of their life stories to a description of their parents' lives. In addition to addressing a general readership and claiming some degree of membership in the deaf community, they reveal dynamics important to understanding clients themselves. These dynamics involve factors such as birth order, number of deaf relatives, and parents' self-concepts. For example, Walker vividly demonstrates the generational legacy of guilt visited upon the hearing child:

> In a family where there is deafness, guilt is a constant undercurrent, tainting relationships, sometimes even shattering that family. My own grandparents constantly exhorted me to "be good," themselves feeling guilty for not doing more for their [deaf] children, hoping somehow I would make up for things. They felt guilty for reasons they couldn't make clear to themselves. Time and again I heard my grandmother Wells say she would give her own hearing to make her daughter "whole." In her mind, deafness was some kind of divine retribution. . . . It breaks my heart sometimes when my father approaches me tentatively with a small request. "Excuse me," he signs . . . . "Could you please make a phone call for me? Would it bother you?" He feels guilty about needing help. And deep inside him, the guilt his own mother felt is still a burden to him. (1986, pp. 20–21)

As a result, Walker took on the guilt of both generations, which manifested itself in the mistaken obligation to "make her parent's whole."

Brody (1990) illustrates how his hearing relatives had both a direct and indirect impact on his life. While young, he resented his hearing relatives for depending on him "by proxy" to hear for his deaf mother. As an adult, he began to realize how his mother's upbringing by a hearing family had affected her and how that upbringing had affected him as well. Having been conditioned to lack initiative and to depend on others, his mother had developed a compensatory sense of gratification. "By depending on me, she had assumed a power close to tyranny," Brody writes. "Weakness served as her strength." Watching his mother "exploiting sympathy," he questioned how much he was "really helping her as a go-between" (p. 301).

ISSUES OF SEPARATION AND IDENTITY FORMATION

While we have focused in the foregoing section on the theme of mediation, all mediation issues focus on the second major theme in hcdp psychological life: identity. Especially during adolescence, what we see is that mediation is precisely the condition that intensifies and complicates the process of creating that initial adult identity. Aspects that complicate this process include de-idealizing already stigmatized parents, turning toward peers and self-selected values, the warmth of the Deaf world versus the untrustworthy hearing world, and liminality in both Deaf and hearing worlds. Delayed or confused identity formation has an impact on all subsequent development, particularly intimacy.

The challenge of mediating two worlds with different values becomes ever clearer in adolescence, for "if group standards differ too greatly from already internalized moral codes, the adolescent may be thrown into tremendous turmoil" (Tyson & Tyson, 1990, p. 225). Because of the difficult task of synthesizing two—sometimes conflicting—sets of cultural values, the hearing child of deaf parents may experience a particularly stressful and even prolonged adolescent rite of passage. For example, the Deaf values of group consensus and reciprocity might not be realistic in a hearing milieu based on individuality and thus would not align with an adult, hearing self-representation; such a misalignment can destabilize self-esteem. How will the adolescent deal with that part of himself that is acculturated to Deaf ways, especially if the adult society of choice does not include adult Deaf peers? How will the hcdp resolve not only different but diametrically opposed (however wrongly so opposed) views of deafness—for example, culture vs. disability. While a Deaf person may reject hearing definitions of deafness as a disability, hcdp cannot so easily dismiss this view. It exists in the reality of a world where hcdp must make their way as adults. Without a clear sense of the group standards that they will choose (from one or both worlds), there may persist a hungering for authority, someone with the answers, yet a distrust of any single authority or view. Moreover, although it is the developmental task of adolescents to de-idealize their parents, hearing children with deaf parents may have difficulty because stigmatization can leave a hunger to idealize the parents that interferes with normal de-idealizing. Alternatively, hearing adolescents might turn away early from their parents and feel acute alienation from them. Perhaps these latter adolescents would turn quickly to others to idealize. Whether a hearing adolescent experiences inhibiting guilt in de-idealizing parents or turns eagerly away from the parents, the underlying dynamic of intensified conflict around this process remains the same. And the price may be high: for too much guilt to devalue, the price is a detrimentally reevaluated self, or low self-esteem (Tyson & Tyson, 1990. p. 115)—"They're ok; it must be me"; for turning away, a fragile but grandiose sense of self.

One way Walker sought to avoid de-idealization and separation was to get her parents to look more hearing. She made up comments to make her father look witty to her hearing girlfriends because "the funny things he really did say weren't all that translatable"; and she tried to get him to join the Masons because members seemed "successful and well-liked" (1986, pp. 115–116). The only way Walker rebelled was in writing and through displacement. An editorial for her school newspaper on the necessary separation of church and state was almost emblematic of her own struggles to make sense of her Deaf and hearing worlds. Going on any and all interpreting jobs in New York City and writing an article on a deaf gang, Walker came to some understanding about a hearing view of deafness she did not want to accept—even among the gang members, she saw a kind of passivity and powerlessness and, perhaps as a result, fatalism and paranoia. Realizing the limitations of being deaf in a predominantly hearing world, Walker was able, through displacement, to de-idealize her parents indirectly. With this epiphany, she was able to give up her special caretaking role (p. 181).

Others rebel against the confusion more dramatically (Erikson, 1968, p. 133; Wolf, 1988, pp. 58–59). Several professionally successful hearing sons and daughters of deaf parents have admitted juvenile delinquent behavior as teens, such as stealing a car, shoplifting, taking and selling drugs, playing hooky from school, and pulling daring pranks. Others became politically rebellious, as indicated in this clinical example: "I felt this desperate need to be involved in civil rights issues for African Americans. I kept saying to my dad, 'How can you not support this movement? These people are oppressed like you are. More even.' Truth is, my argument also was about me. I've been stigmatized and oppressed, too."

A completely different reason separation may be difficult is because their parents' and their own experiences have taught hcdp to distrust hearing people. Sidransky (1990) relates how it was difficult for her to want to take her place in the hearing world that had brought into her life the pain of stigmatized deafness and had contributed to making her an adult prematurely. For example, her mother regularly sent her to the grocer to get some food on credit, but the grocer molested the girl in exchange for the credit. (Inured to the role of representative, Sidransky wonders if her mother had been molested and had sent her daughter in her place.) She also was rejected by her first (hearing) love, Sammy, because he ignorantly feared her having deaf parents meant she would have deaf children.

By contrast, the deaf world of her parents and their friends seemed warmer, in one sense a haven. Nevertheless, it was not "safe" for her psychological development; she was in constant danger of never finding her own self, especially as only a marginalized member of the deaf community.

Walker's minister condescendingly described those "less blessed than we are": "unfortunate blind, the silent deaf, the halt who would walk." The pitying reduction of her parents to a physical disability jarringly contradicted the scene she had just left at home, "a wonderful, storybook Christmas: presents, laughter, kisses, hugs" (1986, pp. 113–114). In addition, when she went to college, she knew she could not continue in a Deaf Education program because the professors treated one deaf graduate student "condescendingly—almost inhumanly. The professors rarely talked to Marion, even though she had had years of experience teaching the deaf—and being deaf" (p. 138). The only way, it may seem, to find a place in the hearing world is by disowning a large chunk of experience.

Through this process of separation and individuation, hcdp often become all the more aware of feeling on the edge of both deaf and hearing cultures. Hcdp recognize that however hearing their world is as an adult, they go about in that hearing world with more intimate knowledge of another world that separates them from this mainstream, even while their ability to hear sets them apart from their intimate deaf world. One analogy might be growing up the white child of African American parents (Shultz Myers, 1991). But such comparisons are faulty and perhaps misleading. We can at least say that awareness of liminality in both deaf and hearing cultures seems to be part of any hcdp's development. Deaf people recognize their own liminality in the mainstream society, but it is also true that their hearing offspring feel liminal with respect to *both* societies.

We cannot overemphasize the intense affect potentially accompanying a hearing child's giving up of his or her deaf parents. This relinquishing can mean giving up a whole community and way of life that is markedly different from the adult hearing world into which the adolescent is making his or her way as an adult. The differences are far greater than generational differences many others face in moving from their families to adult society. Thus "giving up" the parents as love objects for new independence has much higher stakes. Sidransky provides one important metaphor for the conflict between a need to grow up/be hearing and a need to stay connected to the parents that she spun out of the colloquial term for profound deafness: stone deaf. Addressing the pillars of Stonehenge as her parents, she cried, "you did not make me of stone, so I must leave you." Yet afterwards, "I awakened angry, time and again. I pushed my anger away, mindful of its destructive power. . . . I couldn't leave the ring of silent stones" (1990, pp. 200–201). Many hcdp may live solely in the hearing world but carry a sense of emptiness and loss they don't fully understand. Many, as the film *Passport Without a Country* makes clear, share a "lifelong search for acceptance and identity."

This identity confusion then has an impact on all subsequent development, most notably on intimacy. As Erikson (1968) notes, "It is only when identity formation is well on its way that true intimacy—which is really a counterpointing as well as a fusing of identities—is possible" (p. 135). For hcdp, this experience often complicates some aspects of intimacy, such as dependence, independence, and interdependence. One reason is that hcdp have adapted to different standards of interdependence that can be maladaptive for their hearing-world partners. Preston (1994) seems to be talking about this kind of problem when he describes the American mainstream label about the Deaf form of interdependence, reciprocity, as dysfunctional because it does not encourage self-reliance. When one group says it is merely adaptive and the other calls it dysfunctional, the hearing offspring of deaf parents can be left painfully divided. Preston notes a number of his informants were concerned with dysfunctional relationships, particularly co-dependence (cf. pp. 154–161). Even when they do form intimate relationships, hcdp may not want children because they feel the kind of caretaking they performed as children for their parents has exhausted the need or interest for new forms of caretaking (Konner, 1987, p. 232).

Clinical Treatment

In moving from a review of the issues to clinical treatment of hcdp, we seek to connect these issues to two central areas of treatment: mediation and identity. The first step in treating families or individuals is to ameliorate or reduce any biological influences on behavior, such as attention deficit disorder (ADD), depression, or anxiety. At the same time, clinicians need to attend to the individual's and family's cultural experiences and background, the quality of these experiences, and the degree of acculturation to both hearing and Deaf cultures. This information allows clinicians to see how values and meanings conflict and how these conflicts affect the personal life of each hearing child of deaf parents (Preston, 1994). Initially, it may not be easy to address these mediation and identity themes directly, but they can be addressed as they unfold in the context of the presenting problem.

CLINICAL CASE STUDIES

Anecdotal and clinical reports published over the years unfortunately have not taken into account the role of cultural identities. Instead, they often reflect negatively upon the emotional stability of deaf parents who have hearing offspring (Arlow, 1976; Bene, 1977; Halbreich, 1979; Robinson & Weathers, 1974) and suggest that unavoidably stressful interaction patterns in the family will necessitate pathological adjustments. A hearing cultural bias is evident in several published psychoanalytic and other case studies by hearing clinicians with no knowledge of deafness. These clinicians claim that serious deficits in the hcdp's development are a result of the parents' (particularly the primary caregiver's) lack of audition during the early years.

Halbreich (1979) states that hcdp suffer from a serious auditory and verbal communication deficit that has a profound, probably pathological, psychological impact. Dent wonders if the need to keep the child in view harms sensorimotor development and concludes, "Growing up in a world without words may have profound effects on both ego and cognitive development" (1982, pp. 428, 440). Agi Bene (1977) follows the traditional assumption that vocal/verbal interaction between mother and child is the sole primary need, at least after the first year. He assumes that lack of auditory contact and verbalization lead to cognitive and ego deficits (pp. 178, 183–184). (He also virtually ignores the particular history of the individual's parents, a mistake we discuss with regard to doing a clinical interview—see below.) In contrast, Wagenheim (1985) recognizes that deficits in mothering result from the way the mother herself was raised rather than her deafness (pp. 415, 432). But she also asserts that some of her client's difficulties stemmed from the first seven months because the mother could not hear her child cry out of hunger (p. 433). This view about the need for auditory contact the first year contrasts with Bene's contention that problems arise after the first year, "when, in normal circumstances, auditory contact gradually replaces body contact" (1977, p. 178). Overarching these contradictory ideas about when audition is important are the unexamined assumptions that audition or the parents' ability to hear is a necessary part of normal development and the lack of it causes psychological problems.

Only one psychoanalytic case study discusses the traditional emphasis on the voice for bonding and challenges it (Arlow, 1976). From his experience with a hearing child of deaf parents in analysis, Arlow concludes what every deaf mother knows intuitively, that "what seems to be important is the nature of the total object tie. Communication by nonverbal means, especially touch, may convey the necessary warmth, affection, reassurance, and gratification to foster normal development of psychic structure and character formation" (p. 161). What object relations theorists call "good enough" mothering, the best anyone can expect, in fact, happens if the mother is attuned to and invested in her child.

We cannot imagine that anyone, once cognizant of the issue, would argue against Arlow's challenge to the necessity of vocal and verbal interaction for normal maturation and development. Our experience reveals that when problems occur, they result from inadequate connectedness, not from a lack of speech. Any child can experience an impoverished relationship with any mother for any number of reasons. But our point here is that, contrary to a number of published case studies, problems in the earliest mother-child relationship are by no means inherent and inevitable because of the biological fact of deafness. The mother's sensitivity to other modalities—most probably touch and sight—can substitute for hearing.

These examples of hearing cultural bias point to the critical impact that clinicians' varying levels of knowledge and awareness of the two worlds of the hcdp can have on treatment. A recognition of Deaf culture and consciousness distinct from the hearing population allows a more accurate understanding of families with deaf members. This understanding is reflected in the observation that "beliefs, values, attitudes, feelings and behavior of ethnic group members have a direct impact on their psychological functioning, their concept of illness and their expression of symptoms" (Aponte & Barnes, 1995, p. 19). Most important, therapists must understand that the hearing child is not hearing like most of the general public; the hearing child is both hearing and Deaf.

HEARING STATUS OF THE THERAPIST

In addition to the complex interplay between hcdp bicultural identity and the issues hcdp bring to therapy, a critical aspect is the therapist's own level of awareness of Deaf culture. Deaf parents with a young hearing child tend to go to a therapist who is familiar with deaf clients, whether that therapist is hearing, deaf, or a hearing child of deaf parents. By contrast, adult hcdp must choose their therapists, and the hearing status of the chosen therapist reveals where the hcdp is in terms of dealing with issues of mediation and identity. For example, if hcdp clients are driven by a need for comfort or familiarity, even trust or safety, they might choose a therapist who is deaf or the hearing child of deaf parents. If they are motivated by a need to make their way in the hearing world, to strengthen their hearing side, and/or to address issues that they find too difficult or risky to bring up with a deaf or hcdp therapist, they might choose a therapist who can hear and has no connection or knowledge of deafness at all. There are many other possible reasons other than the ones we present here; the therapist should explore the client's choice of therapist because this information might provide significant insight into the client's issues and state of mind.

Hearing therapists must remain cognizant of the dangers of stereotyping the unique experiences of hearing children of deaf parents (Smith, 1981; Sue, 1981). These therapists need to acquire knowledge about the culture of the people they will be treating (Pederson, 1987). In the case of hcdp, therapists must know about the deaf community, including its culture, language, channels of communication (sign or oral), and what it means to grow up bilingually/biculturally. Combined with a substantial degree of self-awareness, this knowledge should increase the success of the therapy. Hcdp may be uncomfortable about expressing emotions (especially those habitually suppressed by both deaf and hearing people) and may not be able to get to the underlying dissociation between deaf and hearing ways. These clients need informed therapists who can draw on their own knowledge of the deaf/hearing dichotomy to intervene.

Hearing therapists who are hcdp should keep in mind that their experiences are *not* universal. Moreover, transference/countertransference issues can emerge from competition about the role or status the client had in the family system. Hence, care should be taken whether to reveal the fact that the therapist also has deaf parents. Finally, it is important to be flexible about the language used in the therapy session and to establish and maintain clear and appropriate boundaries with the client and his family.

The deaf therapist must keep in mind that not all hearing children of deaf adults know sign language. The therapist must avoid making other assumptions as well: for example, that a client shares the therapist's worldview because he or she signs fluently. Indeed, the client may resent having to sign all the time. The therapist can explore this resentment as a way to get into the pulls the hearing child faced/faces growing up and can work toward acknowledgment of *both* deaf and hearing parts. As a part of this work, therapists need to explore the client's degree of assimilation into the majority (hearing) culture and amount of involvement in the deaf community.

Finally, transference and/or countertransference issues can be overwhelming to the hcdp client and the deaf therapist. An hcdp may see a deaf therapist as incompetent because he or she is deaf. He or she may try to protect the therapist from the client's own anger about having deaf parents or the pulls he or she lived with, or overemphasize how enriching it was to have deaf parents. The therapist's own feelings about his or her own parents and/or children can significantly affect the treatment.

THE CLINICAL INTERVIEW

Several signing and nonsigning clinicians in a focus group we conducted, all of whom work with hearing children of deaf parents, reported that in the initial family interview, it is vital to gather an especially detailed social history of the deaf parents themselves (Jacobs, 1996; Myers & Shultz Myers, 1996; Schlesinger & Meadow, 1972). A therapist might discern these dynamics through observing or participating in discussions with extended hearing family members, as well as in therapy with the individual child or adult. The therapist could discover, for instance, overprotective or overcontrolling grandparents who talk about removing the hearing child because they perceive the deaf parents as not being able to parent (Hoffmeister, 1985). With these kinds of situations, it's not too hard to imagine the stress and division in the family.

The way deaf people are raised by their hearing parents has a profound effect on the way they as deaf parents raise their hearing children (Frankenburg et al., 1985; Harvey, 1989; Rienzi, 1990). Even deaf adults with deaf parents have ideas and fantasies about hearing people, which affect how they raise their hearing children (Jacobs, 1993). Hearing parents' reactions to learning their child is deaf "range from denial to overprotection" (Frankenburg et al., 1985, p. 98). In addition, parents may withdraw from the child because of communication problems, doubly isolating and depriving the deaf child (Schlesinger & Meadow, cited in Frankenburg et al., 1985), or may communicate superficially "with possible negative psychological and social consequences" (Vernon, cited in Frankenburg et al., 1985, p. 98). Not surprisingly, a poor connection or bond between deaf adults and their hearing parents can result in a poor connection between these deaf adults and their hearing children. Complicating connection issues,

QUESTIONS FOR CLINICAL INTERVIEWS WITH HEARING CHILDREN OF DEAF PARENTS

- the hearing status of siblings, parents, and extended family members;
- hearing children's experience of their grandparents' feelings about having deaf children;
- the feelings of other extended family members about deaf relatives;
- the parents' understanding of their deafness and hearing family members' experience of them;
- hearing children's view of how the deaf parents fit in and interact with the extended family, as well as their view of their own fit;
- hearing children's experience of their own parents' understanding of their deafness and the influence this understanding has had on their lives;
- the parents' involvement in the Deaf community/culture and the extent to which they involved the hearing child in the Deaf world experience;
- communication modes used in the home among family members (explore all possible relationships) and the attitudes of immediate and extended family members towards speaking and towards signing;
- encouragement the hearing child received around getting involved in activities that were oriented towards hearing people (a good indicator might be involvement with music).

Figure 1. Clinical Interviews

deaf people with hearing children may project old, unresolved issues with their own hearing parents onto their hearing children. Here is where we might see the deaf parents put up their hearing children as "know-all" hearing authorities and yet envy that position, or we might see them rear their hearing children to be the sensitive hearing people their own parents were not. Fitts (cited in Goldenberg et al., 1979) asserts that an adequate self-concept on the parents' part is instrumental in an adequate self-concept in the child.

Because most deaf people have hearing parents and family members who do not sign, it is very likely that there were communication barriers (Mallory et al., 1991–1992) and that deaf people had little opportunity to learn the subtle nuances of interacting with hearing people (Wilbur & Fristoe, 1986). (Indeed, we might question whether deaf people with deaf parents would have any better ability to interact with hearing people.) Furthermore, if the deaf child went to a residential school and was separated from the family for many of the developmental years, the clinician may question how that dynamic affected relationship(s) with hearing family members. In the clinical interview the therapist must discern the nature of the relationships not only between the hcdp client and his or her family but also between the hcdp and extended family (see figure 1). While no two hearing children of deaf adults are alike, we suggest that the central themes and issues we have discussed throughout this chapter remain constant and need to be worked through.

TREATMENT ISSUES

The biopsychosocial and cross-cultural treatment approaches we have presented form the backdrop for not only therapist considerations and clinical interview suggestions but also a couple more treatment issues, such as the structure of the therapy and the use of interpreters during therapy. Cultural competence is the foundation for all other treatment issues.

Cultural Competence

Several models in the literature attempt to explain the process by which individuals and groups develop competence in the majority culture (summarized in La Fromboise et al., 1993, pp. 396–401). These models include *assimilation,* a continual absorption into a dominant or desirable culture; *acculturation,* competent participation in the majority culture while remaining identified with a minority culture; *fusion,* the melting pot concept whereby cultures sharing the same political and economic conditions as well as the same geographic space will fuse until they are indistinguishable and a new culture will arise; and *alternation,* a sense of belonging to two cultures without compromising cultural identity, combined with the ability to alter behavior to fit a particular social context. Suggesting bicultural competence and identification with two different cultures, the alternation model seems to make the most sense for hcdp.

Parallel to code-switching in bilingual (ASL/English) individuals, alternation is additive; that is, a person does not replace one culture with another, as in assimilation, but functions in both cultures. Hence, the relationship individuals develop between their culture of origin and a second culture in which they may be living is bi-directional instead of linear. The two-way interchange also means that there is no hierarchical relationship between the two cultures as there would be in assimilation; instead, they have equal status, even if the individual does not prefer them equally. In fact, individuals may choose the manner and the degree to which they will affiliate with either culture. Individuals who can alternate their behavior according to the targeted culture will be less anxious than people trying to assimilate or acculturate.

Therapists working with hcdp need to consider the degree to which their client has incorporated both the Deaf culture and the hearing world. Using the alternation model, the therapist would encourage clients to accept both cultures as equal while allowing personal preferences to emerge.

Structure of Therapy with Children and Adults

One part of determining the approach in therapy is to understand the roles people have in the family and how those roles contribute to the dysfunction that may exist (Harvey, 1989; Robinson & Weathers, 1974). In clinical situations involving a child still living with deaf parents, the goal of therapy may be to improve parent-child communication, to shift caretaking responsibility back to the parents, or to support the child through a critical developmental stage. We suggest the therapist must find a way to empower the family in a way that promotes communication and interaction among the members. This work includes educating Deaf members about "hearing culture" and hearing members about Deaf culture.

The child's transition from home to school seems marked as a particularly intense one because it is one time when mediation between different values is most clear. Although normally the school-age child begins to identify with others outside the family, the differences between life at home and at school may make that process difficult. Experiences and reactions vary from child to child and can include enduring ridicule for signing and not talking much (Crowe, 1993), refusing to sign to the mother after starting school, and refusing to talk and only signing. Nevertheless, most children seem to live with the contradictions between their two worlds and to derive sustenance from both. In fact, some hearing children even blossom in new ways, as potentialities not evoked by the family may develop at school. In any case, therapists should acknowledge and encourage this bicultural adaptability.

In addition to language differences, the way the family functions may not fit in with classroom expectations (see Rienzi's observations in the section "Issues of Mediating Different Values and Managing Stigma"). In the classroom, the child may not respond to the teacher's authority in the same way that others in the classroom do. For example, it may seem acceptable to counter teacher directives with other suggestions. If the flexibility and cooperation that the child is used to is not forthcoming, the child may act out his frustration and appear defiant, withdraw, or regress to earlier (perhaps more familiar and less intimidating) conflictual behavior at home.

Interventions by the therapist must involve parents, school personnel, and any others in the community who may be involved. Specifically, therapists should gather information about family interactions, school performance, and social behavior to gain a better understanding of their clients' peer relationship skills, attitudes toward authority, study habits, and degree to which primary needs are being met (Rivers & Morrow, 1995). Therapists also should obtain information about school behavior and performance as a way of assessing the hcdp's adjustment to the school, hearing environment, and relationships with hearing peers. If problems are occurring at home, don't assume the cause is there, too—children may act out adjustment problems at school in the safety of the home.

If behavior problems do show up in school, the child needs to be assessed by a psychiatrist or psychologist to rule out biological causes such as ADD, ADHD, or a learning disability. Once this assessment is completed, other factors may be considered. Possible areas of concern include how the school is accommodating the parents' communication with the teachers and the child's communication needs in the classroom. For example, due to the visual nature of sign language, hcdp are accustomed to maintaining direct eye contact when communicating. In this case, it might be helpful for the teacher to face the students and make eye contact when speaking.

Deaf parents must have the ability to communicate in their native language about their children like any other parent. Schools need to make phone lines and interpersonal communication accessible via TTYs (telecommunication devices for people who are deaf) and interpreters. School-related activities must be made accessible so parents can participate. Cultural awareness activities sensitizing students, teachers, and staff to the needs of deaf people and their family members may be useful. Some deaf parents have done this awareness work themselves with very positive results (Duhon, in press).

Adult children of deaf parents have very different therapeutic needs from children. They most often need help on identity issues in relation to the presenting problem. In the therapeutic process, they often reframe their perceptions of their parents and even hearing people, particularly if hearing people have been experienced as untrustworthy. Reconciling the conflicting perceptions of deaf and hearing people within themselves may also be a central theme. The points made earlier about cultural competence speak to these adult concerns in particular, although certainly they apply to all issues of all hcdp.

Using Interpreters during Therapy

At times the therapist may notice that the hcdp, child or adult, expresses himself or herself better in sign language than in spoken English. Such expression needs to be supported and should not be taken as resistance or a hostile act toward the therapist. (The same may be said for the client's breaking out in speech when the therapist is deaf.) The therapist is advised to discuss communication issues and explore how they can best be handled. One way might be occasionally using an interpreter; another might be allowing the client to sign/speak and then waiting for the client's own interpretation afterwards. Regardless of how this issue is handled, the healing factor involves facilitating the emergence of both the hearing and deaf parts of the individual.

Consideration also needs to be made regarding the use of interpreters in family therapy. The communication assessment may include observing how the family communicates without any facilitation. If communication stress prevents effective work, the guiding principle is that interpreting services should be introduced. Using an interpreter naturally disrupts and distorts the natural communication flow in a family. On the other hand, an interpreter can help the therapist understand the family system and can be therapeutic by creating communication channels that previously were not clear and open. In line with this therapeutic value, when the therapist finds that the child is not fluent in sign language, it is important to understand why this is and how the parents and other family members cope with communication gaps. Above all, it should be obvious that hearing children cannot be used to interpret in the therapeutic setting.

Conclusion

The overarching themes of the hcdp experience are mediation between deaf and hearing world paradigms and identity issues as a result of mediation issues. Preston (1994) suggests that a dichotomy between deaf and hearing is a "social creation." Thus, hearing children of deaf parents are "neither completely deaf nor completely hearing" (p. 237). But he also suggests that hcdp might be able to transcend the pulls between the two or at least place them on a continuum that allows some flexibility and overlap so that "We are not deaf. We are not hearing. We are neither deaf nor hearing. We are both deaf and hearing" (p. 236). We agree that a healthy adjustment for hcdp is living with this dual or alternating identity, but we do not think this identity develops without encountering some clashes, or pulls from different directions, that are irreconcilable and thus create emotional stress. We have attempted here to map those bumpy parts on the hcdp culturally two-way road as well as the detours and dead-ends that may necessitate professional help. Our hope is that with this map, the professional treatment hcdp seek may truly be the most helpful and healthful.

Although our focus is on hearing offspring of deaf parents, what this chapter contains may also apply to hearing children whose parents are hard of hearing, deaf-blind, and late-deafened. Indeed, there are quite a few variables to keep in mind. These include both the intergenerational influences we discussed and other factors we did not, such as amount of hearing loss, age of onset of deafness, intermarriages between deaf and hearing couples, number of siblings, and gender (identity, role, and preference), physical differences, and stigmatizing conditions (poverty or ethnicity). In order to refine our map of clinical issues and approaches offered here, these other groups and variables warrant additional study.

References

Aponte, J. F., & Barnes, J. M. (1995). Impact of acculturation and moderator variables on the intervention and treatment of ethnic groups. In J. F. Aponte, R. Y. Rivers, & J. Wohl (Eds.), *Psychological interventions and cultural diversity* (pp. 19–39). Boston: Allyn and Bacon.

Arlow, J. A. (1976). Communication and character: A clinical study of a man raised by deaf-mute parents. *The Psychoanalytic Study of the Child, 31,* 139–163.

Ashby, W. R. (1956). *An introduction to cybernetics.* London: Chapman and Hall.

Bahan, B. (1994). Comment on Turner. *Sign Language Studies, 84.*

Bateson, G. (1972). *Steps to an ecology of mind.* New York: Ballantine.

Becker, G. (1980). *Growing old in silence.* Berkeley: University of California Press.

Bene, A. (1977). The influence of deaf and dumb parents on a child's development. *Psychoanalytic Study of the Child, 32,* 175–194.

Brody, R. (1990, October). The reluctant go-between. *Glamour Magazine, 88* (10), 288, 301.

Buchino, M. (1988). Hearing children of deaf parents: Personal perspectives. Ph.D. dissertation, University of Cincinnati.

Bunde, L. T. (1979). *Deaf parents—hearing children: Towards a greater understanding of the unique aspects, needs, and problems relative to the communication factors caused by deafness* [Monograph 1]. Washington, DC: R.I.D.

Chess, S., & Thomas, A. (1996). Temperament. In M. Lewis (Ed.), *Child and adolescent psychiatry: A comprehensive textbook* (pp. 170–181). Baltimore: Williams and Wilkins.

Crowe, D. I. (1993). *Dummy's little girl.* New York: Carlton Press.

Davie, C. (Director). (1992). *Passport without a country* [videotape]. Queensland, Australia: Griffith University.

Dent, K. (1982). Two daughters of a deaf mute mother: Implications for ego and cognitive development. *Journal of the American Academy of Psychoanalysis, 10,* 427–441.

Dicker, E. B., & Barash, H. L. (1991). *Our father Abe: The story of a deaf shoe repairman.* Madison, WI: Abar Press.

Duhon, S. (In press). Strengthening home and school relationships for deaf parents and their hearing children. In *Proceedings of Building Bridges.* Washington, DC: Gallaudet University, College for Continuing Education.

Engel, G. L. (1977). The need for a new medical model: A challenge for biomedicine. *Science, 196,* 129–136.

———. (1980). The clinical application of the biopsychosocial model. *American Journal of Psychiatry, 137,* 535–544.

Erikson, E. H. (1968). *Identity, youth, and crisis.* New York: W. W. Norton.

Fitts, W. H. (1972). *The self-concept and psychopathology* [Monograph IV]. Nashville, TN: Dede Wallace Center.

Fleischman, A. (1996). Wanted: CODA who's who. *Deaf Life, 10* (1), 7.

Frank, H. (1978–1979). Psychodynamic conflicts in hearing children of deaf parents. *International Journal of Psychoanalytic-Psychotherapy, 7,* 305–315.

Frankenburg, F. R., Sloman, L., & Perry, A. (1985). Issues in the therapy of hearing children with deaf parents. *Canadian Journal of Psychiatry, 30* (2), 98–102.

Goldberg, M. M. (1941). A qualification of the marginal man theory. *American Sociological Review, 6,* 52–58.

Goldenberg, M., Rabinowitz, A., & Kravetz, S. (1979). The relation between communication level and self-concept of deaf parents and their normal children. *American Annals of the Deaf, 30,* 472–478.

Goodman, A. (1991). Organic unity theory: The mind-body problem revisited. *American Journal of Psychiatry, 148* (5), 553–563.

Green, A. W. (1947). A re-examination of the marginal man concept. *Social Forces, 26,* 167–171.

Greenberg, J. (1970). *In this sign.* New York: Holt, Rinehart, and Winston.

Halbreich, U. (1979). Influence of deaf-mute parents on the character of their offspring. *Acuta Psychiatrica Scandinavica, 59* (2), 129–138.

Harvey, M. A. (1989). *Psychotherapy with deaf and hard-of-hearing persons: A systemic model.* Hillsdale, NJ: Lawrence Erlbaum.

Higgins, P. (1980). *Outsiders in a hearing world: A sociology of deafness.* Beverly Hills, CA: Sage Publications.

Hoffmeister, R. J. (1985). Families with deaf parents: A functional perspective. In S. K. Thurman (Ed.), *Children of handicapped parents* (pp. 111–130). Orlando: Academic Press.

Institute of Medicine. (1989). *Research on children and adolescents' mental, behavioral, and developmental disorders: Mobilizing a national initiative.* Washington, DC: National Academy Press.

Jacobs, S. (1993, September). Double Pride [Workshop]. Washington, DC: Gallaudet University.

———. (1996, August). Interview with Sheila Jacobs regarding clinical work with hearing children of deaf parents [Unpublished].

Jones, E. G. (1995). Deaf and hearing parents' perceptions of family functioning. *Nursing Research, 44* (2), 102–105.

Keeny, B. P. (1983). *Aesthetics of change.* New York: Guilford Press.

Konner, L. (1987, May). I was my parents' radio. *Glamour Magazine, 85,* 228–230.

Kramer, S., and Akhtar, S. (1988). The developmental context of internalized pre-oedipal object relations: Clinical applications of Manler's theory of symbiosis and separation-individuation. *Psychoanalytic Quarterly, 57,* 547–576.

LaFromboise, T., Coleman, H. L. K., & Gerton, J. (1993). Psychological impact of biculturalism: Evidence and theory. *Psychology Bulletin, 3* (114), 395–412.

Link, C. (Director). (1996). *Beyond silence* [Film]. Munich: Claussen Wobke Filmproduktion.

Lynch, E. W. (1992). Developing cross-cultural competence. In E. W. Lynch & M. J. Hanson (Eds.), *Developing cross-cultural competence: A guide for working with young children and their families* (pp. 35–59). Baltimore: Paul H. Brookes.

Mallory, B. L., Schein, J. D., & Zingle, H. W. (1991–1992). Parenting resources of deaf parents with hearing children. *Journal of the American Deafness and Rehabilitation Association, 25* (3), 16–30.

Matorin, S., & Greenberg, L. (1992). Family therapy in the treatment of adolescents. *Hospital and Community Psychiatry, 43* (6), 625–629.

Meadow-Orlans, K. P., Erting, C., Day, P. S., MacTurk, R., Prezioso, R., & Gianino, A. (1987). Deaf and hearing mothers of deaf and hearing infants: Interaction in the first year of life. In R. Ojala (Ed.), *Program, X World Congress of the World Federation of the Deaf, Espoo, Finland.* Helsinki, Finland: Finnish Association of the Deaf.

Mindel, E. D., & Vernon, M. (Eds.). (1987). *They grow in silence: Understanding deaf children and adults.* Boston: College Hill Press.

Myers, R. R. (Ed.). (1991). *CODA sixth international conference/retreat proceedings: CODA: At the Oasis, July 19–22, 1991.* Chicago: CODA.

Myers, R. R., & Marcus, A. (1993). HEARING. MOTHER FATHER DEAF: Issues of identity and mediation in culture and communication. In *Proceedings of Deaf Studies III: Bridging cultures in the 21st century* (pp. 171–184). Washington, D.C.: Gallaudet University, College for Continuing Education.

Myers, R. R., & Shultz Myers, S. (Facilitators). (1996, July). Focus group with social work clinicians on clinical issues: Hearing children of deaf parents. [Unpublished transcript].

Padden, C., & Humphries, T. (1988). *Deaf in America: Voices from a culture.* Cambridge, MA: Harvard University Press.

Park, R. E. (1928). Human migration and the marginal man. *American Journal of Sociology, 5,* 881–893.

Pecora, P. J., Despain, C. L., & Loveland, E. J. (1986). Adult children of deaf parents: A psychosocial perspective. *Social Casework: Journal of Contemporary Social Work, 67,* 12–19.

Pederson, P. B. (1987). Ten frequent assumptions of cultural bias in counseling. *Journal of Multicultural Counseling and Development, 15,* 16–24.

Preston, P. (1994). MOTHER FATHER DEAF: *Living between sound and silence.* Cambridge, MA: Harvard University Press.

Rayson, B. (1987). Deaf parents of hearing children. In E. D. Mindel & M. Vernon (Eds.), *They grow in silence* (pp. 103–110). Boston: College Hill Press.

Rienzi, B. M. (1990, December). Influence and adaptability in families with deaf parents and hearing children. *American Annals of the Deaf, 135,* 402–408.

Rivers, R. Y., & Morrow, C. A. (1995). Understanding and treating ethnic minority youth. In J. F. Aponte, R. Y. Rivers, and J. Wohl (Eds.), *Psychological interventions and cultural diversity* (pp. 164–180). Boston: Allyn and Bacon.

Robinson, L. S., & Weathers, O. D. (1974). Family therapy of deaf parents and hearing children: A new dimension in psychotherapeutic intervention. *American Annals of the Deaf, 119,* 325–330.

Rothbart, M. K., & Ahadi, S. A. (1994). Temperament and the development of personality. *Journal of Abnormal Psychology, 103* (1), 55–66.

Sacks, O. (1989). *Seeing voices: A journey into the world of the deaf.* Berkeley: University of California Press.

Sadler, J. Z., & Hulgus, Y. H. (1992). Clinical problem solving and the biopsychosocial model. *American Journal of Psychiatry, 149* (10), 1315–1323.

Schlesinger, H. S., & Meadow, K. P. (1972). *Sound and sign: Childhood deafness and mental health.* Berkeley: University of California Press.

Schwartzman, J. (1982). Normality from a cross-cultural perspective. In F. Walsh (Ed.), *Normal family processes* (pp. 383–398). New York: Guilford Press.

Shultz Myers, S. (1991). In silence: Growing up hearing in a deaf world [Review of Ruth Sidransky's 1990 autobiography]. *The CODA Connection, 8* (1), 1.

Sidransky, R. (1990). *In silence: Growing up hearing in a deaf world.* New York: St. Martin's Press.

Smith, E. J. (1981). Cultural and historical perspectives in counseling Blacks. In D. W. Sue (Ed.), *Counseling the culturally different: Theory and practice.* New York: Wiley.

Sue, D. W. (1981). Evaluating process variables in cross-cultural counseling and psychology. In A. J. Marsell & P. B. Pederson (Eds.), *Cross-cultural counseling and psychology.* New York: Pergamon.

Thurman, S. K. (Ed.). (1985). *Children of handicapped parents.* Orlando: Academic Press.

Tyson, P., & Tyson, R. L. (1990). *Psychoanalytic theories of development: An integration.* New Haven: Yale University Press.

Walker, L. A. (1986). *A loss for words: The story of deafness in a family.* New York: Harper and Row.

Wagenheim, H. (1985). Aspects of the analysis of an adult son of deaf-mute parents. *Journal of the American Psychoanalytic Association, 33* (2), 413–435.

Watzlawick, P., Beavin, J. H., & Jackson, D. D. (1967). *Pragmatics of human communication: A study of interactional patterns, pathologies, and paradoxes.* New York: W. W. Norton.

Watzlawick, P., Weakland, J. H., & Fisch, R. (1974). *Change: Principles of problem formation and problem resolution.* New York: W. W. Norton.

Wilbur, R. B., and Fristoe, M. (1986). I had a wonderful, if somewhat unusual, childhood: Growing up hearing in a Deaf world. In J. B. Christiansen & R. W. Meisegeier (Eds.), *Papers for the Second Research Conference on the Social Aspects of Deafness* (pp. 1–48). Washington, DC: Gallaudet University.

Wolf, E. S. (1988). *Treating the self: Elements of clinical self psychology.* New York: Guilford Press.

Appendix 1: Resources

Mallory, Schein, and Zingle (1991–1992) explored the availability of parenting resources for deaf parents with hearing children and found that the deaf parents could identify few parenting programs and services suitable for themselves and their hearing children. While resources continue to remain limited, the following are some resources deaf parents and their hearing children can use for information and support.

1. CODA (Children of Deaf Adults International) is a thirteen-year-old organization with members throughout the United States and several foreign countries. The organization's mission is to "address bicultural experiences through conferences, support groups and resource development." The support of finding others like oneself cannot be underestimated; as one participant said, "I walked into the room my first time, and in five minutes I knew: these are my brothers and sisters. I belong somewhere after all." Walker (1986) felt grateful to trade stories: "Hearing that daughter tell me of her own guilt and embarrassment and her intense identification with her mother gave me chills. It also gave me a particular relief. It was the first time another child of deaf parents had ever talked about the experience to me. I no longer felt so odd" (p. 185). Voting membership is restricted to adults (over the age of eighteen) who have at least one deaf parent. CODA publishes a quarterly newsletter as well as proceedings from the annual conferences. The organization also sponsors the Millie Brother Scholarship Fund, a one-year higher education scholarship for hcdp. For additional information write to: CODA, P.O. Box 30715, Santa Barbara, CA 93130-0715.

2. KODA (Kids of Deaf Adults) is a grassroots organization run by deaf parents in different parts of the United States and internationally (Chicago; Washington, D.C.; Denver; and Australia). Deaf parent leaders have hosted formal and informal activities that provide an opportunity for deaf parents and their hearing children to socialize and learn together. At present, there are no officers or a mailing address. CODA tries to keep a running list of active KODA groups. For more information, contact CODA.

3. *Bringing Two Worlds Together.* An award-winning parenting videotape, available from Northern Virginia Resource Center for the Deaf and Hard of Hearing (NVRC). This videotape includes interviews with several deaf parents and hcdp. The videotape comes with a manual that helps deaf parents understand the challenges of raising hearing children in a deaf family. To get a copy, contact the NVRC: 10363 Democracy Lane, Fairfax, VA 22030.

4. *Passport Without a Country* (1992): A forty-seven-minute videotape written and directed by Cameron Davie and produced in Australia by Griffith University. This fine documentary provides an intimate and emotional glimpse into the lives of seven hearing adults, from their earliest memories of childhood to where they find themselves now. There are many happy recollections, but there are also painful ones. The viewer gradually learns of the dilemmas facing hcdp who are searching for their identity and learns about the experience of knowing but not fully belonging, as the title's analogy indicates. For more information, contact CODA or the Centre for Deafness Studies and Research, Faculty of Education, Griffith University, Nathan, Queensland, 4111, Australia.

5. *Mother Father Deaf: Living Between Sound and Silence* (Preston, 1994). This excellent book was based on 150 interviews with adult hearing children of deaf parents throughout the United States. It is rich in anecdote and analysis, providing insights into a family life normally closed to outsiders. Interviewees describe their family histories, their

childhood memories, their sense of themselves as adults, and their life choices. The anecdotes illustrate the drama of belonging and being different.

6. *On the Edge of Deaf Culture: Hearing Children/Deaf Parents* (1998) is a comprehensive, annotated bibliography edited by Thomas Bull.

Part Three

The Ethnic Dimension

7

Mental Health Issues for African American Deaf People

CAROLYN A. CORBETT

African American Deaf people are a minority group within a minority group.[1] As a result, they may experience not only discrimination by the majority White culture, but also biases within the African American community based on assumptions about their deafness. Although the media has increased attention to issues of the Deaf community, African Americans remain, for the most part, uneducated about deaf people within their own communities. This often leads to misunderstandings and marginalization of deaf people who have strong African American identities. African American Deaf people are also a minority within the Deaf culture, a group that considers itself a minority in comparison to the hearing majority. The Deaf community is not immune from the influence of racism in the larger society; many African American Deaf people have experienced prejudice within Deaf culture as well.

African American Deaf adults are often an undetected group. The average African American Deaf person is often not identifiable through traditional methods of statistical record keeping used in the United States. Although data is collected on race and hearing status, there is no category that classifies both. The average African American Deaf person is employed and may therefore not come to the attention of agencies that keep statistics, such as schools, social service offices, and vocational rehabilitation agencies. Finally, many African American Deaf people are employed in situations where they work in isolation or at night, which reduces their chances for interaction with others.

The lack of published information about this community also contributes to its "unseen" status. To date, Hairston and Smith (1983) have written the only historical account of the African American Deaf community. Research on African American Deaf people has focused on the educational problems and deficits of individuals from this community (Stewart & Benson, 1988). The few existing articles on the mental health needs of the African American Deaf community are primarily descriptive, not data-based (Anderson, 1992; Anderson & Grace, 1991).

Historically, African American Deaf people, similar to other racial and ethnic minority groups, have had negative experiences with mental health professionals. A disturbing example is the African American Deaf man who was misdiagnosed and hospitalized in a mental institution for seventy years in North Carolina (Mitchell, 1996). Although a single incident, this type of news serves to underscore the fears of the African American Deaf community about mental health treatment. Few mental health professionals are trained to work within the cultural context of African American

1. This chapter follows the Multicultural Counseling Competencies and Standards of the Association for Multicultural Counseling and Development (Sue, Arredondo, & McDavis, 1992, 1995).

clients. Fewer still can sign and are familiar with cultural aspects of the Deaf community. Communication barriers and lack of cultural awareness and expertise have placed severe limits on African American Deaf people's access to quality services.

In order to increase quality services to the African American Deaf community, mental health professionals must be culturally competent. They must also understand that the African American Deaf person is a member of at least three cultural groups: the African American community, the Deaf culture community, and the African American Deaf community. Cultural competence has been found to have a significant impact upon the therapeutic relationship. Clients rate culturally competent psychotherapists as significantly more credible, caring, trustworthy, and effective than therapists perceived as being culturally unresponsive (Atkinson et al., 1992; see Leigh & Lewis, this volume).

Experts in the area of cross-cultural psychology have begun to operationally define cultural competence. For example, Pope-Davis and Dings (1995) provide constructs for multicultural counseling competency:

> a. Understanding the different experiences of members of various cultural groups;
>
> b. Understanding the barriers to communication across cultures that exist as a result of these differences, and possessing a specific set of abilities that can potentially make a counselor culturally skilled. (p. 288)

Sue, Arredondo, and McDavis (1992, 1995) add the following: counselor awareness of his/her own assumptions, values, and biases; counselor understanding of the worldview of the culturally different client; and active development of appropriate intervention strategies and techniques with respect for the client's linguistic, religious/spiritual, and community needs. This chapter will explore the issues most relevant to mental health professionals' understanding and treating African American Deaf clients.

Characteristics of the African American Deaf Community

Members of the African American Deaf community describe themselves as being caught between several identities (Younkin, 1990). Although part of the larger African American community, members perceive some separation and differences from this group because of their hearing loss. In addition, the demographic statistics suggest that what is known as the African American Deaf community is a specific subgroup of the larger African American population with hearing loss. This community is also a subgroup of the larger Deaf community, which has its own culture and is predominantly White. Research on White Deaf culture has revealed specific criteria for membership in the Deaf community:

- hearing loss prior to age seventeen;
- education in a school or educational program for the deaf;
- self-identification as "Deaf," not "hard of hearing" or "hearing impaired";
- fluency in American Sign Language (ASL) and an attitude known as "Deaf Pride" (Benderly, 1980; Higgins, 1987).

Individuals who do not meet these criteria may not always be considered members of the Deaf community.

Many members of the African American Deaf community meet these membership criteria. However, as a whole, the African American Deaf community is a bit more flexible in its definition of members. Although the majority of members of this community received their education in programs specifically designed for deaf students, there are many members of the African American Deaf community who lost their hearing after the age of seventeen. African American Deaf people can describe themselves as "deaf" or "hard of hearing," as long as it is clear that they are committed to the community. While ASL is the primary language of the African American Deaf community, it is possible to see a variety of sign language types within the community, including Contact Sign. There are also sociolinguistic variations of ASL unique to the African American Deaf community (Aramburo, 1992; Lewis, 1997; Reed, 1995; Woodward, 1975). Finally, African American Deaf people have "African American Deaf Pride."

Membership within the African American Deaf community may be more flexible for a number of reasons. Although deafness is considered a low-incidence condition, it is a relatively rare occurrence in the African American community (Holt & Hotto, 1994). In addition, very few African American deaf children have deaf parents. In the larger Deaf community, the culture is passed primarily through deaf children of deaf parents and at residential schools for the deaf.

For African American Deaf children, entry into the educational arena is often delayed significantly compared to White deaf children (Kluwin, 1994; Kluwin & Corbett, 1996), leading to delays in exposure to the culturally Deaf community. Access to African American Deaf adults and role models is also very limited. The potential for social isolation in African American deaf children and adults is extremely high. As a result, the African American Deaf community makes significant efforts to include as many potential members as possible.

However, some members of the African American Deaf community are not as flexible about membership. Aramburo (1992) found that African American Deaf people who had Deaf parents were more likely to identify with the Deaf community first and the African American community second. For these individuals, the criteria used by the White Deaf community to denote cultural Deafness may be considered most important for making decisions about social, educational, and political behaviors (Perkins, 1997).

DEMOGRAPHICS OF THE COMMUNITY

It is difficult to obtain an accurate picture of the quality of life for the average African American person with a significant hearing loss because traditional methods for defining or describing deaf people do not include questions about race. According to the National Center for Health Statistics, however, the incidence rate of hearing loss in the African American population (4.2%) is less than half of that reported (9.4%) for the White population (as cited in Holt & Hotto, 1994). In 1983, Hairston and Smith estimated that there were 22,000 Black members of the Deaf community. More recent statistics either overestimate or account only for a small portion of the community. For example, Valentine (1996) reported the membership of the African American Deaf community to be 240,000, but failed to acknowledge that the African American Deaf community does not include all individuals who have a hearing loss.

The most commonly reported statistics for African American Deaf people are related to education. The Annual Survey of Deaf and Hard of Hearing Children and Youth reported that 17% of students (approximately 7,800 people) attending educational programs for the deaf are African American (Schildroth & Hotto, 1996). These students are potential members of the African American Deaf community. There are approximately 400 African American Deaf people attending Gallaudet University, the National Technical Institute for the Deaf, and California State University at Northridge (Gallaudet University Office of Enrollment Services, 1997). Unfortunately, the average African American Deaf adult, who has been long separated from the formal educational setting, cannot be accounted for in the above statistics.

The National Black Deaf Advocates (NBDA), founded in 1982 to advance the needs of the African American Deaf community, currently has seventeen chapters and more than 700 members (NBDA, 1996). However, the average African American Deaf adult is not a member of NBDA. Although the person may be employed, in receipt of state rehabilitation services or federal assistance (e.g., Supplemental Security Income, Aid to Families with Dependent Children), there is no uniform way of maintaining statistics. Therefore, much of the information about the African American Deaf community is lost.

These facts underscore the importance of outreach by mental health professionals serving the African American Deaf community (Guest-Emery, 1992), particularly because it can be very easy for a mentally ill deaf person to become "lost" or isolated from others. The community knows who its members are, and there are methods each local community uses to maintain communication with its members. For example, a number of cities have Deaf social and athletic organizations that consist primarily of African American members (Aramburo, 1992; Hairston & Smith, 1983). Many churches within the African American community have ministries that serve Black Deaf members. In 1986, the National Baptist Conference of the Deaf was established to assist in the development and enhancement of ministries serving the African American Deaf community (Valentine, 1996). Establishing relationships with these social, athletic, and religious organizations can enhance the clinician's understanding of the community.

IDENTITY ISSUES

African American Deaf people view both their race and their deafness as important aspects of their identities. Yet very often, they are asked to choose between these two components in order to get important needs met (Younkin, 1990). Ideally, they do not wish to separate the two, viewing the African American Deaf community as a group with a culture of its own, separate from that of the White Deaf and African American hearing cultures (Anderson & Grace, 1991; Guest-Emery, 1992). African American hearing and White Deaf mental health professionals can potentially underestimate the importance of both identities to the client, which might have a negative impact on the therapeutic relationship (Anderson, 1992; Corbett & Leigh, 1995; Leigh & Corbett, 1996).

African American Deaf community members frequently discuss the existence of an African American/Black Deaf culture. Though very little has been written about this community (see Hairston & Smith, 1983), storytelling and oral histories have been used to pass on important information from one generation to the next. In addition, characteristics and values unique to the African American Deaf community are revealed and passed on through social, educational, and communication settings

(Aramburo, 1992). For example, many members participate in activities involving music and dancing, something that is downplayed in the White Deaf culture (McCaskill, 1996). Many older African American Deaf people attended segregated residential schools, in which unique aspects of the African American Deaf culture were cultivated and passed on to future generations (Aramburo, 1992; Stewart & Benson, 1988).

As for communication, there are aspects of ASL that are unique to the African American Deaf community. These involve the actual sign handshapes used, hand-body position, use of space, and physical distance. Research has found evidence of code-switching: African American Deaf people vary their sign language production based on the race and hearing status of the receiver (Aramburo, 1992; Reed, 1995). Recent research has found that similar to the African American hearing community, African American Deaf people have incorporated Ebonics into their sign language communication style (Lewis, 1997).

Understanding the Worldview of African American Deaf People

The worldview of African American Deaf people is influenced by four major issues—racism, economics, spirituality, and the physical health/mental health relationship.

RACISM AND MENTAL HEALTH

Racism is a fact of everyday life for African American people living in the United States. According to Turner and Kramer (1995), "inordinate power is held by one racial group; society is stratified according to race; and the dominant racial group uses its power to maintain this system and to oppress those who have been subordinated against their will" (p. 5). Racism affects an individual's daily behaviors, decision making, and information gathering.

Many African American Deaf people report that both White people and other African Americans respond to them first on the basis of race, unaware of their hearing status until communication is required (Aramburo, 1992). Although this may seem to be something that happens to all deaf people, there are some unique situations that may particularly arise for the African American Deaf person. First, within the African American community, it is extremely important to greet others in a way that is *culturally specific.* The manner of the greeting may change depending upon the age, status, and relationship between the persons. Failure to make an appropriate initial remark or response to a greeting may result in severe social consequences (Some, 1998). Very often, an African American Deaf person may be considered rude or snobbish due to failure to "speak" to others. Second, when African American Deaf persons are interacting with members of the majority culture, they may encounter racism or assumptions because of their skin color.

Racism and Mental Health

Racism and mental health have been interrelated in a number of ways in the history of provision of services to minority clients (Turner & Kramer, 1995). Throughout history, the attitudes, values, and behaviors of a society's dominant racial group have been used as standards of normalcy. Anything or anyone who differed from these standards was considered to be exhibiting psychopathology. As a result, many African American people—both deaf and hearing—have been erroneously labeled as mentally ill. Before 1980, many mental health professionals judged use of sign language as aberrant behavior, evidence of diminished mental capacity. In clinical records, it was not unusual to see statements such as:

> The patient used crude gestures and hand signals;
>
> The client communicates by using home-made signs that are evidence of his psychosis;
>
> The patient pointed and made inarticulate noises in order to gain the attention of staff members;
>
> The patient was often loud in vocalizing his wants and needs.

After 1980, an increasing number of publications began providing information on manual forms of communication, such as ASL, to the majority community.

Racism has also influenced perceptions regarding the etiology of mental illness in the African American community. Within the mental health profession, many attempts have been made to prove that African Americans are more genetically inclined to severe mental illness and inferior intelligence. African Americans were believed not to be capable of depression because of genetic deficits in thinking capacity (Turner & Kramer, 1995; Townsend, 1995). African American Deaf people who use sign language have been mistakenly labeled as mentally retarded, schizophrenic, or disordered.

When doing formal assessments of African American patients, psychologists have used psychological tests not normed on African Americans. They have made decisions using tests known to have different validity based on race. Psychologists have also knowingly included stereotypical or biased observations as part of their clinical interviews. There has also been a tendency to apply White middle-class values in determining errors on test items (Comas-Diaz, 1994; Townsend, 1995). These problems have lead to diagnostic and treatment errors with African American clients, especially in the diagnosis of schizophrenia (Leong et al., 1995; White & Parham, 1990).

When examining the impact of racism on the treatment process, African American clients have been more likely to receive the most restrictive forms of mental health treatment, namely, inpatient hospitalization (Dana, 1993; Townsend, 1995; White & Parham, 1990). Drug therapy has been the primary treatment offered to African American patients in these institutions, with little opportunity for psychotherapy. When referred for psychotherapy, they are more often slated for treatment by untrained lay people or crisis intervention counselors (Dana, 1993; Geller, 1988). In addition to these race-based problems, the lack of mental health professionals who also sign has left the African American Deaf community severely underserved.

The advent of managed care has led to tracking low-income minority patients into state mental hospitals. Their stays at these facilities are longer than those at private institutions. For African American Deaf people, these lengthy stays can lead to a "blemish" on their reputations and potential isolation from their community at large. Additionally, many of these institutions have policies that support subtle and sometimes obvious forms of institutional racism. For example, one particular hospital ward designed to serve the special needs of minority clients eventually became known among staff as a dangerous, violent place, even though the number of incident reports on this ward did not differ from any other ward in the hospital. At first the staff included both White and minority professionals, but as time progressed, White personnel began to request transfers and new White employees refused to accept assignments to the vacant positions on the ward. African American professionals with expertise in serving minority clients became isolated from colleagues. African American patients were labeled, rejected, and isolated by hospital staff (Turner & Kramer, 1995).

The African American community has a history of being ill-used by the research community and has specific fears regarding research. The Tuskegee syphilis experiments (conducted from 1932 to 1972) have been cited as one of the primary reasons that African Americans distrust medical and mental health personnel (Jones, 1993). The little research that has been done has highlighted the community's deficits rather than its strengths. The African American Deaf community is particularly wary of hearing researchers with no background in deafness who come in to gather information that may be used against them.

Traditional schools of psychotherapy proposed that special training, techniques, or methods were unnecessary for serving minority clients. The consequence of such "cultural erasure" was that clients who did not continue in treatment or who raised issues about racism or culture were considered to be resistant at best; at worst they were considered too intellectually limited to benefit from psychotherapy. During the 1980s, the American Psychological Association (APA) suggested that individuals training to become psychologists take some coursework on multicultural issues. However, the attitude at that time was that only individuals interested in serving those populations needed training in multicultural issues, and that most of these individuals were minority members themselves. This attitude prevailed despite the fact that most training opportunities for psychologists occurred in public institutions where the majority of patients were people of color. Not until 1992 did the APA require multicultural training as an ethical requirement (APA, 1992). In 1996, the APA revised its standards for accreditation of psychology doctoral programs, requiring documentation of infusion of multicultural information into the curriculum. Gallaudet University has the only clinical psychology doctoral program that specifically trains psychologists to work with Deaf clients (Leigh et al., 1996). Deaf Options, a community mental health center in Detroit, Michigan, has been the only program to provide training for work with African American Deaf clients (Anderson, 1992).

Racism in Education

Many older members of the African American Deaf community were educated in racially segregated programs for the deaf. This had both positive and negative effects. The schools were places where standards for African American Deaf culture developed and were passed on to subsequent generations (Maxwell & Smith, 1986). Many aspects of ASL that were unique to the African American community were lost when the schools were integrated during the 1970s. Although these programs nurtured African American Deaf culture, they were substandard because the administrators and teachers in these programs typically received no training in ASL or in educating deaf students. Because there was no consistent level of communication between teachers and students, the students did not develop English proficiency (Hairston & Smith, 1983).

Even in many of today's schools for the deaf, racial segregation is a continuing artifact of legal practices within the special education system. The fact that minority hearing parents are reluctant to seek help outside of their communities (Dana, 1993) leads to significant delays in diagnosis of deafness, initiation of special education programs, and delays in language acquisition. In contrast, White hearing parents tend to get help soon after their child's deafness is diagnosed. The outcome of these differences is that African American Deaf children are placed in classes for "slower" children rather than receiving the same education as their White Deaf peers. Unfortunately, African American Deaf children often do not overcome these educational lags during their entire educational experience (Christiansen & Delgado, 1994; Kluwin, 1994; Kluwin & Corbett, 1996; Moores, 1996).

The Individuals with Disabilities Education Act of 1990 (IDEA) requires that education take place within the least restrictive environment, which for most deaf children means within a public school. However, studies show that African American Deaf students are the least likely to be placed in mainstreamed educational programs. This significantly decreases the likelihood that they will be exposed to the coursework that would prepare them for college. African American Deaf students also have a higher dropout rate from secondary education (Stewart & Benson, 1988). Within this community there have been significant problems with unemployment (Smith, 1971) and underemployment (Barnartt & Christiansen, 1985).

Corbett (1991) conducted an examination of social and academic adjustment in African American Deaf students at Gallaudet University. At the time, the dropout rate for African American students at Gallaudet University hovered around 90%. African American Deaf students endorsed items on surveys that suggested significant feelings of alienation at the university. These included significantly lower scores of attachment, and social, emotional, and overall adjustment to the university as compared to White students. African American students also obtained significantly lower person-environment fit scores and satisfaction with social support scores. A social support network analysis revealed that African American students had significantly less school-based support, a factor that has predicted persistence in college (Mallinckrodt, 1988). African American students who dropped out obtained significantly higher scores on internalized Black identity compared to those who stayed. It is possible that the university environment did not provide sufficient support for Deaf individuals with a strong Black identity. The final outcome of high dropout rates is a decrease in the available pool of African American Deaf people qualified for professional employment. This, in turn, has had a significant impact on the economic advancement of members of the community (Anderson & Grace, 1991; Dunn, 1992). At present, there is not one African American Deaf person with a doctoral degree in social work, or in clinical, counseling, or school psychology.

Implications for Mental Health Service Providers

In order to provide African American Deaf people with culturally competent services, it is important to provide an environment where the client feels comfortable discussing issues of race and culture. To prepare for this, mental health professionals need to do some self-work (Tyler et al., 1991). The process of working through one's own racial psychohistory helps therapists understand their own experiences may relate to racial issues and affect the therapeutic relationship. A racial psychohistory can be done in a written narrative form, over a period of several sittings (see figure 1).

The client brings a racial psychohistory to the therapeutic relationship as well. The client and the therapist form a racial ecosystem where their two sets of experiences will

AREAS TO EXAMINE IN RACIAL PSYCHOHISTORY

1. *Racial attitudes.* Conscious understanding of their feelings about race, including feelings about one's own race, the role of race in self-definition, perspectives on racial harmony/disharmony, and strengths and weaknesses of their race.

2. *Earliest memories and associations regarding racial identification and stereotype.* This process may include acknowledging the first time and circumstances surrounding one's own self-identification as a person with a racial status and identity, personal experiences with racism and prejudice, and acknowledgment of one's own prejudices, stereotypes, and biases.

3. *Experiences with cross-race relationships.* Therapists may consider successes and failures in cross-race relationships, feelings of trust toward people of other races as colleagues and/or friends, and how much risk they are willing to take to initiate and maintain relationships with people of other races.

Figure 1. Racial Psychohistory

either converge, diverge, or conflict. When client and therapist are in convergence, their experiences, worldviews, and beliefs are similar or in agreement. Divergence occurs when the therapist and client differ in these three areas, but in such a way that it enhances discussion and exploration of the differences. In other words, the therapist and the client agree to disagree. The challenge of psychotherapy is to work through these issues so that both the therapist and the client experience growth.

When the therapist's and client's worldviews, experiences, and beliefs differ in such a way that there is no possible resolution or compromise, conflict results. If a therapeutic relationship is dominated by conflict, it is necessary for the therapist and client to evaluate the feasibility of continuing to work together. Through the racial psychohistory exercise, the therapist may become more self-aware and may be able to identify a conflictual therapeutic relationship early enough to make an appropriate referral (Tyler et al., 1991).

When working with African American or other minority deaf people, it might be important to include issues of hearing status in the racial psychohistory process. The therapist should explore his or her own views of him or herself as deaf, hard of hearing, or hearing using the same three-step process just presented. Two examples of such a process follow.

* * *

An African American hearing therapist was self-trained in providing services to deaf people. She obtained this training through sign language classes, interaction with the Deaf community, research using relevant literature, and supervision by professionals knowledgeable about the field. One of her clients, who was African American, Deaf, and female, discussed feeling oppressed by the fact that she had a hearing therapist. That the therapist was African American did not alleviate the client's feelings. The therapist was appalled at the idea of being an oppressor, due to her overwhelming feelings of being oppressed as an African

American. The therapist did some self-work as to which aspects of herself were oppressive to deaf people. This included an examination of the some of the issues of privilege related to hearing status, the power of being in the therapist's chair, and the feelings of powerlessness associated with racism.

* * *

A young African American was an interpreter at a large African American church that had a deaf ministry. She arrived late for church on a Sunday when she was not interpreting. At this church, it was customary for interpreters, sign language students, and Deaf members to sit together. That day, however, there were a large number of Deaf people present and only one seat was left in the three rows designated for the deaf ministry. Because the interpreter was accompanied by her husband, who was hearing, she asked some of the Deaf members if they could move down in order to make room for the two of them. One of the Deaf members became angry, stating "Hearing people—you can sit anywhere in the church. Why should the Deaf people have to move for you?"

In a situation where seats for Deaf people were at a premium, an African American interpreter with established ties to the community became an oppressor who was not welcome in the section. As a result, an African American hearing therapist who had witnessed the event began revisiting issues of privilege and oppression. In addition, the therapist began to explore issues related to being both an outsider and an insider in the African American Deaf community. She found that one possible implication of the event is that when you are a hearing person working within the Deaf community, membership in that community is not assumed or guaranteed. Membership may be bestowed temporarily, depends upon the circumstances, and is by invitation only.

Economics and the African American Deaf Community

African Americans come from a variety of economic backgrounds. Mental health professionals should be responsible for taking accurate histories about the economic realities of the African American clients they serve. African Americans are more likely to be employed in positions easily affected by economic events (such as budget cuts and layoffs). Many people believe that, in the United States, people of color are more likely to live in poverty (Anderson, 1996). However, recent researchers point out that the majority of African American families are at least working class and that one-third are middle class (Boyd-Franklin, 1994; Burlew et al., 1992).

African American Deaf people also come from a variety of socioeconomic backgrounds. Some individuals support themselves through government programs such as Supplemental Security Income; others work for the city, state, or federal government; and others have advanced degrees. The African American Deaf community has not yet addressed issues of socioeconomics and their impact on the cohesion of the community. It is important to point out, however, that individuals who are African American, Deaf, and poor may face additional difficulties. For example, many African American Deaf people are too poor to afford some of the assistive devices common in the homes of middle-class Deaf people. For example, they cannot afford a TTY (telecommunications device for people who are deaf) or they may not even have a telephone. Many poor deaf people do not know about flashing signal systems or the responsibility of landlords to provide such devices.

African American Deaf people who are college educated may have difficulty finding employment because of their race and hearing status. As mentioned in the demographics section, very few African American Deaf people attend college and even fewer receive their bachelor's degrees. Those who complete their education may have difficulty finding peers in their home communities. The result of all these factors can be isolation and alienation.

Spirituality in the African American Deaf Community

The literature on mental health and African Americans consistently points out the importance of religion and spirituality in their personal lives and communities (Leong et al., 1995; Valentine, 1996). Religion has been a primary source of social support, social activities, and information for the African American community and a primary method for African Americans to cope with stress (Dressler, 1991; Serafica et al., 1990). Many African Americans who experience a problem prefer to consult first with their pastor (Dana, 1993).

The relationship between the African American church and the mental health profession is confusing at best. It is not uncommon for pastors to indirectly dissuade parishioners from seeking mental health treatment by using statements such as: "You don't need to talk to a counselor, all you need is the Lord," or "In the words of an old hymn, just a little talk with Jesus makes it right." On the other hand, many pastors are overwhelmed with the mental health needs of their parishioners. Many of these same churches have formed large counseling ministries, utilizing mental health professionals who are members of the church as mental health educators, prevention specialists, and therapists.

Many African American churches have large deaf ministries, and these serve an important role in the African American Deaf community. As stated previously, it is a place where deaf people receive not only social support, but important information about what is going on in their communities. Frequent topics are health concerns, political activities in the community, and financial planning.

It is not uncommon for African American Deaf and hearing people to report feelings of guilt over seeing a mental health professional. They believe that they are going against their religion by seeking therapy; that they do not trust God enough to handle things. It is not unusual for clients to be afraid that the therapist will try to turn them against God or forbid them to talk about God.

Therapists providing culturally competent mental health treatment to African American Deaf people must be prepared to facilitate discussions about religious issues as part of the treatment process. The therapist must anticipate that the client may ask questions about personal religious beliefs. The therapist should provide an environment where the client can explore his or her concerns about the conflicts between religion and psychotherapy. However, a therapist should not assume that church attendance is a prerequisite for the client's need to engage in this discussion. Although many African American people do not attend any formal religious activities; however, they may nevertheless have a strong sense of spirituality that necessitates this type of discussion in treatment.

The Physical Health/Mental Health Relationship

Current health statistics indicate that African Americans are more likely to have severe health problems than are White Americans. The occurrence rates of cancer, hypertension, diabetes, and Acquired Immune Deficiency Syndrome (AIDS) are all higher for African Americans than for White Americans (American Society for Hypertension, 1997; National Cancer Institute, 1995; National Commission on AIDS, 1992; National Institute of Diabetes and Digestive and Kidney Disease, 1997). Discrimination, poverty, inadequate health care, and education are barriers to meaningful prevention messages and to treatment (Banks et al., 1994). These barriers are compounded by deafness.

Given the fact that African Americans are more likely to experience health concerns, the mental health professional must also be attentive to issues of physical health. Culturally competent mental health professionals should include a detailed medical history in clinical interviews with African Americans. Psychotherapeutic interventions should include attention to compliance with medical recommendations, stress management, and supplemental education/support. In the following case study, a medical problem impacted the identified patient and the family dynamics.

* * *

The Robinson family was referred for in-home services through the County Community Mental Health Clinic.[2] Ciara Robinson was a fifteen-year-old African American who was hard of hearing; she was the person identified as needing mental health services. Ciara attended a residential school for the deaf, returning home on the weekends. Ciara strongly identified with the Deaf community. She communicated primarily through sign language at school and orally at home.

Ciara was the youngest of eight children in the Robinson family. There was a large age gap between herself and her next sibling. When the clinician met with the family, Ciara's mother boasted that she had twelve grandchildren and had helped raise all of them. This was a sore point with Ciara, who resented having to share her mother with all of these people.

Ciara was hospitalized for three weeks for suicidal ideation after witnessing the murder of her favorite cousin. In fact, her cousin pushed her out of the way when he noticed a car with a gun sticking out of the window coming toward them. Within the past two years, Ciara had lost two cousins (twins) and two close family friends to violence. While Ciara was at the local mental health hospital, the family moved to an apartment across town from the area where the violence occurred. Although the apartment was more physically appealing than the old one, the new neighborhood was just as dangerous.

Mrs. Robinson, Ciara's mother, was fifty years old. She suffered from chronic renal failure due to long-term severe hypertension and diabetes. She went for dialysis three times per week. The previous year, Mrs. Robinson's condition had deteriorated and she had to be hospitalized. Since her hospitalization, she had been having significant difficulty managing Ciara's behavior at home. Problem behaviors included tantrums, frequent arguments with visiting siblings and grandchildren, curfew violations, and "running away to the old neighborhood." Ciara also began to skip school, which was very disappointing for her mother, who was looking forward to Ciara's graduation later that year.

2. Names and identifying information in this chapter's case studies have been changed to protect client confidentiality.

Within the past month, things had been rather tense around the home because Ciara's siblings had been arguing about which one of them should donate a kidney to their mother. Because Ciara was the youngest and hard of hearing, she was excluded from the discussion and ruled out as a donor. Ciara was extremely worried and depressed over her mother's condition. When her siblings argued, Ciara would make homicidal threats and then barricade herself in her room.

Mental Health Treatment of African American Deaf People

As mentioned earlier, African American Deaf people are often working through at least three aspects of their identities: their African American selves, their deaf or Deaf selves, and their African American Deaf selves. Because very few mental health professionals are trained to provide services to Deaf people, there is a high likelihood that the African American Deaf client will work with a therapist of a different racial background. That therapist also brings a racial identity to the treatment process. To better serve their African American Deaf clients, therapists must have a clear understanding of Black identity development, White identity development, and Deaf identity development. The therapist should not make assumptions as to what racial identity means to the client, but facilitate exploration of this issue in treatment.

BLACK IDENTITY DEVELOPMENT

Most of the literature on Black identity development uses the Cross model of psychological *Nigrescence* as a theoretical basis (Cross 1980, 1995; Hall et al., 1972). Nigrescence is the term used to denote the "process or psychology of converting from Negro to Black." The Cross model was formulated during the late 1960s and early 1970s at a time when Black Americans were beginning to establish a new identity for themselves. Cross studied the process of change from the identity of Negro, which was considered to be based on negative concepts given to the race by White individuals, to a more positive Black identity based on self-definition and racial pride.

The original Cross model proposed five stages of development: pre-encounter, encounter, immersion-emersion, internalization, and internalization-commitment (Hall et al., 1972; see fig. 2). Researchers in the 1980s found little difference between the fourth and fifth states and therefore combined the two (Parham & Helms, 1985). However, in recent writings, Cross (1995) challenges current researchers to again visit the unique aspects of the internalization-commitment stage. The five stages are outlined in figure 2.

The majority of research on Black identity has used the Racial Identity Attitude Scale (RIAS-B) developed by Helms (1990). One of the difficulties with this measure is that the majority of individuals who complete the scale score within the internalized range of Black identity, which indicates efforts to respond in socially desirable ways. Researchers have discussed the issue of the lifelong cyclical nature of identity development. Parham (1989) suggests that racial identity may be worked through during particular development tasks of young adulthood, middle adulthood, and late adulthood. Parham also raises the issue that an individual may be at different levels of identity development depending upon the environment. For example, an individual may be at different levels of identity development at home, church, and work. Salience, or importance of racial identity issues, may also differ by environment. Current researchers are examining the multidimensional aspects of racial identity and are in the process of validating a measure of this construct (Thompson, 1992).

THE CROSS MODEL OF AFRICAN AMERICAN IDENTITY DEVELOPMENT

1. The *pre-encounter* stage is considered to be the most representative of old world "Negro" thinking. During this stage, the individual believes that the world is, and should be, guided by concepts established by the White majority. White people are considered to be superior and the standards they set are considered to be the most important. The pre-encounter individual accepts the idea that Blacks are inferior, does not trust other Black people, and believes it is important for Black individuals to incorporate, integrate, and assimilate the ideals of the majority culture.

2. The *encounter* stage begins with a shocking personal or social event that forces the person to re-evaluate his or her Negro worldview. Usually, the beginning of this stage is a race-related incident (Cross, 1980). The person decides that his or her old Negro worldview is inappropriate and makes a conscious decision to find his or her Black identity. Social support from others who have also been through this journey is an important part of the encounter stage.

3. The *immersion-emersion* stage is considered to be the most difficult period in the process of psychological Nigrescence. During the *immersion* period, the individual is extremely focused on Blackness and withdraws from everything associated with the White majority. Everything associated with the majority culture is scorned, everything associated with Black culture is idolized. There is an emphasis on attending Black social and political activities, reading Black literature, and acknowledging African heritage. During the *emersion* period, the individual becomes less reactionary and begins to conduct a more realistic, personal assessment of his or her racial identity. The individual evaluates experiences that occurred during the immersion stage, accepting ideas that are personally relevant and rejecting ideas found not to be applicable to his or her personal Black experience. In resolving this stage, the person establishes a lifestyle consistent with the beliefs formulated during the emersion period.

4. During the *internalization* stage, the individual resolves his or her racial identity conflict. Tension is reduced and the individual is seen as secure and confident in his or her Black identity. The internalization stage is also characterized by psychological openness to new ideas and the reestablishment of relationships with Whites.

5. The *internalization-commitment* stage is characterized by a resolved Black identity coupled with continued political and social activities aimed at improving the lives of Black people. Some researchers consider this to be a natural activity that is part of the internalization stage. However, Cross (1995) points out that once some individuals resolve their racial identity, it becomes a less salient part of their lives. Other people negotiate these stages of racial identity development and begin a plan of action or sense of commitment to improving the lives of others. Cross points out that there has not been much research on psychological differences between those who lose interest and those who sustain interest in political commitment.

Figure 2. African American Identity

THE HELMS MODEL OF WHITE IDENTITY DEVELOPMENT

1. *Contact.* In a "color-blind" state, the person may profess not to "see" color and may claim to treat everybody as equal, yet has minimal contact with African Americans, which tends to perpetuate the person's feelings of fear and distrust. The person uses society's rules to evaluate African Americans and unknowingly benefits from the privileges of being White.

2. *Disintegration.* The person uncomfortably "discovers" their Whiteness and the privileges obtained by virtue of race. The person may feel morally conflicted about this position of privilege and attempt to avoid all people of color, advocate the view that minorities are not inferior, deny the existence of racism, or downplay the responsibility of White people in societal inequalities.

3. *Reintegration.* The individual passes through the disintegration stage and decides to return to old ways of thinking. The person begins to endorse White superiority and enjoy the rewards of privilege. The person also believes African Americans are responsible for their current negative circumstances.

4. *Pseudo-independence.* The process of defining a positive White identity begins. The person engages in self-exploration of his or her ideas about racism and how he or she has participated both actively and passively in perpetuating these ideas. People in this stage may become uncomfortable about their "Whiteness" or may help African Americans to meet the standards of White society.

5. *Immersion-emersion.* The person begins to explore his or her own racial identity and become a better White person. The person struggles with how to feel proud about his or her racial identity without perpetuating racism. Instead of changing Black people to conform with White standards, the person attempts to change him- or herself and other White people (Carter, 1995).

6. *Autonomy.* The last stage is characterized by the individual's formulation of a new definition of Whiteness that is positive and non-oppressive. The person who has worked through the stages to autonomy is no longer afraid of racial discussions. The person seeks out interactions with other people from a variety of cultures and sees this as beneficial to his or her personal development.

Figure 3. White Identity

DEAF IDENTITY DEVELOPMENT

Glickman's (1993) theory of deaf identity development (see Leigh & Lewis, this volume) incorporates only the deaf-hearing dimensions of identity while excluding race and ethnic aspects. Most of the research on deaf identity has used the Deaf Identity Development Scale developed by Glickman (1993). However, similar to the RIAS-B, most deaf people who complete this measure score within the bicultural range (Friedburg, 1996; Leigh et al., 1998). For this reason, future research is moving to a focus on culturally hearing and culturally deaf identity levels within individuals as a measure of biculturalism (e.g., Maxwell, 1998). For Black Deaf identity, most of the current literature tends to be anecdotal or from oral histories (Valentine, 1996).

WHITE IDENTITY DEVELOPMENT

Helms's theory of White identity development is based on two major assumptions. First, in American society, White people are socialized to feel superior to people of color or ethnic groups on the basis of skin color. Second, White people rarely think about their Whiteness, and do not usually use race when describing themselves (1990, 1995). The consequence of these attitudes is racism on individual, institutional, and cultural levels (Carter, 1995). Helms's theory of White identity development has six stages (see figure 3).

THE IMPACT OF IDENTITY ISSUES ON THE PSYCHOTHERAPY PROCESS

Racial identity can have a significant impact on the therapeutic relationship. Both the therapist and the client are at specific stages of racial identity when they initiate treatment (Carter, 1995). Four potential therapeutic dyads may result: parallel, crossed, progressive, and regressive.

In the parallel relationship, the African American therapist and African American client are at the same level of racial identity. In cross-racial dyads, the client and therapist share similar views about Blacks and Whites. When both parties in the parallel relationship are at the lower stages of racial identity development, both the client and therapist are confused about the impact of race on their lives; they might experience some difficulty discussing race during the session, and the pair may become frustrated.

In a crossed therapeutic relationship, the therapist and the client are at opposing levels of racial identity development. The crossed dyad is characterized by a lack of empathy between therapist and client where racial attitudes are concerned. Each tries to educate the other to their point of view. However, this has a detrimental effect of the establishment of rapport and the therapy may terminate prematurely (Carter, 1995).

The progressive relationship occurs when the therapist's racial identity is at least one stage higher than the client's. In the progressive relationship, the counselor is able to facilitate the exploration of racial issues in the client. In contrast, the regressive relationship is characterized by a dyad where the client is at least one stage higher than the therapist. This type of relationship may be conflictual, and power struggles between client and therapist are not uncommon. The therapist may downplay the importance of race in the client's worldview and experiences. Attempts by the client to bring up racial issues may be viewed by the therapist as forms of resistance. The client may feel misunderstood by the therapist and may spend time in sessions trying to justify his or her position.

In-Home Psychotherapy Services: A Multicultural Model for Intervention with African American Families with Deaf Members

Within the past five years, many mental health professionals have returned to a form of treatment that was very popular during the 1970s: home-based services. Based on a community mental health philosophy, in-home psychotherapy services have been found to be particularly effective with traditionally underserved populations. Several major urban centers have instituted in-home services as part of "wrap-around" support services for young children and adolescents with emotional difficulties. Intervention at the family level is a significant component of home-based services. In-home services have been used successfully with African American families in which either a parent or a child/adolescent is deaf (Corbett, 1997).

PHILOSOPHY OF IN-HOME SERVICES

The underlying principles of in-home treatment are to empower the family, increase accessibility of mental health treatment, and ensure continuity of care by increasing the family's access to/knowledge of community-based resources (Wasik et al., 1990). Home-based psychotherapy services empower the family by meeting them where they live. In contrast to office-based services where the clinician is "in charge," the clinician is a "guest" in the home where the family is "in charge." In a familiar atmosphere, family members may be more comfortable and may express information or ideas that they might not in a formal setting. Another benefit is that families may feel that they have more privacy when expressing their concerns at home. As treatment progresses, the family gets the opportunity to immediately transfer knowledge gained about themselves to their everyday interactions.

Home-based psychotherapy services also make mental health treatment more accessible for the consumer. There is a decreased likelihood that the consumer will slip between the cracks while making the transition from in-patient to outpatient support services. Often families have difficulty maintaining continuity in mental health treatment because of the expense involved in getting to their appointments. For example, a family with several young children may not be able to afford to hire a babysitter in order to attend their weekly sessions. Families without reliable transportation often cannot afford taxis or public transportation fares required for the entire family to come to the therapist's office. In-home services also improve accessibility to treatment by not limiting the respondents. The therapist is able to talk with parents, extended family, and other major caretakers of the child or adolescent. As an in-home service provider, the clinician is a therapist as well as an educator, informing the family of available community resources. Using a multidisciplinary approach, the clinician facilitates the family's connections to programs that will provide continued support after formal treatment is concluded.

CULTURALLY VALIDATING FEATURES OF HOME-BASED SERVICES

There are several culturally validating features of in-home family therapy. First is the acknowledgment of the importance of community in meeting the needs of the family. Making the community-based intervention first leads to earlier treatment. Second, in-home services necessitate that the clinician work with the family's definition of its members. Clinicians are likely to encounter nontraditional families, stepfamilies, extended families, adoptive families; in other words, whomever the family defines as its members. Third, in-home services allow for the integration of the family therapy process with other supportive cultural activities when available. This may be as either continued mental health treatment or a community resource.

One popular activity that has been used with African American adolescents, both hearing and deaf, has been the "Rites of Passage." Based on African coming-of-age ceremonies, adolescents are trained in the roles and responsibilities expected of them in the future as adult members of the community. Another culturally validating feature is that in-home service is provided by a culturally competent therapist. The therapist treating African American families with Deaf members should be familiar with significant landmarks and important community leaders and organizations, as well as issues of importance in the African American hearing community, African American Deaf community, and Deaf community. The clinician serves as an educator to family members who do not know about all three of these cultures. The therapist is also involved in the continuous self-work that is required to maintain his or her own cultural competence.

Finally, in-home therapy services are culturally validating in that families have the freedom to discuss controversial issues that are relevant in the community as part of the therapy process. Topics may include racism, spirituality, and even politics.

Components of Home-Based Treatment

The major components of the home-based treatment approach are illustrated in the following clinical case study.

* * *

The Burgess family was referred through the Social Services Department at the County Courthouse for in-home family therapy services. The identified patient, Zenia Burgess, was an African American Deaf female, age fourteen, whose mother brought her in on a PINS (person in need of supervision) petition. Annessa Burgess, Zenia's mother, was having significant difficulty controlling Zenia at home. Before the legal process would be set in motion through the courts, it was hoped that a family therapy intervention would help alleviate problems in the home.

Zenia was quite tall (approximately 5'10"), very physically developed, and looked much older than her age. The apartment she shared with her mother was close to the junior high school where Zenia was a ninth grade student in the deaf program. Zenia was an honor student and made the top 5% of the honor roll each term. For this reason, Zenia was placed in many mainstream classes. Most of her deaf peers were bussed to school, which made after-school activities with them nearly impossible. She did not have much interaction with hearing classmates.

Mrs. Burgess (hearing) was approximately forty-five years old and unemployed. She knew some basic sign language, and communicated with her daughter using sign and speech. She had a long history of mental illness, but had not been hospitalized in the last ten years. Although Mrs. Burgess would not disclose the nature of her mental illness, at times she made up words and had some pressured speech. Mrs. Burgess was originally from the island of St. Vincent. She described herself as "a good Christian woman, not about to be beaten by the devil," who she said was "trying to get to me through my child." Before agreeing to an in-home appointment, Mrs. Burgess quoted scriptures to the clinician on the phone in an attempt to discover the clinician's religious beliefs.

The Burgess family were members of the Glory Christian Ministries church, a very strict Pentecostal church. Zenia was very active in the church's sign language ministry; her mother only allowed her to interact with the deaf Christians at church, most of whom were college age. Mrs. Burgess said that the trouble started in church. "The child caught the devil in church. Can you believe it?" she asked the clinician.

Zenia had befriended a man named Alfred at the church. Alfred, age twenty-two, had just graduated from a college for the deaf. Zenia had been caught talking with him on the phone at 3 a.m. Although Mrs. Burgess wanted to know "what is that old man doing hanging around my daughter?" Zenia absolutely refused to give up the friendship. She cried hysterically whenever her mother mentioned breaking off the relationship. Mrs. Burgess tried to have their pastor intervene, and he met with Alfred twice (with church interpreters); Alfred claimed that they were just "friends."

The weekend before the clinician's first session with the Burgess family, Zenia stayed out until 1 a.m. with Alfred. When her mother confronted her upon her return, Zenia became violent and tore the door to her room off the hinges. Mrs. Burgess called the court social worker the first thing the next morning and told her of the events. When the social worker suggested that Mrs. Burgess consider making Zenia a birth control appointment, Mrs. Burgess angrily made it clear that she didn't want to hear about that "demonic" birth control idea again. When the clinician arrived at the Burgess home for the first appointment, Mrs. Burgess informed him that Alfred was on the way and she wanted the clinician to take care of the situation.

Using a multidisciplinary approach, the Burgess family was referred for three service components: behavior management/family therapy, parent training in the home, and a Rites of Passage activity.

BEHAVIOR MANAGEMENT/FAMILY THERAPY

In initial behavior management/family therapy sessions, the clinician establishes rapport with the family by letting the family members tell their own stories. Very often, minority families test clinicians to make sure that they are listening. If this aspect of the test is failed, then the family will not allow the clinician to return to the home. Although clinicians are often required to fill out initial assessments and interview sheets, a skilled clinician can let the family tell their story and get their paperwork completed at the same time.

The second portion of the intervention relates to improving/enhancing communication skills. The therapist and family discuss the rules for communication within the sessions, making sure that everyone can participate in the mode that is most comfortable for them. In families where the adolescent is ASL fluent and the parents know only a few signs, it may be important to discuss the use of a sign language interpreter (trained in mental health) in the session. Issues related to communication accessibility should be discussed prior to the initial session, to make sure that everyone can participate. The safety of the therapeutic environment is also important. The therapist states the ground rules of the session regarding safety of all participants in treatment. The therapist models appropriate communication and provides reinforcement/encouragement to family members who engage in appropriate communication behaviors.

In prosocial family therapy (Blechman et al., 1997), each session consists of four tasks: discovery, reunion, role-play, and plan. During the discovery task, the family works on defining the problems they have been having and prioritizing the areas (home, community, personal) that need to be worked on. The reunion task involves establishing rapport between the family and the clinician. The clinician facilitates appropriate communication between family members. During the role-play task, the family role plays situations related to the current focus area while the clinician observes. Afterwards, the clinician provides feedback to the family about what was observed so that the family can learn more about themselves. Through the role-play task, the family learns and rehearses skills related to behavior management.

In the third week and beyond, the family engages in the plan task. The family negotiates a contingency contract that is acceptable to all members. This means the family sets minimum standards as to what constitutes a "good day." The goal is to increase the number of good days in a week. Clinicians generally ask about the number of good days during the discovery task after the plan has been developed.

* * *

A cognitive behavioral specialist performed this portion of the treatment with the Burgess family. The goal was to reduce acting out behaviors in the home. The therapist used a multicultural modification of prosocial family therapy to assess Zenia's problems in three major areas: home, community, and personal. Zenia's home problems were frequent arguments with her mother and her destruction of household property. Her community problem was that she was staying out too late, which led to court involvement. Failure to improve might have led to placement in a more restrictive environment. Zenia was also involved in a relationship with an older man, although she denied that there was a sexual involvement. Sexual activity might have become a legal problem for Alfred, because Zenia was underage. Zenia was also experiencing a number of personal problems. She was depressed by her mother's restrictions, and socially isolated from others her age. Because of the strictness of her home environment, Zenia was concerned that her mother might not permit her to go to college.

During the family therapy/behavior management component of Zenia's case, two issues became apparent: Zenia had very limited interaction with Deaf peers, and she was struggling with issues related to her African American Deaf identity. For her, Alfred provided an opportunity to interact with a Deaf college graduate, something she considered prestigious.

Secondly, Zenia's mother was so overprotective that she rarely allowed Zenia to engage in activities outside of the home or church. Mrs. Burgess was attempting to raise her using traditions from her native culture of St. Vincent, but was experiencing cultural conflicts. First, she came to the United States in order to improve her economic conditions and to raise her child in an environment where she would have additional advantages. Zenia's failure to follow the rules jeopardized her mother's dreams for her future. Because American culture is more permissive than St. Vincent's, activities that Zenia wanted to be involved in would be considered inappropriate in St. Vincent. Mrs. Burgess felt she would be reprimanded by the Black community there for being a bad mother. Although Zenia and her mother never agreed on Alfred's role, Alfred decided to terminate the relationship with Zenia because of the amount of strife it was causing both him and Zenia at home and at church.

Zenia continued to attend church services, which were a primary source of the family's social activities and support. These interactions were especially important for

Mrs. Burgess, whose unemployment had led to some social isolation. Zenia stated that her mother's mood improved significantly after attending church services.

During the sessions, the family role played typical interactions and received feedback from the therapist. The use of a sign language interpreter during the sessions made Mrs. Burgess aware of how much Zenia relied on sign language. As a result, Mrs. Burgess enrolled in a sign language course at her local community college.

PARENT TRAINING IN THE HOME

The parent training module is based on a problem-solving approach (see Mabry, 1996). The training begins with a session on cognitive empowerment of parents. Key phrases are "I am a parent who is able to solve problems" and "There is a solution to this problem and I am able to find it." There are five modules in the parent training curriculum.

1. *Identifying problems:* Parents learn to be specific about the who, what, when, why, and how of the problems. Breaking down the problems into smaller chunks increases the perceived manageability of the problem.
2. *Brainstorming solutions:* Parents generate a variety of solutions to the problem. The goal is to think up as many solutions as possible without thinking about quality. This empowering activity assists the parent in realizing that there are a variety of ways to solve problems.
3. *Weighing the alternatives:* Parents evaluate the proposed solutions and eliminate some of the items on the list. Parents also work on establishing rewards for desired behaviors and consequences for undesired ones.
4. *Implementing solutions:* In order to choose a solution, parents return to the identifying problems module and recall specific aspects of the problem. A solution is chosen from their list that matches those aspects of the problem. Parents are encouraged to consistently implement rewards and consequences.
5. *Evaluating solutions:* Parents are encouraged to explore the positive and negative outcomes of the particular strategy they chose.

* * *

With Mrs. Burgess, two major issues were addressed in the parent training module—her tendency to be overprotective of Zenia and Zenia's potential for violence. The clinician worked with Mrs. Burgess on establishing a list of activities that she would consider age-appropriate for Zenia and how she would work with Zenia on increasing her activities away from home and church. A strict no-violence policy was enacted, leading to severe consequences such as no telephone and no money if there were any incidents or threats of violence.

RITES OF PASSAGE ACTIVITY

As discussed earlier, Rights of Passage activities are based on African coming-of-age ceremonies. Depending on the client's needs, activities may include rap sessions on important topics, academic skill building, African American history, African American Deaf history, African dance and drumming for self-esteem building, and development of community and political awareness.

* * *

During the Rites of Passage activity, Zenia engaged in age-appropriate activities with peers. This included trips to cultural activities in the community, rap sessions about important topics such as African American Deaf identity, and self-esteem building exercises. At the Rites of Passage activity, several of the group leaders were African American Deaf people, so that Zenia was able to have exposure to African American Deaf adults.

Conclusion

Awareness of cultural values and historical information provides a foundation for understanding the worldview of the African American Deaf community. The specific contributions of racism, economic issues, spirituality, and the physical/mental health relationship all must be considered when planning mental health intervention. Also, the knowledge of strategies for examining factors that impact the therapeutic relationship—including racial identity, deaf/hearing identity, and self-awareness—improve the provision of culturally competent services.

References

American Psychological Association. (1992). Ethical principles of psychologists and code of conduct. *American Psychologist, 47,* 1597–1611.

American Society for Hypertension. (1997). *Hypertension statistics.* [On-line]. Available: www.ash.org.

Anderson, G. B., & Grace, C. A. (1991). Black deaf adolescents: A diverse and underserved population. *Volta Review, 93,* 73–86.

Anderson, N. B. (1996, April). *Why African Americans get sick and die faster than other people.* Paper presented at Gallaudet University, Washington, DC.

Anderson, R. P. (1992). Black, deaf and mentally ill: Triple jeopardy. In *Proceedings of the Empowerment and Black Deaf Persons Conference* (pp. 89–103). Washington, DC: Gallaudet University, College for Continuing Education.

Aramburo, A. J. (1992). Sociolinguistic aspects of the Black deaf community. In *Proceedings of the Empowerment and Black Deaf Persons Conference* (pp. 67–88). Washington, DC: Gallaudet University, College for Continuing Education.

Atkinson, D. F., Casas, A., & Abreu, J. (1992). Mexican-American acculturation, counselor ethnicity and cultural sensitivity, and perceived counselor competence. *Journal of Counseling Psychology, 39,* 515–520.

Baldwin, P. (1996, August). *History of the Black deaf community.* Paper presented at the 17th Annual Conference of the National Black Deaf Advocates, Los Angeles, CA.

Banks, M. E., Ackerman, R. J., & Corbett, C. A. (1995). Feminist neuropsychology: Issues for physically challenged women. In J. H. Chrisler & A. H. Hemstreet, (Eds.), *Variations on a theme: Diversity and the psychology of women* (pp. 29–49). Albany, NY: State University of New York Press.

Barnartt, S. N., & Christiansen, J. B. (1985). *The socioeconomic status of deaf workers: A minority group perspective.* Greenwich, CT: JAI Press.

Benderly, B. L. (1980). *Dancing without music: Deafness in America.* New York: Anchor Press/Doubleday.

Blechman, E., Hall, K., & Mabry, H. O. (1997). *Culturally competent prosocial family therapy.* Unpublished manuscript.

Boyd-Franklin, N. (1994). *Black families in therapy: A multisystems approach.* New York: Guilford Press.

Burlew, A. K. H., Banks, W. C., McAdoo, H. P., & Azibo, D. A. (1992). *African American psychology: Theory, research and practice.* Thousand Oaks, CA: Sage Publications.

Carter, R. T. (1995). *The influence of race and racial identity in psychotherapy: Toward a racially inclusive model.* New York: Wiley.

Christiansen, K. M., & Delgado, G. L. (1993). *Multicultural issues in deafness.* White Plains, NY: Longman.

Comas-Diaz, L. (1994). An integrative approach. In L. Comas-Diaz & B. Greene (Eds.), *Women of color: Integrating ethnic and racial identities in psychotherapy* (pp. 287–318). New York: Guilford Press.

Comas-Diaz, L., & Greene, B. (1994). *Women of color: Integrating ethnic and racial identities in psychotherapy.* New York: Guilford Press.

Comer, J. P. (1980). White racism: Its roots, form, and function. In R. L. Jones (Ed.), *Black psychology* (2d ed.) (pp. 361–366). New York: Harper and Row.

Corbett, C. A. (1991). *Dual minority status and college adjustment: An examination of social and academic adjustment in Black deaf college students.* Ph.D. dissertation, Pennsylvania State University.

———. (1995). Standards of care for minority deaf clients. In R. R. Myers (Ed.), *Standards of care for the delivery of mental health services to deaf and hard of hearing: Model State Plan* (Chapter 7: pp. 10–13). Silver Spring, MD: National Association of the Deaf.

———. (1997a, May). *In-home family therapy services: A model for intervention with African American families with deaf members.* Paper presented at the National Conference of the American Deafness and Rehabilitation Association, Milwaukee, Wisconsin.

———. (1997b, November). *Parent training in the home: A multicultural model for intervention with minority families with deaf members.* Paper presented at the Second Biennial Multicultural Deaf Conference, Beaumont, Texas.

Corbett, C. A., & Leigh, I. W. (1995, June). *Culturally competent mental health counselors.* Paper presented at the National Conference of the American Deafness and Rehabilitation Association, Kansas City, Missouri.

Cross, W. E. (1980). Models of psychological Nigrescence: A literature review. In R. L. Jones (Ed.), *Black psychology* (2d ed.) (pp. 81–98). New York: Harper and Row.

———. (1995). The psychology of Nigrescence: Revising the Cross model. In J. G. Ponterotto, J. M. Casas, L. A. Suzuki, & C. M. Alexander (Eds.), *Handbook of multicultural counseling* (pp. 93–122). Thousand Oaks, CA: Sage Publications.

Dana, R. H. (1993). *Multicultural assessment perspectives for professional psychology.* Boston: Allyn and Bacon.

Dressler, W. W. (1991). *Stress and adaptation in the context of culture: Depression in a southern Black community.* Albany, NY: State University of New York Press.

Dunn, L. M. (1992). Intellectual oppression of the Black deaf child. In M. Garretson (Ed.), *Viewpoints on deafness: A Deaf American monograph* (pp. 53–58). Silver Spring, MD: National Association of the Deaf.

Equal Employment Opportunity Commission. (1978, 25 August). Uniform guidelines on employee selection procedures. *Federal Register, 43* (166), 38295–38309.

Friedburg, I. (1995). Personal identity and reference group orientation of deaf and hard of hearing college students. Unpublished manuscript.

———. (1996). Self-esteem and reference orientation of deaf and hard-of-hearing college students. Unpublished master's thesis. Washington, DC: Gallaudet University.

Gallaudet University Office of Enrollment Services. (1997). *1996–1997 enrollment statistics.* Washington, DC: Gallaudet University.

Geller, J. D. (1988). Racial bias in the evaluation of patients for psychotherapy. In L. Comas-Diaz & E. E. H. Griffith (Eds.), *Clinical guidelines in cross-cultural mental health* (pp. 112–134). New York: Wiley.

Glickman, N. (1993). Deaf identity development: Construction and validation of a theoretical model. Ph.D. dissertation, University of Massachussetts, Amherst.

Guest-Emery, S. (1992). Cousin Hattie's sister's people: The ties between identity and leadership within the Black deaf community. In *Proceedings of the Empowerment and Black Deaf Persons Conference* (pp. 16–19). Washington, DC: Gallaudet University, College of Continuing Education.

Hairston, E., & Smith, L. (1983). *Black and deaf in America: Are we that different?* Silver Spring, MD: T. J. Publishers.

Hall, W. S., Cross, W. E., & Freedle, R. (1972). *Stages in the development of a Black identity.* Iowa City, IA: American College Testing Program.

Helms, J. E. (1990). *Black and White racial identity: Theory, research, and practice.* Westport, CT: Greenwood Press.

———. (1995). An update of Helms's White and people of color racial identity models. In J. G. Ponterotto, J. M. Casas, L. A. Suzuki, & C. M. Alexander (Eds.), *Handbook of multicultural counseling* (pp. 181–199). Thousand Oaks, CA: Sage Publications.

Higgins, P. C. (1987). The deaf community. In P. C. Higgins & J. E. Nash (Eds.), *Understanding deafness socially* (pp. 151–170). Springfield, IL: Charles C. Thomas.

Holt, J. A., & Hotto, S. A. (1994). *Demographic aspects of hearing impairment: Questions and answers* (3rd ed.). Washington, DC: Gallaudet University Center for Assessment and Demographic Studies.

Individuals with Disabilities Education Act Amendments of 1997. [On-line]. Available: www.ed.gov/offices/OSERS/IDEA/regs.html.

Jones, J. H. (1991). *Bad blood: The Tuskegee syphilis experiment* (2d ed.). New York: Free Press.

Klima, E. S., & Bellugi, U. (1979). *The signs of language.* Cambridge, MA: Harvard University Press.

Kluwin, T. N. (1994). The interaction of race, gender and social class: Effects in the education of deaf students. *American Annals of the Deaf, 139,* 465–471.

Kluwin, T. N., & Corbett, C. A. (1996, September). *Predicting minority parent participation in educational programs for the deaf: Preliminary findings.* Poster presented at University of Virginia Medical School's Sixth Annual Virginia Beach Conference, Virginia Beach, Virginia.

Leigh, I. W., & Corbett, C. A. (1996, June). *Multiculturalism: The way of the future.* Paper presented at the International Convention of the Alexander Graham Bell Association for the Deaf, Snowbird, Utah.

Leigh, I. W., Corbett, C. A., Gutman, V. A., & Morere, D. A. (1996). Providing psychological services to deaf individuals: A response to new perceptions in diversity. *Professional Psychology, 27* (4), 364–371.

Leigh, I. W ... 8). Deaf/Hearing cultural identity ... ment Scale. *Journal of Deaf Studies a*

Leong, F. T ... ethnic variations in help-seeking ... uzuki, & C. M. Alexander (Eds.), ... Thousand Oaks, CA: Sage Publicati

Lewis, J. G. ... *tylistic variations of African American* ... 2000—Unity and Diversity, Gallaude

Mabry, H. ... *ning module.* Unpublished manuscr

Mallinckroc ... and dropout intention: Compari ... *tudent Development, 29* (1), 60–64.

Maxwell, D., & Zea, M. C. (1998, August). *The Deaf Acculturation Scale (DAS): Development, reliability, and validity.* Poster session presented at the annual convention of the American Psychological Association, San Franscisco, CA.

Maxwell, M. M., & Smith, T. (1986). Black sign language and school integration in Texas. *Language and Society, 15* (1), 81–94.

McCaskill, A. (1996, February). *The African American deaf community.* Workshop presented at Deaf Awareness Day, Ebenezer A.M.E. Church, Camp Springs, MD.

Mitchell, K. B. (1996). *Life emerges from a world of silence* [On-line]. Available: www.starnews.wilmington.nct/showcase/wilson.html.

Moores, D. F. (1996). *Educating the deaf: Psychology, principles and practices* (4th ed.). Boston: Houghton Mifflin.

National Black Deaf Advocates. (1996, August). *Program of the 17th Annual Conference of the National Black Deaf Advocates,* Los Angeles, CA.

National Cancer Institute. (1995). *Cancer fact book 1995.* [On-line]. Available: www.nci.nih.gov/public/factbk95/c5yr.htm.

National Commission on AIDS. (1992). *The challenge of HIV/AIDS in communities of color.* [On-line]. Available: gopher://gopher.niaid.nih.gov.

National Institute of Diabetes and Digestive and Kidney Disease. (1997). *Diabetes statistics.* [On-line]. Available: www.pharminfo.com/diseases/diabetes/diabstat.

Parham, T. A. (1989). Cycles of psychological Nigrescence. *Counseling Psychologist, 17* (2), 187–226.

Parham, T. A., & Helms, J. E. (1985). Attitudes of racial identity and self-esteem in Black students: An exploratory investigation. *Journal of Counseling Psychology, 28,* 250–257.

Perkins, K. P. (1997). *Signing sisters: The convergence of race, deaf culture and gender in Black deaf women.* Unpublished manuscript.

Pope-Davis, D. B., & Dings, J. G. (1995). The assessment of multicultural counseling competencies. In J. G. Ponterotto, J. M. Casas, L. A. Suzuki, & C. M. Alexander (Eds.), *Handbook of multicultural counseling* (pp. 287–311). Thousand Oaks, CA: Sage Publications.

Reed, R. (1995, October). *Unique aspects of American Sign Language in the African American Deaf community: Preliminary findings of a national research project.* Paper presented at Gallaudet University, Washington, DC.

Schildroth, A. N., & Hotto, S. A. (1996). Annual Survey of Deaf and Hard of Hearing Children and Youth: Changes in student and program characteristics, 1984–85 and 1994–95. *American Annals of the Deaf, 141* (2), 68–71.

Serafica, F. C., Schweibel, A. I., Russell, R. K., Isaac, P. D., & Myers, L. B. (1990). *Mental health of ethnic minorities.* New York: Praeger.

Smith, L. D. (1971). *The hardcore deaf Negro adult in the Watts area of Los Angeles, California.* Unpublished manuscript.

Stewart, D. A., & Benson, G. (1988). Dual cultural negligence: The education of Black deaf children. *Journal of Multicultural Counseling and Development, 16,* 98–109.

Sue, D. W., Arredondo, P., & McDavis, R. J. (1992). Multicultural counseling competencies and standards: A call to the profession. *Journal of Counseling and Development, 70,* 477–486.

———. (1995) Multicultural counseling competencies and standards: A call to the profession. In J. G. Ponterotto, J. M. Casas, L. A. Suzuki, & C. M. Alexander (Eds.), *Handbook of multicultural counseling* (pp. 624–644). Thousand Oaks, CA: Sage Publications.

Thompson, V. S. (1992). A multi-faceted approach to the conceptualization of African-American identification. *Journal of Black Studies, 23,* 75–85.

Townsend, J. (1995). Racial, ethnic and mental illness stereotypes: Cognitive process and behavioral effects. In C. V. Willie, P. P. Rieker, B. M. Kramer, & D. S. Brown (Eds.), *Mental health, racism and sexism* (pp. 119–147). Pittsburgh, PA: University of Pittsburgh Press.

Turner, C. B., & Kramer, B. M. (1995). Connections between racism and mental health. In C. V. Willie, P. P. Rieker, B. M. Kramer, & B. S. Brown (Eds.), *Mental health, racism and sexism* (pp. 3–26). Pittsburgh, PA: University of Pittsburgh Press.

Tyler, F. G., Brome, D. R., & Williams, J. E. (1991). *Ethnic validity, ecology, and psychotherapy: A psychosocial competence model.* New York: Plenum Press.

Valentine, V. (1996, December/January). Being Black and deaf. *Emerge, 7* (3), 56–59.

Wasik, B. H., Bryant, D. M., & Lyons, C. M. (1990). *Home visiting: Procedures for helping families.* Thousand Oaks, CA: Sage Publications.

White, J. L., & Parham, T. A. (1990). *The psychology of Blacks: An African American perspective* (2d ed.). Englewood Cliffs, NJ: Prentice-Hall.

Woodward, J. (1975). Black Southern signing. *Language and Society, 5,* 211–218.

Younkin, L. (1990, January/February). Between two worlds: Black and deaf in America. *Disability Rag,* pp. 30–33.

8

Culturally Responsive Psychotherapy with American Indians Who Are Deaf

NANCY M. ELDREDGE

In recent years, interest has increased in the problems of cross-cultural psychotherapy with Deaf individuals from various minority groups, paralleling trends within the general field of psychotherapy. This chapter explores the comparative cultural values of Deaf people, Indian groups, and the hearing Anglo society as a framework for identifying potential conflicts that may impact the psychotherapeutic relationship. It offers practical suggestions for making psychotherapeutic intervention culturally responsive and affirmative.[1]

The Need for Cultural Training and Cultural Awareness

In general, researchers have assumed that members of a particular ethnic group have unique social and cultural heritages in common. Yet this is not always the case, particularly with American Indians who are Deaf. In general, the data regarding ethnicity have been based on self-identification, which is problematic when an individual must have a certain "blood quantum" to be identified on the register for various tribes, in which quantum requirements vary. Ethnicity has been "confounded with minority group status" (Dix, 1996, p. 268), sometimes referred to as the culture of the poor.

Sue, Chun, and Gee note that "it is important to have treatment approaches consistent with clients' cultural lifestyles," but effective treatment needs to move beyond "vague notions of being culturally sensitive and knowledgeable about the clients' culture" (1995, p. 269). Culturally responsive therapy is being defined, and its effectiveness is being tested, despite the difficulties in finding representative samples and adequate research design. Much of the research continues to be exploratory, however, because of the "lack of baseline measures" (ibid.) and significant misconceptions on the part of some researchers. For example, some studies associate utilization rates with effectiveness or satisfaction, which is not necessarily the case. Other studies have used the length of time in treatment as an outcome measure, yet the studies' results vary, perhaps due

The author thanks the following people for their helpful comments regarding the Deaf and Indian cultural characteristics presented in this chapter: Jeff Davis, Ph.D.; Carol Locust, Ph.D; Byron L. Sanderson; Sam Supalla, Ph.D., and Cindy Volk, Ph.D.

1. In this chapter, Anglo is used to denote the dominant ethnic and hearing community. This is common nomenclature used in the Southwest to refer to Caucasian individuals. The uppercase *Deaf* is used to designate the cultural group, whereas the lowercase *deaf* refers to the audiometric condition of hearing impairment resulting in an inability to perceive the sounds of speech (Rutherford, 1988). *Native American* refers to Native peoples in the contiguous United States and Alaska and Hawaii. *Indian* is accepted nomenclature to describe Native peoples of the contiguous states. Also, the chapter is intended to address all therapeutic professions such as counselors, social workers, psychologists, and psychotherapists.

to region, the particular service system involved, and the time period during which the research was conducted (Sue et al., 1994). Some studies have noted that ethnic match tends to increase the number of sessions, yet this alone does not necessarily point to satisfaction or outcome results associated with demonstrable psychological change.

Darou (1987) states that "counseling, in particular, and American culture in general, may be seen by Natives as a practical form of cultural racism" (p. 34) because standard psychotherapeutic practices often violate accepted forms of behavior for many American Indian groups. For similar reasons, the psychotherapeutic process may also represent cultural oppression for Deaf individuals. Oppression can result from unconscious biases therapists bring to the counseling setting or an inability to use cross-cultural techniques well.

Some therapists may argue that cross-cultural psychotherapy is synonymous with good psychotherapy. No legitimate therapist knowingly creates an oppressive environment for a client, yet oppression occurs. For many therapists, "what comes naturally may be construed as insulting" (Choca, 1996). While the only way to discuss cultures is to talk about them in general ways, a single culture can vary greatly depending on region, family, status, and the individual.

In a 1996 (unpublished) lecture for mental health workers in Arizona, Clay Dix stated that awareness typically should lead to sensitivity, and that with the appropriate techniques, cultural competence can be maintained. His concern is that if we offer something that does not fit, then clients go away. When therapists blamed the high dropout rate on clients by saying, "They shouldn't be here anyway," or "they are just not *ready*," therapists found they had "fewer and fewer [minority] customers." Dix described this as majority (typically Anglo) therapists "gloating in ethnocentric incapacity and making further decisions to remain incapacitated."

Many cross-cultural therapists recognize that the process of transcultural psychotherapy is significantly different from the typical methodology taught in most graduate school programs (LaFromboise et al., 1990). For example, even with a thorough discussion or investigation of specific cultural attributes, there never emerges a template that can be applied to the individual seeking services. Dix reported that the process of transcultural counseling involves "asking more than giving." The therapist becomes a sojourner rather than an expert. Dix likened this to a business merger rather than a takeover. The process of transcultural psychotherapy is a dynamic one with the cultural attributes, characteristics, behaviors, expectations, and resentments of each individual client and therapist serving as a thread throughout the psychotherapeutic process.

Self-Awareness and Oppressive Practices

Oppression, though usually a result of economic competitiveness and fear, can be "enacted with varying degrees of awareness, intensity, and malice" (Harvey, 1993, p. 45). Even good psychotherapy can be disturbed by the unconscious processes resulting from the experiences the therapist brings to the session. Trust and rapport-building are not impeded merely because the therapist comes from a different ethnic background or does not share the disability (Haley & Dowd, 1988; LaFromboise & Dixon, 1981; Lazarus, 1982), nor are they hampered merely by ineffective techniques. Rather, the therapist's underlying assumptions and attitudes also affect psychotherapy outcomes. Sometimes the therapist's "guilt"—his or her desire to right the wrongs of history—can impair the therapy (Ferriera, 1975).

Therapist sensitivity to cultural norms, both the therapist's own and those of the client(s) may, therefore, be one of the most important variables affecting the initial success or failure of the psychotherapeutic experience (Lee, 1991). Such sensitivity lays the foundation for a deep and trusting psychotherapeutic relationship. In order to establish rapport successfully in a cross-cultural intervention, a therapist needs more than empathy to enter the perceptual framework of the client. "The nature of the healing relationship is inextricably bound to the cultural system in which it was developed, that is, certain types of mental disorders are indigenous to a culture and therefore require compatible forms of therapeutic approaches" (Benesch & Ponterotto, 1989, p. 25).

Hughes (1993) provides a series of questions that can be used for a therapist to assess his or her own cultural biases that may impact the therapeutic process (see figure 1). Michael Harvey (1993) explores this question of self-analysis in cross-counseling relationships by asking how counseling someone from the same gender, racial, socioeconomic status, and religious background differs from counseling someone from a different background. His question parallels that asked in a number of texts addressing nonminority counselors: "As a member of a White group, what responsibility do you hold for the racist, oppressive, and discriminating manner by which you personally and professionally deal with minorities?" (Satel, 1996).

QUESTIONS TO ASSESS ONE'S OWN CULTURAL BIAS

1. What is it about the client's appearance or behavior that makes me think that what I am seeing and hearing is pathology?
2. What are the sources of the pathologic characterization?
3. What label(s) am I subconsciously applying to this client and where did they come from?
4. What social class or group am I assuming the client belongs to, and what do I know about that group?
5. What are my own prejudices about that group and where do such characterizations come from—childhood directives and role modeling, family inculcated out-group attitudes, scanning of current events that may have reinforced preexisting stereotypes?
6. Other than "pathology," what other hypotheses come to mind to explain this behavior and/or mentation?
7. What other label could I use to describe this behavior instead of pathology?
8. What are the circumstances of the referral . . . and what are the [descriptive labels] used by other healthcare providers in conveying information about this client?
9. What do I know about the person or persons making such comments in the referral information?

Figure 1. Cultural Bias. *Note.* Selected from Hughes, 1993, p. 5.

The question "What do I know about oppression?" is an important one and relates to understanding of the oppressive experiences clients may have had, as well as to our own experience of oppression. This question has been an integral part of my evolution as a therapist, from the perspective of my own growing awareness, and the assumptions that the clients have made about me during the course of our relationships. One of the more interesting and unpredictable developments when working with American Indians who are Deaf has been their response to me as a person whose great-great grandmother was Huron. Often clients have noticed my skin color and have remarked that I did not look like other white people. At times, they remarked that I looked like someone from their families.

* * *

A number of years ago a healing art therapist and I co-led an art therapy group for American Indians (Eldredge & Carrigan, 1992). In this group, the participants initially identified themselves as "Indian." During one of the sessions, they asked my co-leader what her background was. She named the Indian tribe to which she belonged. At that point, the participants turned to me expectantly, asking about my background. I told them that I was Anglo, and explained where I had grown up. At one point, one of the young men, who was Yaqui, said that I looked like his father because of my dark skin and green eyes. When I told them that my great-great grandmother was Huron from Canada, they all broke out into smiles and looked around the room, remarking, "We're all Indian here."

That identification was an important step in the initial bonding of that group. Later, as the participants became stronger in their individuation, they dropped the "Indian" referent and began to refer to themselves as Navajo, Yaqui, Hopi, and so on. My ethnicity, and that of my co-facilitator, receded in importance at that point. (For further information regarding this process in identity change see Atkinson et al., 1989; Corbett, this volume; Cross 1991; Helms 1993.)

Diversity Among Indian and Deaf Groups

It is only within the last several hundred years that the land restrictions and barriers were set up under government control and regulation. Walker and LaDue (1986) review the medical treatment of these tribal groups during the "pre-contact period."

The majority of Indian populations in the United States presently live in Oklahoma, California, Arizona, New Mexico, Alaska, North Carolina, and Washington State (U.S. Bureau of the Census, 1990). According to the 1990 census, there are 1,959,234 Native American individuals in 328 tribes, villages, bands, groups, and pueblos in the contiguous states, and another 224 groups in Alaska. Hammond and Meiners (1993) report that most Deaf American Indian individuals live in Arizona, New Mexico, and Oklahoma, reflecting the population rates for American Indian individuals in the general population.

Population figures for American Indian people who are Deaf vary considerably. The published incident rates of hearing impairments indicate that about 6% of all people are deaf or hard of hearing (Hammond & Meiners, 1993). However, several authors report conflicting data suggesting that these figures may underrepresent the population of deaf and hard of hearing people among Indian groups. For example,

O'Connell (1987) reports that American Indian children are three times more likely to be hospitalized than Anglo children for conditions associated with the ear.

The high incidence of deafness among American Indian populations is complicated by both geographical and medical considerations. Congenital deafness is often undetected, and perhaps unacknowledged, until a much later age than in industrialized societies. Alternatively, a patient may seek help for a fever or illness that causes deafness, but audiology and other specialized services are rarely part of the usual follow-up. For Indians who live on reservations, intervention and remediation services are sparse, so families frequently have limited medical assistance, speech and language training, or education about hearing impairments.

Generalizing cultural characteristics to frame therapeutic interventions is inherently problematic for both American Indian and Deaf populations. The wide variation of cultural characteristics among Indian populations has been clearly demonstrated. Yet, although there are clear differences among American Indian tribes, clans, and pueblos (Richardson, 1981; Sage, 1991), there also are a number of cultural characteristics that appear to be common to many of the groups (Joe & Miller, 1987; Lazarus, 1982; Lowrey, 1983). Many of these particular American Indian values differ significantly from Anglo values. In a similar fashion, many Deaf cultural characteristics differ from hearing Anglo cultural characteristics.

There is also a great heterogeneity within the Deaf population. Deaf individuals vary relative to etiology, age of onset, degree of loss, first language, hearing status of parents, and educational background, not to mention individual personalities and the degree to which they identify themselves as culturally Deaf. Joseph Brown, in the *Spiritual Legacy of the American Indian* (1982), warns that "to ignore such diversity of origin, place, language, and resulting cultural forms, as is so often done under a plethora of stereotypes, is to do great disservice to the American Indian peoples and their history" (xi). Yet he also notes the pan-Indian concept, stating that recent political/social/religious practices and ceremonies have resulted in cross-participation and a blending of practices. As Aramburo (1989) found with Black Deaf individuals and Page (1993) found with Hispanic Deaf individuals, a multicultural identity may dominate rather than a primary ethnic or primary Deaf identity. For example, the Deaf Indians in an art therapy group frequently shifted their identification between their Deaf and tribal cultures. And, although their deafness was always important, it was often not the primary cultural identity (Eldredge & Carrigan, 1992).

This blending of cultural practices among American Indians who are Deaf typically starts in the residential deaf schools that most Indian children attend, schools which are often miles away from their homes. Although there has been a recent interest in establishing a greater degree of cultural awareness within the schools for the Deaf, the children are typically known as "Indian" rather than by their tribal affiliations. In some schools the use of a school "pow wow" is established where all students can participate in learning more about the various practices. These events may include lectures, demonstrations of dances, crafts, storytelling, and the opportunity to try different foods. There is little emphasis, however, placed on establishing specific ceremonies or even awareness of ceremonies that are unique to each tribe that may be represented. Even so, a benefit of such grouping is that it creates opportunities to learn from other Deaf Indian individuals and to develop a group consciousness that reduces isolation. It also allows greater socialization within the Deaf school environment, which allows students to develop strong communication bonds with other Deaf people.

Assessing Acculturation Patterns

American Indians who are Deaf seldom use psychotherapeutic services, and this lack of involvement may be tied to both communication and cultural issues (Backenroth, 1992; Freedman, 1994). Therapists skilled in working with Indian groups are not typically trained in the cultural and psychosocial aspects of deafness, nor in the use of American Sign Language (ASL). Professionals, such as rehabilitation counselors, who work with the deaf community may be trained in ASL but typically lack the understanding of Indian cultures necessary to make culturally appropriate interventions. Other critical factors in providing culturally appropriate psychotherapy is the careful assessment of cultural identity and its dynamics for each client, and the use of psychotherapeutic strategies that are consistent with that identity (Glickman & Carey, 1993; Lee et al., 1992).

> Knowledge of and respect for an Indian worldview and value system—which varies according to the client's tribe, level of acculturation, and other personal characteristics—is fundamental not only for creating the trusting counselor-client relationship vital to the helping process but also for defining the counseling style or approach most appropriate for each client. (LaFromboise et al., 1990, p. 628)

To assess a client's acculturation patterns,[2] it may be important to explore the following areas:

1. *Languages spoken.* One of the primary ways to assess clients' involvement in their native culture is whether or not they are able to speak their tribal language. However, monolingualism vs. bilingualism is a much more complex issue when working with American Indians who are Deaf. Many deaf individuals may use only ASL because they have been raised away from home and are therefore unable to develop their tribal languages. It is important to keep in mind that assessing the individual alone may be possible only within the urban environment, because it is almost a requirement to include the family or other tribal groups if working on the reservation. Language may become an issue in working with a family whose elders either do not know English or choose not to use English around the Anglo therapist.
2. *Names.* While Indian children often have given names that are not culture specific, such as Mary, John, Elmo, Michele, and so on, they also have ceremonial names different from the birth name. The ceremonial name given to an American Indian is a source of information regarding their acculturation pattern. However, American Indians who are Deaf may not have participated in some of the ceremonies in which they are given an "Indian name" (Lone Wolf, 1996; Thomason, 1991). Therefore, the client's having been given or not given an Indian name gives the therapist much information in terms of the client's involvement in tribal customs.
3. *Place of residence.* The place of residence—not only where the client resides within the urban setting, but also where the family is from—is certainly important. It can give valuable information as to the client's proximity to a town compared to relative isolation from the rest of the community. In urban areas there tends to be more homogeneity, deculturation, and assimilation in the majority culture than in the rural, reservation setting.

2. Acculturation has been defined by Thompson, Walker, and Silk-Walker as "deculturation (the loss of traditional ways) and reculturation (the assumption of the ways of the majority)" (1992, p. 190).

4. *Involvement with extended family.* Among American Indian groups, family is considered to be of primary importance in the social structure. However, American Indians who are Deaf may have limited ties to their family of origin because the practice of sending Deaf individuals to a residential school, often miles away from their home. Moreover, the degree of communication difficulty inherent in their involvement with their families may have encouraged them to develop stronger ties within the Deaf community. These issues can be discussed openly with Deaf individuals who may come in for psychotherapy.

5. *Trips to the extended family.* Often Deaf American Indians who live in urban settings yearn for their tribal practices and their native "identity" (Eldredge and Hammond-McCreery, 1994). One way to assess clients' level of acculturation, therefore, is to ask how often and when they return to visit their families.

6. *Employment and work practices.* There are limited vocational opportunities for American Indians who live on the reservations. The opportunities for Deaf people on reservations are even more limited because of communication issues and all of the other social and political practices that create underemployment and unemployment in the general Deaf community. Consequently, the relative value of work and employment can be quite different from that in Anglo communities (Eldredge, 1993), and therefore needs to be interpreted differently. For example, a Deaf American Indian who has had very limited work history with the exception of service employment or helping with the family should not be perceived as lacking motivation or skills. Rather, the employment can be viewed as an effort by the individual to participate in and give back to the community. The type of employment therefore gives a view of the acculturation pattern.

7. *Involvement in spiritual activities.* Assessing the individual's involvement in church or spiritual activities can help define acculturation. Religious practices may include involvement in Christian or Jewish settings, the Native American Church, Indian ceremonies, expressions of traditional beliefs, or a combination of practices.

8. *Food.* The food individuals choose to eat is highly representative of their acculturation pattern, whether they choose traditional dishes or are more eclectic in their taste.

9. *Degree of contact with public institutions.* Although other traditional American Indians may not be involved in larger social or political systems established in Anglo culture, American Indians who are Deaf typically have had a number of contacts with these institutions. If they have attended a school for the deaf, they have not only been involved with the educational system, but also have very likely been referred to audiologists, counselors, speech pathologists, otologists, or other occupational or physical therapists. The individual's perception of these professional involvements is a useful part of assessing acculturation.

It is important to use an awareness of cultural characteristics as a basis for thought and dialogue as opposed to a basis for intervention. Often, the values and cultural practices of Deaf culture conflict with those of the dominant hearing culture, as well as with Indian cultures. Because of these cultural incompatibilities, and the fact that at times the Deaf Indian client may exhibit traits of all three cultures, the evaluation of acculturation patterns is not only an important initial goal but a critical ongoing task as the psychotherapeutic relationship develops.

One mistake that therapists often make when working cross-culturally is assuming clients consciously recognize that behavior patterns or individual responses are a mark of their culture. However, this is often not the case (Thompson et al., 1993), particularly when working with Deaf clientele, because their families may not be able to communicate adequately with them.

* * *

> When I worked with B.C., a Hopi woman whose mother died during the course of the psychotherapy, she described the family's burial rituals and other ways in which they honored her mother.[3] I asked if the practices were a part of her culture, whether other Hopi families performed the same rituals. B.C. responded, "I don't know if it is cultural or not, I just know that it is the way my family has always done it." Further discussion revealed that these practices were widely shared among her mesa community.

Clients need to be aware of their culture to know when an issue is cross-cultural or when their therapists are behaving in ways that are cultural, as opposed to acting with bad manners. Some clients may respond with anxiety or shame if the therapist shares cultural knowledge about the client's culture, so although sensitivity here is very important, "the advantage of learning about the culture far outweighs this occasional reaction." (Thompson et al., 1993, p. 205). However, Makabe (1996) also cautions that "it is not [the therapist's] place to teach [the client's] culture" (1996, unpublished) because our knowledge is still likely to be superficial and static. Asking questions is probably safer and more respectful.

Spiritual and Cultural Characteristics

It is important to consider the interpretation, sometimes spiritual, that each person gives to the concept of their deafness and "Indian-ness." For example, personnel of the University of Arizona Native American Rehabilitation Research and Training Center conducted extensive interviews and reviews of the literature concerning American Indian perspectives on disability (Joe & Miller, 1987; Locust, 1985). They found that among many Indian groups, the concept of a disability was often defined only as a difference in the individual's ability to contribute to society. In other words, although the physical condition might be characterized descriptively, for example, in Navajo language, *"diné doo da' diits'a'ígíí dóó doo yadaati'ígíí,"* or "people who do not hear or speak," no handicap is implied. Therefore, if a deaf person could fulfill a contributing role in the society as a weaver, shepherd, or in some cases as a medicine man or woman, or diagnostician, he or she is not disabled. These individuals may be disabled only within the wider societal context, such as a school for the deaf or, more pointedly, in the rehabilitation or mental health system.

However, contrary to research findings that people with disabilities are fully accepted by their tribes, conflicting information is vividly recounted by Deaf American Indian individuals and their families, indicating that people with disabilities may in fact be less accepted than was previously reported (Eldredge and Hammond-McCreery, 1994). Deaf American Indian respondents report feeling left out within their families, excluded from important ceremonies, ashamed at being "exiled" to the Deaf school, and sad and frustrated that their parents do not sign; they also reported experiences of being beaten up by White peers at school.

3. Names and identifying information of clients presented in this chapter have been changed to protect clients' confidentiality.

In almost all instances when I have worked with American Indians who are Deaf, two different descriptions of the cause of their deafness have emerged: a cultural interpretation and a Western medical interpretation.

* * *

> One woman believed that her deafness was caused by her mother having seen an owl during her pregnancy. The owl is a powerful animal, an evil omen. The Western medical interpretation associated her condition with a high fever and infection shortly after birth (that in her view also could have been a sequela to having witnessed the owl).

* * *

> A young Navajo man said that his deafness resulted from his father having fought in World War II in Germany and being exposed to so many White people, in addition to contact with the dead. The Western medical interpretation was that the deafness was a result of maternal rubella, or German measles.

* * *

> Another woman believed her deafness to be the result of her mother overhearing violent fights between her grandparents. Her mother was so concerned that her daughter would be harmed by overhearing these fights, that the daughter became deaf as a way to protect herself. In her case, the medical documentation identified the cause of deafness as "unknown" (still the most common etiology).

IDENTIFYING CULTURAL IDENTITIES

Despite the finding that about 40% of all children with hearing impairments are from cultural minority groups (Schildroth & Hotto, 1996), there is a striking lack of research done on these populations. Existing studies indicate prejudicial attitudes within the Anglo Deaf community toward Deaf people who are not white (Anderson & Bowe, 1972; Aramburo, 1989; Jones, 1985; Lane et al., 1996). Studies also indicate dismal achievement and employment statistics within the non-White Deaf community (Anderson & Bowe, 1972). There is also limited research on the ethnic identification or primary acculturation pattern found among Deaf individuals who are members of an ethnic minority group. Aramburo (1989) found that minority group members may identify initially with their ethnicity because skin color or other physical characteristics are immediately perceived by others, as compared to deafness, which is invisible. Contradictory anecdotal evidence suggests that for other Deaf ethnic minority members their primary identity and acculturation is with the Deaf community, perhaps because of the ease of communication with other Deaf people through ASL.

A research study conducted in Arizona (Eldredge & Hammond-McCreery, 1994) clarified this issue among American Indians who are Deaf. Through interviews both on the reservation and in urban environments, a striking pattern became clear. American Indian Deaf individuals who resided in the city identified their tribal affiliation as the most important, whereas the individuals on the reservation identified their deafness as being most important. This observation is noteworthy in that the individuals on the reservation tended to be isolated and had few interactions, if any, with the Deaf community or with other Deaf individuals; individuals who lived in the city had few, if any, affiliations with tribal practices (with the exception of a group that gathered periodically to have a "sweat" ceremony). One possible interpretation for this finding is that people perceive their primary identity in terms of what is missing.

Once again, however, it is important to avoid rigid expectations on the basis of cultural study. The process of ethnographic interviewing suggests that hypotheses are developed after the fact of the interview rather than imposing a hypothesis before the study starts. The therapist needs to accept that certain conclusions of the client may be different from those of the therapist, but both can work together to find areas of commonality.

Cultural Competency with Deaf American Indians

Our psychotherapeutic profession has moved beyond the stage when it was enough to have awareness of our own or other cultures. We must apply cultural sensitivity and avoid using techniques that may be class- and culture-bound (Darou, 1987; Sue & Sue, 1977, 1981). Otherwise, according to Usher, "Even if the treatment goals transcend cultural differences, the techniques themselves may be a form of cultural insensitivity and oppression, resulting in client alienation, early termination, and an overall lack of counseling effectiveness (1989, p. 62).

American Indians who come in for psychotherapy will often be unfamiliar with the psychotherapeutic process itself. If they are traditional in their practices, they may have been accustomed to going to spiritual healers who diagnose and prescribe without asking any personal questions (Thomason, 1991). According to Thomason, directness from the therapist who is working cross-culturally is virtually impossible because of lack of cultural intimacy. Therefore, he suggests that in order to do cross-cultural psychotherapy successfully, even after having studied a number of different American Indian cultures, it is important to get an advisor who can help the therapist decide when to refer and also to help assess or predict what expectations the client might bring to the setting. In some ways, it is better to create a context in the psychotherapeutic setting for asking questions of the client and then serving as a catalyst to help him or her determine the appropriate path or decision. This process is not dissimilar from what happens in "good" therapy. The philosophical standpoint should be that the individual client is the expert because the therapist's expertise is limited by the therapist's parameters of knowledge. The American Indian client who comes into the counseling setting may not be asking "What should I do?" but rather "What should I know . . . and where can I go to find it out?" The therapist should be the guide for the last part of that question.

The problem of dual relationships also needs to be addressed (Smith, 1990). In many cases, the therapist will need to participate in social or ceremonial aspects of the community in addition to providing counseling services. This is particularly true in working with American Indians who are Deaf. Clarifying what will be discussed in the therapy session and asking how your clients prefer that you interact with them if you meet in the community is a necessary first step.

For the therapist, the challenge is to mediate the interpersonal stress, the issues that the client brings to the psychotherapeutic setting that may conflict with our own values, as well as the intrapersonal stress arising from conflicts that may occur between members of the client's community. An American Indian Deaf individual may come to the counseling session for a specific problem. He or she may not fully voice that problem, and when attempts are made to get him or her to identify the issue at hand, the client may make comments that appear to be off the point. Attempts to elicit feelings and even background to the problem may result in the client becoming frustrated and upset. A therapist may try other tactics to focus on the problem and the client may continue to get upset, perhaps voicing concern that psychotherapy will not be productive for him or her.

This type of behavior in the initial interview could be misinterpreted to mean that the client does not want to take responsibility, that he or she is being evasive and not coming to the point, hiding something, or is out of touch with his or her feelings and may have underlying hostility or aggressiveness. In essence, the therapist's expectations in approaching this session violate the expectations of many Indian cultures. There is a lack of directness in these cultures, where meaning is derived from the context. Frequently, when I have had meetings with family members, particularly outside of the office or in nonurban settings, many seemingly unrelated issues were discussed before directly addressing any type of a problem. In some cases the problem was never discussed until the very end. Once, when I was consulting the medicine man of one tribe in order to obtain guidance and make sure I was not violating any of the expectations of the elders or community, the conversation centered around everything from the weather to sports, to family histories. At the end of the hour, without my even asking any direct question, the Medicine Man turned to me and said, "What you're doing is important." That was the end of the interview.

Assessing and Responding to the Multicultural Identity

An article on culturally affirmative counseling with Deaf American Indians reviewed Deaf and Indian cultural characteristics as they may apply to the counseling setting (Eldredge, 1993). Excerpts from that article, particularly the recommendations for using cultural concepts to work with American Indian Deaf clientele, are reiterated in this section. For comparison, table 1 presents a cross-cultural comparison of various Indian, Anglo, and Deaf characteristics.

ORIENTATION TO TIME

Because of the emphasis on the present time among American Indians (Everett et al., 1983; Katz, 1981; Richardson, 1981; Sweezy 1972) and also among Deaf individuals (Padden & Humphries, 1988), doing personal planning for the future and developing a long-term treatment or rehabilitation plan might be difficult or even viewed skeptically. In addition, American Indian Deaf clientele may not initially come to the appointment on time, though they are typically willing to accommodate to the schedule of the therapist. However, they may also want to continue talking long after the typical "fifty-minute hour" is spent. One recommendation is to schedule appointments with these individuals later in the day so that some flexibility can be maintained.

For example, one woman was clearly startled and disoriented by my reminders that the hour was almost over, and she slowly educated me about the importance of the story over the time pressure. We negotiated a schedule to set the appointments later in the afternoon but with an understanding that there would be some time limits. Coming late and wanting to stay longer were not necessarily indicative of resistance or manipulation, but rather an expression of cultural differences.

Table 1. Cultural Characteristics

American Indian	Anglo	Deaf
Present-oriented	Future-oriented	Past-or present-oriented
Group emphasis	Individual emphasis	Group/individual emphasis
Respect for age	Emphasis on youth	Emphasis on success
Family-oriented	Self-oriented	Community-oriented
Lack of time consciousness	Extreme time consciousness	Relationships more important than time
Learn through legends	Learn through school	Learn through stories
Work for a purpose	Work for retirement or to maintain lifestyle	Work for money
Land/nature-oriented	Possession-oriented	People-oriented
Personal information is private	Some personal information is private	Personal information is public
Touch and eye contact are avoided by acquaintances	Touch and eye contact not commonly used by acquaintances	Touch and eye contact are commonly used even among acquaintances

Note: From Bellah, et al., 1985; Carlson, 1975; Darou, 1987; Everett et al., 1983; Glickman, 1983; Good & Good, 1986; Hall, 1986; Hardaway, 1984; Henrich et al., 1990; Herring, 1990; Herring & Meggert, 1994; Joe & Miller, 1987; Katz, 1981; Lazarus, 1982; Lowrey, 1983; Padden & Humphries, 1988; Richardson, 1981; Rutherford, 1988; U. S. Department of Health and Human Services, 1980.

Also, in both Deaf and American Indian cultures, more emphasis is placed on people and relationships rather than on the time clock (Katz, 1981; Padden & Humphries, 1988). As a result, making it to work or the counseling appointment on time may be less important than completing a conversation with friends.

Within Deaf and American Indian cultures, the past is important as a teacher for the present, usually in relation to experiences of individuals. Stories that are told "are carriers of history, ways of repeating and reformulating the past for the present" (Padden & Humphries, 1988, p. 38). Legends are also the teachers for American Indian people; therefore, the use of storytelling and metaphor is a good counseling tool to use (Herring & Meggert, 1994). For example, a story about another client with a similar problem is one way to develop insight and problem-solving skills by objectifying the problem (Pedersen, 1977).

ORIENTATION TO SPACE

It is common among most American Indian groups to value life in harmony with nature. Many groups see pain, disease, and disability as a consequence of disharmony (Locust, 1985; Olson & Wilson, 1984). American Indian parents frequently direct children's attention outward toward the land, the sky, the tribe and its past, its customs and traditions. Many clients often want to meet outside, the preference representing more than an idiosyncratic choice.

In the Deaf community, at least in an industrialized society, spatial orientation tends toward urban settings and buildings. Because of the low incidence factor, deaf people are often geographically isolated from one another. At least 90–95% (Lane et al., 1996) of all deaf people are born of hearing parents; the majority are deaf from no known cause and they are usually the only deaf person in the family. As a result, the "deaf school," or residential state school for people who are deaf, usually located in the city, becomes the cultural center (Padden, 1980) where children learn ASL and Deaf traditions from other children. After graduation from the school, Deaf people tend to stay in the same area and build a tight community with their friends (Padden & Humphries, 1988). Orientation is to the Deaf club (Bragg & Bergman, 1981), the Deaf community center, and their homes; in other words, the places where Deaf people gather and share their lives.

Two clients frequently missed appointments to attend events that were considered more valuable culturally than their jobs or appointments with a counselor. Alonso would miss appointments to attend pow wows, and Ben regularly canceled appointments to attend the sports events involving the Deaf school. Once again, interpretation of this behavior as simply irresponsible or evasive was incorrect. In both cases, we discussed the cultural differences in expectation and eventually both men agreed to let me know in advance before missing an appointment.

Orientation to Family and Social Groups

Among writers making observations about diverse American Indian groups, an almost universal characteristic is that they tend to be group- and family-oriented rather than individual-oriented (Everett et al., 1983; Joe & Miller, 1987; Locust, 1985; U.S. Department of Health and Human Services, 1980). Most American Indian groups, because of the emphasis on the group and the importance of familial relationships, venerate elders for their wisdom and experience (Everett et al., 1983). Elders often serve a function similar to an advisor.

These values contrast with those of the dominant culture, which may place emphasis on individual achievement and competition. To some extent the emphasis on the family may also conflict with the values of the Deaf culture because most Deaf people have hearing parents who never learn to fully communicate with their children. It is common for Deaf people to develop their closest relationships within the Deaf community, where they can communicate freely and easily. In psychotherapy, a functional application of the dominant society's values is to encourage independence from the group and family of origin, and to discourage so-called co-dependence and enmeshment. Clients are encouraged to develop an internal locus of control and to take responsibility for themselves. These practices may, in fact, represent a form of cultural oppression for an individual who is culturally Deaf and Indian.

* * *

> When Mary discussed her concerns about her husband's drinking, she said she had told him he could have two beers each day and could start drinking at six each night; he was also to begin looking for work each morning and not spend the day at home. When I naively asked about her willingness to take responsibility for his behavior, she responded, "Well, it's my house." She was operating within her Hopi expectations of behavior: that it was her house, while the man's role was to earn money for the family to live.

In the psychotherapeutic relationship, the practitioner needs to be open to allowing the client to consult elders, tribal healers, or trusted friends. Alonso was adamant that he wanted me to work with a tribal healer, and on numerous occasions I have sought advice from elders. Mary frequently brought other family members to the sessions, and Ben sometimes asked a close Deaf friend to participate. This group approach or individual consultation with healers and elders was usually beneficial and was also welcomed by the tribe.

Another difference between Anglo and American Indian communities is that decision making may take much longer (Everett et al., 1983), so the usual expectations for client "progress toward goals" may need to be readjusted. Holland, Lee, and Lee, writing about providing services to Navajo individuals on the reservation, state, "If you must have a decision on an important matter, expect to wait for a few days, weeks, or months. The family will want to discuss a decision with the clan (extended family) before giving a final response" (1983, p. 121).

CONVENTIONS FOR GREETINGS AND INTRODUCTIONS

It is common for tribal members to introduce themselves by establishing their identity within the fabric of their families—that is, to disclose their lineage, clans, tribes, or pueblos. This practice gives each individual roots and a secure place in the larger group.

Among Deaf individuals, a similar practice is followed for introductions, except that the relevant information usually contains their full name, the city or state they are from (Padden, 1980), the name of the school attended (usually residential), and if their parents are Deaf (Padden & Humphries, 1988). The introductions serve a similar function of establishing an identity within the culture and providing an opportunity for members to share news about acquaintances they might have in common. In contrast, introductions among many hearing Anglo individuals may be more cursory, perhaps with only first names being exchanged. At most, individuals will exhange a brief statement pertaining to the meeting or socioeconomic status, such as, "I'm a friend of Bill's from Vermont," or "I teach biology at Cholla High School."

Both Indian and Deaf clients may be confused by the latter type of introduction and interpret it as rude or disengaged. And, in fact, all of the Deaf Indian clients with whom I have worked have asked for more personal information than my Anglo and hearing clients. Of particular concern to clients has been my background: where I grew up, how long I worked in the field, how I learned ASL, how and why I first became involved in working with Deaf and/or Indian people. To be sure, the questions of background or involvement in the field were important at some point in the therapeutic process to establish trust and credibility. Rather than deflecting the question it has been more helpful to discuss these points early in the relationship.

ATTITUDES TOWARD DISCLOSURE OF PERSONAL INFORMATION

According to Locust (1985), among many Indian groups, personal information is considered private, and "Indians are reluctant to discuss such personal matters . . . such as beliefs, philosophies, religions . . . with anyone, particularly non-Indians" (p. 19). Speaking about problems may violate tribal customs and could possibly result in retaliation from other members.

By contrast, among Deaf individuals, most information is public and open. Marital concerns, salary amounts, and physical characteristics are but a few of the topics that are openly addressed. The visible nature of sign language makes secrets hard to keep. At a community lecture, M. J. Bienvenu (1991) discussed the way that hearing people close doors to offices for routine privacy. In the Deaf culture, however, this practice is more likely indicative of secrecy. Also, it is common for Deaf people to notice weight changes and scars. Often "name signs" are assigned on the basis of a physical characteristic such as height, hairstyle, big ears, or buck teeth. This type of name sign, although intended to be descriptive (Supalla, 1990), often causes hearing people some discomfort.

A non-Indian hearing therapist may feel uncomfortable with both Indian and Deaf behaviors because in Anglo culture only select information is public and openly discussed (at least with the person directly). This value may present the greatest challenge to a therapist because of the extreme difficulty in determining how to question or explore a problem. An Indian client may find the process of questioning in therapy intensely personal and threatening (Lujan & Dobkins, 1978), whereas the Deaf client may become skeptical or alienated if topics are not addressed directly. In other instances, however, more initial reticence may be found. Mary told her story in layers over about a six-week period. She responded readily to direct questions, but as time passed, she would add details that were clearly more intimate. Once trust was established, she no longer seemed vulnerable in disclosure. Alonso, however, did not want questions but responded more fully to paraphrase and interpretation. In general, however, I have found that Deaf American Indians gravitate toward the Deaf customs regarding disclosure, perhaps as a result of the socialization process in the Deaf school and the lack of ethnic culture role models.

DIFFERENCES IN EYE CONTACT AND TOUCHING

Another cultural characteristic that may be challenging for therapists is the conflict involving the use of touch and eye contact in Indian and Deaf cultures. Among many tribes, touch and eye contact are avoided by acquaintances. Everett, Proctor, and Cartmell (1983) recount the danger of a counselor insisting on eye contact as part of a behavioral program when this objective conflicts with the Navajo creation myth called "He-Who-Kills-With-His-Eyes." Eye contact was in clear violation of the Navajo cultural mode of conduct. Conversely, avoidance of eye contact is often considered a sign of respect, particularly respect of elders and authority figures. In a similar fashion, a firm handshake might be considered a sign of aggression and disrespect (Everett et al., 1983).

In the Deaf community, however, touch is common as a way of getting someone's attention and is a warm gesture. Hand-shaking is not a required part of a greeting—instead, new acquaintances may sign "nice to meet you"—although hugging is common among friends or closer acquaintances. Eye contact, on the other hand, is always important, clearly because of the need to "see" the communication. The "speaker" may look away briefly, but the "receiver" maintains steady eye contact with the speaker (as opposed to looking at the hands signing).

Therapists may find it helpful at first to mirror the eye contact behavior of the client, although because of the "authority" inherent in the professional role, younger clients may expect the therapist to have more direct eye contact. But all of the Deaf American Indian people I have worked with have shown the Deaf cultural preference for eye contact, so this has not been an issue as discussed in the literature.

With regard to touch, there continues to be widespread debate about this issue within the psychotherapeutic profession (Kertay & Reviere, 1993). Touch may be more acceptable among the Deaf community, and to some extent among hearing groups, a "pat on the back or head, or a hug as a friendly behavior . . . may facilitate rapport, [but] these same behaviors may be interpreted by an Indian client as inappropriate, aggressive, and disrespectful" (Everett et al., 1983, p. 593). It may be wise to convey friendliness and acceptance, but initially excluding touch as a way to develop rapport. For example, after a trusting relationship was established with Mary, she frequently requested a hug. The men, however, never initiated nor requested any physical touch. There may also be gender factors that should be considered as well.

ORIENTATION TO WORK AND EMPLOYMENT

There are differences between cultures originating from their views of the purpose of working (Eldredge, 1993). Katz (1981) identifies a potential conflict for Anglo therapists because of the value Indian individuals may place on work as it relates to the practice of sharing earnings; that is, a client may not be motivated to get up every morning and go to work, because friends and relatives use the earnings. Other individuals may be willing to share earnings without first paying rent, bills, which may be seen from the Anglo perspective as showing a lack of responsibility. Another potential source of conflict for Anglo therapists is the Indian client who, after being trained for a vocation in the city, perhaps at great expense, may return without warning to the reservation to assume an entirely different role in the tribe. Returning home to live with the family should not necessarily be considered enmeshment or dependency.

Among Deaf individuals, because most working environments are filled with hearing people and the Deaf person is comparatively isolated in terms of communication, work does not usually have the Anglo significance of fulfillment or emotional gratification. Work, rather, provides money, which can be used to buy things or support the family.

* * *

> Alicia is Tohono O'odham. After graduating from high school, she got her first job and routinely spent much of her paycheck to pay for activities for herself and friends who were not working. Her Vocational Rehabilitation Counselor thought she was being irresponsible and that she needed money management courses. In actuality, however, she was responding consistently with her culture(s).

Anglo therapists may become frustrated by the relative lack of significance placed on working by the Indian and Deaf client. At different points in the psychotherapy most of the Deaf American Indian clients have valued tribal ceremonies or their high school's sports events over showing up for work. All of these individuals experienced the pull of the tribe in relation to their sense of personal value. So, while it may be helpful to discuss with each client the potential consequences of and majority perception toward leaving work, it is important not to interpret their behavior as being disloyal or unmotivated, but rather as being consistent with their cultural values.

CREATING A CULTURALLY RESPONSIVE ENVIRONMENT

Given the history of oppression of Indian and Deaf individuals over the last several hundred years, it is tempting to assume that the psychopathology within this population results from alienation from the tribal culture, stigmatization, or stereotyping from the dominant hearing culture, sometimes known as postcolonization stress disorder (Locust, 1977). Research conducted with American Indian groups has identified high rates of alcoholism, depression, and suicide (Thompson, Walker & Walker, 1993). In a similar fashion, in their review of the incidence of psychopathology among the Deaf, Lane, Hoffmeister, and Bahan (1996) found that the scientific literature has historically ascribed various pathological labels to Deaf individuals. They concluded that these labels are typically a product of inappropriate research methods, researcher bias, or a lack of understanding of Deaf cultural characteristics. More recent research into the mental health functioning of deaf individuals, using ASL and more appropriate assessment methods, has clarified that the degree, incidence, and range of mental illness and psychopathology among the Deaf community is roughly consistent with that of the hearing communities. Without an understanding of linguistic and cultural issues—including facets of the languages, mores, and values—hearing people may evaluate behavior as pathological when it is in fact quite consistent with that culture.

The DSM-IV (1994) has attempted to address the issue of culturally influenced behaviors by discussing "Culture Bound Syndromes." Those syndromes ascribed to American Indian populations include "*ii ch'aa* (among the Navajo): a dissociative episode characterized by a period of brooding followed by an outburst of violent, aggressive, or homicidal behavior directed at people and objects" (p. 845) and "ghost sickness: A preoccupation with death and the deceased . . . frequently observed among members of many American Indian tribes. . . . [S]ymptoms . . . attributed to ghost sickness [include] bad dreams, weakness, feelings of danger, loss of appetite, fainting, dizziness, fear anxiety, hallucinations, loss of consciousness, confusion, feelings of futility, and a sense of suffocation" (p. 846).

However, there are many more idiosyncratic—though not necessarily pathological—behaviors prevalent among American Indian groups that are not covered by the diagnostic categories presented in the DSM-IV. In general, American Indian clientele who have come to therapy are typically referred by an agency, family member, or friend who has also been involved in counseling. The primary reason they are coming for therapy are for the usual types of problems that are common to most individuals. The role of the therapist is to use the cultural context to determine what is "normal" for the Indian or Deaf individual and what is "not normal." Furthermore, the role of the therapist is to decide when it is the cultural condition, as described in the culture bound syndrome, that is at the forefront of the therapeutic intervention, or when the culture is merely interacting with the problem at hand.

* * *

One young woman who was a member of the Yaqui tribe was hospitalized in a local mental hospital for suicidal ideation and an attempt. The staff psychiatrist at this hospital determined that she was depressed, primarily as a result of her inability to communicate adequately with her family. She had had a child before she was married and had given that child to her mother and older sister to raise. The child stayed on the reservation while she had moved to the city. The psychiatrist felt that this woman's inability to be an effective parent for her child and also her guilt over having given her child up contributed to the suicidal feelings. He also determined that the frustration of being deaf and having to communicate with the hearing society was so emotionally difficult and stressful that it brought out suicidal feelings. In addition, he determined that the stories this woman was telling of having been "witched" were psychotic, in that the woman had seen spirits and felt as though she had been cursed.

I subsequently interviewed this woman at the request of the hospital staff, because the psychiatrist did not know ASL and was using a mixture of written communication and a staff member at the hospital who could sign. During the interview, the woman indicated that she had been sexually abused as a child by one of her "uncles," and was beginning to experience some flashbacks and nightmares. She also was involved in a new relationship with a man who was using alcohol and drugs, was verbally abusive with her, and who was also having relationships with other women. In addition, money was tight and she felt as though she was barely making it financially. Regarding her child being raised by her mother and sister, this was a common practice among Yaqui women and for her it represented a very safe place for her child to be reared, particularly given the current instability of her own life at this time. The curse was also consistent with her cultural beliefs and was therefore not pathological.

Clearly, the treatment plan developed by the psychiatrist was based on preconceived notions and biases from a dominant hearing cultural perspective, as opposed to understanding aspects of American Indian and Deaf cultures. In this case, the deafness and Indian cultural attributes were secondary to the very real and significant stressors she was experiencing, in addition to the post-traumatic symptoms that were emerging associated with early abuse. As a result, the treatment plan that was eventually identified for this woman was quite different from the initial one.

Another comment regarding cultural attributes concerns the use of alcohol within this population. Although it is a common stereotype that all Indian groups are alcoholic or have problems with alcohol, this is clearly not the case. At the same time, however, one Anglo therapist working in the field misunderstood the use of peyote by the Native American Church as part of their religious ceremonies, thinking these ceremonies could also include alcohol. To my knowledge, alcohol is not considered a ceremonial substance among any of the Indian groups with whom I have worked.

Zitzow and Estes (1981) term the degree to which people identify with their ethnic heritage as "heritage consistency." Despite pressure from the dominant culture to conform to "majority" standards for behavior and thereby subjugate their Native heritage, most Indians have learned to survive by becoming bicultural in a functional sense.

CREATING A CULTURALLY RESPONSIVE ENVIRONMENT

1. Listen for opportunities to show desire to learn about American Indian and Deaf cultural traditions. Be willing to discuss openly what you have already studied about the culture(s). It may also be helpful to add a statement to the effect of "If I say something that seems strange or offensive, please tell me. . . . It may be my own culture that is showing."
2. Determine what importance cultural considerations may assume in ongoing care.
3. Design interventions that are sensitive to cultural value expectations for tribal, Deaf, and multicultural influences.
4. Frame interventions that consider the restoration of physical and spiritual harmony. Ask in the session, "What do you need to recover balance and harmony?"
5. Emphasize the client's internal ability to develop coping and problem-solving skills.
6. Allow for the involvement of tribal elders, extended family members, and community members when appropriate or requested.
7. Make efforts to understand the individual's concept of mental health or illness, and work within that definition.
8. Refer the client for tribal ceremonies, rituals, or consultation when appropriate.
9. Find a mentor or advisor and consult tribal healers for assistance in guiding your work.
10. Follow the code of ethics to assure all individuals of confidentiality. Allow the client to lead in deciding what information is to be shared and with whom.
11. Approach the therapeutic relationship humbly. Locust (1997) recommends the therapist keep these questions in mind to guide the process: "What am I here to learn? What am I here to teach?"

Figure 2. Cultural Responsiveness

Deaf people are also able to survive in the dominant culture by accommodating the majority societal norms and practices. With Deaf Indians, then, their survival may depend on their ability to become multicultural to some degree. This cultural fluency has implications for psychotherapy in light of recommendations from certain practitioners that therapists "go Native" or "go Deaf" when counseling cross-culturally. It has been my experience that such practices are likely to have a negative effect on the psychotherapeutic relationship. If an Anglo therapist attempts to use Native practices, such as burning herbs during psychotherapy, conducting rituals, building a sweat lodge, or wearing Native jewelry and clothing, it is likely that the Indian client will be offended or alienated by the practices. They will, perhaps, view these pseudo-Indian practices with distrust or disdain, which would be injurious to the psychotherapeutic relationship. It is also important to use caution with office furnishings. For example, pottery or art work that depicts owls would be very offensive to a number of tribes for whom this bird is a symbol of evil and has the power to harm.

Similar recommendations that therapists who are working with American Indian clients dress informally and that women therapists use subtle makeup may also be negatively perceived by the client. Littrell and Littrell (1983) conducted a study of Indian clients that included therapist dress as a variable in client perceptions of empathy, warmth, genuineness. The results indicated that clients who are bicultural may perceive such "dressing down" in a negative way. These clients, because of their ability to survive in two, or perhaps three, cultures are aware of Anglo values of professional dress and may feel insulted rather than comfortable (Trimble & Fleming, 1989). Some practical recommendations to help create a culturally responsive environment appear in figure 2.

Cultural characteristics and intervention as described in this chapter should be viewed as starting points to help the therapist become more sensitive to the influences of culture, to challenge internal expectations and behaviors, and to develop strategies that are effective with American Indians who are Deaf. The general principles of assessing acculturation patterns, identifying spiritual affiliations and definitions of mental health and harmony, evaluating the potential sources of conflict—both inter- and intrapersonal—that frame the psychotherapeutic intervention will help to guide the therapist so that a culturally responsive environment can be created.

References

American Psychiatric Association. (1994). *Diagnostic and statistical manual of mental disorders* (4th ed.). Washington, DC: American Psychiatric Association.

Anderson, G. B., & Bowe, F. G. (1972). Racism within the deaf community. *American Annals of the Deaf, 117,* 617–619.

Aramburo A. J. (1989). Sociolinguistic aspects of the Black deaf community. In C. Lucas (Ed.), *The sociolinguistics of the deaf community* (pp. 103–119). San Diego: Academic Press.

Atkinson, D. R. (1985, October). A meta-review of research on cross-cultural counseling and psychotherapy. *Journal of Multicultural Counseling and Development,* 138–153.

Atkinson, D. R., Morten, G., & Sue, D. W. (1989). *Counseling American minorities: A cross-cultural perspective* (3rd ed.). Dubuque, IA: William C. Brown.

Ayers, G. E. (1970). The White counselor in the Black community: Strategies for effecting attitude change. *Journal of Rehabilitation, 36,* 20–22.

Backenroth, G. A. M. (1992). Resources and shortcomings in deaf clients' social networks. *International Journal of Rehabilitation Research, 15,* 355–359.

Benesch, K. F., & Ponterotto, J. G. (1989). East and West: Transpersonal psychology and cross-cultural counseling. *Counseling and Values, 33,* 121–131.

Bellah, R. N., Madsen, R., Sullivan, W. M., Swidler, A., & Tipton, S. M. (1985). *Habits of the heart.* San Francisco, CA: Harper and Row.

Berkhofer, R. F. (1978). *White man's Indian.* New York: Alfred A. Knopf.

Bienvenu, M. J. (1991, March). *Oppression: Who, what, how, why?* Unpublished lecture sponsored by Deaf Empowerment Advocacy Focus (D.E.A.F.) Network, Tucson, AZ.

Bowe, F. G., Jr. (1974). Non-White deaf persons: Educational, psychological, and occupational considerations. *American Annals of the Deaf, 116,* 357–361.

Bragg, B., & Bergman, E. (1981). *Tales from a clubroom.* Washington, DC: Gallaudet University Press.

Brown, J. E. (1982). *The spiritual legacy of the American Indian.* New York: Crossroad.

Burn, D. (1992). Ethical implications in cross-cultural counseling and training. *Journal of Counseling & Development, 70,* 578–583.

Carter, R. T. (1991). Cultural values: A review of empirical research and implications for counseling. *Journal of Counseling & Development, 70,* 164–173.

Choca, P. (1996, November). Implications for cross-cultural work. An unpublished lecture presented at the Cultural Awareness for Addictions Treatment training workshop for Arizona Biodyne, Inc., Phoenix, AZ.

Cross, W. E. (1991). *Shades of black: Diversity in African-American identity.* Philadelphia: Temple University Press.

Cumming, C. E., & Rodda, M. (1988). Advocacy, prejudice, and role modeling in the deaf community. *The Journal of Social Psychology, 129* (1), 5–12.

D'Andrea, M., Daniels, J., & Heck, R. (1991). Evaluating the impact of multicultural counseling training. *Journal of Counseling & Development, 70,* 143–150.

Darou, W. G. (1987). Counselling and the northern Native. *Canadian Journal of Counseling, 21* (1), 33–41.

Davis, J., & Supalla, S. (1991, October). *A sociolinguistic description of sign language use among the Navajo.* Paper presented at New Ways of Analyzing Variation in English (NWAVE 20), Georgetown University, Washington, DC.

Dix, C. (1996, November). African Americans. An unpublished lecture presented at the Cultural Awareness for Addictions Treatment training workshop for Arizona Biodyne, Inc., Phoenix, AZ.

Driver, H. E., (1969). *Indians of North America* (rev. ed.). Chicago: University of Chicago Press.

Eldredge, N. (1993). Culturally affirmative counseling with American Indians who are deaf. *Journal of the American Deafness and Rehabilitation Association, 26* (4), 1–18.

Eldredge N., & Carrigan, J. (1992). Where do my kindred dwell? . . . Using art and storytelling to understand the transition of young Indian men who are deaf. *The Arts in Psychotherapy, 19,* 29–38.

Eldredge, N., & Hammond, S. A. (1992, April/May). Distant visions: Two studies of deafness and Navajo traditional life. *Hearing Health: The Voice on Hearing Issues,* 10–13.

Eldredge, N., & Hammond-McCreery, S. A. (1994) *Spiritual and cultural beliefs among Navajo deaf individuals.* Unpublished manuscript.

Everett, F., Proctor, N., & Cartmell, B. (1983). Providing psychological services to American Indian children and families. *Professional Psychology: Research and Practice, 14* (5), 588–603.

Ferreira, L. O. (1975). Counseling Native American children. *Contemporary Education, 46* (4), 305–306.

Fischgrund, J. E., Cohen, O. P., & Clarkson, R. L. (1987). Hearing-impaired children in Black and Hispanic families. *Volta Review, 89* (5), 59–67.

Frank, L. W. (1986). *American Indians and vocational rehabilitation: A case review study of former clients.* Paper presented at the National Research Symposium on Native American Rehabilitation, Scottsdale, AZ, 9–12 September.

Freedman, Paul. (1994). Counseling with deaf clients: The need for culturally and linguistically sensitive interventions. *Journal of American Deafness and Rehabilitation Association, 27* (4), 16–27.

Glickman, N. (1983). A cross-cultural view of counseling with deaf clients. *Journal of Rehabilitation of the Deaf, 16* (3), 4–14.

Glickman, N. S., & Carey, J. C. (1993). Measuring Deaf cultural identities: A preliminary investigation. *Rehabilitation Psychology, 38* (4), 275–283.

Goldstein, G. S. (1974). The model dormitory. *Psychiatric Annals, 4,* 85–92.

Good, B. J., & Good, M. D. (1986). The cultural context of diagnosis and therapy: A view from medical anthropology. In M. R. Miranda & H. H. L. Kitano (Eds.), *Mental health research and practice in minority communities: Development of culturally sensitive training programs* (pp. 1–27). Rockville, MD: National Institute of Mental Health.

Haley, T. J., & Dowd, E. T. (1988). Responses of deaf adolescents to differences in counselor method of communication and disability status. *Journal of Counseling Psychology, 35* (3), 258–262.

Hall, R. L. (1986). Alcohol treatment in American Indian populations: An indigenous treatment modality compared with traditional approaches. In T. F. Baber (Ed.), *Alcohol and culture: Comparative perspectives from Europe and America* (pp. 168–177). New York: The New York Academy of Sciences.

Hammond, S. A., & Meiners, L. H. (1993). American Indian deaf children and youth. In K. M. Christensen & G. L. Delgado (Eds.), *Multicultural issues in deafness* (pp. 143–166). White Plains, NY: Longman.

Hanson, W. D., & Eisenbise, M. D. (1982). *Social work methods of intervention with American Indians.* San Francisco: San Francisco State University.

Hardaway, B .D. (1984). *Explorations into a community and its culture.* Paper presented at the Eastern Communication Association, Philadelphia, PA.

Harvey, M. A. (1993). Cross cultural psychotherapy with deaf persons: A hearing, White, middle class, middle aged, non-gay, Jewish, male, therapist's perspective. *Journal of the American Deafness and Rehabilitation Association. 26* (4), 43–55.

Heinrich, R. K., Corbine, J. L., & Thomas, K. R. (1990). Counseling Native Americans. *Journal of Counseling and Development, 69,* 128–133.

Helms, J. E. (1993). *Black and White racial identity.* Westport, CT: Praeger.

Herring, R. D. (1989). The American Native family: Dissolution by coercion. *Journal of Multicultural Counseling and Development, 17,* 4–13.

———. (1990). Nonverbal communication: A necessary component of cross-cultural counseling. *Journal of Multicultural Counseling, 18,* 172–179.

Herring, R. D., & Meggert, S. S. (1994). The use of humor as a counselor strategy with Native American Indian children. *Elementary School Guidance & Counseling, 29,* 67–76.

Hoare, C. H. (1991). Psychosocial identity development and cultural others. *Journal of Counseling & Development, 70,* 45–53.

Holland, S. L., Lee, B., & Lee, J. (1983). Networking services to deaf individuals on the Navajo reservation. In W. P. McCrone, R. L. Beach, & F. R. Zieziula (Eds.), *Networking and Deafness: Proceedings of the national conference* (pp. 118–126). Silver Spring, MD: American Deafness and Rehabilitation Association.

Hughes, C. C. (1993). Culture in clinical psychiatry. In A. C. Gaw (Ed.), *Culture, ethnicity & mental illness* (pp. 3–41). Washington, DC: American Psychiatric Press.

Joe, J. R., & Miller, D. (1987). *American Indian cultural perspectives on disability.* Tucson, AZ: University of Arizona, Native American Research and Training Center.

Jones, P. A. (1985). Issues involving Black interpreters and Black deaf. In M. L. McIntire (Ed.), *Interpreting: The art of cross-cultural mediation: Proceedings of 1985 Registry of Interpreters for the Deaf Convention* (pp. 85–106). San Diego: Registry of Interpreters for the Deaf.

Kaplan, B., & Johnson, D. (1964). The social meaning of Navaho psychopathology and psychotherapy. In A. Kiev (Ed.), *Magic, faith, and healing* (pp. 203–229). Glencoe, NY: Free Press.

Katz, P. (1981). Psychotherapy with Native adolescents. *Canadian Journal of Psychiatry, 26,* 455–459.

Kleinfield, J., & Bloom, J. (1977). Boarding schools: Effects on the mental health of Eskimo adolescents. *American Journal of Psychiatry, 134,* 411–417.

Kertay, L., & Reviere, S. (1993). The use of touch in psychotherapy: Theoretical and ethical considerations. *Psychotherapy, 30,* 32–40.

LaFromboise, T. D., & Dixon, D. N. (1981). American Indian perception of trust-worthiness in a counseling interview. *Journal of Counseling Psychology, 28,* 135–139.

LaFromboise, T. D., Trimble, J. E., & Mohatt, G. V. (1990). Counseling intervention and American Indian tradition: An integrative approach. *The Counseling Psychologist, 18,* 628–654.

Lane, H., Hoffmeister, R., & Bahan B. (1996). *A journey into the Deaf-world.* San Diego: Dawn Sign Press.

Lazarus, P. J. (1982). Counseling the Native American child: A question of values. *Elementary School Guidance and Counseling, 17,* 83–88.

Lee, C. C. (1991). Cultural dynamics: Their importance in multicultural counseling. In C. C. Lee & B. L. Richardson (Eds.), *Multicultural issues in counseling: New approaches to diversity* (pp. 11–17). Alexandria, VA: American Association of Counseling and Development.

Lee, C. C., Oh, M. Y., & Mountcastle, A. R. (1992). Indigenous models of helping in nonwestern countries: Implications for multicultural counseling. *Journal of Multicultural Counseling and Development, 20,* 3–10.

Leong, F. T. L., & Kim, H. W. (1991). Going beyond cultural sensitivity on the road to multiculturalism: Using the intercultural sensitizer as a counselor training tool. *Journal of Counseling & Development, 70,* 112–118.

Littrell, M. A., & Littrell, J. M. (1983). Counselor dress cues: Evaluations by American Indians and Caucasians. *Journal of Cross-Cultural Psychology, 14* (1), 109–121.

Locke, D. C. (1990). A not so provincial view of multicultural counseling. *Counselor Education and Supervision, 30,* 18–25.

Locust, C. S. (1985). American Indian beliefs concerning health and unwellness. *Disability and rehabilitation.* Monograph supported by the National Institute of Native American Research and Training Center. Tucson, AZ: University of Arizona.

———. (1997). *American Indian cultural characteristics.* Unpublished lecture sponsored by the Native American Research and Training Center, Tucson, Arizona.

Lone Wolf, W. (1996). *Native Americans.* An unpublished lecture presented at the Cultural Awareness for Addictions Treatment training workshop for Arizona Biodyne, Inc., Phoenix, AZ.

Lowrey, L. (1983). Bridging a culture in counseling. *Journal of Applied Rehabilitation Counseling, 14* (1), 69–73.

Lujan, P., & Dobkins, D. (1978). *Communicative reticence: Native Americans in the college classroom.* Paper presented at the Annual Meeting of the Speech Communication Asssociation, Minneapolis, MN, 2–5 November.

Makabe. (1996). Unpublished lecture presented at the Tapestries in Progress conference, San Francisco, California, 18 July.

Melick, A., & Herbert, J. (1995). Rehabilitation counseling with the deaf: Considerations for counselors with general caseloads. *Journal of Applied Rehabilitation Counseling, 26* (1), 3–8.

Miller, A. G. (1973). Integration and acculturation of cooperative behavior among Blackfoot Indian and non-Indian Canadian children. *Journal of Cross-cultural Psychology, 4,* 374–380.

Miller, A. G., & Thomas, R. (1972). Cooperation and competition among Blackfoot Indian and urban Canadian children. *Child Development, 43,* 1104–1110.

Morgan, J., & O'Connell, J. C. (1985). *The rehabilitation of disabled Native Americans* [unpublished manuscript].

O'Connell. J. C. (Ed.). (1987). *A study of the special problems and needs of American Indians with handicaps both on and off the reservation* (vols. 1–3). Flagstaff, AZ: Northern Arizona University, Native American Research and Training Center.

Olson, J. S., & Wilson, R. (1984). *Native Americans in the twentieth century.* Provo, UT: Brigham Young University Press.

Padden, C. (1980). The deaf community and the culture of deaf people. In C. Baker & R. Battison (Eds.), *Sign language and the deaf community* (pp. 89–103). Silver Spring, MD: National Association of the Deaf.

Padden, C., & Humphries, T. (1988). *Deaf in America: Voices from a culture.* Cambridge, MA: Harvard University Press.

Page, J. M. (1993). Ethnic identity in deaf Hispanics of New Mexico. *Sign Language Studies, 80,* 185–222.

Pedersen, P. B. (1977). The triad model of cross-cultural counselor training. *Personnel and Guidance Journal, 56* (8), 94–100.

Rehabilitation Brief: Bringing Research into Effective Focus. (1991). *Indigenous Americans and Rehabilitation* (vol. XIII, no. 8). Washington, DC: National Institute on Disability and Rehabilitation Research/Office of Special Education and Rehabilitative Services/ Department of Education.

Richardson, E. H. (1981). Cultural and historical perspectives in counseling American Indians. In D. W. Sue (Ed.), *Counseling the culturally different* (pp. 216–255). New York: Wiley.

Rutherford, S. D. (1988). The culture of American deaf people. *Sign Language Studies, 59,* 129–147.

Sage, G. P. (1991). Counseling American Indian adults. In C. C. Lee & B. L. Richardson (Eds.), *Multicultural issues in counseling: New approaches to diversity* (pp. 23–35). Alexandria, VA: American Association for Counseling and Development.

Satel, S. (1996, 8 May). Psychiatric apartheid. *The Wall Street Journal,* p. A14.

Saville-Troike, M. (1984). Navajo art and education. *Journal of Aesthetic Education, 18,* (2), 41–50.

Schildroth, A., & Hotto, S. (1996). Changes in school and program characteristics, 1984–85 and 1994–95. *American Annals of the Deaf, 141,* 68–71.

Schinke, S. P., Orlandi, M. A., Botvini, G. J., Gilchrist, L. C., Trimble, J. E., & Locklear, V. B. (1988). Preventing substance abuse among American-Indian adolescents: A bicultural competence skills approach. *Journal of Counseling Psychology, 35,* 87–90.

Smith, M. A. (1990). Psychiatric function and roles in an Indian health program context. *American Indian and Alaska Native Mental Health Research, 4* (1), 41–52.

Sue, D. W., & Sue, D. (1977). Barriers to effective cross-cultural counseling. *Journal of Counseling Psychology, 24* (5), 420–429.

———. (1981). The politics of counseling. In D. W. Sue (Ed.), *Counseling the culturally different* (pp. 3–26). New York: Wiley.

Sue, D. W., Arredondo, P., & McDavis, R. J. (1992). Multicultural counseling competencies and standards: A call to the profession. *Journal of Counseling & Development, 70,* 477–486.

Sue, S., Chun, C., & Gee, K. (1995). Ethnic minority intervention and treatment research. In J. Aponte, R. Rivers, & J. Wohl (Eds.), *Psychological interventions and cultural diversity* (pp. 266–282). Boston: Allyn and Bacon.

Sue, S., Zane, N., & Young, K. (1994). Research on psychotherapy with culturally diverse populations. In A. E. Bergin & S. L. Garfield (Eds.), *Handbook of psychotherapy and behavior change* (4th ed.) (pp. 783–817). New York: Wiley.

Supalla, S. (1990). The arbitrary name sign system in American Sign Language. *Sign Language Studies,* 67, 99–126.

Sweezy, C. (1972). The Indian concept of time: A cultural trait. In V. J. Vogel (Ed.), *This country was ours* (pp. 263–266). New York: Harper and Row.

Tedlock, B. (1992). *The beautiful and the dangerous.* New York: Viking Penguin.

Thomason, T. C. (1991). Counseling Native Americans: An introduction for non-Native American counselors. *Journal of Counseling & Development, 69,* 321–327.

Thompson, J. W., Walker, R. D., & Silk Walker, P. (1993). Psychiatric care of American Indians and Alaska Natives. In A. C. Gaw (Ed.), *Culture, ethnicity, and mental illness* (pp. 189–242). Washington, DC: American Psychiatric Press.

Trimble, J. E., & Fleming, C. M. (1989). Providing counseling services for Native American Indians: Client, counselor, and community characteristics. In P. B. Pedersen, J. G. Draguns, & W. J. Lonner (Eds.), *Counseling across cultures* (pp. 177–204). Honolulu: University of Hawaii Press.

U.S. Bureau of the Census. (1990). United States population estimates by age, sex, race, and Hispanic origin: 1980–1988 (p. 25, no. 1045). Washington, DC: U.S. Government Printing Office.

U.S. Department of Health and Human Services. (1980). *What life will we make for our children?* (DHHS Publication No. ADM 81-1010). Washington, DC: U.S. Government Printing Office.

Usher, C. H. (1989). Recognizing cultural bias in counseling theory and practice: The case of Rogers. *Journal of Multicultural Counseling and Development, 17,* 62–71.

Walker, R. D., & LaDue, R. (1986). An integrative approach to American Indian mental health. In C. B. Wilkinson (Ed.), *Ethnic psychiatry* (pp. 143–194). New York: Plenum.

Wasinger, L. (1993). The value system of the Native American counseling client: An exploration. *American Indian Culture and Research Journal, 17* (4), 91–98.

Zitzow, D., & Estes, G. (1981). *Heritage consistency as a consideration in counseling Native Americans* (ERIC Document Reproduction Service No. ED 209 035). Aberdeen, SD.

9

Asian American and Deaf

CHERYL L. WU AND NANCY C. GRANT

This chapter offers perspectives on the meaning and impact of deafness on ethnically Asian deaf and hard of hearing individuals and their families in the United States. Mentally healthy Asian American deaf individuals develop integrated ethnic/cultural identities; that is, they acknowledge and understand the ways in which they are shaped by Asian ethnicity, Americanness, and deafness, and integrate these influences into their own healthy individual identity. They are able to code-switch, to adapt communication and behavior appropriately when in each environment (Atkinson et al., 1983; Phinney, 1990, 1991, 1992; Sue & Sue, 1999, Tajfel, 1981). Most important, they do not have to "choose" one part of their identity over another, to be "deaf [or Asian, or American] first." To deny any part of their identity would be to deny a part of themselves.

An individual cannot be "educated" to become part of a different culture; however, one can develop skills and resources to communicate and function across cultures. In the context of cross-cultural work and deafness, professionals have the advantage of training, insight, experience, and systems to develop those skills and resources. Asian American deaf/hard of hearing individuals and their families may not have such access. It is the responsibility of professionals to develop effective cross-cultural skills and resources.

It might give the reader some perspective to know that the authors work in a private, nonprofit, multiservice agency for deaf and hard of hearing people of all ages and their families. Our program, started in 1982, currently works with about 150 deaf and hard of hearing children in the San Francisco Bay Area; 95% of our clients are "minority," about 50% are recent immigrants, about 50% are Asian American, and about 50% have additional disabilities. Most of our clients are in special day classes in the public schools; some attend the Northern California School for the Deaf.

Demographics

According to the 1990 census, 2.9% of Americans are of Asian/Pacific Island origins. Asians represent the nation's fastest growing population, with 107% growth between 1980 and 1990. Recent data from the Immigration and Naturalization Service indicate that half of all legal immigrants during the past ten years have come from Asia (Lynch & Hanson, 1992; Specht, 1996; Uba, 1994). Recently arrived immigrants face more cultural and language differences (Leung, 1996).

We wish to respect the collectivist spirit and generosity of those who reviewed and offered guidance on this paper. We thank these teachers and colleagues: Sam Chan, Ph.D., California School of Professional Psychology; Deborah Chen, Ph.D., California State University at Northridge; Li-Rong Lilly Cheng, Ph.D., San Diego State University; Nancy Lim-Yee, Chinatown Child Development Center; and Stanley Sue, Ph.D., University of California at Davis and National Research Center on Asian American Mental Health.

After noting the diversity and complexity of the "Asian/Pacific Island" category, Lane, Hoffmeister, and Bahan (1996) note: "Many Deaf immigrants arriving on U.S. shores find that their signed language is utterly unknown in the U. S. DEAF-WORLD. Still others arrive without any signed language" (p. 166). In a national study for National Institutes for Disability Rehabilitation and Research, Ing and Tewey (1994) show 3.7% of hearing impaired youth as Asian/Pacific. Half of all Asian and Pacific Islander students come from homes where a primary language other than English is spoken (Chan, 1983). Asian and Pacific Islander language students are underrepresented in special education, bilingual education, and other programs (Trueba et al., 1993). Compounding this is the fact that given cultural and political factors, many Asian Americans would likely decline to identify their own or a family member's deafness.

Asian American Deaf are barely mentioned in *Disability and Demographic Association Among Race/Ethnic Minority Populations in the United States: Implications for the 21st Century* (Asbury et al., 1991). While some books and articles have been published in recent years on African American Deaf and Hispanic Deaf, there are hardly any specifically addressing Asian American Deaf issues.

Model Minority and Dominant Culture

Despite their increasing visibility, Asian Americans are still the most poorly understood cultural/linguistic group. They are seen either as high achievers who fit into the dominant culture or as enigmatic and exotic. (Huang & Ying, 1989; Sue & McKinney, 1975; Trueba et al, 1993). Contrary to model minority stereotypes of Asian Americans (Kitano, 1969), studies show that Asian Americans do have mental health needs (Sue et al., 1995), and that some of those present with even more severe problems than Euro-American clients (Durvasala & Sue, 1996; Flaskerud & Hu, 1992; Sue & McKinney, 1975). In addition, there are specific mental health disorders that some Asian ethnic groups are prone to experience (Kinzie et al., 1990).

Racism and prejudice reflected in restrictive American immigration laws, from the 1880s Exclusion Acts to the 1990s anti-immigration initiatives, have had a profound impact on the perception and treatment of Asian Americans. Such initiatives reflect social and political agendas that affect availability of health care, welfare, disability benefits, even educational opportunities (Ridley, 1995). Deaf and hard of hearing people from these groups are at even greater disadvantage because of the added cultural, linguistic, and accessibility issues.

Asian American Deaf

"Deaf" refers to a very diverse group of people, including individuals representing a wide range of audiological, linguistic, cultural, political, and personal characteristics. Asian American deaf people reflect the same diversity within deafness as American deaf, as well as ethnic diversity within "Asianness." This diversity incorporates recent arrivals plus those whose families have been in the United States for many generations. The deaf individual's and family's beliefs and practices about the etiology and meaning of disability in general and of deafness in particular reflect the diversity of identity and experience. Yet when Asian American deaf people get together through organizations like the (San Francisco) Bay Area Asian Deaf Association (BAADA), Greater Washington Area Asian

Deaf Association (GWAADA) or national Asian deaf conferences, there is a clear sense of community, identity, "coming home." Deaf visitors from Asian countries manage to find Asian American deaf individuals and groups, just as deaf people traveling outside their home country find other deaf people.

In 1994, the U.S. national conference of Asian deaf people in the United States, called "Access Silent Asia: The Asian Deaf Experience," was held in the heart of San Francisco's Chinatown.

> This conference was a celebration of Asian/Southeast Asian and American Deaf Cultures, and symbolized the "first step" in our "thousand mile journey" of cultural enrichment and empowerment as Asian American deaf people, their families, and the professionals who work with us. For too long, our voices have gone unheard, our hands unseen, our silence misunderstood, and our identities denied. (Wu, 1995)

One result of the conference was the inception of a national association. The identity problems for Asian American deaf people was evident in the struggle to determine the association's name—the struggle continued at the second national conference held in Los Angeles, in March 1997. Conference attendees repeatedly asked: Are we first Asian or Deaf or American? What is most important? Are hard of hearing people included? Are family members to be included in our organization?

The struggle for identity was well expressed by a young person at the first conference who noted, "I always knew I was deaf, but I didn't realize how Asian I am!" He stayed up all night with other young Asian Deaf Americans talking about their "Asian Deaf" characteristics and community. It was the first time they had been in the company of hundreds of people who looked like them, whose nonverbal communication was like theirs, whose way of using signs and facial expressions was familiar, whose life experience was like theirs. For many parents, it was the first time they had ever seen an Asian American deaf adult. It was their first opportunity to ask questions of these role models through interpreters in several Asian languages, English, and American Sign Language (ASL). For deaf community and hearing Asian community professionals it was a rare opportunity to network cross-culturally and to learn from one another about Asian, Asian Deaf, and American Deaf cultures. The Asian American Deaf community is still in the formative stages of development. While the conferences resulted in a national organization, developing a community identity will take time.

This chapter will not address every Asian group, but will focus on Chinese American people in the United States deaf community. They are the largest Asian American group, coming from Hong Kong, Taiwan, mainland China, and Vietnam. Their languages include Cantonese. (used in the southern mainland, Hong Kong, Vietnam, Singapore, and other areas), Mandarin (the national language of China and Taiwan), and local dialects (Toisan, Fukien, and others). Adult deaf immigrants who were educated at schools for the deaf are likely to know their own signed language. Like spoken dialects, Chinese signed languages are not identical, though they may share some characteristics. Chinese deaf immigrants may have oral/aural skills. Some may know Chinese characters; the written language is standardized across China. Deaf children who have been in schools for the deaf may (or may not) have some signed and written language; those coming from rural areas or who have never been in school may have only "home signs" or gestures, no language per se.

Core Values: The Three Teachings

An individual's perceptions and his or her understanding of and reactions to those perceptions, ways of thinking, emotions, behavioral patterns, and morality are informed by the values inherent in his or her culture. Culturally competent assessments and interventions require an understanding of these values.

The core values of Chinese culture have been principally influenced by the doctrines and philosophies of Taoism, Confucianism, and Buddhism. Taoism teaches balance in all things, avoidance of imbalances (intrapersonally, interpersonally, socially), and implies harmony in relationships rather than conflict. The forces of nature and society (yin and yang) are seen as counterbalancing, cyclical: both are necessary for survival (Chan, 1992), whereas American culture tends to think in terms of dichotomy, polarity, opposition, and individual identity rather than this more ecological balance of a larger whole. As in every culture, there is an undercurrent of indigenous values and religion. Ancestor worship is a powerful and influential value and practice for many Asian subcultures. It links the world of living people to the world of spirits. More importantly, it fits with the ecological view of living and dead being part of a larger whole; both have needs; each is able help (or harm) the other.

CONFUCIANISM

Confucianism defines a hierarchical social structure, which implies appropriate social behavior in relationships. It reinforces a sense of group-oriented propriety and behavior (as opposed to American culture's stress on individual rights, opportunities, and responsibilities). Five specific relationships and moral obligations are delineated: ruler and subjects, husband and wife, father and son, older and younger siblings, friend and friend. Balance, reciprocity, and mutuality are assumed. The person who has more overt power is given the higher position because of spiritual worth; it is assumed he or she has responsibility to those in lower positions. Those with less overt power expect to defer to the wisdom and guidance of the powerful, but also expect to receive support and stability from them. A person in either position who does not fulfill his responsibilities is subject to feelings of shame and guilt, powerful indicators of imbalance or disharmony.

Position supersedes gender roles; if individuals are horizontally similar, then males supersede females (Yacobacci-Tam, 1987). "Ruler and subjects" implies employer/employee and teacher/student relationships. This social order directs communication in one direction, from the higher position to the lower. The person in the lower position is expected to receive and utilize advice or teaching that is given to him or her (Chan, 1992). Traditionally, these roles and relationships are powerful in structuring family relationships, especially considering that the spousal relationship is secondary to the parent-child relationship. Filial piety is highly cherished; respect and shame are means of social teaching and social control (Shon & Ja, 1982).

BUDDHISM

Buddhism, which originated in India, is ecological in that it explains the individual's place in the universe through the four noble truths: suffering; desire or attachment to the world; emancipation from suffering and desire; and the middle, or eightfold, path. The eightfold path teaches a set of paths or behaviors that will lead to "nirvana" (calm, insight, enlightenment). The eight aspects of the path are right understanding, right thought, right speech, right action, right livelihood, right effort, right mindfulness, and right concentration. Living these practices helps one develop compassion and wisdom. Buddhism reinforces a sense of integration and relationship, and helps to explain suffering and desire, that they are a natural part of evolution. Evolution and ecology here encompass the spiritual as well as material universe. What is often termed "fatalism" is actually an acceptance of one's experience and place, a pragmatic approach to difficulties (Chan, 1992; Ruhala, 1974).

The integration of these practices influences the traditional Chinese collectivist core values: balance (harmony, place in a larger context); avoiding conflict; fatalism; correct behavior; filial piety (family relationships and obligations); saving face (of self and others); and the resultant shame and guilt when roles or obligations are not fulfilled. These values are the cultural lens through which deafness and mental health issues and the counselor/client relationship will be understood and played out (Chan, 1992).

Cultural Views Toward "Disability," Health, and Mental Health

In order to address mental health issues in Asian American deaf individuals and their families, the clinician must be aware of how clients are likely to understand the concepts, practices, and professional roles related to disability, health, and mental health. Specific disabilities may be attributed to specific causes in a metaphysical or even supernatural point of view. There tends to be greater stigma associated with visible physical, developmental, and especially mental impairments, rather than health or disabling conditions that are not so easily apparent. There is a tendency to somatize emotional or psychological problems, as it is generally more acceptable to express, talk about, and treat anything related to health through medical or physical body approaches. A family might frame a child's problems more easily in terms of deafness rather than mental illness, because the deafness is more acceptable and less stigmatizing. Treatment approaches may include acupuncture, therapeutic massage, therapeutic diet, and herbal medicines, as well as Western approaches to medical treatment (Chan, 1992; Lee, 1997b; Shon & Ja, 1982).

In the United States, parents must combine Eastern and Western views to deal not only with the impact of deafness on the child, but to cope with their own sense of responsibility for the child's condition. Their way of reacting to deafness may not be the same grieving process that happens in the American cultural framework. It is important for both parents, even the extended family, to be involved with treatment; the importance of the family must not be minimized even with an adult patient.

The family's acculturation level influences their hopes and expectations for their deaf child, which in turn influences parenting strategies and styles. Parents deal with these hopes and expectations within their cultural context. For example, a young adult is expected to remain at home, contributing to the family as appropriate to his or her place (birth order, gender, etc.) until he or she is married.

A traditional family is concerned about safety and survival. They hope for their child to learn skills to provide for his or her future. In a traditional Chinese family, it is not appropriate to praise a child verbally or directly because this could result in the child not trying so hard or becoming lazy; the parental role is to encourage the child by pushing him/her to strive ever harder. The American method of affirming the child's potential or giving individual attention and praise may be contrary to the Chinese parents' beliefs regarding what is best for their child. A teacher or clinician could be helpful by addressing the parents' viewpoint and helping to reframe expectations for the child (Chan, 1992).

Chinese culture's unique blend of Taoism, Confucianism, and Buddhism stresses a fatalistic approach to problems. Fatalism is not denial, resistance, or an unwillingness to see the positive aspects of deafness; it is rather a practical coping strategy that fits with high-context, indirect communication that enhances social harmony. One saves face by not directly expressing negative feelings or thoughts. Direct questioning and self-disclosure conflict with cultural etiquette and values; patient indirectness and slow identification of topic and focus can be expected (Yacobacci-Tam, 1987). For example, nodding the head may indicate affirmation of the person (not necessarily of what he or she is expressing); noncommittal responses may stem from misunderstanding or disagreement and preserve harmony by avoiding direct questioning or conflict (Chan, 1992).

The amount of information transmitted through the situation, relationship, and physical cues is much greater than that transmitted through verbal explanation, negotiation, or discussion (Hall, 1976, 1984). The child knows of his or her parents' love through concrete actions (such as working hard for the benefit of the child and family, driving the child to extracurricular activities). Subtle, nonverbal cues such as a "look" from a parent express judgments about right and wrong. These high-context means of communication condition social relationships and values through an individual's lifetime (Chan, 1992). Directly thinking, questioning, or talking about a problem, even in positive ways, may be seen as causing, reinforcing, or even exacerbating it.

A primary parental coping strategy, especially when children are diagnosed, is to seek out medical means to control or "cure" the perceived problem. Medical means involves "doing something" (rather than just calling attention). Teaching is another acceptable way of doing something. Offerings to the gods or ancestors may be a way of doing something. When mental health issues are present, the family may look for ways to "do something," starting within the family system. There are implications here for the use of cognitive-behavioral therapeutic approaches in combination with family systems interventions, especially those more structural in nature (McGoldrick et al., 1996). These approaches are also often utilized successfully with American deaf clients and families (see Greenberg & Kusche, 1993; Harvey, 1989).

Peer and ethnic community supports are critical in assessing the strengths and needs of the family. Part of the professional's strategy can be to reach out to community and religious leaders, elders, educators, and healers who represent authority and respect within the community, and who can help reach out to an Asian American deaf individual or family. A bilingual/bicultural provider who can read and express the high-context cues, play an appropriate provider role, and serve as a bridge between the cultures is likely to be most effective. Role models, especially for children, are important in American and deaf approaches to education and socialization. However, even if interpreters are available, the family may not be responsive to a deaf provider, especially at first, and especially if the provider or intervention is not culturally familiar.

Framing Mental Health Issues Multiculturally

There is a growing literature on the psychology of difference (Chin et al., 1993) that depathologizes cultural differences, integrates cultural characteristics, and synthesizes diversity with approaches of Western psychological frameworks. Multicultural counseling theory (Sue et al., 1996) acknowledges different worldviews, of Western and non-Western cultures, to be inherently neither right nor wrong. It incorporates diverse cultural healing methods and multiple healing roles, with an expanded understanding of the individual (including the healer) in relation to self, family, group, and organization.

Phinney, Lochner, and Murphy (1990) describe how identity development and self-concept of people from racial/ethnic minority groups are affected by the presence of at least two different sets of norms and values: those of their native culture, and those of the larger and dominant culture. Two cultural sets, Deaf and hearing, affect a person who is deaf. Leigh and Stinson (1991) describe biculturalism in Deafness as the ability to maintain ties and effective interaction and relationship with both Deaf and hearing. It follows that a minority deaf person has multiple identity sets to cope with: American and family hearing cultures as well as American and ethnic Deaf cultures. Glickman and Carey (1993), Holcomb (1997), Leigh and Lewis (this volume), Mindel and Vernon (1987), Schlesinger and Meadow (1972) speak to deafness as part of that identity, and its importance in mental health. Acculturation and ethnic identity influence mental health, and specifically racial/ethnic minority clients' attitudes toward Western mental health services and overall levels of mental health functioning (Atkinson & Thompson, 1992; Goodstein, 1994; Leong & Chou, 1994; Ponterotto & Pederson, 1993; Uba, 1994).

When working with an Asian American deaf client, the clinician needs to address potential conflict between "Asian" values (Eastern, group identity, family values, worth as reflection of group) and "American" values (Western, individualism, "pull yourself up by bootstraps," self-esteem, legal focus on rights of individuals over groups). The clinician further needs to address Deaf identity and cultural factors. The clinician must also look for cross-culturally shared values and strengths (for example, parents' love and sense of responsibility for children, strength of family ties, importance of education). The client's ultimate goal is to achieve an integrated Asian American deaf identity. As of yet, there is no research that directly addresses how this process takes place.

Underutilization of Mental Health Services

Underutilization of mental health services by Asian Americans is well documented (Sue & Sue, 1999; Tracey et al., 1986; Uba, 1994). Help-seeking and utilization behaviors are significantly different from those of Euro-Americans, and are primarily based on cultural patterns of perceiving and coping with problems. Problem solving tends to have an internally oriented focus: the individual first struggles within the self to resolve any problem or conflict. The next levels of assistance are immediate family, then extended family, then very close friends. Next are advisors within the cultural community: community and spiritual leaders or individuals with positions of respect (a teacher, for example). The last level of help seeking is outside the community, by which time the original problem has likely escalated to a crisis situation (Chan, 1992; Huang & Ying, 1989; Lee, 1997b; Shon & Ja, 1982). Crisis implies that the situation cannot be ignored by American health, mental health, education and legal systems, especially where children are involved.

The parents, family, friends, and community of a deaf Asian child may have little knowledge about the medical or developmental implications of deafness, or otherwise lack the information they need to make informed decisions about the child. Somatization is a culturally legitimate way to get help, support, and attention (Ishisaka & Takagi, 1982; Marsella et al., 1973; Sue & Sue, 1971; Uba, 1994). An adult client or a parent is more likely to seek medical treatment or technology other than Western mental health or social services, which may be culturally unfamiliar. Speech therapy or teaching a specific skill is seen as educational and therefore acceptable. Education is a powerful value and motivator; however, the family may not ask about special education, seeking to avoid special attention given to the child. Even if the family has little linguistic communication with the child, they probably do have strong bonds, a strong sense of family, and a desire to be effective parents. Sending their child away to a residential American school for the deaf may be seen as not only overwhelming and frightening, but as an abdication of parental responsibilities and boundaries.

Support systems for both the Asian deaf person and the family are critical. The importance of family cannot be emphasized enough as support, validation, and stabilization of the individual, whatever the age (Lee, 1997b). The clinician needs to recognize and help the family find supports for all angles on identity and the integration of them. Lack of supports leaves clients and families without tools, helpless, dependent on an outside value and service system that they don't understand, and can create or exacerbate mental health problems. Learning about culture and working with cultural and language issues is an ongoing process for the clinician and the mental health system. It is critical for mental health workers to connect with resources, exchange cross-training, develop systems for collaborative counseling, be able to model appropriate cross-cultural behaviors, and handle multiple language communication. Through these efforts, the American and deaf mental health worker can work with ethnic community and service providers to develop appropriate supports for Asian deaf people and their families.

Available supports depend on the family's specific culture and country of origin. Relatives may live with the client's family, or extended family living in the area may help the client's family bridge the culture/language gap. Important and basic family supports include childcare, feeding, shared economic base, and shared living space. While ethnic community centers may provide resources regarding more prevalent disabilities or severe mental health issues, these centers are rarely helpful for deafness issues because of their lack of knowledge about deafness.

The mental health system in the United States shape American clinician's views (Matsumoto, 1994; Ridley, 1995; Sue et al., 1996; Sue & Sue, 1990). Funding systems determine the eligibility, means of diagnosis, treatment options, choice of clinician, language(s) in which services are delivered, define the clinical relationship, decide whether only the individual or the (extended) family can receive services, and determine the place, time, and cost of treatment.

With Asian American clients, the clinician must go outside the boundaries of American viewpoints and make significant efforts to connect with and include the family, not just the deaf individual. Professionals may need to advocate for support within our service delivery system for flexible or additional time to work with clients/families, interpreters for phone calls and in-person meetings, and home visits. It can be difficult to sort out cross-cultural conflicts from deaf/hearing issues, and then to analyze the interaction of the two.

SELF-IDENTITY

Collective versus individual identification is a critical factor in addressing the mental health of the Asian American deaf individual. One's name is an important part of identity. Like other ethnic minorities, Asian American Deaf people are often encouraged by their Deaf peers to have an "American" name and name-sign, and may be teased or mocked or put down if they persist with their given name or a name-sign that looks foreign. They may even pronounce their name in an Anglicized way rather than the way their parents pronounce it. To be American and Deaf, does one need to give up one's ethnic identity? To answer yes quite wrongly implies that internalized oppression and fragmented or suppressed identity development is mentally healthy.

Because an Asian American deaf person values the family or workplace or peer group above the self, this does not mean the person has "low self-esteem." Indeed, this may reflect a sense of identity and belonging. Self-esteem is a Western concept that views the individual as primary, separately from the group. An Eastern view reflects one's worth not as an individual, but rather in terms of how the group values one, and how the individual reflects the group. Achievement and value have to do with group or family: there may be a "most valuable team" but not a "most valuable player." The player has no value without the context of the team.

However, in the United States, the focus is primarily on the individual. An American deaf individual has a legal entitlement to assistance that can include interpreters, special education from skilled educators, accommodation on the job or in the classroom via interpreters or technology, and systemic supports such as Supplemental Security Income (SSI) or vocational services. Asian cultures tend to perceive deafness as a disability. The Asian American deaf individual/family may experience conflict with the idea of Deafness as a cultural/language group and not as a disability within American Deaf values. Writing of Deaf children and their culture, Lane, Hoffmeister, and Bahan (1996) observe: "In ethnic minorities, where culture and constitution are usually congruent, one's first loyalty may be to the family, which is the setting for acculturation as well as nurture; loyalty to the ethnic cultural/language group comes second. But most children in the deaf world cannot communicate with their parents who know no signed language, and while their home may be nurturing, it cannot be substantially acculturating" (p. 161). This is a powerful statement that the deaf person's family may find disrespectful and frightening. The very strength of "Deaf pride" may alienate parents who must ultimately decide their child's path, and effectively deny that child entry into the Deaf world.

The challenge for those working within the Deaf community and Deaf culture, and for those working with the multiple Asian American and mainstream communities, is to find a common ground where different viewpoints, beliefs, languages, skills, strengths, and needs are all respected. We must forge cross-cultural (Deaf, hearing, ethnic, and American) relationships and communication so that all deaf people may grow and live in a nurturing and acculturating environment.

MENTAL HEALTH ISSUES IN ASIAN AMERICANS

Contrary to the model minority stereotype, Asian Americans do manifest mental health and adjustment problems despite low utilization rates of mental health services (Leong, 1986). It is crucial that symptoms and behaviors be examined in the client's cultural and developmental context (Huang & Ying, 1989; Matsumoto, 1994). Interethnic differences are relevant in how psychopathology is manifested among different Asian subcultures (Enright & Jaeckle, 1963; Marsella et al., 1973), and how these intercultural differences can affect responses on different assessment tools, few of which are for specific Asian subgroups.

The lack of culturally appropriate assessment procedures and instrumentation leads to misinterpretations and misdiagnoses of observed behaviors and symptomology. There are few psychological tests and assessment instruments developed and normed for American deaf people (Heller, 1987), and none for Asian American deaf individuals. For these two groups, response sets to psychological measures are likely to be different than the response sets for Euro-Americans (Lee, 1997b) or Euro-American deaf individuals.

For Asian American deaf people, risk factors will differ somewhat, depending on whether the client is an adult or youth. The adult deaf Asian immigrant is less likely to be able to work in this country than his or her hearing counterpart, resulting in financial pressures and dependence on family. Preparation for work is likely to be limited: in China, less than 10% of deaf children receive an education, and most of these begin school at age nine and leave at age sixteen; the education is primarily vocational training for work in sheltered workshops (Cheng, 1993). For the adult, gender and birth order roles may already be skewed because of the deafness, which can impact self-concept. (For example, a younger sibling may be expected to take care of a deaf older sibling. An adult "should" be working to help support the family financially, and instead is dependent because of lack of job skills.) The expectations regarding behavior, academics, and career of a deaf Asian female may be less than of a deaf Asian male; a female is more likely to get sympathy and support than a male. Families are also likely to be very protective of the female deaf family member no matter what her age.

Social isolation is common for an Asian American deaf person. Those who are foreign-born are likely to have a smaller peer group, limited communication with others, limited sense of community, and less opportunity for acceptance by the American Deaf community. The child may be isolated at home and in the community but will probably have an opportunity to develop a peer group and accepting environment within his or her school program. Problems begin to arise when the child begins to acculturate as American more quickly than the parents and extended family. Family intercultural as well as intergenerational differences can result in problems including hearing/deaf issues within the native culture; American/native culture issues, and American Deaf/native Deaf cultural/language issues. From a developmental context, younger children may be more likely to show oppositional behavior, attention difficulties, and conduct disorders; with adolescents, issues related to identity, individuation, and adjustment may be more relevant, and parent-adolescent conflicts more frequent. For the older adult, the problems can become more intrapsychic. Regardless of the client's age or whether they raise the issue, therapists need to be sure to address actively all aspects of identity formation (Phinney, 1990, 1992; Ridley, 1995; Uba, 1994).

Relatively recent immigration can be a major risk factor. Because of major political changes and wars in China in the past several decades, families may have experienced a series of separations and losses. Families migrating with young children can be vulnerable to role reversals. People acculturate at different rates depending on time in the new culture, where they live (Chinatown, the inner city, suburbia), their age, education, professional affiliation, and language skills. Work and financial status are additional potential stressors.

Approaching and Treating Asian American Deaf Clients

Therapists need to consider how to integrate ethnic and Deafness-related cultural information and practices into their own professional role and framework for assessing, diagnosing, and treating clients (see Armour-Thomas & Gopaul-McNicol, 1997; Canino & Spurlock, 1994; Chan, 1992; Kim, 1985; Lynch, 1992; Uba, 1994). Here are some areas to consider.

Communication style: A clinician is likely to be seen as a respected professional and thus in a power position (though this may be affected by the clinician's race, age, and gender). Knowing the professional's educational background and experience gives the family confidence in the professional's ability to truly help them. As part of building a relationship, the client or family may ask personal questions about the clinician's roles and status, especially family; answering these questions can help develop trust and rapport (Chan, 1992; Lee, 1997b). The individual/family may expect a relatively brief interaction with the professional. A manner that is confident, unambiguous, relatively direct, and clear is most likely to be effective.

To find a starting point, the therapist needs to get information about the deafness, including etiology (both medical and family's beliefs), age of onset, cultural perspectives on deafness, how the individual and family understand deafness, and how the individual and family feel about the deafness (shame and guilt are more common than grief and anger as in American families). Information about family communication in general, communication with the deaf individual, and what the family knows about American views on deafness/disability, education, parenting, and resources is also important.

The provider's basic mental status examination should include such cultural factors as the individual/family's migration and immigration history, level of acculturation, ethnicity, language skills and preferences (signed, spoken, and written), family structure (age, birth order, gender roles, parenting values, etc.), family support systems, additional environmental strengths or stressors, and treatment history (including ethnic and American helpers in whatever fields the family finds relevant—medical, spiritual, educational, etc.).

In assessing an Asian deaf individual, even an adult, the family must be involved if at all possible. The individual's and family's understanding and framing of the problems and issues may be similar or may be different from each other's and from the clinician's. It can be difficult to understand the different perspectives, especially if the family is monolingual and non-English-speaking. Working with foreign-born Asian deaf adults can be difficult just in terms of communication; they may be fluent in their country's written or sign language and not in English or ASL. They may have no standard language. Interpreters may be needed, and their awareness of boundaries, roles, and confidentiality must be assessed.

Therapists should not ignore sibling relationships. With some families, a hearing sibling may be expected to be the deaf person's interpreter. In our experience, these siblings may have mental health issues of their own in relation to their deaf sibling. Because they are typically "good" children, it may be difficult for the family to see the sibling needs help (or even recreation or social opportunities).

In our work with families from many different linguistic backgrounds, we find that even if we can manage a conversation in English with family members, they may not be confident that they understand or are expressing themselves accurately. They may use English words but not understand the cultural meanings or implications. Conversational fluency in home language or English also should not be assumed to imply literacy in either language. Because of high-context communication patterns, it may be difficult to "read" whether a client is understanding, agreeing, not understanding, or disagreeing but just being polite. Having bi- or multilingual professionals or interpreters easily available makes offering language supports more acceptable.

Asian perspectives on parenting and communication patterns are very different from traditional Westerm views. Just as the client is culturally bound, so is the clinician (Matsumoto, 1994; Ridley, 1995; Sue et al., 1996; Uba, 1994). American and American Deaf ethnocentrism could cause the Asian client to misunderstand. The client's self-esteem, ways of understanding, and ways of thinking and being in the world may be judged as wrong, bad, and dysfunctional. The client may be misunderstood as unable to express emotions. He or she may be seen as weak, passive, too dependent, or lacking self-identity and autonomy. Families may be seen as enmeshed and overprotective (Huang & Ying, 1989).

The clinician can, in effect, make the clients feel that unless they become "like an American," they are failures. Consider an Asian American deaf person, especially a young person dealing with identity and self-esteem issues. He or she may feel he or she must be like an American Deaf person and must deny any Asian-ness. It is analogous to a naive hearing clinician wanting a deaf person to be "like hearing" with the good intentions of helping him or her fit in and cope, but denying the strengths of his or her Deaf culture, language, ways of thinking, feeling, expressing, and behaving. At the same time, incorporating the perspectives and skills of complex adaptive systems into one's own framework is a difficult and demanding (and creative and expanding) challenge for the clinician and his or her working environment (Leong, 1996).

Our treatment framework takes into account the high-context cultural structure, which involves cultural and family systems and expresses an ecological perspective. The starting point of treatment is likely to mean stretching one's professional boundaries by playing multiple roles. The therapist can develop rapport and credibility by providing or negotiating concrete resources, which is a powerful trust-building process. Offering a reciprocal exchange or "working alliance" in which parents share history and the worker shares information or education can be helpful (Chan, 1992; Huang & Ying, 1989; Lee, 1997a).

Most parents will see their child's excitement about participating in a group, going to school, and so on as concrete, identifiable progress. Framing work with a child or young adult as preparing for that young person's future is also a useful approach. The therapist can help by "interpreting" the purpose of the therapy (Huang & Ying, 1989). For example, play therapy is not "just playing"; it has a process, purpose, and meaning. Individual therapy, especially when it separates children from their parents, can be seen as prying, secret meetings, or isolation of a family member—all of which might be viewed as violating intrafamilial communication patterns. Family work, which is generally the treatment of choice (Harris & Moran, 1986; Lee, 1997a), may even be framed as educational or "helping with communication." The clinican should wait until trust and credibility are established before moving to a wider range of treatment strategies, including individual and therapeutic group work, psychoeducational work, social cognition, and various types of support (Ho, 1992).

It's also important to recognize that people in many Asian cultures are inner-oriented in problem-solving and help-seeking behaviors. Therefore, it is not realistic to expect Asian clients to come to a therapist for help unless they already have some familiarity and trust in that therapist. It is crucial to be aware of the appropriate entry points into the Asian communities and, more specifically, the formal and informal communication networks and established social relationships within selected Asian communities that play major roles in determining how a family in need may initially view an available public service.

When the client and family use a dialect or come from an ethnic background different from the clinician's, it helps to utilize co-workers, consultants, and interpreters from Asian mental health resources. Most agencies do not have an Asian deaf mental health provider immediately available. In such situations, Ridley (1995) suggests that building a therapeutic alliance also includes handling potential mistrust by overtly talking about the racial or ethnic difference between the client and therapist, and what that means in their communication and roles. With adults especially, this could be a useful therapeutic tool in not only building trust but looking at Asian Deaf identity issues. Lee (1997a) cautions that clinicians of cultural backgrounds similar to their clients may also have difficulties and blind spots, and that transference and countertransference issues should be handled carefully.

Therapists who encourage an individual deaf Asian young person to express his or her feelings to his or her family can set that person up for being perceived as inappropriate and disrespectful. Rather, the therapist can help the youth identify and understand his or her feelings and behavior, and help him or her to find culturally appropriate ways to get support and guidance from the family. When working on common developmental issues, therapists can encourage clients not to go off on their own (disrespecting and ignoring family wishes and fears), not to keep their Supplemental Security Income for themselves (and therefore not contributing to their family's well-being), and not to tell their parents directly how they feel (blaming parents for overprotectiveness, lack of sign language skills, not understanding, etc.). The therapist needs to consider ways to provide support without having to antagonize the clients' internalized self-perception or removing their family support. If the approach or change is too different, the client may withdraw from conflict, experience increased inner tension, and be at even higher risk for depression and suicide. The therapist needs to do a lot of reframing in addition to deconstruction of internalized oppression. It can help to analyze what success means in the person's and parents' eyes and help them (all) understand what that means within the context of mainstream American society. Interdependence is not enmeshment; nonverbal communication is a real form of communication.

Families with a deaf member need to understand the impact of deafness within a cultural framework. The family's obligation and commitment to caretake is their role and duty, and is not seen as overprotection or "enabling." Rather, it is responsible and appropriate parenting. All members of the family have some role to play in coping with disability within the family. This is a potential asset, rather than something to be undermined. There is often tremendous anxiety on the part of parents, especially for teens and young adults. Parents have long-term fears about what will happen when they are not able to monitor and take care of their children. Family communication "classes" can address communication issues that may be more relational or therapeutic in nature. That concern for the future can help the clinician frame independence skills as active tools for the future: "You won't have to worry in the future if your child is able to take care of him/herself."

* * *

First case study: Jun

Jun (age seventeen) had arrived a year and a half ago from rural southern mainland China.[1] She was the only deaf person in her family, which was very close-knit. Deafness etiology was measles with a high fever in infancy. Jun had lived in a residential part of Chinatown with two younger siblings and working-class parents, all of whom were monolingual Cantonese speakers. Her family used gestures and home signs to communicate with her. In China she was very social, independent, and happy; she enjoyed playing outside and had friends. She had life skills and knew how to cook, clean, and run errands. She had stayed at home until age nine because there was no special school for her. From age nine to seventeen, she went with her brother to his hearing school but did nothing but copy things.

When she arrived in America, Jun found San Francisco's noise and chaos overwhelming. The environment of rural China was much quieter, slower, a smaller community where she knew and was known by everyone. She was afraid of African American people because she had never seen people of other races before. She thought it strange for men to have long hair: "they should cut it!"

When she first arrived at her American school (a special day class for deaf/hard of hearing students in a public school), Jun refused to enter her classroom. She was fearful, shaky, cried, and displayed post-traumatic stress symptoms as a reaction to her move to the United States. She did not have her brother to help her adjust at school as she had in China. She had never been around deaf people before, and feared other students—deaf or hearing—because they moved too aggressively and were visually noisy. Her parents reported no problems at home. At school, however, she continually carried an album of photographs of her home in China that gave her the only concrete sense of security aside from her family. When fitted for hearing aids, she found them too overwhelming to use. The process of adjusting to American culture had to be slowed down.

Our program had a well-established relationship with the local educational programs, and Jun's teachers welcomed our assistance. Our Chinese American clinician was not fluent in the family's Cantonese dialect, so our primary methods for communicating with Jun were gestures and visual aids. Our work with Jun at school focused on giving her some private space and the time she needed to adjust at her own pace. This included setting up her desk in a way that created a "safe" place, an isolated environment, away from other students. She could observe, but was not forced to engage actively with others in the classroom, which itself was too foreign and threatening an environment. Individual therapy was behaviorally oriented, and involved modification of experiential desensitization techniques to facilitate her adjustment to her new environment. Art therapy techniques provided a means by which Jun could express her fears and her desire to return to her homeland.

1. Names and identifying information have been changed in case studies to protect the clients.

She initially felt more comfortable and safe with adults—especially her Chinese American teacher, classroom aide, and Chinese American therapist—than with non-Asian professionals. Once she developed some comfort with adults, Jun was able to connect with a few of the Asian American deaf students. As she became better at socializing, she initiated interactions with people who were familiar and safe. In structured peer group situations, she began to take minimal risks. When overwhelmed, she retreated to a Chinese adult with whom she felt comfortable.

Despite Jun's gradually improving behavioral and social understanding, her language development remained very limited. Communication needed to be very concrete and visual. There was no indication of additional disability but, given the lack of formal education for most of her early years, there was a limited prognosis for Jun's ability to realize her academic potential. One-to-one instruction and structured socialization opportunities were the most effective interventions at this time.

Working with Jun would have been impossible without first having cooperation and approval from her family. (To work with the family, our clinician used an interpreter who was fluent in Cantonese, English, and ASL.) At the onset, the family was in need of, and receptive to, our program's social work support services. This gave us the entry point we needed when Jun was at her peak time of emotional crisis in adjustment. The family eventually used our program services to handle case management and home-school liaison issues, calling us as problems arose.

* * *

Second case study: Tong

Tong, who was twelve years old and hard of hearing, was experiencing auditory and visual hallucinations, extreme restlessness and anxiety, difficulty sleeping, paranoid ideation, and obsessive and compulsive letter writing and phone calling (violent and sexually explicit in content) to his teachers and classmates at school. He was suspended from school due to his inappropriate aggressive behavior, and his behavior at home became increasingly unmanageable. After a brief psychotic episode, he was hospitalized for two weeks in the acute inpatient deaf adolescent unit of a psychiatric hospital. He was referred to our program as part of discharge planning.

Tong's very traditional Chinese family adhered strictly to Chinese customs, beliefs, and values. His parents had limited English skills, and Cantonese was the primary language spoken in the home. Tong's older brother was also hard of hearing. The family had very limited sign language skills, although Tong's brother had intermediate signed English skills. The parents had a fatalistic attitude toward both sons' hearing impairments, and placed great value on Tong's speech and bilingual verbal skills.

Tong's parents acknowledged his special needs. Yet given their very limited understanding of the concept of Western mental health, their lack of understanding of psychological issues could easily have been mistaken as resistance and denial of Tong's problems. The family consistently maintained a strong traditional commitment to protecting and advocating for Tong. His needs became the whole family's responsibility.

When Tong was experiencing difficulties in school, the family tried their own immediate and extended family resources, and appealed to resources in their ethnic community (church, cultural center, etc.). Although his teachers requested help from the school's psychologist, principal, and districtwide resources, no resources had actually been brought in. Numerous referrals to Deaf community and "hearing" Asian community resources were made. However, as is often the case with diverse cultural/language group deaf referrals, neither the Asian community or Deaf service agencies could provide care that reflected both the ethnic, cultural, and Deaf needs of the client and his family. This weakness contributed greatly to the delay in diagnoses early in Tong's life, and functionally further delayed access to the proper services and educational placements. The family was referred to many different places with little coordination or communication among them. The miscommunication and misunderstanding adversely affected the family's trust of these professional services.

Tong's hospitalization presented similar difficulties. His parents felt the hospital was neither linguistically accessible to them nor culturally sensitive to their needs. According to the family, they did not see any active intervention by the hospital staff that benefited their son, whom they "observed doing nothing at the hospital but sit and watch TV." They claimed the physicians never met with them to explain the treatment plan or the problems that Tong had. Finally, they felt the hospital breached confidentiality in sharing information with Tong's school without their permission. All of these factors created a strong mistrust for the "system."

Once Tong was referred to our program, we took on a multifaceted role involving advocacy, mental health counseling, and case management. We also acted as the primary liaison between the family, other service providers, and the educational system. During intake, it was extremely important to address the family's immediate and specific concerns related to Tong in order to build a therapeutic alliance with the parents. We covered the primary issues and background information with a minimum of time focused on family history aside from the basic migration background.

The clinician observed considerable emotional stress and conflict between the parents, as well as additional family issues of concern. It was paramount at that time to observe family dynamics, get a feel for the family structure and act within the family power structure, maintain a directive and problem-oriented focus consistent with parents' expectations and comfort level, and address concretely their specific requests for services for Tong. The parents had clearly come to the meeting with very specific objectives, none of which related solely to services for their son.

The family sought assistance in several areas: first, an explanation for Tong's hospitalization, which they had initially understood to be related to physical symptomology, not mental health. Prior to Tong's hospitalization, he had been expelled from summer school for his aggressive and threatening behavior to other students. The issue of when and to what school placement he would return needed resolution, and the family needed advocacy assistance on this matter. Given Tong's social isolation, the family was interested in our psychosocial group program, which would connect him with deaf and hard of hearing peers. Finally, the family was also open to receiving individual counseling to address Tong's behavioral and social-emotional issues.

We were able to provide concrete action for each service. Equally important, all of these services were provided or managed by a culturally competent, multilingual Chinese American clinician/social worker, a factor that helped significantly in strengthening the therapeutic alliance and gave credibility to our overall program services.

As the family saw the positive impact our interventions had on Tong, their trust and reliance increased. This gave us the leverage to encourage the parents to utilize other services more effectively, and to deal more directly and openly with the mental health issues that Tong presented. An Asian community mental health agency took over supervision of Tong's medications, conducted couples therapy with the parents, and provided family therapy in a co-therapy arrangement with us. This arrangement assured that both deafness and ethnic cultural sensitivity were attended to in a therapeutic milieu.

Individual therapy with Tong, using a cognitive behavioral orientation, helped him identify and organize his thoughts and emotions, and focus his attention on one topic or task at a time. Clear limits and expectations had to be firmly established with regard to persevering behaviors and personal space/boundaries. Tasks had to be broken down into simple concrete steps given Tong's cognitive and visual spatial processing deficits. Communication with Tong involved spoken and signed English and spoken Cantonese. Tong's identity issues concerning his ethnicity and hearing status also needed to be addressed during therapy.

The school did not have the resources to work intensively with Tong. After he was transferred to a specialized school for severely emotionally disturbed students, which had a classroom for deaf youth, he showed improvement. However, the school's initial reports only discussed changes that were for the most part positive. The parents assumed that all of Tong's negative behaviors had stopped, and wanted him to return to public school. When they found this was not true, they felt (as they had with the first hospitalization situation) that they had not been fully informed. They insisted he be given a chance to return to his former school.

The transfer resulted in Tong's mental decompensation, which led to another psychiatric hospitalization. Following the second hospitalization, Tong returned to the specialized school. Because communication expectations were clearer on both sides, and the parents had a growing understanding of Tong's problems, the second time around was much more effective in helping Tong.

Although his school setting provided stable control with regard to Tong's emotional and social behaviors, the home environment was still "out of control." It was eventually decided that placement at a long-term residential treatment facility over sixty-five miles away from home would be in Tong's best interest. The referral was prepared by the case manager at our agency in conjunction with the county mental health system and a co-therapist from the Asian community mental health agency. Continuation of family therapy would be maintained by our agency's worker in co-therapy with the Asian community mental health agency. Tong would occasionally participate in our psychosocial group activities when he visited home on weekends.

The treatment center provided a much needed, highly structured environment. Overall, Tong began to do well academically and demonstrate greater impulse control. His parents gained a much better understanding of their son's needs and his likely future. They gained skills to act in concert rather than being "split" by their son's behavior. They gained much more understanding of and ability to utilize resources available to them.

The treatment center's empowerment of Tong as a Deaf person reinforced Tong's sense of his rights as an eighteen-year-old in America to make his own decisions and be on his own. However, this empowerment pitted him against his family and against the ethnic cultural values, identity, and way of life in which he was raised. There was little progress in helping Tong integrate the positive aspects of his identity as a Deaf individual and as an Asian American, and develop the skills of listening, discussing, and negotiating. The parents felt they had lost their son, who would probably move to an adult deaf residential vocational placement in another part of the state.

Perhaps the ultimate professional and ethical question that remains in this case is how sensitive and respectful the mental health system was in improving Tong's overall well-being and in acknowledging all the components of his identity—not merely the ones the "system" deemed most important to address.

* * *

Third case study: Fong and Lan

Fong and Lan were profoundly deaf adolescent sisters, aged sixteen and twelve, respectively. There was a hearing middle sister, aged fifteen. The etiology of deafness in this family was genetic; the mother's brother was also deaf. The family came to the United States in 1994 from mainland China to live in San Francisco's Chinatown with the father's parents. The family spoke two Chinese dialects (Cantonese and Toisanese). The parents and grandparents had no English skills, and communicated with the girls through home signs; the middle sister sometimes interpreted.

The girls' schools referred them to our program. Their teachers determined that the girls needed support in acculturation and adjustment, and the family needed social work support services. The family claimed they had few problems with either girl in China. They recognized acceptable differences in the girls' personalities and characters. However, they did not understand why, since the move, the younger girl had grown increasingly oppositional and noncompliant with the family's cultural expectations of socially appropriate behavior. They recognized that Lan is more outgoing and adventurous than Fong. However, they still expected Lan to be obedient, respectful, and attentive to her parents, and especially to her grandparents. Instead, Lan often chose not to follow directions or orders, and occasionally questioned the authority of her grandparents and her parents. She frequently "*faht pay hay*" (pouted, whined, cried) when she didn't get what she wanted.

It was first crucial to understand the family structure and hierarchy of authoritative power in order to be able to act within it. In our initial family meeting, communication patterns revealed the specific roles of the various family members. It was clear from the outset that the grandfather held the highest position of authority and respect in the family. He did most of the talking and appeared to take on responsibility for the welfare of his son's entire family. The others acted in accord with whatever the grandfather expressed. Following him in the hierarchy was his wife (the children's grandmother), then the father, the mother, and lastly the three girls.

The family was a very closely knit, traditional Chinese family with each member having a clearly defined role and responsibility. Their strong unity and deep sense of family obligation were strengths that, when utilized in a culturally appropriate manner, could therapeutically aid the family's adjustment to dealing not only with the two girls' deafness, but also facilitate a smooth acculturation process.

Intervention included family and individual counseling, working within the family's perceptions of the mental health issues and with respect for the family hierarchy. The parents' power in an American family would naturally (culturally) be the strongest. In this case, it was essential initially to form an alliance with the grandfather given his decision-making power in the family. This process did not neglect the issues of the parents or of the girls themselves; rather the emphasis was on order, the timing of interventions, and the manner in which issues were raised or challenged.

During counseling, it was helpful to "normalize" many of the behavioral differences the grandparents and parents saw between the eldest and youngest girl, and to put these behaviors in a developmental context that made cultural sense to the family. Using a psychoeducational structure and format, the clinician explained and discussed with the family the American lifestyle of teenagers in contrast to the Chinese perspective on adolescent development. Understanding the pressure on Lan from her school peer group and the general pressure of acculturation to an American lifestyle were very foreign concepts. Repeated discussion of these issues slowly helped to elevate the parents' and grandparents' awareness and understanding of Lan's experience as a foreign-born adolescent. They could see her as tempted, as so many foreign-born young people are, by the attractions of the American lifestyle.

Lan's identity issues had more to do with "fitting into" American culture than with Deaf culture per se; she wanted to have an American name, clothes and other material objects, a boyfriend, and more independence. Many of the issues that the family identified as problems would not have come up if they were still in China. Conceptually, it was especially difficult for the family because the older girl behaves the way they culturally expect. The hearing middle sister was more bicultural, able to code-switch between home and the outside world.

Interventions with Lan helped her understand the difference between her family's expectations and her experience. Her peer group in China would have been thinking and behaving differently, more as her family expected. The clinician helped her to identify her feelings and why they came up. She helped her to gauge her family's responses (by reading facial expressions and body language) and understand her family's perspective. Lan began learning practical coping strategies, including how to express her questions or desires more appropriately and effectively to her parents and grandparents. She began doing well academically and in learning both English and ASL. Her sister Fong, while emotionally more mature, had a harder time with sign language and English.

The family members felt bad because they could not communicate more easily with the girls. Facilitating communication between the girls and the grandparents was very powerful for all of them, and opened the door to dealing with some of their intergenerational and cross-cultural issues. Realistically, this family was not in a position to learn sign language easily or fluently. For them, learning English was a much more critical survival skill. Our communication intervention was critical in preventing problems: as issues came up, the family came to us to serve as communication facilitators. Because of the trust developed over time, the family was open to our suggestions, explanations, and advice.

Language and Interpreting Issues

Language obviously is a critical tool for communication. In working with Asian families with a deaf family member, there could be as many as four languages involved: the signed and spoken language or dialects of the home country, ASL, and English. Because Chinese languages are tonal (they have a range of musical-type pitches that carry meaning), they especially affect a hard of hearing Asian person's understanding, and therefore English is sometimes easier to decode. Utilizing each person's own communication comfort and strength is most effective, but can be tricky when there are several communication systems required. The more links (interpreters) there are in the communication chain, the more likely the message is to become muddled, misunderstood, or distorted, like the child's game of "telephone."

To manage difficulties and be an effective part of the intervention team, interpreters receive training in confidentiality, boundaries within a mental health setting, and cross-cultural communication. They need to understand American mental health concepts and terminology in order to convey these to Asian clients. Interpreters should interpret verbal and nonverbal responses, and provide culturally relevant information so that the clinician can make culturally accurate interventions (Yacobacci-Tam, 1987). An interpreter who is bilingual but not bicultural may know the language but not the cultural information; the client may see them as less knowledgeable or reliable. Finally, it is critical that the interpreter be skilled in the dialect of the client/family member (not just assume that it will be spoken Mandarin or Cantonese, or Beijing-style sign language). The interpreter should also be sensitive to the match between family and interpreter in terms of politics. For example, if an interpreter with a Khmer Rouge background is assigned to a Cambodian refugee family, the consequences could be traumatic.

Realistically, many agencies are not able to hire staff who are fluent in all languages and knowledgeable about all cultures. Developing co-therapy, consultation, and cross-training relationships with ethnic community agencies can give one access to their clinicians and/or interpreters. Our nonprofit agency has a very small pool of multicultural volunteers who serve as community workers. They are usually well-educated immigrants who have an interest in deafness or sign language, know some sign language, and have good English skills. With very careful training and supervision, they can be of great assistance in maintaining communication with family (for example, setting up appointments, interpreting for therapy sessions, and relaying messages to and from families).

Conclusion

Many of the issues concerning mental health and Asian American deaf clients parallel those of other diverse ethnic and cultural groups within the deaf context. This chapter has focused on the competencies, strategies, and skills necessary to work effectively with Asian American deaf people and their families.

The collectivist orientation of Chinese culture naturally lends itself to collaboration. Professionals in the field of deafness should address their own efficacy in two directions: first, by minimizing the individual, community, and systemic barriers between and among hearing and deaf, and Asian and American groups; and second, by actively building bridges between and among our respective communities.

References

Aramburo, A. J. (1989). Sociolinguistic aspects of the black deaf community. In C. Lucas (Ed.), *The sociolinguistics of the deaf community* (pp. 103–119). San Diego: Academic Press.

Armour-Thomas, E., & Gopaul-McNicol, S. (1997). Bio-ecological approach to cognitive assessment. *Cultural Diversity and Mental Health, 3* (2), 131–144.

Asbury, C. A., Walker, S., Maholmes, V., Rackley, R., & White, S. (1991). *Disability prevalence and demographic association among race/ethnic minority populations in the United States: Implications for the 21st century.* Howard University Research and Training Center for Access to Rehabilitation and Economic Opportunity, Washington, DC.

Asian American Health Forum. (1990). *Healthy people 2000 fact sheet.* San Francisco: Asian American Health Forum.

Atkinson, D., Morton, G., & Sue, D. (1983). *Counseling American minorities.* Dubuque, IA: William C. Brown.

Atkinson, D., & Thompson, C. E. (1992). Racial, ethnic, and cultural variables in counseling. In S. D. Brown & R. W. Lent (Eds.), *Handbook of counseling psychology* (2d ed.) (pp. 349–382). New York: Wiley.

Axelson, J. A. (1993). *Counseling and development in a multicultural society* (2d ed.). Pacific Grove, CA: Brooks/Cole.

Baker, C., & Battison, R. (1980). *Sign language and the deaf community: Essays in honor of William Stokoe.* Silver Spring, MD: National Association of the Deaf.

Baker, C., & Cokely, D. (1980). *American sign language: A teacher's resource text on grammar and culture.* Silver Spring, MD: T. J. Publishers.

Becker, G. (1980). *Growing old in silence.* Berkeley: University of California Press.

Canino, I. A., & Spurlock, J. (1994). *Culturally diverse children and adolescents: Assessment, diagnosis, and treatment.* New York: Guilford Press.

Chan, K. S. (1983). Limited English speaking, handicapped, and poor: Triple threat in childhood. In C. C. Mae (Ed.), *Asian- and Pacific-American perspectives in bilingual education: Comparative research* (pp. 153–171). New York: Teachers College, Columbia University.

Chan, S. (1992). Families with Asian roots. In E. W. Lynch, & M. J. Hanson (Eds.), *Developing cross-cultural competence: A guide for working with young children and their families* (pp. 181–257). Baltimore: Paul H. Brookes.

Cheng, L. L. (1993). Deafness: An Asian/Pacific Island perspective. In K. M. Christansen & G. L. Delgado (Eds.), *Multicultural issues in deafness* (pp. 113–126). White Plains, NY: Longman.

Chin, J. L. (1983). Diagnostic considerations in working with Asian-Americans. *American Journal of Orthopsychiatry, 53,* 100–109.

Chin, J. L., De La Cancela, V., & Jenkins, Y. M. (1993). *Diversity in psychotherapy: The politics of race, ethnicity, and gender.* Westport, CT: Praeger.

Cohen, O. P. (1991). At risk deaf adolescents. *Volta Review, 93* (5), 57–72.

Cohen, O. P., Fischgrund, J. E., & Redding, R. (1990). Deaf children from ethnic and racial minority backgrounds: An overview. *American Annals of the Deaf, 135,* 67–73.

Committee on Cultural Psychiatry. (1989). Suicide among the Chinese and Japanese. In Committee on Cultural Psychiatry (Ed.), *Suicide and ethnicity in the United States* (pp. 58–71). New York: Brunner/Mazel.

Christensen, K. M., & Delgado, G. L. (Eds.). (1993). *Multicultural issues in deafness.* White Plains, NY: Longman.

Delgado, G. L. (Ed.). (1984). *The Hispanic deaf: Issues and challenges in special education.* Washington, DC: Gallaudet College Press.

Durvasula, R., & Sue, S. (1996). Severity of disturbance among Asian American outpatients. *Cultural Diversity and Mental Health, 2* (1), 43–51.

Enright, J. V., & Jaeckle, W. R. (1963). Psychiatric symptoms and diagnosis in two subcultures. *International Journal of Social Psychiatry, 9,* 12–17.

Flaskerud, J. (1988). Mental health needs of Vietnamese refugees. *Hospital and Community Psychiatry, 39* (4), 435–437.

Flaskerud, J. H., & Hu, L. (1992). Racial/ethnic identity and amount and type of psychiatric treatment. *American Journal of Psychiatry, 149* (3), 379–384.

Fong, R., & Mokuau, N. (1994). Not simply "Asian Americans": Periodical literature review on Asian and Pacific Islanders. *Social Work, 39* (3), 298–305.

Glickman, N. S., & Carey, J. C. (1993). Measuring deaf cultural identities: A preliminary investigation. *Rehabilitation Psychology, 38* (4), 275–283.

Goodstein, R. (1994). *Racial and ethnic identity and their relationship to self-esteem.* Ph.D. dissertation, Fordham University at Lincoln Center, New York.

Greenberg, M. T., & Kusche, C. A. (1993). *Promoting social and emotional development in deaf children: The PATHS project.* Seattle, WA: University of Washington Press.

Hall, E. T. (1976). *Beyond culture.* Garden City, NY: Anchor Books.

———. (1984). *The dance of life: The other dimension of time.* Garden City, NY: Anchor Books.

Harris, P. R., & Moran, R. T. (1986). *Managing cultural differences* (2d ed.). Houston, TX: Gulf Publishing.

Harvey, M. A. (1989). *Psychotherapy with deaf and hard-of-hearing persons: A systemic model.* Hillsdale, NJ: Lawrence Erlbaum.

Heller, B. (1987). Mental health assessment of deaf persons: A brief history. In H. Elliott, L. Glass, & J. W. Evans (Eds.), *Mental health assessment of deaf clients: A practical manual* (pp. 9–20). Boston: Little, Brown.

Higgins, P. (1980). *Outsiders in a hearing world: A sociology of deafness.* Beverly Hills, CA: Sage Publications.

Ho, M. K. (1992). Differential application of treatment modalities with Asian American youth. In L. A. Vargas & J. D. Loss-Chioino (Eds.), *Working with culture: Psychotherapeutic interventions with ethnic minority children and adolescents* (pp. 182–203). San Francisco: Jossey-Bass.

Holcomb, T. (1997). Development of deaf bicultural identity. *American Annals of the Deaf, 142* (2), 89–93.

Huang, L. N., & Ying, Y. W. (1989). Chinese American children and adolescents. In J. T. Gibbs, L. N. Yuang, & Associates (Eds.), *Children of color: Psychological interventions with minority youth* (pp. 30–66). San Francisco: Jossey-Bass.

Humphries, T. (1993). Deaf culture and cultures. In K. M. Christensen & G. L. Delgado (Eds.), *Multicultural issues in deafness* (pp. 3–15). White Plains, NY: Longman.

Ing, C. D., & Tewey, B. P. (1994). *Chartbook summary of data on children & youth with disabilities in the United States.* Falls Church, VA: Conwal Incorporated.

Ishisaka, H., & Takagi, C. (1982). Social work with Asian- and Pacific-Americans. In J. Green (Ed.), *Cultural awareness in the human services* (pp. 287–315). Englewood Cliffs, NJ: Prentice-Hall.

Kim, S. (1985). Family therapy for Asian Americans: A strategic structural framework. *Psychotherapy, 22,* 342–356.

Kinzie, J. D. (1985). Overview of clinical issues in the treatment of Southeast Asian refugees. In T. Owan (Ed.), *Southeast Asian mental health: Treatment, prevention, services, training, and research* (pp. 113–135). Washington, DC: U. S. Department of Health and Human Services.

Kinzie, J., Boehnlein, J. K., Leung, P. K., Moore, L. J., Riley, C., & Smith, D. (1990). The prevalence of post-traumatic stress disorder and its clinical significance among Southeast Asian refugees. *American Journal of Psychiatry, 147,* 913–917.

Kinzie, J. D., & Manson, S. (1983). Five years experience with Indochinese refugee psychiatric patients. *Journal of Operational Psychiatry, 14,* 105–111.

Kitano, H. H. (1969). Japanese-American mental illness. In S. C. Plog & R. B. Edgerton (Eds.), *Changing perspectives in mental illness* (pp. 256–284). New York: Holt, Rinehart and Winston.

Lane, H., Hoffmeister, R., & Bahan, B. (1996). *A journey into the Deaf-world.* San Diego: Dawn Sign Press.

Lee, E. (1988). Cultural factors in working with Southeast Asian refugee adolescents. *Journal of Adolescence, 11,* 167–179.

———. (1997a). Chinese American families: In E. Lee (Ed.), *Working with Asian Americans: A guide for clinicians* (pp. 46–78). New York: Guilford Press.

———. (1997b). Overview: The assessment and treatment of Asian American families. In E. Lee (Ed.), *Working with Asian Americans: A guide for clinicians* (pp. 3–36). New York: Guilford Press.

Leigh, I. W., & Stinson, M. S. (1991). Social environments, self-perceptions, and identity of hearing-impaired adolescents. *Volta Review, 93* (5), 7–22.

Leong, F. (1986). Counseling and psychotherapy with Asian Americans: Review of the literature. *Journal of Counseling Psychology, 33,* 196–206.

Leong, F. T. L. (1996). MCT theory and Asian-American populations. In D. W. Sue, A. E. Ivey, & P. B. Pedersen (Eds.), *A theory of multicultural counseling and therapy* (pp. 204–216). Pacific Grove, CA: Brooks/Cole.

Leong, F. T. L., & Chou, E. L. (1994). The role of ethnic identity and acculturation in the vocational behavior of Asian Americans: An integrative review. *Journal of Vocational Behavior, 44,* 155–172.

Leung, P. (1996, Spring). Asian Pacific Americans and Section 21 of the Rehabilitation Act Amendments of 1992. *American Rehabilitation,* 2–6.

Lynch, E. (1992). Developing cross-cultural competence. In E. W. Lynch & M. J. Hanson (Eds.), *Developing cross-cultural competence: A guide for working with young children and their families* (pp. 35–62). Baltimore: Paul H. Brookes.

Marsella, A., Kinzie, D., & Gordon, P. (1973). Ethnic variations in the expression of depression. *Journal of Cross-Cultural Psychology, 4,* 435–458.

Matsumoto, D. (1994). *People: Psychology from a cultural perspective.* Pacific Grove, CA: Brooks/Cole.

Matsushima, N. M., & Tashima, N. (1982). *Mental health treatment modalities for Pacific/Asian-American practitioners.* San Francisco: Pacific Asian Mental Health Research Project.

McGoldrick, M., Giordano, J., & Pearce, J. K. (Eds.)., *Ethnicity and family therapy* (2nd ed.). New York: Guilford Press.

Mindel, E. D., & Vernon, M. (1987). *They grow in silence: Understanding deaf children and adults.* Boston: College Hill Press.

Padden, C. (1978). The deaf community and the culture of deaf people. In C. Baker & R. Battison (Eds.), *Sign language and the deaf community: Essays in honor of William C. Stokoe* (pp. 89–103). Silver Spring, MD: National Association of the Deaf.

Padden, C., & Humphries, T. (1988). *Deaf in America: Voices from a culture.* Cambridge, MA: Harvard University Press.

Phinney, J., Lochner, B., & Murphy, R. (1990). Ethnic identity development and psychological adjustment in adolescence. In A. Stillman & L. Davis (Eds.), *Ethnic issues in adolescent mental health* (pp. 53–72). Newbury Park, CA: Sage Publications.

Ridley, C. R. (1995). *Overcoming unintentional racism in counseling and therapy: A practitioner's guide to intentional intervention.* Thousand Oaks, CA: Sage Publications.

Schlesinger, H. S., & Meadow, K. P. (1972). *Sound and sign: Child deafness and mental health.* Berkeley: University of California Press.

Specht, J. (1996, 16 December). Record flow of immigrants into U.S. *Marin Independent Journal,* pp. A-1, A-12.

Sue, D. W., Ivey, A., & Pedersen, P. (1996). *A theory of multicultural counseling & therapy.* Pacific Grove, CA: Brooks/Cole.

Sue, D., & Sue, D. W., (1995). Asian Americans. In N. Vacc, S. DeVaney, & J. Wittmer (Eds.), *Experiencing and counseling multicultural and diverse populations* (3rd ed.) (pp. 63–89). Bristol, PA: Accelerated Development.

Sue, D. W., & Sue, D. (1990). *Counseling the culturally different: Theory and practice* (2d ed.). New York: Wiley.

Sue, S., & McKinney, H. (1975). Asian Americans in the community mental health care system. *American Journal of Orthopsychiatry, 45,* 111–118.

Sue, S., Sue, D. W., Sue, L., & Takeuchi, D. T. (1995). Psychopathology among Asian Americans: A model minority? *Cultural Diversity and Mental Health, 1* (1), 39–51.

Sue, S., & McKinney, H. (1975). Asian Americans in the community mental health care system. *American Journal of Orthopsychiatry, 45,* 111–118.

Tajfel, H. (1981). *Human groups and social categories.* New York: Cambridge University Press.

Takaki, R. (1989). *Strangers from a different shore: A history of Asian Americans.* Boston: Little, Brown.

———. (1993). *A different mirror: A history of multicultural America.* Boston: Little, Brown.

Tracey, T. J., Glidden, C., & Leong, F. T. (1986). Help seeking and problem perception among Asian Americans. *Journal of Counseling Psychology, 33,* 331–336.

Trueba, H. T., Cheng, L., & Ima, K. (1993). *Myth or reality: Adaptive strategies of Asian Americans in California.* Washington, DC: Falmer Press.

Tung, T. M. (1985). Psychiatric care for Southeast Asians: How different is different? In T. Owan (Ed.), *Southeast Asian mental health: Treatment, prevention, services, training, and research* (pp. 5–40). Washington, DC: U. S. Department of Health and Human Services.

Uba, L. (1994). *Asian Americans: Personality patterns, identity, and mental health.* New York: Guilford Press.

Wu, C. (1995). Foreword. In S. E. Ouellette, K. Dolan, & J. Vander Meer (Eds.), *Access Silent Asia: The Asian Deaf Experience Conference Proceedings, March 11–14, 1994, San Francisco, CA* (pp. vii–viii). DeKalb, IL: College of Health and Human Sciences, Northern Illinois University.

Yacobacci-Tam, P. (1987). Interacting with the culturally different family. *Volta Review, 89* (5), 46–58.

10

The Role of Therapeutic Groups in Working with Latino Deaf Adolescent Immigrants

MARGARITA HERNÁNDEZ

Moving to a foreign country is a most challenging experience in any adolescent's development. This is especially true for the deaf adolescent Latino immigrants with whom I have worked. The stressors of adolescence and migration are further compounded by the adolescent's deafness. Feelings of uprootedness, confusion, loss, and anger at adult caretakers are not uncommon. A small group approach appears to be an effective way to reach out to such adolescents. This approach can enhance adolescents' adjustment to the experience of relocation. They are helped to acknowledge and discuss their migration journey on a cognitive, linguistic, and emotional level. Issues specific to their struggles in coping with their new life, as well as typical adolescent concerns and issues related to family, peers, language, and academics need to be addressed within the context of the Latino, new host country, and the Deaf and hearing worlds. This chapter highlights the meaning and implications of this context and describes a small-group approach that was developed to address the unique needs of this population.

Demographics

The U.S. Census Bureau projects that by the year 2000 the nation's Latino population may well reach 31 million, 11.4% of the United States population. By the year 2010, Latinos are expected to be the largest ethnic minority group in the country (U.S. Bureau of the Census, 1996). Hearing-impaired Latinos make up 4.2% of the general Latino population in the United States (National Center for Health Statistics, 1994, as cited in Holt & Hotto, 1994, p. 6). According to the Center for Assessment and Demographic Studies at Gallaudet University, in 1990 there were approximately 20 million hearing-impaired individuals in this country, of whom 550,000 were described as deaf. Within educational programs serving deaf children, the Latino population is rapidly growing, having increased by 39% in the past ten years. In 1996–1997, Latinos (ages three to nineteen) comprised 18% of this population (Holden-Pitt & Díaz, 1998).

The themes in this chapter were first presented at the Fourth National Conference on Habilitation and Rehabilitation of Hearing Impaired/Deaf Adolescents: Puzzles, Problems and Promises, at Boys Town National Research Hospital, Omaha, Nebraska, in November, 1990. The author extends much appreciation to the following individuals for their helpful comments and review of the manuscript: Kathleen Friedman, C.S.W.; Gladys González-Ramos, Ph.D., C.S.W.; Irene W. Leigh, Ph.D.; Deborah Rubien, C.S.W.; and María Isabel Santiviago, M.Ed. I especially wish to acknowledge my colleague Ms. Santiviago for her contribution in our mutual endeavor to address the needs of the Latino deaf immigrant adolescents described in this chapter.

Hispanic is the term the U.S. Census Bureau uses to classify those individuals born in the United States of Hispanic heritage and those individuals born in any of the Spanish-speaking countries of the Caribbean (Cuba, the Dominican Republic, and Puerto Rico) or South America, or Mexico, Central America or Spain who now live in the United States. Increasingly the term "Latino" or "Latina" has come into use as a preferred term of self-identification (Chapa & Valencia, 1993; Dana, 1993; Sue & Sue, 1999).[1] It is important to recognize that Latinos are a heterogeneous group comprised of individuals of diverse racial, ethnic, cultural, linguistic, religious, and socioeconomic backgrounds (Castex, 1994; Guarnaccia & Rodríguez, 1996; Sue & Sue, 1999).

Migration and Associated Stressors

People migrate for different reasons, ranging from a desire to rejoin family members, a desire to improve their economic situation, a wish to pursue educational goals, to avoid political persecution or civil unrest, or because of factors related to family or personal difficulties. Some individuals and families make the decision to migrate voluntarily, while others are forced to leave their country. Children and adolescents are not usually involved in making the final decision to migrate. Regardless of the reason, the experience of separation involves leaving behind one's family and relatives, a home, and belongings, as well as familiar surroundings and social network. This experience brings up feelings of loss and mourning (Castex, 1992, 1997; Espin, 1987; Levy-Warren, 1987).

When people migrate, they do so with certain expectations of a better life in their new country. When discrepancies arise between their dreams and the realities of the actual life they encounter, they may feel disappointment, anger, and disillusionment, paving the way for possible adjustment difficulties (Fitzpatrick, 1987). Even though some immigrants may actually experience an improvement in their socioeconomic status, they nevertheless lack the familial and social support they once had in their homeland.

The degree of stress on the individual will vary according to the immigrant's previous level of functioning in the native country and circumstances confronted within the new host country. Availability and access to employment, to family, to a social support network, and to community resources in the host country are critical indicators of how the immigrant will fare in his or her adaptation (Sluzki, 1979). The immigrant's legal status is another possible stressor. Immigrants who do not possess legal documentation to reside in the host country experience hypervigilance in their daily activities because of fear of possible deportation. Other stressors that confront immigrants relate to experiences of discrimination and prejudice because of their ethnic, racial, linguistic, or religious background. The immigrant's feeling of being "welcomed" and accepted depends on the host country's perceptions of the immigrant's racial and ethnic status. In the United States, a fair-skinned, English-speaking European immigrant's experience will differ markedly from the dark-skinned, non-English-speaking immigrant's experience (Smart & Smart, 1995).

1. The gender-specific ending has become a political issue within the community, with the feminine form "Latina" often preferred for referring to a woman. In order to avoid awkwardness and to facilitate understanding, this chapter uses the masculine or neutral ending "o" when discussing a general population or group of people. When a reference is made to a specific female individual, she is referred to as Latina.

POTENTIAL STRESSORS FOR DEAF ADOLESCENT IMMIGRANTS

1. Psychological turmoil of adolescence;
2. Ensuing family disruption and reshifting;
3. Pressure to learn new languages;
4. Low socioeconomic status or poverty;
5. Feelings of uprootedness, loss and mourning, confusion;
6. Anger at the adult caretaker.

Figure 1. Adolescent Stressors

The need to learn a new language while learning to navigate the different systems—political, employment, legal, educational, and social services—compound the stress. Immigrants often find that their traditions, values, and belief systems are not only different from those of the host country but that they are not held in high regard and may be misunderstood. This can lead to demoralizing feelings of devaluation, affecting both a person's self-esteem and self-concept.

The Latino deaf adolescent immigrant must contend with a number of unique and formidable challenges (see figure 1). Upon entering the host country, specifically the United States, the Latino deaf adolescent is relegated to "minority" status, not only because of the individual's ethnic or racial group but also because of the deafness (Humphries, 1993). The Latino deaf adolescent has been described as possessing "dual minority group membership" (Cohen & Grant, 1983) or "multicultural status" (Humphries, 1993), or as being a "multicultural minority" (Rodríguez & Santiviago, 1991).

The Latino deaf immigrant adolescent must contend with the external societal forces of discrimination and racism within both hearing and deaf communities, while attempting to cope with the internal emotional demands made by individual and familial issues brought on by the acculturation process. For a discussion of racism, see Corbett, in this volume. Suffice it to say that very little has prepared these adolescents for such difficult experiences.

* * *

Miguel, a thirteen-year-old, had been in this country less than a year.[2] He came to his counseling session one day and wrote down on a piece of paper the word "rasims," meaning racism. The counselor learned that some of his deaf classmates were calling him a "drug dealer" because he came from a country that was receiving a lot of media attention related to drugs. This boy was very upset by his classmates' remarks, experiencing them as assaults to his already vulnerable sense of identity. This occurred at the same time that he was trying to adjust to living in a new country with his father and a new stepmother, whom he perceived as rejecting.

2. To protect client confidentiality, all client descriptions are composites that reflect the experiences of several of the Latino deaf immigrant adolescents. Names and countries of origin have been altered.

Latino deaf adolescent immigrants, like their hearing counterparts, must cope with feelings of loss for the caretakers, family, and friends who remain in their native country. They must cope with reentry into a family that they might not have lived with for several years. Many confront these challenges without the benefit of being informed or prepared in a manner consistent with their linguistic or cognitive skills. Most of the adolescents that the author has worked with have had to cope with the issues of loss and adaptation within the context of very limited communication with non-signing hearing parents or family members.

In many families, the trend has been for one of the parents to migrate first, to seek employment, and work toward bringing the remaining family members, sometimes in stages, to the new country (Castex, 1997; González-Ramos, 1990). My impression, based on my clinical practice, is that the mothers are usually the first to migrate. Regardless of who leaves or who remains, all family members experience disruption in their accustomed family life as a result of migration. Some families reconstitute as their former family unit; others do not. It was not uncommon for parents to separate or divorce after such a separation. One student, who had not lived with her mother for five years, said that upon arriving at her new home she was introduced to a new stepfather and two new half-siblings. This adolescent had to deal with the painful reality of migrating to a new country and making a transition to a "new family." The deaf adolescent immigrant often harbors resentment toward the parent or parents for real or imagined reasons for the family separation and changes in the family's circumstances. One deaf adolescent expressed anger at his hearing mother for having departed for the United States with one of his younger hearing siblings, while he remained with his father. This boy experienced the younger sibling as being his mother's favorite, valued and loved, while he was unloved and abandoned, which he also related to his being deaf.

An additional stressor that the deaf adolescent experiences is that of feeling burdened or confused by the parents' own ability to cope with the relocation. Is the parent satisfied or dissatisfied with his or her new circumstances? How are these feelings and reactions manifested and expressed to the deaf adolescent? Can the parent communicate his or her feelings adequately in sign language? Many parents say the primary reason they immigrate is to obtain a good education for their deaf child. What happens then when the family finds itself living in a poor inner-city area or working at menial jobs? Does the adolescent feel his or her deafness is responsible for the family's plight? Does the deaf adolescent internalize the parent's disappointment and possible distress as stemming from disappointment in the child because he or she is deaf, rather than on external circumstances? These issues need to be addressed by the helping professional.

Even "minor" stressors, like the change in climate, need to be addressed (Santiviago, personal communication, June, 1988).

* * *

> One deaf adolescent, a native of a Caribbean island, described how he arrived in New York in January. He had been told about cold weather by relatives who had once lived in that city. However, because he had always lived on a tropical island, as much as he tried to imagine what cold weather might feel like, he was not prepared for the cold weather that greeted him at the airport. He described disembarking from the airplane wearing a heavy sweater, his hands becoming "stiff"

and "frozen" from the cold air. Once enrolled in school, his attendance was sporadic during the first fall and winter term.

These stressors exact a range of emotional responses. It is often difficult for a hearing immigrant who has language to acknowledge and identify experienced distresses. I believe that it is even more difficult and complex for Latino deaf adolescent immigrants, particularly those with limited language skills.

Language/Communication

The Latino deaf adolescent immigrant often arrives in the United States without any knowledge of American Sign Language (ASL) or English. His or her sign language will vary depending on the country the deaf adolescent hails from, and communication modes will be influenced by the school for the deaf that the adolescent attended (if he or she attended a school for the deaf at all). Most schools for the deaf in Latin America strongly adhere to the oral tradition, although some do use their native sign language as the vehicle for instruction (Gerner de García, 1993). Adolescents from rural areas often do not have easy access to a school for the deaf because the school may be situated several hours away in an urban area (Jackson-Maldonado, 1993). Some parents may then resort to enrolling their deaf child in a school for hearing children, usually with minimal or nonexistent services for deaf and hard of hearing students. Some do not send their children to school at all.

Deaf children who do not possess adequate language skills often exhibit behavior problems because they do not have an outlet for their frustration and aggression (Litoff & Feldman, 1981; Schlesinger & Meadow, 1972). Language deprivation affects academic learning, the ability to conceptualize, and the evolution of interpersonal relationships (Marschark, 1993; Meadow, 1980). The Latino deaf immigrant child and adolescent is at risk for adjustment and educational difficulties upon arriving in the new host country and new school by virtue of his or her unfamiliarity with new and foreign languages (ASL and English) and/or limited educational experience. In addition to the physical and emotional upheaval of migration, he or she is now being asked to learn, think, and interact in unknown languages, a formidable challenge for any individual.

Adolescence during Migration

For the Latino deaf adolescent immigrant, the normal stress of adolescence is exacerbated by the migration and acculturation process, and compounded further by deafness. Adolescents find themselves in a state of flux on several different levels. Physically, emotionally, and cognitively their world is changing and expanding. They experience internal and external pressures and demands, often perplexing and stressful. During this developmental stage there are specific tasks that need to be navigated, including psychological separation from parents and identity formation (Blos, 1979; Erikson, 1968). As the parents' importance recedes, peers become more important. Questions of self-identity and group identification begin to emerge. In the quest for a sense of self-identity the question "Who am I?" in relation to family, peers, other adults, and self is most characteristic of this developmental state (Lidz, 1983). For the Latino deaf adolescent immigrant, additional questions are posed: How do I fit in with my hearing family?

Do I identify myself as deaf or hard of hearing? (Cohen, 1978; Glickman, 1983); as a member of the new host country's hearing and/or deaf community? How do I gain entry into these worlds? Can I become a member of the larger non-Latino deaf community without giving up my ethnic identity? Do I and can I enter the mainstream hearing Latino and/or non-Latino cultures? (Hernández, 1990).

In the country of origin the Latino deaf adolescent may have identified as a rural person or urban person, with his or her socioeconomic group, and as a member of his or her national group. Upon arriving in the United States, the adolescent is no longer identified by his or her nationality (Dominican, Mexican, Argentinean, Puerto Rican, etc.) by the new host country, but is now a "Hispanic" or "Latino" deaf adolescent. The distinctiveness of his or her nationality/ethnicity is lost. One adolescent felt pressured by his deaf peers to identify as Deaf only. This sixteen-year-old adolescent had strong ties to his country of origin and family members who remained behind. His wish was to return to his homeland after high school graduation. He felt as if he was being asked to dismiss his ethnicity, adding another stressor to the adolescent struggle of identity formation.

The psychological process of individuation from parents and the gradual redefinition of one's sense of self is often characterized by conflicted feelings. There is a pull to be dependent on the caretakers and an opposing pull to be independent. Latino deaf immigrant adolescents are placed in a precarious position, feeling the developmental pull to be independent in a foreign country where they can not communicate in the languages of either the hearing or the Deaf world. "Home signs" and gestures may be the only language skills these adolescents have, unless they had attended a school for the deaf or associated with deaf peers in their country of origin.

Regardless of the level of language skills, the initial experience upon arriving in the new host country generally is that of not understanding and not being understood. The adolescent depends much more on adult caretakers (parents, stepparents, extended family) to help him or her navigate through the uncharted waters of the foreign environment. This can create emotional conflict for adolescents striving to develop individuation.

Parental Perspectives

Some Latino parents have a difficult time encouraging independence and autonomy in their deaf children because of the parents' traditional cultural values; limited perception of a deaf person's capabilities; wish to make up for the time that they and their children were separated; and, unknowingly at times, because of their own fears and anxieties about the new host county. Some parents are reluctant to permit independent exploration and socialization on the part of their deaf adolescent children because of their own fears about the deaf adolescent's ability to function and interface in the new culturally different hearing environment, the new foreign city.

* * *

One Dominican family had resided in the city for two years, but continued to feel isolated. The mother referred her deaf adolescent daughter for counseling because her daughter was making "demands" to go out with peers. The mother explained, "We come from a small town where everyone knew each other. If I wasn't around, I knew that others would keep an eye on her. Here in New York, I don't know anyone and no one knows my daughter. How would I know if something happens to her?"

This mother said that her daughter was too young to go out on dates unchaperoned, a custom still followed in her country. She felt that because her daughter was "*así*" ("like that," alluding to her daughter's deafness), her daughter would not know how to protect herself from the dangers of the big city and the negative implications related to the custom of dating. The mother's perception of her daughter's deafness and inability to talk, intertwined with her traditional cultural values about dating and family interdependence, was in sharp contrast to the different cultural messages her deaf daughter was being exposed to in the new host country and school. This mother felt she needed to protect her deaf daughter from potentially dangerous situations; that was her perception of her role as a good mother. As her daughter pushed for increasing independence, the mother's perceptions and concerns about her daughter's deafness became more defined and conflicted as she, the mother, contended with living in a new environment that promoted cultural perspectives and values different from hers.

Deaf Latino immigrants begin to acquire skills in ASL and oral/written or signed English as they interface with the cultures of their new host country, school for the deaf, and Deaf community. They become less anxious and freer to interact with non-Latinos or Latinos born in the United States. Peer acceptance and approval is very important to any adolescent. Hence, the Latino deaf adolescent immigrant begins to identify with peers and takes on some of the values of the "new peers" and school culture. Conflict between parent and adolescent emerges as a result of the difference in values and belief systems among the traditional Latino family's culture and the host country's culture and Deaf cultures, both of which are found in the school program for the deaf. The intergenerational conflict that usually arises from this growing identification with peers and the host country's values places the Latino deaf adolescent at risk for acting out behavior and other serious problems (García-Preto & Travis, 1985; Matsuoka, 1990).

Cultural Considerations

It is important for professionals providing mental health services to develop an awareness and understanding of the cultural values and beliefs of the individual Latino deaf immigrant adolescent and family. As mentioned earlier, many authors in the field of cross-cultural counseling warn of the dangers of categorizing all Latinos as if they are one homogeneous group, sharing the exact same values, traditions, and ideologies, regardless of their ethnic, socioeconomic, racial, linguistic, or religious differences (e.g., Dana, 1993; Vásquez, 1994). The inherent danger is in applying and utilizing counseling interventions designed specifically for the "Latino client," without looking at the uniqueness of the individual (Guarnaccia & Rodríguez, 1996). There will be differences distinguishing the newly arrived immigrant from the individual who has resided in this country for many years and adheres to traditional Latino values, and from the second- or third-generation Latino born in the United States, even though all may identify themselves as Latino or Hispanic. The differing levels of acculturation must be assessed and considered in one's work with this population (Bernal & Flores-Ortiz, 1982).

Despite the differences among the different Latino national groups, a major cultural value shared by all Latino groups is the emphasis on the centrality of family—including the extended family and kinship system, which includes individuals not related by blood—in the life of the individual (Sue & Sue, 1999). Embedded in this emphasis is the concept of family interdependence. The traditional Latino cultural perspective of family and interdependence differs markedly from the emphasis on the nuclear family and values of independence and individualism found in the United States culture (Baumeister, 1991).

Perceptions about hearing impairment will be influenced by culture as well as by level of education and socioeconomic factors, and will vary from culture to culture (Christensen & Delgado, 1993; Yacobacci-Tam, 1987). Some parents view deafness as a disability, a condition that imposes limitations on their child. Other parents view their child's deafness as punishment for some past action or thought, or as an act of God that they must resign themselves to for the remainder of their lives. This fatalistic view prevails in many Latino cultures (Fischgrund et al., 1987; Rodríguez & Santiviago, 1991). Some parents seek the help of folk healers to ascertain the possible reasons and remedies for their child's deafness. One parent told me that she had consulted with a folk healer about her concern that her child's deafness was caused by a *"mal de ojo"* (evil eye), placed on the child by an envious neighbor. She requested help to undo the hex. Knowing the parents' perceptions of deafness can be useful to professionals in their clinical work. The following vignette illustrates this point.

* * *

> A middle-class Ecuadorean parent told his counselor that in his country, his deaf son would be viewed as *"un inútil"* (a useless person), a person incapable of functioning productively in society. He was afraid that his son would be treated as the "town idiot," relegated to running errands for friends and neighbors.
>
> The father decided to relocate to the United States, where his son could learn academic and social skills that would foster his ability to live independently and productively. His hope was to return to his native country with a son who would not be perceived as a "defective" individual by family or community. This father, along with his wife, had sought out counseling because of their insecurities and anxiety about raising a child who is deaf, even though they did not identify this as the motivating reason for seeking this service.

The Challenge

In recent years there has been an increase in the number of immigrants entering this country. Approximately 1.1 million immigrants enter this country annually (Fix & Passel, 1994; National Immigration Forum, 1994). (This number does not account for those individuals who are undocumented.) This increase is also reflected in the educational and social services arenas. At the Lexington School for the Deaf in New York City, the Latino population in 1997 was approximately 40% of the student body (O. Cohen, personal communication, 21 October 1997). The school's mental health team, a staff consisting of social workers, counselors, and psychologists, provided counseling service to those students identified as needing this service. One such student was a Latino deaf adolescent immigrant, Juan, who had been in this country less than one year. He was referred to me for individual counseling because he exhibited serious behavior problems at home and his school attendance was poor. He was in a special program designed for immigrant students to address their language and educational needs. The early contacts with this adolescent marked the beginning of a journey for both student and therapist in discovering and understanding the emotional impact of his migration. Meeting this goal led to identifying other Latino deaf immigrants who might benefit from preventive psychotherapeutic intervention.

Counseling and mental health services as generally defined in the United States would not have culturally similar meanings for these adolescents and their families, particularly for those from rural areas or low socioeconomic background who tend to perceive mental illness as stigmatizing. These low-income or rural families often lack access to mental health services. According to Dana (1993), cultural preconceptions as to what problems warrant mental health intervention and what mental health services consist of might keep families from accessing these services. Cultural practices are often resorted to as ways to deal with such problems. Mental health services in the United States have been traditionally underutilized by low-income Latino immigrants (Miranda et al., 1996; Rogler et al., 1989; Vásquez & Ling Han, 1995). Yet it is this very segment of the Latino population—those who experience a multitude of stressors often related to their migration—who could benefit greatly from appropriate intervention.

The challenge was to devise ways to effectively help adolescent immigrants who were at risk for developing, or were already exhibiting, adjustment difficulties. Referrals for individual counseling only did not appear to be the most effective way to reach out to this population. A small group in a school setting with a psychoeducational focus designed to address adjustment difficulties related to the migration experience seemed to be a more viable approach. Because peers play a major role in the adolescent's life, it was thought that a "peer discussion group" would provide the Latino deaf adolescents with the opportunity to meet other adolescent immigrants trying to cope with the experience of relocation and adaptation.

This approach seemed to be the least threatening and most natural because it closely approximates a class setting within the school, but with a different orientation, focus, and goals. There was a better chance of the idea of group therapy being more acceptable and comprehensible to the adolescents and their immigrant parents, in contrast to making a referral to a community mental health program. According to González-Ramos (1990), the school is viewed as "in loco parentis" by traditional Latino parents. The role of the school is respected and understood. The role of the traditional community mental health clinic is less known and less understood. For many parents, because of cultural perceptions, referrals to mental health clinics might carry some degree of stigma of mental illness for their child and/or themselves.

The Group

The remainder of this chapter focuses on a group developed to address the needs of Latino deaf adolescent immigrants who were identified as being at risk by the very nature of their recent relocation to a new country, in this case, the United States. All the participants were attending a school for the deaf.

The goals of the group were several: to provide these Latino deaf adolescent immigrants with a supportive environment in which they could discuss and process, in their native language or preferred communication mode, their migration experience and current concerns; to decrease their sense of isolation by universalizing their experience; to facilitate their adjustment to a new country, new school, new cultures, and new languages; to facilitate their adaptation in living with their families for those who had been separated from their families due to the migratory process; and to help them maintain a sense of self and cultural identity as they faced the challenges of acculturation. It was hoped that the group process would help the adolescents begin to identify, acknowledge, and integrate (on both a cognitive and emotional level) the recent changes in their lives. The ultimate goal was for the adolescents to develop a more cohesive sense of self and surrounding environments (family, school, and their new country's hearing and Deaf cultures). Another crucial goal was to decrease the likelihood of the adolescent developing severe adjustment difficulties or prevent existing difficulties from escalating further.

GROUP LEADERS

Leading the group were a clinical social worker and a teacher, both hearing. The leaders spoke both English and Spanish, and used English-based signs with some ASL structural concepts. Most of the adolescents already knew the teacher in her previous capacities as an intake and language evaluator and Spanish language/culture teacher. She herself had emigrated from South America as an adult. The clinical social worker was known to only one student prior to the formal group sessions; her parents had migrated from Puerto Rico as adolescents. The goal of this collaborative relationship was to address the identified needs of the group members and offer appropriate interventions as optimally as possible. Each group leader brought to the group both personal and professional experience with migration/acculturation issues.

Integral to the group leaders' approach was an understanding and appreciation of the Latino deaf adolescent immigrant's cultural values, traditions, and beliefs. The leaders conceptualized the group as a culturally sensitive and culturally competent model (Guarnaccia & Rodríguez, 1996; Rogler et al., 1987, 1989). Although the group leaders were hearing, their years of experience in the field of deafness had exposed them to Deaf culture, the issues inherent in working with hearing families with a deaf family member, and the many diverse issues related to the deaf/Deaf and hearing worlds. There was no attempt to hasten the adolescent's acculturation but rather to help each one understand what they were going through and to give a name, a framework, to the phenomena of the recent whirlwind changes they were experiencing. The group met weekly for a period of two academic years.

GROUP COMPOSITION

The group members ranged in age from fourteen to twenty. All were severely and profoundly deaf. Each had been living in the United States for two years or less. They came from the Dominican Republic, Mexico, Honduras, Ecuador, Venezuela, and other South American countries. They were of different cultural, racial, and ethnic backgrounds. All except one were from low socioeconomic family backgrounds. The majority were now living in a big city for the first time. One group member had experienced a double migration, having migrated with her family as a young child from an Asian country to South America, and then as a young adolescent to New York.

All of the adolescents who participated in the groups displayed a range of linguistic and cognitive skills. All were learning English and ASL, and continuing to develop their native Spanish-language skills. A major challenge was to encourage those adolescents to identify their concerns and feelings, and be able to discuss them, in the group with their peers. They struggled to find words and concepts, whether in Spanish, English, or ASL, to represent their thoughts and feelings.

The language needs of these adolescents had to be addressed in order for them to process what they were experiencing within the context of migration. Through language we organize our thoughts and emotions (Pérez Foster, 1996). Without language, a person is deprived of the most essential tool by which to understand one's internal (self) and external world (family, friends, the larger society, rules, etc.). Without the use of symbols (words or signs), the individual is unable to identify his or her inner thoughts or emotions. This places severe limitations on cognitive, social, and emotional functioning. Once the adolescents had more words and concepts, it was hoped they would be increasingly able to identify, acknowledge, and discuss their experiences. This ability would initiate a process of integration of their experiences with the associated feelings, coalescing into a stronger sense of who they are, of "self."

GROUP PROCESS

The group leaders began by carefully listening to the concerns raised by the members through their stories, anecdotes, comments, and questions. It meant integrating theory, professional, and life experiences to conceptualize the struggles inherent in each adolescent's life based on past and current family history, current academic and social functioning, expressed concerns by group members, and the group leader's observation of each adolescent member.

The group leaders explained that they were not performing the role of teachers. All communication modes were acceptable. The group was not a language class: discussion or assignments would not be graded. Mistakes could be made without fear of criticism or ridicule; this was a group rule. The material discussed would be confidential unless permission was given by the group member to discuss a pertinent matter with a teacher or parent.

The group went through different stages. The content, themes, and process varied accordingly. Keep in mind that there were no clear lines of demarcation between the different group stages. Even in later stages of group evolution, there was often overlap with immediately preceding issues, as well as a return to themes that had emerged in earlier stages.

INITIAL STAGE

The initial goals were to make the group members feel as comfortable as possible in the new group setting, and for them to understand that the group provided a special place and time to discuss specific concerns unique to Latino deaf immigrant adolescents.

"*¡Bienvenidos!*" (Welcome!) read the poster in the classroom decorated with maps and travel posters of the students' native homelands. "*¡Hola!*" (Hello!) was the customary salutation, and "*adios*" (good-bye) the customary farewell, at each group meeting. Oral Spanish was the dominant language, plus English-based signs, and a combination of gestures and home signs. The group leaders voiced in Spanish and used English-based signs. Written language was in Spanish and English. Some students voiced in Spanish (all had limited vocabulary in Spanish), and also used gestures, home signs, and English-based signs if they knew any.

The beginning was characterized by the group members getting to know each other. They initially asked one other: WHERE FROM (*Which country are you from?*), WHEN COME (*When did you come here?*), FAMILY HERE (*Does your family live here in this country?*), and FLY HERE (*How did you get here?*). Equally meaningful were the adolescents' asking the same of the group leaders. The adolescents also wanted to know about each group leader's ethnicity: WHERE FROM (*Where are you from?*), HERE LONG TIME (*Have you lived here a long time?*), SCHOOL AMERICA (*Did you go to school in the United States?*). These were important questions for the group. The answers also helped to place both leaders in a social context.

Each member initially interacted more and identified with the group leader who had emigrated. "She's been through the same as us" seemed to be the sentiment. This leader had also lived on the same Caribbean island that several of the adolescents were from, although she was not a native of that island. Her knowledge and familiarity with that culture helped to make the adolescents feel that there was someone who really knew "their home" and understood them culturally.

The second leader, whose parents had migrated from Puerto Rico, shared anecdotes about her parents' experiences as adolescent immigrants who attended high school with minimal knowledge of English. This provided the adolescents with the understanding that others, including hearing people, have experienced the challenge of being an immigrant.

At this initial stage the commonality that the group members shared was the experience of emigrating and the new beginnings being encountered. The initial content focused on these new beginnings and transitions. Discussion about life in their native countries and the differences encountered between the new host country and the native countries predominated. The most-often used expression was the Spanish word "*diferente*" and the ASL sign DIFFERENT.

The adolescents were encouraged to recount, in whatever way they could, how they came to this country. They were asked why they came to this country, who accompanied them on their trip, who was the first person in their family to come to this country, which family members stayed behind, how long had they been separated from their parents and siblings before rejoining them or the "new family" they now were a part of. It became apparent that some of this information was missing. There were gaps in knowledge, in facts about their family and reasons for migrating to this country. They also spoke of what and whom they missed in their country of origin.

* * *

- Miguel mentioned missing his dog very much. He also spoke of having lived within walking distance of a beautiful beach (a very popular tourist area known for its beauty); now he lived in a poor urban area, far from any beach.

- Rosa, a shy fifteen-year-old, lived with her mother and siblings, but her father still remained in her country of origin. She was told her father would rejoin the family, but she had no information about when and what steps were being taken to do this.
- María, a fifteen-year-old female, shared that she had been eight years old when her mother left for the United States. She had lived with her maternal grandmother while her mother was working to send for her. Her mother visited her once a year. Even though she was now living with her mother, she missed her grandmother very much. Now she had a new stepfather and two new half siblings. Because she was rejoining her family as an adolescent at a different developmental stage, she and her mother were having difficulties readjusting to each other and finding a new fit. She could no longer relate as an eight-year-old to her mother; she needed to relate as a teenager, and this was causing problems at home.
- Antonio, a twenty-year-old, felt frustrated and angry. He had held a job in his native country. His mother's decision to emigrate meant a change in his status. He was now a student. He felt resentful being in a student role, which made him feel dependent. He preferred being independent and at work, earning money. Yet he was keenly aware of the need to learn ASL and English in order to participate in the workforce in his new country.

The theme of where and how do I fit in, so typical of the adolescent drama, was prevalent in the discussions. "Where do I fit in," they asked, "in this new country, in this new school, in these new cultures and languages, and in my 'new family'"? The feelings of loss and mourning, sadness, disappointment, and longing for the familiar were a major theme. Missing one's relatives and missing one's country, home, friends, neighborhood sweetheart, pet dog, or accustomed tropical climate were all identified and acknowledged as losses. By giving as much time as was needed to discuss these experiences and the feelings of loss they engendered, the group members were allowed to grieve and mourn.

How was this done, taking into account the linguistic limitations that some exhibited in their native language, in addition to facing the challenge of learning new languages? The group used a variety of tools, including maps, family photos, postcards of their country, drawings they made of their homes, a chronological chart of life events, family genograms (a three-generation family map discussed in McGoldrick & Gerson, 1985), and videotape presentations of the family genograms.

Assignments such as the family genogram were given to encourage communication between adolescent and parent. Misconceptions were identified and corrected by working on these projects. Some adolescents did not know the names of extended family members or were not aware of their kinship with certain individuals. These exercises, along with further discussion, helped some members to obtain a clearer understanding of their family system and their position in the family constellation. The family genogram specifically helped track the many changes in the family system as a result of the migration. In a concrete and visual manner the genogram first helped the adolescent to obtain factual information, consider and reflect on the different pieces of information obtained, and then begin to integrate the changes that had taken place within their family system (Freedman, 1994).

The group meetings served to identify other mistaken assumptions. One such assumption was that the school for the deaf they attended had no rules because the students were not required to wear uniforms. All of the students reported that in their countries, school uniforms were required, even at the public schools. The adolescents seemed genuinely surprised to learn that not wearing an official school uniform did not mean there were no rules or expectations about conduct at their school. "Why no uniforms?" they asked. After some discussion, the response was, "because the new school in the United States is different."

Juan said he had never known or seen so many deaf people in one place at the same time as he had at his current school. He, as well as some of the other group members who had never attended a school for the deaf or who had came from rural areas in their country of origin reacted similarly. It was not uncommon to be told that they did not know other deaf adolescents or that they were the only deaf individual in their small community or knew very few, if any, deaf adults in their country of origin. The concept of a deaf community and Deaf culture was novel to some of the group members. This led to discussion and sharing of information about the diversity of the deaf community and opportunities for exposure to Deaf social and cultural events.

The group leaders assumed a very active and didactic role at this beginning stage. They served as role models, language brokers, and culture brokers. They helped frame the adolescents' migration experiences as universal and normal. Frequent comments included YOU TOO, SAME ME, REALLY, FRUSTRATING, and HARD.

Teaching words in Spanish, English, and sign language was paramount at this stage. The relationship between group leader and each adolescent took on the quality of nurturing early parent-child interactions as the group leader introduced words in either Spanish or English and sign language to the group. The group leaders taught the new words in all three languages or translated from one language to another. Any question the adolescent member brought to the group meetings about not understanding a word or a sign or an event was acknowledged and answered. If the adolescent was observed not to understand, or stated that he or she didn't understand the word or sign, the word was then written, signed, and defined. Different tools and strategies were used to convey meaning. If one of the other group members knew the word or sign, he or she would then try to help out by explaining the meaning; sometimes these moments were humorous and other times they were not, especially when one of the adolescents could not grasp the meaning. One could see the frustration on their faces. Labeling words and concepts and explaining these in addition to reviewing them were strategies used in combination with encouragement, acknowledgment, praise, and recognition from the group leaders as incentives and reinforcers.

SECOND STAGE

Gradually there was a shift in language and communication modes. The group members were acquiring more language and thus had more tools at their disposal to express their thoughts and identify their feelings. There was an increase in the use of labeling and identification of feelings attached to the material discussed. The issues that emerged during this second stage were related to the process of learning new languages, the fear of forgetting their native language, and being confronted with academic and social demands in school. The underlying theme was separation and related anxiety.

The anxiety about learning languages manifested itself in different ways. For example, there were times when group members pressed Rosa and another shy group member to participate and elaborate more in the discussions. However, they were unable to do so because of their linguistic limitations. Such interactions were then used to talk about the difficulty and frustration they might be experiencing not only in the group, but outside the group as well, in their attempts to communicate with family members, teachers, and deaf peers.

With increasing frequency the group members came in asking about the meaning of signed or written English words they had just learned. At other times some of the members introduced newly learned words, emoting pride as they signed or wrote the new word. They wanted to practice signing, writing, or vocalizing these new words. While Spanish continued to be the preferred mode of communication, oral and written English and ASL were used more and more frequently. The group leaders maintained their roles as language brokers and supporters of the adolescents' efforts to learn languages.

The following three vignettes typify some of the group members' issues.

- Carlos, a sixteen-year-old member, shared that he could not understand his deaf classmates because they signed too fast. Even though he wanted to socialize with his deaf peers, he felt overwhelmed by the rapidity and fluency his fellow students exhibited in ASL. Because other group members were experiencing this problem as well, the group leaders utilized role play to model different ways to handle that situation. Role-playing provided the group members with concrete strategies on how to communicate one's lack of fluency in ASL to deaf classmates and ask that they slow down their signing. The group members watched and observed how the two group leaders enacted Carlos's description of the situation and tried to resolve it. The group members were encouraged to practice and expand on the different strategies to negotiate this situation.

- Another issue that emerged was concern about forgetting one's native Spanish language. One concerned member said, "If I learn English, I'll forget Spanish. What will I do? I won't be able to communicate with my family [the remaining family members in his country of origin]." There was an underlying fear that the familial bond would be severed. This adolescent was struggling with the potential loss of connection/closeness with relatives. He was trying to make sense out of his new worlds: life in the new host country and the memories of his life in his mother country and loved ones left behind. Learning a new language had emotional significance. Other group members concurred. They were concerned about the widening gap in communication among themselves and their monolingual Spanish-speaking hearing parents and family members. These Latino deaf adolescent immigrants were learning ASL and English, while their parents and family members were either not learning these languages at all or were learning them more slowly.

- Another issue had to do with a skit the group members were required to perform in a school assembly. They were anxious about performing in front of a large group, making mistakes, and dealing with resulting embarrassment. As the members described the skit and attempted to read and sign their lines, it became clear they did not understand the meaning of many of the words. They shared perceptions of feeling awkward and too embarrassed to ask their teacher for help or to admit that they did not comprehend the words or ideas.

A significant turning point occurred at this juncture in the group process. The group members turned to the group leaders and the group as a place to share their anxiety and distress about performing and not understanding the words and concepts. The group took on a special meaning for these adolescent immigrants. They had begun to view the group as a special place for emotional and concrete support, a place separate from family and school, where they could touch base and practice linguistic and social skills that were still new and challenging. The group became a safe haven, and the group leaders took on the role of the accepting and understanding mother who could acknowledge the adolescent's need for nurturing, language, information about the world, safety, and dependency, as well as support their striving for separation and individuation. This turning point in the group process led to further identification and discussion of more complex affect-laden issues.

THIRD STAGE

The group continued to meet, and the content gradually shifted from the migration journey to typical adolescent concerns. The group members were now nearing graduation from their special program in the middle school and anticipating entering high school. This new transition provoked anxiety for the members. Would they understand the new teachers and the other students? Did they know enough English or ASL to communicate effectively with them? What would be expected of them? They were unsure of what to expect. Topics of discussion increasingly began to encompass academic performance, expectations, and responsibilities, socialization with peers, appropriate behaviors and consequences of inappropriate behaviors, developing problem-solving skills, communication issues with hearing people, consideration of future educational and employment goals, and emerging parent-adolescent issues. All of these issues were addressed within the backdrop of the existing cultural differences of the Latino, the new host country, the school, and Deaf culture.

The group also markedly increased its use of English and sign language, with a corresponding decrease in the use of oral and written Spanish. The adolescents said they wanted to practice their English and ASL and not use Spanish in the group; the request was honored. A shift in the relationship with the group leaders occurred at this time. Initially, the group members had interacted most frequently with the group leader who had emigrated. Although they also had a teacher-student relationship with her outside the group, she seemed to have served as a representation (albeit unconsciously) of the group members' experience as newly-arrived immigrants. Now, as they were gradually adapting to the new host country and school, the Latina group leader who had been born in the United States acquired a different significance.

They asked her more questions about the city they lived in: its geography, information about other ethnic groups, and how to use public transportation and public libraries. Some were curious about schools for hearing children because they had siblings in public schools. They also wanted to know more about some of the country's customs and traditions, such as Halloween. The group leader became the culture broker who could clarify the differences among the new host country's culture, the school's culture, and the traditional Latino culture. This shift in the relationship with, and perceived attributes of, the group leaders seemed to parallel the adolescents' own growing adaptation and acculturation to life in the United States.

The group leaders became less active and didactic at this stage. The adolescents initiated discussions and brought in personal concerns about school-related activities, family, or peers. They raised issues related to communication difficulties with hearing people, including family members, functioning in a hearing work world, employment choices, growing up and becoming an adult, and whether to return to one's native country after graduation. They discussed how they felt about their job placements and the difficulties they encountered communicating with hearing employees or supervisors. They began to talk about what they would like to do in the future. Dating, how one chooses a person to go out with, the qualities one wants in friends or in a future spouse, finishing school, and current family problems were the overriding subjects of discussion. These discussions took into account the need to develop problem-solving and negotiation skills. At this time one member, María, became involved in the high school student government, and another announced that he received a "merit certificate." The group members expressed a growing sense of mastery of the challenges they were contending with as they transitioned into high school life.

FINAL STAGE

At this stage, two new events occurred: first, a newly arrived eighteen-year-old male immigrant joined the group; soon after, one of the leaders announced that she would be leaving. The new member's entry into the group and the co-leader's pending resignation simultaneously reactivated themes of separation, loss, and new beginnings. Some of the adolescents reverted to using Spanish, along with English, on behalf of the new member, Ricardo. They were very curious about him and his reasons for immigrating. They in turn reviewed with him their migratory journeys. They took on a big brother/big sister role and reassured him that he would progress and learn the new languages of the Deaf and hearing worlds, ASL and English. The supportive message given was, "We're doing it. You can do it too!" The new immigrant adolescent, although in a different school program, sought out the group members outside the meetings.

Presented with the co-leader's upcoming departure, the adolescents were encouraged to discuss their feelings about her leaving. During this last stage, the theme of ending, being left behind, saying good-bye, and acknowledging feelings of sadness and loss was critical and poignant. The departing co-leader acknowledged her own feelings of sadness and shared these with these adolescents. It was important to provide the group members with a different way to experience separation, loss, and transitions. The group members experienced a planned event: separation in which they actively participated.

They were prepared for the separation by being given information beforehand and most importantly by having the opportunity to share and discuss their feelings. Prior separation experiences from family, friends, and homeland were reviewed and compared. Active involvement of the group members in the discussion of this planned separation process was crucial. For some of the group members, this was a different experience of separation and ending. They were considered significant participants in this major event.

Ending the group meetings, yet another separation, had been discussed earlier. The remainder of the sessions easily flowed into reviewing their experiences in the United States, with family, and in school. The sessions highlighted the progress and gains students made, such as learning ASL and English, further Spanish-language development, graduation to high school, and making new friends. As termination was discussed, issues of previous separations and losses due to their migration also became part of the discussion.

Observations of the group members as they prepared for termination presented a striking contrast to the beginning group sessions two years earlier. The group members were able to discuss and reflect on their migration experiences. These experiences were recounted in a less fragmented and more coherent manner, compared to the earlier attempts made when the group first began. There were more factual details and information evident in the telling of their stories with spontaneous references to feelings and emotional reactions, a significant achievement for several of the adolescents. These impressions were a validation of the important role the group played in addressing the cognitive, emotional, social, and language needs of these Latino deaf adolescent immigrants. The group members displayed a much more cohesive and coherent sense of their migratory experience and current life events and circumstances.

A final group project was assigned. Each member began to work on an "autobiography" so that each could recount his or her story about leaving the homeland and coming to a new country. The project culminated with each group member videotaping their personal account of their migration journey. Juan, the sixteen-year-old mentioned at the beginning of the chapter who had initially been referred for individual counseling, gave the following account of his migration to the United States:[3]

> My name is Juan. I'm eighteen years old. I'm from a small town in Mexico. My father lives in Mexico, my grandmother, aunt, and sister, too. My mother lives in the United States. I'm the only deaf person in my family. My mother and stepfather are hearing. I grew up deaf. I speak Spanish. I know very little sign language. My mother moved to New York. I stayed with my father. She came back to Mexico to visit one or two times. She was away for a long time. One day my father told me I would go to the United States to live with my mother. I was surprised. My sister and I traveled by plane to the United States. I remember when the plane landed. I walked and looked for my mother. When she came up to me, I didn't recognize her because she looked different. I asked her to show me a picture of herself. She said I would have to wait until later. I picked up my suitcase. When I arrived at my mother's home I asked her again to show me a picture of herself, and she did. When I saw her picture she looked the same like when she lived in Mexico. I said, "Okay, now I believe that you are the same mother."
>
> When I attended school for the first time [in the United States], I only knew Spanish. I didn't know English or sign language. I now go to school regularly. Before I was absent often. I hated school. As time went on I improved. Things became easier. I would show up. I began to learn English. It's good to learn English and ASL. I feel better now. I have a job at the hospital that I like. I file and sort out papers. I have friends in school now. I know how to travel and take the subway. It's easy.

This young man, who had been referred for counseling because of frequent school absenteeism and serious behavior problems at home, went on to complete his high school program and enter the workforce.

3. This is the English translation of his ASL account.

Conclusion

Latino deaf adolescent immigrants are faced with major challenges. They are an at-risk population given the very nature of the psychosocial stressors encountered in the migration and acculturation process and the developmental stage of adolescence. These stressors are further compounded by the adolescents' deafness, new host country, and a new school system, as well as their exposure to Deaf and hearing American cultures, new languages, and possibly even a changed family unit. The role of therapeutic groups can be instrumental and valuable in facilitating the deaf adolescent immigrant's entry into and adaptation to their new environments.

Some considerations that should be taken into account when working with Latino deaf adolescent immigrants include the following: the therapist should have some knowledge of the Latino deaf adolescent immigrant's country of origin, culture, and traditional values, as well as the cultural perceptions of deafness. The helping professional should be sensitive to the emotional impact that migration can have on the adolescent's psychosocial functioning. It is crucial to obtain a history from both adolescent and parent about the migratory experience. Each individual's experience will be unique.

The adolescent should be encouraged to describe the circumstances that led to the migration and what is remembered about the actual journey to the new host country. This is particularly important because some adolescents may have experienced trauma in fleeing political persecution or civil war in their home countries. Other adolescent immigrants may have entered the host country undocumented, through means that put their safety at risk. The parents of these adolescents may live in fear of deportation. This information can alert the helping professional regarding the possible degree of trauma and anxiety that the adolescent may be experiencing in addition to the stressors that have already been described in this chapter so that appropriate interventions can be made. It is crucial for clinicians working with these adolescents to show sensitivity to their conflict, confusion, or struggle about self-identity. Most importantly, deaf adolescent immigrants need help in identifying their losses and must be provided with support as they mourn those losses.

The roles and functions of the group leaders can take a number of forms. Initially, they may fulfill a parental-teacher role in which they teach and label words and concepts in three different languages, simultaneously encouraging, acknowledging, and validating the group members' efforts to identify and communicate their thoughts. The varied and fluctuating roles of language broker, culture broker, teacher, counselor, role model, mentor, adult friend, and parental figure are therapeutically critical in the work. This process supports Phelan's (1974) view that group leaders wear different hats depending on the group's needs at various times.

The culturally-sensitive, supportive group environment provides group members with the opportunity to reflect and bring together the different aspects of their migratory experiences and ongoing struggles with adaptation to their new surroundings. A further benefit of the adolescent's participation in the group is that it facilitates referrals for individual and family counseling. The adolescents in the group began to learn concepts related to "emotions," "feelings," "problems," "upset," "family," and "life change," to name a few. Talking about problems and concerns was no longer a concept foreign to them. Many of the adolescents' parents readily identified with the difficulties and stresses of migration and saw value in their adolescent son or daughter participating in such a group that would focus on these issues. They were subsequently more accepting of recommendations for family therapy or individual counseling for their deaf adolescent if and when the need emerged.

Although the group samples were small in number, and related specifically to Latino deaf immigrant adolescents, I believe that the small group approach described here could be broadly applied to other deaf ethnic adolescent immigrant groups. I have also found the issues that emerged and the interventions used also to be applicable to individual and family therapy treatment modalities.

References

Anderson, G., & Bowe, F. (1972). Racism within the deaf community. *American Annals of the Deaf, 117,* 617–619.

Anderson, G., & Grace, C. (1991). The Black deaf adolescent: A diverse and underserved population. *Volta Review, 93,* 73–86.

Anderson, R. (1972). The importance of an actively involved therapist. In I. Berkovitz (Ed.), *Adolescents grow in groups* (pp. 31–36). New York: Brunner/Mazel.

Baumeister, R. (1991). *Meanings of life.* New York: Guilford Press.

Bernal, G., & Flores-Ortiz, Y. (1982). Latino families in therapy: Engagement and evaluation. *Journal of Marital and Family Therapy, 8,* 357–365.

Blos, P. (1962). *On adolescence: A psychoanalytic interpretation.* New York: Macmillan.

Bonham, H. E., Armstrong, T., & Bonham, G. (1981). Group psychotherapy with deaf adolescents. *American Annals of the Deaf, 126,* 806–809.

Canino, I., Earley, B., & Rogler, L. (1980). *The Puerto Rican child in New York City: Stress and mental health.* New York: Hispanic Research Center, Fordham University.

Caplan, G. (1964). *Principles of preventive psychiatry.* New York: Basic Books.

Castex, G. (1992). Soviet refugee children: The dynamic of migration and school practice. *Social Work in Education, 14,* 141–152.

———. (1994). Providing services to Hispanic/Latino populations: Profiles in diversity. *Journal of Social Work, 39,* 288–296.

———. (1997). Immigrant children in the United States. In N. Phillips & S. Straussner (Eds.), *Children in the urban environment* (pp. 43–60). Springfield, IL: Charles C. Thomas.

Chapa, J., & Valencia, R. (1993). Latino population growth, demographic characteristics, and educational stagnation: An examination of recent trends. *Hispanic Journal of Behavioral Sciences, 15,* 165–187.

Christensen, K., & Delgado, G. (Eds.). (1993). *Multicultural issues in deafness.* New York: Longman.

Cohen, O. (1978). The deaf adolescent: Who am I? *Volta Review, 89,* 265–274.

———. (1991). At risk deaf adolescents. *Volta Review, 93,* 57–72.

Cohen, O., Fischgrund, J., & Redding, R. (1990). Deaf children from ethnic, linguistic and racial minority backgrounds: An overview. *American Annals of the Deaf, 135,* 67–73.

Cohen, O., & Grant, B. (1981). Ethnic heritage and cultural implications in a school for deaf children. In F. Solano, J. Dodd-Eggleston, & E. Costello (Eds.), *Focus on infusion* (pp. 72–78). Rochester, NY: Convention of American Instructors of the Deaf.

Dana, H. R. (1993). *Multicultural assessment perspectives for professional psychology.* Boston: Allyn and Bacon.

Delgado, G. (1984). *The Hispanic deaf: Issues and challenges for bilingual special education.* Washington, DC: Gallaudet College Press.

Eldredge, N. (1993). Culturally affirmative counseling with American Indians who are deaf. *Journal of the American Deafness and Rehabilitation Association, 26,* 1–18.

Erikson, E. (1968). *Identity, youth, and crisis.* New York: W. W. Norton.

Espin, O. (1987). Psychological impact of migration on Latinas: Implications for psychotherapeutic practice. *Psychology of Women Quarterly, 2,* 489–503.

Fischgrund, J., Cohen, O., & Clarkson, R. (1987). Hearing-impaired children in Black and Hispanic families. *Volta Review, 89,* 59–67.

Fitzpatrick, J. (1987). *Puerto Rican Americans: The meaning of migration to the mainland.* Englewood Cliffs, NJ: Prentice-Hall.

Fix, M., & Passel, J. (1994). *Immigration and immigrants: Setting the record straight.* Washington, DC: Urban Institute.

Freedman, P. (1994). Counseling with deaf clients: The need for culturally and linguistically sensitive interventions. *Journal of the American Deafness and Rehabilitation Association, 27,* 16–28.

García-Preto, N., & Travis, N. (1985). The adolescent phase of the family life cycle. In M. Mirken & S. Koman (Eds.), *Handbook of adolescence and family therapy* (pp. 21–37). New York: Gardner Press.

Gerner de García, B. (1993). Addressing the needs of Hispanic deaf children. In K. Christensen & G. Delgado (Eds.), *Multicultural issues in deafness* (pp. 69–90). New York: Longman.

Glickman, N. (1983). A cross-cultural view of counseling with deaf clients. *Journal of the American Deafness and Rehabilitation Association, 16,* 4–14.

Glickman, N., & Harvey, M. (Eds.). (1996). *Culturally affirmative psychotherapy with Deaf persons.* Mahwah, NJ: Lawrence Erlbaum Associates.

Goldberg, E. (1980). Relocation and the family: A crisis in adolescent development. In G. Coelho & P. Ahmed (Eds.), *Uprooting and development: Dilemma of coping with modernization* (pp. 211–231). New York: Plenum Press.

González-Ramos, G. (1990). Examining the myth of Hispanic families' resistance to treatment: Using the school as a site for services. *Social Work in Education, 12,* 261–274.

Guarnaccia, P., & Rodríguez, O. (1996). Concepts of culture and their role in the development of culturally competent mental health services. *Hispanic Journal of Behavioral Services, 18,* 419–443.

Hardy-Fanta, C., & Montana, P. (1982). The Hispanic female adolescent: A group therapy model. *International Journal of Group Psychotherapy, 32,* 351–365.

Hernández, M. (1990). *Group and the Hispanic deaf adolescent immigrant.* Paper presented at the Fourth National Conference on Habilitation and Rehabilitation of Hearing Impaired and Deaf Adolescents: Puzzles, Problems and Promises. Boys Town National Research Hospital, Omaha, Nebraska, November.

Holden-Pitt, L., & Díaz, J. (1998). Thirty years of the annual survey of deaf and hard-of-hearing children and youth: A glance over the decades. *American Annals of the Deaf, 143,* 72–76.

Holt, J., & Hotto, S. (1994). *Demographic aspects of hearing impairment: Questions and answers* (3rd ed.). Washington, DC: Center for Assessment and Demographic Studies, Gallaudet University.

Hulewat, P. (1996). Resettlement: A cultural and psychological crisis. *Journal of Social Work, 41,* 129–135.

Humphries, T. (1993). Deaf culture and cultures. In K. Christensen & G. Delgado (Eds.), *Multicultural issues in deafness* (pp. 3–15). White Plains, NY: Longman.

Jackson-Maldonado, D. (1993). Mexico and the United States: A cross-cultural perspective on the education of deaf children. In K. Christensen & G. Delgado (Eds.), *Multicultural issues in deafness* (pp. 91–112). White Plains, NY: Longman.

Kamya, H. (1997). African immigrants in the United States: The challenge for research and practice. *Journal of Social Work, 42,* 154–165.

Levy-Warren, M. (1987). Moving to a new culture: Cultural identity, loss, and mourning. In J. Bloom-Feshbach & S. Feshbach (Eds.), *The psychology of separation and loss* (pp. 300–315). San Francisco, CA: Jossey-Bass.

Lidz, T. (1983). *The person* (2d ed.). New York: HarperCollins.

Litoff, S., & Feldman, V. (1981). Treatment issues with deaf children. In L. Stein, E. Mindel, & T. Jabaley (Eds.), *Deafness and mental health* (pp. 65–77). New York: Grune and Stratton.

McKinley, V. (1987). Group therapy as a treatment modality of special value for Hispanic patients. *International Journal of Group Psychotherapy, 37,* 255–268.

Marschark, M. (1993). *Psychological development of deaf children.* New York: Oxford University Press.

Matsuoka, J. (1990). Differential acculturation among Vietnamese refugees. *Journal of Social Work, 35,* 341–345.

McGoldrick, M., & Gerson, R. (1985). *Genograms in family assessment.* New York: W. W. Norton.

McGoldrick, M., Pearce, J., & Giordano, J. (Eds.). (1982). *Ethnicity and family therapy.* New York: Guilford Press.

Meadow, K. (1980). *Deafness and child development.* Berkeley: University of California Press.

Meeks, J. (1971). *The fragile alliance: An orientation to the outpatient psychotherapy of the adolescent.* Baltimore: Williams and Wilkins.

Millan, F., & Chan, J. (1991). Group therapy with inner city Hispanic acting out adolescent males: Some theoretical observations. *Group, 15,* 109–115.

Mindel, E. (1981). Therapy in the office or classroom. In L. Stein, E. Mindel, & T. Jabaley (Eds.), *Deafness and mental health* (pp. 79–84). New York: Grune and Stratton.

Miranda, J., Azocar, F., Organista, K., Muñoz, R., & Lieberman, A. (1996). Recruiting and retaining low-income Latinos in psychotherapy research. *Journal of Consulting and Clinical Psychology, 64,* 868–874.

National Immigration Forum. (1994). *Fast facts on today's newcomers* [handout]. Washington, DC: National Immigration Forum.

Pedersen, P., Dragus, J., Lonner, W., & Trimble, J. (Eds.). (1995). *Counseling across cultures* (4th ed.). Thousand Oaks, CA: Sage Publications.

Pérez Foster, R. (1996). Assessing the psychodynamic function of language in the bilingual patient. In R. P. Foster, M. Moskowitz, & R. Javier (Eds.), *Reaching across boundaries of culture and class: Widening the scope of psychotherapy,* (pp. 243–263). Northvale, NJ: Jason Aronson.

Phelan, J. (1974). Parent, teacher, or analyst: The adolescent-group therapist's trilemma. *International Journal of Group Therapy, 24,* 238–244.

Portner, D. (1982). Clinical aspects of social group work with the deaf. *Social Work with Groups, 4,* 124–133.

Rodríguez, O., & Santiviago, M. (1991). Hispanic deaf adolescents: A multicultural minority. *Volta Review, 93,* 89–97.

Rogler, L., Malgady, R., Costantino, G., & Blumenthal, R. (1987). What do culturally sensitive mental health services mean? The case of Hispanics. *American Psychologist, 42,* 565–570.

Rogler, L., Malgady, R., & Rodríguez, O. (1989). *Hispanics and mental health: A framework for research.* Malabar, FL: Krieger.

Sarlin, B. (1967). Group therapy with adolescent deaf students: Film and presentation. In J. D. Rainer & K. Z. Altshuler (Eds.), *Psychiatry and the deaf* (pp. 95–105). Washington, DC: U.S. Department of Health, Education, and Welfare, Social and Rehabilitation Service.

Sarlin, B., & Altshuler, K. (1968). Group psychotherapy with deaf adolescents in a school setting. *International Journal of Group Psychotherapy, 18,* 337–344.

Sarti, D. (1993). Reaching the deaf child: A model for diversified intervention. *Smith College Studies in Social Work, 63,* 187–198.

Schildroth, A., & Hotto, S. (1996). Changes in student and program characteristics, 1984–85 and 1994–95. *American Annals of the Deaf, 141,* 68–71.

Schlesinger, H., & Meadow, K. (1972). *Sound and sign: Childhood deafness and mental health.* Berkeley: University of California Press.

Simoni, J., & Pérez, L. (1995). Latinos and mutual support groups: A case for considering culture. *American Journal of Orthopsychiatry, 65,* 440–445.

Sluzki, C. E. (1979). Migration and family conflict. *Family Process, 18,* 379–390.

Smart, J., & Smart, D. (1995). Acculturative stress of Hispanics: Loss and challenge. *Journal of Counseling and Development, 73,* 390–396.

Sue, D. W., & Sue, D. (1990). *Counseling the culturally different.* New York: Wiley.

Twilling, L., & Bock, N. (1989). Team up for school-sponsored parent support groups. *Perspectives for Teachers of the Hearing Impaired, 7,* 2–6.

U.S. Bureau of the Census. (1996). Population projections of the United States, by age, sex, race and Hispanic origin: 1995 to 2050 (Current Population Reports, Series P 25–1130). Washington, DC: U.S. Government Printing Office.

Vásquez, M. (1994). Latinas. In L. Comas-Díaz & B. Greene (Eds.), *Women of color: Integrating ethnic and gender identities in psychotherapy* (pp. 114–138). New York: Guilford Press.

Vásquez, M., & Ling Han, A. (1995). Group interventions and treatment with ethnic minorities. In J. Aponte, R. Rivers, & J. Wohl (Eds.), *Psychological interventions and cultural diversity* (pp. 109–127). Boston: Allyn and Bacon.

Verdonk, A. (1979). Migration and mental illness. *International Journal of Social Psychiatry, 25,* 295–305.

Williams, C. (1991). Teaching Hispanic deaf students: Lessons from Luis. *Perspectives in Education and Deafness, 10,* 2–5.

Yacobacci-Tam, P. (1987). Interacting with the culturally different family. *Volta Review, 89,* 46–58.

Yalom, I. (1985). *The theory and practice of group psychotherapy* (3rd ed.). New York: Basic Books.

Part Four

Special Issues

11

Deaf People with HIV/AIDS: Notes on the Psychotherapeutic Journey

DANIEL J. LANGHOLTZ AND RICHARD RUTH

Since its emergence in the early 1980s, the AIDS epidemic has affected people all around the world, young and old, male and female, from every ethnic and cultural community. While in the United States, Europe, and some parts of Asia and Latin America, HIV infection is more prevalent among gay men than heterosexuals (this is not the case in Africa), there are large numbers of both gay and heterosexual people with HIV/AIDS (Blattner, 1997; Mann, 1989). People who are culturally Deaf, deaf people who are not part of the Deaf community, and people who are hard of hearing are all equally susceptible to the HIV virus. Further, the opportunistic infections that often occur in people with HIV infections can lead to hearing loss, so that significant numbers of people with HIV/AIDS become deaf during the course of their illness (Friedman, 1995; Kalichman, 1995). Some of these people are gay, and the experience of being gay and deaf is at the heart of their experience; some of these people are not gay.

There is an emerging mental health literature on the treatment of people with HIV/AIDS, and many of its findings and recommendations are of relevance to work with deaf individuals with HIV/AIDS. These findings will be discussed later in this chapter (Cadwell et al., 1994; Kalichman, 1995; Wicks, 1997; Winiarski, 1991). The chapter will also affirm the importance of not pathologizing adaptive coping strategies that are nonmainstream, and the need to understand and not whitewash the many difficulties of people living with HIV/AIDS while also acknowledging their many areas of strength—themes that echo throughout the literature. However, materials that specifically examine the issues that emerge in psychotherapeutic work with deaf people with HIV/AIDS are scarce, thus making this work like a journey without a map.

Background Issues

While the focus of this chapter will be on psychotherapeutic work with deaf people with HIV/AIDS, several background issues deserve brief examination at the outset. Each individual affected by HIV/AIDS is psychologically complex and unique, so that not all of these issues will apply to each person equally. Rather, we would consider these issues domains that clinicians need to consider during the assessment and formulation process, along with the other traditional areas to be considered in the process of a psychosocial evaluation.

PSYCHOLOGICAL DIMENSIONS OF HIV AND DEAFNESS

Neither HIV/AIDS nor deafness is viewed by the majority of people in this society as a psychologically neutral experience. While culturally Deaf people would take issue with the view that deafness is a disability, few would contest that society at large views it as such. Added onto this construction is a negative valorization, similar to the way society views disabilities in general (Blotzer & Ruth, 1996; Bogdan & Taylor, 1982). Deaf people and people with disabilities are perceived as embodying vulnerabilities that people in the mainstream cannot bear to think about. This view can provoke an unconscious fear of perceived disability or differentness, which is projected onto deaf people and people with disabilities, and then defensively transformed into hatred and rejection of those people (Blotzer & Ruth, 1996; LeMaistre, 1993) and internalized into a source of self-deprecation (Sinason, 1986).

Similarly, gayness has been viewed as embodying the unspeakable unconscious wishes of a sexist and sexually repressed society. In this context, homophobia is conceptualized as a reaction formation: people hate in others a dissociated part of themselves experienced as shameful (Bird, 1957; Isay, 1989; Moss, 1997). Lewes (1992) argues that homophobia is involved in the pervasive fear of AIDS, and thus the slow, uneven, and inadequate social response to the epidemic. He also suggests that the psychological underpinnings of homophobia lead the society in some ways to view all people with HIV/AIDS as if they were gay.

However, there is a further, social-psychological dimension involved in these phenomena. Once a social group becomes stigmatized (Cain, 1991; Goffman, 1963; Herek & Glunt, 1988), internal psychological processes become an objective reality that then develops its own dynamics and consequences. In the context of our current discussion, deaf people with HIV/AIDS can be perceived as doubly stigmatized, and psychologically tasked with the double burden of serving as a target of the unconscious projections of powerful and privileged others and combating an objective, powerful, sociopolitical prejudice.

The attempt to frame a response to these circumstances is also conditioned by psychological factors. Among these, for people who are both gay and deaf, are needs to combat internalized homophobia (Isay, 1989; Malyon, 1982; Paradis, 1991), develop an integrated gay identity (Coleman, 1982; Paradis, 1991, 1997), and develop a cultural identity and sense of community (Isay, 1996; Lukes & Land, 1990; Paradis, 1997). Such tasks are inherently developmental in nature, and thus would interact with the particular developmental tasks and challenges of all deaf people in a disempowering society (Vernon & Andrews, 1990). Painful psychological issues particular to having a fatal illness, including its many uncertainties (Blotzer & Ruth, 1996), thus become experienced through a very particular set of filters.

This cursory review of psychological aspects of HIV/AIDS highlights, first, that the disease itself is as much a psychological experience as it is a medical one, and second, that there are aspects of the disease that have very specific impacts on people who are deaf.

IMPACT ON THE DEAF COMMUNITY

There are no readily available statistics that can help us understand how HIV/AIDS has impacted the deaf community. Deafness is still not identified on most forms used by HIV testing sites and the Centers for Disease Control, and information about hard of hearing people with HIV/AIDS is even harder to gather. We do not know how many deaf people have HIV/AIDS or how many have died.

Anecdotal reports have suggested a higher incidence of HIV/AIDS among deaf people than in the general population. There are several possible explanations for this. Earlier in the AIDS epidemic, deaf people had insufficient access to basic information on the subject. Language, communication, and community culture factors were barriers in accessing general community education programs, or accessing services once informed (Langholtz, 1996; Van Biema, 1994). Uneven access to sex education in Deaf communities, to some extent a function of disempowering cultures within traditional residential schools, has been suggested as another factor (Langholtz & Rendon, 1991/1992). Paralleling a phenomenon in the general population, it is thought that a number of deaf men who have sex with other men, deaf women who have sex with other women, and deaf women with lesbian identities who also have sex with men, have difficulties in developing a clear sense of gay identity. Among each of these subpopulations, these complexities of behavior and identity can become incorporated into frameworks of denial, leading to risky behaviors that have spread the disease.

Further, many of the grassroots organizations that have arisen to deal with HIV/AIDS have come from the gay community. These organizations have not always been sensitive and responsive to the Deaf community, very much as gayness has often been a "hot potato" in institutions serving deaf populations, Deaf organizations, and the Deaf community.

STIGMA AND PROGRESS

Homophobia in the Deaf community has put the population at risk for acquiring HIV infection and for not getting proper information, treatment, or care (Barthell, 1983; Langholtz & Rendon, 1991/1992, 1994). The deaf community has had a long history of denial that HIV/AIDS could affect its members. In community institutions, homophobia among deaf and hearing administrators, educators, and community leaders has created a tragic history of resistance and denial.

In other populations impacted by HIV/AIDS, widely respected and influential public figures revealing their HIV status has helped combat stigma and encouraged more people to seek adequate care. Deaf equivalents of Magic Johnson, Rock Hudson, and Arthur Ashe have played similar roles within the Deaf community. These people include

- Sam Edwards of New York, a Deaf actor, playwright, and man of the arts;
- Mike Eisele of San Diego, who created materials and programs for drug and alcohol recovery geared for Deaf people;
- Sam Feliciano, who lived in both Boston and San Francisco, and was a selfless supporter for many people with AIDS;
- Mike Felts and Tom Kane of Washington, D.C., who advocated greater awareness among the general public and helped create specialized services for deaf people with HIV/AIDS;
- Paul Isaac, who did the same in the San Francisco Bay area;
- Tommy Saavedra, of San Jose, who starred in the video *Hot and Safe* (McBride, 1990) and challenged the Gallaudet University student government after it denied a request to establish a gay student club; and

- Dennis Schemenaur, from Nevada, who shared his experiences in one of the Sign Enhancers videotapes (Schemenauer, 1989).

By sharing their insights and experiences openly, these individuals and others have begun to break down barriers and reduce stigma within the deaf community. At the Deaf Women United conference in Seattle in 1996, for example, an African-American woman sharing her HIV/AIDS experiences on a panel captured the hearts of the audience and changed the way a sector of the community saw HIV/AIDS.

Still, there continue to be many challenges when it comes to linking deaf people with HIV/AIDS concerns with adequate services. Services may not exist at all in some communities; in others, available services have unacceptable limitations in accessibility or quality of care. Even when potentially useful services exist, significant numbers of deaf people do not want to make themselves known to deaf-oriented service programs. Their concerns about anonymity and confidentiality are understandable but have a regrettable impact in that they lead to inaccurately low estimates of the size of affected populations, making it difficult to obtain needed funds and create necessary services. One AIDS program in a major southern city saw no need for a deaf case manager because few deaf clients had been identified as needing AIDS-related services.

SEXUAL BEHAVIOR AND SEXUAL ORIENTATION

Many, if not most, people find it difficult to discuss their sexual behavior with medical and mental health professionals (Kalichman, 1995). In traditional therapeutic relationships, a long period of trust-building is often required before relevant dimensions of sexual feelings and behaviors can be discussed comfortably and productively. In work with people with HIV/AIDS and other sexually transmitted diseases, external circumstances may telescope this process in a way that can be uncomfortable for both clinician and client. This may be an even more acute problem if clients see their sexual behavior as outside the mainstream or ego-dystonic.

For gay, lesbian, and bisexual clients, issues of sexual behavior are typically wrapped up with issues of sexual orientation. Living openly as a gay, lesbian, or bisexual person involves the process of "coming out," a complex interpersonal and emotional process (Gutman, this volume; Isay, 1989, 1996). When HIV/AIDS becomes a factor in their lives, the psychological space for the coming out process may be constrained when clients are effectively "outed" by the virus (Cadwell, Burnham & Forstein, 1994; Winiarski, 1991). The crisis caused by such complications can make the therapeutic engagement more problematic. Alternatively, it can make a person more reluctant to seek needed mental health treatment.

THE DEAF VIEW OF MENTAL HEALTH SERVICES

Historically, mental health services for deaf people have often been problematic or harmful (Rainer & Altshuler, 1971; Vernon & Andrews, 1990). Not surprisingly, stigma, myths, resistance, and mistrust toward mental health services can easily prevail among many members of the Deaf community (Galloway, 1968; Steinberg et al., this volume).

However, in the past three decades, a better appreciation of the mental health issues of deaf people has developed, and more appropriate mental health services for deaf people, including services using accessible forms of communication, have begun to become available (Steinberg et al., this volume; Willigan & King, 1992). All of this has helped Deaf consumers change attitudes toward mental health treatment.

Yet for people who already have a negative self-concept about being deaf, having HIV/AIDS can be experienced as an additional source of shame that becomes internalized into a negative facet of identity. Confidentiality may be a particular concern in professional and social Deaf contexts. Service recipients may not want to be identified as having HIV/AIDS when they come to Deaf-oriented agencies; they may ask clinicians to consider alternatives to the standard clinical practice of office visits.

* * *

> One client initially asked to be seen outside an agency's facility at the beginning of his treatment because many of the staff members knew him from other contexts. His therapist, a hearing signer who was also gay, came to see the client at his apartment. After several sessions, the client admitted feeling distracted and awkward having the therapist in his home. They moved the sessions to a café in the neighborhood, which facilitated treatment.
>
> After the therapist left the agency, a female Deaf clinician continued working with the client at the café. The client eventually became less concerned about his privacy. When the sessions were moved to the office, the client noted that the clinical work was more intense, in the positive sense of the term, than the work in the alternative meeting places. However, the transition of meeting outside to later meeting at the office appeared to have facilitated the therapeutic process.

NONDEAF CULTURAL ISSUES

HIV/AIDS shows greater prevalence rates in impoverished, disempowered communities that have less access to information, education, and services (Kalichman, 1995; Myers, 1992; Winiarski, 1991). In particular, infection rates among urban African-Americans and Latinos are higher than in European-American communities (Blattner, 1997). Deaf people within these ethnic minority communities may have even less access to information and services than other members of the community. One of us, working in a large, urban hospital, has encountered deaf Latino immigrants with HIV/AIDS who have never been educated. These clients communicate only with informal signs and gestures, and live marginal lives disconnected from both mainstream and Deaf communities. Even among more empowered members of ethnic minority groups, the belief that mental health providers (in both Deaf and mainstream health settings) are not culturally sensitive can impede the client's ability to access services and form therapeutic relationships (Hernández, this volume; Leigh & Lewis, this volume; Wu and Grant, this volume).

HIV/AIDS Service Programs

PROGRAM MODELS

As HIV/AIDS service programs have proliferated, questions have arisen about what kinds of services are most useful for deaf clients. Existing HIV/AIDS agencies with no

PROGRAM MODELS FOR PROVIDING HIV/AIDS MENTAL HEALTH SERVICES

1. HIV/AIDS agencies provide services through their own mental health staff using interpreters, and supplement these services with outside consultation with professionals with Deaf expertise.
2. HIV/AIDS agencies hire in-house staff with specialized training to handle the deaf caseload.
3. Deaf agencies hire staff to focus on HIV/AIDS, often funded through Ryan White CARE funds.
4. Deaf agencies work out collaborative relationships with outside HIV/AIDS programs.
5. Private mental health practitioners provide services based on their experience in serving Deaf people with HIV/AIDS.

Figure 1. HIV/AIDS Program Models

programs geared for Deaf people may feel at a loss as to how to work with Deaf clients; Deaf-oriented programs with no training in the area of HIV/AIDS may be equally at a loss in serving these individuals. Across the country, innovative efforts have arisen to help resolve the gap in services. These tend to fall into five program models (see figure 1). Optimally, deaf people should be able to select any of these program models. Good access to services in general HIV/AIDS programs and mental health programs is a legitimate expectation, and Deaf-oriented mental health programs should also be able to respond to HIV/AIDS.

However, it is important to acknowledge and understand the obstacles. Service providers unfamiliar with working with deaf people may experience what Schlesinger calls "shock-withdrawal-paralysis" (Schlesinger & Meadow, 1972, p. 213). While some professionals may have no trouble modifying their services, others may experience snags. Interestingly, snags may be more likely in HIV/AIDS service organizations, where the intensity of everyday experience—entailing frequent crisis situations and having to deal with the loss of multiple clients and friends—may make the prospect of learning a new area of expertise overwhelming. When one such agency was approached with an offer of in-service training, a staff member commented, "We can't handle another special focus group, we're swamped with so much to do." Some deaf professionals seeking training in HIV/AIDS may experience barriers because training experiences are not communication accessible, although the Americans with Disabilities Act has facilitated the provision of interpreter services as a legal right.

A solution would involve more consultation, collaboration, and competency training. Provisions for this kind of work would need to be ongoing, given the rapidly changing nature of scientific discoveries about HIV/AIDS and the rapid staff turnover in many service agencies dealing with the epidemic, where burnout is a constant challenge. Efforts have begun in this direction. In San Francisco, staff members at the Deaf AIDS Project offer competency training and consultation to personnel at other agencies when a deaf person is involved. A HIV/AIDS training video geared to service providers working with Deaf people is available from Sign Enhancers in Portland, Oregon (Veltri et al., 1996).

THE BOUNDARY BETWEEN CLINICAL WORK AND CASE MANAGEMENT

Hoffman (1996) states that work with deaf people with HIV/AIDS differs from more traditional kinds of clinical work because the work of self-discovery cannot take place at the usual pace and with the same sense of safety. The issues of people with HIV/AIDS usually need to be evaluated and addressed with a greater degree of urgency. Clinicians can feel pulled in many directions when multiple crises and unmet needs for concrete services get in the way of trying to maintain a focus on psychotherapeutic issues as such. Dealing with purely defined therapeutic issues can at times feel like an unattainable luxury.

This is true in mental health work with deaf people in general, because of the limited human services resources available to the Deaf community, but it takes on a particular edge in working with people with HIV/AIDS. As Hoffman (1996) emphasizes, in this work we must be truly interdisciplinary and incorporate knowledge from multiple fields. We need to stay abreast of ongoing findings of effective interventions dealing with psychosocial consequences as we continue to work through the power of empathy, compassion, and the therapeutic alliance.

In many cases, clinicians are called upon to serve simultaneously as case managers and therapists. They usually embrace this role because it enables them to help clients obtain the highest level of independence and quality of life consistent with their functional capacity and preferences of care (Hoffman, 1996; Kalichman, 1995; Winiarski, 1991). HIV/AIDS is life-threatening and debilitating; a narrow focus on psychotherapeutic issues when unmet medical or survival needs could cause death would make neither clinical nor moral sense.

Therapists working with deaf people with HIV/AIDS also have to be sensitive to the limits of how far their roles can expand beyond traditional therapy and toward case management. Because HIV/AIDS can be so incapacitating, both client and clinician can develop strong feelings about what is best for the client during his or her course of care and treatment. Problems of mutual expectations can develop; clients can look to clinicians to provide more than they reasonably can be expected to provide, and clinicians who have formed an empathic attachment to a client can be caught in a difficult situation when clients make treatment choices the clinician may not endorse. Clinicians may identify certain issues as problematic, while their clients may not see things the same way. Two brief vignettes capture some of these dilemmas.

* * *

> A flamboyant Puerto Rican man in his mid-thirties maintained a fast-lane lifestyle. He frequently went to bars, partying and staying up all night. In addition to drinking, he also used recreational drugs. When urged to consider the negative effects these choices had on his health, he said, I WILL DIE SOON, WHAT FOR GIVE UP PLEASURE? NOT WORTH PARANOID WORRY, WASTE TIME; DEATH WILL COME SO I GRAB ALL THE FUN UNTIL I GET BURIED.

* * *

> Another client wanted to continue caring for his cat. Even though cats can transmit toxoplasmosis, an infection that can be very serious for compromised immune systems, the client adamantly refused to let somebody else handle the litter box.

Faced with these kinds of circumstances, therapists are well advised to assert the primacy of their role as clinicians rather than as advocates, concrete services providers, or case managers. Therapists can help people process their thoughts and feelings about concrete issues, or participate on multidisciplinary care teams where others take the lead in arranging concrete services. Sometimes therapists can be most useful as helping professionals with whom clients can vent their complaints about other service providers. Faced with such intense and complex issues, clinicians should seek out consultation and supervision as needed; in this work it is essential (Cadwell et al., 1994; Cournos & Bakalar, 1996; Kalichman, 1995; Wicks, 1997; Winiarski, 1991).

ISSUES OF COMMUNICATION

Communication issues are crucial to all effective mental health work with deaf people. One needs to be particularly astute about the assessment of mental health issues in deaf clients with HIV/AIDS because of language and cognitive considerations.

Those not familiar with writing considerations when assessing deaf people may draw inaccurate conclusions (Leigh et al., 1996). One Deaf man was being assessed for potential HIV dementia by a hearing psychologist, and both were writing notes to each other. When the psychologist looked at the client's notes, she felt his "broken English" suggested distorted thinking processes, when limited English fluency would have been the more accurate assessment.

Writing notes in a clinical situation will rarely make for clear understanding between client and clinician. In one case with which one of us was familiar, misinterpreted writing led to an inaccurate impression of psychosis and a regrettable medication decision.

Signers using a lot of facial and body movement have been misperceived to be agitated, rough, violent, or even a danger to self or others, when this was more accurately a part of their communicative style (Altshuler & Abdullah, 1981). Such misperceptions are a particular risk for clinicians interviewing clients through an interpreter, particularly if the interpreter does not convey an impression of "normality."

Communication problems can at times manifest themselves indirectly. A Deaf individual was perceived as irresponsible and indifferent to AIDS in initial contacts. As the clinician got to know him better over time, it emerged that the client was genuinely naive on the subject because he had had insufficient access to information.

Even excellent speechreaders can have less than perfect understanding, and this can have serious consequences. In one case, a client was following medication instructions incorrectly because he believed he had been told he could take his medication with dairy products. However, the speaker had said "can't," not "can"; both words appear similar on the lips.

In some instances, staff members communicate with hearing partners or family members of deaf clients, rather than the client him or herself. This can create situations where not all information is communicated to the client; there can be additions, deletions, and filtering, and the deaf client may end up not knowing what is going on. One Deaf client did not know for a full year that he had AIDS symptoms because his partner was not conveying crucial information obtained at medical appointments they attended together.

Clinicians have an obligation to check on the quality of deaf clients' communication ability and signing skills, and cannot make assumptions about what clients understand. Particularly when discussing sensitive and potentially embarrassing information, such as alcohol and drug use, sexual behavior, and suicide issues, it is not uncommon for deaf people to tell therapists what they think the therapist wants to hear, or to pretend to understand when they do not.

Deaf clients will sometimes communicate in long monologues. While this may reflect therapeutic resistance, it may also be a function of a communication issue. It may be easier for the client to feel a measure of control if there are no changes in conversation flow; it may be too hard for the client to struggle with speechreading, following signs, listening, and/or processing information. This tendency toward communication-by-monologue, in our clinical experience, is most frequent in oral clients, deaf-blind clients, clients who are hard of hearing, or clients who are losing their hearing.

Use of interpreters is not necessarily a remedy for all communication problems. Unless interpreters are skilled and trained in mental health interpreting and are fluent in the client's preferred mode of communication, they may "clean up" the client's communication (Leigh et al., 1996; Stansfield & Veltri, 1987). There have been reports of adverse clinical consequences when self-proclaimed interpreters did not do their jobs properly, omitting or confusing crucial information (Hiraga & Langholtz, 1996). In one case, an interpreter put a client's jumble of thoughts into coherent and sensible sentences, and the clinician thus missed out on important clinical clues. The consequence was that appropriate and adequate treatment was tragically delayed.

If interpreters are used, the interpreter must have significant exposure to both mental health and HIV/AIDS issues. Therapists need to take time with interpreters in advance to review their comfort and skill with these issues, and also need to check in with clients regarding their feelings about the interpreter and the interpreting process. As is the case with therapists working in this area, interpreters should have access to supervision or similar opportunities to examine their feelings about this emotionally charged work. Because some agency personnel may express qualms about the costs of professional interpreting—there are many other AIDS-related funding needs, and many HIV/AIDS services are provided on a volunteer basis—therapists and allied professionals may have to advocate for deaf clients' rights to accessible services and quality interpreting.

One HIV testing center adamantly asserted that confidentiality prohibited using outside certified ASL interpreters, even though the interpreters themselves were legally bound to confidentiality. Staff members with substandard signing skills, or without signing skills, were used, with disastrous consequences. The following vignettes are far from uncommon.

* * *

> One deaf client explained that a hearing staff person at an HIV testing office had appeared impatient while passing notes back and forth regarding the client's HIV antibody test results. The staff person wrote "negative" and shook his head. Confused, the client left thinking he had not "passed" the test and was infected

by the virus. For several months, he was frightened about his HIV status. Later, he participated in a captive group at a postsecondary program for deaf people where a Deaf expert on AIDS, communicating using ASL, explained the meaning of positive and negative test results. When he realized he had had it all wrong, the client felt betrayed and angry about the serious misunderstanding.

* * *

Another client, informed of his positive status, mistook it as a good sign; in his school days, when teachers put positive signs on his papers, it meant he had done well. Much later, through a casual conversation with a peer, his misperception of his result was corrected. He then realized that some minor medical problems he was experiencing could be HIV-related, and sought help from the counseling service at his educational setting. The misunderstanding delayed necessary medical attention.

To prevent misunderstandings, it is helpful to use open-ended rather than forced-choice questions, and to have clients paraphrase or rephrase what is communicated to check on mutual understanding. This can also model how ideas can be phrased clearly, which is helpful to many clients. Mirroring the client's feelings by using reflective listening techniques and using analogies and metaphors can also help enhance communication.

We want to emphasize that we do not advocate that all deaf people should accept HIV/AIDS-related treatment only from Deaf or signing professionals. Given the great imbalance between available services and existing needs, such a position could get in the way of some people accessing the services they need. With adequate safeguards—including good self-advocacy skills—some deaf clients can obtain good services from agencies unable to provide assessment and therapy through Deaf or signing professionals. General mental health and HIV/AIDS agencies should not be let off the hook, however. Particularly when ongoing counseling or psychotherapy is needed, there may be no adequate substitute for a Deaf or fluently signing hearing therapist, if these are available.

Psychotherapy

GENERAL CONSIDERATIONS

While some have argued that people with HIV/AIDS do not need psychotherapy other than short-term intervention (Crimp, 1988), many psychotherapy clients benefit when they identify, express, and work through their concerns; set priorities; and develop better problem-solving skills (Kalichman, 1995; Winiarski, 1991). Not all HIV/AIDS therapy work is about crisis and intense unmet needs. Coping with emotions becomes a critical component when one's sense of self has been attacked by HIV/AIDS. This is particularly true when clients are dealing not only with the physical manifestations of the illness, but also the painful political and social realities of HIV/AIDS. While experiences of deaf people with HIV/AIDS are certainly not solely defined by their deafness, sexuality, or illness experience, their global subjective experiences are fundamentally informed by these categories.

Therapists need to help clients, particularly those belonging to stigmatized social groups, consider ways in which their cultural, social, and political contexts influence their psychological experience and in turn how these psychological experiences influence their acts (Altman, 1995; Blotzer & Ruth, 1996; Hoffman, 1992). Sometimes this process takes a long time and requires therapists to have a greater empathic understanding. Behavioral, cognitive, psychodynamic, psychoeducational, and systems interventions all have useful places within this framework. We need to keep in mind that HIV/AIDS tends to challenge all manner of psychological therapies because of its unpredictable nature and the intensity and particularities of its tragic impact.

PSYCHOEDUCATION

Despite the foregoing discussion, many clients do not come to therapy with the kinds of issues people traditionally bring into treatment, issues cast in psychological terms. A significant number of clients come specifically seeking information and guidance that can help them deal with the ramifications of HIV/AIDS. Yet the AIDS prevention research literature argues strongly that simply presenting information rarely leads to reductions in risk behaviors or an improvement in illness management behaviors (Coates & Greenblatt, 1990). Psychoeducational work with people with HIV/AIDS can be extremely important in facilitating personalization and navigation of the information.

Both of us have found that in our work with people from the target population, we often find ourselves taking on more of a teaching role than we typically do in other kinds of clinical work. This often involves discussing specifics of sexual behavior necessary to prevent new HIV strains and/or any opportunistic infections from being transmitted between existing HIV carriers. It also means discussing clients' rights to quality services, benefits to which they are entitled, and current HIV/AIDS treatment choices. This line of work can particularly benefit deaf clients who have not always had the opportunity to participate in planning and decision making, perhaps because they have grown up in disempowering hearing families or because educators or service providers have assumed the right to make decisions for them earlier in their lives.

Sometimes, this involves clinical work typical of counseling relationships as opposed to other kinds of psychotherapy. For example, clients may have a need to sort out what to do about personal aspirations that have gone unmet. Examples might include discussing whether to travel overseas while a client is still healthy enough to do so, or whether to make a major purchase with savings for a "rainy day" that has now arrived.

DEATH AND DYING ISSUES

Discussing death, mortality, and dying issues with deaf people may present specific problems. Communication barriers and disempowerment earlier in life may have impeded clients from acquiring a foundation for understanding these issues. The following vignette gives examples of how these dynamics can play out in therapy.

* * *

A thirty-two-year-old Caucasian man was referred for therapy during a seventy-two-hour-hold hospitalization. He had been found unconscious after excessive use of amyl nitrate "poppers" (a recreational inhaled drug used to obtain instant rushes, particularly during sexual activities).

The client was living in a tent as part of an encampment of people dying of AIDS in front of San Francisco City Hall. He was a personable man with borderline intelligence who had attracted a lot of helpers both on the streets and in several agencies. Through a case management program that coordinated collaborations among several agencies, he was placed in a group home for people with borderline intelligence and AIDS complications.

He faithfully attended all the mental health appointments arranged for him. The client lived a sexually active lifestyle, and needed intervention about the importance of practicing safe sex. The work was done on a concrete level and was often quite direct, using a lot of visual demonstrations—for example, practicing putting condoms on phallic-shaped objects. Despite the client's positive attitude toward therapy, it took months of work to help him understand his critical medical condition and its implications.

During the course of therapeutic treatment, early signs of dementia were detected when there was a noticeable drop-off from his baseline communication and language functioning. His signing became disorganized. Late one night, the client was found roaming around his block naked. He was then placed in a local hospital ward for people with AIDS-related dementia. Even at this point, mental health intervention remained important and useful. Frequent visits to the hospital gave him further understanding of what was going on; more generic services would likely not have reached this man with multiple areas of dysfunction and need. He did not appear agitated or disturbed by his increasingly serious symptoms. He died soon after admission.

In this client's case, societal communication barriers had, over the course of his life, gotten in the way of his ability to acquire information about health and many other basic social realities and personal needs. His homeless existence and his nonmonogamous sexual lifestyle seem to have represented not a grounded or informed choice to live as a free spirit, but a less-than-adaptive way of trying to cope with a more broad-scale sense of social disempowerment. By the time he entered therapy, the client's communication difficulties had become internalized and habituated. Thus, he had difficulty taking in information during therapy, just as he had had difficulty taking in information in other areas of his life.

Therapy, however, was able to provide a safe, generative space where the client could overcome this history of disempowerment, at least to some extent. Therapy was not able to keep him from engaging in behaviors that may have hastened his death, but at least his involvement with treatment allowed him to accept support services and personal assistance that softened the psychological impact and eased the process of his dying.

While there can be few generalizations, we have both been impressed by the variety of death and dying issues our clients present. For some, grief is complicated because clients realize they are dying while they are still working on coming-out issues and before they have a chance to consolidate a gay identity and an openly gay lifestyle. Others face their own mortality issues while grieving the death of a lover; some, with longer histories in gay communities, may have lost multiple friends and lovers. Panels commemorating deaf people who have died of AIDS are part of the renowned quilt.

Visiting the quilt in different cities or making panels for the quilt has been important to the psychological healing of several of our clients.

AIDS has its own humor, and clients may bring this in as a resource to help them deal with loss and grief issues. One extremely tall client played with the idea of ordering an extra-long coffin. Another client, who paid a lot of attention to his appearance, liked to joke about having his corpse covered with Oil of Olay. Sometimes we have observed close friends "compete" over who would get to the graveyard first, sharing fantasies about their funerals—flamboyant attire to be worn, absurd and intimate memories to be included in the eulogy. A client once said he would rise from his casket to scare away funeral attendees on his blacklist. While such humor can present as resistance in a therapeutic dialogue, it can also be a vital coping resource, which therapists should not be quick to belittle or dismiss. Rather, therapists should be willing to listen to gallows humor from a position of empathy, attentive to ways it can be adaptive. Often it can be helpful to ask the client about the meaning of a humorous statement, to help discern whether it is a useful survival defense that needs to be supported or a resistance to working through a feeling or experience that could benefit from further exploration in therapy.

ENTITLEMENT AND VICTIMIZATION

For some therapy clients, the experience of being gay, deaf, and diagnosed with AIDS contributes to an attitude of denied personal responsibility. While it is legitimate to observe that deaf people are cut off from information that others may pick up from television, radio, and informal conversation, both hearing and deaf people with HIV/AIDS often feel at a loss for adequate information about their illness and the life complications it often triggers. This can lead to a kind of reaction formation, where the absence of information and a perceived lack of self-efficacy become defensively transformed into a sense of entitlement.

* * *

A bright man who had not completed college wanted more public assistance. "It's hard for me to get a job, I'm Deaf, not White, and I have HIV," he said. Even though this man had substantial financial assets and remained asymptomatic for several years, he felt slighted when an agency denied him emergency funding for people with AIDS. "Your program is funded through the Ryan White CARE program—you should give me some," he insisted.

The client seemed to have considerable difficulty accepting and understanding his HIV illness and its implications for him. Rather than seeking to work through the complex and painful realization that his illness (thus far asymptomatic) and his deafness may not have been what was preventing him from working, or from feeling that he was being provided for adequately, he cast himself, unconsciously, in a victim role. Role assumptions and behavior then further contributed to his disempowerment and sense of entitlement. Through a projective mechanism, the client seemed to have displaced onto a service program an underlying sense that he had needs that were not being met; the request for financial assistance may have been a defensive cover for a more powerful, unconscious sense that he was in need of emotional assistance. However, this feeling seems to have felt too threatening to the client to allow into conscious awareness. His defensive maneuver thus had a counterphobic quality.

BODY IMAGE

Many clients bring into their therapy sessions concerns about their appearance and body image. Particularly when HIV infection becomes AIDS, people in their twenties, thirties, and forties can suddenly look like they have aged twenty or thirty years. They become frail, develop wrinkles and thinning hair, lack energy, and begin to walk like elderly people. Body parts sag. One client complained that his buttocks looked like pancakes. Men can lose the ability to have erections and ejaculations. Clothing can become too big and too baggy. The body can lose flexibility and agility; it can become physically difficult to get dressed. Transportation can be an exhausting ordeal. Constant digestive problems can make it hard for people to leave home for too long, because of the embarrassment of not being able to quickly locate a toilet. Wasting syndrome can take a major toll on the body, energy levels, and mental ability.

When a person loses body fat and muscle, it can be hard to stay on one's feet for long times, chronic pain can develop, and a client may need to carry around pillows because it can be painful to sit on hard surfaces. Some clients need to learn to live with overt physical problems, such as Kaposi's sarcoma lesions; scars on the face, arms, or legs; blackened teeth; emaciation; and wearing a catheter tube sticking out of the chest to receive medications. Clients may feel uncomfortable talking about these concerns, worried that they may sound like hypochondriacs or that they are obsessing about bodily ailments.

Clients may also become overly alarmed about symptoms, and at times may benefit from reminders that some symptoms are the minor, ordinary problems that everyone develops from time to time, with no more malign implications. They may need assistance in learning to ask for physical help, or learning to manage the offers of help and the stream of providers and other outsiders who may quickly begin to appear in their lives. Keeping track of medications—sometimes so many they can cover a kitchen countertop, each with its own exacting dosing schedule and many with uncomfortable side effects—can be even harder when medication becomes associated with embarrassing body images or painful bodily sensations. The cost of medications and the physical demands of obtaining them can be overwhelming. Venting feelings about these horrors in therapy is crucial to sustaining treatment compliance. This can be true whether or not a symptom is likely to improve. Unvented rage and unmourned feelings of loss can also get in the way of learning how to cope with and compensate for residual, disabling symptoms. In each instance, creative adaptations are unlikely to emerge without a measure of emotional release and working through (Hoffman, 1996; Kalichman, 1995; Winiarski, 1991).

FAMILY AND SUPPORT SYSTEM ISSUES

Significant numbers of Deaf people no longer maintain close contacts with their families of origin, due to communication, language, and cultural differences (Jacobs, 1974; Langholtz & Rendon, 1994). Family ties can be further strained and often ruptured when gay people come out. When these already charged phenomena converge with the disclosure of HIV-positive status, the impact on families can be powerful. There is diversity among both hearing and Deaf families; some accept the disclosure, some experience the disclosure as a crisis but manage to work through to a good resolution, while others reject it or may attack aggressively. Some higher-functioning clients find therapy a crucial venue in which to work out their issues and feelings about their families, and in which to learn how to frame attempts at reconciliation, especially if fear of rejection due to cultural or religious biases is involved.

All-Deaf families are often seen as a kind of elite within Deaf culture. As the following vignette illustrates, such families are not exempt from the impact of these phenomena.

* * *

A bright Gallaudet University alumnus in his mid-twenties, living on the East Coast, learned he had AIDS. He was from a large family, where the nuclear family and grandparents, aunts, uncles, and cousins were all Deaf. He had a large support system and was active in numerous community organizations. However, he did not share with any of his family or friends that he was developing AIDS-related symptoms. He did not want anyone to know what had happened to him.

He fled to San Francisco and enrolled in a hospice on his own. After several days of solitude, he agreed to allow the hospice staff to link him with specialized mental health services for Deaf people. In contacts with his therapist, he would apologize profusely when he missed an appointment or was late, as if he had done something terribly wrong and had put himself to shame. It took several sessions for him to be able to talk about his illness and its impact more openly. The unfolding process was slow and painful.

Eventually, the client became less resistant to having contact with those close to him. He identified great fear and a perceived sense of pressure not to upset his all-Deaf family or sully their reputation, yet realized the importance of reaching out to them and not letting his pride and shame take such a toll on him.

He finally called his two siblings, who flew out to see him immediately. Soon afterwards, he was relocated to a medical facility closer to his family and friends. He wrote the mental health program a thank-you note for "helping me to accept and face what needs to happen."

It is important for therapists to realize that a significant portion of those with HIV/AIDS do not have supportive or functional family systems. One of us works in San Francisco, which has a reputation not just as a "gay mecca," but as a city with many AIDS programs. Both deaf and nondeaf people from around the country flock to the city to access these programs.

* * *

Two clients were deaf men who lived in single-room-only hotels in the poorer section of downtown. Neither had been in contact with their family for several years. Both were isolated and without friends. Support staff at the mental health center, therapists, and volunteer buddies became their support system. The clients started referring to these people as members of their families: "you're my mom; you're my uncle." They also personalized their stuffed animals, giving them names and treating them as if they were their children.

In therapy, the clients at first denied any desire for reconciliation with their families. However, as their health deteriorated, they expressed fear of dying and being totally cut off from life, including family. At this point, they started reaching out to their families.

One client's brother flew up to meet him after twelve years of no contact. However, they were together for merely an hour. The brother spent more time talking with health-care providers and arranging funeral plans than with his sibling, and he soon left. Still, the client was not upset and appeared more at ease after the contact was made.

The other client's mother, after we had made extensive efforts to track her down, had no means of coming to see her son. She wrote a long letter instead. The client held the letter for days and never let go of it. He died with the letter in his hands.

As shown in the following vignette, therapists must be sensitive to the particular family configurations and experiences of people who have been disempowered because of their deafness.

* * *

One Deaf individual had chronically low self-esteem as a result of growing up in a noncommunicative family and attending a rural program with insufficient support services. In the transition from school to employment, a rehabilitation agency sent him to a large midwestern city, where he first socialized with Deaf peers. However, they ostracized him because of his limited intelligence and social skills. He further struggled with limited understanding of his gayness. These issues were compounded further when he had to grapple with his HIV-positive status. His counselor at an all-Deaf agency shared the client's feelings of loss and helplessness, which decreased the success of the treatment.

While an HIV diagnosis would be a powerful stressor for anyone, this client's sense of bereftness was not just an automatic reaction to this painful discovery. Rather, he experienced his diagnosis against a preexisting psychological template. His experiences of helplessness, isolation, and disempowerment in his family had made it difficult for him to link up with and take advantage of potential sources of personal support in an urban Deaf community, or to feel joy of discovery and self-pride in his sexuality.

When the client entered therapy, he re-created in his therapist the sense of helplessness and bereftness he himself had experienced earlier in his life. For the therapy to succeed, the therapist had to work through the countertransference feelings evoked in him by the client's experience, and the client had to work through some of his feelings of sadness and suppressed anger related to his earlier family experience. These were the prerequisite steps to coming up with effective ways of responding to the psychological and pragmatic challenges of the client's HIV status, and possibly also the local community service systems' inability to make adequate provisions for his care.

For other clients, feelings about the loss of friends who have become family-by-choice can be more intense and focal than feelings about families of origin. Particularly for people with HIV/AIDS who are openly gay and culturally Deaf, the losses may run into the dozens. They may wonder who will be next. As one man put it when he was asked at intake about his support system, "Nobody now, all of my friends have died. I'm all alone, on my own."

GROUP THERAPY

Group support and the group process can be useful for many, either as an adjunct to individual psychotherapy or as a preferred modality (Gabriel, 1996; Kalichman, 1995; Winiarski, 1991). Group members exchange information, share individual experiences, offer insights and education, reaffirm or refine understandings, and validate feelings. People with HIV or AIDS have powerful common experiences, and thus there is a particular power to homogeneous groups with this population. A variety of group formats are utilized, including groups hosted by an agency and led by a facilitator and nonclinically focused groups and unstructured groups meeting in living room-type settings.

Even though group approaches do benefit deaf people, the main difficulty involves language and communication barriers. There is no easy or uniform answer to these concerns. In some large metropolitan cities there may be enough interested Deaf or signing group members to meet on a regular basis; in other areas, this may not be possible. Even if there are enough interested members, it may be difficult to locate a qualified group facilitator who can sign. In some situations, insistence on only being involved with an all-Deaf group can isolate people from community resources that might be helpful to them. Also, in groups of Deaf people, issues of confidentiality and boundary issues about what can and cannot be expected from the support group may arise.

Those who opt for all-hearing groups may run into other kinds of snags. Funding for interpreter services is often an issue, particular in underfunded grassroots agencies. Deaf participants and interpreters may have difficulty keeping up with rapid, back-and-forth group conversation, particularly when subcultural language specific to the gay community is utilized in all-gay groups.

Alternative group modalities, such as meditation and relaxation exercises, are not always considered for the deaf population, but they have been helpful with other populations affected by HIV/AIDS and should not be ruled out. The presumption that deaf people cannot benefit because exercises must be done with the eyes closed, or because instructions must be whispered, is incorrect. Steve Kennedy, a Deaf AIDS advocate and educator in Los Angeles, has done many metaphysically oriented groups with Deaf people in which he uses creative ways to communicate. These have been well received (Kennedy, personal communication, 1996). Visualization and guided imagery about energizing one's being have been used very powerfully. However, it is important to assess potential group members to screen out those who might be frightened or at risk of entering altered or dissociative states.

BUDDY SERVICES

Providing buddies to assist people with HIV/AIDS is one form of service delivery, originally created by the gay community as a response to the AIDS epidemic (Hoffman, 1996; Kalichman, 1995). As an adjunct to therapy, clinicians may recommend that a client consider obtaining a buddy through an AIDS service organization. The clinician may also need to help the client process his or her feelings about the emotionally intense, but often unfamiliar, relationships between clients and their buddies.

Once again, these relationships take on a particular edge when the people involved are Deaf. Careful screening and matching are necessary for successful buddy situations. One Deaf man objected that the non-signing hearing people assigned to him treated him as if he were an invalid because of his deafness. Others, who insist their buddies be Deaf, signing, HIV-positive, have personal experience with HIV/AIDS, or be a certain gender, may find that none who meet their criteria are available, and thus can lose out on an otherwise valuable service. Interestingly, one Deaf man did not want a Deaf or signing buddy, saying it took too much energy for him to socialize or talk with anyone; he only wanted someone to come help out with errands.

AIDS-RELATED VISION ISSUES

Among the several opportunistic infections that AIDS can bring, cytomegalovirus (CMV), which can cause vision loss, causes the most fear in Deaf people. Severe loss of vision for deaf people means decreased vital communication and access to information, and can close off the possibility of independent functioning (see Miner, this volume). Because of this, many deaf people may feel a special and significant discomfort when they are with deaf-blind individuals. Deaf clients with CMV describe blurring and double vision during acute episodes of infection. The struggle to decipher direct visual communication with blurred vision, combined with the disorientation and fatigue from other AIDS complications and from medication effects, can be staggering. Therapists can help by providing reassurance that these visual symptoms are often transient; by emphasizing the importance of rapid access to good medical and vision care, and advocating for this if needed; and by helping people express and process these powerful feelings.

HIV-RELATED HEARING LOSS

It is suspected that, in addition to hearing loss caused by opportunistic infections and medication side-effects, the HIV infection itself can lead to hearing loss (Friedman, 1995). In some cities, people with such a hearing loss are likely to be referred to Deaf AIDS programs. When referred, they may need particular kinds of assistance. Referring professionals sometimes think these people would benefit from learning sign language, but this may not benefit them, as there may be few, if any, in their environment who communicate in ASL or other sign systems. Rather, such clients can benefit from learning practical communication tips, such as learning good listening and communicating strategies (e.g., learning to look at the speaker or eliminate background noise), practicing self-advocacy around hearing needs, and learning about assistive listening devices, doorbell and telephone light signaling systems, and TV captioning devices. They may also need advocacy in securing access to good medical and audiological services.

* * *

A Latin American gay man was referred for therapy for depression. The referral materials noted that he was hard of hearing, but this was not seen as relevant to his psychological difficulties. However, in therapy it quickly became apparent that the hearing loss was one of his most subjectively devastating symptoms. Already sensitized to communication struggles because of his weak English skills, he was particularly distressed by the waning of his already limited receptive capacity. Venting these intense feelings to an empathetic therapist was a crucial first step.

The therapist encouraged the client to describe his hearing difficulties, and modeled how this could be done nonjudgmentally. The therapist mentioned, in nonjudgmental language, that the client often spoke in monologues rather than admitting it was hard for him to understand the therapist (who was also Spanish-speaking).

Therapist and client were then able to problem-solve about what they could do together to ease the communication difficulties. They came up with a number of simple methods, such as sitting closer together, maintaining direct eye contact, checking to be sure communications were grasped, and practicing self-advocacy skills. The client was able to generalize these coping strategies after a few weeks, leading to a lessening of depressive symptoms.

SPECIAL CONSIDERATIONS

Therapists working with deaf people with HIV/AIDS must take special care to be sensitive to the within-group diversity of the population. Sometimes, when therapist and client share ethnic minority group membership, and especially when they communicate in a minority language, the sense of solidarity can blind either member of the dyad to important issues (Leigh & Lewis, this volume; Ruth, 1986). When dealing with Deaf people who are members of double minorities, therapists must take extra care to develop cultural competencies and to attend to the issues likely to enter the therapy from the client's experience as a member of multiple minority groups.

Among the population of deaf people with HIV/AIDS, our impression is that there will be a larger than average representation of people who are homeless; who are transgendered; who use intravenous drugs; and who do not associate with the Deaf community. Therapists not aware of the issues such people are likely to experience are advised to seek appropriate supervision and consultation.

Countertransference

As therapists, we ourselves are the principal tool in our clinical work, and thus no psychotherapeutic journey can be understood without examining the therapist. In few clinical situations is this more important than in work with deaf people with HIV/AIDS.

Many of us become involved in this work when our friends, family members, colleagues, or we ourselves have been affected by HIV/AIDS. All therapists are compelled to work hard to try to bring about change in our clients' difficult situations, but these difficulties can be especially intense in working with deaf people with HIV/AIDS, who are often facing a terminal condition with grossly inadequate resources or supports. Therapists can easily become overwhelmed by the variety and intensity of clients' needs—emotional, physical, spiritual, and practical. We can have fantasies of curing our clients, eradicating all discomfort, stopping and reversing the epidemic. For Deaf and nondeaf signing providers, the risk of overidentification with clients with inadequate support systems may be especially intense. As the following vignette illustrates, countertransference can get in the way of clearly assessing our clients.

* * *

> A gentleman in his fifties had been experiencing a gradual progressive hearing loss over many years as the result of a war injury. He had recently lost much more hearing, most probably because of his HIV. An interpreter could not be present for the intake appointment at the client's home, but the therapist and client agreed to go ahead, communicating through speechreading and writing.
>
> The therapist had a strong speechreading background, and therefore valued good dental hygiene for communication purposes. When he noted the client's heavily chipped and smeared front teeth, he found himself thinking the client was probably negligent in his general health care, and therefore probably did not take his HIV/AIDS seriously. In his apartment, there were only a few pieces of haphazardly placed furniture, including milk cartons used as shelves. This added to the therapist's impression that the client was an insubstantial, careless person.
>
> It turned out that the patient had recently been mugged. His teeth were damaged during the mugging, and everything had been stolen from his storage while he was away for a lengthy period recovering.

All therapists working with this population have to confront their own moral and mortality issues. Clients may present us with reports of sexual identifications, sexual practices, drug and alcohol use, and fast-lane lifestyles—"Why should I deprive myself of pleasures if I'm going to die soon?"—that conflict deeply with our own values. Morally, we may feel at odds with our patients; but our patients need our support, not judgment. Particularly when working with gay clients, we may be asked to help meet needs for affirmation—to help clients develop gay awareness, consolidate a gay identity, and forge links with the gay culture and community. To be prepared for this work, we need to understand our own beliefs and values with particular clarity, and then learn, perhaps, to leave them aside in the interests of helping our clients.

There are particular issues facing therapists who are both Deaf and HIV-positive (Langholtz, 1996). For such therapists, it is vital to monitor one's own needs so as to be able to offer appropriate clinical support. Even with optimal professional and personal support, coming to terms with being HIV-positive can be a long, painful process. Many therapists are by inclination private people, and it can be difficult to sort out how much to share in the clinical situation, and whether, how, and how much to serve as an ambassador, spokesperson, or catalyst in community efforts. It can take a lot of energy, when energy is in preciously short supply, to stay informed about treatment choices, sort out controversial and contradictory information, and decide whom to confide in or not confide in, while continuing to meet the demands of clinical life.

Many other stressors also face the HIV-positive Deaf therapist. There can be fears of going public, fears of reprisals from homophobic people. The loss of friends and clients to AIDS can take a heavy toll. There are likely to be few, if any, role models; the therapist him- or herself may inadvertently become a role model, locally or beyond.

The combination of uncertainty over one's own prognosis and the need to be attuned to clients' uncertainty and pain can be volatile. Ongoing self-monitoring, close clinical supervision, and finding a viable balance between clinical work and other activities is essential in order to avoid feeling emotionally or physically swamped. Therapists must care for themselves if they are to be able to serve the population.

Therapists involved with this population who are not Deaf or who are not HIV-positive may find themselves dealing with a kind of survivor guilt. This guilt can be experienced directly, as immobilizing, or it can be readily displaced onto other feeling constellations. It can feel disconcertingly odd to be able to circulate socially without communication or resource barriers when one's clients cannot, or to feel personally unconcerned with health and survival when the modal experience of clients and friends seems to be illness and death.

Unless these countertransference feelings are understood and worked through, therapeutic effectiveness can suffer. It is easy to lose the neutral qualities and distanced capacity to assess, and even to lose an empathetic connection. Nondeaf, HIV-negative therapists can succumb to feelings of helplessness, or unconsciously translate their personal health and hearing into fantasies of omnipotence. Even more frequently and more powerfully than in other kinds of clinical situations, therapists' emotional availability to clients and their ability to contain powerful affects can become compromised. It is easy for therapists to feel constraints in their empathy for their clients if they respond to their feelings by distancing, or to get into boundary problems if they respond by getting over-involved. Once again, close self-monitoring and good access to consultation and supervision are essential to prevent these strong feelings from turning into countertransference impasses.

Where Is HIV/AIDS Going?

As the HIV/AIDS epidemic is changing, so is the nature of psychotherapy with people with HIV/AIDS. In the early 1980s, early in the epidemic, many clients had to deal with rapid health deterioration and impending death (Blattner, 1997; Winiarski, 1991). Therapy focused on helping individuals make critical medical and legal decisions and face a roller coaster of changing health status and frequent hospitalizations, worries about financial strains and keeping up with daily demands, and problems of disclosure to friends and family (Kalichman, 1995; Winiarski, 1991). For those with long asymptomatic periods, the focus was often on maintaining well-being, staying abreast of the medical and political climate contextualizing treatment choices, and feelings about the health of others impacted by the epidemic. Therapists found themselves walking a fine line between helping clients not give up on life activities prematurely and helping them prepare for death. Other therapeutic goals included helping instill a sense of hope, helping clients become comfortable with uncertainties, and helping clients cope with bureaucracies.

These issues remain, but new and effective treatments for both opportunistic infections and HIV itself have changed the clinical course of HIV/AIDS (Blattner, 1997). This can itself be a stressor, as clients who burned bridges, exhausting personal, professional, and financial resources in preparing themselves for death, now may have to struggle to revise their self-image and life plans because they will be healthier longer. They may need help in complying with treatment regimens and making informed and grounded choices about new treatment strategies, which may be offered without the long pipeline of experimental and clinical trials that was formerly an obstacle. They may also fear losing benefits and the peer and professional supports on which they had come to rely.

Other clients, however, may not respond to these new treatments and may need help coping with the awareness that they may not be among the fortunate ones. And still, too many people in our circles of friends, colleagues, and families continue to die, and are forever gone.

Concluding Thoughts

We have used the word "notes" in the title of this chapter to reflect the fact that our experiences working with deaf people with HIV/AIDS, and the state of our knowledge, are still fragmented and incomplete. Work like this is like work on the front lines of a war, where understandings develop and shift rapidly in response to changes in our field's knowledge base and to changes in external conditions.

There are two overarching themes we would like to draw out from our experience, by way of closing. First, we hope we have demonstrated in this chapter that there is much in our traditional frameworks and intervention modalities that can be of substantial use in work with deaf people with HIV/AIDS. Much of what we know about deafness, what we know about HIV/AIDS, and what we know about general clinical work can be applied. However, it needs to be applied through a framework of thoughtful consideration of the ways that having this particular illness changes clients' realities. Application, but not automatic or uncritical application, may be the watchword.

Second, it is also our strong feeling that there is little room for purism in this work. Both specialized Deaf services and accessible nonspecialized services can play an important role. There is no reason to have a sense of inevitable gridlock in mental health work with deaf people with HIV/AIDS. With creativity and collaboration, much can be accomplished despite the limitations in resources, knowledge, and energies.

References

Alford, C. F. (1989). *Melanie Klein and critical social theory.* New Haven: Yale University Press.

Altman, N. (1995). *The analyst in the inner city: Race, class, and culture through a psychoanalytic lens.* Hillsdale, NJ: Analytic Press.

Altshuler, K. Z., & Abdullah, S. (1981). Mental health and the deaf adult. In L. K. Stein, E. D. Mindel, & T. Jabaley (Eds.), *Deafness and mental health* (pp. 99–112). New York: Grune and Stratton.

Anzieu, D. (1984). *The group and the unconscious.* London: Routledge and Kegan Paul.

Barthell, C. N. (1983). Deaf and gay: Where is my community? *Readings in Deafness, 9,* 147–157.

Belenky, M., Clinchy, B., Goldberger, N., & Tarule, J. (1986). *Women's ways of knowing: The development of self, voice, and mind.* New York: Basic Books.

Berman, E. (1987). Relational psychoanalysis: A historical background. *American Journal of Psychotherapy, 51,* 185–203.

Bird, B. (1957). A consideration of the etiology of prejudice. *Journal of the American Psychoanalytic Association, 5,* 490–513.

Blattner, W. A. (1997). *Worldwide epidemic of HIV/AIDS: Current trends and future directions.* XI International Conference on AIDS, Vancouver.

Blotzer, M., & Ruth, R. (1996). *Sometimes you just want to feel like a human being: Case studies in empowering psychotherapy with people with disabilities.* Baltimore: Paul H. Brookes.

Bogdan, R., & Taylor, S. (1982). *Inside out: The social meaning of mental retardation.* Toronto: University of Toronto Press.

Cadwell, S. A., Burnham, R. A., & Forstein, M. (Eds.). (1994). *Therapists on the front line: Psychotherapy with gay men in the age of AIDS.* Washington, DC: American Psychiatric Press.

Cain, R. (1991). Stigma management and gay identity development. *Social Work, 36,* 67–73.

Catalan, J., & Hedge, B. (Eds.). (1996). *The impact of AIDS: Psychological and social aspects of HIV infection.* London: Harwood.

Coates, T. J., & Greenblatt, R. M. (1990). Behavioral change using interventions at the community level. In K. K. Holmes, P. A. Mardh, P. F. Sparling, P. J. Wiesner, W. Cates, S. M. Lennon, & W. E. Stamm (Eds.), *Sexually transmitted diseases* (2d ed.) (pp. 1075–1080). New York: McGraw-Hill.

Coleman, E. (1982). Developmental stages of the coming out process. In J. C. Gonsiorek (Ed.), *Homosexuality and psychotherapy: A practitioner's handbook of affirmative models* (pp. 31–44). New York: Haworth Press.

Cournos, F., & Bakalar, N. (Eds.). (1996). *AIDS and people with severe mental illness: A handbook for mental health professionals.* New Haven: Yale University Press.

Crimp, D. (Ed.). (1988). *AIDS: Cultural analysis, cultural activism.* Cambridge, MA: MIT Press.

Deeks, S. G., Smith, M., Holodniy, M., & Kahn, J. O. (1997). HIV-1 protease inhibitors: A review for clinicians. *Journal of the American Medical Association, 277,* 145–153.

Friedland, G. H., & Klein, R. S. (1987). Transmission of the human immunodeficiency virus. *New England Journal of Medicine, 317,* 1125–1135.

Friedman, J. (1995). HIV/AIDS related hearing loss: Beyond the biomedical model. *ADVANCE for Speech-Language Pathologists and Audiologists,* 9 May, 11–12.

Fromm, E. (1941). *Escape from freedom.* New York: Avon.

———. (1955). *The sane society.* Greenwich, CT: Fawcett.

———. (1970). *The crisis of psychoanalysis.* New York: Holt.

Gabriel, M. A. (1996). *AIDS trauma and support group therapy: Mutual aid, empowerment, connection.* New York: Free Press.

Gallo, D., George, J. R., Fitchen, J. H., Goldstein, A. S., & Hindahl, M. S. (1997). Evaluation of a system using mucosal transudate for HIV-1 antibody screening and confirmatory testing. *Journal of the American Medical Association, 277,* 254–258.

Galloway, V. H. (1968). Mental health: What it means to a deaf person. In K. Z. Altshuler & J. D. Rainer (Eds.), *Mental health and the deaf: Approaches and prospects* (pp. 51–61). Washington, DC: U. S. Department of Health, Education and Welfare.

Goffman, E. (1963). *Stigma: Notes on the management of spoiled identity.* New York: Simon and Schuster.

Grey, A., Ortmyer, D., & Caligor, L. (1972). Research issues for psychotherapy with blue-collar patients. In G. D. Goldman & D. S. Milman (Eds.), *Innovations in psychotherapy* (pp. 134–145). Springfield, IL: Charles C. Thomas.

Herek, G. M., & Glunt, E. K. (1988). An epidemic of stigma: Public reactions to AIDS. *American Psychologist, 43,* 886–891.

Hildebrand, H. P. (1992). A patient dying of AIDS. *International Review of Psycho-Analysis, 19,* 457–471.

Hiraga, M., & Langholtz, D. (1996). The challenges of interpreting in HIV settings. *RID Views, 4,* 31.

Hoffman, I. Z. (1992). Some practical considerations of a social-constructionist view of the psychoanalytic situation. *Psychoanalytic Dialogues, 2,* 287–304.

Hoffman, M. A. (1996). *Assessment, intervention, and prevention: Counseling clients with HIV/AIDS disease.* New York: Guilford Press.

Isay, R. (1989). *Being homosexual: Gay men and their development.* New York: Farrar, Strauss, Giroux.

———. (1996). *Becoming gay: The journey to self-acceptance.* New York: Pantheon.

Jacobs, L. M. (1974). *A deaf adult speaks out.* Washington, DC: Gallaudet University Press.

Jacoby, R. (1983). *The repression of psychoanalysis.* New York: Basic Books.

Jaques, E. (1955). Social systems as defence against persecutory and depressive anxiety. In M. Klein (Ed.), *New directions in psychoanalysis* (pp. 478–498). London: Tavistock.

Kalichman, S. C. (1995). *Understanding AIDS: A guide for mental health professionals.* Washington, DC: American Psychological Association.

Kaplan, H. I., Sadock, B. J., & Grebb, J. A. (1994). Neuropsychiatric aspects of human immunodeficiency virus (HIV) infection and acquired immune deficiency syndrome (AIDS). In H. I. Kaplan and B. J. Sadock (Eds.), *Kaplan and Sadock's synopsis of psychiatry* (7th ed.) (pp. 374–382). Baltimore: Williams and Wilkins.

Langer, M. (1989). *From Vienna to Managua.* London: Free Association Books.

Langholtz, D. (1996). Members' communique. *ADARA Update,* Spring, 8–9.

Langholtz, D., & Rendon, M. E. (1991/1992). The deaf gay/lesbian client: Some perspectives. *Journal of the American Deafness and Rehabilitation Association, 25,* 31–34.

———. (1994). A minority within a minority: Deaf and gay. In J. Sears (Ed.), *Bound by diversity* (pp. 89–94). Columbia, SC: Sebastian Press.

Leigh, I. W., Corbett, C. A., Gutman, V., & Morere, D. A. (1996). Providing psychological services to deaf individuals: A response to new perceptions of diversity. *Professional Psychology: Research and Practice, 27,* 364–371.

LeMaistre, J. (1993). *Beyond rage: Mastering unavoidable health changes.* Oak Park, IL: Alpine Guild.

Lewes, K. (1992). Homophobia and the heterosexual fear of AIDS. *American Imago, 49,* 343–357.

Lifson, A. R., Rutherford, G. W., & Jaffe, H. W. (1988). The natural history of the human immunodeficiency virus infection. *Journal of Infectious Disease, 158,* 1360–1367.

Lukes, C. A., & Land, H. (1990). Biculturality and homosexuality. *Social Work, 35,* 155–161.

Malyon, A. K. (1982). Psychotherapeutic implications of internalized homophobia in gay men. In J. C. Gonsiorek (Ed.), *Homosexuality and psychotherapy: A practitioner's handbook of affirmative models* (pp. 59–70). New York: Haworth Press.

Mann, J. M. (1989). *Global AIDS into the 1990s.* (Publication GPA/DIR/89.2, English). Geneva: World Health Organization.

McBride, J. (1990). *Hot and safe* [video]. Toronto: AIDS Committee of Toronto.

Menzies, I. E. P. (1975). A case study in the functioning of social systems as a defense against anxiety. In A. D. Colman & W. H. Bexton (Eds.), *Group relations reader I* (pp. 281–312). Jupiter, FL: A. K. Rice Institute.

Moss, D. (1997). On situating homophobia. *Journal of the American Psychoanalytic Association, 45,* 201–215.

Myers, M. T. (1992). The African American experience with HIV disease. *Focus: A Guide to AIDS Research and Counseling, 7,* 79–82.

Paradis, B. A. (1991). Seeking intimacy and integration: Gay men in the era of AIDS. *Smith College Studies in Social Work, 61,* 260–274.

———. (1997). Multicultural identity and gay men in the era of AIDS. *American Journal of Orthopsychiatry, 67,* 300–307.

Rainer, J. D., & Altshuler, K. Z. (1971). A psychiatric program for the deaf: Experience and implications. *American Journal of Psychiatry, 127,* 1527–1532.

Ruth R. (1986). Being a bilingual therapist. In J. Berry & R. A. Annis (Eds.), *Ethnic psychology* (pp. 315–322). Berwyn, PA: Swets.

Schemenauer, Dennis [Director]. (1989). *Deaf culture autobiographies: Dennis Schemenauer* [video]. San Diego: Sign Enhancers.

Schlesinger, H. S., & Meadow, K. P. (1972). *Sound and sign: Childhood deafness and mental health.* Berkeley: University of California Press.

Sinason, V. E. (1986). Secondary mental handicap and its relationship to trauma. *Psychoanalytical Psychotherapy, 2,* 131–154.

Stansfield, M., & Veltri, D. (1987). Assessment from the perspective of the sign language interpreter. In H. Elliott, L. Glass, & J. W. Evans (Eds.), *Mental health assessment of deaf clients: A practical manual* (pp. 153–163). Boston: Little, Brown.

Van Biema, D. (1994). Society: Silence really does equal death. *Time,* 4 April, 76–77.

Veltri, D., Duffy, K., & Langholtz, D. (1996). *AIDS in the deaf community/deaf in the AIDS community: Creating partnerships* [video]. San Francisco: University of California Center on Deafness.

Vernon, M., & Andrews, J. (1990). *The psychology of deafness.* New York: Longman.

Volberding, P. A., & Cohen, P. T. (1990). Clinical spectrum of HIV infection. In P. T. Cohen, M. A. Sande, & P. A. Volberding (Eds.), *The AIDS knowledge base* (pp. 4.1.1-1–11). Waltham, MA: Medical Publishing Group.

Wicks, L. A. (Ed.). (1997). *Psychotherapy and AIDS: The human dimension.* Washington, DC: Taylor and Francis.

Wilber, J. C. (1990). HIV antibody testing: Methodology. In P. T. Cohen, M. A. Sande, & P. A. Volberding (Eds.), *The AIDS knowledge base* (pp. 2.1.2-1–8). Waltham, MA: Medical Publishing Group.

Willigan, B. K., & King, S. J. (Eds.). (1992). *Mental health services for deaf people: 1992 edition.* Washington, DC: Gallaudet University Research Institute, Mental Health Research Program.

Winiarski, M. G. (1991). *AIDS-related psychotherapy.* New York: Pergamon.

12

Treatment of Deaf Survivors of Sexual Abuse: A Process of Healing

FLORRIE BURKE, VIRGINIA GUTMAN, AND PATRICIA DOBOSH

Sexual abuse of children is currently recognized as a widespread problem that has numerous effects throughout the survivor's life. While much is known about sexual abuse and its impact, Deaf survivors have been largely invisible, both in the professional literature and in the Deaf community itself.

This chapter reviews what is currently known about Deaf survivors of sexual abuse, including the incidence of such experiences, their ramifications, and appropriate treatment methods. Where specific information about Deaf survivors was not available, we have extrapolated from the literature on the general population. However, such extrapolations must be viewed with caution because they are primarily based on experiences of hearing clients, and may not be applicable to Deaf clients in some respects.

Definitions and Prevalence

Lack of legal and clinical consensus on what specifically constitutes child sexual abuse creates confusion for victims and their families, which is compounded by the fact that child sexual abuse is invariably secretive, often unacknowledged, and always difficult to prosecute. In addition to the confusing family dynamics that often surround abuse, recognizing abuse can be obscured by the fact that legal definitions vary from state to state (Morgan, 1987); clinical definitions may vary depending on the clinician's training, experience, and orientation.

Sorting out different perspectives into a coherent definition of childhood sexual abuse is not an easy task. The National Research Council's Panel on Research on Child Abuse and Neglect (1993) defines child sexual abuse as a subgroup of child maltreatment, which includes behaviors such as "incest, sexual assault by a relative or stranger, fondling of genital areas, exposure to indecent acts, sexual rituals, or involvement in child pornography" (p. 59). In general, child sexual abuse may occur with or without physical contact, and may also include voyeurism, exhibitionism, verbal insinuation or seductiveness, obscene behavior, and any sexually explicit or subtly sexual activities. Faller (1993), in her report for the National Center on Child Abuse and Neglect, expands on this by suggesting that three factors are the hallmarks of child sexual abuse: a differential in power, knowledge, and gratification.

Without an agreed-upon definition, the literature provides varying estimates of prevalence and incidence of childhood sexual abuse (Alpert, 1990). Precise figures on incidence are hampered by the secrecy and sense of breaking a social taboo, which may inhibit disclosure (Morgan, 1987), and because abused children and their parents may vacillate about whether what occurred could be considered abuse. According to Finkelhor (1986), from 6% to 62% of adults have been abused as children. The incidence rate has been reported to be 2.1 to 6.3 per 1,000 children up to age 17 per year (Finkelhor & Dziuba-Leatherman, 1994). However, the true incidence rate (including unreported cases) may be four to ten times higher (Alter-Reid et al., 1986; Briere, 1992; Massie & Johnson, 1989). In terms of sex ratios, it is widely reported that one in four girls and one in ten boys are sexually abused prior to adulthood (Finkelhor, 1986). Furthermore, child sexual abuse appears to be a pervasive social problem in all cultures and at all socioeconomic levels.

Victims may reinterpret or deny the significance of what has happened to them, even when the abuse has been severe and has continued for years (Rieker & Carmen, 1986).

* * *

Miranda was a Deaf woman who was sexually abused by her older brother and severely beaten on many occasions by her mother.[1] She later stated, "I wished it would stop, but I thought everyone knew what was happening and no one wanted to do anything about it. After I went to [a foster home] I had other problems and I didn't think about it any more. I wouldn't really call it abuse." This client did not consider herself "abused" because she had not suffered injuries as severe as those of another sibling.

It is difficult to work with this particular dynamic. Clients who spent much of their childhood and adolescence confused about what was happening to them may, for various reasons, come to believe it should not be considered "abuse." Working with such a habitual way of thinking requires going back in time and dealing with complex, abstract concepts. Many clients, Deaf or hearing, are unable to do this easily. A similar kind of confusion can be seen in the case of Carolyn.

* * *

Carolyn was a college freshman who was in therapy because of a history of failed relationships. She repeatedly got into relationships with men who "needed" her. She provided stability, financial support, and other practical assistance to these men, and then felt devastated when they invariably left. For many years she had believed that if she did what a man wanted her to do, the relationship would be fine, and she blamed herself for each failed relationship. She had many sexual partners, but reported that she had never had a satisfactory sexual experience. In therapy, Carolyn revealed that her father had molested her for many years. She thought it was something that happened in all families. For her, this was the only way to get her father's approval. She did not consider herself abused, and did not recognize any ill effects from the abuse. She was unable to connect her current problems to her past.

If Carolyn had been a hearing client, a referral to a therapy or support group dealing with sexual abuse issues would have been appropriate, perhaps in conjunction with individual therapy. A group would have given her an opportunity

1. The clinical vignettes described in this chapter are drawn from our own practices. These are often composites in which the experiences of several individuals have been combined. In every case, names and other important details have been changed in order to protect the privacy and identity of the people involved.

to develop a sense of herself in the context of knowing about the experiences of others. She might have begun to see her experiences through others' eyes and then broadened her understanding of what abuse means. This expanded perspective is especially important for Deaf survivors; groups can provide a "reality check" that is often missing from previous situations where communication was very limited. For Deaf clients, however, there are often not many therapeutic options available, and no group experience was available to Carolyn.

Childhood Abuse and Individuals Who Are Deaf

Ammerman and Baladerian (1993) suggest that children with disabilities may be more at risk of experiencing many types of abuse. They cite incidences ranging from four to ten times that of the general population; prevalence reports vary from 3% to 70%. According to Sullivan et al. (1991), the wide range in prevalence reflects the variety of definitions of both "disability" and "child sexual abuse." As a further complication, many studies do not differentiate between disabled children who are abused and children who developed disabilities as a result of their abuse. Such a distinction can be difficult even in individual cases. For example, a male client reported: "I was hard of hearing as a child. Later I became deaf. A doctor told my mother I lost my hearing because of a fall, but I think it was because of her hitting me on the head so much."

Sobsey's (1994) literature review suggests that risk for sexual abuse may vary with type of disability, and that for disabled children, abuse tends to be chronic and severe. Individuals with mental retardation and hearing loss were frequently reported among those who had experienced child sexual abuse. It might be inferred that vulnerability and the lack of clear and easy communication put children with these disabilities at special risk.

No studies of deaf children in a representative range of locations and settings have been done. Rather, observations regarding abuse of deaf children come from particular clinics or regions. Thus, findings may be heavily influenced by the setting where the observations were made, or by local events that may have created an interest in the topic or a need for intervention. The available published reports generally reinforce the idea that the incidence of sexual abuse is higher for deaf children than for the general population. For example, Sullivan, Vernon, and Scanlon (1987) reported that 75 of 150 Deaf children at a residential school stated that they had been sexually abused. Of these reports, 19 were of incest in the childrens' homes.

Dobosh (1996), studying a general university Deaf population, found that almost one-third of her subjects reported sexual abuse. However, because some subjects gave ambiguous responses when asked about abuse, the prevalence in this population might have been as high as 50%.

Sullivan and her colleagues extrapolate that 54% of deaf boys report abuse (as compared to 10% of hearing boys); 50% of deaf girls report abuse (as compared to 25% of hearing girls) (Sullivan et al., 1987). Thus, not only does the incidence rate appear to be higher for deaf youth but the proportion of girls to boys may be different from that in the hearing population, in which girls are two to three times more likely to report sexual abuse than boys (Finkelhor & Dziuba-Leatherman, 1994). It should be noted that Sullivan et al. studied a residential school population; the generalizability of their extrapolations to other settings is not known.

On the other hand, Skinner (1991) found the male-female ratio for Deaf adult survivors of sexual abuse to be similar to that for the general population, based on questionnaires to therapists serving the deaf community. Her results indicate that survivors of sexual abuse who sought mental health services include a larger percentage of women than men. This finding, however, may be influenced by women's greater willingness to seek therapy. In support of Skinner's findings, Dobosh's (1996) study, while not a study of prevalence, found 62% of Deaf female subjects and 24% of Deaf male subjects in a general college sample reporting sexual abuse.

Skinner (1991) also found that reports of abuse and neglect varied inversely with degree of hearing loss, with hard of hearing individuals most likely to have experienced abuse. Dobosh (1996) however, did not find a significant difference among levels of hearing loss or presence of additional disabilities in rates of reported abuse. Like hearing survivors, deaf survivors were more likely to have subsequent rape experiences than nonabused subjects.

Settings of Abuse

A 1994 study by the National Center on Child Abuse and Neglect (NCCAN) indicated that the primary caretakers of children with disabilities were involved in the reported maltreatment in only 14% of the cases, while primary caretakers were involved in 24% of the cases pertaining to children without disabilities. In other words, compared to children without disabilities, children with disabilities appear to be more at risk for abuse by someone other than their parents.

Similar results were reported by Sullivan, Vernon, and Scanlan (1987). In interviews with one hundred deaf sexually abused children they found that those from a residential program were more likely to report that abuse occurred at school, while those in mainstreamed programs were more likely to report having been abused at home or near home. Dobosh (1996) also found an interaction between settings and reports of sexual abuse.

In the 1994 NCCAN study, the caseworkers reported that they believe the disabilities "directly led to or contributed to child maltreatment" in 47.2% of their cases involving children with disabilities. It is not known what they thought the connection to be. A number of possibilities come to mind: perhaps the disabled child was more likely to be placed in a situation in which abuse could happen, less able to remove him, or herself from the abusive situation, or possibly less able to report the abuse. Another factor may be prior abuse on the part of the perpetrator. According to Friedrich (1995) and Vernon and Rich (1997), both hearing and deaf sexual offenders typically were victims of similar abuse during childhood.

* * *

Charles was a Deaf man charged with abusing a multiply disabled adolescent whom he was supposed to be taking care of after school. Charles explained, "I learned how to do this from a volunteer who came to my school. He showed me how by doing it to me." As a child, this client had attended a residential school far from home. He was one of only a few children left on campus at this school on weekends, and was often in the care of temporary staff or volunteers during that time. He recollected that the volunteer had "disciplined" him for disobedience by tying him up and making him drink urine and engage in sexual activities with the volunteer. It never occurred to him to complain about the abuse because he thought he was lucky to have anyone taking care of him on weekends. When Charles later found himself in the position of having a younger person dependent upon him and under his control, he repeated his own victimization, this time in the role of perpetrator. He was amazed to be charged with a crime, as he had not considered his behavior to be particularly unusual.

Consequences of Child Sexual Abuse

There is a limited amount of research on the effects of childhood sexual abuse on the Deaf individual. Thus, we first discuss the effects that have been described in the general population in order to provide a context. Conte and Berliner (1988) found that 21% of a community sample of sexually abused children were reported by their social workers to be asymptomatic. Most children show some symptoms, however. Initial effects that have been empirically substantiated for the general population cover an enormous range, including fear, anxiety, depression, anger, hostility, and inappropriate sexual behavior (Browne & Finkelhor, 1987).

Faller (1990) divides the early effects into two groups. Sexual symptoms can include excessive masturbation; developmentally unusual sexual interaction with peers, younger children, and adults; and seductive behavior, promiscuity, precocious sexual knowledge, and sexual comments. The second group of symptoms is very diverse and reflects the destructive and overwhelming nature of sexual abuse on the child's coping capacity. Regression in toilet training, elimination problems, fears of sleeping, nightmares, sleepwalking, anorexia, and bulimia have been reported. Also seen are social withdrawal, anxiety, aggressive behavior, running away from home, suicidal acts, drug and alcohol abuse, and involvement in illegal or forbidden behavior (stealing, staying out late, fire-setting). Faller also describes cognitive/academic problems, school failure, and deficiencies in language development and fine and gross motor control.

Briere (1992) suggests that sexual abuse involves the greatest trauma if the following factors are present: the abuse is frequent and continues for a long period of time; there are multiple perpetrators; there is penetration or intercourse; physical force is used to make the child engage in sexual activity; the abuse occurs at an early age; the perpetrator is significantly older than the victim; there is also additional physical abuse; the abuse is bizarre (for example, when the perpetrator is psychotic); the victim feels personally responsible for the abuse; or the victim experiences powerlessness, betrayal, and stigma related to the abuse (pp. 5–6).

Also well documented are long-term effects including depression, self-destructive behavior, anxiety, feelings of isolation and stigma, poor self-esteem, later revictimization, substance abuse, dissociation, experience of many stressful life events, and interpersonal and sexual problems (Becker-Lausen et al., 1995; Browne & Finkelhor, 1987). However, not all adults who were sexually abused as children report long-term sequelae. Those who do may not experience symptoms continually (Bolen, 1993; Kilpatrick, 1986; Maltas & Shay, 1995).

Additional effects may include difficulty trusting others, sexual maladjustment, feelings of powerlessness, compulsive disorders, impulsivity, parenting and relationship difficulties, problems sleeping, weight concern, thoughts of hurting self or others, and suicide attempts (Braver et al., 1992). And as illustrated above in the case of Charles, some sexually abused adults—in both the Deaf and hearing communities—will eventually abuse others (Friedrich, 1995; Vernon & Rich, 1997).

Sexually abused deaf adults report symptoms similar to those found in hearing survivors (Dobosh, 1996), with a similar clinical presentation of these symptoms (Cowgell & Fields, 1983). The kinds of problems experienced by Ruth illustrate the potential range of effects.

* * *

Ruth, a twenty-year-old Deaf woman, was badly abused by a drug-addicted mother and gang-raped at the age of twelve. She recalled that her mother stood by and laughed. Ruth was also forced to work as a prostitute. She had a history of self-mutilation and suicidal gestures. In addition, she had many somatic symptoms. When she entered therapy, she began talking extensively to her therapist about what had happened to her. Having no experience with boundaries or privacy, she also talked about her childhood experiences to anyone who would listen.

As Ruth recalled events, she became very anxious and vulnerable. She could not allow herself to be aware of emotional pain, but she had developed a huge tolerance for physical abuse. Anger, neediness, disappointment, fear, self-blame, and experiences of rejection all touched on deep reservoirs of pain, and all felt unmanageable to her. An insensitive remark from a peer could set her off, and then she would attempt to injure herself. She felt she gained some control over the inchoate emotional pain when she injured herself physically.

Therapists in such situations must take a strong stand for abstinence from self-injuring behavior. Ruth, like many clients who have experienced severe and repeated abuse, did not see anything wrong with hurting herself. Therapist and client may want to work out a detailed contract about self-abusive behaviors, and make sure each keeps a copy. This method lets the client know that his or her well-being is important to someone (in this case the therapist), and that the therapist wants to protect him or her from injury. These may be new ideas to the client. Further healing cannot take place until the self-injurious behavior is stopped. However, for many clients, stopping such behavior requires a long period of effort, with advances and relapses to be expected and constant reinforcement needed from the therapist.

Ethnic Minority Issues

Ethnic minority individuals, Deaf or hearing, may suffer especially high levels of symptoms (Dobosh, 1996, Russell et al., 1998). These may reflect especially severe and violent abuse experiences (Russell et al., 1998). However, because dual-minority individuals (i.e., a person who is both Deaf and African American) face discrimination from multiple sources (Anderson & Grace, 1991) and lack adequate social and educational support (Reagan, 1990), this may compound the after-effects of abuse. Both protection against abuse and services to facilitate recovery may be lacking.

Diagnostic Issues

Fitting wide-ranging symptoms and concerns into any simple diagnostic pattern has proved difficult. Major sampling, design, and measurement problems plague the field and make generalizations difficult. Herman (1981) comments that the insight of a skilled clinician cannot be matched by any questionnaire or survey instrument currently available. Subtle forms of emotional damage, suggested in clinical and first-person reports, may not be easily detectable by standardized measures.

The symptoms may change over time, depending upon life circumstances. Diagnostic issues cannot be ignored, however, because finding diagnostic descriptors that accurately reflect the extent and severity of difficulties a client is experiencing is important in managed care settings in order to obtain appropriate services. An example of the diagnostic difficulty involved can be seen in situations like Millie's.

* * *

Millie's mother had been hospitalized several times for "mental breakdowns." On several occasions before a hospitalization her mother tried to kill herself and her children. Millie was also physically and sexually abused by at least two male relatives. Millie was the only Deaf person in her family and felt that most of the members of her extended family wanted to be supportive but did not understand her situation. She left home at a relatively early age and began supporting herself. A very bright, responsible, and personable young woman, she was able to get and hold good jobs and was thinking about going to college.

During her twenties she had feelings of despair, feelings that she did not belong on earth, difficulty asserting herself in relationships with friends and lovers, several bereavements, suicide attempts, aggressive and destructive behaviors that she later could not remember, episodes of heavy drinking, episodes of prolonged fasting, and overwhelming urges to hurt herself. She had also been attacked by an unknown assailant. It seemed that each time she was able to gain mastery over a troubling symptom, a new set of problems would emerge. Over the course of several years of treatment, many different symptoms appeared at different times. The diagnostic understanding of what she was struggling with internally had to change as well to fit her changing experiences.

One way to conceptualize the wide-ranging effects of childhood sexual abuse is to think of it as a traumatization leading to symptoms of post-traumatic stress disorder (PTSD). In fact, many sexual abuse survivors show symptoms suggestive of PTSD (e.g., flashbacks, nightmares, numbing of affect, a sense of estrangement, and sleep problems) (Finkelhor, 1990). However, PTSD does not cover all of the effects of child abuse. Finkelhor suggests that the PTSD conceptualization is too narrow, overemphasizing affect while ignoring cognitive effects, and that it fails to explain the survivors who do not show PTSD symptoms but do display other effects. The PTSD conceptualization may also give insufficient attention to the importance of the child's developmental level during the abusive situation, and the impact on the child's mastery of later developmental stages.

The advantage of using PTSD as a diagnostic conceptualization is that it allows a wide range of symptoms to be encompassed in a single framework. It may fail to acknowledge the client's survival spirit, however, and may inappropriately suggest an inevitability of certain behavioral and emotional consequences following abuse. The cornerstone of this diagnosis is a trauma so destructive that it must be recognized as the cause of problems. The coping methods a child uses to manage the trauma may later produce their own difficulties. However, we view a mechanistic cause-and-effect formulation to be only a partial explanation. Acknowledging the individual creativity and resourcefulness that allowed survival can be essential to the healing process.

A trauma-healing approach provides a model for therapy that may differ in some respects from models used for other kinds of problems. For example, traditional models view symptoms as pathologies to be removed, while a trauma-healing approach sees symptoms (including life-threatening behaviors) as understandable responses to trauma which may have initially assisted in physical or emotional survival. Therapeutic goals may differ as well. Validation of the survivor's emotional pain and integration of the trauma may be primary goals. Medications are de-emphasized if they make the survivor numb to certain feelings. This differs from the traditional therapeutic approach of trying to quickly increase functioning and decrease signs of distress. An additional difference from current standard approaches is in length of treatment. In a trauma-healing approach, the length of treatment is dictated by the client's emerging recovery process rather than determined in advance.

VULNERABILITY

Westcott (1991) describes characteristics that may make children who have disabilities more vulnerable. These characteristics include: having little control or choice over their own lives; being taught that compliance and obedience are equivalent to good behavior; feeling isolated and therefore very responsive to attention and affection; and having difficulty communicating with adults in general.

For deaf children, the communication issues are especially salient. Sullivan, Vernon, and Scanlan (1987) suggest that in addition to the possibility that a report of abuse may not be believed, a deaf child may find his or her report is not even understood. Communication barriers increase a child's vulnerability because the child may lack access to information about sexuality, have a limited number of people with whom to communicate, or have trouble even describing the event. Prosecution may be hampered by the difficulty of a deaf child witness giving court testimony that would be considered credible. Furthermore, if communication is difficult within the family, the child may not have a good support system to aid in recovery after the abuse has stopped.

Other possible factors that may contribute to vulnerability to abuse include parental stress and social isolation (Fontes, 1995). In addition to the potential stress of having a child diagnosed as deaf, raising the child can require increased time and resources. Another factor is the difficulty a parent may have in learning the many new skills necessary in order to raise a deaf child in a hearing family (Long, 1983). Parents may experience guilt, difficulty in accepting that the child is not "perfect" (Brookhouser et al., 1986), isolation, depression, fatigue, and blame. All of these factors might in some cases compromise their ability to attentively protect the child and to provide support if abuse occurs. Indeed, for certain perpetrators, family stress may increase the likelihood of sexual behaviors with children (Faller, 1990).

DEVELOPMENTAL ISSUES

What is the link between child sexual abuse and adult symptoms? Why does it appear to cause distress continuing into adulthood for many (but not all) survivors? Several theories have been advanced to explain the effects of sexual abuse upon a child's development.

Finkelhor (1984, 1990) and Finkelhor and Browne (1985) identify four characteristics of child sexual abuse that produce adverse impacts upon a child's development: betrayal, traumatic sexualization, powerlessness, and stigmatization. These elements are proposed as constituting the core trauma of sexual abuse (in addition to any additional physical abuse that may also be present).

An important feature of Finkelhor's model is that it takes into account the power of the child's social environment (family and others with whom the child interacts) to directly affect the degree of trauma the child experiences. If the family assists the child in feeling less powerless and stigmatized, trauma is lessened. Familial or institutional reactions that heighten powerlessness or stigmatization will increase the trauma for the child. The family configuration, particularly the presence of reliable authority figures, may also mitigate the experience of betrayal. Thus "traumagenesis" is a function not only of the abuse event but also of the child's environment before and after the abuse occurs.

Finkelhor's emphasis on the child's powerlessness is especially meaningful when considering a Deaf population. Because there may be communication problems between Deaf children and their families, and because Deaf children interact with a large number of other adults in authority positions, the Deaf child's environment is replete with opportunities to increase the child's feeling of powerlessness. It is often the case that Deaf children have no reliable, knowledgeable person available to help or to "take their side," thus partially redressing the children's lack of power.

Becker-Lausen, Sanders, and Chinsky (1995), studying child maltreatment (not limited to sexual abuse) in a nonclinical population, found evidence supporting the idea that both depression and dissociation are common effects of abuse. These reactions then lead to a variety of other problems. Depression was particularly associated with interpersonal problems, while dissociation was associated with the occurrence of repeated victimization and a number of other stressful life events. When the maltreatment was associated with later depressive symptoms, the individual suffered from low self-esteem, preoccupation with his or her faults, lack of enjoyment, and a sense of hopelessness, all of which interfered with maintaining stable and satisfying relationships. The depressed survivor could not attend sufficiently to either his or her own needs or the needs of a relationship partner, and many interpersonal difficulties were reported in family and work relationships.

On the other hand, when dissociation predominated, these survivors reacted to anxiety by withdrawing their attention from what was occurring around them. This appeared to be associated with exposure to risk, and to increased instances of revictimization such as sexual assaults. Becker-Lausen, Sanders, and Chinsky (1995) suggest that the dissociation itself makes it difficult for an individual to be alert to risks and dangers and to take necessary action to avoid them. By entering a trance, numbed, or other dissociative state, an individual may avoid experiencing an intolerable feeling or memory; but such a state also impairs accurate scanning of both the internal and external world in order to detect danger. An individual in a dissociative state who does recognize danger may feel paralyzed, weak, disconnected/unconcerned, or unable to escape or resist.

Treatment

Because the impact of sexual abuse can be so pervasive, treatment of survivors is complex (Briere, 1992; Burke, 1987; Courtois, 1988; Friedrich, 1995; Gil, 1988; Mieselman, 1990). It is often lengthy, although some clients may request help with goals that can be attained in one or more courses of time-limited therapy. Because clients often do not report a history of sexual abuse until the client-therapist relationship has been well established, initial treatment goals may have to be modified to accommodate new issues. In managed care settings, repeated reauthorization of treatment can be facilitated when therapists are specific about current problems and new symptoms and how they will be addressed in therapy.

Outcome research on therapy with survivors of sexual abuse presents significant methodological problems (Beutler & Hill, 1992). A rare study reviewed the effects of a psychotherapeutic intervention in Deaf survivors of sexual abuse at a residential school. A number of the children received treatment, while the parents of other children did not consent to treatment: thus treated and untreated groups could be compared. All therapists had appropriate communication skills. Thirty-five students received psychotherapy that dealt with alleviation of guilt and treatment of depression. The students learned about appropriate expressions of anger, normal human sexuality and interpersonal relationships, sexual preference and homosexuality, maltreatment issues, and self-protection techniques. The program covered the development of a vocabulary to label emotions, establishing a stable identity, developing personal value systems, and developing a capacity for lasting relationships and both tender and genital love. Although the authors did not explicitly state the basis for the treatment offered, one can assume that the treatment was tailored to match the symptoms exhibited by the participants. Blind raters assessed the children before and after receiving therapy using the Child Behavior Checklist (Sullivan et al., 1992).

The results of this study demonstrated that there were significantly fewer behavioral problems in those children who received therapy compared to the group that did not. This study was methodologically limited by the development of the control and experimental groups from convenience rather than by either randomized assignment or a controlled matching technique. Therefore, there may be other factors involved with the improvement in the treatment group. However, the findings support the idea that counseling or psychotherapy can be helpful to Deaf children who have experienced sexual abuse. There is no comparable research on treatment of adult Deaf survivors. There is no reason, however, to assume that treatment will be less effective.

Treating Deaf adults who have been sexually abused is not fundamentally different from treating hearing individuals who have had similar experiences. However, deafness has many dimensions that may increase vulnerability and impede healing. Some areas that may be important, both at the time of the abuse and later as the adult survivor tries to cope, are family relationships, access to medical and psychological services, access to the legal system, exposure to information about sexuality and abuse, and language/communication variables.

One additional area of difficulty for Deaf survivors can be finding appropriate treatment.

* * *

Sandra had experienced childhood sexual abuse over a period of years. After moving out of her mother's house, Sandra sought treatment. She obtained referrals to several therapists, but none had a background in Deaf culture. With each therapist, Sandra attempted to engage in therapy through speechreading; however, she found this led to many misunderstandings. An additional problem was that the person who had abused Sandra was a Deaf man who still lived in the area and was very involved in Deaf sports and social activities. Any time Sandra participated in any Deaf community activities, she might see him. Her therapists, not understanding this, found it difficult to understand why Sandra could not easily avoid seeing the abuser.

Finally, Sandra insisted on a referral to a therapist who could sign. However, this professional did not have much background in trauma and recovery. He recognized her depression, but she felt he was uncomfortable hearing about her abuse and thought she should not "dwell on the past." She also hesitated to tell him much about the abuse experience because she feared he would be able to identify the abuser, whom he knew socially through some advocacy activities. She wasn't sure what would happen if her therapist figured out who had abused her.

What could Sandra's therapists have done to provide more effective treatment? Several possibilities come to mind. Those who were unfamiliar with the Deaf community could have educated themselves about it by reading, supervision, and consultation with Deaf professional peers. Each of her therapists could have discussed with Sandra the effects of the "small world" phenomenon in the Deaf community on her coping with the sexual abuse. Also, the last therapist could have obtained information, consultation, or supervision to improve his skills in working with sexually abused clients. This would have helped him recognize the fact that sexual abuse does not "fade away" no matter how long ago it occurred, but must be dealt with repeatedly as the client encounters new developmental milestones and life challenges.

Several prevention/intervention programs to assist Deaf children with issues of avoiding or dealing with sexual abuse were developed and used in the 1980s and 1990s. Examples include the *Children's Self-Help Project Manual* developed at the University of California Center on Deafness in San Francisco and described in Moser and Burke, 1989/1990; NO-GO-TELL developed by Krents and Atkins at the Lexington Center for the Deaf in New York; Seattle Rape Relief's *Choices: A Sexual Assault Prevention Workbook for Persons who are Deaf and Hard of Hearing* (Shaman, 1985); and Achtzehn's (1987) *PACES: Preventing Abuse of Children through Education for Sexuality,* developed at Gallaudet University. Unfortunately, data on the effectiveness of such programs in preventing abuse are not available.

Even today, large numbers of deaf children do not have the language skills necessary to prevent or report abuse. While early language intervention programs are widespread, deaf immigrant children, for example, may not start learning language until age five or six or even later. Not long ago this was true for most native-born deaf children as well, and many of today's Deaf adults grew up with no usable exposure to language until they entered school. Trauma that occurs before the development of language can be especially difficult to resolve, as more mature coping skills (often language-mediated) cannot be used.

Sometimes a new loss or stressor will "bring back" traumas that were never resolved at the time.

* * *

Dina, a Deaf client from a large and troubled family, suffered a series of losses during her young adulthood. Among these were the death of a supportive grandparent, the murder of two cousins, a fatal car accident that killed an uncle who had abused her as a child, and a miscarriage. Dina was able to maintain her stability fairly well when not acutely stressed, and in general performed well in college and in professional employment. However, each time a loss occurred she suffered severe symptoms: she became fearful of leaving the house; she cut and/or burned her legs and arms; she became dissociative and refused to look at or interact with others; and she was preoccupied with thoughts of dying, death, and dead bodies. At these times she appeared to be in a trance and described herself as "in another world."

During her episodes of severe distress Dina needed support and help in restabilizing her life. On several occasions she needed psychiatric hospitalization. Reassurance, placement in an environment in which she could be kept safe, and medication to temporarily moderate the intensity of her feelings were helpful. The therapist's presence as someone who bridged her "normal" times and her "other world" times was important, as she had little memory of her acutely ill periods when she was functioning well.

The relationship with the therapist and the therapist's ability to promote the client's safety can be a novel experience.

* * *

Edward was a young Deaf man who had been sexually abused by several hearing male cousins he looked up to. He was also physically abused by his father. Feeling he had no place to turn, Edward ran away from home as a young teenager. He got involved with a group that sold drugs. He felt they treated him very well and he was happy to help them by functioning as a look-out and making deliveries.

In the course of this involvement he received some serious injuries, although somehow was never arrested. He eventually decided he wanted a "straight life" and left the gang. However, he continued to have no concern for his own safety and over the course of a year he was badly beaten while walking alone late at night in a neighborhood controlled by gangs, seriously injured in an automobile accident, and robbed several times by people he trusted.

Edward was amazed at his therapist's expressions of concern for his safety. He did not want to talk about his injuries and mishaps, and when he did, he used a very rapid, abbreviated, sloppy sign language that the therapist found difficult to understand. When she persisted in showing interest in his safety, he decided she must want something from him, or that she wanted to get "evidence" to get him into trouble. Then he said she was foolish to be concerned over dangers that he himself did not think about. He eventually was able to recognize that she did not think it was fair or right for him to be repeatedly injured, and that it disturbed her when this happened. For a while Edward used this insight to try to get the therapist to help him get out of various scrapes. When she did not cooperate in this regard, he became angry. After a long period in therapy he began to be able to explore the difference in the therapist's beliefs about the kind of life he had a right to expect, and his own low expectations.

A different type of disregard for safety had been learned by Jill.

* * *

As a Deaf high school student, Jill had been abused by her stepfather. She told her mother, who took legal action against the abuser, and the parents subsequently divorced. Jill left home to attend a residential school. Jill's mother worked long hours at a professional position to support herself and her daughter, but they saw little of each other. Jill and her mother used speech, speechreading, and written notes to communicate; discussing nuances or complex topics was difficult. There had been almost no discussion between mother and daughter about the legal charges or the divorce, and Jill assumed her mother resented her for breaking up the family. She also assumed that she had been placed in residential school because taking care of her was wearing her mother out. During her junior year of high school, Jill was raped by an older student. Her mother was called, and came to the school the next day. However, she talked with her daughter for only an hour and a half, and then brought Jill back to continue the school year.

In therapy, Jill was bland and not very forthcoming. She talked in a very uninvolved way about topics the therapist brought up. She talked about her previous sexual abuse and the rape in the same unemotional way that she described her classes or her friends. The therapist assumed that she was numb because her feelings were so frightening to her and because she did not think anyone was interested in them. Jill might have also assumed that she had "made trouble" for her mother by her previous complaint and so did not want to be perceived as complaining further. The therapist's challenge was to deal with the numbing of her experiences in a way that would allow her to experience her feelings without being overwhelmed by them.

The therapist got her involved in drawings, doll play, and other less verbal ways of expressing herself. A program of active exercise and physical self-defense training was helpful in giving her more of a sense of physical efficacy and being a physical presence in the world.

Therapy Goals

There are many ways to conceptualize the goals of therapy for those who have been abused. Those proposed by Faria and Belohlavek (1984) are worth mentioning in summing up treatment approaches for the wide-ranging problems that survivors of sexual abuse may experience.

The first goal is for the therapist and client to establish a commitment to be involved in the healing process.

The second is to identify old patterns by which the client leaves relationships. Because the therapy process can be difficult, the client will be tempted to leave therapy. It is imperative to engage the client as an active participant in the therapy process so that there is a feeling of empowerment rather than helplessness or passivity.

A third goal is to develop a mutual working relationship in which the client becomes aware of his or her strengths and skills and can start to regain a sense of control.

The fourth goal is for the therapist to build the client's self-esteem about survival. This can be accomplished by assuring the client of his or her value and strength, as evidenced by survival to this point; alleviating shame about past experiences; and accepting and supporting the survivor's intense feelings, especially anger.

The fifth goal is for the client to be able to find constructive ways to express anger. It is necessary to be able to express the rage felt against both the perpetrator and the person or people who were in positions to protect but did not. The rage does not have to be expressed directly to these people, but it must be expressed. The survivor might also be angry at the therapist. This can be an important stage, as it allows the client to see that anger will not drive the therapist away and can be expressed appropriately. Mastering anger is one of the most critical parts of the healing process. Clients often either cannot externalize anger (and become suicidal, self-mutilating, etc.) or inappropriately dump anger (perhaps verbally, physically, or sexually abusing others).

The sixth and most immediate goal of therapy is to help the client identify and gain control over self-destructive and self-defeating behaviors. If the self-destructive behaviors are dangerous to the client or to others, such as suicide attempts, self-mutilation, uncontrollable rage, or substance abuse, the clinician must address these behaviors immediately. Therapists must work with clients to understand that therapy cannot progress until some of the life-threatening behaviors are under control.

A seventh goal is networking for and with the client to make other support systems available. This can be a significant challenge with Deaf clients because there are so few resources, and confidentiality concerns or past experience with a service agency can be a barrier.

The eighth goal is to increase self-esteem through improving body image and understanding of sexual response. With Deaf clients, no previous sex education may have been provided and basic information sharing can be important (Achtzehn, 1981). Therapy may have to address issues of physiological response, sexual dysfunction, intimacy, sexual preference, separating sex from affection, and other related areas.

The ninth goal of therapy is to address specific sexuality concerns with the hope of having clients reclaim their sexuality for themselves.

Group Treatment

Whether a client should be referred for group or individual therapy or some combination of the two depends, in part, on the availability of a suitable therapy group and the client's particular needs. Much of the literature suggests that a combination of individual therapy with a long-term, process-oriented survivors' group is a particularly powerful approach to healing. Many clients seem to need and benefit from the experience of being with others who have been abused. Clients often begin the group feeling abnormal, burdened by a secret that makes them feel different from everyone else. During the group process, this feeling shifts and members begin to feel connected. The experience of sharing the secret of the abuse with a group and having it acknowledged and believed is one of a group's most healing aspects.

Group treatment is always problematic with Deaf clients, however. Communication becomes a major issue when a Deaf person participates in a group with hearing people who do not sign. In all-Deaf groups, lack of anonymity can be a concern (Leigh &

Lewis, this volume). It is possible to work with these issues constructively (Morton & Marcus, 1998). Several steps can be taken to make group interventions more feasible for Deaf participants. First, if a Deaf member joins a hearing group, the leader or facilitator and the other members must be informed about basic communication issues (such as the importance of only one person talking at a time) and receive some information on the role of the interpreter if one is used. Payment for the interpreter may be an issue, especially in low-fee therapy groups or mutual support groups that have no fee at all. The difficulty of interpreting in such a group must be recognized; the interpreter should have both the requisite technical skills and no other relationships with the Deaf participant(s) that could compromise the Deaf client's feeling of emotional safety and privacy in the group.

For groups with several Deaf members, each member must make an informed commitment to maintain the confidentiality of the other members. The group leaders must be adamant and firm in enforcing the confidentiality requirements. Communication can become an issue even within all Deaf groups, as communication skills and preferences may vary. The group members can establish ground rules for communication to assure that each member has an opportunity for full participation (Morton & Marcus, 1998).

In other respects, groups for Deaf survivors have many of the same characteristics as the survivor groups that have been reported in the literature (Herman & Schatzow, 1984). The therapist must help the members establish an environment of mutual trust and support. The group experience should be one in which the survivor is supported in discussing concerns, but not pressured to reveal more than he or she is comfortable with. The goal is for each member to feel less stigmatized and less alone, knowing that others deal with similar experiences. They can receive the concerned attention that may have been lacking at the time that the abuse originally occurred. The opportunity to help another survivor can also give group members a sense of their own worth and their ability to contribute to the well-being of others.

Family Relations

A particularly difficult question in work with survivors, whether in group or individual therapy, is what goals are appropriate for the client's relationships with various family members. Many survivors of abuse wish to confront the abuser, especially if the perpetrator is a family member or someone who is still in their lives. We have heard of therapists who encourage or require a confrontation with the abuser. Our position on this is different: we believe that it is of the utmost importance for therapists to remember that confrontation does not start the process of recovery, nor is it necessary for recovery. A survivor may do it if he or she wants to, when he or she is ready. This is often better done late in the healing process when the client is very strong. Some clients never wish to do it at all. In many cases the outcome of the confrontation is not what the client hoped, and for a fragile client at a vulnerable stage in therapy this can be devastating.

With Deaf clients, not only the history of abuse, but the adult survivor's deafness may drive a wedge between family members. A history of poor communication can make dealing with sensitive emotional issues, such as previous abuse and how the family responded to it, difficult.

* * *

Mary was a young Deaf college graduate in her twenties. She had been sexually abused by a cousin who babysat for her as a child. When she tried to tell her mother about the abuse at the time, her mother either did not understand her or did not believe her. Later Mary told a teacher, and the matter came to light. She had never discussed this with her mother, but wanted to find out why her mother initially reacted as she did. She asked for a joint therapy session with her mother and asked for an interpreter to ensure good communication. However, when her mother arrived for the session, she objected vigorously to the presence of the interpreter, saying that she and her daughter had always understood each other and that Mary sometimes tried to avoid blame or work by pretending not to understand.

The therapist had to choose whether to first pursue the client's immediate goal of getting some clarification with the mother regarding the earlier abuse, or attend to the obviously unresolved family communication issues. The therapist decided that Mary's preference for having the interpreter present would take precedence, as that way full communication would be more assured. She then allowed Mary to persevere in her original intent of questioning her mother about the childhood abuse. The mother attempted to remain cooperative, but seemed angry and defensive. She denied that her daughter had ever told her anything about the abuse and simply reiterated, "I never knew anything about it until [the principal] called me." At the next individual session, Mary said, "See, she will never change." The client was not interested in further exploration of whether the break in the mother-daughter relationship might be repaired.

Adult survivors who "confront" perpetrators or others about their abuse are often disappointed in the response they get. If Mary's therapist had been thinking about this possibility, she might have more effectively guided the client to explore her goals for the conversation with her mother. What might she reasonably hope to achieve? What reactions might she expect from her mother? How would she respond to the different reactions she might anticipate? Had necessary groundwork been done?

It might also have been possible to develop a gradual process of increasing communication between mother and daughter on personal topics so as to lay a foundation for such a difficult discussion rather than jumping into it without much preparation. A gradual process might also have allowed the two of them to develop some mutual skills and techniques for communicating with each other, especially in emotionally sensitive areas. The communication issues (which involved not only the interpreter but questions of the mother's skill in sign language and the daughter's skill in speechreading) in this example contributed to derailing the therapeutic purpose of the session, and might have been more fruitfully addressed before the "confrontation" was attempted.

Flashbacks and Memories

Sexual abuse survivors are often in acute distress when they seek therapy. They may be involved in life crisis situations, or they may be re-experiencing the helplessness, terror, and pain associated with the abuse, with or without direct memories of the abuse.

* * *

Julie, a Deaf client in her fifties, reported flashes of memory ("like would be seen by a flashbulb") of being horrified and seeing blood. She could not identify what was occurring, and felt overwhelmed by fear every time this happened. Certain apparently innocuous scenes or words would trigger these feelings. Julie remembered little of her childhood, but recollects having these flashes throughout her adult life. Initially she thought they were hallucinations; later, as she explored these in therapy, she began to think of them as memories.

The origins of Julie's fear—now close to panic—could not be determined. Her most acute need was to find ways to maintain her internal self-regulation in the face of these disregulating experiences. Julie found relaxation/imagery techniques difficult. Cognitive restructuring and assertiveness training (stating her needs to others) worked better for her and allowed her to build up her feelings of control over herself and her environment.

"Flashbacks" are frequently encountered in work with clients who have experienced sexual abuse or other types of trauma. Flashbacks are usually defined as memories (perhaps fragmentary, displaced, or distorted) that are not well integrated with the client's daily life. When they are experienced, they tend to arise unexpectedly and suddenly, and to bring the feeling of reliving the original experience. Flashbacks can be terrifying and disruptive. Clients may find themselves in tears or in flight and not know why. They are afraid they will do something dangerous or harmful while having a flashback, or that they are "going crazy." In dealing with traumatized individuals, it is often helpful to talk about flashbacks as fragmentary memories that are trying to push their way to the surface. The implication is that they are not current events, but memories of past events, and that they can be understood. Further, once the emotions associated with them are explored and the triggering events understood, the sense of immediacy and danger can be expected to subside.

Working with flashbacks requires time, encouragement, reassurance, and sensitivity on the part of the therapist. Such memories don't necessarily pop up at opportune times; in fact they frequently emerge once a different "presenting problem" seems nearly resolved. Once these issues come into consciousness, they cannot easily be "put back in the box." They make an imperative claim on the client's feelings and attention, often seem overwhelming, and must be dealt with. In time-limited therapy, it may not be wise to encourage exploration of partial or fragmentary memories. Therapists have a duty to inform clients that abuse-related material frequently cannot be resolved in a limited time frame and that beginning such an exploration may in fact make the client feel worse, at least temporarily.

Many Deaf adults in therapy have been trying to avoid thinking about the abuse so that they won't be debilitated or preoccupied with it. A common response is "It's over . . . finished!" While it is true that in most cases (although not all!) the abusive situation has ended by the time the survivor seeks therapy, there still can be considerable value to the client in discussing these events in therapy. One benefit is that by doing this the client can have more sense of coherence about his or her life history. Confusing events or feelings may become clearer. The survivor may find less personally disruptive ways to deal with fear, anger, and other emotions.

Like hearing survivors, Deaf clients may feel they caused the abuse or that they should have been able to stop it. Others feel generally guilty for reasons that they do not fully understand. This is especially common if the abuse happened at a time when the child had little language competence, the abuse and surrounding events were never sufficiently explained to the child, and if the child felt blamed or shamed for the abuse or its aftermath.

TOOLS AND TECHNIQUES

A number of tools and approaches can help clients deal with traumatic or abusive events that happened in childhood, and many techniques used with the general hearing population can be modified in order to be effective aids to healing for Deaf clients. This discussion will focus on some that we have found to be helpful, but is not intended to be exhaustive. Some of these methods assist in developing cognitive clarity about what happened in the past, and how it effects everyday life. Other techniques mentioned here may help with conveying feelings the clients may not know how to express in words or signs. Many of the techniques help clients keep track of their thoughts and feelings through some kind of record. This helps with the feeling of discontinuity experienced by many survivors. They learned in childhood to break their experience up into pieces to make it less painful, and they have to learn as adults to put the parts back together to feel whole.

Reconstructing the Childhood Context

Images from childhood can be very powerful and may bring about an appropriate sense of outrage about things that happened to a child. These images can also be used to help regain a sense of self-love, self-care, and self-protection. The following methods may be helpful techniques for helping a client reconstruct the childhood context of a remembered trauma.

1. The client chooses an age; the therapist asks about the family when the client was that age. Start talking about activities that are pleasant or "normal" and follow the client's lead in moving to more disturbing or threatening areas.
2. The client draws a family map; the therapist asks the client to tell who each person is and the stories and rumors/myths about them.
3. The client brings in pictures of himself or herself as a young child. Pictures of family members can also be helpful. The therapist encourages the client to talk about the child in the picture in different places, such as at home, at school, or at other places. Again, following the client's lead, include the place where the abuse occurred.
4. The client draws a floor plan of the house or school or other site of abuse. The therapist gives the client a paper doll of appropriate gender so the client can "walk" it through the house. Have the doll engage in child behaviors.

* * *

Jane, a young Deaf woman, had been molested and mistreated by her father and had intense anger that she displaced onto those around her in a way that interfered with successful relationships and caused multiple school and work problems.

For a long time she was unable to place the abuse in its rightful time frame. She was a very visual person who enjoyed activities related to art. Developing her own floor plans, dolls, and other visual tools gave her a sense of participation and control in the therapy, as well as a way to situate herself as a child and look at the abuse. These activities allowed Jane to connect with her earlier self, her history, and her emotions. After drawing the sites where molestation had occurred, she could finally understand why the smells of dust and sweat triggered strong feelings for her. Her father had molested her while working in the fields.

Expressing Emotions and Images

A patient, creative therapist who is willing to be flexible in approach can help a client with the healing process despite the absence of extensive language skills. Drawings, collages, and related techniques can constitute a dialogue between client and therapist within which change can occur and be recorded. Power can be regained by any method by which the client feels in greater control of his or her life and experiences, and stronger in his or her ability to have an influence on the world. The following tools can help clients express emotions and images that may be hard for them to put into words.

1. Drawings. Without much instruction, ask the client to draw about the experience: feelings, people, a depiction of the abuse, dreams, and so on. Drawings, such as those in figures 1 and 2, can be an important part of therapy and can show the progression of mood and feeling. They can put the client in an active and powerful role vis-à-vis the subject of the drawing.

* * *

Maria, a twenty-two-year-old Deaf woman, experienced multiple rapes and abuse. She learned to dissociate while the abuse was taking place. She was also a gifted artist and in therapy used drawings to recreate the traumatic experiences. She then used sign language to explain the "captions" for the drawings. The therapist wrote these for her on the computer. As she thought more specifically about the abuse, some of her physical symptoms increased. However, she felt very strongly about the drawings; they provided a way for her to reduce the powerlessness she felt during the abuse.

2. Collage making. Materials are provided to assist a client with explaining, elaborating, or mastering a theme. Collages seem especially useful for clients working with body image issues and reclaiming of their sexuality as part of the healing process.

* * *

Sandy, a nineteen-year-old Deaf woman with limited language skills, made dozens of collages during her therapy. Originally the themes were repetitive: pregnancy and glamour. She cut out pictures of models from magazines and then cut out rounded shapes and added them to the models to make them look pregnant. She also cut out images of fingernail polish, lipstick, eye makeup, clothing, jewelry, and so on. This client was providing information to the therapist in the only way she could. The collages (in addition to other nonverbal techniques such as drawings, sand tray, and psychodrama) helped to reveal that Sandy's father had given her mixed messages over the years he had molested her. He gave her all the trappings of an adult female (makeup, sexy clothing) and then told her she was his baby.

Figure 1. Maria's drawings of her assault and subsequent unsuccessful attempts to get help enabled client and therapist to overcome language barriers.

Figure 2. Prior to therapy, Maria viewed her life as a series of dissociated events. After more than a year of therapy, her drawings began to reflect the integration of these events.

3. Sand tray therapy. This is a very old Jungian-based therapy that utilizes a small sandbox and small figures chosen and arranged by the client to reflect the client's feelings at the time of the session (Kalff, 1980). The completed sand tray can be seen as providing a glimpse into unconscious processes, as well as providing a way for a client to describe a feeling, thought, or sensation without language. The client is asked to make his or her own interpretation of the sand tray, and the therapist can assist in the process. A photograph should be taken of each completed sand tray so that the client and therapist can review what has happened at various stages of healing.

* * *

Elizabeth was a twenty-four-year-old woman who was repeatedly molested by male family members and then physically abused by school authority figures. She had an extremely negative body image and her weight fluctuated greatly. During treatment, she lost over forty pounds and became quite androgynous-looking. She said that the goal of her weight loss was to lose her breasts, which were a constant painful reminder to her of abuse.

One of her sand trays had at the top two mounds of sand covered by small plastic insects. At the bottom of the sand tray was a snake head and an indentation representing the vagina. This tray was made at a point in therapy when body image was a major theme. Constructing this powerful sand tray provided her with a concrete image to look at and talk about. She and the therapist referred back to the photograph in later stages of therapy.

Techniques That Can Be Used by Clients Outside of Therapy

Often clients need to know that they have support and contact at other times than during the therapy hour. One way of bridging the gap between the therapy sessions and the rest of the client's life is to encourage keeping a journal. Many Deaf people find writing exercises too academic and not helpful. However, journals can include not only writing but also drawings, pasted-in pictures, or anything else that will help with self-expression and the healing process. The journal can be a way for clients not only to keep track of feelings and thoughts between sessions, but to provide a private means of expression for those who find it too difficult or painful to communicate directly with the therapist. Clients who need specific guidelines can be given a set of questions (such as those shown in figure 3) to help them write about a specific abuse situation.

* * *

Carol, a twenty-six-year-old Deaf client, loved to read and write, so journal keeping was a tool she liked. She initially used a diary approach, writing about things that were happening currently. She then shifted to writing about the past after a trusting relationship with the therapist was established. Carol's life became more real to her when she wrote about it—previously she had seen her life as a fantasy, a fictional event. She saw the little girl she had been and saw how her stepfather had taken advantage of her and prevented her from having any friends among her peers. She saw other relationships around her for what they were, not as she fantasized them to be. Carol started putting love letters from her stepfather into the journal and was able to look at their relationship more realistically.

A PAGE FROM MY JOURNAL

At (time, date) ______________________________.

I was (tell where you were) ______________________________.

I was (tell what you were doing) ______________________,

I was feeling ______________________________________,

And I was thinking ________________________________.

The perpetrator (tell who hurt you) __________________,

Was (tell what he/she was doing) ____________________.

He/she came to me and said _________________________.

Then he/she (tell what he/she did) ___________________.

He/she also ____.

I felt ____.

I thought ____.

I wanted him/her to ___________________________________.

When he/she stopped, I (tell what you did) ______________.

I thought ____,

And I felt ____.

Now I think ____,

And I want to tell him/her (the person who hurt you) that

____.

Figure 3. Sample Journal Questions

Issues for the Therapist

Dealing with sexual abuse is difficult for therapists (Briere, 1992; Courtois, 1988). It requires a flexible range of skills and a commitment to therapy that may extend beyond the usual short-term interventions. The therapy itself can be emotionally draining, as the client repeatedly suffers through childhood terrors or continues to experience revictimizations. The therapist may be called upon to handle emergencies or to negotiate with third-party payers for coverage of needed services.

Countertransference issues can include over-identification with the client. Therapists can see themselves as the client's only hope, or as the rescuer who will undo all the harm done to the client. These reactions provoke levels of responsibility that can lead therapists to burnout, as well as to poor decisions based on fatigue and over involvement. Hearing therapists working with Deaf clients have been described as especially prone to seeing themselves as the client's "rescuer" (Hoffmeister & Harvey, 1996). This could occur as a result of the lack of other support services that Deaf clients can use, and the need for therapists sometimes to become more involved in advocacy and provision of adjunctive services than they may with hearing clients. It may also be in part an outgrowth of the historical disenfranchisement of Deaf people and the consequent role of professionals even in the lives of Deaf adults.

Whether the client is Deaf or hearing, work with survivors of sexual abuse is challenging and personally demanding for therapists. The therapist must be able to hear about horrifying events that occurred in the client's childhood, without either becoming overwhelmed by outrage and sadness, or numb and indifferent to the suffering perpetrated on the client. Furthermore, the therapist must be able to remain a supportive and reliable figure for a client who may be at times angry, self-destructive, and facing numerous crises. When the client is Deaf, the lack of supportive services, mental health services, and specialized health services in the community add to the issues the therapist must face in order to assist the client's healing process.

Finally, clients dealing with issues resulting from sexual abuse often do not fit the short-term therapy models currently predominating in managed mental health care, so therapists may be faced with continual anxiety over whether the client will be able to continue therapy or not. Individual or group supervision (preferably with peers or supervisors experienced in working with sexual abuse survivors) and other kinds of personal and professional support for the therapist are imperative for us to be able to provide sexual abuse survivors with the quality, intensity, and continuity of services that will allow healing to occur.

References

Achtzehn, J. (1981). *The analysis of three approaches in assessment cognitive sexual information among deaf college students.* Ph.D. dissertation, Syracuse University.

———. (1987). *PACES: Preventing abuse of children through education for sexuality.* Workshop presented at a conference on Preventing Incidence of Sexual Abuse among Hearing Impaired Children and Youth, Department of Education, Gallaudet University, Washington, DC.

Alpert, J. L. (1990). Introduction to special section on clinical intervention in child sexual abuse. *American Psychologist: Research and Practice, 21* (5), 323–324.

Alter-Reid, K., Gibbs, M. S., Lachenmeyer, J. R., Seigal, J., & Massoth, N. A. (1986). Sexual abuse of children: A review of the empirical findings. *Clinical Psychology Review, 6,* 249–266.

American Psychiatric Association. (1987). *Diagnostic and statistical manual of mental disorders* (4th ed.). Washington, DC: American Psychiatric Association.

Ammerman, R. T., & Baladerian, N. J. (1993). *Maltreatment of children with disabilities* (Working paper No. 860). Chicago: National Committee to Prevent Child Abuse.

Anderson, G. B., & Grace, C. A. (1991). Black deaf adolescents: A diverse and underserved population. *Volta Review, 93* (5), 73–86.

Becker-Lausen, E., Sanders, B., & Chinsky, J. (1995). Mediation of childhood abuse experiences: Depression, dissociation, and negative life outcomes. *American Journal of Orthopsychiatry, 65* (4), 560–573.

Beutler, L., and Hill, C. (1992). Process and outcomes research in the treatment of adult victims of childhood sexual abuse: Methodological issues. Special section: Adult survivors of childhood sexual abuse. *Journal of Consulting and Clinical Psychology, 60,* 204–212.

Blume, E. S. (1990). *Secret survivors.* New York: Wiley.

Bolen, J. (1993). The impact of sexual abuse on women's health. *Psychiatric Annals, 23,* 226–253.

Braver, M., Bumberry, J., Green, K., & Rawson, R. (1992). Childhood abuse and current psychological functioning in a university counseling center population. *Journal of Counseling Psychology, 39* (2), 252–257.

Briere, J. (1992). *Child abuse trauma: Theory and treatment of the lasting effects.* Newbury Park, CA: Sage Publications.

Briere, J., & Runtz,, M. (1989). The trauma symptom checklist (TSC-33): Early data on a new scale. *Journal of Interpersonal Violence, 4,* 151–163.

Brookhouser, P. E., Sullivan, P. M., Scanlan, J. H., & Garbarino, J. (1986). Identifying the sexually abused deaf child: The otolaryngologist's role. *Laryngoscope, 96* (2), 152–158.

Browne, A., & Finkelhor, D. (1987). Impact of child sexual abuse: A review of the research. In S. Chess, A. Thomas, & M. Hertzig (Eds.), *Annual progress in child psychiatry and child development* (pp. 66–77). New York: Brunner/Mazel.

Burke, F. (1987). Treatment issues of deaf adolescent victims of sexual abuse. In G. B. Anderson & D. Watson (Eds.), *Innovations in the habilitation and rehabilitation of deaf adolescents* (pp. 156–168). Little Rock, AR: University of Arkansas and Arkansas Division of Rehabilitation Services.

Cole, P., & Putnam, F. (1992). Effect of incest on self and social functioning: A developmental psychopathology perspective. *Journal of Consulting and Clinical Psychology, 60* (2), 174–184.

Conte, J., & Berliner, L. (1988). The impact of sexual abuse on children: Empirical findings. In L. Walker (Ed.), *Handbook on sexual abuse of children* (pp. 72–93). New York: Guilford Press.

Courtois, C. (1988). *Healing the incest wound.* New York: W. W. Norton.

Cowgell, V., & Fields, R. (1983). Incest and sexual abuse: Treatment of the young adult victim. In B. Heller & D. Watson (Eds.), *Mental health and deafness: Strategic perspectives* (pp. 147–155). Proceedings of the National Conference of the American Deafness and Rehabilitation Association. Little Rock, AR: American Deafness and Rehabilitation Association.

Dickman, H. (1983). Intrafamilial sexual abuse and deafness. In B. Heller & D. Watson (Eds.), *Mental health and deafness: Strategic perspectives* (pp. 156–165). Proceedings of the National Conference of the American Deafness and Rehabilitation Association. Little Rock, AR: American Deafness and Rehabilitation Association.

Dobosh, P.K. (1996). *Symptomatology of deaf adults reporting a history of childhood sexual abuse.* Predissertation report, Gallaudet University, Washington, DC.

Faller, K. (1990). *Understanding child sexual maltreament.* Newbury Park, CA: Sage Publications.

———. (1993). *Child sexual abuse: Intervention and treatment issues.* (Report No. S105-89-1730). McLean, VA: The Circle, Inc.

Faria, G., & Blohlavek, N. (1984). Treating female adult survivors of childhood incest. *Social Casework, 65,* 465–471.

Feldman-Summers, S., & Pope, K. (1994). The experience of "forgetting" childhood abuse: A national survey of psychologists. *Journal of Consulting and Clinical Psychology, 62,* 636–639.

Finkelhor, D. (1984). *Child sexual abuse: New theory and research.* New York: Free Press.

———. (1986). *A sourcebook on child sexual abuse.* Beverly Hills, CA: Sage Publications.

———. (1990). Early and long-term effects of child sexual abuse: An update. *Professional Psychology: Research and Practice, 21,* 325–330.

Finkelhor, D., & Browne, A. (1985). The traumatic impact of child sexual abuse: A conceptualization. *American Journal of Orthopsychiatry, 55,* 530–541.

Finkelhor, D., & Dziuba-Leatherman, J. (1994). Victimization of children. *American Psychologist, 49,* 173–183.

Fontes, L. (1995). Introduction. In L. Fontes (Ed.), *Sexual abuse in nine North American cultures: Treatment and prevention* (pp. 1–9). Thousand Oaks, CA: Sage Publications.

Friedrich, W. (1995). *Psychotherapy with sexually abused boys.* Thousand Oaks, CA: Sage Publications.

Gil, E. (1988). *Treatment of adult survivors of childhood abuse.* Rockville, MD: Launch.

Herman, J. (1981). *Father daughter incest.* Cambridge, MA: Harvard University Press.

Herman, J., and Schatzow, E. (1984). Time limited group therapy for women with a history of incest. *International Journal of Group Psychotherapy, 34,* 605–616.

Hoffmeister, R., & Harvey, M. (1996). Is there a psychology of the hearing? In N. Glickman & M. Harvey (Eds.), *Culturally affirmative psychotherapy with Deaf persons* (pp. 73–98). Mahwah, NJ: Lawrence Erlbaum Associates.

Kalff, D. (1980). *SandPlay: A psychotherapeutic approach to the psyche.* Santa Monica, CA: Sigo Press.

Kilpatrick, A. (1986). Some correlates of women's childhood sexual experiences: A retrospective study. *Journal of Sex Research, 22,* 221–242.

Krents, E., & Atkins, D. (nd). NO-GO-TELL. New York: Lexington Center for the Deaf, Research Division.

Loftus, E., Garry, M., & Feldman, J. (1994). Forgetting sexual trauma: What does it mean when 38% forget? *Journal of Consulting and Clinical Psychology, 62,* 1177–1182.

Long, G. (1983). Deafness and family therapy. In B. Heller & D. Watson (Eds.), *Mental health and deafness: Strategic perspectives* (pp. 132–146). Proceedings of the National Conference of the American Deafness and Rehabilitation Association. Little Rock, AR: American Deafness and Rehabilitation Association.

Lytle, L., & Lewis, J. (1996). Deaf therapists, deaf clients, and the therapeutic relationship. In N. Glickman & M. Harvey (Eds.), *Culturally affirmative psychotherapy with Deaf persons* (261–276). Mahwah, NJ: Lawrence Erlbaum Associates.

Maltas, C., & Shay, J. (1995). Trauma contagion in partners of survivors of childhood sexual abuse. *American Journal of Orthopsychiatry, 65,* 529–539.

Massie, M. E., & Johnson, S. M. (1989). The importance of recognizing a history of sexual abuse in female adolescents. *Journal of Adolescent Health Care, 10,* 184–191.

Meiselman, K. (1990). *Resolving the trauma of incest: Reintegration therapy with survivors.* San Francisco: Jossey-Bass.

Morgan, S. R. (1987). *Abuse and neglect of handicapped children.* Boston: College Hill Press.

Morton, D., and Marcus, A. (1998). *Mixed gender psychotherapy with Deaf survivors of sexual abuse.* Presented at the World Conference on Mental Health and Deafness, Washington, DC.

Moser, N., & Burke, F. (1989/1990). *The children's self-help project manual.* San Francisco: University of California Center on Deafness.

National Center of Child Abuse and Neglect. (1993). *Understanding child abuse and neglect.* Washington, DC: National Center of Child Abuse and Neglect.

———. (1994). *A report on the maltreatment of children with disabilities* (Contract No. 105-89-1630). Washington, DC: National Center of Child Abuse and Neglect.

Okamura, A., Heras, P., & Wong-Kerberg, L. (1995). Asian, Pacific Island, and Filipino Americans and sexual child abuse. In L. A. Fontes (Ed.), *Sexual abuse in nine North American cultures: Treatment and prevention* (pp. 67–96). Thousand Oaks, CA: Sage Publications.

Poole, D., Lindsay, D., Memon, A., & Bull, R. (1995). Psychotherapy and the recovery of memories of childhood sexual abuse: U.S. and British practitioners' opinions, practices, and experiences. *Journal of Consulting and Clinical Psychology, 63,* 426–437.

Pope, K. (1995). What psychologists better know about recovered memories, research, lawsuits, and the pivotal experiment. *Clinical Psychology: Science and Practice, 2,* 304–315.

———. (1996). Memory, abuse, and science: Questioning claims about the false memory syndrome epidemic. *American Psychologist, 51,* 957–974.

Priest, R. (1992). Child sexual abuse histories among African American college students: A preliminary study. *American Journal of Orthopsychiatry, 62,* 475–476.

Reagan, T. (1990). Cultural considerations in the education of deaf children. In D. F. Moores & K. P. Meadow-Orlans (Eds.), *Educational and developmental aspects of deafness* (pp. 73–84). Washington, DC: Gallaudet University Press.

Rieker, P., & Carmen, E. (1986). The victim-to-patient process: The disconfirmation and transformation of abuse. *American Journal of Orthopsychiatry, 56,* 360–370.

Russell, D., Schurman, R., & Trocki, K. (1988). The long-term effects of incestuous abuse: A comparison of Afro-American and White American victims. In G. E. Wyatt and G. J. Powell (Eds.), *Lasting effects of child sexual abuse* (pp. 119–134). Newbury Park, CA: Sage Publications.

Shaman, E. (1985). *Choices: A sexual assault prevention workbook for persons who are deaf and hard of hearing.* Seattle, WA: Seattle Rape Relief.

Skinner, S. K. (1991). *Child abuse and the deaf clinical population: Reported prevalence and associated factors.* Ph.D. dissertation, University of Arkansas.

Sobsey, D. (1994). *Violence and abuse in the lives of people with disabilities: The end of silent acceptance?* Baltimore: Paul H. Brookes.

Sullivan, P. M., Brookhouser, P. E., Scanlan, J. H., Knutson, J. F., & Schulte, L. E. (1991). Patterns of physical and sexual abuse of communicatively handicapped children. *Annals of Otology, Rhinology, and Laryngology, 100,* 188–194.

Sullivan, P. M., Scanlan, J. M., Brookhouser, P. E., Schulte, L. E., & Knutson, J. F. (1992). The effects of psychotherapy on behavior problems of sexually abused deaf children. *Child Abuse and Neglect, 16,* 297–307.

Sullivan, P. M., Vernon, M., & Scanlan, J. H. (1987). Sexual abuse of deaf youth. *American Annals of the Deaf, 132,* 256–262.

Vernon, M., & Rich, S. (1997). Pedophilia and deafness. *American Annals of the Deaf, 142,* 4, 300–311.

Wescott, H. (1991). The abuse of disabled children: A review of the literature. *Child Care Health and Development, 17,* 243–258.

Williams, L. (1994). Recall of childhood trauma: A prospective study of women's memories of child sexual abuse. *Journal of Consulting and Clinical Psychology, 62,* 1167–1176.

Wyatt, G. E. (1990). Sexual abuse of ethnic minority children: Identifying dimensions of victimization. *Professional Psychology: Research and Practice, 21,* 338–343.

Zitter, S. (1996). Report from the front lines: Balancing multiple roles of a deafness therapist. In N. Glickman & M. Harvey (Eds.), *Culturally affirmative psychotherapy with Deaf persons* (pp. 185–246). Mahwah, NJ: Lawrence Erlbaum Associates.

13

Psychotherapy for People with Usher Syndrome

ILENE D. MINER

People who have Usher syndrome comprise more than half of all deaf-blind adults (Smith et al., 1994; Vernon, 1969; Vernon & Hicks, 1983), and they make up two aspects of the deaf-blind spectrum: people involved in the Deaf community and people involved in the hearing community.[1] The subject of deaf-blindness is broad and the repercussions so different, however, that it is impossible to cover the entire subject in one chapter. This chapter is therefore limited to issues presented by people with Usher syndrome.

All people with Usher syndrome are deaf or are mildly to moderately hard of hearing, and have deteriorating vision loss as a result of retinitis pigmentosa. Retinitis pigmentosa (RP) is a degenerative eye disease marked by night blindness in the early stages, retina pigment changes, loss of peripheral vision, and eventual blindness. Parents often recount that their children seemed to be bumping into things or tripping frequently before the RP diagnosis was made. Vision loss for any person changes every sphere of life and compromises membership in the person's community of primary identification. In a person who is deaf or hard of hearing, however, it can be a catastrophe.

There are three types of Usher syndrome:

1. People with Type I are born profoundly deaf, have no internal sense of balance, and begin to show symptoms of retinitis pigmentosa (RP) in early childhood, although it is not usually recognized until later (Kimberling & Möller, 1995; Smith et al., 1994). As children, they have delayed motor milestones (Davenport, 1995, personal communication) and experience night blindness in infancy or early childhood. They can be legally blind by adolescence (Miner & Cioffi, 1997). About 3–6% of children born deaf will have Type I (Kimberling & Möller, 1995).

2. People with Type II are born hard of hearing and have moderate stable hearing loss. They have normal balance. They develop blind spots by late childhood or teens, and can be legally blind by late adolescence to early adulthood (Miner & Cioffi, 1997). Their RP is usually diagnosed in adolescence, and sometimes not

I would like to thank the many deaf-blind people who have been so willing to share parts of their lives. I also wish to thank McCay Vernon, Ph.D., for his support and guidance during all the time I have been working with and writing about people with Usher syndrome. He has been a source of help, clarification, and understanding, and has been one person consistently concerned with mental health access and service to deaf-blind people.

1.There are four basic categories of deaf-blindness: congenital deaf-blindness, acquired deafness and blindness, congenital or early deafness with acquired blindness, and congenital blindness with acquired deafness (Adler, 1987; Ingraham et al., 1994).

until early adulthood (Kimberling & Möller, 1995; Smith et al., 1994). About 3–6% of children who are hard of hearing are born with Type II (Davenport, 1995, personal communication; Guest, 1994, personal communication).

3. Type III involves progressive hearing loss and RP. The status of the balance system is still being determined. A person with Type III will experience night blindness in childhood or as a teenager, and can be legally blind by early- to mid-adulthood. (Miner & Cioffi, 1997; Pakarinen et al., 1995).

Working effectively with people with Usher syndrome requires knowing about this condition and its "natural history" over the course of the lifespan. (The rate of progressive vision loss due to RP in any one person is not predictable. I have seen people as young as sixteen who must use tactile sign language to communicate, and people in their seventies still using visual sign language.) It is also important to have contact with people with Usher syndrome to understand how they gain some mastery over their progressive vision loss. It involves being aware of the pitfalls of countertransference and being open to a different experience. One must also feel comfortable working in what is essentially a small town because of the very small size of the total population.

Different Life Experiences and Primary Group Identification

Because each type of Usher syndrome is autosomal recessive, both parents are carriers of the condition but do not have it themselves (Kimberling & Möller, 1995; Smith et al., 1994). While they are young, people with Usher have little contact with others like themselves. Because of a total lack of exposure to adults with Usher, young adults don't really understand what they will be facing (Miner, 1995). Despite the fact that they have both hearing loss and vision loss, the lives of people with Type I and Type II are quite different from one another,

For people with Type I, deafness is the core of their identity. They are almost always culturally Deaf, use American Sign Language (ASL), and feel positive about being Deaf. They do not view deafness as a disability because within the community of culturally Deaf people, a Deaf person is not disabled (Baker & Cokely, 1980; Lane, 1992; Lane et al., 1996; Padden & Humphries, 1988). Many people with Type I have gone to schools for the deaf and are strongly identified as members of the culturally Deaf community.

Deaf people with Type I grow up like other deaf people, most of whom use ASL to communicate. Because many of their families never learn ASL, they may also use speechreading and note-writing as methods of communication. As teens, they may start to miss signed communication coming at them from the side. Then, as their vision deteriorates, they may need to have people sign to them in a smaller space. As their vision continues to deteriorate, they slowly change to "tracking": resting their hands lightly on the wrists of a signer to follow communication by keeping the signer's hands in the "window" of the tunnel of vision left to them. As their field of vision narrows further, they change to tactile communication, hand-over-hand signing. When their vision becomes compromised, easy and comfortable communication with the family will first become strained and then nearly impossible. People with Type I may also feel estranged from the Deaf community and from old friends (Chiocciola et al., 1994).

People with Type II almost always grow up as members of the majority hearing community, and they view hearing loss as a problem for which they must compensate.

Overcoming the disability is a source of pride and allows them to participate in the hearing world. Most people with Type II have no contact with culturally Deaf people, although some do go to schools for the deaf and use ASL. (To my knowledge there has been no study of why some people with Type II attend schools for the deaf and some don't.) Because most people with Type II do not use ASL, there is no reason for their families to learn it either.

Some people with Type II have said that they have never felt so hearing impaired as the day they found out about their RP. An early impact of RP is that speechreading becomes more difficult under certain circumstances, such as dim light or bright sunlight. As their vision fails, a small number of people with Type II learn ASL to help communication flow more smoothly. Some parents are not able to accept these changes and do not learn ASL themselves. As a result, communication with the family becomes difficult and strained. Because people with Type II are well integrated into the majority culture, both vision and hearing loss feel like assaults on the self from the outside (Miner, 1997). They grow up without role models or having met anyone like themselves, and therefore have no idea of the kind of life they can have or what to expect (Miner, 1995, 1996, 1997).

Beginning in childhood and adolescence, RP interferes with life in gradually increasing ways. It limits communication, socialization, activities, and group membership. Friends start to withdraw. Some adolescents self-isolate, knowing early that they are different. Their fears about the future are often overlooked because of family and professional unwillingness to discuss the issue. Depression and suicidal ideation are seen in teens and adults (Miner, 1995, 1996, 1997).

As people with RP get older, they grow concerned about losing their place in their identified cultural community and losing friends and significant people in their lives. Some friendships and marriages do not survive. There are obvious financial threats, job losses, and significant changes in roles and social lives (Miner, 1997). There seems to be a correlation between the degree of visual loss and the upheaval in relationships, but there has been no study that actually has looked at this.

People in both groups grow up without a disability identity; they learn to compensate for Usher's initial effects. The transition to using the visible markers of vision impairment—such as a cane, a sighted guide, and tactile sign—is therefore particularly painful. People with Type I or Type II begin to feel marginalized. The person with Type I wants to hold on to a place in the community of culturally Deaf people, while the person with Type II wants to hold on to a place in the majority hearing community. This difference is crucial to understanding the experience of the person with Type I or Type II. Isolation, loneliness, decreased mobility and independence, difficulty getting information, and periodic "re-grieving" are part of the lives of deaf-blind people (Miner, 1995, 1996, 1997; Tedder, 1987).

At this point, the needs of people with Type I and Type II converge but, ironically, they often lack a common language and don't realize that they have common goals. Except for those people with Type II who have grown up in schools for the deaf and are familiar with ASL, these two groups of people generally do not know each other. And although the impact of vision loss on people with Type I or Type II is similarly devastating, the two groups don't see their needs and desires as being congruent.

Illness, Acquired Disability, and the Independent Adult

The literature on illness and acquired disability (Budman & Gurman, 1988; Druss, 1995; Gunther, 1994; Langer, 1994; Padrone, 1994; Rolland, 1990, 1994) helps to clarify the issues presented by Usher patients and their families who come for consultation. After catastrophic illness and disability, no person or family feels totally safe; the unthinkable and impossible have happened and can happen again (Gunther, 1994). "Catastrophic illness has severe and permanent consequence to the degree that restoration to pre-illness functioning is impossible. This results in limitation of life activities, cognitive disorganization and fragmentation of the cohesive self and feelings of rage, anxiety, panic and despair" (Gunther, 1994, p. 208).

People living with a disability experience concerns about independence, money, staying healthy, guilt about demands placed on others, and fear of abandonment (Pollin, 1995; Rolland, 1990, 1994). Involvement with systems such as hospitals and rehabilitation agencies means a loss of privacy, limited choices, and a loss of dignity. People with serious illness feel unloved and unlovable (Druss, 1995). Asking for help often feels like the final proof of one's mental and physical deterioration.

Druss (1995) discusses the importance of touch to people who are chronically and seriously ill. He describes a leading plastic surgeon who always embraces his patients, regardless of their visible deformity, when they return to appointments because this "did more to make them feel worthwhile and was worth more than words alone" (p. 5). Druss reminds us that tactile and visual techniques address the sense of physical deficit, and that human beings cannot survive without human contact (p. 6). These techniques take on special meaning when applied to people who are deaf-blind, whose only stimulation and contact comes through touch.

Acquired disability and illness impact differently at different life stages (Budman & Gurman, 1988; Pollin, 1995; Rolland, 1990, 1994). With RP, people may have long quiescent periods in between phases of deteriorating vision. Each progressive stage of vision loss brings more limitations, as well as new challenges and accommodations that must be made. People may experience a significant change in their activity level, and may lose not only their careers but also their friends. It is these past, present, and future losses that bring people to psychotherapy (Budman & Gurman, 1988, p. 63). Taking a good history and an assessment of how each patient has handled stress, catastrophe, illness, and challenge in the past is crucial (Druss, 1995; Rolland, 1990, 1994).

The family is affected in many ways over long periods of time, and these impacts must also be addressed (Budman & Gurman,1988; Druss, 1995; Padrone, 1994; Pollin, 1995; Rolland, 1990, 1994). For adults who are married or in a relationship, progressive disability means spouses and partners have to assume new duties. Shifting family roles may result in resentment, exhaustion, and/or significant financial hardship (Rolland, 1994).

Even normal events can bring up feelings of loss, grief, stress, anxiety, and depression (Rolland, 1990, 1994). These normative life transitions may include the birth of a grandchild, a child going to college, or the death of a parent. The event reminds the person with Usher syndrome that, in their family, most events do not proceed at the same pace as those in "normal" families.

When working with clients who have Usher syndrome, it is important to understand the role of denial. Druss (1995) discusses what he has termed pathological denial and healthy denial. "Once regarded as a sign of serious psychopathology, denial has been rehabilitated to the status of a 'healthy' defense for patients with serious illness" (p. 74). The therapist must be prepared to give the client permission to express loss and anger at the illness, while maintaining optimism and hope.

Therapeutic Work with People Who Have Usher

There is no one method that works best with people with Usher, although knowledge, familiarity, and comfort with the issues are most important. Short-term therapy can be useful as long as the therapist understands that patients may want to return for further treatment as they undergo the transitions that occur with a degenerative disease. It is important to discuss this reality and to let patients know they are welcome to come back. The therapist must draw upon multiple modalities and methods, culling from each what is most appropriate. Active participation in the process is necessary, as is a willingness to ferret out information and contacts on the client's behalf.

Change and loss are recurrent themes in the lives of people with Usher syndrome (Miner, 1995, 1996, 1997). Some people do well with brief time-limited intervention. Others need more support and a longer course of treatment depending on such variables as their available supports, ego strength, degree of disorganization and depression, ability to cope with the reality of what is happening, and emotional readiness for psychotherapy.

Some of the more useful aspects of short-term therapy models are that they allow and demand an active and involved therapist who is aware of the patient's life outside of the confines of the therapist's office (Budman & Gurman, 1988; Pollin, 1995; Rolland, 1994). The therapist is encouraged to be fully aware and knowledgeable about the course of the particular disability (Budman & Gurman, 1988; Druss, 1995; Gunther, 1994). This is crucial to the person with Usher syndrome and can make the difference in whether or not a patient and therapist connect. Some authors also discuss the importance of working not only with the identified patient, but also with family members who often present with parallel issues, such as dislocation, depression, and fears about the future (Druss, 1995; Padrone, 1994; Pollin, 1995; Rolland, 1990, 1994). Some patients and therapists might prefer long-term treatment, but in this age of cost-cutting managed care, this is often no longer an option.

The therapist working with any person with Usher syndrome must be comfortable with touch. If the patient's vision loss has progressed to total or near-total blindness, then touch will be necessary for even the most basic communication (MacDonald, 1994). A therapist who is not comfortable with tactile sign language will not be able to work with a person with advanced Usher syndrome. A person with Type I is often deprived of sensory input, information, communication, and comfort. Perhaps because of this, people with Usher syndrome and their friends and colleagues hug on meeting and hug on separating. This practice is widespread because many people with Usher syndrome live isolated lives and that hug might have to last a long time.

A young woman with Usher syndrome told me, "It's important to live today and prepare for tomorrow. I guess I am really hoping for the best and preparing for the worst." I have yet to hear a better description of the work that needs to be done. Balancing hope and optimism and the range of real possibilities is delicate because no one can predict what will happen to the vision of any particular person with Usher.

People with Usher syndrome seeking psychotherapy are often experiencing noticeable vision loss and significant impact on their daily lives for the first time. Although they may have been living with the impact of RP for years, many are still remarkably unaware of what needs to be done, how to do it, and where to find help. The only information they may have about Usher syndrome is its name, that it is genetic, and that it results in tunnel vision and night blindness. It is likely that they have never met another person with Usher syndrome and are terrified because they cannot conceptualize the future, cannot imagine being deaf-blind, and have no idea what will happen to them or how they will continue to live (Miner, 1995, 1996, 1997). This is often the case because adolescents almost never receive any services prior to graduating secondary school. There is wide variability in terms of when services are first received: a person with Type I may be diagnosed in infancy and not receive services until age twenty-one; a person with Type II might be diagnosed as an adolescent and not receive any rehabilitation services until their late thirties.

For people with Usher syndrome, the active work involves an acknowledgment that RP is causing a significant visual problem and that help is necessary in effectively dealing with what is happening. Clients must confront the real tasks that need to be accomplished in order to regain a sense of mastery and start to actually master those tasks. They will need to understand that there will be intermittent mourning throughout life.

* * *

> Annie is a young woman in her late twenties with a college degree who works full time.[2] She was referred by a mental health program after becoming extremely upset when she was separated from a friend while leaving a movie theater. For a few terrible minutes, she was blind, lost, and without help. Despite having known about having Type I since she was a child, she knew nothing about the condition and had learned only three months earlier that it is genetic. This patient is actively working with a vocational rehabilitation agency and a service agency for people who are deaf and hard of hearing. Although her vocational rehabilitation counselor knows the client has Usher syndrome, it is not noted on her record and has never been discussed, despite its impact in the workplace. Of course, the client could have sought out information, but the client's friends, family, mental health counselor, and vocational rehabilitation counselor had all contributed to making this a topic that no one dared discuss.

Once clients are encouraged to discuss the topic, the comments can be quite overwhelming for even an experienced therapist. Some examples from patients just starting treatment are: "I feel like I am hanging over a deep hole and I want to let go;" "I will commit suicide when my vision goes because I can't continue to live if I can't see;" "There is no reason for me to continue to live;" "I hate this Usher syndrome and want to rip out my eyes;" and "I must be a very evil person inside to deserve such a fate."

Trust is most easily built with a therapist who knows about Usher syndrome, knows people who have it, and can deal with these kinds of feelings.

2. Names and identifying information have been changed to protect clients' anonymity.

* * *

Jill, age twenty-six, has Type II. When she called for an appointment, she told me that she had heard that I knew many people with Usher syndrome, and asked if it were true. When she came in for her first appointment, she said she had left two other therapists after several visits because she knew they didn't really understand what was happening to her. "Couldn't they see that I am deaf and slowly going blind?" she asked me. She and others have explained that the fact they are going blind is the primary thing that brings them to a therapist in the first place.

Many clients have gone through an extended period of bumping into people; falling in the street; missing communication; and feeling vulnerable and under attack because of accidental collisions with people, objects, and sometimes with motor vehicles. Hopes and plans for the future are dashed.

The issues for psychotherapy include fear of the unknown and grief over the loss of the person that was. The work involves discovering how to develop a new identity that respects the person that was, accepts the person that is, and begins to incorporate what will be. Then, therapy can shift to gaining and mastering the necessary skills and information to be able to accomplish these tasks. For a person who is in despair about the first signs of eventual blindness, seemingly small tasks—picking up the phone and calling for information, setting up a meeting, or finding another person with Usher syndrome—can be the beginning of building a sense of mastery. Boundaries must be relaxed, because touch is often necessary for every conversation, depending on the lighting and the degree of visual loss.

Some patients reorganize, take steps quickly, and do well with brief intervention. These patients may come back for further treatment when there are new challenges or frustrations to meet and overcome. Both grief and anxiety increase at times of further visual deterioration and at times of normal developmental transitions that must be delayed, postponed, or modified because of the impact of Usher syndrome. Some examples include not being able to drive, postponing college to get braille and mobility training, being unable to help one's own child with homework, or not being able to baby-sit for a new grandchild. Any one of these circumstances may bring someone to therapy.

Issues for the Beginning Phase

In the beginning of treatment it is important for the therapist to be aware of and explore some of the common experiences of many people with Usher syndrome. For example, young adults worry that after their vision has deteriorated, communication with parents and siblings will be impossible. Many adults still have very strong feelings attached to these events even though they may have happened years before, often in childhood. Five topics to examine immediately are highlighted in figure 1.

It is still fairly common for parents to learn of their child's Usher diagnosis and withhold the information for years. The patient then has the double shock of getting the diagnosis and learning that his or her parents have, in some cases, known for more than a decade. In some cases the patient's teachers had also known, although the student remained ignorant of the problem. These situations cause a significant disruption of the trust relationship between patient and parents (Collins et al., 1994; Miner, 1995).

TOPICS TO EXPLORE DURING INITIAL TREATMENT

1. The age at which the patient found out about the diagnosis;
2. Whether the parents found out first and withheld the information for some period of time;
3. Whether the patient has received misinformation from a care provider or responsible adult;
4. Whether the patient has been around any other people with Usher syndrome since the diagnosis; and
5. Whether the patient can adequately communicate with his or her family (especially if the patient is a young adult still living at home or the family is regularly involved with the patient).

Figure 1. Initial Treatment

* * *

Kelly is a forty-two-year-old woman whose parents found out about her Usher syndrome when she was eight. She was not told until she was twenty-one, and then by a doctor who thought she already knew. She was furious with her family for keeping this secret, and it was years before she was able to understand that her parents wanted her to have a "normal" life for as long as possible. Shortly after her mother died, Kelly met an old friend from her residential school who revealed that she had been told about Kelly's Usher syndrome during their school years by Kelly's mother, had been asked to keep an eye on Kelly, and had been sworn to secrecy. This came as a shock and brought back a lot of the anger Kelly had felt as a younger woman. This is a typical experience in the lives of people with Usher syndrome and needs to be addressed in therapy. Asking new patients about when they were diagnosed and who told them the diagnosis is often crucial to understanding affect attached to the topic.

Another common experience is having doctors miss RP for years, telling the family that there is nothing wrong. Many medical providers are unaware of the relationship between the patient's hearing and vision loss (Boughman et al., 1983). Later, when the diagnosis is made, the patient or family is told that the person will be blind within a very short time or given some other incorrect prediction.

* * *

Mary Jane came to the Helen Keller National Center at the age of sixteen for a two-week educational program. She was diagnosed with Type I at age twelve, and her parents were told that she would be blind within a year. She described her mother crying for days on end. Because she still had vision at the time of her next annual check-up, her physician modified his prediction, saying that she would become totally blind by age sixteen. One of her classroom teachers took it upon herself to tell Mary Jane that she would be totally blind by the age of twenty. According to Mary Jane's mother, this upset her greatly. The fear and anger generated by these incorrect comments to patients and families are palpable and form the basis for much of the early work in therapy. Because neither Mary Jane nor her parents had ever met another person with Usher syndrome, they had no way to evaluate the validity of such predictions.

The impact of never meeting another person like themselves is significant for people with Usher syndrome (Miner, 1995, 1996, 1997). Culturally Deaf people cherish vision for many reasons, one of which is that it is required for understanding ASL. Just as medically ill people are often avoided in hospitals or by friends (Druss, 1995), people with vision loss are often avoided by those who are culturally Deaf (Chiocciola et al., 1994). People with Usher syndrome who are just beginning this process of loss are unable to imagine what kind of life they could possibly lead. They see themselves in the future as old, abandoned, and alone.

* * *

Miriam arrived at the Helen Keller National Center having never spoken to anyone with Usher syndrome. When she was introduced to her braille teacher, who also has Usher syndrome and uses tactile communication, Miriam recoiled and said she couldn't communicate. Although she had seen deaf-blind people at Deaf community events, she had never actually spoken to them. Her parents said several times that they could not understand why she was not suicidal. It would be impossible for this young woman not to have sensed her parents' thoughts and fears.

Contact with adults and children with Usher syndrome and their families throughout childhood and adolescence is recommended (Adams, 1993; Guest & Roper, 1988; Miner, 1995, 1996, 1997; Smith, 1993) along with early supportive counseling for those families who want it (Hicks & Hicks, 1981; Singh & Guest, 1991). Unfortunately, neither of these things usually occur. A young adult may be disturbed by his or her first contact with somebody who is visually impaired, but the discomfort passes quickly as all kinds of questions are asked and answered, perhaps for the first time.

Therapeutic Work

Hope plays an important part in the thinking of people with RP. Patients who still have vision hope for a cure for RP before they lose their remaining vision. They also hope they will lose no more vision. They are aware of how having little or no vision will impact their mobility and therefore their independence. The therapist must encourage the patient to remain optimistic and must balance this encouragement with a realistic discussion of possible outcomes.

Some patients have asked me directly, "Will you make me give up my hope for a cure?" Clearly some overzealous therapist or counselor had been talking to them about the need for "acceptance." As therapists, we should not attempt to destroy this hope, nor should we attack this defense as long as these patients continue learning the skills they need. If a client believes that his or her vision will not worsen, and yet is learning more about needed skills like mobility and braille and meeting other people with Usher syndrome, that denial should be left alone. This is functional denial, or what Druss (1995) refers to as "healthy denial."

The focus of the work differs depending on the client's life stage and degree of depression or disorganization. Although visual loss is progressive and inexorable, there may be long periods when deterioration is slow and therefore not much change in lifestyle is necessary. During these quiet times, many patients may hold to the belief that deterioration of vision has stopped; denial and minimization work well during these periods of little change. When deterioration recurs, they are thrown once again into depression and anxiety. Continued loss brings up past losses that need to be reexamined and reworked.

A recurrent complaint of young people with Usher syndrome is that no one has been willing to broach the subject of their pain.

* * *

> Joyce, who has Type I, visited the Helen Keller National Center while she was still in high school. During the past two years, she had been psychiatrically hospitalized three times for depression with suicidal ideation and attempts. At the age of eighteen she had very little vision left. After she sat in on the Usher syndrome weekly group meeting, she said, "This is so different from school. In our group there, they only let us discuss information about Usher. As soon as we start talking about feelings, the leader starts handing out those brochures again."

Many professionals who work with teens are loathe to discuss vision loss for fear of upsetting them, but teenagers with Usher have already thought a lot about their futures (Miner, 1997). When teenagers and young adults learn that no one will discuss Usher, they bear their pain alone, often because they feel they must protect their families (Miner, 1996). One patient felt she had caused her mother to have a nervous breakdown, and another told her parents that she had caused their divorce. Both of these patients felt that they could not discuss their fears about Usher syndrome with their parents for fear of hurting them more. In these situations work with the family is also recommended.

Professionals and families who think that teenagers and young adults are not thinking about the implications of having Usher syndrome are wrong. Thoughts of the future are always on the surface, ready for work. At my first meeting with the mother of a fifteen-year-old with Type I, the mother told me that the word *blind* was not permitted in the home. I then watched this fifteen-year-old discuss with two other teenagers who also have Usher syndrome when they thought they would become blind. The conversation was taking place in ASL, which the mother did not understand.

Many teenagers are concerned about their future spouses, especially about whether they should be told about Usher syndrome. They fear that prospective mates could also be carriers, thereby introducing the possibility of having a baby with Usher syndrome.

* * *

> Jen, who is nineteen and has Type I, said, "I am in so much pain now. I wouldn't want to do that to my own child. I see my mother's pain at watching my pain because I am almost blind. For me, having a child with Usher would mean triple pain: my own pain, the pain of having given this to my child, and watching that child go through the pain I am going through now. I couldn't do that to a child." She also mourns the things she will literally never see, such as the rest of the world or the faces of her own children and grandchildren.

* * *

> Edward, a seventeen-year-old visiting the Helen Keller National Center, spoke about his fears of never finding a spouse, or if he is lucky enough to find a woman who will marry him, he said he will soon not be able to see her anymore. "I will have to hold her face in my hands and really look and look at her and hold that in my memory because that memory will have to last me forever." He expressed sadness that he might never see nieces and nephews born to his siblings and may never see the faces of his own children if he is fortunate enough to have them. He had never revealed these feelings to anyone.

Young adults are sometimes angry at parents for giving them Usher, even though rationally they know that their parents could not have known they were each carriers of the gene for Usher syndrome. A number of young adults do not understand the genetic transmission of this condition—they need explanations and are helped by discussions with other people with Usher syndrome and with geneticists.

The issues faced by adults are just as complicated. Some adults fear that their children will develop Usher, even when these children have normal hearing. This fear often extends to their grandchildren, because the person with Usher syndrome understands that their children are carriers. Adults with deteriorating vision have guilt and anger about their increased dependence on their spouses, parents, and children. They worry that their needs may drive their families away from them.

* * *

> Bob spoke eloquently about the isolation and loneliness imposed by his vision loss. He said when his wife came home from work every day, he demanded to know everything that was going on in the world. He wouldn't let her eat or cook or relax until she had told him everything. He said that his children were avoiding discussions with him, and he missed the closeness that he had felt with them.

Job retraining or adaptation is often necessary. Some people can not be retrained for the job they have been doing and have to leave their position and even their career. This threatens the family's financial security (Miner, 1995; Vernon et al., 1982). Necessary changes in family functioning and disruption of roles in the unit have a profound effect on self-esteem and self-concept. Securing a new position after becoming blind is difficult, and some people never work again. Even with job retraining, the process of starting all over again in a new field in mid-life is a daunting task. Maintaining one's equanimity and self-esteem under such circumstances is extremely difficult.

Some people with Usher syndrome are significantly depressed and embarrassed at having to ask for help. Suicidal ideation and attempts are common (Miner, 1995, 1996, 1997). Clinical experience with Usher patients has shown that if the therapist does not ask questions about suicidal ideation and past attempts, the patient will rarely volunteer the information. Therefore, it is extremely important to ask about this topic openly and directly.

* * *

> The first Usher syndrome support group at the Helen Keller National Center had seven members, four of whom were totally blind. In this group of seven, four

people had made suicide attempts; three of these four had been hospitalized. Two other members considered suicide every day.

Betty, who has Type I, made a serious suicide attempt resulting in hospitalization while in her early forties after losing her remaining vision. She felt unneeded and unloved; her husband had taken over all her household duties, and her daughters were almost finished with high school. She felt there was no reason for her to continue to exist.

Daniel, now age twenty-six, made a serious attempt at age sixteen shortly after he was diagnosed with Usher. He was overwhelmed with a feeling that he had lost everything and would not be able to realize his goal of college. He was hospitalized for several weeks and, unfortunately, discharged without follow-up.

Grief, loss, and fears about the future are inherent in an Usher diagnosis. These feelings are cyclical, recurrent, and to be expected, even at times that would be considered joyful. Georgina was very depressed after becoming a grandmother for the first time because she knew she couldn't "do the things that normal grandmothers do." Talking about grief, loss, and feeling damaged are an integral part of the work in therapy.

Older adults with Usher syndrome worry about abandonment and being left alone to die (Miner, 1995). These are feelings normally experienced by all older adults, but to an older deaf-blind person, the debilitation or death of a sighted spouse or a child's moving some distance away may also signal the loss of home or loss of the ability to live independently. Even if there are adult children, the older adult with Usher may not wish to impose upon them or may feel guilty about impositions already made (Miner, 1995). Some families may not be able to discuss these issues among themselves. An awareness of the common concerns and issues of older adults with Usher is important for any therapist working with this age group.

* * *

Maria, age fifty-five, has Type I. Her husband Julio is seventy and deaf. She was concerned that her husband would die before she did, and she wanted to discuss plans for the future with him and her adult daughters. She was afraid that Julio would be upset if she raised these issues. In separate interviews with Julio and with one of the adult daughters, it was discovered that both Julio and the daughter had the same concerns as Maria but each had been afraid to raise the issue with the others.

Having Usher syndrome does not in itself confer a psychiatric diagnosis on the patient. The job of the therapist is to balance and build on the unique strengths of the person with Usher syndrome in a way that encourages growth and reintegration. Neither Usher nor any concurrent psychiatric issue should be the only focus.

WORK WITH OTHER FAMILY MEMBERS

It is important to address the needs of parents, spouses, significant others, and children if they are old enough (Ingraham et al., 1994; Rolland 1990). There are tasks that each needs to do and information that each must secure. Connecting parents to other parents and to adults with Usher syndrome is crucial, because parents often feel totally alone. The following vignette illustrates a widespread problem with services for parents of children, youth, and young adults with Usher.

* * *

> Mrs. W. is a woman in her mid-forties who approached me at a meeting for more than seventy-five parents with deaf-blind children, some of whom had Usher syndrome. Yet despite the purpose of the meeting, there was no adult with Usher or other deaf-blind condition present. The message from the organizers seemed to be, "You have nothing to learn from people like your children."
>
> Mrs. W., who had been attending meetings like this for years, told me that she had ordered a videotape on which I appeared with a colleague who has Usher and is totally blind. I asked Mrs. W. why she had ordered this particular video, never expecting the answer she gave me: "I ordered it because I have never met or seen another adult with Usher except my son, and I have no idea what to expect as my son ages."

Parents of children with Usher syndrome are concerned about the future, and may fear that their child will never be able to live independently. They may be overprotective and reluctant to let the young adult grow up and leave home, wondering how they will survive (Ingraham et al., 1994). If their child is an adult, the parents may be devoting time to being available to their child and perhaps to grandchildren as well. As their adult child's vision is finally failing, parents may be unable to help as much as they would like because they are aging themselves. Some of these parents have been caregivers for forty years, have never received appropriate services, and find themselves old, exhausted, and perhaps very angry or full of guilt.

Spouses, who thought they understood what would happen, invariably find that they really didn't understand the demands that would be made on them. When discussing these issues, sighted spouses relate that when they were first young and dating, they too, like their spouse with Usher, held on to the hope that vision would not deteriorate.

* * *

> B. T. was married, had two young children, and Usher I. He worked in a major corporation for ten years before being laid off in a round of downsizing. He knew he should give up driving, but he couldn't bring himself to do it. He thought his wife resented the fact that he depended on her so much for transportation and running errands. "I am sure that one of the reasons she married me was that I am assertive and have always taken care of the family's interaction with the outside world," he said. "Now I am pushing her to do these things and she doesn't want to."

Some couples feel anger, depression, and confusion (Miner, 1995, 1997), while other couples and families are more aggressive in seeking out information and help. Once presented with the tools, such as mobility instruction and rehabilitation teaching, they proceed to integrate these skills into their lives.

Because the rehabilitation system is set up to wait until help is requested, people with Usher syndrome and their families who are asking for concrete help in living independently end up making this request after there has already been significant dislocation. All of the information that families and people with Usher syndrome need should be given to them early on, not just once but repeatedly. This body of knowledge can be drawn upon as needed, rather than waiting until things have fallen apart. Rehabilitation teaching should be looked upon as a source of techniques and skills to keep people independent rather than as a necessity to compensate for what people have lost.

Issues for Counselors Working for the First Time with Patients with Both Vision and Hearing Loss

Getting appropriate mental health counseling or psychotherapy is not as easy at it should be because few professionals are knowledgeable about vision and hearing loss (Miner, 1995, 1996, 1997; Stiefel, 1991; Tedder, 1987; Vernon & Green, 1980; Vernon & Hicks, 1983). Because professionals come to deaf-blindness work from working with either deafness or blindness, integrating information about the other condition is complex. Many rehabilitation counselors and mental health professionals who work with culturally Deaf people are not aware of the issues and needs of people with concurrent vision loss. At the same time, those who work with blind people are not aware of the issues or the needs of people with concurrent hearing loss. The result is that meetings with therapists are often less helpful than they could be and replete with misinformation.

Furthermore, even therapists who are aware of both deafness and blindness issues do not understand that deaf-blindness is an entirely different entity (Stiefel, 1991). Most counselors aren't aware that when working with a person with Usher who is still visual there is a need to be at a distance greater than usual and to sign in a manner smaller than usual. When working with a person with Usher syndrome, one is never just dealing with a deaf or Deaf person or blind or visually impaired person. For example:

• One blindness counselor suggested to a mobility instructor that he could save money by holding group classes for people with Usher syndrome, forgetting that each totally blind client would need an interpreter.

• A deafness counselor fluent in ASL could not understand why a student would need a one-to-one interpreter, despite the student's description of always missing what was happening in the classroom because she could not find a speaker behind her in her "window" of vision before the next student started signing.

• A counselor for the blind connected a young man with Usher to a support group for people with RP but never asked about the availability of an interpreter.

TREATMENT GAFFES

Some inexperienced therapists want the patient to "get on with it" and "accept" what is happening.

* * *

A twenty-one-year old man in a residential rehabilitation center was discussing his unwillingness to use his cane. The young man clearly understood that he had Usher syndrome and was taking action to master the necessary skills. He wished to maintain some decision-making power as to when he needed to use his cane. In response, his rehabilitation counselor loudly demanded: "You have to stop denying, and accept that you have Usher and are going blind."

The counselor didn't want to discuss the client's impending blindness in any depth; she wanted him to accept it so they would not have to discuss it any further. The counselor simply wanted her client to follow the dictates of the teacher and to end the discussion. Her thinking was that "if the client accepts, then these issues will not have to be dealt with again." This supposition is incorrect; these issues and topics are always being reworked. The therapist was attempting to meet her own needs, perhaps because of her own discomfort in discussing impending blindness.

COUNTERTRANSFERENCE: "I DON'T LIKE THOSE DEAF-BLIND PEOPLE"

Countertransference is an issue that is interwoven in everything we do and, of course, is not limited to deaf-blind people and their therapists. However, the issue of countertransference is rarely discussed in the professional community working with deaf-blind people. I have been unable to turn up anything in the literature about countertransference related to professionals in this field. Drawing upon what has been written about work with people with other disabilities is useful.

All of us have a need to distance ourselves from the horrible effects of overwhelming disability (Rolland, 1990). But, "since none of us is immune to tragedy, and almost all of us will be faced with grief, crises, and losses over the course of our lives, the barrier between the therapist and patient in the treatment of such situations is a very fine line indeed" (Budman & Gurman, 1988, p. 95). The result is that professionals sometimes minimize the pain that patients feel, distance themselves from it, or ignore it because of their own inability to deal with the effects of overwhelming catastrophe (Druss, 1995). This kind of response to the patient can hurt instead of help (Gunther, 1994).

It is very important to look at "what and whose needs are being served and what would happen if denial were to be punctured" (Langer, 1994, p. 189). Discussing how to approach a patient's denial, Langer cautions against pushing too hard and fast. He says a therapist should do an "analysis of whose needs would be met by having the patient faced with external reality, the family? The patient? The therapist?" This analysis applies in situations where the patient has Usher syndrome because the material is depressing, and it may be less painful for the therapist to consciously or unconsciously avoid the subject. It's also easier for the therapist to believe that this acceptance process has already been completed.

This "acceptance," however, is not an isolated event. It is, rather, an ongoing process of adaptation throughout life; dealing with Usher syndrome is a daily activity, and change is incremental in vision and in feelings. The therapist must look for signs of mourning and depression and allow these feelings to surface while at the same time not forcing the patient beyond what is possible at a given moment. "Healthy denial" must always be supported (Druss, 1995).

I have seen psychotic or significantly depressed adults who were known to mental health or rehabilitation agencies, who had therapists and counselors who could sign, but who were nevertheless undertreated or underdiagnosed.

* * *

> Deb is an older teenager who arrived at a rehabilitation center to learn skills to help her stay in school. She had a full delusional system, including a "family" who lived on a star who visited periodically. Her "family" members all had names and personalities. She refused to respond to her name or talk to her mother or siblings, and was extremely depressed because her "family" had not visited recently. Additionally, she had mealtime rituals that included not allowing any of the different foods on a plate touch each other and eating foods in a particular order. If these rituals were disrupted, she would demand a new plate of food. Each meal took two hours or longer. Interestingly, before this young woman arrived at the center, her therapist sent a psychological evaluation that did not mention her second "family" or rituals. When the psychologist was later asked about this, he said he thought her psychosis was a normal part of becoming deaf-blind.

* * *

> Rina, age forty-five, had made two suicide attempts that resulted in hospitalization. She never received treatment and when she arrived at Helen Keller National Center, she was depressed, feeling that she had already lost everything. She has an older sister with Usher who is totally blind and who returned to live with their elderly mother, and she thought this was the only thing that life had to offer her. She was significantly helped with psychotherapy and medication.

These two examples illustrate the point that because of stereotypes of what deaf-blind people feel, think, or do, some mental health clinicians take less than adequate action in dealing with their patient's symptoms. This may be compounded by the therapist's countertransference. Depression or psychosis should not be assumed to be the "normal" mental state of any person with Usher syndrome. These symptoms must be addressed directly and taken seriously.

Clinicians who work with deaf-blind people are often deaf themselves and/or involved in the culturally Deaf community. Deaf people cherish their vision, fear losing it, and have assimilated many of the attitudes in the community about people who are blind or who have lost their vision (Chiocciola et al., 1994). A client with Usher syndrome represents the incarnation of their worst fears. Some are aware enough of their own feelings and fears to be able to discuss these issues in supervision. Others are not.

* * *

> L.V. is a culturally Deaf rehabilitation counselor who attended an in-service Usher syndrome training session held at her agency. When comments from the audience were solicited, she raised her hand and said, "I don't like those deaf-blind people; they should have their own counselors and their own clubs, and I don't like doing that tactile sign language—it makes my arms tired."

Most comments are not so blatant, but a milder version of this kind of attitude has been seen and heard. A deaf mental health professional once said to me, "If I lose my vision, just shoot me please." Hearing professionals may also feel they learned ASL to work with deaf people, not deaf people who are slowly becoming blind. Some hearing and deaf professionals have said that they avoid people with Usher syndrome because they feel totally responsible for the interaction. They also feel they have to do much more for people with Usher than they do for patients who are just Deaf or just hard of hearing.

I have heard professionals ask, "My God, what kind of life can they have?" If professionals can't move beyond this feeling and reach out to find out about the lives of deaf-blind people, then they must ask themselves whether in fact they can be effective therapists for a client with Usher syndrome. Deaf-blind people seeking help can quickly pick up on a therapist's discomfort in using tactile communication or attitudes of pity and patronization.

Hearing people who have no experience working with deaf-blind people may not be able to understand how communication occurs if they have not seen it before. In a situation in which some mental health professionals tend to distance themselves for many reasons, communication with deaf-blind people may be very overwhelming. The very need to touch may be threatening to some therapists.

* * *

> I worked with a particularly difficult psychotic adventitiously deaf-blind man on an inpatient psychiatric unit where this patient was the only one who was deaf. The patient's threats of violence, his many attempts to strike out, and screamed insults made him quite unpopular with staff. I saw the patient daily and then went to a morning meeting to report on progress made. The patient used an expressive voice and his receptive mode was fingerspelled English. Despite the fact that I was obviously communicating with the patient, some staff had not thought about how this was occurring. One day while I was fingerspelling to the patient in the hall outside his room, a psychiatrist walked by, was stunned, and loudly blurted out with obvious disgust, "Oh, no! You have to touch him."

Supervision is imperative, and professionals should be willing to look at their own feelings in working with deaf-blind people. In working with this degree of loss on a regular basis, we all start to feel vulnerable. The pain of the inexorable progressive loss of vision experienced by people with Usher syndrome is awesome, and therapists who cannot tolerate the expression of this pain should consider referring to others who have chosen to work with this population.

The grief work is not unlike the work of people who are living with life-threatening illness, balancing fear and hope and the recurrence of painful thoughts and feelings. In the meeting of a support group for people with Usher syndrome, one twenty-year-old woman, who had lost her sister to leukemia less than a year before, brought up the following issue for discussion. "Which would you rather have, cancer or Usher syndrome?" She and another young woman agreed they would rather have cancer and die in five years than live with a slow death of vision over a lifetime; they felt that their daily loss was just too acute, too painful, to be tolerated indefinitely.

There is wear and tear on a therapist dealing with this much grief every day, and there needs to be an outlet for it. One does not want to become inured to the patients' feelings as a defense and then miss opportunities to intervene. It is easy to stop offering small bits of hope. There needs to be a neutral objective place to think and reflect and get feedback. Some therapists will learn in supervision that working with people who are experiencing continuous losses is just too painful and may choose not to do this kind of work. Supervision allows this kind of exploration of one's feelings in a climate that is safe and nonjudgmental and encourages further learning.

Finding Life Again in the Community of Deaf-Blind People

For many people it takes years of isolation before they try to reach out to other people with Usher syndrome. Teens grow up without role models and ego ideals. Clients almost always remember in great detail the first time they met another person with Usher syndrome. Young adults have discussed this topic and relate that this was the first time they really knew they were not alone.

Recently some state deaf-blind children's programs around the country have developed special weekends or camps in which teens with Usher syndrome interact and learn from adults with Usher syndrome. There they have the opportunity to discuss careers, lifestyles, families, vision loss, and communication modes. This is a way of providing positive role models and examples of available future choices and opportunities. Involvement in these kinds of activities should be encouraged both for teens and adults with Usher syndrome and their families. In 1996, the American Association of the Deaf-Blind (AADB) sponsored its first teen program, bringing together twenty teens, most with Usher syndrome, for a special meeting within the larger AADB convention.

Unique Aspects of Working with the Deaf-Blind Community

When working with a client who is a member of the deaf-blind community, the therapist must actively consult with the client about issues such as lighting, seating, and rate and style of signing, and then make appropriate modifications. In cases where vision is already seriously compromised, a therapist must feel comfortable literally touching people, which may be difficult after so many years of being trained not to. Without touch, there is no communication. Learning about sighted guide, mobility, and other techniques is an important part of communicating interest to deaf-blind people who sense when their therapists don't understand or can't imagine their lives. It also requires an ability to deal with the intense grief and pain of a deaf or hard of hearing person who is slowly and inexorably becoming blind.

The community of deaf-blind people is heterogeneous and not easy to characterize. (For a more comprehensive discussion of this subject, see T. B. Smith, 1994.) The community is comprised of people who have both vision and hearing loss and communicate in different ways and live in different places. There is a large community of deaf-blind people in Seattle, Washington, regarded by many as a model community because of its services, job opportunities, public transportation, and highly skilled deaf and hearing interpreters who have chosen to work in this field. There are state associations of deaf-blind people in many, but not all, states. In some places, people are very isolated and only see each other at AADB conventions every two years or at regional conferences.

One of the most noticeable aspects of interpreting work in the deaf-blind community is the high number of Deaf interpreters. Many people with Type I use ASL visually or tactilely. Although many people with Type II use spoken English, they also use ASL in a more English-like word order. In the deaf-blind community, the pace of communication is slower than in the Deaf community to accommodate individual communication differences and the time lag inherent in multiple layers of relay interpretation. Large meetings have an array of one-to-one interpreters, individual and small group, platform, tactile and visual, and relay interpreters. There is often a liberal use of assistive devices, including FM systems and computers with braille output.

In any group where there are deaf-blind people, support people are a necessary addition. The support service provider, or SSP, is essential to the functioning of any deaf-blind community. It is this person, in some places paid and in others volunteer, who helps to make communication happen in large meetings. Often SSPs help deaf-blind people get the business of daily life done, shopping, paying bills, doing errands. SSPs are often culturally Deaf.

The Internet has had a tremendous impact on members of the deaf-blind community who are knowledgeable and who can afford computers. People with limited access to the outside world can now meet other deaf-blind people from all over the world on the Deaf-Blind List on the Internet (send an e-mail to listserv@tr.wou.edu with the message "subscribe deafblnd first name last name"). People who have some hearing, like those with Type II, use a computer that talks, so that what is on the screen is converted to voice for the user. In situations where the person has Type I, voice output would be useless. These people use a refreshable braille output, so that text that appears on the screen appears on a braille output that has a metal braille display that is continually displaying what is on the screen. This allows access to e-mail and to the Internet.

A therapist working with people with Usher syndrome is much like a therapist who lives and works in a small town. It is a norm of the community that professionals from different disciplines work as volunteer support service providers, guiding and interpreting, for example, at meetings of the American Association of Deaf-Blind. Guiding, interpreting, and just basic communication all necessitate touch. There is also a lot of hugging that happens among people who have known each other for years. Touch is critically important to deaf-blind people who can't connect to people with their eyes any more. One can no longer see a smile or a wink and return it. All of these feelings—the light-hearted, good and loving ones or the sad and angry ones—are communicated by touch. This may feel strange to those who are unaccustomed to doing more than shaking hands or patting a shoulder of a client. It can be uncomfortable at first, and yet it quickly becomes normal and feels right, such that it becomes hard to remember the awkward feelings that were present when starting to work with deaf-blind clients. Boundaries are not necessarily sacrificed at all. We do the same work we do with other patients, despite the fact that we have to rely on different ways of communicating and relating.

People fortunate enough to be involved in the community of deaf-blind people quickly find it to be the most warm and caring of communities. Smith (1994) defines the deaf-blind community as encompassing the hearing and deaf people who live and work with deaf-blind people as part of this community of people who share common experiences and values (p. 166). As Smith says, "The courage of deaf-blind people is physical, intellectual, and emotional. It is an inspiration (it fills me with breath) which gives me courage" (p. 165). It is a rich learning experience, one from which we gain much understanding about the grace and dignity of the human spirit.

References

Adams, J. (1993). Self-determination: Presentation. In J. Reiman & P. Johnson (Eds.), *Proceedings of the National Symposium on Children and Youth Who Are Deaf-Blind* (pp. 223–228). Monmouth, OR: Teaching Research Publications.

Adler, M. (1987). Psychosocial interventions with deaf-blind youth and adults. In B. Heller, L. Flohr, & L. Zegans (Eds.), *Psychosocial interventions with sensorially disabled persons* (pp. 187–207). Orlando, FL: Grune and Stratton.

Baker, C., & Cokely, D. (1980). *ASL: A teacher's resource text on grammar and culture.* Silver Spring, MD: T. J. Publishers.

Boughman, J., Vernon, M., & Shaver, K. (1983). Usher syndrome: Definition and estimate of prevalence from two high risk populations. *Journal of Chronic Diseases, 36* (8), 595–603.

Brennan, M. (1994). The deaf-blind community: A tale of two cultures. *Usher Family Support Newsletter, 2* (1), 5–7.

Budman, S. H., & Gurman, A. S. (1988). *Theory and practice of brief therapy.* New York: Guilford Press.

Chiocciola, T., Harrison, S., Herrada-Benites, R., Kesner, B., Lejeune, J., Levine, F., Lugo, J., Stender, A., & Tunison, W. (1994). An open letter to the deaf community. *Usher Family Support Newsletter, 1* (4), 4.

Collins, M., Delgadillo, D., Frawley, M., Kinney, G., Lugo, J., Lundgren, J., Price, K., & Rybarski, S. (1994). An open letter to our parents: What we wish you had known. *Usher Family Support Newsletter, 2* (3), 4–6.

Corr, C. A. (1991–1992). A task-based approach to coping with dying. *Omega: Journal of Death and Dying, 24* (2), 81–94.

Druss, R. G. (1995). *The psychology of illness, in sickness and in health.* Washington, DC: American Psychiatric Press.

Guest, M., & Roper, F. (1988). *Usher syndrome in the school population.* Usher Syndrome: Awareness and Education Project. London, England: SENSE (The National Deaf-Blind and Rubella Association).

Gunther, M. S. (1994). Countertransference issues in staff caregivers who work to rehabilitate catastrophic-injury survivors. *American Journal of Psychotherapy, 48* (2), 208–220.

Gzesiak, R. C., & Hicok, D. A. (1994). A brief history of psychotherapy and physical disability. *American Journal of Psychotherapy, 48* (2), 240–250.

Hammer, E. (1978). Needs of adolescents who have Usher's syndrome. *American Annals of the Deaf, 123* (3), 389–394.

Hicks, W., & Hicks, D. E. (1981). The Usher's syndrome adolescent: Programming implications for school administrators, teachers, and residential advisors. *American Annals of the Deaf, 126,* 422–431.

Ingraham, C. L., Carey, A., Vernon, M., & Berry, P. (1994). Deaf-blind clients and vocational rehabilitation: Practical guidelines for counselors. *Journal of Vision Impairment and Blindness, 88* (2), 117–127.

Kimberling, W. J., & Moller, C. (1995). Clinical and molecular genetics of Usher syndrome. *Journal of the American Academy of Audiology, 6,* 63–72.

Lane, H. (1992). *The mask of benevolence: Disabling the deaf community.* New York: Alfred A. Knopf.

Lane, H., Hoffmeister, R., & Bahan, B. (1996). *A journey into the Deaf-world.* San Diego: Dawn Sign Press.

Langer, K. G. (1994). Depression and denial in psychotherapy of persons with disabilities. *American Journal of Psychotherapy, 48* (2), 181–194.

MacDonald, R. J. (1994). Deaf-blindness: An emerging culture? In C. J. Erting, R. C. Johnson, D. L. Smith, & B. D. Snider (Eds.), *The Deaf Way: Perspectives from the international conference on deaf culture* (pp. 496–503). Washington, DC: Gallaudet University Press.

Miner, I. D. (1995). Psychosocial implications of Usher syndrome, Type I, throughout the life cycle. *Journal of Vision Impairment and Blindness, 89* (3), 287–296.

———. (1996). The impact of Usher syndrome, Type I, on adolescent development. *Journal of Vocational Rehabilitation, 6,* 159–166.

———. (1997). People with Usher syndrome, Type II: Issues and adaptation. *Journal of Vision Impairment and Blindness, 91,* 579–589.

Padden, C., & Humphries, T. (1988). *Deaf in America: Voices from a culture.* Cambridge, MA: Harvard University Press.

Padrone, F. J. (1994). Psychotherapeutic issues with family members of persons with physical disabilities. *American Journal of Psychotherapy, 48* (2), 195–207.

Pakarinen, L., Karjalainen, S., Simola, K. O., Laippala, P., & Kaitalo, H. (1995, June). Usher's syndrome Type III in Finland. *Laryngoscope, 105,* 613–617.

Pollin, I. (1995). *Medical crisis counseling: Short-term therapy for long-term illness.* New York: W. W. Norton.

Rolland, J. S. (1990). Anticipatory loss: A family systems developmental framework. *Family Process, 29* (3), 229–244.

———. (1994). *Families, illness, and disability.* New York: Basic Books.

Singh, R., & Guest, M. (1991). *Parents answer back.* Usher Syndrome: Awareness and Education Project. London, England: SENSE (The National Deaf-Blind and Rubella Association).

Smith, R. J. H., Berlin, C. I., Hajtmancik, J. F., Keats, W. J., Lewis, R. A., Moller, C. G., Pelaiz, M. Z., & Tranebjaerg, L. (1994). Clinical diagnosis of the Usher syndromes. *American Journal of Medical Genetics, 50,* 32–38.

Smith, T. (1993). Psychosocial services: Reaction. In J. Reiman & P. Johnson (Eds.), *Proceedings of the National Symposium on Children and Youth Who Are Deaf-Blind* (pp. 113–127). Monmouth, OR: Teaching Research Publications.

Smith, T. B. (1994). *Guidelines: Practical tips for working and socializing with deaf-blind people.* Burtonsville, MD: Sign Media.

Stiefel, D. H. (1991). *The madness of Usher's: Coping with vision and hearing loss (Usher syndrome, Type II).* Corpus Christi, TX: The Business of Living Publications.

Tedder, N. (1987). Counseling issues for clients with Usher's syndrome. *Journal of Rehabilitation,* April/May/June, 61–63.

Torrie, C. (1978). Families of adolescent children with Usher's syndrome: Developing services to meet their needs. *American Annals of the Deaf, 123* (3), 381–388.

Vernon, M. (1969). Usher's syndrome, prevention, theory, and literature survey. *Journal of Chronic Diseases, 22,* 133–151.

Vernon, M., Boughman, J., & Annala, L. (1982). Considerations in diagnosing Usher syndrome: RP and hearing loss. *Journal of Visual Impairment and Blindness, 76* (9), 258–261.

Vernon, M., & Green, D. (1980). A guide to the assessment of deaf-blind adults. *Journal of Visual Impairment and Blindness, 74* (6), 229–231.

Vernon, M., & Hicks, W. (1983, February). A group counseling and information program for students with Usher syndrome. *Journal of Visual Impairment and Blindness,* 64–67.

Wortman, C. B., & Silver, R. C. (1989). The myths of coping with loss. *Journal of Consulting and Clinical Psychology, 57* (3), 349–357.

14

Clinical Case Management with Traditionally Underserved Deaf Adults

KATHLEEN DUFFY

The traditional therapeutic process assumes, for any client, the right to make decisions, to explore options, to experience and express a range of emotion, to experiment, to fail, and to succeed. The therapist/social worker/case manager/counselor[1] witnesses the pain, the growth, and the treading water. Therapeutic interventions include asking questions, mirroring the client, and being genuinely empathetic. Basic needs must be met before a client will be able to address and work toward more traditional therapy goals, including a more cohesive sense of self, improved relationships, and meaningful work (Maslow, 1968). Some people, whether hearing or deaf, for whatever reason, need assistance to access services that are available to them. For some of these clients, more extensive interventions are needed.

Working with traditionally underserved people who are deaf often requires other skills in addition to more traditional psychotherapeutic interventions. These people may present with such factors such as mental illness, trauma, cognitive impairment, illiteracy, economic disadvantage, and debilitating and/or catastrophic illness. The complexity of their needs nearly always contributes to service delivery problems.

One pervasive problem exhibited by deaf clients who are traditionally underserved is their limited ability to take the initiative in procuring services. It is essential to explore the etiology of this apparent apathy for each client. Knowing whether the etiology is related to a personality trait, a symptom of schizophrenia, or a demonstration of learned powerlessness helps clarify the client's service needs. Clients may also exhibit substantial deficits in social skills, such as poor language skills or a limited ability to form interpersonal attachments. The inability to take another person's perspective or to actively initiate relationships makes it difficult for clients to maintain housing, employment, or friendships.

The low incidence of deafness combined with the low incidence of severe/persistent mental illness means that people who have both of these traits are a very small segment of both the Deaf community and the mental health community. Aphasia, developmental or learning disabilities, and cerebral palsy are also low incidence but critical factors (Vernon, 1982). Specialized services for clients with multiple problems such as these are difficult to obtain, and so the population has been traditionally underserved by mental health, social, education, welfare, and other professions.

Whatever therapeutic method or approach we choose it is imperative that we work *with* such clients, regardless of the multiple challenges they present, regardless of the time it takes. In California, mental health services for deaf people in California have expanded since 1967 when Hilde Schlesinger began the Mental Health Services for

1. Hereafter referred to as case manager.

the Deaf program at the Langley Porter Neuropsychiatric Institute in San Francisco (Elliot et al., 1987; Schlesinger & Meadow, 1972). Nationally, however, the need for such services still vastly exceeds their availability (Heller, 1987). The full range of mental health services must be an option for everybody, particularly those traditionally underserved people who are deaf. We need to ask ourselves: what can good clinical practice offer to these clients?

Describing the Traditionally Underserved Population

How does one define this group? The descriptive nature of the characteristics and the heterogeneity of the population make definitions difficult. Northern Illinois University Research and Training Center personnel surveyed rehabilitation professionals and educators regarding shared characteristics of group members. The center concluded that an assessment must evaluate five areas of functioning: academic achievement, communication skills, vocational skills, independent living skills, and social skills. In essence, while an individual may function at a higher level for any one factor it is the *overall level of functioning* that is the most important factor when determining a classification of traditionally underserved (Long, 1993).

For traditionally underserved people who are deaf, communication deficits are all too common. In the past members of this group might have been called "low functioning" or "low verbal." Essentially, many rely on a strongly visual mode of learning and information exchange that may include the use of idiosyncratic language, mime, gesture, or drawing to convey messages. Some clients may lack extensive vocabulary in ASL but may proficiently use some of its grammatical aspects, such as size and shape specifiers, directionality, and the use of space. Other clients may have the ability to communicate information clearly as long as the content is concrete, yet have difficulty conveying abstractions.

One particular client illustrates some of the potential complexities involved in linguistic and communication aspects. She had some vocabulary in four languages: Chinese, the language of her home; Vietnamese, the language of her country of origin; English, the spoken language of her adopted country; and American Sign Language (ASL), the visual language of her adopted country. It was difficult for her to express herself and to be understood fully in any of these languages.

Some clients with reasonably good language skills lack communication skills that incorporate knowledge of, and fluency in, social and cultural rules for interaction. They will have problems with the appropriate use of touch or eye contact, talking out of turn, or going "off the point," sometimes with dire social consequences. Some clients may be functionally illiterate, unable to use a TTY (telecommunications device for people who are deaf), benefit from closed captioning, or process written transactions independently.

While communication skills are critical, it is imperative that client assessment not be solely focused on language and communication skills. This sometimes can be used as a smokescreen for other equally important areas such as independent living skills and vocational skills that need to be assessed. Many traditionally underserved people have strengths that go unnoticed, such as adaptive strategies developed to deal with daily living issues. Such strategies may be greatly beneficial, even though at first glance some of these strategies may seem unusual or maladaptive.

Many traditionally underserved deaf people are marginalized within the Deaf community. One of the most frequently cited requirements of membership in the Deaf community is language (Padden, 1980), and a high value is placed on American Sign Language (ASL) fluency. However, many traditionally underserved people experience substantial linguistic deficits, in addition to exhibiting impulse control problems and "inappropriate" social behavior. Consequently, they are rejected from what could have been their "true" community.

The social ethic that distances people based on difference, disability, or "aberrant behavior" is often based on fear (Goffman, 1963). People, hearing or deaf, are made uncomfortable by what they do not understand. Even though "outsider status" can be painfully familiar to members of the Deaf community (Higgins, 1980), they may fear that those unfamiliar with the Deaf community will generalize the behavior of an apparent outsider who does not fit the mold to the group at large. This social phenomena is by no means limited to this community. It is important to note that many hearing people are also marginalized by mental illness, developmental disabilities, substance abuse, and poor social skills. The stakes are higher for deaf people who are marginalized, because resources are comparatively limited. For this group of people, family and/or service providers may be the sole source of social support in dealing with a world that they cannot fully comprehend or connect with.

Some deaf, traditionally underserved people have strengths that are noticed by others and an effort might be made to include the person in social/cultural activities. "Good enough" social skills are a positive attribute that will increase the client's sense of belonging and relatedness. Some clients take great pride in being Deaf or in their racial or ethnic identity. They may seek out Deaf or other cultural events. It is important to understand how the client views him or herself, and if and where the client feels a sense of belonging. It is imperative that service providers understand the dynamics of the community and cultural group that they serve, and the impact that Deaf culture may have in relation to the culture of the individual client who is deaf. Within this paradigm, working with Deaf clients requires a multicultural perspective, a perspective that has been elaborated on in the Leigh and Lewis chapter, in this volume.

Service Needs

Service needs emerge in relation to the problems clients are dealing with. In general, members of this group tend to need assistance and a system of support, formal or informal, to ensure that they are able to live as independently as possible, achieve at their greatest potential, and attain a quality of life that is satisfying.

If a deaf client demonstrates limited initiative or motivation in procuring services, it is essential to explore the etiology of this apparent apathy for each client. Knowing the source of the apathy helps clarify the client's service needs. Substantial deficits in social skills might be related to poor language skills and/or limited ability to form interpersonal attachments. This aspect must be evaluated. A deficit in any one area will impact other areas and readily contribute to a sense of failure.

Another critical area of need is reflected by the concern of aging family members for the continued welfare of a beloved son or daughter who is deaf and meets the criteria for those who are traditionally underserved. Some families who previously coped adequately with deaf family members that have special needs may become overwhelmed and frustrated after years of trying to manage alone without adequate resources. The desperation of these families is difficult to imagine.

* * *

Audrey is a thirty-five-year-old deaf Caucasian woman with deteriorating vision.[2] She presents with dystonic movement and dementia, etiology unknown. Her history includes hospitalization for catatonic-like behavior. She remains ineligible for services for people with developmental disabilities because, even though there were premorbid indications of more severe impairment, it was determined the onset of her neurological impairment occurred after the age of eighteen.

She has lived at home with her mother and stepfather since obtaining a "certificate of completion" from a residential school. She has never been employed and is currently not considered competitively employable. Her ability to capitalize on any funding source for deaf-blind or habilitation services is extremely limited. She is becoming increasingly aggressive toward her family members, who are complaining about her attention-seeking behavior. She does not express any dissatisfaction with her situation. She has been denied mental health services through her county because dementia is considered a medical condition.

* * *

Jose, a Central American deaf man, arrived in the United States after being displaced and perhaps traumatized by war. He sits in the corner of his room, looking out of his window, for hours at a time. His family is concerned, but because "he doesn't cause any trouble" they hesitated to seek help. He bathes and dresses independently, and will prepare simple meals for himself. The family reports that in their country of origin Jose played with other children and was able to both fish and farm. He has no expressive language skills, despite having Deaf siblings who were able to successfully take advantage of various educational and vocational opportunities in this country.

Estrangement from family members is not uncommon. Some clients may come from families that are ill-equipped to provide care to any of their children or family members. Within these families, domestic violence, alcoholism, neglect, and abuse are multigenerational issues. People with special needs are not protected from being born into families with severe psychosocial problems. An adult client may choose to distance him or herself from the family, or family members may distance themselves because they do not approve of the client's choices. In essence, family dynamics are lifelong negotiations made more complex by the multiple challenges of communication and other special considerations such as cognitive ability and independent living skills.

* * *

Mike was raised in a series of foster homes. He is not fluent in English or ASL, but uses vocabulary from both languages. He appears relatively disconnected from his environment most of the time. He has a history of psychiatric hospital-

2. Clients discussed are composites of typical clients, and/or their identifying information has been changed to protect their identities.

ization with a diagnosis of Psychotic Disorder NOS and substance abuse (in remission). He also has an AIDS diagnosis.

* * *

Cecilia is a twenty-seven-year-old African American Deaf woman who has been brought to the clinic on several occasions by a friend. Her mother has been diagnosed with schizophrenia. A history of neglect was documented through Child Protective Services, and Cecilia attempted suicide on several occasions during adolescence. Cecilia's friend is concerned because since Cecilia left residential school at age thirteen, she spends her days watching television. Her Supplemental Security Income (SSI) barely covers her expenses and the money is managed by a distant relative. Cecilia herself is unmotivated for change, and does not follow through with further appointments at the mental health clinic, with vocational rehabilitation, or other local educational programs.

Enmeshed relationships with parents/caregivers are not uncommon. Families with poor differentiation may find it difficult to recognize the separateness of individual family members. The culture of such families may prevent members from functioning independently or "leaving home." For some families the deaf member has become an "identified patient" who serves as a lightning rod for attention, allowing other relationships to be neglected and other needs to be unmet.

* * *

Mae, a forty-five-year-old female of European American background, has schizophrenia. Her family says she has "the mind of a child" and needs to be protected. Mae cannot read or write English. While quite streetwise in some situations, she is naive and overly trusting in others. Mae's mother manages all of Mae's finances, provides for her needs, and cares for Mae's daughter.

Traditionally underserved people who are deaf often lose out in terms of getting their service needs met because they are unaware such services exist, and because of the lack of culturally competent services. It is estimated that only 2% of deaf Americans in need of mental health services actually receive them (Vernon, 1983). Clients who are referred often "fall through the cracks" of social safety nets. In some instances, clients are well known to a multitude of health and social service agencies but are not served effectively because of deficiencies in the coordination of care. They bounce from one agency to another, causing replication of services, and many essential needs are left unmet. In an age of shrinking social service budgets and managed care, eligibility for services is often based on criteria that exclude, rather than criteria that are inclusive.

Some clients are self-referred, having received help from a mental health agency in the past, or because they heard from other clients that they can receive help from the agency. More typically, members of this group are referred for mental health services when they come to the attention of a medical provider, law enforcement/courts, regional center services for developmentally disabled people, or other social service agencies. Usually the client has some need that exceeds the ability of a specific service provider or because others are overwhelmed by the deaf client's unique way of viewing the world. Traditionally underserved people who are deaf are often referred for psychological assessment in order to obtain a diagnosis, to determine eligibility for other services, to determine capacity to parent, for conservatorship evaluations, or to assist in planning for treatment or vocational and educational planning. However, the most frequent reason for referral is poor social skills. The client may be aggressive, have low frustration tolerance, have difficulty establishing social support, poor emotional control and/or poor problem-solving skills (Long, 1993).

Some clients are never referred. There are a variety of reasons for this: clients could be paranoid, mistrustful of service delivery systems (particularly after a history of poor and inadequate service provision), or they might be clinically depressed and withdrawn from others but still manage to survive on a day-to-day basis.

* * *

A woman called the clinic to ask about counseling services and independent living training for her forty-year-old brother. The brother was increasingly depressed after the death of his mother, with whom he had lived most of his adult life. The sister described longstanding symptoms that indicated her brother could be severely mentally ill. Because the family lived in a rural location and did not know any other deaf people, the man's unusual behaviors were attributed solely to his deafness. The man "didn't bother anyone," received SSI, and contributed in a limited manner to the household. The client had gotten along "well enough" until the stressor of his mother's death and his subsequent decompensation. The social isolation the man experienced no doubt contributed to his longstanding mental health issues.

Some clients seek mental health services to address life transitions, and for short-term assistance in looking at obstacles that prevent them from attaining their goals.

* * *

Deborah came to the clinic requesting counseling when the imminent closing of the group home she lived in necessitated a change in her living situation. Deborah has borderline intellectual functioning and was determined to be eligible for services for people with developmental disabilities. She is financially self-supporting and is employed though a supported employment program. She felt that everyone was telling her what to do and that no one was paying attention to what she wanted or felt. She wanted to be able to tell her mother and social worker that the thought of leaving her friends at the group home made her feel sad and she felt nervous about leaving the support of the group home. Nonetheless, despite these feelings, she perceives herself as capable of independent living.

Other clients seek out mental health services for assistance in finding a job. While the Department of Rehabilitation or the Employment Development Department might be appropriate adjunct referrals, the client may have significant mental health issues that require supportive linkage to these employment programs in order to make employment a truly viable option.

* * *

Charlie is a deaf African American man who has lived in single-room occupancy hotels for most of his adult life. His sister manages his monthly disability check. He does not spontaneously initiate conversation but will respond in a concrete manner when addressed. He often pauses when he is signing, giving the impression he is "freezing" his thought in mid-air. He has in the past worked in supported employment until a series of disasters, specifically a bad relationship, an earthquake, and a psychotic break, forced his layoff. Since that time he has drifted from hotel to shelter. Sometimes he is homeless; sometimes he is victimized. He is generally pleasant and well groomed, given his circumstances. He has no friends and he visits his family on a weekly basis. He does not use drugs or alcohol. He is currently considering the possibility of going back to work.

Case Management

Since the deinstitutionalization movement in the 1970s, clinical case management has tried to help people remain in their communities. The case management approach has provided a link in the continuum of care between weekly therapy sessions and hospitalization. The approach aims to meet the needs of the client in a rapidly and radically changing mental health system.

Over the past three decades, clinical case management has become a recognized treatment modality for people with severe and persistent mental illness. It is a process that includes "double vision" in addressing immediate practical concerns—such as food, housing, medical care, vocational training, literacy, and obtaining adaptive equipment—while simultaneously building a collaborative relationship. The combination of these two approaches hopefully enhances the potential of achieving long range goals related to increased independence, more satisfying interpersonal relationships, meaningful work, or symptom management. When people are able to obtain what they need, the capacity for a more satisfying life increases exponentially.

In addressing the mental health needs of traditionally underserved people who are deaf, case management offers comprehensive, coordinated services that may best address a client's needs. Case management services are provided in many arenas. Typically, services are provided to a targeted population. Child welfare services, substance abuse treatment facilities, elder care, and services for people with developmental disabilities have long incorporated case management as part of their respective programs. More recently, case management services have been included in services for people with HIV/AIDS (Brennan, 1996; Langholtz & Ruth, this volume). Many agencies serving deaf people have traditionally provided case management services that involve assessing client needs, linking clients to services, advocating with and for clients, and following up to ensure that clients have received necessary services. There are many definitions of case management and different models of case management service delivery. This chapter addresses a model of service delivery and not, as the term is sometimes used, solely the authorization of services such as treatment of medical conditions.

Moxley (1989) defines case management as "a client level strategy for promoting the coordination of human services, opportunities, or benefits" (p. 11). Austin (1983) states that "case management is widely viewed as a mechanism for linking and coordinating

MODELS FOR PROVIDING CASE MANAGEMENT SERVICES

1. The *brokerage model* emphasizes referral, advocacy, linkage, and service coordination (Johnson & Reuben, 1983). The client or client's family is responsible for the procurement of specific direct services.

2. The *strengths model* emphasizes the utilization and development of the client's strengths in a wide range of spheres through community based resources (Modrcin et al., 1988; Rapp & Chamberlin, 1985).

3. The *PACT model* focuses on establishing a primary clinical relationship with the client and family. Within this model, meeting the basic needs of the client and improving social functioning is considered to be critical (Rapp & Kisthardt, 1996). Symptom reduction and symptom management receive significant attention. The case manager provides direct assistance with meeting the basic needs of the client.

4. The *rehabilitation model* utilizes the client's specific goals and identifies strengths, evaluates barriers both personal and environmental, and takes necessary steps toward achieving identified goals.

Figure 1. Service Delivery Models

segments of a service delivery system . . . to ensure the most comprehensive program for meeting an individual client's need for care" (p. 16). Case management is a dynamic process that reflects the client's strengths and needs, evolving social network, living environment, economic circumstances, and relationships with service and care providers. It also reflects the shifting of societal priorities and funding for service delivery.

The philosophies driving various case management models of service delivery are essentially the same, although each model has a somewhat different focus. Rapp and Kisthardt (1996) identify four predominant models of case management: the brokerage model, the strengths model, the Program for Assertive Community Training (PACT) model, and the rehabilitation model. All of these models share core functions, including client identification/outreach, individual assessment, service planning, linkage, monitoring of service delivery, and client advocacy. However, each model differs in its emphasis on service delivery. In general, clinical case management includes all of the facets outlined in figure 1, and also emphasizes the importance of the therapeutic relationship between client and case manager. It is important to recognize that psychotherapy is included in the services provided by case managers (Kanter, 1989; Lamb, 1980; Manoleas, 1996; Surber, 1994).

The clinical case manager is a member of a team who works in close collaboration with other clinical staff. The clinical case manager is a therapist, advocate, crisis worker, consultant, care provider, and interpreter. Ethical questions arise repeatedly and great care must be taken to maintain appropriate and clear boundaries in often murky situations. Zitter (1996) addresses the expanded role of therapists working with deaf clients and explores the difference between rigid boundaries and more flexible parameters in clinical work. The clinical case manager relies on the guiding principles of autonomy, beneficence (acting in the best interest of the client), nonmalfeasance (doing no harm), justice/fairness, and fidelity in determining a course of action.

As in any therapeutic relationship, establishing rapport is essential to creating a partnership. The first task of clinical case management is to engage the client. The initial meeting focuses on what the client wants. This approach offers a radical departure for many clients who may have experiences with involuntary hospitalization or overinvolved caretakers who feel they know what is best for the client. This initial encounter may take place on the streets, in the client's home, in a psychiatric emergency room, or at a social service agency. Generally, in therapy a therapist will meet the client "where the client is at" because that is the necessary starting point of a collaborative relationship.

In cases that require clinical case management, the therapist/case manager may take this task literally. A client discharged from psychiatric emergency services may disappear into the streets again without adequate follow up, and subsequently experience repeated hospitalizations. To prevent this from happening, a case manager may need to meet a client at the hospital to begin developing a post-hospitalization plan, as well as to establish rapport and create a link to out-patient services. The case manager may meet the client again at the time of discharge to facilitate transportation home. Home may be a transitional housing program, a house or apartment shared with family, a board-and-care home, or a homeless shelter.

By working with the client in the client's own environment, the case manager begins to gain understanding of the client, his or her current situation and motivation, and other environmental circumstances. This flexibility is one of the facets that sets clinical case management apart from more traditional models of therapy.

The assessment commences with the first client contact. During this phase the client's current concerns are discussed. The case manager reviews any available records pertaining to prior treatment and the psychosocial history, as assessment includes an appraisal of prior and current functioning. The case manager also assesses the client's formal and informal support network and evaluates strengths and gaps in this system, taking into account cultural considerations and the reality of the client's situation. The presenting issue is often tangible and external to the client. Even though many clients in a counseling setting will present a concrete issue as the presenting problem, underlying issues or themes can be expected to emerge. The impact of coexisting conditions, such as severe mental illness, substance abuse, developmental disabilities, visual impairment, medical conditions, and being educationally disadvantaged, must be assessed and eventually addressed. The emphasis is on the strengths of the whole person. A realistic assessment should never underestimate the abilities of a client.

It may be important to work with the client to identify sources of assistance for independent living issues. The clinician must be comfortable with either providing the necessary services or referring the client to other experts. Together, the client and the clinician can then develop a comprehensive plan that hopefully will enable the client to achieve or take steps toward his or her goals. In the plan, agreements are made and tasks delegated. For example, if a client wants to live independently, he or she may agree to begin looking at apartments available in the neighborhood. The client and case manager may begin to work out a budget for moving. The client may agree to save 15% of his or her income over the next six months for an apartment deposit. The case manager might agree to assist with obtaining listings, or refer the client to an agency that assists in finding housing.

Care is taken not to do what clients can do for theselves, but rather to assist in areas where assistance is needed. Services are adapted to the clients' abilities. For example, a case manager may accompany a client who does not travel independently to the Social Security office to discuss a plan for economic self-sufficiency. Later, with new skills and confidence, the client may meet the case manager at the Social Security office. Over time, the client will travel to and attend the meeting independently and then report back to the case manager. After a client is stabilized and linked to appropriate services, the need for such intensive ongoing support may be reduced.

The case manager continues to monitor the success of placements or other interventions, and evaluates the need for any changes in the plan with the client on an ongoing basis. Sometimes the case manager is called upon to assist with environmental interventions that make the difference between having a home and being homeless, living independently or returning to a board-and-care home or the hospital. The case manager is available to the client in the client's own environment. Interventions are often made "in vivo," in the situation where the issue arises, and/or the client may come to the case manager's office for regularly scheduled appointments.

Clinical issues are interwoven through all facets of the work together. Awareness of the client's motivation, defenses, and clinical status facilitates the clinician's ability to make informed decisions and recommendations. The clinical case manager is aware of the client's internal, less readily identifiable needs and resources, as well as the more readily identifiable external resources and needs, in order to more appropriately match interventions that will work for the client. For some clients, ongoing intensive case management will always be needed. This should not be considered a "failure" on the part of the client or the service provider. Rather, this level of service should be perceived as an ongoing endeavor that supports a least restrictive environment for the client.

Increasingly, case management services are needed to help clients access services whose eligibility requirements appear to be based on exclusion rather than inclusion. Depending on insurance coverage or available community resources, decompensation is no longer enough to admit one to a hospital. One must be a danger to oneself or others or gravely disabled to obtain emergency services. Because of the additional barrier of communication access, case managers all too often have to fight for a client despite legislation that mandates access. If the client's right to access a program is resented by the program's staff, ultimately the question arises as to whether the program will be helpful for the client.

Just as we assess the needs of the client we must evaluate the service delivery systems available and any barriers the client may encounter when trying to access these systems. Some of the barriers are obvious, such as sign language or English language issues. Other barriers involve lack of awareness on the part of service providers. It is not unusual for a deaf client to try to contact a public agency that is listed as TTY accessible only to have whoever answers the phone hang up. When planning to give out the number of the local hospital, suicide prevention, or social service agencies it might be helpful to first call the TTY number to verify that the number is correct and that a TTY call will be answered. The call gives the agency the opportunity to take corrective action before the client calls. Again, this kind of intervention depends on the client, being careful not to manage for the client what the client is able to manage for him or herself.

Simple oversights can adversely impact a deaf client's ability to obtain his or her own services. For example, a deaf client may wait in a public office for assistance, visually vigilant for the signal that it is her turn to be served. If the receptionist forgets or is unaware that the person is deaf, and does not cue her visually, the client may wait for hours. If the client does not have the tools to assert herself, the impact is magnified. Such oversights exacerbate dependency and negative self-evaluation based on hearing status, particularly for clients who do not have solid ego functioning.

While evaluating the needs of traditionally underserved clients who are deaf, it is also important to look at their resiliency. So often we look at clients' deficiencies, but then fail to wonder at their achievements. The clinical case manager must delve deeply into internal resources and maintain a vision bigger and healthier than the system will allow. When a client on a fixed income comes to us with the desire to move from substandard housing, we must not only think in terms of what is realistic. We must also hold the ultimate vision that adequate, affordable housing is a right. Just as we hold for any client the belief that things can and will change, and that they hold the ability and the power to make change, we must hold that belief for ourselves even while working with too few resources.

Therapeutic Approaches within Clinical Case Management

It is important in any therapeutic relationship that the therapist facilitate the client's internal sense of validation, thereby encouraging him or her to maintain the therapeutic relationship. For example, a client may reenact other relationships in the therapy. It is important for the therapist/case manager not to reenact unhealthy responses to the client. If the client and therapist are able to resolve the conflicts that emerge in their relationship, the client can generalize from this new experience and successfully adopt more adaptive responses with others (Teyber, 1992).

Good communication skills and capacity for insight are considered requisites for psychodynamic therapy. In clinical case management we generally address the mental health needs of individuals who have often been perceived as poor candidates for more traditional models of psychotherapy or who have been excluded from mainstream services due to prejudice or service delivery models that do not meet the needs of the client. What happens when clients are able to experience many of the dynamics of the therapeutic experience and yet lack the language to speak directly of their experiences?

When therapeutic insights are more forthcoming than communication skills, issues that may emerge include: How can understanding be fostered and encouraged? Can the beneficial elements of individual psychotherapy practiced at an advanced level be translated to clinical case management? How do we not underestimate the capacity of the client to change or to understand what is happening in their lives? How do we make sure that we as clinicians have the capacity to understand what our client is going through? Do we trust in the client's ability to internalize corrective emotional experiences? Do we dare allow ourselves the empathetic stance of feeling a world so seemingly foreign?

The therapeutic relationship also requires that the partnership respects the client's autonomy. In working with deaf adults who are traditionally underserved it is most important that the client is respected and his or her life experience is valued. Subjective experience has too long been ignored or invalidated in ways that do not encourage clients to trust their own experiences. Empathetic breaks are not uncommon even when two people share a common language. Where different languages are used, for whatever reason, the challenge to mirror the experiences of the self by the selfobject—as represented by the mother or caretaker—are even greater.

The selfobject performs for the infant missing intrapsychic functions that can become his or her own through a process called transmuting internalization (Kohut, 1984). To clarify, the client may transferentially expect the therapist/case manager to "know" his or her inner state or what he or she needs, just as the early selfobject was expected to know the infant's needs (Elson, 1986). This expectation can cause a break in the attunement between the clinician and client. Repairing the break can be difficult with clients whose social cognitions are limited. They tend to be unable to take another person's perspective and may have a more "narcissistic" worldview.

Regardless (or possibly because of) past experiences, these clients seek to be understood *in the present.* Mirroring clients' affect and validating their experiences allows them to more fully own their experiences. The need to be understood, and to understand, are the underpinnings of a corrective emotional experience. This concept is also integral to the healthy development of any child (Jacobs, 1974). To have someone bear witness to our struggles in a compassionate, nonjudgmental manner is beneficial, often healing, and unfortunately, for some, a rare experience.

Too often for a deaf client who is traditionally underserved, misunderstanding is primarily language based. The client's affect and the experience tends not to be attended to in the struggle to understand the manifest content of the message. The client expects empathetic breaks, or, in other words, not to be understood. Being understood in the present sets the healing process in motion (Kohut, 1984). An empathetic relationship with a therapist/case manager who can communicate in the client's own language offers the client the possibility of experiencing and recognizing a stronger sense of self and other empathetic relationships. The client then feels supported and less alone.

* * *

Elana was first referred to mental health services at the age of nineteen. She is Latina, currently in her early thirties, and profoundly deaf. Elana uses ASL clearly, although slowly. English is her family's first language, but her understanding of written English is limited. Elana has never worked, and has no current connections to the Deaf community. Her time at the state school for the deaf is remembered fondly and somewhat unrealistically as a time without any problems.

Her family is very religious. The client is the youngest of five children. Elana lives at home with her parents, both of whom are elderly, and professes that she would like to have her own apartment. She has borderline intellectual functioning and "hears voices." She refers to the voices as "the bad dream" and their relationship to the client is predominantly persecutory, interfering with her ability to participate in daily activities. Despite repeated medication trials, the psychotic symptoms are not well controlled, although medication offers some relief. Elana complains about the "bad mind people" and the fact that they will not go away. Without medication the "bad mind people" become "mean, mean" and Elana becomes violent and threatening to her family.

Her first psychotic break was subsequent to her graduation from residential school. She did not follow through on referrals through the Department of Rehabilitation and her case has been opened and closed countless times. The family was in denial about the nature and extent of her mental illness. She was hospitalized four times within a six-month period as being "gravely disabled and a danger to self or others." (She attempted to harm family members upon instruction from the voices.) After the fourth hospitalization the family feared for their own safety and refused to allow Elana to come home. During routine lab testing, the hospital found that Elana had diabetes and also needed to take insulin regularly. After Elana's referral, the clinical case manager met with the client and psychiatrist to explore day programs, housing, and other services.

The first task was to find a placement for the client, who was distraught and shocked by what she perceived as her family's abandonment. The case manager met the client at the hospital and accompanied her to a board-and-care home not far from where she lived. Intensive services were provided for several weeks, with regularly scheduled visits.

The client had a difficult time adjusting to the board-and-care home placement. It was the first time she had ever lived away from home and the circumstances were difficult. The provider was apprehensive about meeting the needs of a deaf client, despite her extensive experience in providing a safe and comfortable environment for people with major psychiatric disorders. The provider was encouraged to draw on her own expertise. In order to create a working relationship with the board-and-care provider, the case manager avoided "educating" her about the psychosocial impact of deafness but instead supported the provider in obtaining adjunctive and necessary services. Arrangements were made to obtain a TTY and lend the provider sign language videotapes. Such simple supports allowed the provider to feel that she could continue to work with this client. The placement was far from ideal but for the time being the client was safely sheltered. More appropriate and supportive housing would become a long-term goal. This is one example of how the clinical case manager acts as an advocate in a way that elicits and enlists the support necessary to ensure that the client's needs are met in the best way possible.

One advantage of the board-and-care placement was that the client was medication compliant for the first time since the onset of her mental illness. This resulted in a substantial reduction in auditory and visual hallucinations. Nonetheless, Elana was adamant about returning home, and was deeply hurt by her family's rejection. An interesting aspect to this case surfaced while the client was living away from home. The family system shifted dramatically with the daughter's absence, and the parents separated. Elana's role in keeping the parents together while she was at home became clear.

For the client, assistance in making appointments with her primary health care provider was provided. Previously, the client's mother had interpreted all medical appointments. Arrangements were made with the hospital for a certified interpreter to be present at all future appointments. Elana requested that her case manager also be present in case she didn't understand. Released of any primary interpreting responsibilities, the case manager was able to support the client through difficult medical appointments and continue the advocacy role. Consent was given for the primary care physician, the psychiatrist, and the case manager to exchange information. All three consulted regularly about changes in medication.

The case manager initially met Elana at the group home so that they could travel together to meet with her psychiatrist at the mental health clinic. Elana mastered the route and after several weeks felt confident about her ability to travel for other appointments. One day, after traveling alone, Elana missed her appointment at the clinic. The next week she told the case manager she didn't have money for the subway fare; she only had $20! After some discussion it became clear that Elana didn't know how to get change. She waited for coins to be given to her and her understanding of money was random at best. The case manager accompanied Elana to a bank and assisted in obtaining change. Elana had largely depended on her parents for money management, transportation, and for procuring needed services. Care was taken not to fulfill parental functions, and Elana was proud of her increased ability to travel and live somewhat independently.

After exhausting community resources for transitional housing, it became clear that Elana would have more opportunities available to her for supported employment and housing if she were to become eligible for Regional Center services. The Regional Center is a state agency responsible for providing services for people with developmental disabilities or people who have needs similar to those with developmental disabilities. The decision to pursue the eligibility for Regional Center services was based on the premise that the case manager needed to create and to hold opportunities for the client, and the belief that Elana was eligible for and entitled to receive these services. Although the area where Elana lived had a vibrant Deaf community, resources for people like Elana were few. Eligibility for Regional Center services would give Elana a few more options, whether she decided to pursue them or not. A previous referral for those services had been made but Elana's family had not followed through with the referral. This time the case manager and Elana discussed the process and together they followed up on the referral. Initially Elana's application was denied, based on a Performance IQ of 79. (The cutoff point for such services is a Performance IQ of 70, although there is some latitude in functional evaluation.) Elana successfully appealed the decision with the assistance of her case manager.

Over the next four months, Elana struggled with the issues that had caused her expulsion from her family home. Her parents were again living together, and as Elana improved she began visiting them for dinner. Elana decided that she wanted to return home and was welcomed back. The work with Elana continued. She came to the clinic on a weekly basis and participated in a time-limited therapy group for deaf women who were considered traditionally underserved. All but one of the group members were eligible for Regional Center services. Half of the group had Axis I diagnoses that included major depression, schizophrenia, and bipolar disorder. The group shared difficult situations related to family relationships, leaving home, and supported employment. They addressed issues of sameness and difference within the group. Group members also challenged and confronted each other regarding absence from group, tardiness, and other issues related to the group process.

Elana continued regular office meetings with the case manager. During this time she was able to focus more clearly on her internal struggles. She decided that she wasn't ready to leave home and discussed her ambivalence about leaving her parents and her desire to care for them as they became older and more frail. She expressed her concern about what would happen to her if her parents died. She continued to reject many of the options for housing, training, or

> employment. She became more open to discussing her anger and frustration with her mental illness, culture, race, and hearing status, as well as having to inject insulin on a daily basis. Elana addressed her feelings of things being "not fair." Elana and her case manager regularly collaborated with her medical doctor and her psychiatrist, and she began to conceptualize her schizophrenia as an illness not unlike diabetes—an illness that is not curable, but perhaps a bit more manageable than she had originally believed.
>
> Termination with Elana occurred when the case manager left the agency. There were concerns about termination in part because of Elana's longstanding pattern of ending sessions prematurely and her difficulty acknowledging the end of a session. Additionally, Elana had worked for a long time with this particular service provider. She expressed a range of emotion regarding termination, particularly sadness. A significant development at this point was her use of a metaphor: "CRYING CRYING, WATER FLOODING, BUT ME SWIMMING." It became apparent that she not only was addressing the end of her work with this case manager, but had also internalized a sense of her own ability to stay afloat. Also, when Elana was asked shortly before the final termination what had been helpful for her, she paused, looked directly at the clinician and signed, "ALL THESE YEARS, YOU MAD (AT ME) NEVER, EMOTIONAL-AGITATED NOT, ME HERE SAFE."

Merely treading water can be success. The case manager recognized that many of the goals that had been established were essentially unmet. Elana did not have a job; she was still living with her parents, and the "bad dream people" still bothered her. She was beginning to understand that diabetes and mental illness could, however, be more manageable than she once believed. Elana had not been hospitalized in five years, and this too was a success. The relationship with her therapist/case manager had provided a holding environment, a safe place. Elana's work continues with another provider; success is measured incrementally.

Elson (1986) states that clinicians are often their own best tool. As clinicians we have no magic bag of tricks, no special access. What we offer clients is an empathetic attunement. The relationship between the client and clinician is a dynamic relationship, offering both participants in the relationship opportunities for growth and change.

While current research continues to formulate new hypotheses covering biosocial etiologies in psychotic disorders, Kohut's (1984) work in self-psychology continues to offer a psychotherapeutic approach that embraces infinite possibilities within clinical case management. In this respect, Elson summarizes the process of self-psychology:

> The selfobjects [caregivers] of early infancy and childhood perform mirroring, confirming, and guiding functions, and they permit empathetic merger with their idealized strength and wisdom in sufficient amounts and for sufficient duration to allow selfobject functions to be transmuted into self functions. These functions are the capacity to regulate self-esteem, to monitor stress, to define and pursue realistic goals. Deficits occur in the self of the individual when the original selfobjects have been unable to provide such functions in a consistent manner. The self emerges subject to fragmentation and enfeebled rather than cohesive, vigorous, and harmonious. It is with the social worker as the new selfobject in the present that the individual is able to reengage himself in the process of structure building. It is this concept of the social worker as a new selfobject that clarifies what we do. (1986, p. 5)

Interference with the self and selfobject relationship may begin with the lack of parental capacity or skills, as well as through the infant's inability to provide cues to the caregiver (selfobject) regarding needs and desires. Empathetic breaks can and do happen. The self's ability to manage and negotiate those breaks without fragmenting or flying into a rage depends on a cohesive sense of self. A self-psychology framework can make good sense when working with traditionally underserved clients who are deaf. The complementary nature of clinical case management and self-psychology forces the clinician to understand the client in a way that is always dynamic and minimizes paternalism. This framework was utilized in work with Elana.

* * *

The case manager's primary goal was to understand Elana's experience and to reflect that understanding. Confirmation of Elana's own experiences strengthened her sense of ownership of those experiences, as external confirmation was very important to her. The pain and discomfort that she experienced as a result of the "bad dreams" had too often been dismissed. Elana knew that she missed out in many ways. She was the only unmarried member of her family, and she had no children. She was the only deaf member of her family, and communication at home was extremely limited. She also had limited understanding of her needs.

Much of the work focused on the practical aspects of medication management, ensuring that her prescriptions were available, and that she knew when to take the medication. Charts for medication were made; this included drawing the size and color of the medication and the number of pills and time of day that she needed to take her medication. Her blood sugar was charted and the records sent to her physician. It was critical for the clinician to recognize that these aspects were at times tedious, as Elana needed acknowledgment of the difficulties and challenges she faced managing "the bad dreams" and her diabetes.

The loneliness Elana often felt as the only deaf person in her family was also acknowledged. The group she participated in provided additional empathetic and confirming responses for her. Her group therapist was able to provide an additional source of empathetic mirroring. The group also provided a kind of collateral support for the clinical case manager. Consultation with the group therapist confirmed that Elana's group work paralleled what transpired in the individual work with Elana. While much of the group was focused on independent living skills, the egalitarian nature of the group and its emphasis on adult life issues challenged Elana to assume more responsibility for herself as she internalized the belief of the therapists and her peers that she could and would do things for herself.

While a family therapy approach might also have been beneficial, the family was not as motivated for treatment as the client. It is important to remember, however, that interventions can and often must be multidimensional. While working with the client, the family was supported and challenged to recognize the changes in Elana and the impact of those changes on the family. Family changes such as illness or divorce were more openly acknowledged, where previously they had been concealed to "protect" Elana, often with disastrous results.

Sustaining the Work

An in-depth look at occupational stress is beyond the scope of this chapter. However, it is critical to consider these factors when working with traditionally underserved clients, because of the general intensity of both the work and commitment. Exposure to ongoing trauma and crisis can leave clinicians vulnerable to professional burnout and, in some more extreme instances, secondary post-traumatic stress.

There is no end to what needs to be done. Often case management seems simply to be chaos management. Our clients invite us into their lives or we are mandated into their lives. We are with them when their children are taken from them by child protection workers; we sit with them in their rage and grief. We witness grossly inadequate parenting and the failure of a social services system to take action to protect the children. Clients stagger into the office, often victimized or battered. Sometimes the only thing that we can do is witness the client's experience and empathetically provide a mirror.

The provider must utilize internal and personal resources in order to maintain equilibrium. For example, Elana's case manager monitored her own internal feelings of frustration regarding her client's situation and discussed them in supervision. The concept of self-care/nurturance is not new for healthcare providers. However, it seems necessary to remind providers on a regular basis that our ability to care for others is directly related to our ability to care for ourselves. A variety of factors affect the professionals' susceptibility to burnout. Profession, personal skills and characteristics, specific stressors in the workplace, and institutional factors are variables that must be scrutinized in this equation. Among social workers, demands from funding sources, increased bureaucratization, and the inability to participate in decision making have been identified as significant correlates to job dissatisfaction and burnout.

Providers working for democratic managers who promote autonomy, flexibility, and team approach to client care experience less stress than do those working for autocratic managers. (Arches, 1991; Mather & Frakes, 1983). Supportive relationships with supervisors and colleagues buffer stress and burnout and are integral in maintaining workplace morale and "productivity" (Albrecht et al., 1982; Cherniss, 1981; Macks, 1992; McLean, 1985).

Often, the unique aspects of working with deaf clients prevent both clinicians and clients from recognizing that other groups—different cultures, linguistic minorities, or disability groups—share many of the same central issues. Our professional development must reach beyond the scope of "deafness." It is important for providers working with clients who are deaf to participate in and access resources that are available to larger communities. It is equally important for "mainstream" service providers to be aware of and sensitive to the need for accessible services. The ethical stance for providing accessible services must supersede the legal mandate.

Conclusion

At its best, clinical case management is an orientation toward service provision that affirms the value of the client as a whole person. Psychodiagnostic and psychosocial assessment skills, group and family skills, case management skills (including broad-based information and referral resources), and cultural competence are necessary components in the practice of clinical case management. The varied nature of the work and close client and community contact allow for a methodology of clinical practice and case management that offers unique opportunities in the consumer-clinician partnership, in the interest of serving a segment of the deaf community that is traditionally underserved.

References

Albrecht, T. L., Irey, K. V., & Mundy, A. K. (1982). Integration in a communication network as a mediator of stress. *Social Work, 27,* 229–234.

Arches, J. (1991). Social structure, burnout, and job satisfaction. *Social Work, 36,* 202–206.

Austin, C. (1983). Case-management in long-term care: Options and opportunities. *Health and Social Work, 8* (1), 16–30.

Brennan, J. (1996). Comprehensive case management with HIV clients. In C. Austin & R. McClelland (Eds.), *Perspectives on case management practice* (pp. 219–240). Milwaukee: Families International.

Cherniss, C. (1981). *Professional burnout in human service organizations.* New York: Praeger.

Dowhower, D. D., & Long, N. M. (1992). What is traditionally underserved? *Northern Illinois University-Research & Training Center Bulletin, 1* (1), 1.

Elliot, H., Glass, L., and Evans, J. W. (1987). *Mental health assessment of deaf clients: a practical manual.* Boston: College-Hill Press.

Elson, M. (1986). *Self psychology in clinical social work.* New York: W. W. Norton.

Goffman, E. (1963). *Stigma: Notes on the management of spoiled identity.* Englewood Cliffs, NJ: Prentice-Hall.

Heller, B. (1987). Overview of the function of UCCD. In H. Elliot, L. Glass, & J. W. Evans (Eds.), *Mental health assessment of deaf clients: A practical manual* (pp. 3–8). Boston: College-Hill Press.

Higgins, P. (1980). *Outsiders in a hearing world: A sociology of deafness.* Beverly Hills, CA: Sage Publications.

Jacobs, L. (1974). *A deaf adult speaks out.* Washington, DC: Gallaudet University Press.

Johnson, P. J., & Rubin A. (1983). Case management in mental health: A social work domain? *Social Work, 28* (1), 49–55.

Kanter, J. (1989). Clinical case management: Definitions, principles, components. *Hospital and Community Psychiatry, 40* (4), 361–368.

———. (1990). Community based management of psychotic clients: The contributions of D. W. & Claire Winnicott. *Clinical Social Work Journal, 18* (1), 23–41.

Kohut, H. (1984). *How does analysis cure?* Chicago: University of Chicago Press.

Lamb, H. R. (1980). Therapist-case managers: More than brokers of service. *Hospital and Community Psychiatry, 31,* 762–764.

Long, G., and Clark, D. A. (1993). *Defining traditionally underserved persons who are deaf* [NIU-RTC Research Brief]. DeKalb, IL: Northern Illinois University, Communicative Disorders Department, Research and Training Center for Traditionally Underserved Persons Who Are Deaf.

Macks, J. (1992). "Sustaining professional caregivers" in H. Land (Ed.), *AIDS: A complete guide to psychosocial intervention* (pp. 215–325). Milwaukee: Family Service America.

Manoleas, P. (1996). *The cross-cultural practice of clinical case management in mental health.* New York: Haworth Press.

Marschark, M. (1993). *Psychological development of deaf children.* New York: Oxford University Press.

Maslow, A. H. (1968). *Toward a psychology of being.* New York: Van Nostrand.

Mather, C. D., & Frakes, K. (1983). The hospice philosophy: They bring out the best in you. *Nursing Life, 3,* 50–51.

McLean, A. A. (1985). *Work stress.* Reading, MA: Addison-Wesley.

Modrcin, M., Rapp, C. A., & Poertner, J. (1988). The evaluation of case management services with the chronically mentally ill. *Evaluation and Program Planning, 11,* 307–314.

Moores, D. F. (1996). *Educating the deaf: Psychology, principles, and practices.* Boston: Houghton Mifflin.

Moxley, D. P. (1989). *The practice of case management.* Newbury Park, CA: Sage Publications.

Padden, C. (1980). The deaf community and the culture of Deaf people. In C. Baker and R. Battison (Eds.), *Sign language and the Deaf community* (pp. 89–103). Silver Spring, MD: National Association of the Deaf.

Pines, A., & Aronson, E. (1989). *Career burnout.* New York: Free Press.

Pines, A., Aronson, E., & Kafry, D. (1981). *Burnout: From tedium to personal growth.* New York: Free Press.

Pollard, R. Q. (1994). Public mental health services and diagnostic trends regarding individuals who are deaf or hard of hearing. *Rehabilitation Psychology, 39,* 147–160.

Quinn, J. (1993). *Successful case management in long-term care.* New York: Springer.

Radol Raiff, N., & Shore, B. (1994). *Advanced case management.* Newbury Park, CA: Sage Publications.

Rapp, C. A., & Chamberlain, R. (1985). Case management services for the chronically mentally ill. *Social Work, 30* (5), 417–422.

Rapp, C. A., & Kishardt, W. (1996). Case management with people with severe and persistent mental illness. In C. Austin & R. McClelland (Eds.), *Perspectives on case management practice* (pp. 17–45). Milwaukee: Families International.

Ryan, C. S., Sherman, P. S., & Bogart, L. M. (1997). Patterns of services and consumer outcome in an intensive case management program. *Journal of Consulting and Clinical Psychology, 65,* 485–493.

Scott, C. D, & Jaffe, D. T. (1989). Managing occupational stress associated with HIV infection. *Occupational Medicine, 4,* 85–93.

Schlesinger, H. S., and Meadow, K. P. (1972). *Childhood deafness and mental health.* Berkeley: University of California Press.

Surber, R. (Ed). (1994). *Clinical case management: A guide to comprehensive treatment of serious mental illness.* Thousand Oaks, CA: Sage Publications.

Teyber, E. (1992). *Interpersonal process in psychotherapy: A guide for clinical training* (2d ed.). Pacific Grove, CA: Brooks/Cole.

Vernon, M. (1982). Multi-handicapped deaf children, types and causes. In D. Tweedie & E. Shroyer (Eds.), *The multi-handicapped hearing impaired* (pp. 11–28). Washington, DC: Gallaudet University Press.

———. (1983). Deafness and mental health: Emerging responses. In E. Petersen (Ed.), *Mental health and deafness: Emerging responses.* Silver Spring, MD: American Deafness and Rehabilitation Association.

Zitter, S. (1996). Report from the front lines: Balancing multiple roles of a deafness therapist. In N. Glickman & M. Harvey (Eds.), *Culturally affirmative psychotherapy with Deaf persons* (pp. 185–246). Mahwah, NJ: Lawrence Erlbaum.

15

Chemical Dependency: An Application of a Treatment Model for Deaf People

DEBRA GUTHMANN, KATHERINE SANDBERG, AND JANET DICKINSON

The availability of substance abuse prevention and treatment programs for the deaf community is relatively recent, having developed primarily since the late 1980s. Because services and information about substance abuse are not yet widely available within the deaf community, members of the community may be aware that another individual has a problem with alcohol or other drugs but may not know what to do to help the individual. Community members may tolerate substance-abusing behavior, due to their close-knit relationships with one another. As a result of this and the historic lack of substance abuse services for deaf people, the subgroup of deaf individuals in recovery is in its infancy.

A substance-abusing individual's denial of his or her problem may be a strong factor prohibiting him or her from joining the community of recovering deaf people, who themselves face isolation and lack of a true peer group. Because they may have damaged their relationship with the larger community, they may feel left out of the deaf community and left out of the recovering (mostly hearing) community. Many deaf individuals in recovery are brought together for the first time in a treatment program or a self-help support group meeting.

Nationally, a few substance abuse treatment programs have become available that meet the communication and cultural needs of deaf people. The Minnesota Chemical Dependency Program for Deaf and Hard of Hearing Individuals (referred to as the Minnesota Program) provides comprehensive treatment for deaf people. It has served deaf people from forty-five states and Canada and is a key factor connecting deaf people in recovery from across the country. While in treatment, clients develop supportive relationships with each other, an important component in the recovery process. Those individuals who return home to an area where there are other recovering deaf people can continue that type of fellowship with beneficial results to their sobriety. However, too many people return home to areas where there are few, if any, other deaf people in recovery. They face the situation of trying to socialize in places like Deaf clubs or athletic activities, where alcohol is often consumed. They then feel the need to choose between socializing in an unsafe environment or avoiding that environment and dealing with loneliness.

The substance abuse profession is beginning to identify the deaf community as a community in need of specialized treatment approaches, and programs such as the Minnesota Program are training other professionals who work with the deaf community. This chapter will provide information about this model treatment program and clinical approaches that have been effective for members of the deaf community and assisted them in beginning the process of recovery.

Is chemical dependency a serious problem for deaf people? Are deaf people at greater risk for becoming addicted to alcohol and other drugs than hearing people? These questions are often asked but rarely answered. There have been no empirical studies to determine the prevalence of alcohol and drug use among deaf adults for several reasons, including: (a) deaf people's distrust of predominantly hearing researchers; (b) fear of ostracism and labeling within the deaf community; (c) lack of identification of substance abusers within the deaf community; (d) communicatively inaccessible instruments based on English; and (e) the inability to survey this population due to communication barriers.

Some researchers have attempted to extrapolate data from other sources regarding the seriousness of substance use and chemical dependency among deaf people. Based on U.S. Justice Department figures (1992) about the overall incidence of illicit drug use in the United States and assuming that deaf people represent one-half of one percent of the general population, McCrone (1994) estimates that there are approximately 3,505 deaf heroin users, 31,915 deaf cocaine users, 5,105 deaf crack users, and 97,745 deaf marijuana users in the United States today. The National Council on Alcoholism suggests that at least 600,000 individuals experience both alcoholism and hearing loss (Kearns, 1989). Clearly, more research is needed to determine the level of substance abuse and dependency within the deaf community. There is also a need for understanding the risk factors that may contribute to the development of alcohol or other drug abuse problems among deaf people.

Risk Factors That Can Lead to Substance Abuse

Risk factors experienced by deaf people are comparable to those experienced by people with other physical disabilities, who may abuse alcohol and other drugs for reasons related to their disability, and for reasons similar to those of nondisabled people. For youth and adults, the risk factors include:

- Lack of education and other academic problems, low self-esteem, lack of positive deaf role models, communication barriers, lack of appropriate drug education and drug resistance skills, a lack of early intervention resources (Boros, 1983; Dixon, 1987; Ferrell & George, 1984; McCrone, 1982; Stewart, 1991; Zangar, 1990).

- Misuse of medication, health concerns, chronic pain, peer group differences, increased stress on family life, fewer social supports, enabling of alcohol and other drug use by others, excess free time, lack of access to appropriate alcohol and other drug abuse prevention resources (Boros, 1981; Buss & Cramer, 1989; de Miranda & Cherry, 1989).

Deaf adolescents, however, may experience a higher level of stress than their hearing counterparts. For example, their contact with hearing students may be very stressful due to increased potential for social rejection and isolation (Dick, 1996; Leigh & Stinson, 1991; Stinson & Lane, 1994). Drinking and drug use may occur to reduce the stress and/or to fit in with hearing students (Dick, 1996). They may experience risk factors that are often associated with drug abuse, including school failure, low self-esteem, lack of purpose in school, child abuse and neglect, expectations of unemployment, and alienation from family (McCrone, 1994). Additional risk factors include: an external locus of control, the tendency to submit to peer pressure, dependence on the opinions of others, poor impulse control, poor communication skills, depression, immaturity, and intense feelings of isolation and inferiority (Steitler, 1984).

Communication barriers often exist in family systems with a deaf member because more than 90% of all parents of deaf children are hearing (Moores, 1996) and often can not easily communicate with their children (Freedman et al., 1975). Such communication barriers are often a valid predictor of substance abuse (Babst et al., 1976; Carter, 1983). Family members may have difficulty accepting that they have a deaf child and may be overprotective. They may also have difficulty learning American Sign Language (ASL). When the child is older, the family may also overlook classic symptoms of chemical dependency and attribute them to the fact that the person is deaf. Hearing parents and deaf children may identify with two different cultures, with the child acquiring cultural identity from Deaf peers (Greenberg, 1980, 1983; Meadow et al., 1981). Such misunderstanding may lead to limited contact between the deaf child and the family. The problem may be compounded if the child attends a residential school, thereby impeding the family's ability to recognize early warning signs of a substance abuse problem.

Caution must be used, however, as some of these risk factors may be relevant while others are not. For example, deaf people may experience stress and frustration in their lives similar to people with disabilities in areas of family life, interactions with nondisabled people, or discrimination in work or social situations. However, issues such as chronic pain and the use of potentially addictive medication for disability-related conditions have no relevance for most deaf people.

Very few studies have been conducted to identify the variables that predict drinking and drug use among deaf adolescents. Dick (1996) found certain school- and peer-related variables to be predictors of deaf and hard of hearing adolescents' use of alcohol and marijuana. Specifically, low grades in school were the most salient predictor of marijuana use. Additionally, deaf adolescents who attended mainstreamed schools and had high numbers of hearing friends at school reported higher rates of alcohol use than those with smaller numbers of hearing friends at school. On the other hand, marijuana use was found to be more frequent at one residential school for the deaf (Locke & Johnson, 1978). These findings are preliminary and should be retested because these have significant implications for school placement decisions (mainstreamed vs. residential), peer relationships (associating with hearing vs. deaf friends), and the impact of both variables on the use of alcohol and marijuana by deaf and hard of hearing adolescents.

Comprehensive substance abuse prevention programs were implemented in many public schools for hearing students beginning in the 1980s. Epidemiological studies of hearing adolescents have shown that the rates of alcohol and drug use have since decreased (Johnson & O'Malley, 1993; New Jersey Department of Law and Public Safety, 1993). In contrast, there are limited prevention programs within residential or mainstreamed school settings for deaf students. Few schools have a chemical health specialist who offers assessment, intervention, or counseling services appropriate for deaf students. Mainstream schools that may offer prevention programs often do not have materials modified for deaf students. In addition, prevention efforts through the media have been inaccessible to deaf people. Radio public service announcements miss this population entirely, and many TV announcements are still not captioned. Consequently, deaf people may not be well informed about the risks of using alcohol and other drugs, or about addiction, treatment, and various recovery programs such as Alcoholics Anonymous (AA).

Recognizing and understanding substance abuse within the deaf community lags significantly behind the hearing community. In most communities there are few, if any, deaf or hard of hearing counselors specializing in this area. The majority of deaf people socialize through their community Deaf clubs and organized activities like bowling, softball, basketball, and golf. All of these activities may also entail the use of alcohol, and people who abstain from drinking may be viewed negatively. A tremendous amount of peer pressure and constant availability of alcohol exists throughout the deaf community (Guthmann, 1996).

Yet Sabin (1988) indicates that only a few years ago, young deaf people still considered drunkenness to be a "sin" or a character weakness. Once a person's alcohol use becomes sabusive, he or she is ostracized by the community for having a character defect. The Deaf community's attempts to avoid the social stigma associated with an alcohol and other drug abuse make detecting problem use more difficult (Boros, 1981). These kinds of attitudes impede advocacy efforts for additional chemical dependency services for the deaf community.

More than 800,000 people from the general population are in alcohol and drug abuse treatment at any given time (Robert Wood Johnson Foundation, 1993). If deaf people represent one-half of one percent of the U.S. population, there should be 4,000 deaf and hard of hearing people in drug or alcohol treatment on any given day. There appears to be no evidence of this occurring, possibly because of barriers that limit access to such services. Further, when deaf people are able to access care, barriers within the treatment programs may result in reduced treatment effectiveness.

The first such barrier relates to concerns about stigma. Myers (1992) notes that deaf people who are chemically dependent fear discovery within the deaf community. Because its members have suffered various stereotypes such as "deaf and dumb," they may view substance abuse rigidly and harshly. Therefore, deaf individuals who are chemically dependent hide their problems from their friends; likewise, their deaf friends may ignore an obvious problem in order to protect the community. The idea of community confidentiality, which is seen as critical in recovery, is less cherished among deaf people than among hearing people, due to the "grapevine." Fear of gossip reinforces the addicted individual's tendency to keep his or her problem a secret (Dixon, 1987).

A second barrier relates to communication. In order for a deaf person to benefit from services, there must be a sensitivity to the cultural and communicative aspects of this group of people. The majority of deaf people placed in hearing residential programs for chemical dependency treatment recovery receive services contingent upon interpreter availability and funding. An interpreter may be provided on a limited basis for groups, individual counseling, or other specific activities. The absence of an interpreter precludes deaf patients from having equal access to staff and severely restricts interaction with other clients, which are a key part of the treatment process. The optimal placement for deaf individuals is with staff who are fluent in ASL and sensitive to Deaf culture (Guthmann, 1996). Good communication is essential in both the educational-therapeutic and peer-interaction dimensions of a well-designed program.

A third barrier is the limited availability of treatment and recovery resources for deaf people. There is a tendency for deaf clients to mistrust hearing professionals, and few personnel at treatment centers are knowledgeable about both the sociocultural aspects of deafness and chemical dependency (Lane, 1989). Within the population of recovering people, few deaf role models are available to support deaf people who are new to recovery. A common suggestion in recovery is to avoid old acquaintances and environments associated with chemical use. Most hearing people in recovery have a variety of choices of places to go and people to see. They can realistically develop new friendships in the recovering community. In contrast, many deaf people in recovery are isolated and have a limited circle of sober, deaf friends. A tendency to resume associations with friends who may still be using chemicals increases the risk of relapse.

In summary, much about the exact prevalence of substance abuse within the deaf community remains unresearched. Risk factors that contribute to the development of chemical dependency in deaf people are not well defined. What is known is that deaf people face many barriers in learning about and seeking help for substance abuse problems. The need for ongoing research and substance abuse service improvement is clear.

Assessment and Diagnosis of Chemical Dependency

For diagnostic purposes, most agencies that work with deaf and hearing individuals have developed their own assessment protocols, because there are no assessment tools specifically designed for use with deaf people. The following elements, consistent with the biopsychosocial perspective, should be included in a model assessment: "medical examination, alcohol and drug use history, psychosocial evaluation, psychiatric evaluation (where warranted), review of socioeconomic factors, review of eligibility for public health, welfare, employment, and educational assistance program" (Center for Substance Abuse Treatment, 1995, p. 66). The assessment process typically incorporates a structured interview model focusing on major life areas. These life areas may include school/employment, family, social, physical, legal, spiritual, financial, and the impact that substance use has on each area.

Generally, the primary differences in assessing deaf people as opposed to hearing people are related to communication issues. A common problem encountered when assessing deaf people involves the use of chemical dependency language not familiar to the deaf client. For example, a typical question may deal with the experience of a "blackout," which is a significant diagnostic feature of chemical dependency. ("Blackout" refers to a period of time in which you are awake and functioning but after which you have no recollection of what occurred.) In assessing a deaf client, the interviewer may need to explain the phenomenon.

The interviewer who fails to explain concepts or vocabulary risks compromising the validity of the assessment. Few clients will ask for an explanation or clarification of terminology, but instead will respond to the question without understanding it completely. Another common problem area is related to the use of a sign language interpreter. The addition of a third party changes the dynamics and, if the interpreter is not fully qualified, possibly the validity of the interview session. The limited availability of such interpreters is also a factor that continues to be a problem throughout the United States. There are very few interpreter training programs that focus on the specialized substance abuse vocabulary necessary for assessing deaf individuals.

Theoretical Models of Chemical Dependency and Treatment

Deaf individuals have been placed in treatment programs around the country that use the models described below. Yet the only research regarding the effectiveness of such models was a study by Guthmann (1996) on the disease model (also called the Minnesota model). The specific results of this study will be discussed later in this chapter. Keeping in mind that there is no universal treatment model that is effective for every deaf or hearing person, a review of some of the more commonly used treatment models offers some helpful background information.

Moral model: The moral model is the oldest in the field of chemical dependency. This model relies on the belief that chemical dependency results from an individual's moral weakness or lack of willpower. The substance abuser is someone with a weak, bad,or evil character. The goal of treatment is to increase one's willpower in resisting the evil temptation of drugs and/or alcohol.

Learning model: According to the learning model, the substance abuser is a person who learned "bad" habits through no fault of his or her own (Marlatt, 1985). The goal of treatment is to teach new behaviors and cognitions that allow old habits to be controlled by new learning (Brower et al., 1989). Whether the treatment goal is "controlled drinking" or abstinence, the emphasis is on self-control. In this model, a relapse is a loss of self-control resulting in the harmful use of substances.

Self-medication model: According to the self-medication model, chemical dependency occurs either as a symptom of another primary mental disorder or as a coping mechanism for deficits in a person's psychological structure or functioning. People abusing drugs and/or alcohol do so to alleviate the painful symptoms of another mental disorder such as depression or as a way to fill some kind of void left by deficiencies in the psychological structure or functioning (Khantzian, 1985). The goal of treatment, therefore, is to improve this mental functioning.

Social model: In the social model, chemical dependency is believed to result from environmental, cultural, social, peer, or family influences (Beigel & Ghertner, 1977); substance abuse is an outcome of external forces such as poverty, drug availability, peer pressure, and family dysfunction. Using this model, the goal of treatment is to improve the social functioning of substance abusers by either altering the social environment or the individual's coping responses to environmental stresses.

Dual diagnosis model: Dual diagnosis encompasses both a substance dependence diagnosis and an additional Axis I or psychiatric diagnosis (Robertson, 1992). The strategy in dual diagnosis treatment models depends on specific viewpoints but involves focusing on both disorders, with the understanding that substance use must first stop in order to diagnose and treat the coexisting mental disorder (Brower et al., 1989). One viewpoint assumes that the substance abuse problem is primary and the psychiatric disorder is caused by the use. A second perspective is represented by patients whose psychiatric disorders lead to alcohol or other drug use, or a "drugs as the cure" perspective. An example of this pattern would be a depressed individual who medicates the mood disorder with stimulants. A third perspective involves a simultaneous or parallel presentation that emerges because the question of which came first—drug abuse or psychiatric disorder—most often cannot be reliably answered (Batki, 1990). Education focuses on teaching patients about the connections between their use of mood altering chemicals and their mental illness (Batki, 1990).

Therapeutic community model: The therapeutic community model of treatment began in the U.S. in 1958 when Charles Dedrich, a recovering alcoholic, established a community called Synanon to help narcotics addicts who wanted to rehabilitate themselves

(Oakley & Ksir, 1987). The Synanon community was a close, self-contained, self-supportive, and highly structured social system. Although Synanon achieved breakthroughs in developing new therapeutic techniques, excesses and abuses of authority and power also occurred because of the emphasis on regimentation. From Synanon came a modern therapeutic community treatment system that provides comprehensive, holistic, individualized treatment delivered by interdisciplinary treatment teams. Recovering addicts still serve as primary counselors and case managers (Carroll, 1992).

Disease model (Minnesota model): According to Jellinek (1946, 1952, 1960), there are several different types of alcoholism, and some types of alcoholics progress irreversibly through a series of ever worsening stages unless there is a therapeutic intervention. The belief in loss of control over chemical use is an important part of the disease. The Minnesota model is a comprehensive, multiprofessional approach to the treatment of addictions; it is abstinence-oriented and based on the Twelve Step principles of Alcoholics Anonymous (AA)/Narcotics Anonymous (NA), with a strong spiritual emphasis. There are twelve elements commonly included in primary treatment programs following the Minnesota model. These elements include group therapy, lectures, recovering people as counselors, a multidisciplinary staff team, a therapeutic milieu, therapeutic work assignments, family counseling, the use of a Twelve Step program, daily reading (Twelve Step literature) groups, the presentation of a life history, attendance at AA/NA meetings, and the opportunity for recreation/physical activity. These elements are generally integrated into a structured daily routine. Local AA/NA groups provide the mainstay of the aftercare phase (Cook, 1998).

Application/Testing of a Treatment Model with Deaf People

At the Minnesota Program, deaf and hard of hearing individuals acquire information and skills to assist them in making different choices in their lives, including the choice of sobriety. The program is located in a major medical center that has a long history of providing chemical dependency treatment services to hearing people. Its reputation for accepting adults and adolescents who were not successful in traditional treatment settings enabled it to create unique approaches for difficult-to-serve populations, including structured schedules and highly visual materials. The program addresses communication and cultural needs, incorporates aspects of other models and approaches, and utilizes a structured, behavior-based system based on the Minnesota model.

Effective communication is the most essential tool in providing quality treatment services. Of utmost importance is the communication skill of staff members. The program's staff is fluent in ASL and other communication methods used by deaf people; they are also knowledgeable about and respectful of Deaf culture.

The Minnesota Program's highly trained staff provides a full range of treatment services. The treatment team includes a medical director, a program director, certified chemical dependency counselors, interpreters, an outreach counselor, a family counselor, a licensed teacher of the deaf, a chaplain, an occupational therapist, a recreational therapist, nurses, a case manager, unit assistants, and a secretary.

It is important to view substance abuse services as a continuum ranging from prevention/education through intervention, assessment, treatment, and aftercare. With regard to treatment, a variety of services should be available to deaf people, including detoxification, outpatient programming, residential treatment, and aftercare. In the case of the Minnesota Program, chemical dependency treatment means hospital-based residential treatment, one of several services in the continuum of substance abuse treatment. Recovery is most readily achieved and maintained when individuals are able to access all of the services they need. Professionals should understand the full continuum of services to appropriately coordinate services for and with individuals in need of treatment.

At the front end of the continuum is detoxification. Detoxification removes mood-altering chemicals from the individual's system, a process that may require close medical supervision. Often, the individual is referred from detoxification to further treatment.

Outpatient counseling offers a low-intensity treatment, consisting of an hour or more per week of services, and is most appropriate for individuals who have experienced less-serious consequences of chemical dependency. It should be used with individuals residing in safe, supportive living environments. By increasing the number of hours of treatment per week, intensive outpatient programs provide more service and are sometimes used as a cost-saving alternative to residential treatment.

Residential or inpatient treatment programs can be hospital- or nonhospital-based and can vary in the length of stay. Hospital-based programs generally provide more extensive medical services than programs housed outside of the hospital. Some residential programs offer a length of stay of up to two years and usually include educational, vocational, and community reentry components.

Following the completion of primary treatment, most individuals still need support from chemical dependency professionals through an aftercare program. Some individuals may be referred to a halfway house program, which provides a supportive living environment where a person can gain confidence in his or her recovery, practice independent living skills, and receive ongoing support and education. Support groups, relapse prevention groups, and counseling may also be a part of an individual's aftercare plan.

The last component of the continuum involves self-help support groups where people with similar problems come together to help one another. Twelve Step groups such as Alcoholics Anonymous serve as a resource for many individuals in recovery.

At the Minnesota Program, more than 75% of admitted clients have issues related to chemical dependency and additional psychiatric disorders. Although the focus of treatment is chemical dependency, a flexible treatment model is necessary for individuals who present with dual diagnoses. These patients too often receive inadequate separate treatment in both the mental health and addiction treatment settings. Simultaneous treatment or case management is especially important for deaf people, because it is difficult to find service providers familiar with mental health, chemical dependency, and deafness/hearing loss issues.

Similar to many chemical dependency programs for hearing people, the full range of treatment services includes comprehensive assessment, individual and group therapy, educational services, lectures, occupational therapy, recreational therapy, participation in Twelve Step groups, and aftercare planning. Some of the group therapy sessions focus on topics of particular relevance to addicts such as grief and spirituality. There are also separate men's and women's groups.

The program offers patients the opportunity to attend various Twelve Step meetings within the hospital and in the community. Some of these meetings consist of all deaf members, and others are attended primarily by hearing people and are made accessible to deaf people with interpreters. The Disease/Minnesota model is modified to respect and accommodate the patients' linguistic and cultural needs. For example, patients are encouraged to use drawing, role playing, and signed communication in place of the written assignments normally used to complete assignments focusing on the Twelve Steps. Written materials traditionally used in residential treatment programs for hearing people are modified and video materials are presented with sign language, voice, and captions. Furthermore, TTYs, assistive listening devices, and telecaption decoders are examples of equipment provided, so that patients can make the most of their time in the program.

The Twelve Steps are an integral component of the treatment approach in this program, which teaches the steps so that they are meaningful to deaf individuals. For example, clients may be asked to "draw pictures of unmanageable." Although not grammatically correct, the term is both written and signed this way because it will be more understandable (more ASL). This approach is used throughout the program.

Clients use videotapes of the Twelve Steps communicated in ASL (with voice and captions) along with a workbook. With these materials and counseling sessions, clients come to recognize that they are powerless over alcohol and/or other drugs and that their drug use has caused their lives to become unmanageable. Clients explore for themselves what the impact of that use has been. Upon reaching an understanding of the concepts of powerlessness and unmanageability, clients are assisted in seeing that there is hope for changing their lives, and that there are resources for assisting them in doing so.

The Twelve Step approach helps to prepare clients to access important sources of support, Alcoholics Anonymous and other Twelve Step meetings. Viewing each client as unique and striving to meet treatment needs in an individualized, therapeutic manner is emphasized, with attention given to client diversity with respect to ethnic background, education, socialization, cultural identity, family history, and mental health status. In addition, staff members recognize individual variation in clients' degrees of hearing loss, level of functioning, communication preferences, and drug use experiences.

The Minnesota Program's Treatment Phases

PHASE 1: EVALUATION/ASSESSMENT

The Minnesota Program provides treatment in three phases. Phase 1 is the evaluation/assessment phase, using various assessments to gain an understanding of the client and his or her use of mood altering chemicals. The assessments include data on the client's medical background, a social history, a chemical use history, a clinical assessment, and a communication assessment. The communication assessment profiles a client's communication preferences and needs, and facilitates the provision of treatment and support using the client's preferred method of communication.

During Phase 1, clients complete a drug chart assignment. Table 1 explains the rationale and value behind each of the tasks included in the Drug Chart. For the assignment, they use drawings to detail (a) the different drugs they have used, (b) a description of their last use, and (c) examples of consequences of their drug use on major life areas such as physical health, legal, family, social, work/school, and financial. (A sample drug chart assignment appears in appendix 1.) Using drawings removes the barrier the English language creates for many deaf people. It also encourages clients to be in touch with their experiences and, as a result, be more in touch with the feelings connected to those experiences.

Table 1. Drug Chart Tasks and Their Purpose

Task	Outcome
Drugs used/last time used	Client recognizes the extent (in time and quantity) of his or her use of mood altering chemicals.
Consequences	Client recognizes the extent to which the use of chemicals has negatively impacted his or her life. Understanding the relationship between use and consequences is especially valuable.
Total Assignment	Client evaluates the evidence—or lack of evidence—for a diagnosis of chemical dependency and gains a more realistic perspective of his or her use.

When the client completes the drug chart assignment, he or she presents the work in a group of peers who, along with staff, provide feedback to the client. Upon completion of Phase 1, appropriate clients (those diagnosed as chemically dependent using DSM-IV criteria) move to Phase 2.

PHASE 2: PRIMARY TREATMENT

During the primary treatment phase, clients receive education about the Twelve Steps and complete step-related assignments. Ideally, clients will complete the first five steps while in primary treatment. Clients begin attending Twelve Step meetings during this phase and continue doing so throughout the entire program.

Integrating the concepts behind the Twelve Steps into the recovery process is more important than the number of steps completed. The typical step work assignments for hearing people are modified to meet the needs of the clients at the Minnesota Program. For example, clients draw pictures of their experiences related to particular steps that they present in therapeutic groups with staff and peers. Most often, clients present their work using ASL. Task rationale for various portions of step assignments help to identify the objectives of each assignment and help to determine if the client has met the objective.

Step One

During Step One a client confronts his or her denial. Table 2 shows the components of a Step One assignment. Clients give examples of how their use of alcohol or other drugs has hurt others and themselves to help personalize the powerlessness and unmanageability of their own addiction. Following the Alcoholics Anonymous philosophy, clients are asked to admit that drugs/alcohol are more powerful than they are, and that they cannot manage their lives any more. This admission helps to establish a foundation on which to build a sober life through the subsequent steps.

After the client presents the work, peer feedback helps the client develop a sense that he or she is not alone, that others have had similar experiences. The client's work is accepted when he or she demonstrates an understanding of the concepts of unmanageability, powerlessness, and the effects of these on self and others. For clients who

Table 2. Components of a Step One Assignment

Task	Outcome
Pictures of unmanageable	Client identifies aspects of his or her life that are unmanageable related to the use of alcohol and other drugs.
Pictures of powerlessness	Client identifies examples of loss of control over alcohol and other drug use.
Pictures of feelings (related to powerlessness and unmanageable)	Client explores and expresses feelings related to the powerlessness and unmanageability in his or her life.
Pictures of hurting self and others	Client identifies how his or her use has hurt or caused dysfunction with self and others. Client recognizes impact of his or her use.

have not completely understood the concepts, additional assignment(s) may be given to help supply the missing information or understanding. The Step One assignments are related to the tasks specified in table 1. Typical modifications of this assignment would involve breaking the assignment down into smaller parts, limiting the scope of the assignment to a period of relapse, or expecting fewer examples in each task.

Step Two

Step Two assignments (as well as assignments for the subsequent steps) tend to be more individualized. The goal is to allow clients to develop a sense of hope. The staff team develops a task for each client, who later present their assignments in group. (A sample assignment appears in appendix 2; a full list of potential tasks, for each of the steps, can be found in *Clinical Approaches: A Model for Treating Chemically Dependent Deaf and Hard of Hearing Individuals,* from the Minnesota Chemical Dependency Program for Deaf and Hard of Hearing Individuals, 1994.) The assignment helps the clients realize that they are not alone, that there is a power to sustain them in recovery. Because many clients often have had negative or confusing experiences with the concepts of God and religion, they are encouraged in Step Two to identify their own Higher Power as someone or something—not necessarily God—which they believe to be greater than themselves. Many clients identify their sponsors or an AA/NA group as their Higher Power. Asking for and accepting help are vital parts of acknowledging and accepting a Higher Power. Task outlines for this step are shown in table 3.

Step Three

As in the previous stage, Step Three is individualized and may be comprised of a number of tasks. In this step, the emphasis is on action—safe places the clients can go for sober support, people who can help the client stay sober, and so on. At the same time, clients are asked to begin developing their understanding of a Higher Power. The program emphasizes the importance of spirituality, and the people and places that help the individual feel safe and supported. Examples of this may be an AA meeting, sober friends, or a natural environment. Other people may receive support from their belief

Table 3. Components of a Step Two Assignment

Task	Outcomes
Identifying people who can help, places that feel safe, times when help is needed, and places and people to avoid sobriety.	Client recognizes and utilizes sources of support to stay sober and identify those people and places which threaten their ongoing recovery.
Picture of how it feels to ask for help or keep a feelings journal.	Client recognizes and accepts feelings associated with asking for help.
Identifying people the client can trust and places for support.	Client identifies people and places that can be trusted to help support sobriety.

in God. The Serenity Prayer closes each therapeutic group session. Clients use the Serenity Prayer as a tool for coping with everyday stresses of living as well as with efforts to maintain sobriety.

The Serenity Prayer

God, grant me the serenity
to accept the things I cannot change,
the courage to change the things I can,
and the wisdom to know the difference.

While chemical dependency is the primary area of concern, additional problem areas, such as ineffective coping skills and grief/loss issues, receive attention within group and individual counseling. Clients attend educational lectures on health concerns associated with substance abuse. Topics include HIV/AIDS, sexually transmitted diseases, physical effects of mood altering chemicals, birth control, and various types of abuse. Medical testing and consultation is available to all clients.

Clients have a family week experience whenever possible. Often, family members are not fluent in sign language, so through an interpreter the family explores a variety of issues, often for the first time. Clients disclose information about their use and behaviors to family members. Family members share how their loved one's chemical use has impacted them. This sharing of experiences and information happens in the context of family groups where both patients and family members receive support and encouragement. Very often, communication issues also emerge during family week, with feelings of disappointment, frustration, and confusion on the part of all family members. Lectures to families offer help in understanding issues connected with having a family member who is chemically dependent. If family members are unable to attend, materials and phone contact with staff is available. An educational component helps school-aged clients maintain their schooling while in treatment.

The Minnesota Program uses a behavioral approach to therapy that includes education and support designed to help individuals identify and correct self-defeating behaviors. Levels of intervention for negative behaviors are specific to the client's behavior and are modified if the behavior escalates. Clients have the opportunity to learn, practice, and integrate skills developed in treatment. An initial intervention would typically

Table 4. Components of a Step Three Assignment

Task	Outcomes
Explaining/describing Higher Power	Client begins to understand who/what his or her Higher Power is.
Explaining "my will" and my Higher Power's will	Client begins to differentiate between wants and needs; between their own will and the will of their Higher Power.
Explaining communication with Higher Power	Client discovers how to seek help from their Higher Power.

be a one-to-one discussion with the counselor, and often this helps the client recognize and change the behavior. If the behavior continues to be inappropriate or negatively affects the treatment process, behavior contracts may be an appropriate second-level intervention. These contracts cover incidents such as unit rules violations, arguing about staff directives, failure to complete work on time, failure to focus on treatment, or focusing on the needs or issues of other patients. Behavior contracts are not punishment and should specify the behaviors for which the clients are being given the contract, as well as the changes that are expected.

Another behavior management technique is the probation contract, which may help a client recognize behaviors that threaten the success or quality of the treatment experience. Probation contracts are used as a follow-up to a behavior contract in the event that the client does not respond positively or is openly defiant to the terms of a behavior contract. Probation contracts again specify expected changes in the client's behavior and may also include an assignment that helps the client identify and change his or her behavior. Failure to adhere to the probation contract may result in the client being asked to leave the program.

PHASE 3: EXTENDED CARE/AFTERCARE

Phase 3 includes an optional extended care/aftercare program for those clients who need additional support and aftercare in transitioning back into the community. Minnesota residents can receive individual and group aftercare sessions, and work with local resources such as Twelve Step meetings, a Relapse Prevention group, therapists fluent in ASL, an interpreter referral center, vocational assistance, halfway houses, sober houses, and other sources of assistance and support. Networking with other service providers both locally and nationally is an important aftercare activity.

Aftercare for clients residing in states other than Minnesota continues to be a challenge. Staff members attempt to set up a comprehensive aftercare program in the client's home area, offering education and support to the area service providers. However, Twelve Step meetings that currently provide interpreters are minimal in most major metropolitan areas, and practically nonexistent in rural communities. Shortages of professionals trained to work in this discipline exist on a national basis. Developing an aftercare plan for out-of-state clients might be compared to putting together a puzzle—sometimes many of the pieces are missing. In this aftercare phase, Steps Six through Twelve are discussed, and clients are given assignments similar to the format described previously in this section.

Relapse prevention is addressed in primary treatment or in later stages such as aftercare/extended care. It is important to understand that relapse is a process of changing behaviors that culminates in the return to using mood altering chemicals. Clients are offered information about warning signs of relapse in terms of feelings, behaviors, or environment, and are taught to respond to these signs in ways that are likely to support ongoing sobriety. The vignette in the following section provides an example of how the clinical approaches are applied. It depicts a client who entered treatment with an additional diagnosis of major depressive disorder (DSM-IV, 1994), a depressed mood or loss of interest or pleasure in all or almost all activities and associated symptoms for at least two weeks. It is subclassified to indicate single or recurrent episodes as well as the current state of the disturbance.

CASE STUDY: JERRY

Background Information

Jerry is a thirty-five-year-old male born deaf with hearing parents and a deaf sister.[1] He was self-referred to treatment. He had one previous treatment experience with hearing people that he reports as unsuccessful. Jerry attended an oral school from age two to age thirteen. He attended a residential school for the deaf but quit at age sixteen. His parents divorced when he was two years old and his mother has remarried five times. He was raised by his alcoholic father who physically abused and cruelly treated him. He suffered sexual abuse from an undisclosed perpetrator. The family has experienced ongoing turmoil for a number of years, and Jerry currently has contact only with his deaf sister.

Jerry reports that his first sexual experience and use of alcohol occurred at age twelve. His chemical use included cocaine (intravenous and sniffing), crack, marijuana, codeine, PCP, mushrooms, acid, speed, IV amphetamines, Valium, Xanax, Ativan, quaaludes, and painkillers. His drug of choice is alcohol. He has been prostituting for drugs since age sixteen. Jerry has been homeless and transient for the past two years, moving from the streets to his friends' or sister's homes.

Assessment

In addition to chemical dependency, Jerry displays the following indications for a diagnosis of depression: depressed mood, significant weight loss, flashbacks, diminished interest in almost all activities, insomnia and disrupted sleep, flat affect, fatigue, loss of energy, and suicidal thoughts.

Counseling Strategies

Upon Jerry's arrival, staff assessed him for current suicidal ideation and staff began to monitor him for signs of depression. It became evident early in his treatment that Jerry suffered from major depression. After consulting with the program medical director, a decision was made for a trial period of antidepressant medication. Jerry was

1. The client represents elements of actual clients treated at the program. Client names and identifying information have been changed to protect privacy.

provided counseling and education to help him understand the therapeutic implications of a trial period on medication, with emphasis placed on pharmacological effects of the medication, including an explanation of the time necessary for the medication to reach a therapeutic blood level. He was offered further education related to the difference between antidepressant medication and the chemicals he had been abusing. Jerry responded well to this information and appeared to clearly understand the purpose of taking medication.

Staff educated Jerry about depression and how it could impact his day-to-day living, including his chemical dependency treatment. They encouraged him to seek out one-to-one staff time to discuss issues related to his depression, but it was emphasized that chemical dependency was the primary focus of his treatment.

Early in the treatment process, staff provided Jerry with clinical tasks designed to assist him in the process of gaining insight into his chemical dependency and allowing him to experience small successes. Assignments were short and clear to accommodate his short attention span. As Jerry began to experience multiple successes, he seemed to gain a degree of confidence in himself and his ability to do chemical dependency treatment work. As he responded, the tasks assigned became increasingly complex. This process continued developing throughout his treatment stay. Providing case management was vital.

Concurrently matching Jerry's therapeutic tasks while monitoring his depressive symptoms seemed to effectively meet his special needs. Jerry began to show signs of improvement and became more responsive to all aspects of his chemical dependency treatment experience. This cumulative change could be attributed to the combination of medication, appropriate treatment approaches, counseling, and education.

Many depressed individuals are survivors of abuse and Jerry was no exception. Jerry was able to successfully enter into therapeutic relationships with several staff members. These relationships enabled him to process some abuse-related issues during his work on Step Four. Ongoing recovery, particularly for a dually diagnosed client, may depend on the opportunity to process these issues in what is perceived as a safe place. There were times when Jerry became overwhelmed with emotions or feelings of depression. At these times he seemed willing to seek out appropriate peer and staff support.

Step Work Approaches

During his treatment stay, Jerry was able to complete Steps One through Five. The assignments he completed included:

1. A standard drug chart.
2. A Step One assignment. Jerry was asked to provide a minimum number of examples of unmanageability and powerlessness, so as not to exacerbate his depression.
3. A Step Two assignment. In addition to the tasks discussed earlier for this step, Jerry identified ways he can take care of himself and drew a picture of how he would look a year from now if he stayed sober.
4. Two additional Step Two assignments. First, he had to identify fifteen things he liked about himself. He then had to identify twenty skills he has and how they can help him stay sober.

5. A Step Three Assignment. After identifying his Higher Power, he explained ways he gets answers from his Higher Power and twenty things his Higher Power wants for him.

Because Jerry had a history of traumatic stressors in the form of abuse, there was discussion about whether Step Four (a moral inventory) would further traumatize him. A decision was made to go ahead with a modified inventory, and to ask him to confine the inventory to his dependency. Jerry subsequently completed that assignment as well as a Step Five assignment (sharing of Step Four work).

After completing treatment, Jerry was referred to a halfway house program where he now resides and receives aftercare services, including counseling. It was also recommended that he attend a minimum of three AA/NA meetings per week. At last contact with the program, Jerry was still sober.

Treatment Effectiveness and Outcome Data

Guthmann (1996) studied the treatment outcomes of 100 individuals who completed treatment at the Minnesota Program to determine which demographic, attitudinal, and other background variables had the greatest impact upon treatment outcomes. The two outcome variables assessed in this research were general improvement (defined as the client's having fewer problems in all life areas, including physical health) and abstinence from alcohol and other drugs. Each client who successfully completed treatment filled out a pre/post treatment survey. The surveys recorded demographic information; attitudinal, behavioral, and knowledge changes that occurred during treatment; and client satisfaction. A follow-up interview between staff and former clients took place after discharge. The study assessed if positive changes occurred within clients one, three, six, or twelve months after discharge in the following life areas: health/mental health, vocational/educational, functional living, or ability to reduce or stop the use of alcohol/drugs.

The study found that the variables having the greatest positive impact on general improvement and the ability to maintain abstinence were AA/NA attendance, the ability to talk with family about sobriety, and being employed. In essence, "When deaf and hard of hearing individuals receive the same treatment as hearing people, outcomes appear to be the same and aftercare needs are similar and equally important" (Guthmann, 1996, p.15).

Recommendations for Effective Treatment

Effective substance abuse treatment services for deaf people should use the following recommendations as guidelines.

1. *Education and prevention services.* Comprehensive education and prevention services should be provided to deaf persons of all ages, particularly within residential and mainstreamed schools that need to provide alcohol and drug programs comparable to those provided to hearing students.

2. *Accessible language.* Efforts should be made to develop accessible assessment procedures for deaf individuals. Ideally, all assessment of deaf persons should be administered by a substance abuse counselor who is fluent in ASL. If a counselor who is fluent

in sign language is not available, a substance abuse counselor and a qualified interpreter who has training in substance abuse vocabulary and concepts should be used.

3. *Cooperation between state and regional programs.* Cooperative efforts to support regional residential programs combined with local community support for aftercare services are imperative. The cost of providing comprehensive services to deaf individuals in every state is prohibitive.

4. *Improvement of aftercare services.* There is a need to establish additional services related to aftercare. Overall, aftercare continues to be one of the greatest obstacles in assisting clients to maintain sobriety and improve their quality of life. The biggest gap seems to be related to accessing safe and sober living environments upon the completion of residential treatment. Deaf individuals are limited in the availability of safe communities because of diverse communication needs. Most states have gaps in their continuum of services.

5. *Accessible self-help groups.* There is a national need for additional accessible self-help groups such as AA/NA/Alanon, CA, etc. Without these, deaf individuals will not be aware of the positive support and results they may access through Twelve Step meetings. How can counselors and service providers in this field tell their deaf clients they need to attend Twelve Step meetings to stay sober when there are no accessible meetings in the client's area?

6. *Recognition and prevention of deafness-related enabling.* Professionals, caregivers, family members and friends when trying to ease their own pain regarding the client's deafness, often enable the disabled individual to continue his or her chemical dependency. Family, friends and other concerned persons encourage the use of alcohol or drugs believing that this will help the person who is disabled to socialize, obtain happiness or satisfaction, and perhaps even feel equal to nondisabled people (Schaschl and Straw, 1989). These feelings and behaviors displayed by family members and friends must be dealt with if the individual is to maintain sobriety. Hence, they must be included in the continuum of services.

7. *Vocational rehabilitation.* Vocational rehabilitation must be a strong component of treatment and aftercare. Guthmann (1996) indicated that there is a strong relationship between abstinence and employment. This would seem to support the need for emphasis on career exploration by individuals while in treatment and the linkage of vocational rehabilitation services. The vocational rehabilitation (VR) counselor should be responsible for assessing the individual's potential related to employment while in treatment. At the time of discharge, the VR counselor should assist local clients with job training and placement, and assist out-of-state clients by working with their home communities. Counselors providing substance abuse services should spend time on strategies related to employment and job readiness skills.

8. *Emphasis on basic employment skills.* A curriculum must be developed to focus on the importance of employment and teaches some basic skills related to how to seek, access, and retain employment. Many individuals who enter treatment are on some kind of public assistance and are not employed. As the demographic data indicates, 36% of the subjects admitted to treatment were on some kind of public assistance and were not gainfully employed or in school (Guthmann, 1996). This is a societal issue that needs to be addressed since there is little, if any, incentive for deaf people on public assistance to get off of it. In some situations, parents and others before them were on public assistance and it may be a cultural issue. All of this makes the preparation of the curriculum difficult but very important.

9. *Professional training programs.* Training programs need to be established for all service providers who are working with deaf individuals. This training should focus on provision of knowledge about the unique considerations related to this population as well as chemical dependency assessment, how to recognize signs and symptoms of use/abuse, prevention strategies, clinical issues, and the referral process and aftercare options.

10. *Creative and alternative funding sources.* Additional funding through grants and other methods for outpatient treatment, inpatient treatment, prevention services, aftercare, and sober living environments should be sought. With today's economy, organizations need to be innovative and creative in finding ways to fund programs for specialized populations.

11. *Research.* Additional research, including more longitudinal studies, is critical in the area of substance abuse and deafness. A national data base should be established related to demographic and other appropriate research involving substance abuse and deafness. Longitudinal studies offer reassurances of reliability and information on long-term results.

12. *Encouragement of deaf people to enter the field.* Provide opportunities for the training and employment of deaf persons in the substance abuse field. This may foster greater communication and provide positive role models for individuals in treatment. The use of deaf counselors helps alleviate cultural barriers often present in other settings. Individuals who are deaf and also in recovery can also provide additional clinical insight.

Conclusion

The number of facilities emerging to meet the needs of deaf substance abusers is increasing, and existing resources are gradually attempting to make their services accessible. The integration of community models and public health concepts offers promise in addressing problems of addiction. Appropriate training is imperative for service delivery models that accommodate deaf substance abusers.

Ideally, individuals who successfully complete an alcohol/drug treatment program should be able to return to the environment in which they lived before entering the program. However, that environment must include accessible Twelve Step meetings; a sober living option; family and friend support; and professionals trained to work on aftercare issues. When deaf individuals receive the same treatment as hearing people, outcomes appear to be the same. We cannot fairly measure the risk factors for substance abuse until deaf and hard of hearing individuals receive the same consideration as hearing people in regard to prevention, intervention, accessible treatment, and adequate aftercare.

References

Akers, R. L., Krohn, M. D., Lanza-Kaduce, L., & Radosevich, M. (1979). Social learning and deviant behavior: A specific test of a general theory. *American Sociological Review, 44*, 636–655.

Alcoholics Anonymous. (1952). *Twelve steps and twelve traditions.* New York: A. A. World Services. Available: alcoholics-anonymous.org/em24doc6.html.

American Psychiatric Association. (1994). *Diagnostic and statistical manual of mental disorders* (4th ed.). Washington, DC: American Psychiatric Association.

Babst, D., Miran, J., & Koval, M. (1976). The relationship between friends' marijuana use, family cohesion, school interest and drug abuse. *Alcohol Health and Research World, 91,* 23–41.

Batki, S. L. (1990). Drug abuse, psychiatric disorders, and AIDS: Dual and triple diagnosis. *Addiction Medicine, 152,* 547–552.

Beigel, A., & Ghertner, S. (1977). Toward a social model: An assessment of social factors which influence problem drinking and its treatment. In B. Kissin & H. Begleiter (Eds.), *The biology of alcoholism: Treatment and rehabilitation of the chronic alcoholic* (vol. 5, pp. 197–233). New York: Plenum Press.

Boros, A. (1983). Alcoholism and deaf people. *Gallaudet Today, 3* (13), 7–11.

Brower, K. J., Blow, F. C., & Beresford. T. P. (1989). Treatment implications of chemical dependency models: An integrative approach. *Journal of Substance Abuse Treatment, 6,* 147–157.

Buss, A., & Cramer, C. (1989). *Incidence of alcohol use by people with disabilities: A Wisconsin survey of persons with a disability.* Madison, WI: Office of Persons with Disabilities.

Carter, D. (1983, 24 October). Why do kids use drugs and alcohol, and how do we help them stop? *PTA Today,* 15–18.

Carroll, J. F. X. (1992). The evolving American therapeutic community. *Alcoholism Treatment Quarterly, 9,* 175–181.

Center for Substance Abuse Treatment (CSAT). (1995). *Treatment improvement protocol: The role and current status of patient placement criteria in the treatment of substance use disorders.* Rockville, MD: U.S. Department of Health and Human Services.

Cook, C. C. H. (1988). The Minnesota Model in the management of drug and alcohol and drug dependency: Miracle, method or myth? *British Journal of Addiction, 83,* 625–634.

DeMiranda, F., & Cherry, L. (1989). California responds: Changing treatment systems through advocacy for the disabled. *Alcohol Health and Research World, 13* (2), 154–157.

Dick, J. (1996). Signing for a high: A study of alcohol and drug use by deaf and hard of hearing adolescents. Ed.D. dissertation, Rutgers University, New Brunswick, NJ. *Dissertation Abstracts International, 57* (6A), 2675.

Dixon, T. L. (1987, January/February). Addiction among the hearing impaired. *E.A.P. Digest,* 41–44.

El-Guebaly, N. (1990). Substance abuse and mental disorders: The dual diagnosis concept. *Canadian Journal of Psychiatry, 35,* 261–267.

Elliot, D. S., Huizinga, D., & Ageton, S. S. (1985). *Explaining delinquency and drug use.* Beverly Hills, CA: Sage Publications.

Ferrell, R., & George, J. (1984). One community's response to alcohol problems among the deaf community. *Journal of Rehabilitation of the Deaf, 18* (2), 15–18.

Freedman, R., Malkin, S., & Hastings, J. (1975). Psychosocial problems of deaf children and their families: A comparative study. *American Annals of the Deaf, 120,* 392–405.

Gorski, R. (1980). Drug abuse and disabled people: A hidden problem. *Disabled USA, 4* (2), 8–12.

Greenberg, M. (1980). Social interaction between deaf preschoolers and their mothers: The effects of communication method and communication competence. *Developmental Psychology, 16,* 465–474.

———. (1983). Family stress and child competence: The effects of early intervention for families with deaf infants. *American Annals of the Deaf, 128,* 407–417.

Guthmann, D. (1996). An analysis of variables that impact treatment outcomes of chemically dependent deaf and hard of hearing individuals. Ph.D. dissertation, University of Minnesota. *Dissertations Abstracts International, 56* (7A), 2638.

Harris, A. E. (1978). The development of the deaf individual and the deaf community. In L. S. Liben (Ed.), *Deaf children: Developmental perspectives* (pp. 217–233). New York: Academic Press.

Heinemann, A., Keen, M., Donohue, R., & Schnoll, S. (1988). Alcohol use by persons with recent spinal cord injury. *Archives of Physical Medicine and Rehabilitation, 69,* 619–624.

Jaquith, S. M. (1981). Adolescent marijuana and alcohol use: An empirical test of differential association theory. *Criminology, 19,* 271–280.

Jellinek, E. M. (1946). Phases in the drinking history of alcoholics. *Quarterly Journal of Studies on Alcohol, 7,* 1–88.

———. (1952). Current notes: Phases of alcohol addiction. *Quarterly Journal of Studies on Alcohol, 13,* 673–684.

———. (1960). *The disease concept of alcoholism.* New Haven, CT. United Printing Services, Inc.

Jessor, R. (1987). Problem-behavior theory, psychosocial development, and adolescent problem drinking. *British Journal of Addiction, 82,* 331–342.

Jessor, R., & Jessor, S. L. (1984). Adolescence to young adulthood: A twelve-year prospective study of problem behavior and psychosocial development. In S. A. Mednick, M. Harway, and D. M. Finello (Eds.), *Handbook of longitudinal research volume two: Teenage and adult cohorts* (pp. 34–61). New York: Praeger Publishers.

Johnston, L., O'Malley, P., & Bachman, J. (1985). *Use of licit and illicit drugs by America's high school students, 1975–1984.* Rockville, MD: National Institute on Drug Abuse.

———. (1991). *Drug abuse among American high school seniors, college students, and young adults, 1975–1990: vol. 1, high school seniors.* DHHS Publication No. (ADM) 91-1813. Washington, DC: U. S. Department of Health and Human Services.

Kandel, D. B., Kessler, R. C., & Margulies, R. Z. (1978). Antecedents of adolescent initiation into stages of drug use: A developmental analysis. *Journal of Youth and Adolescence, 7,* 13–40.

Kaplan, H. B., Martin, S. S., & Robbins, C. (1984). Pathways to adolescent drug use: Self-derogation, peer influence, weakening of social controls, and early substance use. *Journal of Health and Social Behavior, 25,* 270–289.

Kapp, D. L., Clark, K., Jones, J., & Owens, P. (1984). Drug and alcohol prevention/education with deaf adolescents: A preventative guidance and counseling program. In G. B. Anderson & D. Watson (Eds.), *The habilitation and rehabilitation of deaf adolescents* (pp. 177–186). Little Rock, AR: University of Arkansas Rehabilitation Research and Training Center on Deafness and Hearing Impairment.

Kearns, G. (1989, April). A community of underserved alcoholics. *Alcohol Health and Research World, 13* (2), 27.

Khantzian, E. J. (1985). The self-medication hypothesis of addictive disorders: Focus on heroin and cocaine dependence. *American Journal of Psychiatry, 142,* 1259–1264.

Lane, K. E. (1989). Substance abuse among the deaf population: An overview of current strategies, programs, and barriers to recovery. *Journal of American Deafness and Rehabilitation Association, 2* (4), 79–85.

Leigh, I. W., & Stinson, M. S. (1991). Social environment, self-perceptions, and identity of hearing impaired adolescents. *Volta Review, 93,* 7–22.

Locke, R., & Johnson, S. (1978). A descriptive study of drug use among the hearing impaired in a senior high school for the hearing impaired. In A. J. Schector (Ed.), *Drug dependence and alcoholism* (vol. 2) (pp. 833–841). New York: Plenum Press.

Marlatt, G. A. (1985). Relapse prevention: Theoretical rationale and overview of the model. In G. A. Marlatt & J. R. Gordon (Eds.), *Relapse prevention* (pp. 3–70). New York: Guilford Press.

Massey, J. L., & Krohn, M. D. (1986). A longitudinal study of an integrated social process model of deviant behavior. *Social Forces, 65,* 106–134.

McConnell, J.V. (1986). *Understanding human behavior.* Ann Arbor, MI: The University of Michigan and Holt, Rinehart and Winston.

McCrone, W. (1982). Serving the deaf substance abuser. *Journal of Psychoactive Drugs, 14* (3), 199–203.

———. (1994). A two-year report card on Title I of the Americans with Disabilities Act: Implications for rehabilitation counseling with deaf people. *Journal of American Deafness and Rehabilitation Association, 28* (2), 1–20.

Meadow, K. P., Greenberg, M. T., Erting, C., & Carmichael, H. (1981). Interactions with deaf mothers and deaf preschool children: Comparisons with three other groups of deaf and hearing dyads. *American Annals of the Deaf, 126* (4), 454–468.

Minnesota Chemical Dependency Program for Deaf and Hard of Hearing Individuals. (1994). *Clinical approaches: A model for treating chemically dependent deaf and hard of hearing individuals.* Minneapolis: Deacones Press.

Moores, D. F. (1996). *Educating the deaf: Psychology, principles, and practices* (4th ed). Boston: Houghton Mifflin.

Myers, L. R. (1992). Oppression and identity: The shame addiction connection. In *Proceedings of The Next Step: A national conference focusing on issues related to substance abuse in the deaf and hard of hearing population* (pp. 117–126). Washington, DC: Gallaudet University, College for Continuing Education.

New Jersey Department of Law and Public Safety. (1993). *Drug and alcohol use among New Jersey high school students.* Trenton, NJ: Department of Law and Public Safety.

Oakley, R., & Ksir, C. (1987). *Drugs, society, and human behavior.* St. Louis: Times Mirror/Mosby College Publishing.

Pollard, R.Q. (1992). Cross-cultural ethics in the conduct of deafness research. *Rehabilitation Psychology, 37,* 87–101.

Rasmussen, G., & DeBoer, R. (1980/81, Winter). Alcohol and drug use among clients at a residential vocational rehabilitation facility. *Alcohol and Health Research World, 8* (2), 48–56.

Robert Wood Johnson Foundation. (1993). *Substance abuse: The nations' number one health problem.* Princeton, NJ: Brandeis University Institute for Health Policy.

Robertson, E. C., Jr. (1992). The challenge of dual diagnosis. *Journal of Health Care for the Poor and Underserved, 3,* 198–207.

Sabin, M. C. (1988). Responses of deaf high school students to an "attitudes toward alcohol" scale: A national survey. *American Annals of the Deaf, 133* (3), 199–203.

Schaschl, S., & Straw, D. (1989). Results of a model intervention program for physically impaired persons. *Alcohol Health and Research World, 13,* 150–153.

Sparadeo, F., & Gill, D. (1989). Effect of prior alcohol use on head injury recovery. *Journal of Head Trauma Rehabilitation, 4* (1), 75–82.

Steitler, K. A. (1984). Substance abuse and the deaf adolescent. In G. B. Anderson & D. Watson (Eds.), *The habilitation and rehabilitation of deaf adolescents* (pp. 125–146). Little Rock, AR: University of Arkansas Rehabilitation Research and Training Center on Deafness and Hearing Impairment.

Stewart, L. (1991). Adolescents and prevention: Reaching out and making a difference in a residential and mainstream setting. In F. White, W. McCrone, & C. Trotter (Eds.), *Proceedings of the Department of Counseling's Drug Free Schools and Communities National Training Institute* (pp. 31–37). Washington, DC: Gallaudet University, Department of Counseling.

Stinson, M., & Lane, H. (1994). The potential impact on deaf students of the full inclusion movement. In R. C. Johnson & O. P. Cohen (Eds.), *Implications and complications for deaf students of the full inclusion movement* (pp. 31–40). Washington, DC: Gallaudet Research Institute.

U.S. Department of Justice Bureau of Justice Statistics. (1992). *Drugs, crime, and the justice system.* Washington, DC: U. S. Government Printing Office.

White, H. R., Johnson, V., & Horwitz, A. (1986). An application of three deviance theories to adolescent substance use. *The International Journal of the Addictions, 21,* 347–366.

Williams, D., & Wilkins, J. (1992). Substance abuse and psychiatric disorders. *The Journal of Nervous and Mental Disease, 180* (4), 251–257.

Zangara, M. (1990). Deaf aftercare: Working toward a common goal. In *Proceedings of the Substance Abuse and Recovery Conference: Empowerment of deaf persons* (pp. 144–147). Washington, DC: Gallaudet University, College for Continuing Education.

Appendix 1

DRUG CHART SAMPLE

Do all work in the order written. Get staff to sign before doing the next part.
Drug chart is due on:
Staff initials/Date:

1. Name all drugs you have used.
2. Tell the last time you used. What? When? How much?
3. When I am high or drunk, bad things happen. These things are called consequences.
   Draw seven pictures of body consequences.
   Draw seven pictures of money consequences.
   Draw seven pictures of family consequences.
   Draw seven pictures of legal consequences.
   Draw seven pictures of job/school consequences.
   Draw seven pictures of social consequences.
4. Present your drug chart work in group.

Appendix 2

STEP ONE SAMPLE ASSIGNMENT

Step One tells us: "We admitted we were powerless over drugs and alcohol and that our lives had become unmanageable" (Alcoholics Anonymous, 1952).

Do work in the order written. Get staff to sign before doing the next part.
Step One is due on:
Staff Initials/Date:

1. Watch ASL videotape on Step One.
2. Draw ten pictures of unmanageable from drug/alcohol use.
3. Draw ten pictures of powerless with drugs and alcohol.
4. Draw one picture of how powerless feels.
5. Draw eight examples of how my drug/alcohol use has caused problems for other people.
6. Draw/write examples of how using alcohol/drug has caused problems for me.
7. Two one-to-ones with peers.
8. Two one-to-ones with staff.
9. Present your Step One work in group.

Index

The use of *deaf/Deaf* follows the individual contributors' preferences in their chapters. For further information on contributor preferences, see the preface.